T0311460

A NEW PRINCIPLES OF ECONOMICS

Despite the dynamic development of the discipline of economics, the ways in which economics is taught and how it defines its basic principles have hardly changed, resulting in economics being criticised for its inability to provide relevant insights on global challenges. In response, this book defines new principles of economics and seeks to establish economics as the science of markets.

A New Principles of Economics provides an alternative conceptual framework for the study of economics, integrating recent developments and research in both economics and neighbouring social sciences. Adopting the structure of a standard principles text, it separates the study of markets as mechanisms and markets in their wider contexts. In doing so, a number of new perspectives are introduced, including approaching the economy as part and parcel of the Earth system; directly connecting the analysis of production with an analysis of technology and thermodynamic principles; explicitly treating markets as forms of social networks mediated by the institution of money; and reinstating the central role of distribution in political economy analysis.

Drawing on the latest theories and research on the economy, and including both the natural and social sciences, this text provides a holistic introduction suitable for postgraduates and other advanced students.

Carsten Herrmann-Pillath is Professor of Economics and Permanent Fellow at the Max Weber Centre for Advanced Cultural and Social Studies, University of Erfurt, Germany.

Christian Hederer is Professor of Economics and International Economic Policy at the Technical University of Applied Sciences Wildau, Germany.

To Sigrun, Emil, Hans, Luisa, Otto and Yolanda. CHP
To my father, in gratitude. CH

A NEW PRINCIPLES OF ECONOMICS

The Science of Markets

Carsten Herrmann-Pillath
and Christian Hederer

Routledge
Taylor & Francis Group

LONDON AND NEW YORK

Cover image: © Getty Images

First published 2023
by Routledge
4 Park Square, Milton Park, Abingdon, Oxon OX14 4RN

and by Routledge
605 Third Avenue, New York, NY 10158

Routledge is an imprint of the Taylor & Francis Group, an informa business

British Library Cataloguing-in-Publication Data
A catalogue record for this book is available from the British Library

ISBN: 978-0-367-55720-1 (hbk)
ISBN: 978-0-367-55719-5 (pbk)
ISBN: 978-1-003-09486-9 (ebk)

DOI: 10.4324/9781003094869

Typeset in Times New Roman
by Apex CoVantage, LLC

CONTENTS

Introduction   1

PART I

1 What are markets?   9
   1.   Introduction   9
   2.   Marketplaces   10
       2.1. Marketplaces embody markets   10
       2.2. Markets and market society   11
       2.3. Markets, land, and labour   13
   3.   Market system   14
       3.1. Market infrastructure and arbitrage 14
       3.2. Markets and institutions   15
   4.   Markets: For good or bad?   17
   5.   Market economy versus capitalism   18
   6.   Conclusion   20
   Major chapter insights   21
   Notes   21
   References   23

2 Economics as the science of markets   26
   1.   Introduction   26
   2.   What is science? The first-, second-, and third-person view 27
   3.   Economics, the economy, and markets   29
       3.1. The economy as an object of science 29
       3.2. Performativity and materiality of markets 31
   4.   Economic models as mechanistic explanations 33
   5.   Economic models triangulate cross-disciplinary data and hypotheses 37
   6.   Economics is entangled with its object: Reflexivity 38
   7.   Conclusion   40

	Major chapter insights	41
	Notes	42
	References	43

3	Economics and values	48
	1. Introduction	48
	2. Freedom, values, and markets	49
	2.1. Freedom of choosing preferences	49
	2.2. Freedom and social interdependence	50
	2.3. Freedom and rationality	51
	2.4. Freedom and social justice	53
	3. Efficiency	54
	3.1. Efficiency as progress	54
	3.2. Trade-offs: Efficiency versus values	55
	4. Markets, economists, and values	58
	5. Conclusion	59
	Major chapter insights	59
	Notes	60
	References	61

PART II

4	Evolution, ecology, economy	67
	1. Introduction	67
	2. Physical principles of evolution	68
	2.1. Economic niche, environment, Earth system	68
	2.2. Thermodynamic principles of evolution	70
	2.3. Metabolism and growth	74
	3. Fundamentals of evolution	77
	3.1. Selection, fitness, adaptation	77
	3.2. The VSR mechanism and levels of selection	80
	4. The evolutionary economy of living systems	82
	4.1. Evolving synergy in ecosystems and the human economy	82
	4.2. Cultural evolution, institutions, and human ultra-sociality	84
	5. Conclusion	88
	Major chapter insights	89
	Notes	89
	References	92

5	Specialisation and cooperation	99
	1. Introduction	99
	2. Specialisation and exchange: Gains and limitations	100
	2.1. Comparative advantage	100
	2.2. The specialisation dilemma	102

	3.	Strategic interaction and power	104
		3.1. The archetypes	104
		3.2. Power and forced specialization	108
	4.	Externalities and the efficiency of specialisation	111
	5.	Conclusion	115
		Major chapter insights	116
		Notes	117
		References	119
6		Production and technological evolution	123
	1.	Introduction	123
	2.	Production in the technosphere	124
		2.1. The technosphere	124
		2.2. Production and consumption in the ecological dimension	126
	3.	Specialisation and technology	129
		3.1. Engineering versus economic approaches to production	129
		3.2. Production and use of technology	132
		3.3. Technological evolution	135
	4.	Firms, technology, and specialisation	138
		4.1. The firm as organisational form of specialisation	138
		4.2. Technology and power in firms	140
	5.	Conclusion	142
		Major chapter insights	143
		Notes	143
		References	146

PART III

7		The economic agent	153
	1.	Introduction	153
	2.	Reframing rationality in economics	154
	3.	Brain, reason, and human sociality	155
		3.1. The nature of the brain: Predictive and social	155
		3.2. Reason and rationality	158
		3.3. Emotions	160
	4.	The economic agent	161
		4.1. Agency and agential power	161
		4.2 Identity	163
		4.3. Performativity	165
	5.	Mechanisms of choice and valuation	166
		5.1. Imitation and learning	166
		5.2. Wanting, liking, and happiness	168
		5.3. Creativity and entrepreneurial action	169
	6.	Conclusion	171

Major chapter insights   172
Notes   173
References   177

8   Networks and social interaction   185
    1.   Introduction   185
    2.   A short primer of network analysis   186
         2.1. Fundamental types of network configurations
              in the context of markets   186
         2.2. Dimensions of networks   190
    3.   Network structure and dynamics   194
         3.1. Network structure and agential power   194
         3.2. Social capital   197
         3.3. Boundaries in networks: In-group/out-group   201
         3.4. Network dynamics and frequency-dependent
              mechanisms   203
    4.   Conclusion   207
    Major chapter insights   208
    Notes   209
    References   211

9   Institutions   216
    1.   Introduction   216
    2.   Following an institution   217
         2.1. Cognitive mechanisms of institutionalisation   217
         2.2. Institutions and emotions   220
    3.   Performing institutions   221
         3.1. Performative mechanisms in two dimensions   221
         3.2. Path dependency of institutional evolution   224
    4.   The cost of institutions   226
         4.1. The basic setup   226
         4.2. Economic transaction costs   227
         4.3. Political transaction costs   229
         4.4. Political transaction costs on the constitutional level
              and the social contract   231
    5.   Power and institutions   232
         5.1. Institutions and endogenous agential power   232
         5.2. Institutions and violence   233
         5.3. Evaluating institutions   235
    6.   Conclusion   236
    Major chapter insights   237
    Notes   238
    References   240

10 Money and value   246
    1. Introduction   246
    2. Performing money   247
        2.1. The institution of money   247
        2.2. Money, prices, and arbitrage   250
    3. The psychology of money: Anchoring the performativity
        of monetary institutions   253
        3.1. Agential power and the value of money   253
        3.2. Cognition and money emotions   254
    4. Money, arbitrage, and the objectivisation of subjective value 256
        4.1. Objectification of value as performative rationalisation
             of choice   257
        4.2. Entrepreneurial rent and exchange value   261
        4.3. Money as form of social capital   262
    5. Conclusion   264
    Major chapter insights   264
    Notes   265
    References   267

11 Markets evolving   272
    1. Introduction   272
    2. Characteristics of markets: A reprise   273
        2.1. Elements of markets   273
        2.2. A simple map of a market   275
    3. The evolutionary market process: Competition, endogenous
        niche formation, and growth   277
    4. Money, prices, and market states   280
        4.1. Entrepreneurship and pricing under the shadow of the
             specialisation dilemma   280
        4.2. Beyond equilibrium: Prices, market clearing, and
             market states   282
    5. Entrepreneurs and firms as market makers   284
    6. Markets and institutions   288
    7. Conclusion   290
    Major chapter insights   290
    Notes   291
    References   293

PART IV

12 Money and finance   301
    1. Introduction   301
    2. Private and sovereign money   302

	2.1. Private money as assetified debt	302
	2.2. Sovereign money as public unit of account	305
	2.3. Linkages between primary and secondary monetary communities	306
3.	Money and capital	308
	3.1. Saving and investment relating to types of agents	308
	3.2. Deconstructing the capital market	312
	3.3. Valuing capital	316
4.	Assetification and liability	319
5.	Conclusion	321
	Major chapter insights	322
	Notes	323
	References	325

13	Economic fluctuations and aggregate economic evolution	330
1.	Introduction	330
2.	Schumpeterian dynamics and techno-institutional regimes	331
3.	Economic fluctuations of monetary aggregates: Macroeconomics and accounting balances	335
4.	Expectations as drivers of economic fluctuations	336
	4.1. Individual expectations	337
	4.2. Collective dynamics	338
5.	Patterns of economic fluctuations	340
	5.1. Entrepreneurship and technological change	340
	5.2. Finance and financial crises	341
6.	Fluctuations and economic policy	344
	6.1. Performative measurement and modelling	344
	6.2. Monetary policy	345
	6.3. Fiscal policy and reform	347
7.	Economic fluctuations as shifts in market states	349
8.	Conclusion	353
	Major chapter insights	354
	Notes	354
	References	356

14	The economics of global markets	361
1.	Introduction	361
2.	Transactions and the spatial structure of global markets	362
	2.1. Deconstructing global transactions	362
	2.2. Spatial structure, borders, and costs of global economic transactions	364
	2.3. The exchange rate and arbitrage	367
3.	Market access rights and institutions governing global transactions	369
	3.1. MARs and two-level exchange	370
	3.2. MARs and currency areas	373

4.	The evolution of the global division of labour	375
	4.1. Evolving comparative advantage, capacities to trade, and locational externalities	375
	4.2. Multinational enterprises and the structure of international production	378
	4.3. National payment balances and their evolution over time	380
5.	Conclusion	383
	Major chapter insights	383
	Notes	384
	References	387
15	**Markets and inequality**	**393**
1.	Introduction	393
2.	Concepts and measurement of inequality	394
3.	Structural inequality and multilevel market selection	396
	3.1. Country-level inequality regimes and formal institutions	396
	3.2. Firms and interfirm competition	398
4.	Interpersonal inequality: Individual differences, networks, and social mobility	403
	4.1. Individual differences, nature versus nurture, and path dependency	403
	4.2. Human capital: Educational stratification and labour markets	405
	4.3. Social capital: Interaction in social networks and divergence	406
	4.4. Entrepreneurship and risk-taking	409
5.	Legitimacy and performativity of regimes of inequality	410
6.	Conclusion	412
	Major chapter insights	413
	Notes	414
	References	416
16	**Global economic growth in the Earth system**	**421**
1.	Introduction	421
2.	The evolution of the human economy	422
3.	Economic growth and the technosphere	426
4.	Energy and limits to growth	428
5.	Markets as drivers of growth	432
6.	Anthropocentric versus geocentric conceptions of growth	435
	6.1. The anthropocentric perspective	435
	6.2. The geocentric perspective	438
7.	Conclusion	439
	Major chapter insights	440
	Notes	442
	References	444

PART V

17 Economic policy   453
   1.   Introduction   453
   2.   Economic policy and political competition: An evolutionary
       approach   454
      2.1. Economic policy and the state   454
      2.2. Political competition as an evolutionary process   456
   3.   Realms of political competition   459
      3.1. Competition for public opinion   459
      3.2. Competition for votes within jurisdictions   460
      3.3. Competition for (bottom-up) influence on political
          decision makers   461
      3.4. Interjurisdictional competition   464
      3.5. Occupation of political elite positions and political
          decision making   465
      3.6. Policy implementation and the bureaucracy   467
   4.   Deliberation, values, and economic policy   468
      4.1. Inclusive deliberation as a procedural criterion   468
      4.2. Freedom and human dignity as substantive criteria   469
      4.3. The deliberative policy process in interjurisdictional
          competition   471
   5.   Conclusion   472
   Major chapter insights   473
   Notes   474
   References   476

18 Epilogue: The economist as adviser   482
   Notes   489
   References   490

Index   492

INTRODUCTION

Economics has been evolving rapidly in the recent decades. New subdisciplines have emerged, such as experimental economics, behavioural economics, and mechanism design. Policy stances have changed, such as in central banking, and substantial analysis has been provided with respect to pressing issues, such as economic inequality. Yet many observers believe that modern economics needs radical renewal. How can this be explained? One point undoubtedly is the continued association of economics with the age of so-called neoliberalism, which attributed a dominant role to the discipline in terms of formulating policies with far-reaching societal impact, such as the privatisation of certain public services. There was also widespread disappointment with the failure of mainstream economics to adequately deal with – let alone predict – the 2008/2009 crisis.

In this context, one prominent issue is the status of economics textbooks. The last decade has seen the emergence of a worldwide student movement demanding radical curriculum reform, mostly under the label of pluralist economics; by now, teaching material that incorporates those demands is widely available.[1] However, there are tight constraints on changing textbooks.[2] Economics departments and business schools must adhere to a curriculum that is compatible across different universities, in line with external accreditation requirements, and they must clearly define what an economist represents on the job market. As a result, established economics textbooks not only fail to incorporate pluralist perspectives but also fall far behind the current advances of mainstream economics.

What can be done? The authors of this book revive a genre that has been languishing for long: the *Principles*. Today, this label is almost exclusively used as a title for textbooks. In the 19th century, however, *Principles* were monographic studies of the foundations of a discipline yet without much technical detail and accessibility to the educated reader. Our book takes up this tradition. We perceive the need to reinvent economics as a discipline from scratch, although, of course, building on previous achievements. The format of *Principles* is conducive to this goal. Indeed, in many respects, we take Alfred Marshall's *Principles* as a template.[3] Notably, Marshall, the first

1

DOI: 10.4324/9781003094869-1

professor of economics at Cambridge and distinguished mathematician, advocated the use of ordinary language to explain economics to the reader and relegated formalism to footnotes. He saw mathematics in economics as a tool to test economic hypotheses for consistency and systematic coherence but not as the main medium of generating hypotheses.[4]

Marshall's case for ordinary language in economics can be grounded theoretically: Economics directly affects the actions of economic agents and, thereby, changes their behaviour, potentially in a way that corroborates its hypotheses. This core characteristic of the discipline has been a traditional focus of its critiques as well, reaching from Carlyle's dismal science to modern observers who deplore the impact of economics not only in terms of its policy consequences but also in terms of its societal value stances. The key theoretical concept capturing the interdependence between economics (in fact, all social science) and its object is performativity. Economics is a performative science and, therefore, is fundamentally different from most other disciplines that rely on mathematics, primarily the sciences. Our book takes performativity as one pivot of reinventing economics, implying that economics cannot be defined as an exclusively quantitative science. To be sure, this stance in no way precludes the use of a distinct conceptual apparatus as well as Marshall's point that for testing economic hypotheses, advanced mathematical and quantitative techniques are absolutely necessary. But when it comes to principles, these must be accessible in ordinary language.

We follow Marshall in another way, namely with regard to his focus on markets. In the past decades, and until today, economics has been defined by its basic theoretical principles and its method. This propelled its significant expansion into other disciplinary domains but also diluted its domain more and more towards a mere application of mathematical modelling and econometrics to social problems of all kinds, rather than focusing it on a clearly defined object. For Marshall, that focus was clear: Economics is the science of markets.

This view may appear as naive to some, but in fact, the history of economics, both European and beyond, is mostly about theorising markets – such as the law of one price discovered by the Spanish Jesuits in medieval times or the Chinese treatise of price movements, the *Guanzi*, of seventh century BCE. Most of modern economics since Adam Smith has been preoccupied with defending and designing markets and, since Karl Marx, criticising, attacking, and suppressing them. This directly connects to the performative nature of modern economics which not only analyses markets but also contributes to engineering them and, even more fundamentally, determines their reach and scope. Of course, defining economics as science of markets does not imply that contexts of markets do not matter – most importantly, government, insofar as it shapes and intervenes in markets, and firms, insofar as they co-evolve with market-based allocation.

We therefore argue that markets are a scientific object domain of its own status and require the attention of a specialised scientific discipline.

2

Establishing an autonomous position of economics in this way implies, on the one hand, to keep its performative connection with the real economy at the centre of its methodological development. On the other hand, markets are not mere arbitrary constructs but objects out there, implying a combination of the performative view with a thoroughly materialist or naturalistic perspective. Markets are social entities, made up by living people, artefacts, and natural conditions which are in constant flux. We take account of this by conceiving economics as an evolutionary science, again referring to Marshall who called biology the mecca of the economist.[5]

References to biology are common in modern economics, in particular, game theory, yet they are largely restricted to theoretical modelling (i.e., the mathematical side of modern biology). What is mostly left out is the biologist as naturalist, that is, the keen observer of life and chronicler of its change in its full richness, as famously described in Darwin's concluding paragraphs of the *Origin of Species* depicting the entangled bank. The older tradition of economic principles started out from observing economic realities and built on rich knowledge about practices in economic life.

The conjunction of materialism and biology offers a view of economics as an integral part of the life sciences. A fundamental premise of our book is that the evolutionary view on markets is embedded in a broader evolutionary view on the economy as the specifically human way of living in face of ecological conditions and constraints. Thus, we approach ecology and economy as unity. By implication, we draw a specific distinction between the cross-disciplinary study of *the economy* in the life sciences, broadly interpreted, and *economics* as the *science of markets*. This connection operates via the contextualisation of markets. For example, the growth and development of markets must be contextualised by environmental and ecological conditions; understanding economic agents on markets needs contextualisation by psychology and neuroscience. Yet contextualisation does not mean that there is no theoretical core distinct to economics proper.

The book is divided into five parts.

The first part introduces economics as a scientific discipline. We introduce our object, markets, by presenting a real-life case, the evolution of China's market system over two millennia. In Chapter 2, we discuss basic methodological premises of economics and elaborate on one key consequence of the performativity of economics, namely the character of economics as a values-based science, which is the topic of Chapter 3.

The second part develops the contextualisation of economics in the life sciences. Chapter 4 discusses the relation between ecology and economy on the basis of a generalised evolutionary paradigm. Chapter 5 introduces specialisation and the division of labour as core concepts that bridge evolutionary theory and economics, conceiving of market-based specialisation as a key feature of human niche construction. Chapter 6 presents an ecological view on production and introduces technology and technological evolution.

The third part unfolds the key elements of a newly conceived conceptual apparatus of economics. Chapter 7 starts with the economic agent. Chapter 8 explores relationships between agents and the establishment of agency based on the theory of social networks. Chapter 9 introduces institutions as bringing markets into existence, in the sense of durable structures and material frames for action beyond the dynamism and fluidity of networks. The core institution that separates markets from other institutionalised domains is money; Chapter 10 is devoted to it. Chapter 11 concludes this part by presenting our theory of markets, based on evolutionary thinking and the theoretical recognition of performativity.

The separating line between the third and the fourth part is similar to the distinction of microeconomics and macroeconomics. In Chapter 12, we take a systemic look at monetary systems and finance, understood in a broad sense. Chapter 13 investigates one of the most conspicuous features of modern economies, economic fluctuations. Chapter 14 deals with the global coexistence of various monetary domains, mostly tied to nation states, and its consequences for international trade and investment. Chapter 15 tackles an issue of central concern for understanding the impact of markets on society, namely inequality of market outcomes and its connection to societal power structures. Chapter 16 analyses economic growth in the context of ecology, closing the circle to the second part.

The fifth part focuses on economic policy and the role played by economics as a science. Chapter 17 introduces an endogenous view of economic policy in which specific frameworks and decisions are outcomes of the policy process. Chapter 18 concludes by reflecting on the economist as adviser. Compared to other social scientists, economists play an important role in shaping modern politics, and their advice, if followed, potentially affects the lives of millions. Therefore, economists bear responsibility with respect to the consequences of their advice. At the same time, the discipline has evolved endogenously with economic, social, and political change, which raises doubts about its intellectual autonomy. Economists must always adopt a critical attitude in the sense that they are aware of the performative nature of their theories, and they must also employ their theories on their own roles as advisers. Sometimes they might take an engineering stance, such as in market design, but ultimately, taking a normative position in the wider societal and political context is inevitable. This means that at a certain point, economic advice must go beyond its expert status and understand itself as equal voices in a broader deliberative venture.

We conclude this introduction with a few remarks on how the book can be used. In line with the *Principles* tradition, the book can be read as a monograph on economics. We do not delve deeper in technical aspects or methods; at the same time, we employ didactic techniques that establish a hybrid character as a textbook, in particular, marginal boxes on key points and connections across chapters and chapter summaries. The text is designed to be accessible to undergraduate readers with a minimum background in economics and high school–level knowledge about other fields, such as evolution, technology, and history.

The book develops a completely new approach to the foundations of economics and its application to major fields of the discipline, such as macroeconomics, growth, and international trade. The chapter structure roughly follows the conventional architecture of introductory economics textbooks, first establishing the foundations of the discipline and then moving from lower to higher levels of aggregation. However, the book cannot be used to teach the standard curriculum insofar as we employ a fundamentally different micro-macro distinction. We do not refer to utility functions or aggregate demand functions; our micro perspective is constituted by a naturalistic approach to the economic agent, network structures, institutions, and their evolution; the macro perspective focuses on the role of money in the economy and the resulting aggregate dynamics.

Thus, our book cannot substitute for a standard economic textbook, unless a department is in a truly revolutionary mood. But it can be used for complementary readings showing alternatives to standard accounts. Here, following the common architecture is helpful, as chapters can be used separately as specific contributions. For example, the chapter on the economic agent can be read separately as input to teaching standard microeconomics.

Another use of the book reaches beyond economics. Neighbouring fields often face difficulties in combining economics with their own approaches. Also, for their curricula, standards of teaching economics do not matter much, as both academic and professional careers of graduates follow trajectories different than those of economists. In contrast, economics as presented here easily dovetails with disciplines such as anthropology, psychology, sociology, or political science.

To sum up, we hope that our book will be received in creative ways among a wide range of readers, including, last but not least, professionals and officials who do the economy. In presenting a new view on economics as a performative science, we hope to provide a modest contribution to change economic practice.

* * *

This book has a long history, going back to the first attempt of one of us (CHP) writing a radically new textbook of economics in 2002, in German, the *Grundriß der Evolutionsökonomik* (*Elements of Evolutionary Economics*).[6] At that time, the other author (CH) was a PhD student of the former. CHP is grateful for CH's encouragement and consistent support of heterodox thinking in economics, culminating in the suggestion to try again, resulting in these co-authored *Principles*. CH gratefully owes a core part of his intellectual development to CHP, while entering important experiences of the non-academic parts of his career into the *Principles* as well.

For the final stage of the project, we thankfully recognise generous financial support by Hertha and Dr. Friedrich Bauersachs, which allowed for employing two capable student assistants, Saskia Podzimek and Jonas Plattner. They contributed many valuable suggestions for improvement and did the final formatting, which we gratefully acknowledge.

Notes

1 A landmark was the publication of the Core Team (2017) textbook.
2 Mankiw (2020).
3 Marshall (1920).
4 On Marshall's famous remarks on the role of mathematics in economics, see Pigou (1966, p. 427).
5 Marshall (1920, 636ff) defined 'economics' as a branch of biology, "broadly interpreted".
6 Herrmann-Pillath (2002).

References

The Core Team (2017) *The Economy. Economics for a Changing World*. Oxford: Oxford University Press.

Herrmann-Pillath, C. (2002) *Grundriß der Evolutionsökonomik*. München: Fink.

Mankiw, N Gregory (2020) 'Reflections of a Textbook Author', *Journal of Economic Literature*, 58(1), pp. 215–228. DOI: 10.1257/jel.20191589.

Marshall, A. (1920) *Principles of Economics*. 8th Edition. Reprint Cosimo Classics 2009. New York: Cosimo.

Pigou, A. C. (1966) *Memorials of Alfred Marshall*. New York: A. M. Kelley.

PART I

CHAPTER ONE

What are markets?

1. Introduction

Markets are an emergent social technology that enables economic exchange among large numbers of people. Market actors specialise in terms of skills, knowledge, and equipment to produce goods and services that are sold and bought on the marketplace. They thereby gain relative to a state of autarky: Markets are communities of advantage.[1] Markets are a ubiquitous and pervasive element of complex human societies and, as such, are independent from the level of economic and technological development. Historically, markets emerged from nascent forms of institutionalised barter, often elaborated in the context of long-distance trade, and gradually evolved further to encompass all spheres of the economy.[2] Markets are deeply intertwined with the evolution of the division of labour in human ways of life.[3]

Markets are a universal social technology and communities of advantage.

To a large extent, economics, as practised by economists, is the science of markets. Yet modern economics tends to downplay the crucial distinction between markets as generic objects of study and the specific historical forms in which markets are embodied. This has resulted in a conflation of the economics of markets with the economics of capitalism, implying that the lesson of the 20th century is that capitalism is the most advanced and presumably final form of a market economy.[4] Accordingly, most treatments of economic history employ a vision of progress, in both technological and institutional terms, on the European and Western trajectory of economic growth.[5]

Many economists fail to distinguish between market economy and capitalism.

As we argue in Chapter 3, progress reflects a value stance of economics.

We disentangle the conceptual fusion of markets and capitalism. This will be done by means of a paradigmatic historical case study, namely the market economy of Imperial China (221 BCE–1911). China had developed a complex market economy long before the onset of (European) industrialisation but introduced capitalist institutions only gradually during the 20th century. Analysing key characteristics of the pre-20th-century Chinese economy paves the ground for establishing economics as a science of markets, as we will do in Chapter 2. This posits markets as a universal object of economic inquiry and capitalism as a specific economic, political, social, and cultural form of organising these markets.

China is an important historical case of the dissociation of market economy and capitalism.

9

DOI: 10.4324/9781003094869-3

Accordingly, this chapter provides an overview of key features of markets in Imperial China, such as market systems, market infrastructure, and market management by private and public actors.

2. Marketplaces

2.1. Marketplaces embody markets

In contemporary China, many towns bear a disyllabic name with the element *zhen*. This means "market town". Throughout her history, China has been a country of marketplaces.[6] Markets are physically embodied in marketplaces (today, perhaps on internet servers). In old China, a marketplace was a specific location where people set up stalls to sell goods to customers. Typically, markets were specialised; for example, there were markets for bamboo. Those elements have a long tradition in China and were formalised during the Tang dynasty (617–907), when the government established marketplaces by administrative decree and assigned trades to specific places. In later times, markets grew out of this form of government control yet often retained the pattern of spatial specialisation.

In Chapter 2, section 2, we argue that economics should approach markets as real-world phenomena.

The creation of markets was an entrepreneurial activity.

A market is a social arrangement that allows for buyers and sellers to meet – with a wide range of forms of technological mediation – negotiate over quantities and prices, and eventually settle and realise transactions. In old China, this happened on spatially circumscribed marketplaces, which required investment in market infrastructure. A certain amount of land had to be assigned to the status of a marketplace, and traders had to set up stalls. In Tang dynasty cities, that was mainly done by the government, but in the rural areas, and after the retreat of government in Song times (960–1279), it fell under the realm of private activity. There were many ways to set up a market: A village might invest as a community, or a wealthy family group might allot some of the jointly held land to set up a market. There were various benefits from those activities, reaching from the rents that traders had to pay for setting up a stall to the informal control of trades that were conducted on the market. For example, a merchant family engaging in bamboo trade might set up a regional bamboo market, which opened channels to create competitive advantage over other bamboo traders.[7]

For a systematic treatment of market pricing, see Chapter 10, section 2.2.

On the social network dimension of markets, see Chapter 8.

A common characteristic of markets is that participants mostly conduct trades in the language of prices and quantities, given certain conceptions of the quality of goods traded. On the marketplace, supply of certain goods meets demand, and participants negotiate over deals. Unlike many consumer goods markets today, prices in old China were not publicly announced but always subject to negotiations between the parties: This is sometimes called the bazaar type of markets.[8] However, since sellers and buyers met on the respective physical location and could conduct many negotiations in a sequence, or potential buyers met at dens over lunch, the marketplace assumed another important function: Markets are social networks in which economic information is generated, processed, and communicated. One of the essential outcomes of markets, which was well recognised in China, is that people learn about prices of goods as data informing them about the general state of the economy, beyond particular business deals.[9]

2.2. Markets and market society

Even if marketplaces are specialised, many other goods and services complementary to the product in question were offered. For example, when buyers on a bamboo market bought a larger quantity of bamboo, they needed means of transport. They might own them, but if they were not specialised traders themselves, keeping the equipment over a year without regular need possibly was too expensive.[10] The most important services were transport, accommodation and restaurants, and the loan business, such as pawnshops. In modern parlance, the market town was a local service centre. Typically, marketplaces also attracted many other forms of business, including entertainment and even the religious domain: For example, for planning their business, traders might rely on fortune-telling such that at local temples many fortune-tellers offered their services.

We discuss the role of market information and its aggregation in Chapter 13.

A market town manifested a rich ecology of markets and specialised trade, reaching across all social domains.

The complex division of labour and the variety of goods and services offered on marketplaces were central to safeguarding the livelihood of most Chinese in the agrarian economy of old China.[11] Chinese peasants were engaged in many activities oriented towards markets. Villages and market towns were the fundamental geographical units in old Chinese society and at par in terms of their significance for life. For example, following traditional rules of marriage, villagers often had to find brides from other places since marriage among relatives in the village was prohibited. The local market was the place where matchmakers offered their services, and people had many opportunities for gossiping and exchanging news about other villages. This involved the explicit calculation of bride prices, reflecting the cost of raising daughters.[12]

We distinguish between market niches, markets, and market systems in Chapter 11.

Old China was a market society.

There were other forms of market-related activities for which a specific physical location was not crucial. An example are itinerant petty traders who moved between different marketplaces and villages.[13] Those traders specialised on the buying and selling of goods, without eventually aiming to use them for own consumption or production. Generalising this, three economic activities associated with markets can be distinguished:

We have a special focus on trading in Chapter 14, section 2.

- consumption;
- production;
- trading or, in more abstract terms, transacting.

In the first place, markets allow for the separation between consumption and production: Consumption on a do-it-yourself basis is characteristic for a subsistence economy only. In poor agricultural societies, the subsistence economy has remained significant until today, with market related activities only constituting a marginal phenomenon. In old China, the subsistence economy was in continuous retreat over the centuries and of low significance in late Imperial China. For example, villages were often specialised in a particular trade, such as papermaking, and therefore, had to rely on markets to procure other goods, including even basic staples. This was possible because the network of marketplaces had grown into a market system early.[14]

We look at
specialisation in
Chapter 5.

Households in old China were specialised in both consumption and production, relying on markets for their livelihood.

The other side of the reliance of consumption on markets is that producers specialise to produce goods that they do not need for their own consumption and can sell on the market. Even for poor Chinese farmers, production for the market was a necessary means of survival; often, this was the task of women in agricultural sideline businesses, such as weaving. Agricultural production itself became increasingly specialised, too, such that depending on the local ecology, farmers concentrated on certain cash crops and bought staples on the market.[15] Producing for the market creates specific risks, in particular, price fluctuations and the disappointment of expectations about future income. Even in pre-imperial times, concerns over price fluctuations were widespread among educated elites who reflected on markets.[16]

On the notion of
production, see
Chapter 6.

Traders, in comparison, neither produce nor consume goods that they buy and sell but provide a service. Traders were so essential in the traditional Chinese economy that some scholars labelled it 'commercial capitalism'. Traders are a special type of intermediary in markets. In traditional Chinese marketplaces, intermediators were active in all domains; for example, connecting people in need for transport with suppliers of transport services. The broker was even an officially recognised profession, and in more expert trades and important marketplaces, brokers received official recognition by the local government and had to have a license.[17]

Intermediators of various kinds (traders, brokers, etc.) played a key role in the old Chinese market economy.

Intermediation points to a general problem facing all markets: The larger the market and the larger the number of people involved, the more complex the information problem becomes. Accordingly, markets presuppose a minimum level of trust among market participants that promises will be kept and cheating will be held at bay. One solution in old China was the social role of the middleman (mostly male, indeed, but also female, such as on marriage markets). In simplest terms, a middleman acts as a trusted third person in mediating a transaction: By putting his own reputation at risk, the middleman creates derived trust between two otherwise less-trusting parties. Markets in old China were deeply embedded in social relations or social networks. This is true until today and relates to the ominous term *guanxi* (relationships, networks).[18] In comparison, professional brokers turn social networking into a business, such as via earning fees for doing their service. This comes close to trading but includes many forms of transactions, such as forming business partnerships.

In Chapter 5,
we refer to this
issue of trust and
exchange as the
specialisation
dilemma. Trust as
a social network
phenomenon
is analysed in
Chapter 8.

All these observations can be summarised in approaching old China as a market society: Markets deeply shaped social relations, community life, and individual fates, and many daily activities were centred on markets.

2.3. Markets, land, and labour

So far, we have considered markets for goods and services. In old China, there were markets for other economic assets as well, most importantly, land. Land cannot be physically moved in space; hence, the object of trade is rights in using land and claims to the proceeds of exploiting land. The land market was embedded in social relations, in which demand and supply met in other settings. In prosperous regions of China, land was mostly exchanged among elite families who owned larger stretches of land that was rented out to tenants. The underlying contracts were often sold several times as subletting arrangements.[19]

These arrangements stood in tension with the widely held, and politically endorsed, idea that land is the ultimate source of individual livelihood. Hence, most farmers strived to own at least a minimal swath of land and added additional land via tenancy arrangements. These arrangements often remained local, that is, families reshuffled land ownership via flexible reallocations of land among families (e.g., widows renting out land to families with many able-bodied sons). The land market emerged via the construction of derivative land rights in which the tenants sometimes obtained quasi-permanent status. Buyers of land rights would just buy claims on the rent without changing the existing structure of possession and land management.[20] An important feature of agricultural production in old China was that it was mainly organised in nuclear families, even if landownership was concentrated in some regions or at specific historical periods.

Old China was a country characterised by scarcity of land and abundance of labour. Over the centuries, most forms of slavery and other forms of bounded labour vanished, and the labour market took hold.[21] However, many participants were families who acted as entrepreneurs offering labour as a service, such as transport works. In this case, the distinction between labour and self-employed entrepreneur became blurred: The production unit was mostly the family, which offered productive services in the market environment. Specific forms included labour gangs, where a leading foreman acted as a middleman and guarantor.

A remarkable fact about China's economic history is the secular decline of all forms of larger-scale organisation of production in organisations, such as the manor or the workshop as a factory.[22] The basic unit of production was the family, which combined many sources of market generated income and directly acted on marketplaces or in exchange with itinerant trades. Specific organisational forms included putting-out, where traders would supply families with inputs as advance payment in kind, to be returned as finished

We discuss property in Chapter 10.

A key market was the market for land that was grounded in a complex nested structure of distributed property rights.

The family was the dominant agent in the Chinese economy.

On the firm as distinct form of organising economic activity, see Chapter 6, section 4, and Chapter 11, section 5.

products. This was enabled by the highly efficient infrastructure of market-places. China did not evolve the organisational form of the corporation phys-ically embodied in the factory. Even very large-scale production sites, such as the imperial porcelain works at Jingdezhen, were organised as assemblages of thousands of small family workshops.

3. Market system

3.1. Market infrastructure and arbitrage

As said, itinerant traders moved between various local markets and villages to buy and sell goods. A similar activity also connected larger specialised and regional markets. Here, long-distance traders, which often were special-ised merchant families, connected the empire not only regionally but also transregionally. For example, rice merchants were active all over the country.[23]

We explore arbitrage in theoretical detail in Chapter 10, section 4.

These different groups realised an essential market function: arbitrage. Arbitrage was recognised in early Chinese writings as selling when prices are dear and buying when they are cheap.[24] Traders specialising on arbitrage can make a profit. This is one of the fundamental forms of market dynamics: Prof-its attract other traders, and, for example, they buy more goods when they are cheap. Demand drives prices up to the point that profits are too small to cover the cost of the trade, such as transport and travelling. If arbitrage works well, prices should converge. Indeed, transregional prices for rice did show this tendency in late Imperial China. Government officials developed the view that markets may be the best way to cope with regional price fluctuations, such as resulting from a bad harvest confined to a certain region, and even recommended that public aid should be transferred in cash, as that would be faster and more efficient than in-kind, since traders would balance supply across regions via markets.[25]

The role of geographical space and borders for trade is explored in Chapter 14, section 2.

Therefore, markets in China had grown together to a market system. A market system is a set of markets connected via the activity of arbitrage. If transport cost is too high, local markets can be isolated and manifest inde-pendent price movements. Of course, this applies for all goods and services that cannot be traded for reasons of transport cost or physical impossibility, such as in case of many services which are produced and consumed locally (think of the barbershop), and, most importantly, land.

The market system of China was embodied in a regional network of towns and cities.

In Imperial China, over centuries of continuous trading activities, the mar-ket system became embodied in the geography of towns and cities which were connected via trading routes. The emerging networks were shaped by a com-bination of geographical factors and the establishment of physical infrastruc-ture (e.g., harbours, roads), ultimately determining transport cost. The providers of the infrastructure were either the government or the traders themselves.

For example, rice was an essential good not only with respect to nutrition but also for taxation purposes and national security reasons, given necessities of stabilising political conditions in case of harvest failure or provisioning the military. Therefore, Chinese imperial governments invested in the creation of respective transport infrastructure, most famously the Imperial Grand Canal from Yangzhou to Beijing.[26] In many other cases, such as harbour construction and maintenance, private traders in larger cities formed alliances and invested jointly:[27] In economic terminology, public goods were produced. Markets build on a range of public goods to increase their efficiency and sustainability. Once infrastructure is created, specific locations attract even more economic activity, possibly resulting in a virtuous circle of local development. Indeed, Western visitors until the 18th century were stunned by the prosperity and bustling economic activity in Chinese cities, with many of them much larger than average European cities at the time. At the same time, urbanisation rates were not high because the market system supported the spread of small towns all over the country; rural and urban were not yet separated in sociological terms. Peasant families were integrated into a complex system of division of labour, such as in artisanal production: Required inputs were often traded on local markets, and products were sold there as well, from where they were traded across regions. Sometimes this was even organised by specialist merchants who would buy the products on a piece-rate basis, such as in the previously mentioned putting-out systems.[28]

In general, the scope of arbitrage, and hence, the reach of the market system, is determined by physical characteristics of space and the technologies underlying transactions, in particular, transport and communication technologies which are shaped by both private and public actors. One reason for the decline of China relative to Europe since the 18th century was the comparatively weak role of government investment in infrastructure.[29]

3.2. Markets and institutions

Markets need another type of infrastructure, namely institutions that govern market transactions. Until today, a fundamental issue for market transactions is the presence of cheating, fraud, and faking products and product quality; markets plagued by these phenomena will not be sustainable. Therefore, two kinds of measures are required: One is the improvement of information and transparency before transactions are realised; the other is the development of means of conflict resolution and sanctions after realisation. We already mentioned the role of various types of intermediators, such as professional brokers, as one possible solution.

Concurrently, with the emergence of markets, social norms against cheating emerged and diffused. Confucian philosophers and, later, religious beliefs, such as Buddhism, strongly condemned cheating on the marketplace. Effective social control was provided in groups of traders. At marketplaces, traders

Apart from giant projects, such as the Grand Canal, most market infrastructure was provided by merchants and communities.

In Chapter 16, we approach the city as the key phenomenon in economic growth.

This observation is central to understanding the globalisation of markets that we explore in Chapter 14.

We explore institutions in Chapter 9.

In Chapter 8, we study the role of networks in fostering trust and cooperation.

*Old China had a rich
associational life in
commerce which
fostered trust among
market actors.*

The role of formal
institutions for
the workability
of markets is
analysed in
Chapter 11,
section 6.

*Contracts were
mostly enforced by
private regulations,
not a civil law system.*

We explore
the production
of money in
Chapter 12.

*China never
developed a unified
monetary system.*

On the origin of
money in IOUs,
see Chapter 12,
section 2.1.

We discuss
global economic
linkages in
Chapter 14.

often organised in guilds and other organisations, such as native place associations, which not only created and disseminated norms against cheating but were also involved in punishing cheaters, such as via ostracising them from the community. Whereas, after the Tang dynasty, the imperial government generally adopted a detached attitude towards market regulation, cheating and fraud were explicitly recognised as capital offenses. Merchant practices were, thus, undergirded by law, and in case of unresolvable conflict, courts could be approached.[30]

Another essential element in institutional market infrastructure is property and contracts. In both respects, law is important but not necessarily all-encompassing. This is because, in principle, transaction parties can fix the conditions in detail via contracts so that third parties and more general rules only need to be involved in case of violations that cannot be settled by contract rules. Old China was a society based on contracts. This included the family domain; for example, marriage and inheritance were governed by contractual relations that in rural areas even survived the Maoist revolution. Many contracts included a witness and a guarantor, again highlighting the importance of middlemen. Interestingly, the imperial government also provided a service to testify property rights on land: If a land deed was to be recognised by the local magistrates' red seal, it had to be registered for taxation. In exchange, these rights were safe against challenge before the courts.[31]

In contrast to the European experience, therefore, the law did not play a central role in institutionalising the market system. China never developed a civil law; yet to a certain extent, its legal tradition does resemble common law. But this mainly operated as customary law mostly enforced by private regulation, not public courts.[32]

As a final element, a market system requires a medium of exchange – money. The Chinese developed the idea early that the government should rely on the control of currency to control the level of prices. Yet in late imperial times, government-minted copper coins coexisted with silver coins that flowed in via global trade relations.[33] The Chinese invented paper money during the Song dynasty, emerging from merchant practices to issue IOUs, but they also learned under Mongol rule that paper money can easily be abused by government to fund expenses.

The Chinese monetary institutions also demonstrate the role of the market system in establishing international linkages. When, in 18th-century England, consumption habits emerged that created a strong demand for tea and silk, the market system channelled price signals down to the grassroots level of Chinese peasant families who intensified tea and silk production. This caused a huge inflow of Mexican silver coins into China, as the British traders had developed a global system of long-distance trade in which these served as a medium of exchange.

4. Markets: For good or bad?

1
What are markets?

In pre-imperial times, Chinese intellectuals started to debate the merits and drawbacks of markets.[34] Beginning with Confucius, one of the greatest concerns was the potential erosion of social order, for two reasons.

The first is the general effect of markets on increasing freedom but also the alienation of people from traditional contexts of social and economic life. The growing role of markets contributed to an early erosion of the Chinese feudal order in which personal loyalties and socio-political hierarchies between people loomed large. Indeed, market dynamics, together with the territorial expansion of the empire and huge migration flows within it, undermined any kind of static ascription of people to social classes, castes, or other forms of segregation.[35]

Early Chinese discussion was concerned about social alienation and inequality caused by markets.

The second was the perceived contribution of market dynamics to social inequality, enhancing social dynamics in the earlier sense and resulting in a serious potential of social unrest. This was a major concern of all imperial governments and became pertinent in recurrent episodes of popular uprisings and protests, which were mainly motivated by growing poverty and desperation among large parts of the lower social strata.

We refer such social changes as performative emergence of types of agents; see Chapter 7.

Both aspects generated an ambivalent attitude towards traders and merchants.[36] Merchants were often seen as colluding against the public interest and creating power structures that undermined social order. In contrast, in late Imperial China, voices questioning the overall beneficial effects of markets on the prosperity of the populace were rare. One manifestation of this attitude was that the government kept taxation of economic activity as low as possible and often cooperated with local merchant groups in striking a balance between the interests of government and the locality.[37] Merchant families invested heavily in education to launch successful official careers of gifted sons.

We treat inequality and distribution in Chapter 15.

Although wary of merchant power, the imperial administration was supportive of markets. Governments took measures to contain forces of inequality.

In some periods, the imperial government adopted specific measures to contain economic forces that could contribute to destabilising inequality. One example is the establishment of a system of disaster relief, such as by the countrywide setting up of granaries which could be used to stabilise markets in case of bad harvests or natural disasters. Another example was a policy by which families were provided with a right of subsistence in owning a basic amount of land necessary for survival. Since, theoretically, all land in China was the emperor's, this could have been achieved by direct allocation; but such measures were taken only in times of imperial reconstruction, typically when a new dynasty took the helm, and large tracts of land were without owners after decades of civil unrest and war.[38]

We already mentioned the concern that powerful merchants or groups of merchants might control markets and, thus, accumulate wealth and power. Therefore, rules securing open markets and limiting market power of incumbents became an important element in the market institutions formalised by

Power and markets is a leitmotif in this book; for example, in Chapters 3, 5, and 10.

imperial law and decree. For example, merchant guilds were explicitly prohibited to regulate and constrain market entry of non-members.

A special case was monopoly, established by the government itself, such as the oldest monopoly that existed throughout imperial history, the salt monopoly. In one of the important early documents of the global history of economic thought, a Debate on Salt and Iron was held at the Han imperial court between promoters of strong government (the modernisers) and their critics.[39] The discussion revealed a complex view on markets:

We discuss
the role of
government and
economic policy
in Chapter 17.

*The question on
how markets and the
government relate
has been a perennial
topic in the Chinese
economic discourse
since earliest times.*

- The modernisers thought that strong government is necessary to contain destabilising forces of markets and create a wide range of public goods. For this, buoyant sources of revenue were necessary which could partly be created by government monopolies. But the government should also establish a direct relation to the taxable population, foremostly the peasants. A policy of equity was conceived as condition for establishing a fiscal state.
- The critics of strong government pointed out that government involvement in the economy creates the risk of corrupting the political and administrative elites. The Confucian scholars thought that markets were the medium of livelihood for ordinary people but that political and administrative elites should refrain from pursuing profit. In addition, maintaining a strong state would impose high tax burdens on the populace and, thus, contribute to increasing poverty.

These two basic stances towards markets and government were present throughout Chinese history.[40] They often remained in conflict, and each prevailed at different times. In the prosperous times of the first two centuries of the Qing dynasty (1644–1911), the Confucian stance prevailed, and China adopted an exceptionally low tax regime. This weak fiscal state, however, could not maintain an economic and military infrastructure to withstand the aggression of Western imperialism.[41]

5. Market economy versus capitalism

Why did China fail to develop capitalism endogenously? Many explanations have been provided. For a long time, it was claimed that markets were underdeveloped because of the imperial bureaucracy and traditional, especially Confucian worldviews. As we have seen, the current state of economic history research clearly shows this to be incorrect. So what was different about old China?

Explanations focus on various aspects.[42] One looks at the conjunction of capitalism and industrialisation in Europe. The question, then, is why China did not industrialise, that is, why China did not achieve the transition to the state of continuous, and partly radical, technological innovation that is one important feature of modern capitalism. Some scholars argue that the reason for this does not lie in institutional or ideological factors but the perfection of the Chinese market system itself: China's ecology and geography did not promote increasing use of technology in production; the market system allowed for demographic growth, and families specialised in labour-intensive production across a wide range of goods. In particular, energy was expensive, and coal deposits were located far away from economic centres. In Britain, labour was expensive and coal was cheap.[43] In other words, the fact that China did not industrialise was an economically efficient outcome, not an expression of failure. Specifically, the market system guided China to efficiently adapt to constraints in harnessing and utilising energy.

In other words, this theory would claim that industrialisation in Europe mainly resulted from an exploitation of the opportunity to shift to the carbon economy.[44] However, many economists do not accept this explanation but point to institutions as the main driver of progress. Scholars have meticulously compared Chinese and European institutional conditions, ending up with a short but substantial list:

The first point is that China did not develop the institution of the corporation combined with limited liability. Businesspeople were always personally liable for all their actions. Limited liability can be conceived of as a major means to reduce personal risk in capitalist undertakings. However, scholars have recently argued that in China, large extended kinship groups used the institutional form of the estate to create corporate bodies in many businesses, which would come close to limited liability in substantive terms.[45]

The second point is the lack of modern forms of finance.[46] Indeed, in the Chinese economy, banking was conspicuously absent as an institutional means to provide credit in the economy. Although indigenous banks did exist in Qing dynasty China, they were mostly involved in long-distance trade and did not provide loans to industrial ventures in a systematic way. Some scholars have argued that capitalism systematically builds on the capacities of banks to create money via credit, thereby enabling risky investments without the need to rely on previously accumulated funds.

The third point is the lack of a modern monetary system in China, which needs to be seen together with the lack of institutionalised government debt. The imperial state, after episodes of paper money inflation, always followed the principle of funding expenditures via taxes. This differed fundamentally from the entanglement of high finance and war finance in Europe, which resulted in the emergence of a range of financial instruments that fostered the growth of a new type of market, namely the capital market.[47] Instead, the monetary system and taxation remained coupled in China; the government

One hypothesis on China's failure to industrialise is that the market system enabled an efficient adaptation to ecological constraints.

Chapters 4 and 16 discuss related issues from the perspective of ecological economics.

Major institutional differences between Imperial China's market economy and capitalism are the absence of limited liability; the lack of capital markets, securitised government debt, and banking; and the weak fiscal state.

On limited liability, see Chapter 9, section 4.2, and Chapter 12, section 4.

On banking and the monetary system, see Chapter 12.

managed the production of coinage with the aim of enabling smooth transfers of revenue to the government.

The fourth point is linked to the third: Government in China remained very weak in comparison not only to the advanced European states but even to non-European entities, such as the Ottoman Empire.[48] That would lead to the conclusion that strong government is a defining feature of capitalism, contrary to some libertarian interpretations of capitalism. However, it must be taken into account that government in old China was endemically corrupt and often failed to protect private property rights. Therefore, the diagnosis is difficult to generalise as it may vary across different periods, such as the stages of dynastical ascent versus decline.

The comparison of the European economy with the Chinese market economy in imperial times results in a clear differentiation between the market economy and capitalism. The market economy is a system of markets that is based on institutions, such as free market entry, private property, and restrained government intervention, in particular with respect to pricing. While these conditions also apply for capitalism, capitalism adds specific features – mainly in the areas of finance, including government debt, and the institutionalised reduction of risk. Clearly, these additional elements are not fundamental in defining markets or even market systems; indeed, many economists have argued that they might even be dysfunctional. For example, government debt is often seen in a critical light, some economists have demanded the privatisation of money, and advocates of private property have strongly criticised all forms of limiting liability. Indeed, the market economy of Imperial China appears to resemble the visions of market purists much better than modern capitalism.

6. Conclusion

This chapter introduced the topic of this book: markets. We approach economics as the science of markets and will explore this in more detail in the next chapter. Much of current economics, however, restricts its perspective to our current economic system, which is capitalism, a specific historical form of market economy. We can learn a lot about this crucial distinction when studying historical cases of non-capitalist market economies, of which China is a prime example. A core question is to explain and understand why China did not develop capitalism and industrialisation endogenously. The Whiggish economic history to which many economic theorists subscribe explains this in terms of institutional and cultural failures in developing a market economy, such as weak property rights, and, therefore, presents a narrative of universal progress in Western civilisation against stagnation in China. However, this is in fact an argument about capitalism, not the market economy.

As our references in the framed boxes reveal, the market economy of old China manifested all features that are topical for economics as the science of markets, albeit in technological and institutional forms that differ from the economic systems that prevail in most countries today. The science of markets focuses on those features that are not bound to specific times and places.

Major chapter insights

- The notion of a market economy is not coextensive with capitalism; capitalism is a specific historical form of market economy. The economy of late Imperial China is the case of a mature non-capitalist market economy.
- Old China developed a rich physical infrastructure of marketplaces and market towns shaping her geography and undergirding the regional integration of the market system. China was a market society, with markets permeating all social domains.
- Markets were sustained by a wide range of institutions, such as property rights, contracts, and intermediation, and were embedded in social networks. Markets enabled comprehensive economic specialisation, grounding in the household and family as key units of economic agency.
- Major institutional differences between Imperial China's market economy and capitalism are the absence of limited liability; the lack of capital markets, securitised government debt, and banking; and the weak fiscal state.

Notes

1 This term is used by Robert Sugden who borrowed it from John Stuart Mill (Sugden, 2018).
2 Hodges (1989).
3 Lucassen (2021).
4 Fukuyama (1992). The German economic historian Werner Plumpe endorses this case in his monumental history of capitalism (Plumpe, 2019).
5 Jones (2003); compare with Mokyr (2017).
6 Skinner (1964/1965), Lu (2010).
7 Siu (1989, 62ff).
8 North distinguishes this from modern markets (i.e., capitalism) (North, 1990, 122ff).
9 One of the probably oldest scholarly works in economics worldwide is the *Guanzi* which contains a theory of price movements (Chin, 2014, 31ff). The

Guanzi is roughly dated at the fourth century BCE, though finally compiled in the first century BCE.

10 Naquin and Rawski (1987, 46ff).

11 Tellingly, in the Qing dynasty, China public relief in catastrophes was deliberately channelled via markets (Will, 1990, 212ff, 294ff).

12 Gates (1997, 121ff).

13 For a lively ethnographic account, see Fei (1939).

14 Economic historians and economists have accumulated much quantitative evidence on market integration in old China; see Keller and Shiue (2007).

15 Classical contributions to research on the relationship between households and markets in China include Chao (1986) and Huang (1990).

16 Zanasi (2020, 54ff).

17 Glahn (2016, 268f, 318).

18 There is a huge literature on *guanxi* in the modern Chinese economy; for a survey, see Chen, Chen, and Huang (2013).

19 Important contributions to this topic are in the edited volume of Zelin et al. (2004).

20 Hase (2013).

21 Lucassen (2021, 290ff).

22 Huang (1990) calls this involution, manifest in the absence of more complex forms of economic organisation.

23 Skinner (1985).

24 Chin (2014, 34ff).

25 Keller and Shiue (2007), Will (1990, 294ff).

26 Ball (2017, 115ff).

27 Rowe (1989).

28 Huang (1990).

29 Jones (1988).

30 See various contributions in Zelin et al. (2004).

31 Hase (2013).

32 Classical contributions to traditional Chinese law are Chen and Myers (1976) and Chen and Myers (1978). The comparison with Western development is made in Huang (2019).

33 Glahn (1996). Goetzmann (2017, 137ff) highlights the differences between the Chinese and the European monetary systems.

34 The watershed event was the Han dynasty Discourse on Salt and Iron, a very important event in the global history of economics (Zanasi, 2020, 24ff).

35 Naquin and Rawski (1987, 114ff).

36 Zelin (2004).

37 Mann (1987).

38 Twitchett (1979).

39 Zanasi (2020, 24ff).

40 Zanasi (2020, 109ff).

41 Brandt et al. (2014).

42 A very influential contribution is Pomeranz (2000). For an alternative view, see Brandt et al. (2014).
43 Allen (2009).
44 Herrmann-Pillath (2016).
45 Zelin (2009).
46 On this and the next point, see Goetzmann (2017, 194ff).
47 Ferguson (2008).
48 Brandt et al. (2014).

References

Allen, R. C. (2009) *The British Industrial Revolution in Global Perspective*. Cambridge: Cambridge University Press. DOI: 10.1017/CBO9780511816680.

Ball, P. (2017) *The Water Kingdom: A Secret History of China*. Chicago: The University of Chicago Press. DOI: 10.7208/9780226470924.

Brandt, L., Ma, D. and Rawski, T. G. (2014) 'From Divergence to Convergence: Reevaluating the History Behind China's Economic Boom', *Journal of Economic Literature*, 52(1), pp. 45–123. DOI: 10.1257/jel.52.1.45.

Chao, K. (1986) *Man and Land in China: An Economic Analysis*. Stanford: Stanford University Press.

Chen, C.-C., Chen, X.-P. and Huang, S. (2013) 'Chinese guanxi: An Integrative Review and New Directions for Future Research', *Management and Organization Review*, 9(1), pp. 167–207. DOI: 10.1111/more.12010.

Chen, F.-M. C. and Myers, R. (1976) 'Customary Law and the Economic Growth of China During the Ch'ing Period, Part I', *Ch'ing-shih Wen-t'i*, 3(5), pp. 1–32.

Chen, F.-M. C. and Myers, R. (1978) 'Customary Law and the Economic Growth of China During the Ch'ing Period, Part II', *Ch'ing-shih Wen-t'i*, 3(10), pp. 4–27.

Chin, T. T. (2014) *Savage Exchange: Han Imperialism, Chinese Literary Style, and the Economic Imagination*. Cambridge: Harvard University Asia Center. DOI: 10.1163/9781684170784.

Fei, X. (1939) *Peasant Life in China: A Field Study of Country Life in the Yangtze Valley*. London and Henley: Routledge and Kegan Paul.

Ferguson, N. (2008) *The Ascent of Money: A Financial History of the World*. London: Penguin Books.

Fukuyama, F. (1992) *The End of History and the Last Man*. New York: Free Press.

Gates, H. (1997) *China's Motor: A Thousand Years of Petty Capitalism*. Ithaca and London: Cornell University Press. DOI: 10.7591/9781501721618.

Glahn, R. von (1996) *Fountains of Fortune. Money and Monetary Policy in China, 1000–1700*. Berkeley: University of California Press. DOI: 10.1525/9780520917453.

Glahn, R. von (2016) *The Economic History of China: From Antiquity to the Nineteenth Century*. Cambridge: Cambridge University Press. DOI: 10.1017/CBO9781139343848.

Goetzmann, W. N. (2017) *Money Changes Everything: How Finance Made Civilization Possible*. Princeton: Princeton University Press. DOI: 10.2307/j. ctvc77dzg.

Hase, P. (2013) *Custom, Land and Livelihood in Rural South China: The Traditional Land Law of Hong Kong's New Territories, 1750–1950*. Hong Kong: Hong Kong University Press. DOI: 10.5790/hongkong/9789888139088.001.0001.

Herrmann-Pillath, C. (2016) 'Constitutive Explanations as a Methodological Framework for Integrating Thermodynamics and Economics', *Entropy*, 18(1), 18. DOI: 10.3390/e18010018.

Hodges, R. (1989) *Dark Age Economics: Origins of Towns and Trade, A.D. 600–1000*. London: Bloomsbury Academic.

Huang, P. C. C. (1990) *The Peasant Family and Rural Development in the Yangzi Delta, 1350–1988*. Stanford: Stanford University Press.

Huang, P. C. C. (2019) 'Rethinking "the Third Sphere": The Dualistic Unity of State and Society in China, Past and Present', *Modern China*, 45(4), pp. 355–391. DOI: 10.1177/0097700419844962.

Jones, E. (1988) *Growth Recurring*. Oxford: Oxford University Press.

Jones, E. (2003) *The European Miracle: Environments, Economies and Geopolitics in the History of Europe and Asia*. 3rd Edition. Cambridge: Cambridge University Press. DOI: 10.1017/CBO9780511817700.

Keller, W. and Shiue, C. H. (2007) 'Markets in China and Europe on the Eve of the Industrial Revolution', *American Economic Review*, 97(4), pp. 1189–1216. DOI: 10.1257/aer.97.4.1189.

Lu, H. (2010) 'Small-Town China: A Historical Perspective on Rural-Urban Relations', in Whyte, M. K. (ed.) *One Country, Two Societies: Rural-Urban Inequality in Contemporary China*. Cambridge: Cambridge University Press, pp. 29–54. DOI: 10.2307/j.ctt1sq5t74.5.

Lucassen, J. (2021) *The Story of Work: A New History of Mankind*. New Haven and London: Yale University Press. DOI: 10.12987/9780300262995.

Mann, S. (1987) *Local Merchants and the Chinese Bureaucracy, 1750–1950*. Stanford: Stanford University Press.

Mokyr, J. (2017) *A Culture of Growth: The Origins of Modern Economy*. Princeton: Princeton University Press. DOI: 10.1515/9781400882915.

Naquin, S. and Rawski, E. (1987) *Chinese Society in the Eighteenth Century*. New Haven and London: Yale University Press.

North, D. C. (1990) *Institutions, Institutional Change, and Economic Performance*. Cambridge: Cambridge University Press. DOI: 10.1017/cbo9780511808678.

Plumpe, W. (2019) *Das kalte Herz: Kapitalismus: Die Geschichte einer andauernden Revolution*. Berlin: Rowohlt.

Pomeranz, K. (2000) *The Great Divergence: China, Europe and the Making of the Modern World Economy*. Princeton: Princeton University Press. DOI: 10.1515/9781400823499.

Rowe, W. T. (1989) *Hankow: Conflict and Community in a Chinese City, 1796–1895*. Stanford: Stanford University Press.

Siu, H. F. (1989) *Agents and Victims in South China: Accomplices of Rural Revolution.* New Haven and London: Yale University Press. DOI: 10.2307/j. ctt2250x73.

Skinner, G. W. (1964/1965) 'Marketing and Social Structure in Rural China, Parts I-III', *The Journal of Asian Studies*, 24(1), pp. 3–43; 24(2), pp. 195–228; 24(3), pp. 363–399.

Skinner, G. W. (1985) 'The Structure of Chinese History', *The Journal of Asian Studies*, 44(2), pp. 271–292.

Sugden, R. (2018) *The Community of Advantage: A Behavioural Economist's Defence of the Market.* Oxford: Oxford University Press. DOI: 10.1093/ oso/9780198825142.001.000.

Twitchett, D. (1979) 'Introduction', in Twitchett, D. (ed.) *The Cambridge History of China, Volume 3, Sui and T'ang China, 589–906, Part I.* Cambridge: Cambridge University Press, pp. 1–47. DOI: 10.1017/CHOL9780521214469.

Will, P.-E. (1990) *Bureaucracy and Famine in Eighteenth-Century China.* Stanford: Stanford University Press.

Zanasi, M. (2020) *Economic Thought in Modern China: Market and Consumption, c.1500–1937.* Cambridge: Cambridge University Press. DOI: 10.1017/ 9781108752787.

Zelin, M. (2004) 'Economic Freedom in Late Imperial China', in Kirby, W. C. (ed.) *Realms of Freedom in Modern China.* Stanford: Stanford University Press, pp. 57–83.

Zelin, M. (2009) 'The Firm in Early Modern China', *Journal of Economic Behavior & Organization*, 71(3), pp. 623–637. DOI: 10.1016/j.jebo.2009.03.002.

Zelin, M., Ocko, J. K. and Gardella, R. (eds.) (2004) *Contract and Property in Early Modern China.* Stanford: Stanford University Press, pp. 178–208.

CHAPTER TWO

Economics as the science of markets

1. Introduction

We define economics by markets as its object domain, by its character as a performative science, and by recognising the materiality of markets.

In this chapter, we introduce economics as a scientific discipline. Our approach differs from established views in economics in three ways:

First, we define economics by its object and not by its method. This object is markets: complex, open evolutionary systems that emerged in early stages of human civilisation and have become the core of modern economic systems.[1]

Second, we approach economics as a performative science, and we put performative mechanisms at the centre of analysing markets. This means that economics is co-creating the object of its study. The important implication is that we cannot do economics without critically reflecting its role in shaping markets as a fundamental research practice and theoretical stance.[2]

For example, our theory of economic growth expounded in Chapter 16 differs radically from established economics in highlighting materiality.

Third, we approach markets as material phenomena, involving people and things in patterns of actions that create the economy as we observe it. Materiality implies that we adopt an integrative cross-disciplinary perspective matching our object-oriented approach. This elevates certain sub-disciplinary developments, such as in behavioural economics or ecological economics, to a paradigmatic position.[3]

The chapter proceeds as follows. In section 1, we develop our basic approach to economics as a science, starting out from a distinction of first-, second-, and third-person views on the world. Section 2 presents our guiding idea, which is to approach markets as complex real-world phenomena that form the core of the economy as the subsystem of human society in which production, allocation, and consumption of goods and services take place. We show, however, that this cannot be simply approached from an objective third-person view but requires continuous epistemic interaction between the three views, classically distinguished in the two epistemic

DOI: 10.4324/9781003094869-4

modes of understanding (*Verstehen*) and explaining (*Erklären*). The core principle that defines the relationship of the modes is performativity. Section 3 draws conclusions for economic method: We posit that economic explanations are mechanistic explanations in the sense of identifying real-world mechanisms that generate economic phenomena. Section 4 discusses the role of cross-disciplinary relations in generating knowledge about markets, and section 5 focuses on the role of reflexivity in economics as a performative science.

2. What is science? The first-, second-, and third-person view

Economics emerged as a science in the Age of Enlightenment, which launched the project of establishing an autonomous domain of objective knowledge that would not be subject to interventions by any authorities, be it political, religious, or public opinion.[4] Since Adam Smith, this has motivated economists to rely on scientific methods for achieving an objective view of how economic systems operate, claiming an Archimedean point from which we can improve economic conditions by means of better decision making.

Science strives to achieve an objective view of the world.

However, the meaning of 'science' entails a wide variety across scientific disciplines in terms of methods and fields of inquiry. There is no king's way to objective knowledge, although there is the view that the natural sciences excel in this endeavour whereas the humanities struggle with getting hold of the rich domains of human subjectivity.[5] The complexity and diversity of real-world economies and their actors would suggest that economics cannot be reduced to one methodological paradigm. Nevertheless, since the mid-20th century, economics has mostly pursued the goal of mathematisation and quantification in order to achieve causal explanations, thus following the example of the natural sciences. In contrast, for example, the historical sciences also pursue causal explanations, but they often cannot only rely on quantitative data: In order to understand the events that lead towards World War II, it is certainly of great significance to understand Adolf Hitler's biography. The difference between these approaches has been classically defined in terms of the distinction between explaining and understanding: Explaining aims at regular, even law-like, recurrent occurrences of causal chains, whereas understanding aims at grasping the unique features of individual phenomena, reaching from individual personalities to cultural patterns shared by communities and societies. However, the latter does not preclude causal explanations, as is evident from the historical sciences.[6]

Scientific disciplines differ in methods and topics.

Explaining (Erklären) and understanding (Verstehen) are both forms of causal explanations.

*The first-person view
is the subjective view
of the individual,
the second-person
view is the shared
view of at least two
individuals, and the
third-person view is
the view of external
observers.*

We cut a complex philosophical and methodological debate short by introducing three points of view: the first-, second-, and third-person view (Figure 2.1).[7]

- The first-person view is the domain of subjectivity. For example, feelings are inherently subjective. Standard economics recognises the subjective domain in terms of the key notions of subjective value and utility.
- The second-person view is the view shared with others, resulting from interaction/transaction, communication, and mutual observation. In economics, an example is the perceptions and opinions that drive behaviour on stock markets. Market prices entail an objectified second-person view insofar as they reflect shared quantitative valuations of products subject to market transactions.
- The third-person view is the view that can be shared by any actor, especially including external observers, which establishes universal

The distinction
of views is a
leitmotif in this
book, such as
when considering
externalities
and institutions
(Chapter 5,
section 4),
needs and wants
(Chapter 7,
section 5.2),
market prices
and valuations
(Chapter 10,
section 2.2), and
the notion of
borders in the
global economy
(Chapter 14,
section 2.2.)

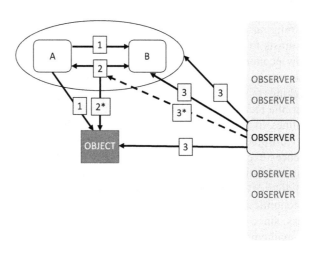

Figure 2.1 The three views on reality

1 The first-person view (1) is A's subjective view on an object or another person, such as a feeling which can be verbalised.
2 In communicating with B and reaching an intersubjective understanding, the second-person view (2) is established. The second-person view (2*) establishes a shared reference to an object.
3 The external observer establishes the third-person view (3) commensurable across any other observer. This can include reference to objects (as in physics), individuals (as in medicine), or the symbolic media in which the second-person view is established (as in linguistics). A special form is (3*) where the observers approach a second-person view as the means to establish the third-person view, as in treating market prices as reflecting objective scarcity (see Figure 2.2).

commensurability of knowledge.[8] In economics, for example, the third-person view is pursued by neuroeconomists who claim to show that subjective values can be measured by patterns of neuronal activity that are observable in the brain scanner.

Science in the conventional sense is often equated with the third-person view. However, we must draw a clear distinction between the third-person view as the only source of objective knowledge and a third-person view that would explicitly recognise the other views in terms of causal explanations. Take, for example, the measurement of economic well-being and welfare, which for a long time mainly relied on GDP per capita: This is a second-person view because it relies on market valuations as a measure of well-being, thus excluding many other factors such as non-market housework. The third-person view is salient in creating alternative indicators, such as the Human Development Index, which directly captures externally measurable features of well-being such as life expectation.[9] In the past decades, though, another approach emerged – the so-called happiness studies, which often directly refer to the subjective feeling of being happy and, hence, entail a first-person view.[10]

The third-person view can recognise first- and second-person view phenomena as causal factors.

Taking all views as possible sources of information and data in economics directly implies methodological pluralism, however, without sacrificing the goal of achieving objective knowledge. Economic knowledge results from the systematic triangulation of the three views.

The triangulation of the three views implies methodological pluralism.

3. Economics, the economy, and markets

3.1. The economy as an object of science

Among the many definitions of 'economics', the most influential was given by Lionel Robbins: "Economics is the science which studies human behaviour as a relationship between ends and scarce means which have alternative uses".[11] This methods-based definition has led economics to vastly expand its domain; for example, to politics and religion. However, economic imperialism[12] has met with fierce criticism by the other disciplines which it invaded.

The methods-based definition of 'economics' has led it to vastly expand its domain.

One solution to these cross-disciplinary tensions is a definition of 'economics' not via its method but via its object. Economics, then, would be conceived as the study of the economy. Yet what is the economy? A relatively intuitive and broad definition could be the following: The economy is a subsystem of human society where resources are spent on production and the allocation of goods, including final consumption. Relating this potential definition to the distinction between the three different points of view, we note that it adopts the third-person view right from the outset: The economy would be a given object of scientific inquiry, just as physics studies stars in space.

*There is a long
tradition in
economics, from
Marx to modern
neoclassical
economics, in
claiming to discover
the true economic
motives and causes
behind what
individuals believe
to be social reality.*

But can we actually approach the economy as a set of facts like the facts that the sciences deal with?

As an example, consider a religious organisation that invests into building a temple. Is this part of the economy? The problem is that there is no human activity that does not involve the use of resources in some way, if only in terms of spending limited time, which in turn would subsume all human activity under the domain of the economy. The question then is whether, if religious believers tell us that they are expressing their beliefs without economic meaning, economists are legitimised in disregarding this view and analyse their activities by employing economic theories.[13] Do we have objective standards for identifying the economy at specific places and times, or do we need to refer to what the involved actors perceive to be the economy and explicitly define as economic motives and actions? Is the second-person view dispensable for economics, or even worse, would it block the discovery of objective knowledge about the economy (Marx's concept of fetishism)? If we do have objective standards, then economists may even be able to show that actors do not fully recognise the true extent and scope of the economy in their specific contexts, whereas economics allows for a third-person view.[14]

*The alternative
view, as pursued
in anthropology,
regards the economy
as a cultural
construct.*

The possibility of a third-person view on economics is rejected by disciplines such as anthropology, which regard the economy as a cultural construct and demand that economics as a science must reflect this cultural contextualisation.[15] The religious believer would vehemently deny being driven by economic motives and might even take explicit measures against the intrusion of economic forces into everyday life, such as the prohibition of interest in Islam. Against this, the economist would point towards the fact that economic practices are constantly eroding such religious stances, revealing a supposedly objective nature of the economy as opposed to the domains of value and beliefs. She could also unveil the true function of a certain practice that purportedly observes non-economic values, such as by showing that certain arrangements in Islamic finance effectively constitute interest.[16]

*Lionel Robbins's
famous definition
of 'economics'
effectively
establishes an
interpretive stance
of understanding.*

How can this conundrum be solved? One solution seems to lie in a restriction of economics to the economic aspects of human activities, such as those involved in building a temple. Yet this cannot resolve the issue of separating analytically between various motivations and judging their relative weight. Rather, it would mean that adopting the economic view is an interpretive stance in the first place and not necessarily an explanatory stance. Indeed, this can be derived from Robbins's definition: The 'as' can be conceived as interpretive stance, which can stand side by side with other interpretive stances, such as considering religious motivations in building the temple. As an implication, the economy would be subject to various interpretive approaches, thus appearing as the proverbial elephant touched by several blind people at different parts. Just like sociologists, anthropologists, and representatives of other disciplines, economists would find themselves among those people without being able to claim any privileged status.

Another approach is to define the 'economic' primarily in terms of market behaviour. That is the stance of most of modern economics, which tends to approach all phenomena outside this domain either as a black box (exogenous) or by applying the same theoretical principles as in the case of market behaviour. The problem with this view is that throughout human history, the relation between the economy and markets was organised in very different ways, depending on which perspectives assumed intellectual and political hegemony. Often, the political system dominated the economy, such as in European feudalism where the rights of the noble warrior class determined the structure of agriculture. Yet the rise of markets also resulted in the emergence of new forms of social organisation in the medieval cities. The dominance of planned economies in Eastern Europe from the 1950s gave way to a strong market orientation from the 1990s, until today.

3.2. Performativity and materiality of markets

Against this background, we propose a definition of economics as the science of markets, relying on two key concepts, namely the performativity of economic science and the materiality of markets.

Performativity is a notion that is essentially tied to the second-person view and refers to the creation of social facts via the mutual recognition of performative acts. A prime example in the economic domain is the creation of fiat money, which becomes real only via the mutual beliefs and affirming actions of the users of money. Is money a fact in the third-person view, too? This is only the case once the second-person view is taken for granted and then proceeding to, say, which changes in the quantity of money affect the economy.

An implication of performativity, as eventually introduced to the sociology of economics,[17] is that economics as a science and the economy as its object stand in a co-evolutionary relationship, with economics co-creating what is deemed economic and the economy. A key example is accounting: Accounting is conceived as a crucial invention supporting the rise of capitalism and is performative in the sense that it creates economic values which can become the objects of economic action.[18] Accounting creates economic objects that do not exist in nature and transforms economic action according to templates that inhere market action, such as the use of prices to organise entrepreneurial decisions and the internal structure of corporations. More generally, this aligns with the role of economics in the history of Western modernisation, where it supported functional differentiation and the growing autonomy of social domains (called value spheres by Max Weber).[19]

The most important performative function of economics is its contribution to the creation of markets, following or accompanying the epistemic recognition of markets as real-world phenomena. This happened, for example, in China during the decline of the feudal order in pre-imperial times or when Spanish Jesuits discovered the law of one price. Existing social relations and

In Chapter 8, we approach money as the archetypical performative phenomenon in economics. Chapter 13 discusses the role of money and credit in generating economic fluctuations.

Performativity in economics refers to the phenomenon that economics co-creates the economy as the object that it claims to explore from a third-person view.

On the case of China, see Chapter 1.

31

*Marketisation
proceeds via the
diffusion of market
templates in society
or via explicit design
by economics.*

*Economics,
in particular,
neoclassical
economics, often
treats the second-
person view
of markets as
mediating the
third-person view.*

On mark-to-
market pricing,
see Chapter 10,
section 4.2.

interactions can be marketised, which is a specific form of economisation, that is, firstly, conceiving of certain actions as being part of the economy and not of other social domains (such as religion, as in our previous example of church building), and secondly, moving into the institutional sphere of markets and interactions mediated by money.[20] Marketisation can also happen by explicit design; today, economists are directly engaged in designing new markets, such as the markets for emission rights in climate policies.[21]

Because of this performative dimension, economics cannot be a purely explanatory science like the natural sciences, which mostly assume a clear line of demarcation between epistemic subject and real-world object.[22] Most of established economic reasoning obscures this by treating the second-person perspective as objective in the sense of assuming that markets generate information which adequately reflects the true status of the world (Figure 2.2). The practical consequences are significant; for example, new accounting standards enforce the valuation of assets according to market prices, assuming that these prices approximate the true value.[23]

At the same time, economics tends to neglect the objective dimension of markets in a third-person view; for example, in the sense of material properties of goods, energetic aspects of production, and technical aspects of transactions. As we showed in the previous chapter, markets are a social technology in which behavioural patterns and ways of thinking are deeply enmeshed with material artefacts that create the capacity for economic transactions. This is in line with recent developments in economic sociology which promoted a material turn in research on markets.[24]

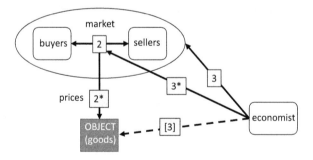

Figure 2.2 Market prices as third-person view in economics
Economists often assume (such as in financial economics) that they have no direct access to objective knowledge about their object (economic value of goods) (3). They assume that the market generates this knowledge via competition among and between buyers and sellers (2), hence establishing an objectified second-person view (2*) as the economist's third-person view (3*). The medium is market prices.

Materiality is essential to define economics as a science. A market is an object, just as the local markets in old China or the digital market established by eBay. Markets include different kinds of real actors, not only human individuals with bodies but also organisations such as a company with a physical location and operating physical processes such as production or computer algorithms in financial markets implemented via digital infrastructure. In contrast, established economics defines markets as theoretical entities in line with certain axiomatic mathematical principles and via sophisticated methods of modelling and empirical testing that are then projected on real-world markets. This direction of analytical moves is reversed by starting out from markets as real-world phenomena.

We approach markets as real-world phenomena constituted by human agents, technologies of transaction, organisations, and embedding environments.

This view implies, again, that economics must be methodologically diverse. Markets are not isolated entities; for example, they include individuals as actors. Thus, if we want to explain market phenomena, we must include knowledge about humans.[25] This knowledge is not economics but knowledge gained in other fields such as psychology, biology, or sociology. In other words, although economics is the specialist science dealing with markets, it is fundamentally cross-disciplinary in terms of its methods.

Economics is a cross-disciplinary enterprise with core analytical principles grounded in the investigation of markets as its main object.

Economics as a discipline is, thus, clearly placed on the larger canvas of the social and the human sciences; a scientific division of labour is established. But there are also consequences for the internal organisation of economics: Traditionally, economists tend to approach markets as generic phenomena, described and analysed in one basic model which is then adapted to various specific markets, such as the financial market or international trade. In contrast, the material view of markets implies the need to describe and analyse specific structures of different markets: For example, financial markets need to be understood on their own terms and analytically distinguished from global commodities markets. In methodological terms, economics must rest on theories of medium range, renouncing universal claims such as posited in general equilibrium theory.[26]

Economic theories are of medium range, without universalistic claims such as advanced by general equilibrium theory.

4. Economic models as mechanistic explanations

In this section, we develop a methodological standard which defines a third-person view on markets without essentialising the second-person view of markets as generators of objectivity. The great challenge that we meet in this endeavour is the overwhelming complexity of markets and market systems. This applies in three senses:

Chapter 11 is devoted to detailing this picture.

* The first sense is internal complexity. Markets are constituted by millions of agents of different types, they follow complicated rules of operation,

and they generate complex evolutionary processes, such as the trajectory of innovation in the internet business.

*Markets are
hypercomplex
evolving open
systems that
endogenously create
novelty.*

- The second sense is that markets are open systems. This means that markets connect with all other domains in human societies, with the biosphere in general, and even with geography and climate. There is continuous and intensive interaction across the boundaries of market systems; therefore, causal explanations always need to include both internal and external factors.

- The third sense is that markets generate endogenous novelty. This means, for example, that markets create new goods and services: This is grasped by the idea that markets and entrepreneurship go along with each other. Technically speaking, an open system manifests a space of possible states that is continuously expanding and changing its internal structure. By implication, this creates uncertainty about future states, as these are never predictable.

*The mechanistic
approach in
philosophy of
science distinguishes
the life sciences
from physics as
a methodological
benchmark for
designing theories.
Mechanisms
generate causal
phenomena in a
specific organisation
of conditions and
structures.*

Those elements confirm the conclusion that we reached at the end of the previous section: There is no way to create a grand theory of markets that would enable us to explain economic phenomena in a similar way as applying physics to predict positions of planets in the solar system; instead, a medium-range approach is needed. We concretise this by advocating a different approach to theorising which has recently been gaining ground in the philosophy of science, the life sciences and in social sciences, namely the so-called mechanistic approach.[27] In this approach, the focus is on mechanisms, that is, real-world structures that produce certain phenomena via sequences of causal effects. Thus, we strictly stick to the principle of causal explanation but drastically downsize our claims about the reach of our theories to limited domains in time and space.

Mechanisms are
ubiquitous in
this book, such
as imitation as
a psychological
mechanism
(Chapter 7,
section 5.1)
which can be
used in explaining
phenomena such
as financial crises
(Chapter 13,
sections 4.2
and 5.2).

Mechanistic approaches so far have mainly been used in two fields: the life sciences, specifically the neurosciences,[28] and analytical sociology.[29] In the philosophy of science, the approach is often referred to as constitutive explanations.[30] The standard model of causal explanation aims at subsuming causal processes under universal laws (often dubbed the covering law approach or deductive-nomological model). In contrast, constitutive explanations study generating mechanisms. The first step is to understand the constitution of a mechanism, that is, its structure and composition, its boundaries, and so on. All these constituents jointly and simultaneously determine the unfolding of a causal process. Therefore, the main research challenge often is to identify the mechanism and describe it accurately, that is, understand how it works.

As in the neurosciences, a mechanistic methodology in economics would mean that a certain phenomenon is clearly identified and described, such as – to take an example common to both disciplines – addiction to gambling.[31] Once this is done, the search for a generating mechanism starts. This would not, as usual in economics, start out from certain general hypotheses of rationality[32] but follow the track of the neurosciences and psychology in the first place, where concrete mechanisms that result in the craving for gambling are identified. Research in these disciplines has shown that the mechanisms are by no means only limited to inner somatic and mental states of the individual but that there is also a strong impact of social context, such as peer behaviour, social norms, and institutions.[33] This is where the economic perspective comes into play, given that behaviour is also driven by economic factors such as pricing schemes in gambling and the institutional organisation of the market for gambling. Therefore, the mechanisms will certainly turn out to be an assemblage of constituents and determinants on many different levels and both internal and external to the individual. Finally, when economists focus on the market for gambling, they are less interested in the individual determinants than the behavioural patterns on the population level, thus heavily invoking statistical methods.

Addiction to gambling is explained via various causal mechanisms on different levels, reaching from neurophysiology to social context. Economics highlights population-level phenomena and the context and impact of markets.

Progress of economic science has always been driven by the discovery and exploration of mechanisms which are, at least to a certain degree, generalisable. The most influential example is the price mechanism which states that if the supply of a good increases, prices will drop, all other things equal. Obviously, the Achilles heel of this is the ceteris paribus condition, which rarely applies in open systems. Yet the mechanism as such is highly plausible on theoretical grounds, and we often can explain observed price movements by relying on it. However, in philosophy of science, the standard depiction of this mechanism would only count as mechanism sketch because it entirely lacks specification in terms of its materiality.[34] For example, it would await specification in terms of its functioning on concrete markets, such as cotton exchanges.[35]

For a discussion of price mechanisms, see Chapter 10, sections 2.2 and 4.2.

Therefore, we should never confuse the theoretical mechanism with the real mechanism. The intermediating element is the model.[36] The mechanism view suggests a different interpretation of this central element of economic methodology. A general mechanism sketch stands at the centre of a model, which is further enriched by including abstract descriptions of its context, such as other intervening variables and exogenous parameters which demarcate the boundary of the mechanism. The model is intended to relate to the real-world mechanism, without however being a description. Yet even an enriched model of this kind often fails to be empirically fully adequate. However, this failure is only apparent and reflects misplaced methodological standards.[37] In an open system, we cannot expect to achieve degrees of exactness which allow for point-predictions of phenomena. Therefore, we need a

Economic hypotheses such as the law of demand are mere mechanism sketches which must be specified in terms of material structures of generating mechanisms.

*Models are
simulations of real
economic processes,
empirically validated
via the match between
patterns generated
by models and those
observable in the real
economy. Models
identify causal forces
as propensities of
patterns.*

Examples for
generalised
forces are wants
and needs as
drivers of action
(Chapter 6,
section 2.2,
and Chapter 7,
section 5.2) or
spatial gradients
relative to agent
capabilities to
trade shaping
the location
of production
(Chapter 14).

*Models must be
systematised in
an empirically
grounded taxonomy
of mechanisms.*

We distinguish
types of
financial agents
in Chapter 12,
section 3.1.

device of epistemological parsimony, which is the model. A model is not at all a description of reality:

- First, an economic model can be compared to a toy model of a complex engineering device. In this sense, a model is a mechanism that simulates the real-world mechanism without implying that the real mechanism works in the same way in all details. Since the real economy is hyper-complex, we can never expect to build exact one-to-one models even of partial aspects. What we can achieve is to construct models which generate patterns that correspond to the real-world patterns in essential respects.[38]

- Second, however, there are also realistic claims generated by the models. As long as the model does not become performative (see section 6), it does not have any ontological status (meaning, being real in some sense). But if we can match patterns between model and reality, we go one step further and posit structural similarities between model and reality that identify forces which, in turn, drive the emergence of patterns.[39] It is those forces that assume the role of central theoretical propositions in economics which claim to be empirically meaningful. Models identify mechanisms that generate forces which result in observable patterns. So if we observe a glut of investment on the real estate markets, we think that this generates a force that will drive housing prices down. How that force precisely operates must be submitted to further empirical scrutiny. Forces are propensities, that is, they never realise deterministically. Markets as open systems are stochastic in a deep and comprehensive sense. Accordingly, one of the essential empirical methods in economics is econometrics.

Combining the notion of model and mechanism in this way, we immediately realise that many, if not most, models of economics today do not fit the bill. Models must closely relate to an empirical taxonomy of mechanisms and, hence, would be akin to an ideal-typical description of a species in biology. Take, for example, the analysis of individual behaviour. Conventionally, economics adopts a generic concept of individual as rational agent. In contrast, a mechanistic approach requires the construction of a typology or taxonomy of individuals. For example, the addict would not be subsumed under the generic model of rational agent but as a type of its own, defined by certain mechanistic features. In other words, a taxonomy of agents in economics would distinguish between various types of agents with certain generic roles in the economy, such as the type of financial professional or the type of adolescent consumer. For achieving such a taxonomy, cross-disciplinary research is a necessary element in economics, as we already learned from our example of addiction.

5. Economic models triangulate cross-disciplinary data and hypotheses

Conventionally, economists think of models as mathematical models. Undoubtedly, mathematical models have the advantage of fixing causal relationships unequivocally and allowing for a tracing of all possible consequences of the assumptions underlying the model. Nevertheless, we posit that models can be of various types and include various kinds of conceptual and qualitative models as well. Famous examples of conceptual models are taxonomies of economic systems, such as the distinction between varieties of capitalism in political science and sociology, which is mostly sidelined in economics.[40] These conceptual models approach economic systems in terms of institutional details, such as the organisation of the labour market or of the financial system, and venture hypotheses about developmental patterns. Models of this type are often cross-disciplinary constructs. For example, economists often assume that the market economy builds on individualism as a universal human feature. However, anthropological and sociological research shows that individualism is a complex cultural phenomenon, and research on human values has revealed a wide diversity of attitudes and resulting behavioural patterns.[41]

Economic models include both mathematical-quantitative models and all kinds of qualitative models, such as conceptual or structural models.

Our approach to culture is developed in Chapter 8, section 3.3.

In this respect, the mechanism approach can avoid a fundamental issue in economic method that has been jokingly referred to as the drunken man who searches his lost key where the light is, while ignoring where he might possibly have lost it in the darkness. As long as economic models are exclusively defined in terms of quantitative and mathematical methods, economists cannot do without data that are quantifiable. But this is a risky research strategy, as economists often employ very sophisticated and sensitive econometric techniques on databases that are highly questionable.[42] This problem includes data that comes from the economic domain. For example, in analysing international trade, economists for decades could only rely on data provided by the customs administration; only very recently, quantitative research has moved forward to unearthing the underlying pattern of value-added trade, that is, trade with embodied services and other inputs in value chains involving intermediary steps of production distributed across several countries. In cases like trade relations between

Quantitative data biases explanatory strategies to building models that can be grounded in available data, sidelining explanations that involve other types of observations.

For more detail on value-added trade, see Chapter 14, sections 2.1 and 4.3.

the US and China, this affects macroeconomic data such as the trade balance in a substantial way.[43]

Accordingly, moving the frontier in data construction and collection has become a major part of economic research. A mechanistic view would take a much broader approach: What counts essentially as well is the identification of structures and contextual determinants of phenomena that are not easily amenable to quantification or might even be impossible to quantify. This directly relates to a core field of economic research, the study of institutions. We approach institutions as mechanisms creating forces that generate behavioural patterns and, ultimately, economic phenomena. This does not mean that institutions cannot be analysed by quantitative methods, but these methods always have to go hand in hand with qualitative analysis. These observations can be summarised in terms of model building by triangulation: Economists systematically combine insights from various disciplines in constructing models, without, however, aspiring to unify these in one grand theory.

Defining and operationalising what are 'data' is a major methodological concern in economics.

On institutions, see Chapter 9.

This approach includes archetypical topics of economics. The supply and demand mechanism normally assumes that demand decreases if prices go up. However, sometimes, this might not work out in the real world: An example is the exploding demand for expensive French red wine in China over the past two decades, with wide-ranging implications for French wineries and luxury business. Does this falsify the hypothesis? No, because it motivates us to look in more detail at the factual mechanism that produces this pattern, starting with a mechanism sketch: We might realise that the good might be a luxury good signalling high social status; once its reputation as a status good is established, producers and sellers may increase prices. But this is a signal further cementing its role as a status good, and therefore, demand might increase because more people crave for buying this good as a status marker.

For example, the law of demand is mechanism sketch that requires substantial modification for the case of status goods, and a model must including sociological and cultural aspects of status.

To summarise, our approach to models differs fundamentally from common approaches in economics, which mostly aim at establishing direct empirical connections between abstract models and real-world phenomena. Most standard models only identify a logic of a situation in principle and often generate a need to show why this logic operates differently in the real world or even fails to materialise.

The social sciences and economics differ from the natural sciences in that the objects of research, human beings, can understand and use the theories in their actions.

6. Economics is entangled with its object: Reflexivity

A fundamental difference between the natural sciences and the social sciences is the presence of reflexivity: The social sciences deal with human agents who can understand scientific theories and may apply them or follow them in other ways, thus changing the very behaviour which is under scientific scrutiny. Theory and action are entangled, implying that there is no independent position for establishing a third-person view. In that sense, the concepts of reflexivity and performativity are closely related, with reflexivity taking the more general perspective: Reflexivity is cognition influenced by theory; performativity is behaviour conditioned and enabled by it. In economics, reflexivity is a particularly serious issue because of its strongly institutionalised role in social engineering, especially with respect to policy advice.[44]

In economics, reflexivity is mainly recognised in the context of the theory of expectations. If they are rational, agent expectations should be informed by the state of the art of economics. Thus, economics will directly influence peoples' behaviour via the way they form expectations. This has been condensed in the famous Lucas critique of macroeconomic models: Economists build macroeconomic models to predict economic development and behaviour, but the prediction and knowledge of the model will directly change the behaviour of the agents and, thereby, make the original prediction irrelevant.[45]

The phenomenon of reflexivity is universal in economics and includes the level of the individual: There are controversial results of economic experiments showing that students of economics become more individualist, rational, and even opportunistic by studying economics.[46] Similar results have even been obtained with reference to professional roles, such as in finance: The same individuals manifest different performances in economic experiments if their professional roles are invoked.[47] This is a crucial theoretical justification of our previous call for creating taxonomies of agents in economics, which would now include even the economist as a type of agent that applies economics on herself.

This does not only apply for economics in the narrow sense but for all kinds of thinking about the economy.[48] A reflective loop between the second- and the third-person view needs to be established which results in the requirement to approach the second-person view as a data source in economic analysis. For example, financial traders are not regarded as people who apply economic theory on markets (quantitative analysts may do so when they design algorithms) but as agents who observe specific behavioural disciplines and maintain certain views on the markets which determine their actions, sometimes explicitly deviating from economics, such as in the approach of chartists.[49] This implies that economists must explicitly refer to the second-person view in order to understand how markets work: For example, they must study the narratives and ideas that people follow in their actions, to which economics is only one contributor. Economists have only recently begun to recognise this, with framing as the key notion.[50] It is essential, and today well established in psychological research, that one central frame is the market: Markets frame cognition in a way to generate behaviour that corresponds to the assumptions of economics. For example, even apparently universal behavioural phenomena such as the endowment effect and loss aversion

Our epilogue in Chapter 18 reflects on economists as advisers.

The Lucas critique of Keynesian macroeconomics recognises the reflexivity of economics.

Reflexivity entails the performative constitution of types of economic agents.

We discuss these phenomena in Chapter 7, section 4.3.

The second-person view needs to be viewed as a data source.

The market is a frame triggering performative actions that may correspond to economic hypotheses about behaviour.

can vanish if the experimental subjects are framed as traders and not as owners of the goods traded.[51]

Consequently, economics as a science must be reflective: Economists need to reflect upon their own role in society, both intentional (economists as advisers) and non-intentional (such as transforming individual values by adopting market frames). This does in no way imply that economics should apply self-censorship, including on results that may stand against a current societal mainstream or zeitgeist. But it means that the idea of the economist standing outside the object she is analysing and, therefore, ultimately bearing no responsibility for the impact of her analyses, needs to be abandoned.

We say more on the necessary neutrality of academic economics in Chapter 3, section 5, and Chapter 18.

Reflexivity implies that the history of economic ideas is an important part of economics.

Our position also implies an increased emphasis on the history of economic ideas in economic analysis.[52] Take, for example, the recent decades of economic liberalisation, deregulation, and privatisation, often dubbed neoliberalism. These policies were strongly influenced by economists and reflected the perceived progress of economic science at that time. However, in hindsight, they contributed to the creation of trends that directly contradict fundamental convictions that most economists uphold, such as the growth of economic nationalism.[53] The question arises whether the original policy advice overlooked something important, namely the embeddedness of the market in society, culture, and politics. The design of markets needs to consider its effects across all domains, and this, in turn, requires cross-disciplinary openness.

7. Conclusion

In this chapter, we defined our understanding of economics as a science. We argued that its scientific nature rests on the pursuit of causal explanations of economic phenomena; however, these cannot follow the physical template of deductive-nomological explanations but need to abide by the mechanistic thinking of the life sciences. This perspective substantially deflates the universalist claims of economics; it favours medium-range theorising and the development of taxonomies of mechanisms that ground in thick descriptions of real-world phenomena.

The language of economics is ordinary language, both as the meta-language of cross-disciplinary triangulation and as the main medium of the reflexivity and performativity of economics.

This has an important consequence for how economic theories should be formulated. We showed that the models economists typically champion are only mechanism sketches, hence, lacking the status of fully fledged theories. A full description of a mechanism will take the form of an ordinary language causal narrative, much closer to causal explanations in the historical sciences.[54] This primacy of ordinary language has also been declared by Alfred Marshall, who relegated mathematical theorising to the status of an auxiliary, albeit indispensable method.[55] What emerged as the preferred method in economics since the 1930s is helpful to clarify precise meanings of concepts or check for hidden implications and for guiding the construction of econometric data analysis, but it cannot be the king's way for formulating economic theories. Two reasons loom large.

The first is that cross-disciplinary triangulation requires a language that is independent from the various specific disciplinary idioms. The most powerful meta-language is ordinary language. Ordinary language can best cope with the complexity and multidimensionality of economic processes and problems.

The second reason is that economics is performative, hence, always must establish a close relationship to the language used by the economic subjects. If economics cuts its direct connection with the second-person view as embodied in the ordinary language of the people acting on markets, there is a growing risk of them misinterpreting economic theories and of theories losing touch with reality, as it happened in the wake of the rational expectations revolution in macroeconomics. In principle, economic theories must be understandable in ordinary language, and, as Alfred Marshall already recommended, translating economic models in ordinary language is one of the most powerful tests of their validity.

Major chapter insights

- We distinguish between the first-, second-, and third-person view: The natural sciences strive to attain the third-person view, whereas the humanities focus on the other two. The social sciences stand in between, with economics often claiming epistemic access to a third-person view established by economic method.
- We define 'economics' in terms of its object domain, namely markets as a fundamental constituent of the economy, where both markets and the economy are conceived in terms of their materiality. Identifying these objects requires the explicit consideration of the second-person view, that is, of how the economic subjects construct and perform markets via their actions and ideas. This includes economics such that economics is a performative science.
- Economic explanations are mechanistical explanations. Economists identify mechanisms that generate certain economic phenomena via a specific organisation of constitutive elements. Mechanisms are described and analysed via models, which can be both quantitative/mathematical and qualitative (e.g., conceptual, structural, or taxonomic).
- Economics recognises reflexivity, that is, the fact that economic agents understand, apply, and respond to economic theories. In extension, how agents reflexively constitute markets by wider ideational constructs is an important type of data in economic analysis.
- Since economics is performative, economists must take responsibility for their research and how it affects real-world phenomena, in particular via the impact on people's behaviour.

Notes

1 Here, we stand in the tradition of Marshall (1920).

2 This view was classically elaborated by Polanyi (2001[1944]).

3 Materiality is a key concern of recent economic sociology; see Callon et al. (2007).

4 On the notion of objectivity, see Daston and Galison (2010).

5 This refers to Snow's famous distinction between the two cultures; Snow (2001[1959]).

6 This was systematically elaborated by the German philosopher Wilhelm Dilthey (Dilthey, 1883). In a classical paper, Stegmüller (1979) has shown that even interpretations of poetry in academic literary studies have a similar logical structure as physical explanations in astronomy.

7 This is familiar from anthropology and the cultural sciences. The third-person view is referred to as 'etics', and adopting the second-person view is referred to as 'emics'; see Headland et al. (1990).

8 Nagel (1989) refers to this as the "view from nowhere". There is a complex debate in philosophy about whether this view is attainable in practice. We can refer to it as aspiration driven by scientific method, as in Popper's (1983) idea of approximating the truth.

9 United Nations Development Programme (2022).

10 Helliwell et al. (2021).

11 Robbins (1934).

12 Radnitzky and Bernholz (1987).

13 There is the field of the 'economics of religion', launched by Iannaccone (1991). For a recent survey, see McCleary and Barro (2019).

14 Levitt and Dubner (2005).

15 Gudeman (1986).

16 For a rich discussion, see Tripp (2006).

17 For a survey, see Boldyrev and Svetlova (2016).

18 Vosselman (2014).

19 Weber (1922, 542ff).

20 Çalışkan and Callon (2009).

21 Roth (2018).

22 However, this is different in fields such as quantum physics, Barad (2007).

23 Perry and Nölke (2006).

24 Callon et al. (2007).

25 Thaler (2016) distinguishes 'ECONS' and 'HUMANS', the latter being in the focus of behavioural economics.

26 On medium-range theories, see Little (1992).

27 Craver and Tabery (2015).

28 Bechtel and Abrahamsen (2005); Craver (2007).

29 Hedström and Ylikoski (2010); Demeulenaere (2011). Elster (2015) is an author close to economics.

30 Harbecke (2014).
31 Ross et al. (2008).
32 The classic paper on the theory of rational addiction is by Becker and Murphy (1988).
33 West (2006).
34 Piccinini and Craver (2011).
35 Çalışkan (2007).
36 Mäki (2009).
37 Hausman (1992).
38 Hayek (1972).
39 Cartwright (1994).
40 Jackson and Deeg (2006).
41 Inglehart (2018).
42 Mayer (1993).
43 WTO (2013, 79).
44 Hirschman and Berman (2014).
45 The Lucas critique is arguably a crucial event in the development of modern macroeconomics, De Vroey (2016, 191ff).
46 Ghoshal (2005); Wang et al. (2011).
47 Cohn et al. (2014).
48 Callon et al. (2007).
49 For an anthropological perspective on trading, see Zaloom (2003) and Zaloom (2004).
50 Shiller (2017) and Shiller (2019).
51 Kahneman (2012).
52 This has been seminally established by Polanyi (2001[1944]).
53 This is counterperformativity in the sense of MacKenzie (2007).
54 For a representative author, see Tilly (1990).
55 See Marshall's much-cited statement in Pigou (1966, 427–428).

References

Barad, K. M. (2007) *Meeting the Universe Halfway: Quantum Physics and the Entanglement of Matter and Meaning*. Durham: Duke University Press.

Bechtel, W. and Abrahamsen, A. (2005) 'Explanation: A Mechanist Alternative', *Studies in History and Philosophy of Biological and Biomedical Sciences*, 36, pp. 421–441. DOI: 10.1016/J.SHPSC.2005.03.010.

Becker, G. S. and Murphy, K. M. (1988) 'A Theory of Rational Addiction', *Journal of Political Economy*, 96(4), pp. 675–700. DOI: 10.1086/261558.

Boldyrev, I. and Svetlova, E. (2016) 'After the Turn: How the Performativity of Economics Matters', in Boldyrev, I. and Svetlova, E. (eds.) *Enacting Dismal Science: New Perspectives on the Performativity of Economics. Perspectives from Social Economics*. London: Palgrave Macmillan, pp. 1–28. DOI: 10.1057/978-1-137-48876-3_1.

Çalışkan, K. (2007) 'Price as a Market Device: Cotton Trading in Izmir Mercantile Exchange', in Callon, M., Millo, Y. and Muniesa, F. (eds.) *Market Devices*. Hoboken: Wiley-Blackwell, pp. 241–261. DOI: 10.1111/J.1467-954X.2007.00738.X.

Çalışkan, K. and Callon, M. (2009) 'Economization, Part 1: Shifting Attention from the Economy Towards Processes of Economization', *Economy and Society*, 38(3), pp. 369–398. DOI: 10.1080/03085140903020580.

Callon, M., Muniesa, F. and Millo, Y. (2007) *Market Devices*. Hoboken: Wiley-Blackwell. DOI: 10.1111/j.1467-954X.2007.00727.x

Cartwright, N. (1994) *Nature's Capacities and their Measurement*. Oxford: Clarendon Press. DOI: 10.2307/2215663

Cohn, A., Fehr, E. and Maréchal, M. A. (2014) 'Business Culture and Dishonesty in the Banking Industry', *Nature*, 516, pp. 86–89. DOI: 10.1038/nature13977.

Craver, C. (2007) *Explaining the Brain: Mechanisms and the Mosaic Unity of the Neurosciences*. Oxford: Oxford University Press.

Craver, C. and Tabery, J. (2015) 'Mechanisms in Science', *The Stanford Encyclopedia of Philosophy*, Summer 2019 Edition. Available at: https://plato.stanford.edu/archives/sum2019/entries/science-mechanisms/ (Accessed: 11 May 2022).

Daston, L. and Galison, P. (2010) *Objectivity*. New York: Zone Books. DOI: 10.2307/j.ctv1c9hq4d

De Vroey, M. (2016) *A History of Macroeconomics from Keynes to Lucas and Beyond*. Cambridge: Cambridge University Press. DOI: 10.1017/cbo9780511843617.

Demeulenaere, P. (2011) *Analytical Sociology and Social Mechanisms*. Cambridge: Cambridge University Press. DOI: 10.1017/CBO9780511921315.

Dilthey, W. (1883) *Einleitung in die Geisteswissenschaften: Versuch einer Grundlegung für das Studium der Gesellschaft und Geschichte*. Leipzig: Duncker & Humblot. DOI: 10.13109/9783666303012

Elster, J. (2015) *Explaining Social Behavior: More Nuts and Bolts for the Social Sciences*. Revised edition. Cambridge: Cambridge University Press.

Ghoshal, S. (2005) 'Bad Management Theories Are Destroying Good Management Practices', *Academy of Management Learning & Education*, 4(1), pp. 75–91. DOI: 10.5465/AMLE.2005.16132558.

Gudeman, S. (1986) *Economics as Culture: Models and Metaphors of Livelihood*. London and Boston: Henley. DOI: 10.2307/2803001

Harbecke, J. (2014) 'The Role of Supervenience and Constitution in Neuroscientific Research', *Synthese*, 191(5), pp. 725–743. DOI: 10.1007/s11229-013-0308-y.

Hausman, D. M. (1992) *The Inexact and Separate Science of Economics*. Cambridge: Cambridge University Press.

Hayek, F. A. (1972) *Die Theorie komplexer Phänomene*. Tübingen: Mohr.

Headland, T. N., Pike, K. L. and Harris, M. (1990) *Emics and Etics: The Insider/Outsider Debate*. Newbury Park: Sage.

Hedström, P. and Ylikoski, P. (2010) 'Causal Mechanisms in the Social Sciences', *Annual Review of Sociology*, 36, pp. 49–67. DOI: 10.1146/ANNUREV.SOC.012809.102632.

Helliwell, J. *et al.* (2021) *World Happiness Report 2021.* Available at: https://happiness-report.s3.amazonaws.com/2021/WHR+21.pdf (Accessed: 17 March 2022).

Hirschman, D. and Berman, E. P. (2014) 'Do Economists Make Policies? On the Political Effects of Economics', *Socio-Economic Review,* 12(4), pp. 779–811. DOI: 10.1093/SER/MWU017.

Iannaccone, L. R. (1991) 'The Consequences of Religious Market Structure: Adam Smith and the Economics of Religion', *Rationality and Society,* 3(2), pp. 156–177. DOI: 10.1177/1043463191003002002.

Inglehart, R. (2018) *Cultural Evolution: People's Motivations Are Changing, and Reshaping the World*. Cambridge: Cambridge University Press. DOI: 10.1093/sf/soz119

Jackson, G. and Deeg, R. (2006) 'How Many Varieties of Capitalism? Comparing the Comparative Institutional Analyses of Capitalist Diversity', *MPIfG Discussion Papers*, 06(2), Köln: Max Planck Institute for the Study of Societies. DOI: 10.2139/ssrn.896384.

Kahneman, D. (2012) *Thinking, Fast and Slow*. London: Penguin Books. DOI: 10.5860/choice.49–5972

Levitt, S. D. and Dubner, S. J. (2005) *Freakonomics: A Rogue Economist Explores the Hidden Side of Everything*. Revised and Expanded Edition. New York: William Morrow. DOI: 10.1111/j.1468-0297.2006.01102_7.x

Little, D. (1992) *Understanding Peasant China. Case Studies in the Philosophy of Social Science*. New Haven and London: Yale University Press. DOI: 10.2307/2163371.

MacKenzie, D. (2007) 'Is Economics Performative? Option Theory and the Construction of Derivatives Market's', in MacKenzie, D., Muniesa, F. and Siu, L. (eds.) *Do Economists Make Markets? On the Performativity of Economics*. Princeton: Princeton University Press, pp. 54–86. DOI: 10.1080/10427710500509722.

Mäki, U. (2009) 'MISSing the World: Models as Isolations and Credible Surrogate Systems', *Erkenntnis,* 70(1), pp. 29–43. DOI: 10.1007/S10670-008-9135-9.

Marshall, A. (2009[1920]) *Principles of Economics; Eighth Edition, Reprint Cosimo Classics 2009*. New York: Cosimo.

Mayer, T. (1993) *Truth versus Precision in Economics*. Cheltenham: Edward Elgar Publishing. DOI: 10.2307/1060161

McCleary, R. M. and Barro, R. J. (2019) *The Wealth of Religions: The Political Economy of Believing and Belonging*. Princeton: Princeton University Press. DOI: 10.1515/9780691185798.

Nagel, T. (1989) *The View from Nowhere*. New York: Oxford University Press.

Perry, J. and Nölke, A. (2006) 'The Political Economy of International Accounting Standards', *Review of International Political Economy*, 13(4), pp. 559–586. DOI: 10.1080/09692290600839790.

Piccinini, G. and Craver, C. (2011) 'Integrating Psychology and Neuroscience: Functional Analyses as Mechanism Sketches', *Synthese*, 183(3), pp. 283–311. DOI: 10.1007/s11229-011-9898-4.

Pigou, A. C. (1966) *Memorials of Alfred Marshall*. New York: A. M. Kelley. DOI: 10.2307/1054226

Polanyi, K. (2001[1944]) *The Great Transformation: The Political and Economic Origins of Our Time*. Boston: Beacon Press.

Radnitzky, G. and Bernholz, P. (1987) *Economic Imperialism. The Economic Approach Applied Outside the Field of Economics*. New York: UNKNO.

Robbins, L. (1934) 'An Essay on the Nature and Significance of Economic Science', *Journal of the Royal Statistical Society*, 97(2), pp. 343–344. DOI: 10.2307/2342397.

Ross, D. *et al.* (2008) *Midbrain Mutiny: The Picoeconomics and Neuroeconomics of Disordered Gambling*. Cambridge: MIT Press. DOI: 10.4309/JGI.2010.24.14.

Roth, A. E. (2018) 'Marketplaces, Markets, and Market Design', *American Economic Review*, 108(7), pp. 1609–1658. DOI: 10.1257/AER.108.7.1609.

Shiller, R. J. (2017) 'Narrative Economics', *American Economic Review*, 107(4), pp. 967–1004. DOI: 10.1257/aer.107.4.967.

Shiller, R. J. (2019) *Narrative Economics: How Stories Go Viral and Drive Major Economic Events*. Princeton: Princeton University Press.

Snow, C. P. (2001[1959]) *The Two Cultures*. London: Cambridge University Press.

Stegmüller, W. (1979) 'Walther von der Vogelweides Lied von der Traumliebe und Quasar 3 C 273. Betrachtungen zum sogenannten Zirkel des Verstehens und zur sogenannten Theorienbeladenheit der Beobachtungen', in Stegmüller, W. (ed.) *Rationale Rekonstruktion von Wissenschaft und ihrem Wandel*. Stuttgart: Reclam.

Thaler, R. H. (2016) 'Behavioral Economics: Past, Present, and Future', *American Economic Review*, 106(7), pp. 1577–1600. DOI: 10.1257/AER.106.7.1577.

Tilly, C. (1990) *Coercion, Capital, and European States, AD 990–1992*. Hoboken: Wiley-Blackwell. DOI: 10.2307/2151823.

Tripp, C. (2006) *Islam and the Moral Economy: The Challenge of Capitalism*. Cambridge and New York: Cambridge University Press. DOI: 10.1017/cbo9780511617614.

United Nations Development Programme (2022) *Human Development Reports*. Available at: https://hdr.undp.org/en/content/human-development-index-hdi (Accessed: 2 March 2022).

Vosselman, E. (2014) 'The 'Performativity Thesis' and Its Critics: Towards a Relational Ontology of Management Accounting', *Accounting and Business Research,* 44(2), pp. 181–203. DOI: 10.1080/00014788.2013.856748.

Wang, L., Malhotra, D. and Murnighan, J. K. (2011) 'Economics Education and Greed', *Academy of Management: Learning Education*, *10*(4), pp. 643–660. DOI: 10.5465/AMLE.2009.0185.

Weber, M. (1922) *Gesammelte Aufsätze zur Religionssoziologie*. Tübingen: Mohr.

West, R. (2006) *Theory of Addiction*. Hoboken: Wiley-Blackwell.

WTO (2013) *World Trade Report 2013: Factors Shaping the Future of World Trade*. Geneva: WTO. Available at: https://www.wto.org/english/res_e/booksp_e/world_trade_report13_e.pdf (Accessed at 17 March 2022).

Zaloom, C. (2003) 'Ambiguous Numbers: Trading Technologies and Interpretation in Financial Markets', *American Ethnologist*, 30(2), pp. 258–272. DOI: 10.1525/AE.2003.30.2.258.

Zaloom, C. (2004) 'The Productive Life of Risk', *Current Anthropology*, 19(3), pp. 365–391. DOI: 10.1525/CAN.2004.19.3.365.

CHAPTER THREE

Economics and values

1. Introduction

In economics as a performative science, there is no contradiction between adopting a value stance and striving to attain a third-person view on the economy.

In this chapter, we explain why the science of economics must explicitly reflect upon values and adopt clear and transparent value stances. These stances would certainly differ among economists and their various research traditions, therefore posing a distinct challenge to the establishment of claims of scientific objectivity that are commensurable even within the research community of economists. We think that this reasoning falsely confronts values and objectivity in the context of economics as a performative science. Performativity implies human freedom in choosing ways on how to perform an economy, with no a priori of what is the best way. This does not mean that we cannot objectively analyse performative mechanisms and markets, in the same way as engineers know how to build a house. But values determine where, when, and how we choose markets as mechanisms of coordinating economic actions. For example, there is no objective criterion on whether we want to allow markets for surrogate motherhood.

If values are an inextricable part of economics, approaching the third-person view means a strive to attain a position of impartiality.

A corollary of this viewpoint is the need to modify our understanding of objectivity. We argue that in a performative science, objectivity is approximated by impartiality.[1] In the first place, impartiality means that one's position is independent from any of the interests involved in a specific situational context, including one's own. Clearly, a third-person view, if attainable, creates a position of impartiality: Take the example of undernourishment and cognitive impairment as a consequence of economic poverty. But how can impartiality be achieved if values, interests, and judgement of the situation remain deeply entangled? The task of this chapter is to present an approach to tackle this quandary.

We come back on these notions in Chapters 17 and 18.

Economists have adopted various stances towards the issue of values. One is to aim at the establishment of sound methodological principles and analytical tools that approximate a third-person view. An example is the recent trend towards evidence-based policy design based on randomised controlled experiments, which often deliberately shuns pre-commitment to

48

DOI: 10.4324/9781003094869-5

established theories in economics.[2] A more radical version of this approach is to focus economics only on those domains where value-free propositions are feasible and to explicitly relegate all other issues to extra-economic disciplines and discourses, such as philosophical ethics or religion. This option is often defended by the argument that economics is about means, not ends: People must define goals as based on their values; economists would inform them about costs and benefits of adopting such goals and efficient ways to attain them.[3]

The contrasting methodological stance is to regard certain values as foundational for economics and at the same time as justifiable and universally agreeable by economic reasoning. As we shall see, an important example is the value of freedom and individual liberty.[4] This may be grounded in ideas on their objective necessity for generating certain results, such as efficiency of economic processes and universal prosperity. But economists may even defend the view that economics *must* be value based. This is often manifest in leading economists-philosophers' stances, most famously Friedrich Hayek.[5] They assert the supremacy of certain values, such as liberty, over other values, such as social justice, and define economics by those values. A softer version of this stance is to accept the diversity of values, which would imply that economics needs to be diverse as well. In this chapter, we endorse the latter view and present arguments why values are an integral part of economic analysis, leaving much leeway in choosing which values we want to adopt and pursue.

In section 2, we discuss the role of freedom as a paramount value in economics, which has been essential in building the theory of choice on the strict assumption of radical subjectivity of preferences, implying that economics refrains from any positive judgement about preferences. Section 3 considers the notion of efficiency, in particular, whether efficiency allows for taking a third-person view in terms of the instrumentalist justification of certain values. Section 4 shows how the results of the previous sections shape the ways economists should approach markets, and section 5 concludes with sketching how economists may safeguard that the economics academia can achieve impartiality of judgement.

2. Freedom, values, and markets

2.1. Freedom of choosing preferences

Since the marginalist turn, economics as a science has tried to separate objective analysis from value propositions. This is done via treating values as preferences.[6] Preferences, in turn, are treated as the domain of subjectivity and freely chosen by individuals. Those choices as such are not subject to further scrutiny: *de gustibus non est disputandum*.[7] The market is regarded as the social domain where these preferences are expressed and translated into

There are various ways in which economics can differentiate between domains of value judgement and of objective claims.

Economics as a performative science recognises the diversity of values.

*Most economists
maintain the
principle of
subjectivity of
preferences as
manifestation of
individual freedom.*

*Allowing for
the autonomous
determination of
preferences is an
achievement of the
Enlightenment, and
freedom of living
one's preferences
often is an issue of
civil rights.*

economic exchange, subject to endowment constraints. The corollary to this is that suppliers recognise and adapt to the preferences of buyers as consumers and that the satisfaction of these preferences is the ultimate objective of economic activity. Economic ethicists have, therefore, concluded that markets only require a minimal consent on values and, in positive terms, that markets are cosmopolitan and emancipatory in terms of expanding the domain of human freedom with mutual recognition.[8]

It can easily be recognised that the idea of individual preference determination and consumer sovereignty rests on a fundamental value proposition itself, namely the idea of freedom.[9] Seen in this view, economics is a genuine product of the Enlightenment, which is the historical period that saw economics emerging as a science: Humans are regarded as equal and endowed with the capacity for rational reasoning; they should enjoy the right to decide over their lives autonomously, given that they also have the ability to use this right in a responsible way. Of course, at the time, these ideas had an immensely liberating effect. For example, before the capitalist revolution, European societies were governed by many codes on consumption, such as prohibiting ordinary people to dress like aristocrats or imposing dress codes on professions.[10] Hence, endorsing freedom of consumption was part and parcel of the secular process of establishing civil rights. Indeed, this process is contested and ongoing, as social and cultural battles across the globe over rights of freely living sexual preferences demonstrate.

2.2. Freedom and social interdependence

One long-standing issue in circumscribing domains of individual liberty is the well-known condition that the exertion of freedom should not do harm to others. The question, then, is how others define 'harm'. One of the most debated issues in economic philosophy in the recent decades has been the paradox of the Paretian liberal, which implies that one cannot simultaneously meet the criteria of minimal freedom of choice and of maximising individual benefit without reducing the benefit of others (the so-called Pareto criterion).[11]

*The impossibility
of the Paretian
liberal results when
individuals are free
to determine their
preferences and form
preferences about
preferences of others.*

The core reason is that freedom in determining one's preferences (subjective value) does not preclude having preferences about what other individuals choose. All societies maintain values about what people should value and teach this via many channels (think of women's dresses in certain Islamic societies). However, once individuals have preferences over preference of others, we cannot achieve coordination via markets which would simultaneously work to the advantage of everyone.

Under this condition, free market transactions or free individual acts of choice can do harm to others because these acts negatively impact on the preferences, or values, that those others have over the preferences of the actors. In economics, this is captured by the externality concept: A negative externality is generated when an individual act is costly to other individuals and takes place without their consent and compensation. Since an externality by definition cannot be endogenously regulated by the market, in order to reach a mutually agreeable arrangement, it is necessary to build a consensus on harm, which establishes a shared second-person view. In finding consensus about conflicting preferences, individuals must form and express meta-preferences over the subjective preferences of others. However, this renders externalities ubiquitous even when there is no direct physical impact at all on individual well-being of the original action (my way of dressing does not directly affect a passer-by physically).

It is well established in economic research today that the formation and evolution of individual preferences is socially embedded, both in the sense of socialisation and the continuous interaction with others. Social preferences include phenomena such as concern for the status of others, both positively (e.g., compassion) and negatively (e.g., envy); direct mutual influence; or the sharing of preferences via shared identities.[12] One approach that covers the resulting dynamics is the economics of identity.[13]

Values and manifested preferences are deeply intertwined with identity, both on a personal and group level. They are often the result of a reflective attitude towards ourselves and the opinions of others. There is also a hierarchical relation between the two in the sense that manifested preferences may reflect more basic value stances: For example, someone may turn vegetarian because he is concerned about the environment and may be ready to give up non-vegetarian food even if he preferred it in terms of taste.[14] Eating vegetarian food in public also expresses those preferences vis-à-vis others, triggering reactions that may confirm the element of personal identity as well as eventually leading to the formation of a group identity. Deviant behaviour then becomes an issue of personal as well as group identity.

All this implies that merely regarding values as preferences that are chosen on an individual basis leaves out essential aspects of understanding individual choice and markets, given the fundamental role of social interdependence in value formation. The normative character of the economic focus on freedom of choice becomes clear once we consider the ubiquity of external effects and their regulatory consequences.

2.3. Freedom and rationality

A corollary of the economic value proposition on freedom of choice and individual autonomy is the focus on rational behaviour. If people are ready and able to take consistent decisions over time, they should be left to do so, particularly in a market context. This view is further strengthened by assuming that rational individuals will also invest into processing an adequate amount of information for enabling rational choice. Therefore, there is no need for directly intervening into their choices, apart from easing access to information.[15]

Measuring externalities presupposes a shared second-person view.

We discuss the concept of externality in Chapter 5, section 4.

Individual preferences are socially embedded.

Preferences manifest individual identity, and identity relates essentially to groups, hence to preferences shared with others.

In Chapter 7, section 4.2, we discuss identity as fundamental for the economic theory of the individual.

Rationality is a corollary of freedom of choice and individual autonomy.

*There is rich
evidence that people
do not always
behave rationally.*

*A core question is
whether rationality
should be imposed
as a behavioural
norm on individuals,
thus making them
responsible for
irrational choices.*

Behavioural economics research has accumulated rich evidence that we cannot assume that people always behave rationally.[16] This is especially true when considering choices over longer time spans, when we might easily rationalise current choices but fail to construct a coherent and consistent rational framework over the entire life span. One example is individual decision making on expending resources to prolong life, for example, by taking out private health or retirement insurance in an early stage of the life cycle.[17] Again, the standard economic approach would be to take individual preferences as given, including acceptance that people would be ready to trade off potential lifetime against other, more immediate enjoyments. The problem, however, is that people can be inconsistent in their preferences over time. When young, they might think that a shorter but joyful and intensive life is preferable, but when approaching death, they might wish to prolong life at any price. But if the former behaviour leads to higher costs in prolonging life, should anybody else take responsibility? More specifically, in a social welfare state setting, should lung cancer caused by smoking be excluded from regular treatment in public health services; that is, should people forced to pay on their own and die prematurely if they cannot?

The deeper question arising from this discussion is that what is deemed rational is a value proposition of its own.[18] If economists define what is 'rational', what is the consequence of diagnosing a certain behaviour as irrational? This creates a trade-off between individual freedom and economic rationality. Should individuals be allowed to behave irrationally in the first place? What if their behaviour does not only harm themselves but also generates negative externalities on others, such as a threat of contagion in the case of an infective disease or herd behaviour on financial markets? Respective decisions, whether explicitly or implicitly, involve trade-offs on value stances. If smokers should pay for their irrationality, what about financial traders who enjoy themselves in irrational exuberance?

*Societies differ
in normatively
demarcating
domains of
rationality versus
irrationality.*

*Economics must
take a value stance
towards where and
when to impose the
norm of rationality
on specific social
domains.*

Societies differ widely in valuing rationality across various social domains. A case in point are marriage markets. In Western societies, there is a pervasive ideal of marriage relying on romantic love based on free mutual consent that is unrelated to material conditions: True love cannot have a price.[19] From the perspective of many traditional and non-Western societies, this is clearly an irrational stance: Feelings can change, the individual opportunity cost of a wrong-headed decision to marry is enormous, economic imbalances remain unaddressed, and the socially destabilising potential of allowing for marriage across social classes or cultures is substantial. Against that, market-based (or at least wealth-focused) concepts of marriage might appear fully rational. Yet it is exactly this approach to marriage that Western culture has rebelled against: There are entire cultural movements, such as 19th-century romanticism and 20th-century sexual liberation, that have been preoccupied with freeing up love and marriage from its social and material, non-emotional contexts.

We conclude that rationality is a value and that economists cannot avoid defining criteria where and to which extent social domains must be subject to this norm with the consequence that individuals must be held fully accountable for behaving irrationally. This is a value judgement.

2.4. Freedom and social justice

Another major issue regarding freedom and individual autonomy as a value stance relates to distribution and fairness. We focus on one specific question: Should we accept the distributional outcomes of markets once the engagement in market transactions is voluntary in the first place? Does freedom to engage in markets render markets and their outcomes value-neutral? The classical economic view on markets tends to marginalise distributional issues based on the assumption that markets create benefits for everyone. If markets are free and competitive, the question of what influences the capacity to generate those benefits is mostly excluded from judging the outcome.

The related notion of agential power enabled by endowments will be discussed in Chapters 8 and 15.

There are many policy debates relating to this class of problem; for instance, with regard to the legitimacy of lower labour standards in developing and emerging countries that can serve as a competitive advantage in international trade. These issues have been haunting economics since the early times of the industrial revolution: Did the peasants who became industrial workers and formed the new urban proletariat gain or lose?[20] As in the case of migration today, many economists would note that the migrants revealed their preferences voluntarily and, hence, gained. Social critics beg to disagree.

A key question is whether, given the voluntariness of market transactions, distributional market outcomes should be accepted.

This shows that there is a specific issue in approaching markets as value-neutral once market outcomes feed back on capacities to transact on markets. A famous example is the deskilling of workers during industrialisation.[21] In early stages, workers may indeed have gained as long as their skills were valuable for employers. But with the increasing role of mechanisation, specific skills became less important and workers easier to substitute. This deteriorated their bargaining position on the labour market. There are many ways market outcomes directly or indirectly affect the capacities to benefit from markets, such as when housing markets produce settlement patterns that reduce the availability of resources for the inhabitants; for example, in the food deserts in some American cities which contribute to lower health status of resident population.

Market outcomes based on free decisions to engage in markets may feed back on capacities to reap the benefits of markets.

However, there is no value-neutral definition of 'fairness' or 'justice' which enjoys unequivocal support in the scientific community, let alone in wider society. As we show later, we can speak of regimes of inequality which are rooted in values and, therefore, are performative in an essential way. Economists, again in line with traditional liberal thinking, often tend to circumvent the question of distributional justice in the narrow sense by focusing on procedural criteria, which corresponds to the *de gustibus non est disputandum* assumption with regard to the choice of preferences. However, in those

No definition of fairness or justice enjoys unequivocal support.

We explore regimes of inequality in Chapter 15.

debates, notions of individual autonomy and rationality alone are not necessarily sufficient for economic judgement. Instead, the notion of efficiency gets centre stage, to which we now turn.

3. Efficiency

3.1. Efficiency as progress

The notion of efficiency is embedded in the broader notion of material progress in human society that emerged in the Enlightenment.

In a most general sense, efficiency is regarded as the attainment of an objective under scarcity of resources with a minimum amount of waste.[22] In economics, this objective is mostly associated with the production of goods and services. At first sight, this is a rather narrow perspective, but it is in fact inextricably associated with an idea that is foundational to all modern economic systems, including the planned economy, namely progress.

On subjective well-being and happiness, see Chapter 7, section 5.2.

Progress was the clarion call of the European Enlightenment and, from there, spread across the world.[23] It is enshrined in the idea of human development which is a central mission of the United Nations: Lifting as many people as possible out of poverty, raising levels of education, and empowering girls and women. Recent cross-cultural studies have shown that there are indeed some material conditions, such as sufficient nutrition, health, and physical security, that universally contribute to an improvement of subjective well-being.[24] Is efficiency the anchor that grounds economics in a third-person view?

Almost all religions and many ethical teachings radically question the human drive towards material improvement.

In contrast, many religions question basic conceptions about progress in emphasising the delusion of pursuing material benefit and, in particular, the distraction from the real essence of life that results from concentrating on getting more. For example, Buddhism would claim that engaging in the business of progress simply means to speed up the wheel of suffering in human life.

In health care, efficiency criteria would imply that an economic value must be assigned to human life, which is often regarded as anathema.

The idea that human lifetime has a sacred character and should be unaffected by efficiency considerations is endorsed by many people, but in modern societies, there are in fact many examples how the notion of economic efficiency, as related to material progress, can undermine this idea. A case in point are health systems, including insurance. In modern societies, it is relatively uncontroversial that an implicit price is put on human life in the context of insurance, such as in private health insurance or life insurance contracts.[25] But efficiency aspects also loom large with respect to the classic scarcity of resources aspect, which of course arose in full force in the recent COVID-19 crisis: To whom should doctors give access to a respirator machine when these are in scarce supply?[26] Should they weigh the expected lifetime of the young against the lifetime of the old? Should the activities pursued by the concerned persons be taken into consideration, such as preferring a doctor to a drug addict, since the doctor is needed in the hospital? The challenge is that a decision must be taken, unless this would be left to a lottery, which most people would reject as well.

Another key characteristic of progress as value is its anthropocentric character, that is, the view that the economy serves human purposes and works for the benefit of humans.[27] This position, which may appear self-evident at first glance, has become increasingly controversial from an environmental protection point of view. An alternative is provided by so-called deep ecology thinking: Proponents take human well-being out of the focus and argue that we are caretakers of the Earth system in toto such that we also must pay respect to the welfare of all forms of life on Earth.[28] Again, those are different value propositions that can have far-reaching, economically relevant consequences.

Take, for example, the question of biodiversity. How should human interests be related to the goal of maintaining species diversity, given that species extinction has always been a regular phenomenon in biological evolution? The anthropocentric approach would look at the economic value of species diversity. For example, we can estimate the economic value of ecosystem services of bees, which include the important function of pollination in human agriculture, and thereby define economic incentives that may drive costly protective measures. But does that imply that once we invent an alternative technology of pollination, we no longer need to care for the bees? Obviously, people maintain different value stances here: For some, nature is sacred; for others, it is just a means.[29]

Economists often approach these issues in terms of externalities. We can treat damage inflicted on bees as an externality that harms owners of fruit orchards and, eventually, their customers. Would the invention of a new technology of pollination substantially reduce the size of externalities and, hence, the priority of protecting bees? Or should we take the interests of bees and ecologically related species into consideration, and if so, with which weight? In other words, do externalities only refer to harm done to other humans or also harm to all other members of the biosphere? The notion of efficiency cannot provide an answer to these questions.

3.2. Trade-offs: Efficiency versus values

Many economists would agree that material progress based on efficiency considerations can lead to trade-offs with the attainment of other values and objectives. We can roughly distinguish two categories here.

The first relates to values that are principally regarded to fall into the economic domain and, therefore, economic analysis. A famous example is the equity-efficiency trade-off, the idea being that a certain amount of inequality is economically necessary to keep up incentives for economic activity,

Economics often takes for granted that the economy serves human purposes. In the context of environmental issues, this can be radically questioned.

We discuss anthropocentrism in Chapter 16, section 6.

Even when approaching environmental issues in terms of externalities, we must decide which entities, potentially beyond human beings, we include as suffering.

*Distributional issues
can be discussed
from an efficiency
perspective,
considering the
implications for
incentivising
activities that drive
material progress.*

*Markets and
efficiency-driven
action can erode
social structures that
sustain cooperation
and social
coherence.*

On the
institutional
design of market
competition, see
Chapter 11.

*As far as generated
by human design,
competition is
value-imbued.*

including risk-taking and innovation.[30] Another fundamental issue is the weighting of well-being of present versus future generations, that is, the determination of a social discount rate. This determination can have far-reaching policy consequences (e.g., with respect to decisions to increase the capital stock or to combat climate change). There is no efficiency criterion on which such a determination can be based.[31]

The second category relates to objectives that are commonly regarded as outside the economic domain, such as the impact of material progress on social cohesion. As an example, consider labour markets and the anthropological distinction between gift exchange and market exchange. In traditional societies, labour exchange is often the rule in village communities. It is seen as a gift, implying that a mutual obligation for help was established to an extent that the gift might not even have been fully desired (such as too many relatives helping with building a house than necessary, creating obligations to pay back later). In this sense, labour exchange is inefficient but sustains community.[32] To what extent this loss is made explicit by economic analysis depends on what is regarded as the subject of economic analysis in the first place and which consequences of economic activity are externalised into other realms, even if those may later feed back into the economy (for example, via negative effects of weaker family structures and high geographical mobility on mental health and crime).[33]

In a dynamic perspective, efficiency is often seen as an endogenous result of competition. This leads to the question whether competition is value-imbued. At first glance, we would certainly have to answer this in the affirmative, given that the question of to what extent economic allocation should be organised along competitive or cooperative principles has always been among the most important issues of the discipline. The extent and structure of competition in the economic realm is channelled by institutions and, in that sense, an artificial human construct; but institutions and systems of institutions are themselves subject to competition on a global scale. In practice, we do observe a wide variety of institutional arrangements with respect to the role and scope of market competition, which are partly explainable by diversity of values. For example, in advanced economies, legal frames create the scope for new types of business entities, such as social enterprises which embody value propositions that are autonomous from the mandate to make profit.[34] Lines between competition and cooperation can also be blurred: For example, even the functioning of competitive markets requires a substantial degree of cooperation (e.g., with respect to the prevention of misinformation and cheating).[35]

There are many instances in which competition tends to enforce efficient behaviour, regardless of intention and motivation. A famous economic hypothesis links competition to rationality: Competition weeds out irrational behaviour since it will result in relative losses to competitors;[36] a loss-making firm will go bankrupt, and losses are indicators of low efficiency. Consider the example of a family business which has a long tradition in a certain trade and wants to keep that tradition. Production cost is relatively high due to partly outdated equipment and a staff that is not particularly productive but personally attached to the family. In consequence, profit is low, and competitive pressure is rising. Thus, although the family may be ready to trade off the maintenance of traditional values, such as employment of certain production methods or loyalty to its staff, against lower income, external competition may enforce rationalisation in the sense of increasing efficiency, and alternative values may become unsustainable.

But does that mean that values become entirely endogenous to the selective force of competition such that, in the longer run at least, only those values would survive that are compatible with efficiency? As we will explain more systematically in later chapters, this is not the case due to great variation in the concrete structure, criteria, and intensity of economic competition.[37] Consider again the family business: It may be able to carve out a market segment in which consumers are actively willing to pay more for the upholding of traditional production methods (e.g., for environmental or cultural reasons); it may also find sources of finance that would keep it sustainable even if economic loss were generated, such as from well-off private financiers or state subsidies. On a higher level as well, economic history has shown that many economic systems, including the German-style social market economy, non-capitalist market economies, and even fully planned economies, have proved sustainable for considerable stretches of time. This coexistence, in turn, can provide ample niches for apparently inefficient structures and the values associated with them; for example, the state-owned company in China or the Scandinavian market economies with a strongly egalitarian component achieved via high tax levels and redistribution.

In evolutionary terms, these observations point towards niche formation in competition. Despite competitive pressure, values are not predetermined or objectified by economic competition; instead, values, including efficiency itself, are subject to active human choice because economic actors can actively shape competitive conditions. Yet competition in many contexts remains a fundamental force towards more efficiency and, therefore, restrains the range of sustainable values in various ways; the decay and death of many traditional social structures as a consequence of economic development bear ample witness to this. In that sense, value change is indeed an endogenous result of progress and can be analysed as such. Values shape how we perform markets, while at the same time, market

We meet this efficiency argument in various contexts, such as Chapter 10, section 4.1, on the rationalising force of money.

Competition is a force that partly endogenises the formation of values.

We discuss the generic evolutionary aspects of competition in Chapter 5 and employ the niche concept on markets in Chapter 11.

Economic competition manifests itself in widely diverse ways.

Despite forces of competition, markets allow for a diversity of niches and domains in which values are manifest.

competition creates forces that change our values or require that we find new ways to express them.

4. Markets, economists, and values

The legitimacy
of market-based
inequality is
discussed in
Chapter 15,
section 5.

Where does all this leave us with respect to markets, as main subjects of economic science, and their relation to values?

A decision for or against markets as mechanisms to allocate scarce resources is not value-free. The market mechanism – partly by its organisation, partly via its effects – is inextricably enmeshed with fundamental value propositions: freedom and individual autonomy; rationality and efficiency; an acceptance of dynamism and social change; and the acceptance of a certain amount of social inequality together with a procedurally oriented and partly meritocratic conception of how that inequality should be grounded. As such, they stand in tension with other values and social models, such as traditional and socially static societies, egalitarian models, and religious concepts related to sacred domains. Markets are an essential element of promoting economic efficiency and progress, enabling the hypercomplex patterns of division of labour, specialisation, and exchange as well as the high rates of innovation that are characteristic of modern economies and societies. Efficiency is not an objective determinant of values but a value itself which is subject to active decision making. Market participants eventually adopt this value and behave accordingly; hence, markets are performative.

*Markets are
performative and
endogenise values.*

The latter aspect often creates tensions between markets and values and should not be framed as tension between efficiency and values but as conflicts of values. For example, in health care, it can make a large difference for a doctor's self-perception whether she works strictly along her Hippocratic oath without explicitly reflecting on the limits of her capacities or whether she sees himself on the supply side of a market-based relationship, including the implied rationalisation and distancing of the doctor-patient relationship. Eventually, therefore, economisation and marketisation can generate identity change.

*The enactment and
design of markets
are decisions
involving values,
which also means
that they can stay in
tension with other
values.*

*Economists must be
explicit about their
values.*

In our view, those considerations have important implications for the way that economics as science and economists deal, and should deal, with values. Economists should be explicit about the values they advocate when making recommendations, or comparative assessments, of different institutional arrangements to allocate scarce resources. More specifically, in their role as responsible participants in public discourse, they should also recognise that in many instances, a decision for or against a market arrangement is primarily a question of values, not of efficiency, and they should reflect upon the eventual performative character of their analyses and recommendations.

Economic
advisership is
the subject of
Chapter 18.

All this does not mean, however, that the aspiration of economics to be a science that can deliver widely accepted results (in the sense of generalising from the second-person to the third-person perspective and, therefore, abstracting over a wide range of values) must be abandoned. The key here is the analysis of trade-offs: If the introduction of markets implies increasing levels of inequality or weakened social cohesion, this can and should be explicitly pointed out and analysed. As outlined in the previous chapter, this requires the embedding of economic analysis into other disciplines and recognising their research methodologies. Such analysis, particularly if directed towards explicit policy considerations, will always be subject to large degrees of uncertainty. In that sense, values are inextricably intertwined with active human decision making.

5. Conclusion

If economists want to adopt a value stance while maintaining scientific claims, this must be governed by impartiality. Given the analysis of this chapter, how can this be achieved? We highlight two ways.

We introduced the impartiality criterion in Chapter 2.

The first is that the organisation of economics academia must allow for expressing diversity of values within the profession and avoid confronting misplaced claims of scientific status with value stances outside academia. Economics must make values explicit and provide an arena to discuss values within its disciplinary domain. Therefore, impartiality requires that economics academia adopts an institutional framework for safeguarding the diversity of values, with important consequences particularly with respect to its stance towards internal competition; for example, on job markets for economists, the role of journal rankings, and the presence of different schools of thought in economics faculties.

Economic academia must recognise the diversity of values in organising research and teaching.

The second way to safeguard impartiality is the creation on a stringent professional ethics for academic economists about their relationship with interest groups in society.[38] That means, while economists working outside academia may openly represent a specific interest, such as economists at trade unions, research economists and academic teachers must be completely independent from any interest group. Further, the education of economists should include nurturing a professional ethics that makes economists sensitive to those issues such that they can act responsibly and independently.

Academic economists must adopt an ethics of professional independence and integrity.

Major chapter insights

- There is a large variety of positions and schools of thought in economics regarding the relative role and significance of values. Being a performative science, economics cannot neutralise the diversity of values by achieving a third-person view, but economists can aspire for achieving impartiality of their judgements.

- The analytical assumption of subjectivity of preferences reflects the fundamental role of freedom in economics. However, once we consider that this includes the freedom to assume preferences about preferences that others have, we recognise that markets cannot meet the Pareto criterion.
- Rationality has the status of a value and cannot be neutralised as a mere analytical principle once we acknowledge that individuals are free to act irrationally.
- Economists cannot blank out the question on how initial endowments affect results of markets and how this distribution is to be judged in value terms. The voluntariness of market transactions does not neutralise this issue.
- Efficiency is closely tied to the Enlightenment notion of human progress. Yet there are deep tensions with widely held ethical and religious values. Although market competition drives efficiency, the diversity of values can be sustained by institutional design.
- Economic academia needs institutional frames to safeguard and enhance the impartiality of academic economists (as different from professional economists).

Notes

1 This was the core ethical principle invoked by Adam Smith (Sen, 2009, 114ff).
2 Duflo (2017, 2020).
3 See the discussion in Hausman and McPherson (1996, 209ff).
4 This is one reason of establishing the distinct field of philosophy and economics, represented by authors such as Nozick, Sen, or Sugden. Overview in Hausman (2021).
5 Hayek (1979).
6 Becker (1976).
7 Stigler and Becker (1977).
8 This is the famous *doux commerce* thesis that was elaborated by Enlightenment thinkers, including Adam Smith (Forman-Barzilai, 2010). On minimalistic morality, see Baurmann (1996).
9 Weizsäcker (2011).
10 Plumpe (2019, 55ff, 158ff).
11 Sen (1970). For an extension and confirmation, see Chung (2019).
12 Bowles and Polanía-Reyes (2012).
13 Akerlof and Kranton (2000), Kranton (2016).
14 Meta-preferences are a key concept in Sen's (2002) conception of rationality.
15 Harrison and Ross (2017).

16 For a survey, see Thaler (2016).
17 Thaler and Benartzi (2004).
18 This is often recognised by psychologists, see, for example, Wiers et al. (2020).
19 Zelizer (1997).
20 Elster (1982).
21 Marglin (1991).
22 The notion of efficiency emerged together with thermodynamics, which explains its apparently objective status; see Daggett (2019).
23 Pinker (2018).
24 This is the subject of happiness research in economics, as documented in the annual World Happiness Reports. For the most recent one, see Helliwell et al. (2021).
25 For a case study, see Hood (2017).
26 Emanuel et al. (2020).
27 This is Adam Smith's original view, maintained by economists also in the context of ecological crisis, such as Llavador et al. (2015).
28 Spash (2013).
29 Dasgupta (2021, 307ff).
30 Okun (1975).
31 Pindyck (2013).
32 This is a central topic in the moral economy theoretical framework; for examples, see Kimambo (2008).
33 The classic on this is Polanyi (2001[1944]).
34 Collier (2019, 77ff).
35 Akerlof and Shiller (2015).
36 Alchian (1977).
37 For a survey of arguments, see Elster (2015, 205ff).
38 On professional ethics of economists, see the volume edited by Dolfsma and Negru (2021).

References

Akerlof, G. A. and Kranton, R. E. (2000) 'Economics and Identity', *Quarterly Journal of Economics*, 115(3), pp. 715–753. DOI: 10.1162/003355300554881.

Akerlof, G. A. and Shiller, R. J. (2015) *Phishing for Phools: The Economics of Manipulation and Deception*. Princeton and Oxford: Princeton University Press.

Alchian, A. (1977) *Economic Forces at Work*. Indianapolis: Liberty Press.

Baurmann, M. (1996) *Der Markt der Tugend. Recht und Moral in der liberalen Gesellschaft. Eine soziologische Untersuchung*. Tübingen: Mohr Siebeck.

Becker, G. S. (1976) *The Economic Approach to Human Behavior*. Chicago: Chicago University Press. DOI: 10.2307/2553078.

Bowles, S. and Polanía-Reyes, S. (2012) 'Economic Incentives and Social Preferences: Substitutes or Complements?' *Journal of Economic Literature*, 50(2), pp. 368–425. DOI: 10.32609/0042-8736-2013-5-73-108.

Chung, H. (2019) 'The Impossibility of Liberal Rights in a Diverse World', *Economics and Philosophy*, 35(1), pp. 1–27. DOI: 10.1017/S0266267118000044.

Collier, P. (2019) *The Future of Capitalism: Facing the New Anxieties*. London: Penguin Books.

Daggett, C. (2019) *The Birth of Energy: Fossil Fuels, Thermodynamics, and the Politics of Work*. Durham: Duke University Press.

Dasgupta, P. (2021) *The Economics of Biodiversity*. Available at: https://www.gov.uk/government/collections/the-economics-of-biodiversity-the-dasgupta-review (Accessed: 17 March 2022)

Dolfsma, W. and Negru, I. (2021) *The Ethical Formation of Economists*. Abingdon and New York: Routledge. DOI: 10.4324/9781351043809.

Duflo, E. (2017) 'The Economist as Plumber', *American Economic Review*, 107(5), pp. 1–26. DOI: 10.1257/AER.P20171153.

Duflo, E. (2020) 'Field Experiments and the Practice of Policy', *American Economic Review* 110(7), pp. 1952–1973. DOI: 10.1257/aer.110.7.1952.

Elster, J. (1982) 'Sour Grapes – Utilitarianism and the Genesis of Wants', in Sen, A. and Williams, B. (eds.) *Utilitarianism and Beyond*. Cambridge: Cambridge University Press, pp. 219–238. DOI: 10.1017/CBO9780511611964.013.

Elster, J. (2015) *Explaining Social Behavior: More Nuts and Bolts for the Social Sciences*. Cambridge: Cambridge University Press.

Emanuel, E. J. *et al.* (2020) 'Fair Allocation of Scarce Medical Resources in the Time of COVID-19', *New England Journal of Medicine*, 382(21), pp. 2049–2055. DOI: 10.1056/NEJMsb2005114.

Forman-Barzilai, F. (2010) *Adam Smith and the Circles of Sympathy: Cosmopolitanism and Moral Theory*. Cambridge: Cambridge University Press.

Harrison, G. W. and Ross, D. (2017) 'The Empirical Adequacy of Cumulative Prospect Theory and Its Implications for Normative Assessment', *Journal of Economic Methodology*, 24(2), pp. 150–165. DOI: 10.1080/1350178X.2017.1309753.

Hausman, D. M. (2021) 'Philosophy of Economics', *The Stanford Encyclopedia of Philosophy,* Winter 2021 Edition. Available at: https://plato.stanford.edu/archives/win2021/entries/economics/ (Accessed: 11 May 2022).

Hausman, D. M. and McPherson, M. S. (1996) *Economic Analysis and Moral Philosophy*. Cambridge and New York: Cambridge University Press. DOI: 10.5860/choice.34-1657.

Hayek, F. A. von (1979) *Law, Legislation and Liberty: A New Statement of the Liberal Principles of Justice and Political Economy, Volume 3: The Political Order of a Free People*. Chicago: University of Chicago Press. DOI: 10.4324/9780203103814.

Helliwell, J. *et al.* (2021) *World Happiness Report 2021*. Available at: https://happiness-report.s3.amazonaws.com/2021/WHR+21.pdf (Accessed: 17 March 2022).

Hood, K. (2017) 'The Science of Value: Economic Expertise and the Valuation of Human Life in US Federal Regulatory Agencies', *Social Studies of Science,* 47(4), pp. 441–465. DOI: 10.1177/0306312717693465.

Kimambo, I. N. (2008) *Contemporary Perspectives on African Moral Economy*. Dar es Salaam: Dar es Salaam University Press.

Kranton, R. E. (2016) 'Identity Economics 2016: Where Do Social Distinctions and Norms Come From?' *American Economic Review*, 106(5), pp. 405–409. DOI: 10.1257/AER.P20161038.

Llavador, H., Roemer, J. E. and Silvestre, J. (2015) *Sustainability for a Warming Planet*. Cambridge: Harvard University Press. DOI: 10.5860/choice.193050.

Marglin, S. (1991) 'Understanding Capitalism: Control versus Efficiency', in Gustafsson, B. (ed.) *Power and Economic Institutions. Reinterpretations in Economic History*. Aldershot: Edward Elgar Publishing, pp. 107–169.

Okun, A. M. (1975) *Equality and Efficiency: The Big Tradeoff*. Washington, DC: Brookings Institution. DOI: 10.2307/1978438.

Pindyck, R. S. (2013) 'Climate Change Policy: What Do the Models Tell Us?' *Journal of Economic Literature*, 51(3), pp. 860–872. DOI: 10.1257/JEL.51.3.860.

Pinker, S. (2018) *Enlightenment Now: The Case for Reason, Science, Humanism, and Progress*. New York: Viking.

Plumpe, W. (2019) *Das kalte Herz: Kapitalismus, die Geschichte einer andauernden Revolution*. Berlin: Rowohlt.

Polanyi, K. (2001[1944]) *The Great Transformation: The Political and Economic Origins of Our Time*. Boston: Beacon Press.

Sen, A. (1970) 'The Impossibility of a Paretian Liberal', *Journal of Political Economy*, 78(1), pp. 152–157. DOI: 10.1086/259614.

Sen, A. (2002) *Rationality and Freedom*. Cambridge: Belknap Press. DOI: 10.5860/choice.40-6342.

Sen, A. (2009) *The Idea of Justice*. Cambridge: Belknap Press. DOI: 10.1177/0191453714553501.

Spash, C. L. (2013) 'The Shallow or the Deep Ecological Economics Movement?' *Ecological Economics*, 93, pp. 351–362. DOI: 10.1016/J.ECOLECON.2013.05.016.

Stigler, G. J. and Becker, G. S. (1977) 'De Gustibus Non Est Disputandum', *The American Economic Review*, 67(2), pp. 76–90. DOI: 10.3917/IDEE.159.0054.

Thaler, R. H. (2016) 'Behavioral Economics: Past, Present, and Future', *American Economic Review,* 106(7), pp. 1577–1600. DOI: 10.1257/AER.106.7.1577.

Thaler, R. H. and Benartzi, S. (2004) 'Save More Tomorrow™: Using Behavioral Economics to Increase Employee Saving', *Journal of Political Economy,* 112(S1), pp. 164–187. DOI: 10.1086/380085.

Weizsäcker, C. C. (2011) 'Homo Oeconomicus Adaptivus – Die Logik des Handelns bei veränderlichen Präferenzen', Preprints of the Max Planck Institute for Research on Collective Goods, 2011/10.

Wiers, R. W., van Gaal, S. and Le Pelley, M. E. (2020) 'Akrasia and Addiction: Neurophilosophy and Psychological Mechanisms', in Harbecke, J. and Herrmann-Pillath, C. (eds.) *Social Neuroeconomics: Mechanistic Integration of the Neurosciences and the Social Sciences*. London: Routledge, pp. 121–147.

Zelizer, V. A. (1997) *The Social Meaning of Money*. Princeton: Princeton University Press. DOI: 10.2307/40183906.

PART II

CHAPTER FOUR

Evolution, ecology, economy

1. Introduction

In this chapter, we develop a general framework for approaching the human economy as part of the Earth system. Against the backdrop of the previous chapters, we aim at establishing criteria and conceptual frames for approaching the economy from a third-person view and in terms of its materiality. This means to build cross-disciplinary bridges to physics, chemistry, and biology in adopting a life sciences perspective.[1] The goal is to abandon the anthropocentric focus of economics and adopt a geocentric view.[2] That means, we approach the human economy as a regulatory layer in Earth system dynamics, which has emerged in the transition to the Anthropocene.[3] We suggest a co-evolutionary conceptual framework for developing the necessary cross-disciplinary synthesis.[4] For co-evolutionary theory, two ideas are basic:

On the distinction between three points of view, see Chapter 2, section 2.

The distinction between an anthropocentric and a geocentric view is further pursued in Chapter 16, section 6.

- First, we posit *ontological continuity* across Earth system domains, in two senses:[5] One is the continuity between ecology and economy, which implies that we must analyse all economic processes in terms of their ecosystem interactions. The other is to approach human agents as biological entities, implying to take an embodied approach to analysing human behaviour.
- Second, we posit formal analogies of evolutionary processes across domains.[6] This corresponds to recent thinking in evolutionary economics and grounds in the recognition that competition is a universal phenomenon in terms of the general formal model of variation, selection, and retention (VSR).[7] At the same time, the co-evolutionary approach recognises the emergence of new evolutionary mechanisms, in particular, culture, technology, and institutions.

The co-evolutionary perspective entails ontological continuity as well as formal analogies of evolutionary processes across domains.

In this chapter, we explore four fundamental aspects which emerge when we approach humans and their economies as a special type of living systems:

- the role of thermodynamics in analysing living systems;
- the concepts of growth and metabolism;

67

DOI: 10.4324/9781003094869-7

- the concepts of ecological system and niche construction;
- the general principles of co-evolutionary analysis.

Accordingly, this chapter moves across three levels of analysis. In section 2, we explore physical foundations of the human economy. We concentrate on one aspect: the thermodynamics of the Earth system and principles that apply across all levels. In section 3, we present basic mechanisms of evolution, which extend to the human domain via emergent cultural evolution. We approach evolution as generating and accumulating functional information in a stochastic process of variation, selection, and retention that causally entangles an uncertain environment with a an open, indeterministic process of information processing. The general model for causation is multilevel selection, that is, selection on the individual level (including levels of selection within individuals) and the group level (with different levels of aggregation). In section 4, we discuss the evolution of the human economy as a manifestation of emergent ultra-sociality, that is, the cooperation of large, genetically unrelated groups.

2. Physical principles of evolution

2.1. Economic niche, environment, Earth system

We approach the human economy as a system that provides humans with the resources necessary for survival, reproduction, and the pursuit of culturally evolved goals. The economy is the human adaptive niche in the Earth system,

For more on the technosphere, see Chapter 6, section 2.

which, however, has grown to a size that now exerts deep and comprehensive impact on the biosphere, that is, the system that encompasses all living systems and their niches. Spatially connected niches are local and regional ecosystems. The vast expansion of the human adaptive niche has been driven by the globalisation of the market system in recent centuries, culminating in the Great Acceleration.[8] As a result, we refer to a new emergent layer in Earth system evolution, the technosphere.[9]

With the emergence of the technosphere, the Earth became a hybrid planet where the interactions between geological, biological, and technological forces determine states of the Earth system such as the climate.[10] The emerging new geological epoch is the Anthropocene.[11]

Living systems endogenously construct boundaries that define the environmental niche specific to that system.

All living systems endogenously create biospheric niches via exploiting species-specific resources and establishing distinct modes of interaction between system and environment.[12] In maintaining a living system in relation to its niche, boundaries are essential, which can be physically manifest (such as cell membranes or the skin of an organism) or generated by various mechanisms that selectively mediate between system and environment, including ways the environment is represented in internal system processes. This results in the distinction between Umwelt as niche and *Umgebung* as environment. In the case of humans, boundaries are established by technological artefacts, such as greenhouses, or fences in husbandry, and by institutionalised exclusionary behaviour, such as property. The latter grounds in general biological dispositions of establishing and defending territories controlled by individuals and groups.[13]

One of the remarkable features of humans is the capacity to construct a great variety of niches via cultural, technological, and institutional adaptation to local conditions, such as the distinct economic systems of sedentary agriculture versus nomadism in Imperial China that shaped its history over millennia, related to various forms of territorial exclusion such as the Great Chinese Wall and recurrent warfare. The establishment of boundaries is especially important when we study the relationship between economy and environment, distinguishing between that part of the environment which is integrated into the economy (the ecosystem) and that which is not, both in terms of material inclusion (such as grassland used by nomads or hills transformed by terracing for rice cultivation) or selective representation. In the economy, the most important form of selective representation is mediated by markets, that is, by either pricing parts of the environment or keeping it out of monetary calculations.

On in-group/out-group boundaries see Chapter 8, section 3.3.

Technically, exclusion from pricing creates an externality, see Chapter 5, section 4.

We can identify boundaries in two different perspectives, inside out and outside in (Figure 4.1). With reference to markets, this corresponds to the distinction between a second-person and a third-person view. Markets are a core medium by which the environment is represented to human agents in the economy via the pricing of environmental resources:

- The internal perspective, or second-person view, is constituted by market agents and market institutions and refers to the notion of internalisation. Of the set of all interactions with the environment, some are internalised and some or not, referring to their pricing in market interactions. Beyond the borderline defined by internalisation is the sink (i.e., waste disposal).[14] By definition, waste transgresses the border between economy and ecosystem, especially once it is no longer traded on markets.
- From the third-person view, the internally determined sink still causally interacts with the economy such that it remains a physical part of it, albeit not internalised in markets. A key example is climate change: For a long time, the atmosphere was perceived as exclusively part of the environment and external to the economy, aside of local effects such as air pollution. But today, we have recognised that via the accumulation of greenhouse gas emissions, the atmosphere has become part of the economy in the sense that economic actions must be taken in managing and internalising these emissions in a global context.

Markets are the medium to internalise the environment via pricing, thus determining what crosses the system boundary as waste.

Yet waste can still causally interact with the economy, thus triggering mechanisms of inclusion (internalisation).

The emergence of the technosphere means that market internalisation becomes an integral part of Earth system regulation. This implies that an

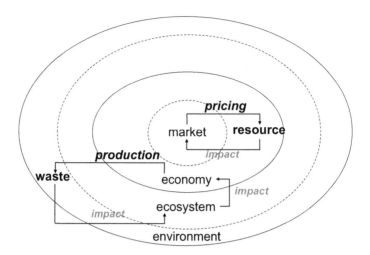

Figure 4.1 Economy and ecosystem: Boundaries and internalisation
The diagram represents mutually embedded system levels. The ecosystem is
that part of the environment which is causally connected with the economy
in physical terms. Via pricing, markets determine internally what counts
as a resource in the human ecosystem, thus transforming it into a part of
the economy (such as fish shoals into fisheries). Wastes are economically
externalised to the environment as a sink but impact on the ecosystem, thus
still exert causal impact on the economy (such as poisonous waste on soils
used in agriculture).

*In ecological
economics,
thermodynamics
is the unifying
framework of
geophysics, ecology,
and economy.*

analysis of markets and the economy must include fundamental geophysical
processes. That perspective is provided by thermodynamics, which in an economic context is mostly seen as an aspect of engineering production processes. However, in ecological economics, thermodynamics is conceived as
establishing the general framework for understanding economic evolution.[15]

2.2. Thermodynamic principles of evolution

In a static sense, the Earth system can be approached as a closed system for
which the fundamental laws of thermodynamics hold, given that there is
almost no material exchange with outer space.[16] In principle, we can approach
all types of living systems as heat engines.[17]

In simplest terms, a heat engine exploits an energetic potential in the environment combined with a temperature differential to generate physical work.
While doing this, the energy potential is depleted. Simultaneously, a certain
amount of heat is produced which constitutes the entropy generated by the
process, in the sense of energy that is no longer usable for work. This means

that heat engines run out unless there is a continuous renewal of the original energy potential, which applies for all living systems, including the human economy. All work in production is enabled by the depletion of energy potentials and necessarily contributes to the increase of entropy in the environment of the system that generates work. Entropy can take various forms, including solid waste of any kind; most universal kinds of waste are emissions of simple chemicals, such as CO_2 or, even more universally, just heat that dissipates in the environment.

Depending on contextual conditions, these outputs can be also used to drive other processes: For example, heat can be used to create another thermodynamic gradient which can be exploited to generate work of another kind (atmospheric temperature gradients cause clouding and rain, and rain drives soil erosion). Once all energetic transformations are concluded, no more work can be generated according to the second law of thermodynamics. The most general concept of efficiency from a third-person view is, therefore, the efficiency of the thermodynamic conversion processes in the sense of maximising the transformation of energy into work and minimising entropy production. This applies to all kinds of processes, such as the thermodynamic efficiency of engines or the efficiency of human food chains, where eating meat, notably, is a thermodynamically inefficient way to generate the energetic input to human metabolism compared to direct consumption of plants.[18]

Living systems differ from mechanical heat engines insofar as the work they produce is directed at restoring their energy potential, that is, they activate work for their own survival and reproduction governed by the information embodied in the system. We define this as autonomous agent.[19] Autonomous agents represent states of order which require constant maintenance, but ultimately, the direction of the life cycle tends towards disorder: senescence, death, and decay.[20] Therefore, physical work can be approached as an activity that maintains states of order in a certain system of reference which can be located on all levels and domains of the Earth system:[21] For example, birds construct nests which would never occur spontaneously in the biological world without their expenditure of work. The most general description of human economic activity is the organisation and realisation of physical work according to certain rules and regularities, resulting in outputs that sustain states of order in the human niche.[22] Notably, physical work is a more general notion than economic work as a goal-oriented activity.[23]

As said, thermodynamic principles universally apply on different levels: For example, the Earth system can be approached as a complex structure with many gradients of free energy which are manifest in processes that generate physical work; for example, temperature differences create the wind systems that shape the weather globally (Figure 4.2). In turn, wind systems are forces that drive erosion, thus generating changes in the physical landscape. In this sense, the Earth system can be conceived as a global heat engine with a border to the outer space and the gradient of incoming versus outgoing radiation

Living systems are heat engines that generate physical work to maintain their metabolism and reproduction.

A third-person view on efficiency is the efficiency of thermodynamic conversions.

Living systems represent states of order maintained by physical work.

The Earth system is a global heat engine with many interlocking thermodynamic gradients which can generate physical work, given structural conditions (constraints).

71

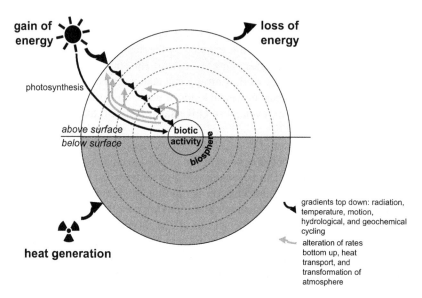

Figure 4.2 The thermodynamics of the Earth system (after Kleidon)
The thermodynamic machinery of the Earth system is mainly driven by inflowing solar radiation and geological forces originating from inner Earth (which we do not detail here). For the human economy, the former matter most, while the latter have been most prominent in terms of technologically exploiting accumulated stocks that embody past solar radiation (i.e., fossil fuels). There is a hierarchy of gradients where lower levels dissipate higher level gradients, such as soil erosion dissipating wind flows. Processes on lower levels feed back on higher levels, such as sediments impacting on river flows and alter the rates of dissipation.

constituting the energy potential that drives it. Eventually, we can approach the biosphere as one of the constitutive subsystems of this heat engine.

What determines the difference between work and heat? If the Earth system mostly produced heat, the Earth surface would be a mass without structure but in constant movement (think of gaseous planets such as Jupiter). Work is generated if there are constraints that channel energy flows in a way that structures emerge. There is a fundamental analogy between living systems and human technology in being goal-directed structures that impose constraints such that systems are maintained and reproduced.

The continuous inflow of solar energy, given structural constraints, drives the emergence of more complex forms of physical organisation and work, including life and technology.

A general phenomenon emerging from this is that flows of energy and matter assume shapes and structures that maximise flow throughput.[24] Living systems represent an important qualitative threshold in this process because they produce structure based on their evolving embodied information and reproduce it. But the more general physical principles of energetic dissipation also apply for them. This is salient in the ubiquity of certain structures, such as the branching of flow systems (river systems, arteries, leaves of trees), which maximises flow throughput in the most efficient way. Human artefacts such as road systems built under economic and political constraints reflect the same principles. We can extend the basic thermodynamic principles by the maximum power principle (MPP) or Lotka's principle (Figure 4.3), which follows from evolutionary analysis, as developed in the next section.[25] This principle states that living systems tend to evolve towards a direction by which the throughput of energy is maximised, implying that the production of entropy is maximised as well (maximum entropy production principle, MEPP).[26] This has a fundamental implication for analysing the Earth system: Since living systems exploit the inflow of solar radiation, they build structures which resist entropy maximisation, while at the same time speeding up the production of entropy even further.[27] The ultimate manifestation of this is the generation of heat (i.e., warming the planet), which, in turn, dissipates to outer space via radiation. This shows, again, that the biosphere is an integral part of the physics of the Earth system.[28] It is important to emphasise that those points refer to tendencies but not equilibrium states: A certain state of the system need not manifest maximisation but only a tendency towards maximisation.

The MPP can be regarded as a natural law of energy transformations in the biosphere. The physical foundation is the energetic enabling of work and the role of work in a selection process that favours those living systems that can invest more work in the process of their reproduction. This does not imply that all parts of the ecological system move in this direction because there are many niches in which various forms of energetic transformations can survive.

Living systems evolve to maximise flow throughput.

For the example of market systems in Imperial China which reflect efficiency and maximisation of resource flows, see Chapter 1.

The maximum power principle states that evolution generates structural change towards the maximal harnessing and flow of energy.

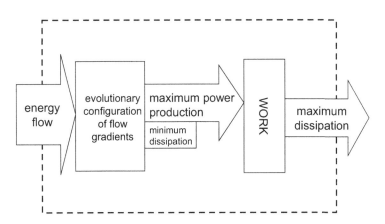

Figure 4.3 Maximum power principle (after Bejan)[29]
Living systems are flow systems in which evolutionary forces on the population level create the tendency to maximise energetic flows generating maximum power efficiently (such as running as fast as possible in predator-prey interactions). This power output generates work that eventually dissipates, entailing maximum dissipation.

But for the entire system, a direction of change is created which favours growth of size and complexity of some living systems and their related eco-systems.[30] Living systems as open, non-linear, and complex systems manifest growth in various senses: growth of complexity, growth of throughputs, expansion of borders and, hence, size, and others.

2.3. Metabolism and growth

All living systems are sustained by a metabolism in which energy and material inputs are consumed while producing certain outputs, which minimally includes behaviour directed at harnessing those inputs and disposal of waste in the environment. Inputs are often transformed in some way before they can be processed by the metabolism (think of cracking nuts or chewing before digesting). In the widest sense, human technology is an extension of the organism, reaching into the construction of technologically altered niches.[31] The physical manifestation of the human metabolism beyond its organismic functions is the technosphere: The technosphere provides the human metabo-lism with processed inputs via a vast and complex network that is mainly governed by markets. For example, eating a hamburger is enabled by a net-work of various agricultural producers, food processing companies, transport agencies, and eventually, restaurants which prepare the food.[32]

Metabolism maintains the functioning of living systems via harnessing energetic and material inputs.

The technosphere extends and scaffolds the human metabolism externally.

Metabolism requires a physical structure of transporting and channelling inputs within a living system, most generally described as a network, such as arteries in the body or rivers in landscapes. Building and sustaining such net-works follows general physical principles which apply across levels, includ-ing the technosphere; the most fundamental being the MPP that drives the evolution of flow gradients.[33] Accordingly, we can distinguish between intra-organismic networks (such as arteries), ecological networks (such as habitat structures), and technological networks (such as roads), which partly obey the same physical principles (Figure 4.4).

Growth in living systems manifests life cycle dynamics and, hence, faces limits on both the organismic and the community level.

Two essential characteristics of living systems are the life cycle and repro-duction: All living systems are embedded in a chain of living systems reach-ing from the past to the present into the future (barring extinction) via reproduction and undergo life cycles of development, maturity, senescence, and death.[34] The time scale or eigentime at which the generational sequence unfolds varies widely across living systems, reaching from minutes to decades and even millennia (think of bacteria or giant sequoias), defining their biolog-ical clocks of reproduction and growth.

For the Great Acceleration and an ecological perspective on economic growth, see Chapter 16.

A fundamental question is whether life cycle dynamics is a principled lim-itation to growth only on the organismic level or whether higher-level interac-tions enable growth without limits (such that, for example, the human economy could grow without limits). Physically, growth without limits is, of course, impossible because it would be constrained by the upper limit to energy inflows into the Earth system (i.e., mostly solar energy). But it can be argued

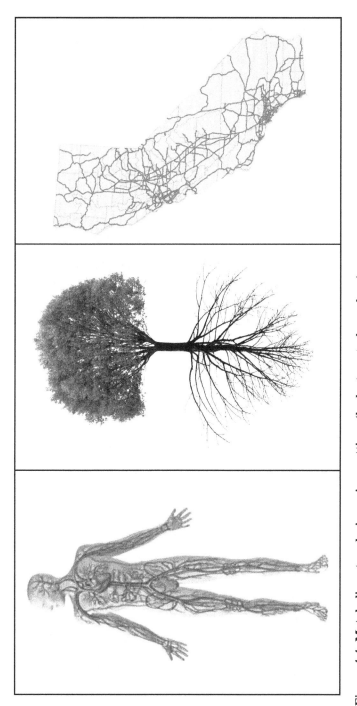

Figure 4.4 Metabolic networks in various settings (body, tree, technosphere)

Metabolism requires physical means of transporting and allocating energy and resources to functional consumers in a living system (such as different organs of the body or different members of an ecological community). These networks assume similar shapes across domains, reflecting universal physical constraints. In the technosphere, these are transport and logistics networks, such as roads.

that the tree of life, as such, manifests growth that overcomes limitations of organismic or ecosystem growth (see subsequent section). Since the mobilisation of fossil fuels, the human economy even shows symptoms of hyperbolic growth (the Great Acceleration), which certainly is impossible to sustain.[35]

All living systems are productive. In the most general sense, this means that populations of living systems tend to grow through time via reproduction, provided that there are sufficient resources available in the environment. This implies the phenomenon of scarcity as the most general condition of evolution: Scarcity results from growth with a limited resource base and creates selective pressure towards increasing the efficiency of resource use. The result is the standard form of logistic growth, with a part of accelerating exponential growth as long as resources are plenty and decelerating growth when resources become scarcer (Figure 4.5).[36] A population of living systems is sustainable if it maintains a certain size within the carrying capacity of its resource base, given constant renewal of population members via reproduction.

Growth creates scarcity and selection pressure towards efficiency once the underlying resource is limited. A general pattern of growth is the logistic curve.

For logistic growth in the context of social networks, see Chapter 8, section 3.4.

The notion of carrying capacity is itself dynamic; as for a specific type of living system, it depends on its embeddedness into the local ecosystem and the way this affects the resource space via the dynamic interaction between various species. Accordingly, the carrying capacity is not a fixed and deterministic physical boundary but dynamically moving and determined endogenously by complex non-linear interdependencies.

The carrying capacity of ecosystems is endogenous to the biosphere; however, complex interactions can result in tipping points which threaten sustainability even before limits have been reached.

A distinct expression of this is the existence of tipping points: Ecosystems can maintain apparently sustainable patterns of growth up to the tipping point,

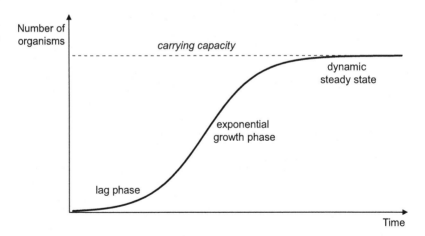

Figure 4.5 The logistic curve
The logistic curve describes a general pattern of growth in which an acceleration with exponential growth is followed by a deceleration when approaching the carrying capacity. It applies across a wide range of phenomena, such as animal populations or products in markets.

when minor further changes trigger sudden and perhaps catastrophic changes within a very short time.[37] Because of the complex dynamics, tipping points cannot be predicted by linear extrapolation, and many possible trajectories reflecting basic parameters of the ecosystem, such as continuous chaotic fluctuations of populations, can be created. In recent research on climate change, this has been treated in the context of planetary boundaries, that is, ecological constraints on the growth of the technosphere which involve the possibility of tipping points when growth approaches them.

We come back on planetary boundaries in Chapter 16, section 4.

3. Fundamentals of evolution

3.1. Selection, fitness, adaptation

As we have seen, living systems maintain a metabolism via input-output flows to pursue the goal of survival and reproduction in sustaining states of thermodynamic disequilibrium (i.e., states of order and complexity). This metabolism is regulated by information embodied in the living system, evolving over time: on the population level via natural selection (phylogeny) and on the organismic level via development and learning (ontogeny). Hence, the meaning of this information is its function in fulfilling the goals of the living system.[38] The generic theory of evolution explains how this information accumulates and changes through time.

Living systems actively maintain a state of embodied information that regulates a metabolism sustaining and reproducing their state of order relative to the environment.

Information in living systems is embodied in system-environment interactions and evolves on various levels.[39] This includes information accumulating within the boundaries of a living system (such as DNA universal to all living systems or memory in brains) and outside it, that is, in stable and embodied structures of the environment (such as the ecological niches of animals or durable artefacts of humans). This means that in the case of humans, evolutionarily significant information is distributed across various levels: For example, information about what we need to eat to sustain our metabolism is stored in our DNA, in the food habits of the group we live in, in information provided on the market, and in the structures of the environment that we partly created by ourselves, such as the vast infrastructure of rice farming.[40]

Information is distributed, stored, and transmitted across levels of evolution.

The general theory of evolution is the framework which integrates these different levels, grounding in the concept of (natural) selection under scarcity of resources. Scarcity is endogenous: In principle, the Earth system, receiving the continuous inflow of solar energy, is abundant in resources, especially the ultimate resource of energy (see section 2.2).[41] However, as said previously, living systems have the inherent tendency to grow and proliferate, which implies emerging scarcity of those resources on which they specialise at a certain point in time. This drives competition over access to resources and the capacities to harness resources efficiently and productively. The core mechanism of competition is selection. Hence, growth, scarcity, and competition are conjugated and constitute evolutionary universals.[42]

Growth, scarcity, and competition / selection are evolutionary universals.

Endogenous growth of living systems creates scarcity of resources and, hence, forces of selection in different modes.

Fitness defines a statistical correlation between the past and the present distribution of traits in a population.

For the closely related concept of heritability, see Chapter 15, section 4.1.

We elaborate this view of market selection in Chapter 11.

Adaptation denotes functional performance and involves intra-individual trade-offs and inter-individual frequency-dependent mechanisms. This results in status or rank competition in selection.

Selection is a complex notion because we cannot simply distinguish between the living system and its environment: As we have seen, the niche its partly determined by the living system and its boundary-constituting processes. Further, ecosystems are delicately balanced and coordinated networks of many living systems, which mutually shape their niches. This implies that one cannot define an absolute measure for two related core concepts in general evolutionary theory, namely fitness and adaptation.[43]

In Darwinian theory, fitness refers to relative reproductive success, which is strictly defined as a statistical correlation between traits across a sequence of generations of a population of living systems.[44] Fitness of a trait means that its share will grow through time, which establishes heredity as a statistical phenomenon: A trait is hereditary if the probability of its occurrence in the current generation is partly determined by its occurrence in the past generation and not only by current causal factors.[45] In this most general formal definition, the evolutionary concepts apply across many levels in terms of formal homologies: For example, the frequency of a product that prevails on a certain market is determined by its fitness, that is, competitive success in the previous periods, since earned profits allow for expanding production. However, as this example immediately reveals, the process of determining fitness is open and indeterministic because we must distinguish between realised fitness (i.e., competitive success) in the past periods, fitness as expected success in the next period, and the factors that determine realised fitness in that period. In Darwinian theory, these causal processes are most generally covered by the concept of adaptation. In our market example, adaptation relates to fulfilling the needs on the demand side, which determines the willingness of customers to buy the product, as well as to economic efficiency in terms of production cost.

Accordingly, adaptation denotes functional performance ultimately related to reproductive success as measured by fitness. Functional performance is multidimensional in two senses:

- First, any single functional performance of a living system is determined by the intra-system interplay between all functional performances relative to the niche. This creates complex trade-offs: For example, performance in intra-species sexual competition may foster traits which are costly in terms of other performances, such as speed and agility, as in the much-cited example of oversized antlers.[46]
- Second, functional performance is always determined by the interaction with other living systems. The simplest but universal phenomenon is the Red Queen competition or evolutionary arms races.[47] The fitness of an adaptation depends on all other adaptations adopted by competing living systems, considering their multidimensionality in the previous sense.

Taking these distinctions together, we conclude that selection is always and necessarily two-pronged. Many standard uses of the term 'natural selection' only refer to selection relative to a stable environment independently from the living system. An example is adapting the shape of fins to the hydrodynamics of water flows. This is an engineering interpretation of adaptation. However, there is also interactive selection via niche creation and, most importantly, intra- and inter-species selection. Competition enforces a regime in which relative adaptation (i.e., fitness) matters essentially. We refer to this as status (or rank) competition, which corresponds to interactive selection. Status competition does not necessarily concur with engineering adaptation but crucially determines reproductive success.

Those observations link the theory of selection to the general thermodynamics of living systems and, hence, are fundamental for the theory of evolution. In status competition, maximising power throughput and output is the selective criterion (running faster than others, being stronger than others, and so on), whereas the efficiency of energetic flows is only a secondary constraint. This corresponds to the general physical observation that power maxima are not the most efficient states;[48] engineering optimality is not identical with performance maximisation. Again, this observation extends across all levels by analogy and has been seminally stated in one of the core hypotheses in Veblen's theory of economic evolution: Market competition is competition over relative status in terms of relative profits and market shares and, hence, does not necessarily result into optimising technology in engineering terms.[49]

At the systems boundary, selection differentiates into two interdependent processes, namely internal and external selection. The former refers to the intra-organismic functional interdependencies which determine organismic-level adaptive performances as a multidimensional phenomenon. This generates macro-level consequences in establishing general structural characteristics of living systems linked by heredity, that is, common ancestry.[50] External selection operates on the organismic performances as a whole, ultimately determining relative reproductive success of individual variants. The interplay of internal and external selection is one reason why evolution tends to proceed gradually: The more radical innovations, the larger the risk of jeopardising internal organismic functioning given the respective degree of interdependency of traits.[51]

Selection alone cannot explain the continuous emergence of novelty because there is always a limit to improving existing functionings. There must be a source of innovation that is functionally independent of selection. This establishes the fundamental distinction between individual and type, or species, in evolution. Species embody accumulated information about functions as types relating to recurrent and similar adaptive needs, such as adapting to a niche with certain resource characteristics, or in the market context, general types of product uses, such as passenger transport by cars. Individuals embody

Competition over relative fitness creates a wedge between efficiency and power maximisation.

We explore these points further in Chapter 6, section 3.1, and Chapter 16, section 5.

Intra-organismic functional interdependencies condition internal selection of variations; inter-organismic competition conditions external selection.

Selection is a population-level process requiring exogenous individual variation.

We explore capabilities and functionings in Chapter 5, section 2.

a variation of capabilities that does not necessarily include or may transcend their current functionings (hidden talents). We conclude that selection is a population-level process which requires exogenous individual novelty to maintain its dynamics.

3.2. The VSR mechanism and levels of selection

The general mechanism of evolution results in the accumulation of embodied information via variation, selection, and retention (VSR mechanism).

We can now approach evolution in terms of a generic mechanism, which is well known in biology: variation, selection, and retention (the VSR mechanism), which drives the statistical interdependencies that define evolution as change of traits in a population.[52] A condition for selection is that living systems differ individually, if only minimally (VSR: variation). This difference is relevant for selection if it alters the capacity of a living system to exploit its resource base, over which it competes with others (VSR: selection). The consequence of selection is that the information stored in living systems evolves and reflects the differential capacity to create and exploit environmental niches (VSR: retention). Heredity as a statistical phenomenon can be explained by many causal factors beyond the genetic domain, such as epigenetic mechanisms or stable features of the environment, and it can be also established in purely non-genetic terms.[53] One important non-genetic mechanism of retention is the cultural transmission of traits.

Accumulation of information proceeds in the modes of evolution and learning, relating to phylogenesis and ontogenesis. In the case of humans, learning is of paramount importance.

In individual development of a living system (ontogenesis), the various causal factors of heredity work together. Living systems differ in the degree to which development involves learning. In the case of humans, learning is of paramount importance both on the individual and the group level. Learning allows for larger phenotypic plasticity and flexibility in adapting to various and changing environments. In principle, we can approach both learning and evolution with the same general VSR mechanism[54]: Learning is a mechanism in cultural selection. For example, in human societies, there are many channels by which individuals learn about constraints on their behaviour and experience social selection for relative status; yet they also test the limits of constraints via creative, entrepreneurial, and deviant behaviour. Both, together, drive cultural evolution, in which certain individual variations will be retained on the population level.[55]

Evolutionary economics employs different versions of the VSR mechanism to analyse market competition and evolution.[56] Market competition is mediated by various signals (such as prices and profits) and is constrained by the availability of resources, such as availability of physical stores of energy or wealth). Individual variation (entrepreneurship) drives the evolution of knowledge embodied in technology, as organised in firms (retention). In the first place, this is a formal homology. However, we can also ask how evolutionary processes in the economy interact with evolutionary processes in other domains of the Earth system. This is the co-evolutionary perspective of ecological economics.[57] As discussed previously, waste is externalised in the economic process but may eventually impact on availability of economic resources, such as harming ecosystems harnessed by human agriculture.

Depending on the various types of living systems, ecosystems, media of information storage, and transmission through time, there are different types of selection mechanisms. Three basic types are the following:

- Natural selection is selection by environmental forces and intra- and inter-species competition over natural resources.[58]
- Signal selection is selection mediated by signals in intra- and inter-species interaction and competition (such as signs, symbols, and language), with specific forms, such as sexual selection, a fundamental type of frequency-dependent selection.[59]
- Cultural selection is group selection mediated by cultural forms of establishing group boundaries and of group-specific patterns of cooperation.[60]

These various basic forms diversify in terms of levels of selection, units of selection, and mechanisms of information transmission.[61] For example, genes are often seen as units of natural selection, whereas units in cultural selection may be stable embodied patterns of meaning (sometimes theorised as memes).[62] Levels of selection reach from intra-organismic entities, such as genes to individuals, intra-species groups, or species.

The concept of selection levels refers to three basic features of general evolution that ground in the formal criterion of partitioning selection into within-group and between-group selection, which is a special case of the differentiation between external and internal selection (see previous section):[63]

- First, evolution manifests evolutionary transitions that result from the tighter integration of previously competing living systems in units that share a boundary to a common niche.[64] An example is the eukaryotic cell that emerged from integrating mitochondria and, in general, all kinds of complex organisms originating therefrom.
- Second, a crucial determinant of sustaining species-level functional adaptation is evolvability as a population-level property which cannot be reduced to individual properties.[65]
- Third, more specifically, both previous features can result in the phenomenon of group selection such that traits can be reproduced which reduce relative fitness within the group but nevertheless expand relative to traits in other groups because the trait contributes to the growth of group size relative to other groups.[66]

An important corollary of group selection is ultra-sociality. In an ultra-social species, group selection is an important form of selection that often dominates individual selection: In humans, this is salient in distinct cultural manifestations, such as group-oriented morality and altruism.[67] Co-evolutionary theory has developed criteria to differentiate levels and units depending on the evolutionary domain.[68]

*Living systems
evolve on different
levels with distinct
temporal dynamics
(eigentimes) that
shape the interactions
across levels.*

When considering the evolutionary dynamics of interactions across the various levels of evolution and across the various living systems constituting an ecosystem, the dimension of time is crucial. On the individual level, the basic pattern is the life cycle (see section 2.2).[69] On the group level, we have various time scales, reaching from generations to the secular dimension of civilisations, in case of humans. For the economy, time scales vary according to the durability of artefacts and to the sustainability and resilience of human-induced environmental changes (for example, there are irrigation systems managed as commons over many centuries[70]).

4. The evolutionary economy of living systems

4.1. Evolving synergy in ecosystems and the human economy

Central questions in understanding economic evolution are how the different levels and constituents of a human ecosystem interact, which mechanisms drive their respective evolutionary dynamics, and which shape the interactions. In most general terms, living systems co-evolve patterns of specialisation in the ecosystems in which they are interconnected, corresponding to the principle of division of labour in economics.[71] This specialisation is creative and productive: Creative in the sense of changing the space of resources, and productive in terms of raising ecological productivity as measured in biomass per unit of space. This applies for the human economy as well, where the market generates the expansion of the possible states of technology relative to the space of resources that can be exploited economically.

We devote
Chapter 5 to
specialisation.

See Chapter 6,
section 3.3.

*The stock of
resources in the
Earth system is
almost fixed and,
thus, subject
to entropic
degradation. Life
is a countervailing
force driven by
solar energy and
its capacity to
trigger chemical
transformations
of the stock of
resources.*

The Earth system is extraordinarily rich in a wide variety of materials, chemical compounds, and sources of energy. The material stock of resources is limited since the occasions are rare and minimal when additional materials arrive on Earth, such as when an asteroid falls down.[72] Thermodynamics implies that the stock erodes qualitatively through time, although the entire amount of matter is fixed: For example, soils erode by the impact of weather. Yet erosion can also become a resource (fertile soil created from erosion of rocks and other materials). The emergence of photosynthesis resulted in a fundamental transformation of the Earth system.[73] The continuous flow of solar energy counteracts stock erosion and keeps the Earth system far from thermodynamic equilibrium: For example, plants can contain soil erosion, and their debris contributes to the chemical reproduction of soil.

Living systems differ in terms of which specific resources they exploit. Hence, we can interpret evolution as a process by which the stock of information grows in exploring the resource space, which is embodied in the entire tree of life, thus linking phylogeny (diachrony) and ecology (synchrony). Since living systems are tightly connected in ecosystems, we can view an ecosystem as corresponding to a local stock of information distributed across all types of living systems in it.

The resource space is not given when we consider that living systems can directly or indirectly exploit other living systems as a resource: We refer to this as synergy.[74] The most general manifestation of this is food webs in ecological systems. The resource space evolves with the emergence of new variants of living systems, too. Eventually, however, the expansion is constrained by the general availability of resources, most universally, energetic flows: It is the specialisation of living systems that allows other living systems to feed on them without being able to exploit their resources themselves, with exploitation taking place indirectly via the food chain. The most significant example is the capacity of plants to conduct photosynthesis, thus enabling other living systems to consume plants: This is how they can exploit the resource base of a continuous flow of solar energy without being able themselves to feed on solar energy. Human agriculture as well as carbon-based industrialisation rest on this principle.

The fundamental principle in the evolutionary dynamics of living systems and ecosystems is the creation of qualitative novelty in exploiting stocks via the use of waste as a resource, thus driving the transformation of the chemical composition of the Earth system. The most dramatic transition of this kind by far was the Cambrian explosion, which was partly, though not predominantly, driven by raising oxygen levels in the atmosphere, a waste product of cyanobacteria. Once this was triggered, the mutual exploitation of waste products could achieve unprecedented scale, in the form of niche diversification via the emergence of new species (Figure 4.6). Accordingly, a fundamental principle of achieving sustainability of the entire ecological system via creating synergies is to achieve a high, if not complete, degree of recycling. This is because

Evolution explores and transforms the space of resources in the Earth system, with information distributed in ecosystems.

On transitions to agriculture and industrialisation, see Chapter 16, section 2.

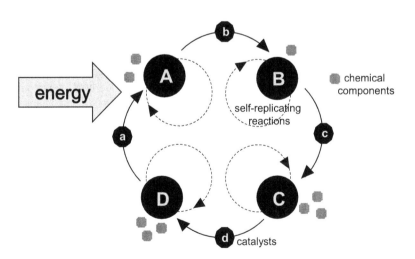

Figure 4.6 The autocatalytic cycle
In chemistry, the autocatalytic cycle refers to cyclically connected reactions that produce catalysts for other reactions as a by-product.

what is waste for one type of living system can become a resource for another system. The fundamental chemical mechanism for this is the autocatalytic cycle, where one chemical reaction produces the catalysts for another reaction as a side product and where a chain of such reactions is eventually closed.[75]

Evolution favours the emergence of autocatalytic network patterns because waste initially is a part of the potential resource space which is not subject to competition with other species. A human circular economy would follow an autocatalytic logic if it succeeds in fully using all wastes productively.

The fundamental problem in the relation between ecology and economy is the temporal disjunction of eigentimes of human waste production and the evolutionary emergence of ecological mechanisms of recycling.

One central issue in the relation between the human economy and ecosystems is that the former produces huge amounts of waste that cannot be recycled in the embedding ecosystems and, because of the high speed of waste accumulation, does not allow sufficient time for the biological evolution of living systems to create the capacity to recycle this waste. There is, thus, a pronounced difference in eigentimes of cultural and technological evolution on the one hand and biological evolution on the other. Accordingly, to render the human economy ecologically sustainable, endogenous forms of the circular economy need to be developed that technologically replicate the circularity of ecosystems.[76]

4.2. Cultural evolution, institutions, and human ultra-sociality

Humans differ from all other species in the important respect that the information about their explored resource space is not mainly stored in the genetic code but in culturally transmitted media of information.[77] In recent biological research, many forms of gene-environment interaction have been identified which build the bridge to human culture as a collection of various forms of heredity, further specified as media such as technology or institutions. In the standard Neo-Darwinian model, the only information storage is the genetic code which is not affected by environmental impacts after reproduction. Modern evolutionary theory recognises other channels such as epigenetic interactions; here, environmental impacts determine which, or how, genes find expression in ontogeny and behaviour, or in (the creation of) the niche and its artefacts as such, which, in endogenising selective forces, becomes a transmission line of information (Baldwin effect; Figure 4.7).[78]

Biological evolution unfolds via genetic and non-genetic channels of information transmission.

Thus, human culture greatly enhances the importance of non-genetic information transmission. The mediator between non-genetic and genetic endowments is the evolution of the social brain. Compared to other mammals, the human brain evolved a significantly different structure and relative size, which enabled more complex and contextualised social interaction in groups. This required even larger flexibility in behavioural adaptations, which was enabled by further differential development of the brain.

We investigate the social brain in Chapter 7.

The human social brain evolved the capacity for cultural learning.

The core biological adaptation to non-genetic transmission in humans is neoteny: Humans are unique in being born in a relatively immature state and going through a long stage in the life cycle (infancy, childhood, and

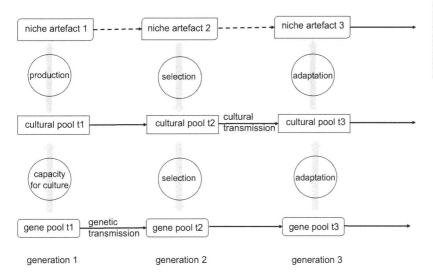

Figure 4.7 The basic co-evolutionary model
The basic channel of evolutionary information transmission is genetic. The human gene pool includes the capacity for culture via learning such that a cultural pool co-evolves with the gene pool. Human culture produces artefacts which construct the human niche. The niche selects cultural variants and ultimately channels genetic evolution that undergirds adaptation to the culturally conditioned niche.

adolescence) in which they accumulate information in their environment by various means, such as observation, teaching, and exploration; for this, they depend on parents, relatives, and peers, that is, there is a development-learning link.[79] More complex societies add other media, such as written texts and schooling. Genetically determined neoteny is a biological adaptation to non-genetic transmission and vice versa.

Another aspect of interaction between non-genetic and genetic transmission is the role of artefacts. For example, humans have no genetically endowed capacity for using fire but eventually learn it by growing up in groups that use fire.[80] While knowledge about fire is not genetically transmitted, the use of fire over a long time (probably 400,000 years) caused many adaptations of the human body, from the digestive track to the teeth, because fire enables cooking.[81] Cooking has greatly enhanced the resource base accessible to humans and has opened new spaces for behavioural innovation. By implication, human technology created a specific niche to which humans are biologically adapted: It is almost impossible to move back to a form of life based on nutrition that is entirely non-cooked, at least on a global scale, and certainly the current size of the human population could not be maintained.

Controlled fire and cooking are cultural artefacts that shaped the human organism in the very long run.

85

Key media of non-genetic transmission are group-based behavioural patterns, language, and artefacts.

On imitation,
see Chapter 7,
section 5.1.

Culture is based on human ultra-sociality and enables mechanisms of group selection via maintaining in-group vs. out-group boundaries.

On groups in a
social network
perspective,
see Chapter 8,
section 3.3.

The most important media of non-genetic transmission are behavioural patterns in the group of which an individual is a member, language, and artefacts. This creates new channels of information transmission and variation, thus leveraging the human capacity for innovation in exploiting the resource space.[82] These include a wide variety of horizontal information transmission channels, especially imitation, as opposed to almost exclusively vertical genetic transmission, and the possibility to recover information that has fallen out of use. Culture is the medium in which human learning is enabled.

The capacity for culture is the precondition for the emergence of human ultra-sociality: Human survival is based on cooperation in groups which, via cultural evolution, could achieve considerable size and complexity.[83] The human economy is an important manifestation of ultra-sociality in enabling a division of labour in terms of skills and knowledge (capabilities) and not only tasks as such (functionings). This kind of flexible cooperation requires the cultural transmission of norms, values, and institutions. The effectiveness of this cultural adaptation is ultimately expressed in biological dimensions as well, especially population growth, health status of populations, and ecological sustainability in the long run.[84] One of the key forms of institutionalised cooperation is the market which expands the reach of cooperation even beyond biologically and culturally circumscribed groups.[85]

Ultra-sociality conditions group selection as a specific form of cultural selection.[86] As we saw, the condition for group selection in living systems is that the interaction between group members creates group-level selective advantages that increase performance relative to individuals that belong to other groups, even if the individual contribution comes at a cost that would lower relative performance vis-à-vis other members of the cooperating group.

Group selection is enabled by mechanisms of distinguishing between in-group and out-group individuals and by mechanisms that monitor and enforce cooperation in the group. Human culture has evolved to enabling such mechanisms, as they are strong forms of expressing and maintaining group identities and of creating moral commitments.[87]

The term 'group selection' is multidimensional rather than confined to the genetic level. Human groups are defined by shared patterns of social interaction, such as norms and institutions, which are media of non-genetic information storage and transmission. Selection operates on these patterns and their adoption by human groups, which ultimately manifest in relative numbers of individuals that show those norms in their behaviour. There is no direct relation to biological measures of reproductive success on the level of individuals.

Given the importance of stabilising and enforcing group-level boundaries sustaining cooperation, the most significant cultural phenomenon for understanding the linkages across evolutionary levels, including markets, is institutions, that is, non-genetic rules that structure social interaction.[88] In concluding this chapter, we suggest a shift in the conceptual framework of co-evolutionary analysis.

So far, we followed the common approach in biology to extend evolutionary analysis to culture, where 'culture' is used as an extremely broad umbrella term which effectively covers all non-genetic transmission channels of adaptively relevant information. Since this appears overly broad and imprecise, in the subsequent chapters, we will reserve the concept of culture for those behavioural and artefactual phenomena that are transmitted across generations and demarcate groups against others, independently from their scale.[89] We treat 'technology' as referring to information embodied in artefacts and relating to lines of technological descent and innovation in the technosphere, and we refer to 'institutions' as the core phenomenon of behavioural coordination in human groups (Figure 4.8). In this view, institutions also figure as the central channel of non-genetic inheritance.

We distinguish between culture, technology, and institutions as distinct forms of non-genetic information transmission.

As a result, institutionalised behaviour manifests much scope for variation on the individual level, given the uniqueness of brains. At the same time, institutions create forces of convergence. Therefore, in terms of evolutionary

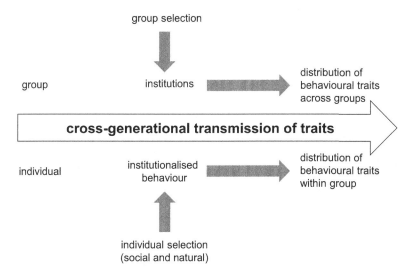

Figure 4.8 Institutions and group selection
The co-evolutionary model suggests that group selection operates on the level of institutions as shared properties in groups, which statistically relate to a distribution of behaviour in a population allowing for individual variation. This results in institutionalised behaviour of individuals which is subject to forces of natural and social selection, and hence, in two different distributions of behavioural traits, within-group and between-group, which is commonly conceived as cultural variety.

mechanisms, groups are carriers of institutions, and group selection is the primary analytical device for the study of institutions. Institutions are the channel by which groups are constituted that assume an autonomous role in selective dynamics. Genetic relatedness, if playing a role at all, can both figure as result and cause of group selection.

To conclude, in the case of humans, there are two new properties of the evolutionary process:

- First, there is the level of cultural or, more precisely, institutional evolution with distinct VSR mechanisms that are at least partly autonomous from the biological level. Variation is variation of symbolic forms, normative and institutional frames of behaviour, or idiosyncratic behavioural stances; selection is multidimensional and includes selection for social status, cultural prominence, or economic productivity; retention is multilevel and includes oral traditions, written media, or architectural artefacts.
- Second, human institutions are embedded in human groups, which implies that group selection is a dominant form of the VSR mechanism. Group selection in institutional evolution proceeds on many levels and via many mechanisms, from the basic biological level of differential population growth and related cultural mechanisms, such as migration, to cultural forms, such as war, cultural diffusion, or economic competition.

5. Conclusion

This chapter laid the foundations for a new materialism in economic analysis: We approached the economy from a third-person view by highlighting the biological, chemical, and physical causal mechanisms that determine its evolution, and we explored universal evolutionary theory as an explanatory framework. Culture, however, is the medium in which the second-person view prevails. One of the most powerful social-cognitive means to establish this view is market prices emerging from exchange in hypercomplex specialisation. Thus, the science of markets must always strive to achieve a reflective equilibrium between the second- and the third-person view. In practical terms, this means to establish tight cross-disciplinary relations of economics with the life sciences and the Earth sciences.

We have seen that there are two major explanatory frames that establish ontological continuity in the study of markets. The first is the formal analogy between evolutionary mechanisms across levels. This is the analytical stance of the evolutionary economics approach to markets, going back to seminal contributions of Veblen, Schumpeter, and Hayek.[90] The second is to ground the material analysis of market processes and outcomes to ecological analysis, which is the perspective of ecological economics.

Major chapter insights

- The human economy is an integral part of the Earth system. The thermodynamics of open evolutionary systems states that evolution tends towards maximising flow throughputs: This is the maximum power theorem. This principle applies on all levels, from the Earth system to the human economy, and explains why evolution goes hand in hand with growth.
- The emerging structures obey physical principles of flow organisation in metabolism, which shape growth processes, such as the unfolding of networks.
- Humans are living systems with ultra-sociality, with markets as a core manifestation. The theoretical framework for understanding living systems is evolutionary theory. Evolutionary theory applies both in terms of ontological continuity and formal homology.
- Evolutionary processes operate on biological as well as cultural levels. Across the levels, the same general type of mechanism applies in causal analysis: variation, selection, and retention (VSR). Selection is triggered and shaped by emergent scarcity in the growth of living systems.
- Living systems interact in ecosystems according to the general mechanism type of hypercyclic autocatalysis: The metabolic waste of one living system becomes a resource for another system. Therefore, the resource space of the Earth system evolves endogenously, only constrained by the inflow of solar energy.
- The human economy evolves via interaction between biological and cultural and institutional evolution, and ultra-sociality conditions a special role of group selection. The market is a special institutional form of social organisation emergent from cultural evolution that allows for the expansion of the division of labour beyond biological constraints, though operating according to homologous evolutionary principles.

Notes

1 This is the program pursued by bioeconomics; seminally, see Vermeij (2004, 2009) or Corning (1983, 2005).
2 The anthropocentric view is explicitly stated in Llavador et al. (2015) or Dasgupta (2021). On geocentrism, see Bohle and Marone (2019).
3 Folke et al. (2021).
4 Donges et al. (2017), Haider et al. (2021).

5 Witt (2003, 15ff).

6 The classic analysis is Boyd and Richerson (1985). For a comprehensive approach, see Mesoudi (2011).

7 Hull et al. (2001).

8 McNeill and Engelke (2014).

9 Haff (2012), Herrmann-Pillath (2013, 485f), Herrmann-Pillath (2018), Zalasiewicz et al. (2017).

10 Frank et al. (2017).

11 Malhi (2017), Zalasiewicz (2021).

12 The seminal approach to the species-centred niche was developed by the ethologist von Uexkuell, von Uexküll and Kriszat (1956). For a Darwinian view, see Odling-Smee et al. (2003). Our concept of living systems is inspired by Miller's (1978) monumental work.

13 This is explored in the biological discipline of behavioural ecology, see Davies et al. (2012).

14 Explicitly including the sink in economic analysis is the hallmark of ecological economics and, more specifically, of "Material Flow Accounting", see Krausmann (2018).

15 This perspective was developed by Georgescu-Roegen (1971) and is widely accepted in ecological economics today, see Costanza et al. (2014).

16 Kümmel (2011) argues that despite energetic exchange with the sun, the Earth system can be analytically approximated as an adiabatic system. The fundamental laws of thermodynamics can be summarised: The principle of the conservation of energy (first law), the impossibility of a perpetuum mobile or heat does not flow spontaneously from a cold to a warm body (second law stating that in a thermodynamic process, entropy cannot decrease), and at absolute temperature of zero, entropy approaches zero (third law). For an excellent introduction, see Atkins (2007).

17 Kleidon (2016).

18 Smil (2008, 297ff).

19 Kauffman (2000), Kolchinsky and Wolpert (2018).

20 Salthe (1993).

21 Kauffman (2000, 96ff), Atkins (2007).

22 This can be conceived in Darwinian terms as the 'extended phenotype', as suggested by Dawkins (1982).

23 Deacon (2013, 316ff).

24 This is the constructal law according to Bejan and Lorente (2010).

25 The maximum power principle was introduced by Alfred Lotka (1922a, 1922b) and plays a central role in some core contributions to ecological economics, such as Odum (2007).

26 Kleidon and Lorenz (2005), Dewar et al. (2013).

27 This corresponds to Schrödinger's (1944) famous definition of life.

28 For this, the term 'gaia' has been coined. Gaia is a global non-equilibrium system or, as mentioned previously, a hybrid planet today Lovelock (1990), Frank et al. (2017).

29 Bejan (2009).
30 For seminal views, see Bonner (1988) and Vermeij (2004).
31 These foundational perspectives on technology have been explored in the philosophy of technology, see Mitcham (1994).
32 Smil (2008, 300ff).
33 Much more detailed analysis considers empirical regularities in network evolution, such as scaling laws, West (2017).
34 Salthe (1993).
35 Smil (2019, 498ff).
36 Smil (2019, 31ff).
37 Turner et al. (2020).
38 Ayres (1994), Kolchinsky and Wolpert (2018).
39 Seminally, see Oyama (2001). There is a complex debate about the locus of biological information, where we adopt a non-reductionist position; overview in Godfrey-Smith and Sterelny (2016).
40 Richerson and Boyd (2005), Altmann and Mesoudi (2019).
41 On the physics, see Kåberger and Månsson (2001). Interestingly, this corresponds to the philosophical views of Bataille (2014[1949]).
42 This is the fundamental tenet of bioeconomics, Vermeij (2009).
43 Adaptation is a very complex notion with many and disputed meanings; for a survey, see Orzack and Forber (2017).
44 This statistical definition has been seminally formulated by Price (1995[1973]) who, thereby, created the foundations of evolutionary game theory which was widely received in economics. For a systematic treatment, see Frank (1995b).
45 For a full discussion, see Downes and Matthews (2020).
46 Zahavi and Zahavi (1997).
47 Robson (2005).
48 Odum (2007, 35ff).
49 Veblen (1990[1914]), Veblen (1983[1921]).
50 Gould (2002) develops this systemic multilevel view in rich detail.
51 Kauffman (1993, 237ff).
52 Frank (1995a).
53 Danchin et al. (2011), Lamm (2021).
54 Campbell (1960), Hull et al. (2001), Mesoudi (2011).
55 Hartley and Potts (2014).
56 Knudsen (2002), Knudsen (2004), Witt (2003).
57 Kallis and Norgaard (2010).
58 Gildenhuys (2019).
59 Zahavi and Zahavi (1997).
60 Mesoudi (2011), Bowles and Gintis (2011).
61 Jablonka and Lamb (2006), Lloyd (2020).
62 Aunger (2000), Hartley and Potts (2014), Schlaile (2021).
63 Sober and Wilson (1998), Frank (2009).
64 Maynard Smith and Száthmary (1995).
65 Gould (2002).

66 The mathematical foundation is the Simpson effect, Sprenger and Weinberger (2021).

67 Wilson (2015).

68 The classic is Boyd and Richerson (1985), followed by works such as Mesoudi (2011).

69 Salthe (1993).

70 Ostrom (1990).

71 Vermeij (2004).

72 This material view was introduced into economics by Georgescu-Roegen (1971).

73 Lenton et al. (2016).

74 Seminally, Corning (1983).

75 Maynard Smith and Szathmáry (1995), Ulanowicz (1997). This often specifically designated as hypercycle.

76 The concept of circular economy is still mainly a policy benchmark and needs further scientific clarification, see Korhonen et al. (2018).

77 Danchin et al. (2011).

78 Odling-Smee et al. (2003), Jablonka and Lamb (2006), Altman and Mesoudi (2019).

79 Zawidzki (2013) suggests the specific human capacity of mind shaping, resulting in group-level shared culture.

80 Ofek (2001), Brown et al. (2009).

81 Wrangham (2010).

82 Mesoudi (2011) gives a comprehensive account of cultural transmission channels.

83 Gowdy and Krall (2016).

84 Corning (1983), Corning (2003).

85 Seabright (2004).

86 Sober and Wilson (1998), Wilson (2015).

87 Bowles et al. (2003), Hartley and Potts (2014).

88 North (1991).

89 This follows the economic definition suggested by Beugelsdijk and Maseland (2010).

90 Veblen (1898), Schumpeter (2006[1911]), Hayek (1945).

References

Altman, A. and Mesoudi, A. (2019) 'Understanding Agriculture within the Frameworks of Cumulative Cultural Evolution, Gene-Culture Co-Evolution, and Cultural Niche Construction', *Human Ecology*, 47, pp. 483–497. DOI: 10.1007/S10745–019–00090-Y.

Atkins, P. (2007) *Four Laws That Drive the Universe*. Oxford: Oxford University Press.

Aunger, R. (ed.) (2000) *Darwinizing Culture: The Status of Memetics as a Science*. Oxford: Oxford University Press. DOI: 10.1093/ACPROF: OSO/9780192632449.001.0001.

Ayres, R. U. (1994) *Information, Entropy, and Progress: A New Evolutionary Paradigm*. New York: AIP Press.

Bataille, G. (2014[1949]) *La part maudite*. Paris: les Éd. de Minuit. DOI: 10.3917/ECOREV.040.0007.

Bejan, A. (2009) 'Science and Technology as Evolving Flow Architectures'. *International Journal of Energy Research*, 33(2), pp. 112–125. https://doi.org/10.1002/er.1427.

Bejan, A. and Lorente, S. (2010) 'The Constructal Law of Design and Evolution in Nature', *Philosophical Transactions of the Royal Society*, 365(1545), pp. 1335–1347. DOI: 10.1098/rstb.2009.0302.

Beugelsdijk, S. and Maseland, R. (2010) *Culture in Economics. History, Methodological Reflections, and Contemporary Applications*. Cambridge: Cambridge University Press.

Bohle, M. and Marone, E. (2019) 'Humanistic Geosciences and the Planetary Human Niche', in Bohle, M. (ed.) *Exploring Geoethics*. London: Palgrave Pivot, pp. 137–164. DOI: 10.1007/978-3-030-12010-8_4.

Bonner, J. T. (1988) *The Evolution of Complexity by Means of Natural Selection*. Princeton: Princeton University Press. DOI: 10.2307/j.ctv173f26c.

Bowles, S. and Gintis, H. (2011) *A Cooperative Species: Human Reciprocity and Its Evolution*. Princeton: Princeton University Press.

Bowles, S., Choi, Jung–Kyoo, J. and Hopfensitz, A. (2003) 'The Co–Evolution of Individual Behaviors and Social Institutions', *Journal of Theoretical Biology*, 223, pp. 135–147. DOI:10.1016/S0022-5193(03)00060-2.

Boyd, R. and Richerson, P. R. (1985) *Culture and the Evolutionary Process*. Chicago and London: University of Chicago Press.

Brown, K. S. *et al.* (2009) 'Fire as an Engineering Tool of Early Modern Humans', *Science*, 325(5942), pp. 859–862. DOI: 10.1126/science.1175028.

Campbell, D. T. (1987 [1960]) 'Blind Variation and Selective Retention in Creative Thought as in Other Knowledge Processes', in Radnitzky, G. and Bartley III, W. W. (eds.) *Evolutionary Epistemology, Rationality, and the Sociology of Knowledge*. La Salle: Open Court, pp. 91–114.

Corning, P. A. (1983) *The Synergism Hypothesis: A Theory of Progressive Evolution*. New York: McGraw-Hill.

Corning, P. A. (2003) *Nature's Magic: Synergy in Evolution and the Fate of Humankind*. Cambridge: Cambridge University Press.

Corning, P. A. (2005) *Holistic Darwinism: Synergy, Cybernetics, and the Bioeconomics of Evolution*. Chicago and London: Chicago University Press.

Costanza, R. *et al.* (2014) *An Introduction to Ecological Economics*. Boca Raton: CRC Press.

Danchin, É. *et al.* (2011) 'Beyond DNA: Integrating Inclusive Inheritance into an Extended Theory of Evolution', *Nature Reviews Genetics*, 12(7), pp. 475–486. DOI: 10.1038/nrg3028.

Dasgupta, P. (2021) *The Economics of Biodiversity*. Available at: https://www.gov.uk/government/collections/the-economics-of-biodiversity-the-dasgupta-review (Accessed: 18 March 2022).

Davies, N. B., Krebs, J. R. and West, S. A. (2012) *An Introduction to Behavioural Ecology*. Oxford: Wiley-Blackwell.

Dawkins, R. (1982) *The Extended Phenotype*. Oxford: Freeman.

Deacon, T. W. (2013) *Incomplete Nature: How Mind Emerged from Matter*. New York: Norton.

Dewar, R. C. *et al.* (eds.) (2013) *Beyond the Second Law. Entropy Production in Non-equilibrium Systems*. Heidelberg: Springer.

Donges, J. F. *et al.* (2017) 'The Technosphere in Earth System Analysis: A Coevolutionary Perspective', *The Anthropocene Review*, 4(1), pp. 23–33. DOI: 10.1177/2053019616676608.

Downes, S. M. and Matthews, L. (2020) 'Heritability', *The Stanford Encyclopedia of Philosophy,* Spring 2020 Edition. Available at: https://plato.stanford.edu/archives/spr2020/entries/heredity/ (Accessed: 18 March 2022).

Folke, C., Polasky, S., Rockström, J. *et al.* (2021) 'Our Future in the Anthropocene Biosphere', *Ambio*, 50, pp. 834–869. DOI: 10.1007/s13280-021-01544-8.

Frank, S. A. (1995a) *Foundations of Social Evolution*. Princeton: Princeton University Press. DOI: 10.2307/j.ctvs32rv2.

Frank, S. A. (1995b) 'George Price's Contribution to Evolutionary Genetics', *Journal of Theoretical Biology*, 175(3), pp. 373–388. DOI: 10.1006/JTBI.1995.0148.

Frank, S. A. (2009) 'Evolutionary Foundations of Cooperation and Group Cohesion', in Levin, S. (ed.) *Games, Groups, and the Global Good: Springer Series in Game Theory*. Berlin and Heidelberg: Springer. DOI: 10.1007/978-3-540-85436-4_1.

Frank, S. A., Kleidon, A. and Alberti, M. (2017) 'Earth as a Hybrid Planet: The Anthropocene in an Evolutionary Astrobiological Context', *Anthropocene,* 19, pp. 13–21. DOI. 10.1016/J.ANCENE.2017.08.002.

Georgescu-Roegen, N. (1971) *The Entropy Law and the Economic Process*. Cambridge: Harvard University Press.

Gildenhuys, P. (2019) 'Natural Selection', *The Stanford Encyclopedia of Philosophy*, Winter 2019 Edition. Available at: https://plato.stanford.edu/archives/win2019/entries/natural-selection/ (Accessed: 18 March 2022).

Godfrey-Smith, P. and Sterelny, K. (2016) 'Biological Information', *The Stanford Encyclopedia of Philosophy*, Summer 2016 Edition. Available at: https://plato.stanford.edu/archives/sum2016/entries/information-biological/ (Accessed: 18 March 2022).

Gould, S. J. (2002) *The Structure of Evolutionary Theory*. Cambridge and London: Belknap.

Gowdy, J. and Krall, L. (2016) 'The Economic Origins of Ultrasociality', *The Behavioral and Brain Sciences,* 39, p. e92. DOI: 10.1017/S0140525X1500059X.

Haff, P. K. (2012) 'Technology and Human Purpose: The Problem of Solids Transport on the Earth's Surface', *Earth System Dynamics*, 3(2), pp. 149–156. DOI: 10.5194/esd-3-149-2012.

Haider, L. J. *et al.* (2021) 'Rethinking Resilience and Development: A Coevolutionary Perspective', *Ambio,* 50(7), pp. 1304–1312. DOI: 10.1007/s13280-020-01485-8.

Hartley, J. and Potts, J. (2014) *Cultural Science: A Natural History of Stories, Demes, Knowledge and Innovation.* London and New York: Bloomsbury Academic. DOI: 1 0.5040/9781849666053.

Hayek, F. A. von (1945) 'The Use of Knowledge in Society', *American Economic Review,* 35(4), pp. 519–530.

Herrmann-Pillath, C. (2013) *Foundations of Economic Evolution: A Treatise on the Natural Philosophy of Economics.* Cheltenham and Northampton: Edward Elgar Publishing. DOI: 10.4337/9781782548362.

Herrmann-Pillath, C. (2018) 'The Case for a New Discipline: Technosphere Science', *Ecological Economics,* 149, pp. 212–225. DOI: 10.1016/j. ecolecon.2018.03.024.

Hull, D. L. *et al.* (2001) 'A General Account of Selection: Biology, Immunology and Behaviour', *Behavioral and Brain Sciences,* 24(2), pp. 511–573. DOI: 10.1017/S0140525X01004162.

Jablonka, E. and Lamb, M. J. (2006) *Evolution in Four Dimensions: Genetic, Epigenetic, Behavioral and Symbolic Variation in the History of Life.* Cambridge and London: MIT Press.

Kåberger, T. and Månsson, B. (2001) 'Entropy and Economic Processes – Physics Perspectives', *Ecological Economics,* 36(1), pp. 165–179. DOI: 10.1016/ S0921-8009(00)00225-1.

Kallis, G. and Norgaard, R. B. (2010) 'Coevolutionary Ecological Economics', *Ecological Economics,* 69(4), pp. 690–699. DOI: 10.1016/J.ECOLECON.2009.09.017.

Kauffman, S. A. (1993) *Origins of Order, Self-Organization and Selection in Evolution.* New York and Oxford: Oxford University Press. DOI: 10.1142/9789814415743_0003.

Kauffman, S. A. (2000) *Investigations.* Oxford: Oxford University Press.

Kleidon, A. (2016) *Thermodynamic Foundations of the Earth System.* Cambridge: Cambridge University Press. DOI: 10.1017/cbo9781139342742.

Kleidon, A. and Lorenz, R. (2005) 'Entropy Production in Earth System Processes', in Kleidon, A. and Lorenz, R. (eds.) *Non – Equilibrium Thermodynamics and the Production of Entropy: Life, Earth, and Beyond.* Heidelberg: Springer, pp. 1–20.

Knudsen, T. (2002) 'Economic Selection Theory', *Journal of Evolutionary Economics,* 12(4), pp. 443–470. DOI: 10.1007/S00191-002-0126-8.

Knudsen, T. (2004) 'General Selection Theory and Economic Evolution: The Price Equation and the Replicator/Interactor Distinction', *Journal of Economic Methodology,* 11(2), pp. 147–173. DOI: 10.1080/13501780410001694109.

Kolchinsky, A. and Wolpert, D. H. (2018) 'Semantic Information, Autonomous Agency and Non-Equilibrium Statistical Physics', *Interface Focus,* 8(6). DOI: 10.1098/rsfs.2018.0041.

Korhonen, J., Honkasalo, A. and Seppälä, J. (2018) 'Circular Economy: The Concept and its Limitations', *Ecological Economics*, 143, pp. 37–46. DOI: 10.1016/J.ECOLECON.2017.06.041.

Krausmann, F. (2018) 'Social Metabolism', in Spash, C. L. (ed.) *Routledge Handbook of Ecological Economics: Nature and Society*. London and New York: Routledge.

Kümmel, R. (2011) *The Second Law of Economics: Energy, Entropy, and the Origins of Wealth*. New York: Springer.

Lamm, E. (2021) 'Inheritance Systems', *The Stanford Encyclopedia of Philosophy,* Spring 2021 Edition. Available at: https://plato.stanford.edu/archives/spr2021/entries/inheritance-systems/ (Accessed: 18 March 2022).

Lenton, T. M., Pichler, P.-P. and Weisz, H. (2016) 'Revolutions in Energy Input and Material Cycling in Earth History and Human History', *Earth System Dynamics,* 7(2), pp. 353–370. DOI: 10.5194/ESD-7-353-2016.

Llavador, H., Roemer, J. E. and Silvestre, J. (2015) *Sustainability for a Warming Planet*. Cambridge: Harvard University Press.

Lloyd, E. (2020) 'Units and Levels of Selection', *The Stanford Encyclopedia of Philosophy,* Spring 2020 Edition. Available at: https://plato.stanford.edu/archives/spr2020/entries/selection-units/ (Accessed: 18 March 2022).

Lotka, A. (1922a) 'Contribution to the Energetics of Evolution', *Proceedings of the National Academy of Sciences*, 8, pp. 147–151.

Lotka, A. (1922b) 'Natural Selection as a Physical Principle', *Proceedings of the National Academy of Sciences*, 8, pp. 151–154.

Lovelock, J. E. (1990) 'Hands up for the Gaia Hypothesis', *Nature*, 344(6262), pp. 100–102. DOI: 10.1038/344100A0.

Malhi, Y. (2017) 'The Concept of the Anthropocene', *Annual Review of Environment and Resources*, 42(1), pp. 77–104. DOI: 10.1146/ANNUREV-ENVIRON-102016-060854.

Maynard Smith, John and Szathmáry, E. (1995) *The Major Transitions in Evolution*. Oxford and New York: Freeman. DOI: 10.1111/J.1558-5646.1995.TB04464.X.

McNeill, J. R. and Engelke, P. (2014) *The Great Acceleration: An Environmental History of the Anthropocene since 1945*. Cambridge: The Belknap Press of Harvard University Press.

Mesoudi, A. (2011) *Cultural Evolution: How Darwinian Theory Can Explain Human Culture and Synthesize the Social Sciences*. Chicago and London: University of Chicago Press.

Miller, J. G. (1978) *Living Systems*. New York: McGraw-Hill.

Mitcham, C. (1994) *Thinking Through Technology: The Path Between Engineering and Philosophy*. Chicago and London: University of Chicago Press.

North, D. C. (1991) 'Institutions', *Journal of Economic Perspectives*, 5(1), pp. 97–112.

Odling-Smee, F. J., Kevin, N. Z. and Feldman, M. W. (2003) *Niche Construction: The Neglected Process in Evolution*. Princeton: Princeton University Press.

Odum, H. T. (2007) *Environment, Power, and Society for the Twenty-First Century: The Hierarchy of Energy*. New York: Columbia University Press.

Ofek, H. (2001) *Second Nature: Economic Origins of Human Evolution*. Cambridge: Cambridge University Press.

Orzack, S. H. and Forber, P. (2017) 'Adaptationism', *The Stanford Encyclopedia of Philosophy,* Spring 2017 Edition. Available at: https://plato.stanford.edu/archives/spr2017/entries/adaptationism/ (Accessed: 18 March 2022).

Ostrom, E. (1990) *Governing the Commons. The Evolution of Institutions for Collective Action*. Cambridge: Cambridge University Press.

Oyama, S. (2001) *The Ontogeny of Information: Developmental Systems and Evolution*. Durham and London: Duke University Press.

Price, R. G. (1995[1973]) 'The Nature of Selection', *Journal of Theoretical Biology*, 175(3), pp. 389–396. DOI: 10.1006/JTBI.1995.0149.

Richerson, P. J. and Boyd, R. (2005) *Not by Genes Alone: How Culture Transformed Human Evolution*. Chicago: University of Chicago Press. DOI: 10.7208/CHICAGO/9780226712130.001.0001.

Robson, A. J. (2005) 'Complex Evolutionary Systems and the Red Queen', *Economic Journal*, 115(504), pp. F211–F224. DOI: 10.1111/J.1468-0297.2005.01002.X.

Salthe, S. N. (1993) *Development and Evolution: Complexity and Change in Biology*. Cambridge: MIT Press.

Schlaile, M. P. (2021) *Memetics and Evolutionary Economics: To Boldly Go Where No Meme Has Gone Before*. Cham: Springer. DOI: 10.1007/978-3-030-59955-3.

Schrödinger, E. (1944) *What Is Life? The Physical Aspect of the Living Cell*. Cambridge: Cambridge University Press.

Schumpeter, J. A. (2006[1911]) *Theorie der wirtschaftlichen Entwicklung*. Berlin: Duncker & Humblot.

Seabright, P. (2004) *The Company of Strangers: A Natural History of Economic Life*. Princeton: Princeton University Press.

Smil, V. (2008) *Energy in Nature and Society: General Energetics of Complex Systems*. Cambridge and London: MIT Press.

Smil, V. (2019) *Growth: From Microorganisms to Megacities*. Cambridge: The MIT Press.

Sober, E. and Wilson, D. S. (1998) *Unto Others: The Evolution and Psychology of Unselfish Behavior*. Cambridge and London: Harvard University Press.

Sprenger, J. and Weinberger, N. (2021) 'Simpson's Paradox', *The Stanford Encyclopedia of Philosophy,* Summer 2021 Edition. Available at: https://plato.stanford.edu/archives/sum2021/entries/paradox-simpson/ (Accessed: 18 March 2022).

Turner, M. G. *et al.* (2020) 'Climate Change, Ecosystems and Abrupt Change: Science Priorities', *Philosophical Transactions of the Royal Society B: Biological Sciences,* 375(1794). DOI: 10.1098/rstb.2019.0105.

Uexküll, J. and Kriszat, G. (1956) *Streifzüge durch die Umwelten von Tieren und Menschen: Bedeutungslehre*. Hamburg: Rowohlt.

Ulanowicz, R. E. (1997) *Ecology, the Ascendent Perspective*. New York: Columbia University Press.

Veblen, T. (1983[1921]) *The Engineers and the Price System*. New Brunswick: Transaction.

Veblen, T. (1898) 'Why is Economics not an Evolutionary Science?' *The Quarterly Journal of Economics*, 12(4), pp. 373–397.

Veblen, T. (1990[1914]) *The Instinct of Workmanship and the State of Industrial Arts*. New Brunswick and London: Transaction.

Vermeij, G. J. (2004) *Nature: An Economic History*. Princeton and Oxford: Princeton University Press.

Vermeij, G. J. (2009) 'Comparative Economics: Evolution and the Modern Economy', *Journal of Bioeconomics*, 11, pp. 105–134. DOI: 10.1007/S10818-009-9062-0.

West, G. B. (2017) *Scale: The Universal Laws of Growth, Innovation, Sustainability, and the Pace of Life in Organisms, Cities, Economies, and Companies*. New York: Penguin Press.

Wilson, D. S. (2015) *Does Altruism Exist? Culture, Genes, and the Welfare of Others*. New Haven and London: Yale University Press and Templeton Press.

Witt, U. (2003) *The Evolving Economy. Essays on the Evolutionary Approach to Economics*. Cheltenham and Northampton: Edward Elgar Publishing.

Wrangham, R. W. (2010) *Catching Fire: How Cooking Made Us Human*. London: Profile.

Zahavi, A. and Zahavi, A. (1997) *The Handicap Principle: A Missing Piece of Darwin's Puzzle*. New York and Oxford: Oxford University Press.

Zalasiewicz, J. *et al.* (2017) 'Scale and Diversity of the Physical Technosphere: A Geological Perspective', *The Anthropocene Review,* 4(1), pp. 9–22. DOI: 10.1177/2053019616677743.

Zalasiewicz, J. *et al.* (2021) 'The Anthropocene: Comparing Its Meaning in Geology (Chronostratigraphy) with Conceptual Approaches Arising in Other Disciplines', *Earth's Future,* 9(3). DOI: 10.1029/2020EF001896.

Zawidzki, T. (2013) *Mindshaping: A New Framework for Understanding Human Social Cognition*. Cambridge: MIT Press.

CHAPTER FIVE

Specialisation and cooperation

1. Introduction

The previous chapter revealed a homology between ecological and economic specialisation: In an ecological network of various niches, living systems both specialise in the exploitation of specific resources in their environment and in contributing to the advantage of other living systems, resulting into productivity enhancement of the entire ecological system. Similarly, in the human economy, individuals specialise on specific skills and enter exchange relations in various arrangements with markets and firms as dominant forms, which increases the productivity of the entire economic system. In this section, we develop the principles of specialisation as an emergent phenomenon in economic evolution that extends the general framework of evolutionary theory. In the case of humans, the strategic perspective on coordination of actions in groups gains key importance. The most general pertinent analytical model is the social contract: The evolutionary condition for sustainability takes the form of voluntary agreement on specialisation and participation in the division of labour.

Ecological and economic specialisation are formally homologous.

Strategic actions to specialise face many issues of coordination and commitment to agreements. One of the core problems of economics is to explain constraints on gains from cooperation in any social form, including markets, and to find ways to overcome these obstacles. Markets, in the first place, are a form of cooperation in which competition is a core organising feature. Specialisation is risk-taking. Accordingly, we highlight the core theoretical complement to the famous invisible hand theorem[1] in economics, the specialisation dilemma.[2] In this view, specialisation always includes the possibility that asymmetric positions of power emerge endogenously which create a wedge between the general gains from cooperation in the group and their distribution among members of the group.

Cooperation is necessary to overcome obstacles to making competition work on markets.

In Chapter 15, we analyse these forms as inequality regimes.

One important consequence is that patterns of social power can determine the externalisation of costs of economic action (think of the power struggles

99

DOI: 10.4324/9781003094869-8

and economic forces driving the deforestation of the Amazonas region). In this chapter, we unfold these arguments, starting in section 2, with the general notion of comparative advantage and gains from cooperation, followed by an analysis of the specialisation dilemma. After looking at basic problems of coordination in cooperation, in section 3, we analyse forced exchange as the counter-pole of ideal typical voluntary exchange on markets. In section 4, we conclude by discussing the efficiency of specialisation in the light of omnipresent externalities.

2. Specialisation and exchange: Gains and limitations

2.1. Comparative advantage

Specialisation in human groups enhances productivity because it allows the single member to become more productive and because group activities become possible which cannot be accomplished individually.

Human ultra-sociality enabled the attainment of adaptive advantages of human groups via specialisation of cooperating group members and changing the nature of work, the division of labour.[3] There are two advantages of specialisation:

- The first is that individuals may be more productive in certain tasks, given their genetically endowed and culturally acquired capabilities, enhancing efficiency of resource use.
- The second is that, in combining these skills, the production of new types of activities and products is enabled that are impossible to achieve by individual activities alone.

For the evolutionary background, see Chapter 4, section 3.1.

The archetypical example, which is important in the context of human phylogeny and the evolutionary emergence of cooperative capabilities, is the group hunt: The group hunt enables the killing of large game, that is, vastly increases the productivity of individual labour time, but is impossible to achieve alone. Thus, an innovation in social organisation radically changed the human adaptive niche.[4]

Specialisation as a form of cooperation is different from individual specialisation. Consider the example of Robinson Crusoe: The only way Crusoe can enlarge the product gained by his labour is to acquire specific skills and to invest into capital. For example, if fish proves to be especially nutritious and easy to get, he might gain in specialising on catching fish and neglecting other activities, following an individual cost-benefit calculus. But only after meeting Friday can he reap additional gains beyond what he could at maximum achieve alone, based now on the comparison between the relative advantages and the possible gains from specialisation of Robinson and Friday.

Specialisation is the subject of one of the most universal economic hypotheses, the law of comparative advantage. This law, originally discovered in the context of international trade theory,[5] applies on all levels of economic activity. In a group of hunters, the skilled marksman may be able to do all other tasks better than a weak member of the group, but that does not mean that he should do any of these tasks by himself. The criterion of assigning tasks to group members is not what she or he achieves in the tasks compared to others who do the same task but what she or he cannot do when assuming a task. This is the opportunity cost principle: A single individual would compare lost opportunities when choosing a course of action and would go for the least cost, and in a group, the pattern of cooperation would follow a comparison between possible gains lost across all members.

The principle of comparative advantage states that specialisation in a group minimises the lost gains (the opportunity cost) from assigning tasks to individual members.

The other core concept for understanding the division of labour in groups is exchange. Once individuals specialise and can no longer survive in autarky, they must exchange the product of their work with others. Exchange can take many forms, but the most fundamental distinction is between voluntary and forced exchange.[6] In economics, the archetypical form of voluntary exchange is the market, and of forced exchange, it is the government, with primordial forms such as sheer physical dominance over others. What unifies all forms of forced exchange is that power asymmetries in any form result in exchange violating the criteria of reciprocity which are met in voluntary exchange. In anthropology and the social sciences, many variations of forms of exchange between these ideal-typical poles are recognised as well as many forms of political organisation of power, such as chiefdoms or empires.[7] However, in all contexts, the question is how we can establish criteria for distinguishing between voluntary and forced exchange, which also relates to the distinction between reciprocal and unequal exchange.[8]

There are two ideal-typical forms of exchange, voluntary and forced, defining a spectrum of variants.

In economics, gains from trade imply that voluntary specialisation meets the so-called Pareto criterion: If members of a group specialise, nobody loses compared to the status quo ante in absolute terms.[9] The Pareto criterion has an ambivalent analytical status because it can be interpreted in both a second- and a third-person perspective. In the second-person view, it is a normative principle of the underlying social contract: If individuals agree to cooperate, this presupposes that everybody gains, that is, nobody can be forced to assume a certain task. Every group member judges the advantages from cooperation and would agree for purely subjective reasons, that is, grounded in the first-person view.[10]

The Pareto criterion states that in absolute terms, nobody loses from specialisation compared to the status quo.

See our discussion of efficiency as value in Chapter 3, section 3.

However, when we look at the situation from the third-person view, the Pareto principle can also serve as a positive criterion of measurement, following the logic of revealed preferences: We know from observing cooperation that nobody receives less product than in autarky as long as participation is voluntary. Therefore, freedom obtains the status of a necessary condition for reaching an assessment of the cooperation from the third-person view, as this view is exclusively based on observation of the fact of cooperation.

The Pareto principle is both a normative and a positive hypothesis that is independent from applying a unified measure of advantage but in both senses presupposes freedom (i.e., voluntary participation).

The analytical significance of freedom is also salient when we evaluate the ex post situation in terms of the change of outside options for the involved

*Capabilities
refer to potential
comparative
advantage, and
functionings to
realised comparative
advantage.*

See, for a
social justice
perspective
on deskilling,
Chapter 3,
section 2.4.

*Specialisation
interacts with
the formation of
capabilities and,
hence, the scope
of outside options
beyond realised
functionings.*

See Chapter 6,
section 4.2.

agents. This is covered by the distinction between capabilities and function-ings in specialisation: The capabilities refer to the range of possible speciali-sations that are feasible to a member of a cooperating group, and the functionings refer to the realised pattern of specialisation;[11] capabilities are potential comparative advantage, and functionings are realised comparative advantage. The point is that either can there be a tight match between capabil-ities and functionings such that realising a certain functioning defines com-parative advantage exclusively, or there is a surplus of capabilities which would allow for realising a broader range of functionings than the realised ones. This wider set of capabilities would define the potential comparative advantage that can be realised by actual functionings adapting to varying eco-nomic circumstances.

Hence, the opportunity cost of realised specialisation includes the potential loss of dynamic capabilities to adapt to new circumstances, thus changing the outside options and the structure of opportunity costs. Patterns of specialisa-tion of functionings and capabilities are interlinked, as the fulfilment of func-tionings goes along with the development of capabilities, such as via on-the-job learning. In the economy, this distinction allows for the possibility that current specialisation, as driven by market signals and possibly persisting over longer time spans, goes too far. For example, a deskilling of human labour has been observed in many contexts, such as in the time of diffusion of industrial facto-ries. Workers specialise on narrowly defined tasks and fulfil them with high accuracy and speed, such as in the context of Taylorism, the doctrine of scien-tific management that emerged in the early 20th century, but never acquire broader skills that would cover more aspects of the production process.[12] This makes them vulnerable to technological change that alters the current pattern of specialisation.

Therefore, in order to judge the outcome of a specific pattern of specialisa-tion, it is crucial to include its effects on capabilities, which define the degrees of freedom that members have in choosing outside options. The larger the scope of outside options, the higher the probability that the current pattern is to the benefit of the respective members and enhances total productivity on the group level. As the formation of capabilities requires investment and costs of sustaining them, this violates static criteria of efficiency in resource use while maintaining degrees of freedom of evolving new patterns of specialisation.[13]

2.2. The specialisation dilemma

Even if individuals know the gains from cooperation, exchange may be blocked by problems of coordinating their actions. The specialisation dilemma stands at the core of this problem.[14] Imagine that Friday and Robinson agree to specialise along comparative advantage: Friday would do the fishing, and Robinson would do gardening, and later, they would share the product via exchange. The problem is that both parties cannot observe whether the other keeps the agreement. If one party reneges and does not fully specialise, he can create a position of power because he is less dependent on the other and can, therefore, shift the terms of exchange in his favour. This entails the possibility that a party specialises less in order to safeguard ex post agential power, thus sacrificing potential gains from trade while increasing their relative share in the joint product. If Robinson continues to fish while Friday fully specialises, Friday will be more dependent on Robinson than vice versa.

As said, specialisation implies that the parties will produce a part of the joint product that they cannot consume by themselves anymore; in most forms of cooperative specialisation on markets, the parties produce goods and services that they cannot use by themselves at all. Hence, the fundamental problem of cooperation is to ensure that the parties will produce the right quality and quantity of the product that is exchanged and that all parties stick to the agreement to specialise. The specialisation dilemma is exacerbated when considering the role of ex ante uncertainty in identifying comparative advantage. Contrary to the Crusoe-Friday example, on markets, suppliers and buyers normally do not agree in advance about specialisation (although there is a range of intermediate forms of exchange, such as in bespoke production of consumer goods or special arrangements in supplier relations about specific tools). At the same time, in temporal terms, agents often must first invest into specialisation, such as by engaging into production or acquiring certain skills, before they can potentially reap the gains from exchange. Thus, uncertainty implies a status quo bias against specialisation because individuals cannot safely predict those gains.[15]

If a party produces exclusively for the market, this implies that the specialisation is highly specific to market opportunity. We refer to this as capability specificity.[16] This notion refers to any kind of capacity to gain advantage from specialisation by means of investing in pertinent capabilities to produce for the market.[17] Several dimensions can be distinguished.

First is the *specificity of capabilities to specialise*. There are two main dimensions here: One is the formation of skills and knowledge; the other is the build-up of specific physical assets. Indeed, specialising on a product does not necessarily mean to specialise capabilities: Growing cabbage may not differ much from growing radish. But building a greenhouse is expensive and cannot be used for all kinds of products.

Second, there is *specificity in the temporal dimension*. A product may lose in value rapidly once the temporal structures of opportunity and product durability differ. The classic example is a fish market where the fish must be sold on the same day.[18] If fishermen offer too many fishes, their bargaining power diminishes since buyers may just wait until the fishermen are forced to sell at bargain prices; in fact, shortly before the fish turns unsalable, they would accept any price above zero.[19] Such a constellation can emerge in many contexts, such as in fashion, where fads can change rapidly and producers may

The specialisation dilemma highlights the fact that specialisation may create incentives to renege on the original agreement to specialise. If parties anticipate that, they are less willing to specialise.

We look at the temporal aspect of market transactions more closely in Chapter 11.

We refer to the specialisation dilemma in various contexts, such as the theory of the firm (Chapter 11, section 5) or international trade (Chapter 14, section 3.1).

In the most general sense, capability specificity refers to the formation of capabilities to specialise that are specific to market opportunity.

overestimate market demand. An important pattern that applies on many markets is the so-called hog cycle, which results from lack of coordination among many suppliers of a good:[20] Raising pigs needs time, and once they mature, market conditions may have changed because everyone jumped on the opportunity. Another market that manifests this problem is the labour market: Qualifications need time to be acquired, but demand may change later, and lack of coordination among individual decisions may lead to oversupply of certain qualifications.[21]

Dimensions of capability specificity include capabilities to specialise, temporal, spatial, and social.

Third, there is *specificity in the spatial dimension*, which is normally intertwined with the temporal dimension. For example, a supplier who sends goods to a remote location may be forced to accept price discounts when demand turns out to be low once the goods have arrived, as the cost of moving the goods to another place would then be too high. Locating a production site close to an important customer saves cost but may put the producer in a weaker position in price negotiations at a later stage. Core markets in the economy that manifest a combination between temporal and spatial specificity are the markets for real estate and construction. Forecasting future demand is as uncertain as knowing the decisions of other real estate investors in advance.[22]

For more on economic cycles, see Chapter 13.

Last, there is the *specificity of social relations*, which adds complexity, as social networks can become endogenous in the specialisation decision (see subsequent section). For example, if someone wants to be successful as a real estate entrepreneur, she must invest in networking with the real estate community, thus building up social capital. Social capital can manifest varying degrees of asset specificity, especially when it comes to specific identities of network members; for example, with respect to consumption or dressing patterns.

We discuss social capital in detail in Chapter 8, section 3.2.

All these types of capability specificity create risks for the specialising party to lose agential power to the other party and, hence, may motivate decisions that limit the degree of specialisation. Possibilities to overcome problems of capability specificity depend on the precise type of asset and pattern of interaction concerned and, in particular, on whether strategic behaviour is involved.

3. Strategic interaction and power

3.1. The archetypes

Canonical games in game theory allow to identify archetypical problems in overcoming the specialisation dilemma.

In this section, we look at the specific role of strategic behaviour in specialisation. In economics, this is the domain of game theory. We cannot introduce the formal apparatus of game theory here but only refer to certain canonical forms of games in distinguishing between different types of strategic behaviour in specialisation.[23] We approach agential power as a relational term: What often counts in considering strategic interaction are not the pay-offs in absolute but in relative terms.[24] Therefore, agents would form expectations about

Party 1	Party 2		
		A	B
	A	1,1	0,0
	B	0,0	1,1

Figure 5.1 Coordination game
In this and the subsequent figures, we show two strategic choices, A and B, for each party, which are symmetric. The boxes show the resulting pay-offs for a specific combination of choices in the order of the numbering of the parties. We count as equilibrium those combinations where there are no incentives to deviate. In the simple coordination game, there are two equilibria, which creates the problem of how to select one of them. In equilibrium, there is no difference in pay-offs, but both parties gain in absolute terms.

resulting differences among them once a round of strategic interaction is concluded. This is well known in military strategy where differences between military capacities matter rather than absolute levels.[25] One general observation is that in games of difference, problems of cooperation are accentuated, such as in arms races.

Let us first consider cooperation that is certain to achieve, provided that it is ensured by appropriate flows of information: Cooperation is a mere problem of coordination (Figure 5.1), even when considering relative status since relative positions of agents do not change across the various joint outcomes.

When we only consider two parties specialising to a degree that they both take part in a joint production in which they cannot consume their own product independently from the other, we have a pure coordination game. The canonical example is Hume's famous parable of several men jointly rowing a boat (strategies A and B in Figure 5.1 correspond to alternative timings of beats). If they fail to coordinate, the boat will wallow. Hence, there is a strong interest in coordination: The men might even be willing to subordinate to a leader who coordinates their actions. There are no incentives to cheat or renege on the cooperation agreement because the individual gains from cooperation are always larger than the individual gains from non-cooperation, once the boat wallows.

.Pure coordination problems, such as the standard example of driving left or right, do not involve differences. But there are problems, often labelled as battle of the sexes (Figure 5.2), where pay-offs differ in the two alternatives. Even if both parties are happy with realising cooperation in any form, one party may relatively gain more and generate status gains that might even accumulate through time. If the other party focuses on this consequence, the coordination game will collapse. In cooperation agreements between firms, a

Coordination problems in specialisation are accentuated if differential pay-offs lead to increasing status differences through repeated interactions.

	Party 2		
Party 1		A	B
	A	3,1 (+2, −2)	0,0 (0,0)
	B	0,0 (0,0)	1,3 (−2, +2)

Figure 5.2 Battle of the sexes

In the battle of the sexes, there are two equilibria that are stable unless the actors focus on differences in pay-offs (shown in brackets), which might induce one party to renege on cooperation since she will realise a loss. However, in absolute terms, the equilibria represent advantages for both and, hence, match the Pareto criterion.

supplier may be satisfied with cooperating with a large producer even though the producer gains relatively more; once other opportunities arise, however, it might decide to cancel the cooperation. This shows that in applying game archetypes to real-world social interactions, it is often misleading to only consider the absolute pay-offs of one specific game structure.[26] Often, what matters is the opportunity cost of playing the game as such, which are the pay-offs of available alternative games.

The case of rowing a boat stands for a type of cooperation in which the failure to specialise is immediately obvious to everybody. Yet there is room for cheating with respect to the actual individual energy and effort spent on rowing below the threshold when the boat starts to wallow. This is another motivation for installing a leader as supervisor because the rowing individuals cannot mutually observe their effort.

In cooperation with opportunities of free-riding, the prisoner's dilemma is an archetypical problem of strategic interaction.

Such constellations can result in another game structure, the prisoner's dilemma (Figure 5.3). An example is the joint exploitation of a shared resource such as a water reservoir. All parties know that if they individually withdraw too much water, the resource may be overexploited. But if most members observe a withdrawal limit and some continue to maximise, they can gain and may even reduce water supply to others. If there is mutual mistrust, all parties will violate the cooperation agreement and the reservoir will rapidly deplete. This is the tragedy of the commons.[27]

Positive externalities inherently involve free-riding of beneficiaries, creating opportunities for exchange if exclusion is possible.

Another important class of cooperation problem concerns the allocation of useful by-products (waste) or, more generally, positive externalities. Positive externalities pose a coordination problem that emerges in sustaining efforts through time, such as motivating beekeepers to continue with their activity that sustains pollination of fruit trees.[28]

A paradigmatic example referring to prehistoric conditions is the maintenance of fire in a co-residing community via organisation of night watches.[29] Fire must be maintained overnight at least by one member of the group to enable all others to light their fire again next morning. While sharing the fire

		Party 2	
		A	B
Party 1	A	2,2 (0,0)	−1,3 (−4,+4)
	B	3, −1 (+4,−4)	0,0 (0,0)

Figure 5.3 Prisoner's dilemma

The prisoner's dilemma describes a coordination problem where there are strong individual incentives to move to an individually higher pay-off, to the detriment of the other party. However, if this strategy is adopted by both parties, a Pareto-inferior outcome for both results, which is the equilibrium. This is exacerbated in the difference scheme.

does not entail any cost to the individual, the effort to keep it does. Of course, the individual who keeps the fire has a strong interest in doing so because she directly benefits from it. But she could gain more if the community agrees on a rotating arrangement in which members take their turn in keeping the fire, which would internalise the externality and preclude free-riding. In this case, the agreement could easily be monitored. The problem of keeping incentives over time is prevalent in many other constellations: for example, at first sight, a successful single hunter could freely share his game because it will rot anyway; but others can free-ride on his hunting efforts, which is why again, internalisation becomes a necessity.

Useful waste is one origin of reciprocal exchange because the individual who controls the waste has incentives to create opportunities for exchange from which additional benefits may be generated. However, there are many forms of cooperation that have a different pay-off structure. The paradigmatic example is the group hunt as seminally analysed by Rousseau, mostly labelled as 'stag hunt' (Figure 5.4).[30] In this case, some individuals specialise on chasing, others on shooting. The problem is that the outcome of the effort is uncertain and that everyone needs to predict whether all others will be dutifully fulfilling their part. For that reason, some chasers might be attracted by catching small fry, such as hares, to be on the safe side. That would jeopardise the success of the hunt due to a lack of available chasers even though everyone would be better off with the large game, such as a stag. One remarkable feature of this pay-off structure is that in the Pareto-optimal solution, there are no differences in pay-offs so that striving for relative gains does not undermine cooperation once the solution is established. Someone who still aims at relative gains (which are substantial) must incur an opportunity cost, which is the loss in comparison to the Pareto-optimal solution. Hence, in the stag hunt, commitment to cooperation matters essentially in launching the cooperation in the first place, but once cooperation works, there are no incentives to deviate.

On fire in human prehistory, see Chapter 4, section 4.2.

On the role of exclusion in sustaining cooperation, see Chapter 8, section 3.3.

The stag hunt is one of the primordial forms of strategic interaction in human cooperation.

Party 1		Party 2	
		A	B
	A	4,4 (0,0)	0,3 (−3,+3[−1])
	B	3,0 (+3[−1],−3)	2,2 (0,0)

Figure 5.4 Stag hunt

In the stag hunt, the parties can fall back to a status of individually attainable pay-offs (hares (BB)) or they can cooperate to attain a higher pay-off (the large game (AA)). In the latter case, the parties may experience ex ante incentives to fall back on the individual strategy, gaining even more than in status quo BB (others don't chase hares, so they can gain more) but losing in relation to full cooperation AA (opportunity cost indicated by [−1], i.e., the loss relative to AA). The perceived risk of relative loss may induce ex ante choice of BB.

Status-based specialisation is a salient pattern in historical transitions to more complex societies.

The stag hunt is of great interest as it reflects a phylogenetically crucial form of human cooperation, given that cooperative hunting of large and often dangerous game was one of the essential sources of sustaining human groups.[31] At its base, this is a coordination problem: Cooperation is a dominant strategy, but uncertainty about behaviour looms large.

In sum, our discussion of canonical games shows that as long as agents maximise relative pay-offs, cooperation is fragile. Beyond this observation, relative status also allows for imposing conditions of cooperation on others. This is clear from the historical record when original cooperation had a strong potential to develop into status-based specialisation, such as in the transition from egalitarian hunter-gatherer groups to tribal societies and chiefdoms, and eventually, kingdoms and empires, with highly unequal distributional outcomes.

See Chapter 9, section 5, and Chapter 15, sections 3.2 and 4.3.

3.2. Power and forced specialization

Forced specialisation includes both distributions of gains that violate the Pareto principle and distributions that match the Pareto principle but assign only a minimal gain to the powerless.

Forced specialisation is possible if some parties in the cooperating group have special power positions that allow them to coerce others into cooperation at conditions that are worse than in the case of purely voluntary cooperation (but not necessarily worse than in the status quo). There are three possible cases:

- In the first case, the Pareto criterion is fulfilled but combined with a high degree of intra-group inequality, which can be upheld by threats of violence (although not necessarily by actually applying violence such that other forms of power are more important for sustaining the constellation).
- In the second case, the Pareto criterion is violated but total output increases. The increase may be appropriated by a relatively small elite whereas the majority of group members loses out. Visible incidence of violence is, therefore, necessary for stabilising this constellation.

- In the third case, the Pareto criterion is violated and total output decreases. In this case, application of violence is widespread and necessary for sustaining the constellation.

Agreeing to a distribution that only provides minimum advantage to some members can potentially be of a voluntary nature since it meets the Pareto criterion (first case). This implies that agreeing with a most lopsided distribution of gains from specialisation would be a rational decision. The classical experimental setup for assessing the real-world sharing behaviour of individuals are dictator and ultimatum games.[32] The result of this research is that most individuals would not accept the offer of a rule that leaves them with only a minimal share; often, proposers go for a 50/50 sharing rule. The question is whether the receivers can build countervailing power to the power of the proposer. If they reject the lopsided offer, they pay the cost of losing the advantage. In some versions of the experiments, the proposer would lose their endowment upon refusal of the receiver, which turns the experiment into a test of cooperation as analysed up to this point.

In many circumstances, agreeing to lopsided distributions of gains from specialisation is rational, yet people refuse to cooperate.

Whether threats to refuse cooperation induce powerful actors to give up their attempts at coercion depends on the advantage they would lose when others threaten not to cooperate. This relates to the different degrees of capacity specificity of specialisation, as outlined earlier. We can connect this with the general definition of power originally suggested by James Coleman: "The power of an actor resides in his control of valuable events. The value of an event lies in the interests powerful actors have in that event".[33] This is a recursive definition of power which clearly establishes a second-person view and focuses on the interdependence between members of a group structured by power relations. It can be connected to the principle of comparative advantage: All members of a group that enacts specialisation principally have an interest in that cooperation; they control not only their own advantage from cooperation but also the advantage that accrues to all others via the threat of withdrawal. Therefore, what matters for establishing power relations is the opportunity cost of cooperation versus non-cooperation for the different individuals because those opportunity costs define individual interests.

Power emerges from differences in the strength of interest that group members have in cooperation and the relative extent of mutual control in actualising those interests.

This is a major basis of intrafirm inequality, see Chapter 15, section 3.2.

Consider, again, a group of hunters. The best marksman controls the advantages that all others can gain from cooperation, particularly if he holds a monopoly as a shooter. All other members have a strong interest in cooperation because the opportunity cost of remaining in the status quo is high. Other members also exert control of the advantage that the marksman gets from cooperation, which, however, is smaller in terms of opportunity cost since the marksman may successfully hunt game alone. As a consequence, the marksman is more powerful than the other members of the group. In the modern economy, workers may suffer more when losing a job than the entrepreneur, who might close the factory and move capital to a new project.[34]

In creating outside options, competition can reduce power differentials in cooperation.

Accordingly, competition is a core feature of market design, see Chapter 11.

A general principle of cultural evolution is that circumscription of outside options fosters unequal distribution of power in groups.

A fundamental form of specialisation is specialisation on violence.

For the relation of violence to institutions and power, see Chapter 9, section 5.2.

This analysis implies that specialisation and power are necessary correlates. We can identify two crucial elements that determine the distribution of power in specialisation. First, there is a collective action issue in terms of the opportunity cost of reneging on cooperation. If the individual chaser threatens withdrawal, the effect on cooperation is minuscule, so the power differential to the marksman is large. But for a group of chasers acting collectively, the effect is much stronger. Therefore, in all arrangements of cooperation, there are embedded issues of cooperating in negotiations over the terms of cooperation (such as whether chasers would be able to cooperate in negotiating collectively with the marksman).[35] Second, competition for power positions plays an important role. The marksman's monopoly can be challenged by others, who eventually may become as proficient as he is. Hence, a fundamental idea in economics is that competition minimises the role of power in specialisation.[36] Competition is a crucial condition for minimising the risk of entering specialisation based on asymmetric exchange because it creates outside options endogenously.

These observations can be generalised as a principle of cultural evolution under conditions of group selection. If group members have the freedom of opting out, in particular, the freedom to join other groups, the probability increases that cooperation tends to level out power differentials within groups and favours the emergence of group regimes which expand the joint product, even with an unequal distribution. The more circumscribed the opting-out options, the higher the probability that regimes with lopsided distributions of the joint product and power emerge. In human history, these mechanisms were salient in the transition from tribal organisations to the first empires which entailed an extremely unequal distribution of power but at the same time produced civilisational breakthroughs by large-scale cooperation, such as in the early river civilisations where outmigration opportunities were limited (e.g., in Ancient Egypt).[37]

In the archetypical hunting group, shooters and chasers differ in the skills of using weapons that can also be directed against humans. Shooters may threaten other members of the group to the point of violence in order to impose an advantage for themselves. Therefore, one key form of specialisation in human societies is specialisation on using means of violence.[38] Theft is always an alternative to exchange, although it, if happening recurrently, may dampen incentives to production. Yet there is a lower limit of survival: Violent appropriation can, in principle, install an unequal cooperation regime in which one larger group just survives on the minimum. Again, the problem is to organise collective action of the oppressed majority facing specialists in violence. There are famous historical examples for these interdependencies, such as the Swiss pike phalanx in medieval times by which the collective could overcome the massive advantage of armoured knights, building on capacities for cooperation and handling the pikes.[39]

Specialisation in violence gains in importance once we consider warfare among human groups.[40] Warfare induces another form of forced exchange yet on the collective level. Specialists in violence can offer the service of protection in exchange for status gains and a larger share of the total product to the level of bare survival for the rest of the population and potentially even less, if warfare also threatens survival.[41] A cooperation problem of a similar kind is the gendered division of labour that is characteristic for almost all human societies in history.[42] In the West, during industrialisation until the mid-20th century, it was sharpened by keeping women mostly in the non-paid sector of domestic work and care. This is not only a coordination problem: Violence can be directed at women, and men can sustain a highly unequal distribution of gains from cooperation.

The sexual division of labour is an example of a status-based specialisation undergirded by violence.

Beyond violence, the patterns and degree of specialisation are crucially determined by emergent power positions in the underlying exchange relations, which directly relate to capability specificity as discussed previously. Capability specificity reduces the range of outside options: For example, women who specialise on housework may lose the capability to access the labour market and, hence, get locked in into the relationship. Threat points differ before and after the specialisation; a party may be locked in an exchange relation ex post if the specialisation closes all alternative options. There is one most general form of capability specialisation with reference to markets: Individuals may differ in terms of their capabilities to sustain their livelihood independent from generating market income, approximated in terms of a market-based measure, namely wealth. Actors with low levels of wealth are more dependent on generating market income even in the short run whereas more wealthy individuals can temporarily stay out of the market. Hence, their relative power in arranging specialisation agreements differs substantially.

We discuss wealth and inequality in Chapter 15.

4. Externalities and the efficiency of specialisation

So far, we have mostly taken for granted that specialisation increases the joint product of cooperators. The Pareto criterion is a measure of efficiency, which, however, is contingent on the reference points and on the allocation of the costs of cooperation. The efficiency of specialisation can be assessed from the three points of view:

Efficiency can be judged differentially from the three points of view.

- In the first-person view, efficiency is judged in terms of the perceived gains for only one single individual. This implies that everybody else in a group can lose in a third-person assessment, unless all members agree based on their own first-person views.
- In the second-person view, efficiency not only reflects consent by the concerned parties but also consent on how to measure the joint gains. This

allows for the possibility that costs are shifted to non-members, even though all members gain.

- In the third-person view, efficiency would be judged by employing a measure that is independent from the valuations of the concerned parties.

In assessing specific forms of cooperation in the second-person view, the various parties must agree on a measure of efficiency. Opting for or enforcing a certain measure has direct consequences on the evolving pattern of cooperation. For example, in traditional societies, the measure may be determined by beliefs that give priority to the benefit, accruing to a god-like leader (such as the Pharaoh in Ancient Egypt), thus generalising a specific first-person view. If this measure is also accepted by all cooperating members, the arrangement may be deemed efficient even if all other members lose (those members would effectively act altruistically towards their leader). Similarly, all members of a cooperation may agree on a shared measure which, however, does not include other living systems in their environment, which may, therefore, become objects of a negative externality. The internalisation of this externality may be deemed necessary from the third-person view to diagnose a pattern of cooperation as efficient.

Specialisation of production is efficient only if all costs of production are internalised in the measure for assessing the gains from specialisation.

Specialisation is globally efficient only if all parties internalise all relevant costs of production in their decisions, which would ultimately require to fix a criterion from the third-person view. In the context of the human economy, the basic question is whether we employ an anthropocentric or geocentric measure of costs. In the latter case, we judge the efficiency of human cooperation, including the costs that it imposes on the biosphere. As we have seen, this is vindicated from the third-person view, considering the role of the technosphere in Earth system regulation. The geocentric view can be conceived as an emergent outcome of co-evolution that moves the human second-person view towards a third-person perspective.[43]

We discuss anthropocentrism and geocentrism in more detail in Chapter 16, section 5.

There are three different types of externalities in cooperative arrangements, which correspond to the three points of view:

The three points of view correspond to three types of externalities and corresponding measures of costs and gains of specialisation.

- First, the arrangement is based on power asymmetries which allow one party to impose (i.e., externalise) costs on the other party (from its first-person view) for which that party cannot demand compensation. For example, in the industrial revolution, wages mostly did not internalise the human costs of factory work to physical and mental health of families. Today, costs of commuting are mostly not covered in wage contracts.
- Second, the cooperating group (having achieved internal agreement in the second-person view) shifts costs to human non-members. For example, consumers in one country buy cheap goods from another country, which shifts environmental pollution to the latter. High-income earners concentrate at a particular location close to their workplace (Silicon Valley, financial centres), thus driving up real estate prices and excluding low-income

earners who still need to commute for providing low-skilled services to the high-income earners.

- Third, the cooperating group shifts costs to non-human entities, that is, the biosphere (third-person view). For example, even if the cost of commuting is included in work contracts, this is ecologically costly as long as greenhouse gas emissions are not priced properly, that is, include the costs of biospheric externalities.

How can we know the true gains from specialisation? We can adopt the third-person perspective and measure the ecological costs and benefits. But there are clearly trade-offs; for example, in setting priorities in investing in certain projects of ecological transformation. The problem is that, ultimately, the category of costs refers to the costs of decisions that must be taken by agents who are responsible for them. Therefore, the third-person view can only become relevant via the internalisation generated by the measure that those agents decide (for example, government may impose a tax on pollution). This shifts the view to the second-person perspective.

In economics, measures of efficiency are divided into two large classes:

- The first is price-based efficiency, which takes market prices as a measure for both production cost and the gains from specialisation. This is the standard economic second-person view as enshrined in GDP.
- The second is inclusive valuation: Here, all costs would be included that are not reflected in market prices. This is the third-person view demanded by many ecological economists who suggest alternative measures to GDP.[44]

We consider two levels of internalisation: One is the design of the measure of gains from specialisation; the other is the negotiations over the inclusion of costs, given the measure.

Hence, there are two levels of revealing the true costs of specialisation. The first is the decision to adopt a specific type of measure, such as incentives for internalising certain costs in terms of market prices. The second is that, given a certain measure, parties may negotiate over the inclusion of costs in the specific arrangement of cooperation. Take the example of costs of commuting:[45] There might be a legal arrangement that costs of commuting must be included in a wage contract; or the commuting party may request for implicit compensation in the wage contract which may not include the full monetary costs of commuting. In the latter case, one important issue is whether the parties in the negotiation would only accept a monetary measure to assess the costs of commuting or whether they would include subjective costs, that is, the first-person view of the commuter; for example, with respect to lost family time. In contrast, there is the question whether the environmental costs of commuting, such as of CO_2 emissions of driving, are internalised in the measure that both parties employ. If there is a carbon tax, the allocation of commuting costs between the parties implies that environmental costs are allocated accordingly. As we see, there are many ledgers by which true costs of specialisation can be approximated.[46]

See, for the
question of
externalities
from a values
perspective,
Chapter 3,
section 3.1.

The measure of
efficiency can be
intentionally designed
to shape comparative
advantage via
externalisation
of costs.

For the related
question of
locational
competition,
see Chapter 14,
section 4.

Transaction costs of
negotiations differ
across members of
a cooperation and
impact on the result,
depending on the
initial assignment
of rights (Coase
theorem).

The determination of measures for internalising externalities is a pervasive issue in economic policy. The dilemma is that the market prices as a measure by definition cannot be employed on externalities that are manifest outside markets. Economists apply complex indirect methods to assign a monetary value to externalities, such as pricing ecosystem services which are ultimately contributions to the human economy, mostly in including longer time horizons and more complex causal chains.[47] This would explore long-run sustainability of agriculture in the region, effects on other sectors such as tourism, or effects on health, which would eventually also result in costs (like medical treatments). The other alternative is to evaluate externalities from an even broader angle (such as biodiversity), without referring them to the human economy.[48] The problem is evident: How can we assign a monetary value in this case, given that interests of non-humans who do not enter an exchange relation with humans count essentially?

In the ecological context, if market prices are declared the reference, actors can externalise costs and thereby shape comparative advantage. For example, in international trade, a firm may simply disregard costs of pollution – with the acquiescence of its government – and therefore drive other foreign competitors out of business who operate under a more inclusive regime of measuring environmental costs. This might create a race to the bottom in environmental standards.[49] In general, we can therefore conclude that imposing a certain measure of the outcomes of cooperation is shaped by the differential capacities of various parties to take part or impact on establishing it. This is a question of power relations. Accordingly, asymmetric exchange implies the imposition of a measure that externalises costs to the less powerful parties.

Can we identify general principles that might explain why a specific pattern of internalisation will emerge during negotiations among concerned parties? The process of internalisation is itself costly, thus potentially blocking some forms of bargaining. That means, in assessing a certain form of externalisation, we face a problem of measuring second-level efficiency: A form of externalisation may be second-level efficient if internalisation is too costly to implement, eventually even jeopardising the benefits of the excluded parties.[50]

This fundamental problem is recognised in a celebrated theorem of economics, the Coase theorem.[51] The central idea is that the outcome of negotiations will be affected by the transaction cost of negotiations. This is important when considering the assignment of rights to claims to the parties. For example, one could give the factory a right to pollute the river, and then farmers may offer compensation to the factory if pollution is stopped. Or farmers have the right to clean water, and the factory needs to pay for the right to pollute.

The Coase theorem states that with zero transaction costs, the assignment of rights does not matter for efficiency of the outcome, which will be the same across various possible arrangements. However, in the real world, assignments differ in terms of the costs of negotiations they induce for the different parties, and power imbalances may matter. Take again the example of a factory polluting the river and harming local farmers who need the river for irrigation. The factory may be the sole non-agricultural employer in the region, and organising the dispersed group of farmers in raising their collective claims may be difficult. Hence, assigning initial rights to pollute water to the factory may lead to the situation that farmers do not approach the factory, despite everyone recognising the costs of pollution shifted to them. If rights to clean water are assigned to the farmers, the factory is a single decision maker and can approach them with a proposal. The problem of power asymmetry still matters: The offer may be low because the factory may threaten to close, thus laying off family members of farmers.

We can analyse this in terms of the opportunity cost of specialisation in relation to Coleman's definition of power. For the farmers, the opportunity cost of claiming the true costs of pollution is relatively higher than the opportunity cost of the factory relocating its operations to another village because the former includes the loss of jobs and the cost of organising collective action whereas the factory may have many outside options of relocating. In sum, the factory is more powerful than the farmers in determining the pattern of internalisation. Therefore, we can conclude that the assignment of rights is not neutral in terms of power structure, even though it might appear to be neutral in terms of efficiency.

Power relationships impact on negotiations and, hence, the pattern of internalisation; rights assignments shape power relationships.

This analysis has an important implication: When we evaluate observed forms of internalisation, we need to take the actual social and political structure into account; we cannot simply assume that the prevailing prices reflect an adequate degree of internalisation. For example, most climate scientists argue that the costs of fossil fuels need to be dramatically increased via a CO_2 tax. However, this is difficult to achieve in the political process, in both democracies and autocracies, since there are serious distributional impacts that can destabilise incumbent governments: After all, in many countries, fuel is even subsidised. In consequence, the current pattern of economic specialisation is governed by the wrong prices: For example, with higher transport cost, local and regional agriculture would become more competitive, with many desirable ecological consequences. But there is no way to discover the right prices via a social bargaining process because of the inherent obstacles to organising relevant interests.

5. Conclusion

This chapter laid the foundations for understanding markets as a form of cooperation. This seems to stay in tension with the common notion of markets being regimes of competition. Yet there are two aspects that loom large in diagnosing markets as cooperative regimes. The first is that the full potential of markets requires overcoming the specialisation dilemma: This is especially challenging when exchange transcends the limits of small groups in which reciprocity can be governed by social norms and direct personal interaction.[52] Specialisation in markets presupposes a strong level of trust into gaining from market opportunity. Creating the conditions for mutual trust is a major achievement in the evolution of human cooperation.[53] The second is that competition and power are deeply entangled. Here, Max Weber's view on market competition is much more on the point than many economics definitions. Weber described competition as scramble over opportunities of monopolising markets, since this is the safest means to increase profits.[54] In other words, markets create incentives for limiting competition endogenously, which implies that market competition must be governed, and setting up the institutions of governance is a cooperative venture.

Therefore, we cannot regard comparative advantage and gains from trade as givens that drive market but to the opposite: It is the institutional setup of markets that determines the potential and degree of specialisation via the specific forms of externalisation. In particular, specialisation and exchange can go along with many different social structures with different distributions of power. One crucial observation on human history is that most regimes manifest a highly unequal distribution of power and a prominent role of violence in enforcing specific forms of specialisation. Free markets and peaceful free societies are a rare achievement in history.[55] This also means that in most cases, markets have always been deeply shaped by power relations in society.

For more on
violence, power,
and institutions,
see Chapter 9,
section 5

This fact about human history and society is of deep significance for the ecology of the economy: We observe that societies with high levels of inequality and asymmetries of power also exert especially harmful impact on the environment (as in the case of socialist planned economies in Eastern Europe). In contrast, in recent history, green movements were often drivers of democratic change. On the global level, the carbon economy is the accomplice of authoritarian, oppressive, and corrupt political regimes.[56] Therefore, political change is a condition for transforming markets into economic regimes that foster sustainability.

Major chapter insights

- Fundamental principles of specialisation apply on both ecology and economy. Specialisation follows the principle of comparative advantage and enables quantitative and qualitative enhancement of productive work. The Pareto principle allows to assess whether all members of a cooperating group gain from specialisation. We distinguish between potential comparative advantage aka capabilities and realised aka functionings: The former determines the scope of outside options.

- The specialisation dilemma refers to problems of enabling cooperation under the condition that specialisation creates asymmetries of agential power that can reduce the benefit from cooperation for a party, which the party anticipates and, therefore, reduces its degree of specialisation to protect its relative power.
- Capability specificity is the cause of the endogenous emergence of power asymmetries in markets in the most general sense of the specificity of capabilities of exploiting market opportunity.
- The specialisation dilemma creates contexts of strategic interaction which can be analysed by means of game theory. Game theory allows for distinguishing archetypical scenarios of cooperation problems, such as the stag hunt, the battle of the sexes, or the prisoner's dilemma.
- A particularly important class of games is games of difference which result from the transformation of standard games by considering relative pay-offs and the results of pay-offs on relative status in repeated games.
- The efficiency of specialisation can be assessed from the three points of view, which is reflected in the patterns of externalisation and the conjugated measure of costs and gains from cooperation.
- This transpires in negotiating externalities, as analysed by the Coase theorem. The Coase theorem shows that once these negotiations are costly (transaction costs), power asymmetries will affect the measurement of the gains from cooperation and the outcome of the negotiations.

Notes

1 The term originated with Adam Smith (1759), however, appeared only once in his *The Wealth of Nations*, hence, had no prominent and systematic status. Only in the course of the 20th century, the term assumed a paradigmatic role in economic discourse.
2 This analytical figure has been developed by Buchanan (1979) and Kliemt (1986).
3 This is, of course, Adam Smith's (1776) foundational contribution to economics.
4 Bowles and Gintis (2011, 93ff), Lucassen (2021, 46ff).
5 Ricardo (1817).
6 Dixit (2004).
7 Bernbeck (2007).
8 For seminal approaches to the taxonomy of exchange, see Sahlins (1972) or Pryor (1977).

9 The Pareto criterion is pivotal in neoclassical welfare economics; for an overview, see Lockwood (2008).

10 This is the contractarian view as deployed in Sugden (2018).

11 This distinction has been introduced by Sen (1984). For an overview, see Robeyns and Byskov (2020).

12 Marglin (1991).

13 This corresponds to the general principle of ascendency in ecology, see Ulanowicz (1997).

14 On the following example, see Buchanan (1979).

15 Fernandez and Rodrik (1991).

16 For the original statement of the concept of asset specificity, see Williamson (1985).

17 Our overview follows similar outlines in the literature, although reaching wider than supplier relations; see Joskow (1988).

18 For an instructive analysis, see Kirman (2001).

19 This reflects the game theoretic analysis of the ultimatum game, Holt (2019, 261ff).

20 See, for example, Rosen et al. (1994).

21 Diebolt and El Murr (2005).

22 Barras (2009).

23 For a short introduction into game theory, see Binmore (2007).

24 For a seminal contribution, see Taylor (1987). It must be noticed that differences in pay-offs are crucial in evolutionary game theory which we do not consider here.

25 Wolford (2019).

26 Bednar and Page (2007).

27 For rich analysis of commons, see Ostrom (1990).

28 Elster (2015, 289ff) distinguishes 'externalities' and 'internalities'.

29 Ofek (2001).

30 Skyrms (2003). This is often also referred to as 'assurance game'.

31 Lucassen (2021, 39ff).

32 Güth and Kocher (2013), Holt (2019, 261ff).

33 Coleman (1990, 133).

34 Dagan (2021, 179ff).

35 The classical contribution is Olson (1965).

36 This is a key point in German ordoliberalism, Eucken (1952).

37 Mann (1986, 105ff).

38 Hirshleifer (2001), North et al. (2009).

39 Mann (1986).

40 Bowles and Gintis (2011, 133ff).

41 Hicks (1969, 16ff).

42 Alesina et al. (2013).

43 Lenton and Latour (2018), Lenton et al. (2018).

44 Overview in Roma and Thiry (2018).

45 Van Ommeren and Fosgerau (2009).

46 For example, estimates of carbon prices vary widely, allowing for much policy discretion, see Auffhammer (2018).

47 Gomez-Baggethun (2018).

48 Dasgupta (2021).

49 Madsen (2009).

50 Dahlman (1979) is a seminal contribution.

51 Coase (1960).

52 Seabright (2004).

53 Field (2001).

54 Weber (1922, 439).

55 North et al. (2009).

56 Wenar (2016).

References

Alesina, A., Giuliano, P. and Nunn, N. (2013) 'On the Origins of Gender Roles: Women and the Plough', *The Quarterly Journal of Economics*, 128(2), pp. 469–530. DOI: 10.1093/qje/qjt005.

Auffhammer, M. (2018) 'Quantifying Economic Damages from Climate Change', *Journal of Economic Perspectives*, 32(4), pp. 33–52. DOI: 10.1257/jep.32.4.33.

Barras, R. (2009) *Building Cycles: Growth & Instability: Real Estate Issues*. Chichester and Ames: Wiley-Blackwell.

Bednar, J. and Page, S. (2007) 'Can Game(s) Theory Explain Culture? The Emergence of Cultural Behavior Within Multiple Games', *Rationality and Society*, 19(1), pp. 65–97. DOI: 10.1177/1043463107075108.

Bernbeck, R. (2007) 'The Rise of the State', in Bentley R. A., Maschner, H. D. G. and Chippendale, C. (eds.) *Handbook of Archaeological Theories*. Lanham, MD: Alta Mira Press, pp. 533–545.

Binmore, K. G. (2007) *Game Theory: A Very Short Introduction*. New York: Oxford University Press.

Bowles, S. and Gintis, H. (2011) *A Cooperative Species: Human Reciprocity and its Evolution*. Princeton: Princeton University Press.

Buchanan, J. M. (1979) 'A Hobbesian Interpretation of the Rawlsian Difference Principle', in Brunner, K. (ed.) *Economics & Social Institutions*. Boston, The Hague and London: Martinus Nijhoff, pp. 59–78.

Coase, R. H. (1960) 'The Problem of Social Cost', *Journal of Law and Economics*, 3, pp. 1–44.

Coleman, J. (1990) *Foundations of Social Theory*. Cambridge and London: Harvard University Press.

Dagan, Ḥ. (2021) *A Liberal Theory of Property*. Cambridge and New York: Cambridge University Press. DOI: 10.1017/9781108290340.

Dahlman, C. J. (1979) 'The Problem of Externality', *Journal of Law and Economics*, 22(1), pp. 141–162.

Dasgupta, P. (2021) *The Economics of Biodiversity: The Dasgupta Review*. Available at: https://www.gov.uk/government/collections/the-economics-of-biodiversity-the-dasgupta-review (Accessed: 22 March 2022).

Diebolt, C. and El Murr, B. (2005) 'A Cobweb Model of Higher Education and Labour Market Dynamics', *Association Française de Cliométrie (AFC) Working Papers*, WP2005–4.

Dixit, A. K. (2004) *Lawlessness and Economics: Alternative Modes of Governance*. Princeton and Oxford: Princeton University Press. DOI: 10.1515/9781400841370.

Elster, J. (2015) *Explaining Social Behavior: More Nuts and Bolts for the Social Sciences, Revised Edition*. Cambridge: Cambridge University Press. DOI: 10.1017/CBO9781107763111.

Eucken, W. (1952) *Grundsätze der Wirtschaftspolitik*. Bern and Tübingen: J.C.B. Mohr.

Fernandez, R. and Rodrik, D. (1991) 'Resistance to Reform: Status Quo Bias in the Presence of Individual-Specific Uncertainty', *American Economic Review*, 81(5), pp. 1146–1155. DOI: 10.1257/0002828041464425.

Field, A. (2001) *Altruistically Inclined? The Behavioral Sciences, Evolutionary Theory, and the Origins of Reciprocity*. Ann Arbor: University of Michigan Press.

Gomez-Baggethun, E. (2018) 'Ecosystem Services', in Spash, C. L. (ed.) *Routledge Handbook of Ecological Economics: Nature and Society*. London and New York: Routledge, pp. 445–454.

Güth, W. and Kocher, M. G. (2013) 'More than Thirty Years of Ultimatum Bargaining Experiments: Motives, Variations, and a Survey of the Recent Literature', *Jena Economic Research Papers*, 2013–2035.

Hicks, J. (1969) *A Theory of Economic History*. Oxford: Clarendon.

Hirshleifer, J. (2001) *The Dark Side of the Force: Economic Foundations of Conflict Theory*. Cambridge: Cambridge University Press.

Holt, C. A. (2019) *Markets, Games, and Strategic Behavior: An Introduction to Experimental Economics*. 2nd Edition. Princeton and Woodstock: Princeton University Press.

Joskow, P. L. (1988) 'Asset Specificity and the Structure of Vertical Relationships: Empirical Evidence', *Journal of Law, Economics, & Organization*, 4(1), pp. 95–117. DOI: 10.1093/oxfordjournals.jleo.a036950.

Kirman, A. P. (2001) 'Market Organization and Individual Behavior: Evidence from Fish Markets', in Rauch, J. E. and Casella, A. (eds.) *Networks and Markets*. New York: Russell Sage Foundation, pp. 155–195.

Kliemt, H. (1986) *Antagonistische Kooperation: Elementare spieltheoretische Modelle spontaner Ordnungsentstehung*. Freiburg and Munich: Alber.

Lenton, T. M. and Latour, B. (2018) 'Gaia 2.0', *Science*, 361(6407), pp. 1066–1068. DOI: 10.1126/science.aau0427.

Lenton, T. M. *et al.* (2018) 'Selection for Gaia across Multiple Scales', *Trends in Ecology & Evolution,* 33(8), pp. 633–645. DOI: 10.1016/j.tree.2018.05.006.

Lockwood, B. (2008) 'Pareto Efficiency', in Durlauf, S. N. and Blume, L. E. (eds.) *The New Palgrave Dictionary of Economics*. London: Palgrave Macmillan. DOI: 10.1057/978-1-349-95121-5_1823-2.

Lucassen, J. (2021) *The Story of Work: A New History of Humankind*. New Haven: Yale University Press. DOI: 10.12987/9780300262995.

Madsen, P. M. (2009) 'Does Corporate Investment Drive a "Race to the Bottom" in Environmental Protection? A Reexamination of the Effect of Environmental Regulation on Investment', *Academy of Management Journal*, 52(6), pp. 1297–1318.

Mann, M. (1986) *The Sources of Social Power, Vol. I: A History of Power from the Beginning to A.D. 1760*. Cambridge: Cambridge University Press.

Marglin, S. (1991) 'Understanding Capitalism: Control versus Efficiency', in Gustafsson, B. (ed.) *Power and Economic Institutions: Reinterpretations in Economic History*. Aldershot: Edward Elgar, pp. 225–252.

North, D. C., Wallis, J. J. and Weingast, B. R. (2009) *Violence and Social Orders. A Conceptual Framework for Interpreting Recorded Human History*. Cambridge: Cambridge University Press. DOI: 10.1017/CBO9780511575839.

Ofek, H. (2001) *Second Nature: Economic Origins of Human Evolution*. Cambridge: Cambridge University Press. DOI: 10.1017/CBO9780511754937.

Olson, M. (2003 [1965]) *The Logic of Collective Action: Public Goods and the Theory of Groups*. Cambridge: Harvard University Press.

Ostrom, E. (1990) *Governing the Commons: The Evolution of Institutions for Collective Action*. Cambridge: Cambridge University Press.

Pryor, F. L. (1977) *The Origins of the Economy: A Comparative Study of Distribution in Primitive and Peasant Societies*. New York: Academic Press.

Ricardo, D. (2015 [1817]) *On the Principles of Political Economy and Taxation*. Cambridge: Cambridge University Press. DOI: 10.1017/CBO9781107589421.

Robeyns, I. and Byskov, M. F. (2020) 'The Capability Approach', *The Stanford Encyclopedia of Philosophy,* Winter 2020 Edition. Available at: https://plato.stanford.edu/archives/win2020/entries/capability-approach/> (Accessed: 22 March 2022).

Roman, P. and Thiry, G. (2018) 'Sustainability Indicators', in Spash, C. L. (ed.) *Routledge Handbook of Ecological Economics: Nature and Society*. London and New York: Routledge, pp. 382–392.

Rosen, S., Murphy, K. M. and Scheinkman, J. A. (1994) 'Cattle Cycles', *Journal of Political Economy*, 102(3), pp. 468–492. DOI: 10.1086/261942.

Sahlins, M. D. (2011 [1972]) *Stone Age Economics*. New Brunswick, NJ: Transaction Publishers. DOI: 10.4324/9781003058762.

Seabright, P. (2004) *The Company of Strangers: A Natural History of Economic Life*. Princeton: Princeton University Press.

Sen, A. (1999 [1984]) *Commodities and Capabilities*. Oxford and New Delhi: Oxford University Press.

Skyrms, B. (2003) *The Stag Hunt and the Evolution of Social Structure*. Cambridge: Cambridge University Press. DOI: 10.1017/CBO9781139165228.

Smith, A. (1759) *The Theory of Moral Sentiments*. London.

Smith, A. (1776) *An Inquiry into the Nature and Causes of the Wealth of Nations*. London: W. Strahan and T. Cadell.

Sugden, R. (2018) *The Community of Advantage: A Behavioural Economist's Defence of the Market*. Oxford and New York: Oxford University Press. DOI: 10.1093/oso/9780198825142.001.0001.

Taylor, M. (1987) *The Possibility of Cooperation*. Cambridge: Cambridge University Press.

Ulanowicz, R. E. (1997) *Ecology: The Ascendent Perspective*. New York: Columbia University Press.

Van Ommeren, J. and Fosgerau, M. (2009) 'Workers' Marginal Costs of Commuting', *Journal of Urban Economics*, 65(1), pp. 38–47. DOI: 10.1016/j.jue.2008.08.001.

Weber, M. (1985 [1922]) *Wirtschaft und Gesellschaft, Studienausgabe, 8. Auflage*. Tübingen: Mohr.

Wenar, L. (2016) *Blood Oil: Tyrants, Violence, and the Rules That Run the World*. Oxford: Oxford University Press.

Williamson, O. (1985) *The Economic Institutions of Capitalism*. New York: The Free Press.

Wolford, S. (2019) *The Politics of the First World War: A Course in Game Theory and International Security*. Cambridge and New York: Cambridge University Press.

CHAPTER SIX

Production and technological evolution

1. Introduction

Via evolving the capacity for cooperation and the division of labour, humans have assumed a dominant position in the biosphere, eventually creating a new regulatory layer in the Earth system, the technosphere. A crucial factor for this was the collective handling of artefacts, such as controlling fire, which would at least require cooperation in surveillance and the maintenance of fire sites. In this chapter, we explore how the human economy culturally transforms principles of ecological production in the biosphere via enhancing productivity by the cooperative use of technology and the generation of technological innovation.

On fire, see Chapter 4, section 3.2, and Chapter 5, section 2.2.

In this context, the notion of production is essential, which, first, summarises core physical processes in the economy. Second, in modern integrated economies, the satisfaction of dispersed and evolving needs requires a vast and hypercomplex division of labour that no actor or planner can oversee in its entirety. To meet the corresponding coordination needs, markets have emerged as the most efficacious cultural form.[1] At the same time, however, markets create a deep wedge between what is internalised by markets, in particular, via prices, and what remains causally relevant in shaping the larger adaptive functionings of the human economy in the biosphere.

We discuss internalisation in Chapter 4, section 2.1, and Chapter 5, section 5.

For understanding production in the technosphere, an analysis of technological evolution is indispensable. We can approach technological evolution with the same conceptual frame as biological and cultural evolution, that is, a generalised VSR mechanism.[2] Of course, there are also important specificities. One is that markets and firms drive technological evolution in combination. Firms are the main form in which production is organised; in the firm, contrary to markets, the division of labour is largely subject to intentional design. As hierarchical structures, firms are embedded in power relations in society, and technological evolution co-evolves with power structures. For example, firms can directly affect the distribution of power via the labour market when bargaining power is redistributed between labour and capital in the course of automation.

We detail the VSR mechanism in Chapter 4, section 3.1.

123

DOI: 10.4324/9781003094869-9

2. Production in the technosphere

2.1. The technosphere

*The biosphere
is evolutionarily
integrated by the
tree of life rooted
in one common
ancestor of all living
systems.*

All living systems are embedded in a unified tree of life that originates in the emergence of life on earth (Figure 6.1). They divide into different species and higher-level groups, such as phylae. Ecosystems are locally and temporarily confined networks of interacting living systems that exploit their resource space. Ecosystems are in turn connected via higher-level forms of interaction. The totality of connected ecosystems on the globe constitutes the biosphere.[3]

For human
characteristics
from an
evolutionary
perspective,
see Chapter 4,
section 4.2.

These basic distinctions also apply for humans. On the one hand, we can approach humans as a generic species with certain species-specific character-istics rooted in phylogeny. On the other hand, humans divide into a large number of groups living in highly variable ecological niches which support distinct economic systems partly corresponding to cultural differences (think of nomads versus sedentary farmers in Africa or the carbon-intensive indus-trial society in the United States).[4] This pattern of ecological niche formation follows the same principles as biological niche formation but is mainly ena-bled by cultural, institutional, and technological evolution.

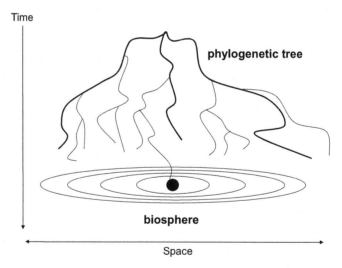

Figure 6.1 Biosphere and tree of life
The biosphere is the result of evolutionary processes in the past that connect current living systems with one common ancestor. Subdivisions in the phylogenetic tree reflect functional similarities, that is, adaptation to similar ecological niches, which are manifest in the nested spatial structure of the biosphere today (such as a local biotope in a tropical ecosystem). However, changed environments in the present may create mismatches which induce further evolutionary changes via natural selection.

Since early times, local and regional economies have been interconnected via flows of trade, migration, and eventually, investment. This resulted in today's globally integrated economy which encompasses almost the entire biosphere and co-evolves with embedding ecosystems, such as in the case of the diffusion of plantation agriculture in South America as a result of colonisation.[5] Economic integration is enabled by various artefacts that humans have created and continue to create, such as cities, roads, and communication networks. The global network of the human economy and its material form is the technosphere (Figure 6.2).

The technosphere has emerged as an evolutionary and regulatory system encompassing the biosphere and, hence, assuming crucial functions in Earth system processes.

Today, technosphere and biosphere are coextensive which implies that both compete over planetary resources (Figure 6.2): The total mass of technosphere artefacts is already larger than the entire biomass of planet Earth.[6] The biosphere has become part of the technosphere in two senses: First, wildlife has lost significant share in global biomass relative to domesticated species, which are biological components of the technosphere; and second, the technosphere increasingly regulates the environment of the biosphere. One most general planetary resource is space, relating to the most fundamental feature of the biosphere that directly affects the human

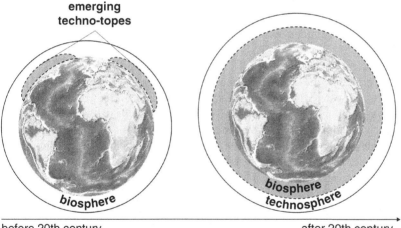

before 20th century   after 20th century

Figure 6.2 Biosphere and technosphere
As a result of the Great Acceleration, the relationship between technosphere and biosphere has reversed in the 20th century. Before the 20th century, emerging techno-topes (left, grey bubbles), especially in Europe and North America, remained part of the biosphere. In most other societies, economies remained embedded in nature, albeit with technological modification (such as irrigation systems in agriculture). In the 21st century, the technosphere is encompassing the biosphere.

economy, that is, the distinction between autotrophic and heterotrophic living systems. The former enact photosynthesis and can, therefore, directly exploit solar energy for sustaining their metabolism, whereas the latter cannot and, therefore, must rely on consuming autotrophic organisms and their products for sustenance.[7] Until most recently, the human economy was no exception: Modern industrial growth relied on the consumption of accumulated stocks of carbon fuels as a product of plant photosynthesis in a distant past. This may change, however, with a widespread use of solar energy technology.

Until today, the technosphere remains heterotrophic in relying on fossil fuels mainly. Photovoltaic energy generation does not reduce competition over space.

Recognising the technosphere as an emerging layer of Earth system regulation implies an approach to the human economy in geocentric terms. The human economy is the core driver of technosphere evolution and, hence, is embedded and subordinate to the Earth system. This results in new ways of approaching production and consumption in the economy.

For a more detailed discussion of geocentrism, see Chapter 16, section 5.

2.2. Production and consumption in the ecological dimension

Production is an analytical concept that pertains to both ecology and economy.[8] In the standard economic notion of production, the ultimate criterion of productivity is whether the product is consumed (i.e., meets a demand), reflecting the anthropocentric view on the economy. 'Consumption' is normally defined as end use on the marketplace, with the product not entering the market again. But this notion of consumption is misleading in many respects. This springs to the eye when comparing the economic concept of production with the ecological one.

On waste, see Chapter 4, section 4.1.

In principle, the ecological concept of production corresponds to the engineering view in terms of approaching living systems as productive and ecosystems as complex webs of production (Figure 6.3).[9] But evidently, in ecosystems, there is no output that is devoted to an end use. Analysis of production in ecosystems is only about intermediate products, which includes waste; for example, plants decay, but debris feeds bacteria, insects, and so on.

The conventional economic view of production and consumption is linear and open; the ecological view is cyclically closed. The economic view is framed by markets.

The conventional economic approach reverses the perspective and does not see waste as product but only treats consumption as end use. This is the fundamental contrast between a circular and a linear view of production, with the latter projecting the market frame on the analysis of material flows (Figure 6.3). Markets frame the human technospheric ecosystem in terms of a linear view on production, which, however, does not adequately reflect the underlying physical and biological interdependencies.

However, once we approach humans as living systems, consumption needs to be treated as intermediate production. The consumption of bread is an intermediate input into reproducing the human metabolism, and this metabolism enables work as part of production. Rather than consumption, the end use is the production of waste, like faeces. But in traditional agriculture, even faeces

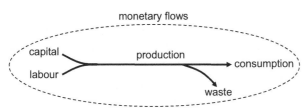

Standard view of production

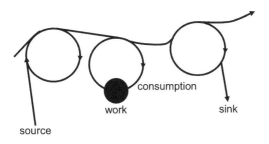

Evolutionary view of production

Figure 6.3 Linear economic and circular ecological view on production and consumption

The economic view on production and consumption suggests a linear process where consumption is the end use that is complementary to waste. In the ecological view, production and consumption are integrated in self-reproducing circuits. The only waste is entropy production by energetic transformations.

In the ecological view, consumption is intermediate production, and only waste is consumed.

might be valuable as fertilisers. In other words, in the ecological view, the distinction between consumption and production becomes obsolete.

For more on needs and wants, see Chapter 7, section 5.2.

The human metabolism is the result of biological evolution, but our food consumption is shaped by cultural evolution. An important corresponding distinction is between needs and wants.[10] For example, sugar is biologically needed for maintaining the human metabolism, but the want for sugar (e.g., in the shape of sweets) is culturally conditioned. The needs category can also be bolstered by technological evolution; for example, the use of sugar in the preservation of food, overcoming seasonal fluctuations in availability.[11] In principle, needs reflect a third-person view whereas wants can only be approached in the other views.

For analysing consumption, the distinction between needs and wants is crucial, with the former approachable in the third-person view, the latter in the second-person view only.

Approaching human needs in terms of human biology and ecology implies their analysis in terms of adaptive functions.[12] Needs include various dimensions, such as the need for adequate nutrition, for shelter, but also for human friendship, love, and recognition; all these can be related to

127

biological indicators of adaptation. There is also a rich literature on needs-based indicators of human well-being related to inequality; for example, with respect to racial discrimination (such as differences in body height, life expectancy, or susceptibility to disease) or different levels of development across countries.[13]

In human niche construction, there are needs that reflect adaptation to the cultural dimensions of the respective human niche, as in the case of sugar. Wants are partly determined by cultural context and may, but do not have to, harmonise with needs. For example, the want for luxury goods may compel us to earn more income, thus jeopardising our need for idleness and companionship with friends; however, it may also reflect a deeper need for social status. Many wants are indirectly determined by needs. An important example is the need for daylight. Energy consumption for lighting is about 10 percent of global energy consumption in buildings (which in turn account for about 40 percent of total energy consumption of the technosphere), and there are no signs of satiation given that reproducing daylight conditions in buildings is still not attainable for most humans worldwide.[14]

Wants and needs tend to convergent evolution, but there is much scope for non-functional wants, especially if economic selection pressure is weak.

We can go a long way in understanding wants in terms of needs when we consider indirect effects of fulfilling wants on adaptive performances.[15] In the example of sugar, the rapid diffusion of sugar as a regular consumption item was driven by the nutritional needs in industrial work governed by strict schedules of working, requiring a simple, quick, and efficacious means to intake huge amounts of calories (such as via bread and preserved fruits in jam).[16] Specific forms of consumption, such as of cultural status goods (visiting the opera house), may fulfil functions in sustaining social hierarchies that stabilise a specific power structure in society.

A fundamental difference between wants and needs is that needs have inherent limits of satiation. For example, in terms of needs, we can only eat a certain quantity of food; only wants can add further expansion via eating food with a high cultural value (such as drinking expensive red wine). This applies for all needs: For example, our cognitive capacities are limited in maintaining deeper relations of affection and emotional closeness with friends such that we cannot maintain an unbounded number of these relations at the same time. The industrial economy emerged together with the cultural element of unlimited wants, rooted in the conception of individual freedom and creativity of lifestyle: Wants can never be satisfied, as new forms of consumption constantly emerge (we maintain social relationships via the internet, which requires the purchase of electronic devices requiring specific inputs such as rare earths).[17] One driver of wants is status competition, with the biological archetype of sexual selection and concomitant runaway selection.[18]

On cognitive limits of social interaction, see Chapter 7, section 3.1.

On status competition, see Chapter 7, section 3.1.

We conclude that in understanding the interaction between production, human needs, and the ecological context, we must explore various mechanisms that involve different levels of evolution. There are cultural mechanisms in the sense of being performative, without underlying biological necessity. Other mechanisms are biological and cannot be changed at whim. For example, there are mechanisms that relate sugar intake causally with obesity and various diseases.

A want is a functional need that is not related to biological adaptation but to the technosphere as the human niche. Since technologies are interconnected, using a certain technology may create derived wants for a complementary technology and all inputs necessary to use that technology.[19] Most forms of human consumption have become leveraged by technological devices, such as using a mixer for making a smoothie or using the microwave to heat ready-made food. Technological developments create new wants once they piggyback on a need: Humans need company and conversation, and smartphones enable the use of social media for meeting that need. However, arguably, before the age of the smartphone, there was no deprivation in meeting that need. In this sense, wants co-evolve with the evolution of the technosphere. Therefore, we cannot approach production as merely instrumental to fulfilling given needs ('consumer preferences' in standard parlance): Production also produces the wants that it aims to fulfil.[20]

The co-evolution of wants and needs is multilevel selection involving mechanisms of various kinds.

Wants are endogenous to technosphere evolution.

See, for the influencing of wants by entrepreneurs on markets, Chapter 11, section 5.

3. Specialisation and technology

3.1. *Engineering versus economic approaches to production*

Specialisation is specialisation in production. As we have seen, production is a thermodynamic conversion process involving physical work, which in turn is mostly enabled and enhanced by the application of technical devices. Production is commonly analysed in terms of inputs and outputs, the latter including services.

On underlying thermodynamic principles, see Chapter 4, section 2.2.

Production can be approached from an engineering or an economic perspective. Input-output analysis stands at the core of both approaches, all the more so since most products of production processes in modern economic systems are intermediate products that are used in other production processes.[21] In the engineering perspective, the production process is analysed in an input-output matrix that describes the relationship between inputs and outputs in physical terms (material balances) and reflects the underlying technology.[22] In the economic perspective, all inputs, intermediate products, and outputs are measured in monetary terms; the great advantage is simplicity of aggregation. Aggregation in the engineering perspective requires alternative and less straightforward approaches such as the definition of Raw Material Equivalents.[23] The advantage here is the possibility to directly connect the economy with the ecosystem, such as analysis of the impact of nitrogen

The engineering view on production specifies the physical view on production, whereas the economic view focuses on the generation of value as measured on markets.

*A crucial difference
between the
engineering and
the economic
perspective is the
treatment of waste
and associated
externalities.*

See, for the issue
of externalisation
in markets and
ecosystems,
Chapter 4,
section 2.1.

carried by fertilisers on groundwater. In monetary calculations, this would only show in case this impact is internalised and, therefore, reflected in market prices.

Consequently, one crucial difference between the engineering and the economic perspective is the treatment of waste: In the former, it is a product, but economically, it is not, unless waste can be sold on markets or recycled in the production process.[24] Clearly, this implies a basic externalisation process: Waste which is not attributed a market value will not be economically relevant for emerging patterns of specialisation in production (this is only true for the cost of waste disposal, which creates strong incentives to externalise waste). However, although the engineering perspective grounds in physical processes, it need not fully include the ecological dimension.[25] Therefore, it is crucial to coordinate the engineering and the economic view in terms of internalisation of externalities: Although physically, all outputs relate with the production process, the way they are treated in the engineering process is at least partly influenced by its economic framing, which is in turn determined by the chosen measures and the degree of internalising effects of outputs. For example, CO_2 emissions have always been universal outputs of human production, but only today, their internalisation has become a major goal in engineering production.

Another key difference between the engineering and economic view on production is that the former allows for the possibility of useless production. This is a fundamental problem in arranging for complex patterns of specialisation in producing for a certain demand. In a factory with division of labour, the engineers can provide precise information about the inputs needed for producing the product that the factory is destined to produce. But if we move beyond the factory and consider an economic system that consists of millions of consumers and producers which are connected via supply chains, how can producers know what they should produce?

*Socialist planned
economies were
organised along
engineering
principles but often
failed to produce
what was needed
in society.*

This was an endemic problem in socialist planned economies, which were basically organised along engineering principles: In a central plan, factories would receive orders for production as if the entire economy was a megafactory. But planners were not able to cope with complexity and constantly changing conditions such that serious imbalances were a notorious feature of socialist systems: Some factories produced goods which were not needed; others would need inputs that were not available.[26] The question then arises on what a product is beyond the mere physical result of the production process, given the possibility that products of a factory are all wasted, if not needed.

Therefore, even the engineering view needs to include consumption as the final stage of production, implying that we only count as a product what is potentially consumed. The engineering notion of production is conceptually incomplete and needs to be complemented by the economic criterion of production. In (standard) economics, this is that someone is willing to pay a price: A product that fetches a market price is needed and, therefore, counts as a product. Hence, the production process is described in terms of monetary valued inputs and outputs. All outputs that consume inputs priced by the market but do not fetch a price are waste.

In classical economics and Marxism, distinctions were made between use value and exchange value as well as between productive and non-productive work.[27] Use value refers to the need that the product meets; exchange value to its valuation in exchange with other goods, such as money. Modern economics argues that valuation is expressed via the market and reduces use value to subjective preferences expressed in the willingness to pay. This notion also underlies the measure of GDP: GDP is the sum of all value added via production processes, priced via the market.[28]

However, there are well-known problems with the use of GDP as a measure of production, of which we highlight two.[29]

The first is that there are many productive activities which meet a need (have use value in the classical sense) but which are not part of the market. The most important example is household production (cooking, gardening, cleaning, etc.). Government is included in GDP via certain measurement conventions. But since government does not sell its products on markets, there are no market prices such that, strictly speaking, government production would have to count as economically unproductive.

The second is the role of externalities. A factory that pollutes the environment may not be economically productive if all externalities are priced in. Therefore, when we evaluate production in a combined ecological-engineering perspective, we may identify a wide range of unproductive activities, which nevertheless catch positive market prices and generate profits (after all, cleaning up an environmental disaster by employing private firms is economically productive). The same reasoning applies for positive externalities: There are many activities that create use value without being compensated by markets; for example, education produced in families which undergirds the operation of the economic system.

Both observations have the straightforward implication that we cannot assume that markets orient production towards its most productive uses in terms of a combined ecological and engineering perspective: The market-mediated second-person view does not match with the third-person view that would consider the larger context of the biosphere and Earth system processes but also the non-market domain in society.[30] For example, some critics point out that the market economy externalises important productive activities by way of a strongly gendered care domain without monetary compensation (think of taking care of elderly in the family).[31] This implies that the way market valuation reflects production is influenced by power structures in society.

In economics, the focus on GDP combines with the common production function approach, which is applied on different levels of aggregation. The production function does not make the structure of intermediates explicit but

If a product in economic terms is only what is priced on the market, this reinstates the classical distinction between productive and unproductive activities, such as when excluding household production from GDP.

See Chapter 4, section 2, on the ecological perspective.

Markets do not necessarily orient production towards its most productive use.

*Economics
commonly applies
highly aggregate
production functions
that relate a small
number of inputs
with aggregate
output, valued in
monetary terms.*

*This allows
formalising and
quantifying essential
concepts, such
as diminishing
marginal returns and
economies of scale.*

*Production
functions implicitly
reflect social and
political structures
of production
and do not detail
mechanisms of
technological
change and
innovation.*

On capabilities,
see Chapter 5,
section 2.

*The use of
technology involves
both producer and
user capabilities.
New applications of
technology are often
discovered by users.*

describes the relationship between inputs and outputs as a mathematical function with very few types of input aggregates. The function reflects the underlying technology of production without detailing the precise flow of activities and processes. Production functions can have various mathematical forms, in the simplest way, either describing the change of product when only one input is varied, with all others kept constant, or the simultaneous variation of all inputs.[32] A typical assumption for the former is that the marginal contribution of additional units of the variable input is declining, eventually even becoming negative (think of adding workers to a fixed pool of machines, with eventual crowding which disturbs work processes). This is one defining feature of neoclassical production function. Varying all inputs simultaneously allows for defining the important concept of economies of scale. Often, the assumption of constant returns is made (again, a neoclassical assumption), which means that size does not matter. But many production processes may manifest increasing returns to scale, which means that with growing size, unit costs of output will decline, thus creating comparative advantage vis-à-vis smaller competitors.

Production functions of the type mostly used in economics have two serious limitations. The first is that they mix the engineering perspective with hidden assumptions about the social structure (such as capital and labour). At the same time, essential physical aspects of the production process are blanked out, in particular, the role of energy.[33] The second is that innovation and technological change are not treated in detail, even though the continuous change of production processes is a key feature of modern economies, including the environmental impact of economic action. We pursue this topic in the next section.

3.2. Production and use of technology

Technology is central to production. The origin of technology is the use of tools. A hunter cutting a flint and using it as a knife employs a technology in two senses: One is the creation of the tool; the other is its usage. Hence, we can distinguish between producer capabilities and user capabilities, which are fused in the case of the hunter but separate in complex patterns of specialisation.[34] Even in the case of simple technologies, the principle of specialisation drives the differentiation of capabilities: Some individuals may have special skills in making stone knives, and others may be very versatile in using it when dissecting game. The maker of knives may not know the details of using the knives, and vice versa. Clearly, there must be some overlap, as those who make knives need to imagine how they can be used. But users may also invent usages that were not envisaged by makers. For example, when the telephone was invented and introduced, the inventors and producers mostly thought that it would be used by government, military, and business;

but rapid diffusion in the United States was strongly driven by the demand for distance communication in the vast rural areas where farms are located far away from each other.[35]

The example also demonstrates another important point: A tool cannot simply be seen as an artefact but constitutes a combination of artefact and capabilities. Technology is a complex action pattern that coordinates artefacts, behaviour, and capabilities.[36] Knowledge about technology is partly tacit in the sense that it cannot be described explicitly and only obtained via observation and imitation, which is true for both making and using it.[37]

Compared to simple tools, more complex technologies include machines. A machine is a mechanism in which many parts work together in combining inputs and energy throughputs towards a specific outcome. Machines can entail simple intermediary artefacts, such as the wheel in relation to the wheel cart: The wheel is a simple tool but can rarely be employed directly in producing a certain output. If four wheels are put together in a cart, however, the cart can be pulled and used as a transport device. The cart is an example of a machine that combines a living system (such as a human pulling the cart) with an artefact. The ultimate transition to a machine occurs when the living system is substituted by a steam engine.[38]

These observations result in a core insight about specialisation: Specialisation is embodied in artefacts and capabilities; technologies partly determine the embodied capabilities that economic actors build up in adapting and using the technologies. In this sense, specialisation is not confined to the domain of human actors but encompasses the domain of artefacts. This results in the fundamental hypothesis of co-evolution of technosphere and human economy, with causal mechanisms working in both directions.

On the micro-level, the interface between the artefactual and the human is defined as design. Design mediates between producer and user capabilities in specifically enabling and constraining the action patterns that involve the handling of the technological artefact.[39] Design creates affordances for action and, thereby, drives and channels the diffusion of technology in the economy.[40] When producers implement technology produced by others, design is often essential for enabling the fit between different elements of technology and their smooth interaction, independently from the original functionality. This applies for simplest technologies. The screw is an excellent example: Basically, every screw could be unique and still would fulfil its function. But the widespread use of screws is strongly supported by standardisation of types of screws.

Standardisation is a specific form of design, which otherwise would also include bespoke designs applying only for one individual case. Standardising over a potentially unlimited number of cases implies that production processes can exploit economies of scale in many stages of production: Think of the custom-made suit compared to the standardised blue jeans sold globally.[41]

A technology is an assemblage of artefacts, behaviour, and capabilities.

Specialisation is embodied in artefacts and capabilities, resulting in the co-evolution of technosphere and human economy.

Design defines the interface between artefacts and capabilities via creating affordances for action.

Accordingly, standardisation is an essential element of many design processes because it determines the frictionless and precise interaction between different technologies. One important implication is that standardisation can favour certain technologies over others: For example, formats in data transmission can favour certain technologies of data processing, such as visualisation technologies.

Standardisation is design applied over a potentially unlimited number of instances that enables productivity gains, such as by economies of scale.

Considering the distinction between the engineering and the economic view on production, standardisation can be driven by concerns in both dimensions. In particular, standardisation can lower costs, activates economies of scale, and may speed up learning processes such that dynamic externalities are created which favour certain trajectories of technological evolution over others via differential rates of profitability (see subsequent section).

We discuss status goods in Chapter 7, section 4.3.

Finally, when we consider the consumer perspective, design also involves other aspects which do not necessarily relate to the engineering functionality as such. Consider the car: The public image of the car was shaped for decades by luxury cars and sports cars as highly appreciated ideals of cars, whose design is influenced by many non-technological factors that, however, also impact on the technical functioning of the car. The centrality of design in the evolution of cars is evident in the strategy that Tesla has adopted in triggering the switch to electric cars (also see subsequent section): The Tesla sedan is a high-end luxury and sports car, thus signalling that the electric car can be a full alternative to the petrol-fuelled car. Generally, the most advanced car technologies are first implemented in high-end cars and then gradually trickle down to ordinary cars.

Design can entail aspects of social stratification and status.

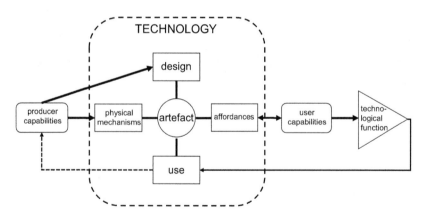

Figure 6.4 The structure of technology
Technology is a complex assemblage that relates the physical mechanisms which enable the generation of a function with the design that creates affordances for user action and the manifest patterns of use, that is, the related behaviour. Producer capabilities enable the production of technology by arranging the mechanisms and creating design interfaces for use. The actual technological function is generated by the interaction with user capabilities. Function is activated by usage. Manifest usage can create new producer knowledge.

To summarise, technology cannot be reduced to the artefact as constituted by the physical mechanisms that are the necessary condition for generating its functions (Figure 6.4). This opens many degrees of freedom for the driving forces of technological evolution.

3.3. Technological evolution

Most complex technologies are combinations of existing artefacts, although modern science can also produce entirely new artefacts such as supra-conductivity. Therefore, to a large extent, we can approach technosphere evolution by similar concepts and theories as biosphere evolution.[42] Technological evolution unfolds in a possibility space that is spanned by all possible combinations of simple technologies into more complex ones.[43] This technology space is structured in two ways. First, there are physical constraints in combining certain technologies, although these can themselves be overcome by innovation. Second, all combinations become themselves elements of new combinations.

Technology evolves in an open space of possible recombinations of existing technologies.

This general view on technology makes clear that technological evolution is open and non-deterministic: We will never fully explore the growing possibility space created by the recombination of simple and composite technologies.[44] There is an almost infinite number of alternative trajectories of technological evolution that have not been realised and are unknown, for if there was a possibility to imagine them, they could potentially be realised. Technological evolution does not optimise globally but locally, which implies that it can be in a suboptimal state.[45]

Technological evolution is open, non-deterministic, and locally optimising, implying that there is a vast diversity of niches in which various functionally similar technologies are sustained.

One of the central features of modern technology is that it combines with the idea of progress, even to the extent of utopian thinking.[46] Particularly in the West, the transition to industrialisation was supported by an emergent societal belief in progress, thus supporting the active promotion of technology by entrepreneurs and the government. As a result, the process of invention and innovation has increasingly been organised in specific organisations, such as research institutes and, most importantly, firms (see next section). These organisations systematically explore the possibility space of technology in two basic ways:

On the notion of progress, see Chapter 3, section 3.1.

- One is trial and error, which is often the main method; for example, in the pharmaceutical industry.[47] The possibility space is defined by possible combinations of chemical elements into new substances, but it is mostly difficult to predict the properties of the substances based on knowing the elements and hypotheses how they interact. Hence, technological evolution closely follows an evolutionary pattern, based on variation and selection, with selection determined by the criteria of application, such as therapeutic efficacy of a new medicine.
- The other way is science and theory based, which means that theory-grounded predictions are made regarding the use of certain

There are two basic modes of technological evolution, trial and error, and projections of science.

technologies, such as the laser. However, one important difference between science and technology remains that technological applications often involve many small-scale adaptations of the artefacts which can only be processed by trial and error, again: This is the domain of engineering as compared to science.[48]

In this sense, technological evolution indeed follows a quasi-Darwinian pattern. This also applies to the notion of a phylogenetic tree of technology: For example, the original bicycle branched out in many forms today, adapted to specific market niches and user patterns. This is expressed in the stability of certain design principles across all variants which may also represent certain physical constraints, as in nature.[49]

In the market context, the basic criterion is that newer technologies must be profitable to overcome old technologies. But there are many factors that may reduce profitability in the state of transition from one to another technology, of which we highlight two:

Technological evolution is shaped by economic mechanisms, such as economies of scale, learning economies, and network effects.

- The first is economies of scale and learning economies.[50] Many technologies require investment in large physical assets to be profitable (think of a chemical plant). This means that the availability of financial resources determines the direction taken by technological evolution. Learning economies have various aspects. One is simply that the use of technology over time increases speed and accuracy of applying it, such as dexterity. The other is more systematic skill development and training. Most technologies require expert knowledge at least during the production process. The capability structure in a certain economy is an important determinant of the direction taken by specialisation of countries or regions in the technological domain. This is demonstrated by the example of Silicon Valley, which relies on a rich workforce of software engineers.[51]
- The second is network effects. Technologies often need to combine with others, and a lack of coordination may hinder their diffusion.[52] Furthermore, there are network effects on the user side, with some technologies directly depending on large numbers of users. Network effects often compare with economies of scale as cost declines with growing size, thus creating a tendency of monopolisation on the market. This is an important impact of technology on markets, which in turn shapes technological development: For example, the monopolist may try to keep competitors out of business, thus also blocking new ideas and technologies.

As said, both economic conditions can constrain the transition to a new technology. Take the development of the electric car: Electric cars were already available in the early days of the automotive industry.[53] However, they were not further developed beyond certain niche applications such as golf carts. The growth of the petrol car technology was strongly shaped by the US market, where oil proved to be a rich resource available. Hence, a coalition of carmakers and the oil industry pushed the growth of the petrol automotive sector and stopped investing in electric cars. This was by no means a necessary development and certainly did not take the externalities into account that we face today in terms of global warming. Yet as we know, it is not easy to switch from the combustion engine to the electric motor. One reason is the lack, or slow development, of complementary technologies such as batteries. The other is the need to install a network of recharging stations. Accordingly, there are huge needs to overcome the stage of initial investment, either by venture capital, as in the case of Tesla, or via the subsidisation of electric cars, as in Germany.

We can summarise our observations on technological evolution in two concepts: technological paradigms[54] and path dependencies.[55]

These economic mechanisms can constrain the transition to a new technology.

- A technological paradigm is a set of basic principles that shapes the composition of elementary technologies in a more complex assemblage, such as the modern car and the related networks of main producers and suppliers. Technological paradigms can achieve the status of general-purpose technologies, which means that they can be applied in various contexts, such as in the case of the steam engine or electricity. Such paradigms have great impact on the evolution of the economy. An example is container transport, which was crucial for driving the growth of international trade in substantially lowering transport costs, thus affecting many other developments such as the growth of global production chains.
- Paradigms, but also single technologies, can manifest path dependency. Take again the example of the electric car: Even though the technology was available at the same time as the combustion engine, and was in fact appreciated in many respects (less noise and pollution), the trajectory was not selected. Subsequently, the trajectory of the combustion engine became superior in terms of profitability because a potential switch would have required huge upscale investment and the writing off of the huge assets invested in the conventional car industry. Thus, initial events can put a technology on a contingent evolutionary track which then stabilises in an almost deterministic way, given economic valuations.

Technological paradigms are configurations of elementary technologies in complex assemblages that can manifest strong path dependencies.

In conclusion, technosphere evolution is a co-evolutionary phenomenon of its own. Technological evolution follows mechanisms that are partly autonomous, such as the existence of complementarities between single technologies or trajectories defined by endogenous problem solving. However, markets shape technological paradigms following different criteria, in particular, profitability.

4. Firms, technology, and specialisation

4.1. The firm as organisational form of specialisation

Our discussion of the firm is continued and complemented in Chapter 11, section 5, and Chapter 15, section 3.2.

In the modern economy, the firm is the central organisational form of arranging patterns of capabilities and artefacts in technology, involving hierarchical coordination in time and space (such as in a factory).[56] Since the industrial revolution, we cannot directly relate markets and technology in the general notion of specialisation. Beginning with Adam Smith's famous example of the pin factory, economics recognises that specialisation of production is mostly arranged within firms. Firms, in turn, are coordinated via the market in higher-level patterns of specialisation, defining industries as niches of technology use that evolve in dynamic markets.[57]

In Imperial China, technology was directly embedded in markets, see Chapter 1.

Many firms arrange complex technological networks of production which process a huge number of inputs, intermediary products, and outputs. A classic example is chemical industry: Vast chemical complexes combine many factories on one site, which are connected via the use of thousands of products resulting from a limited number of chemical processes; thus, high levels of efficiency of resource use and the avoidance of waste in the form of side products are achieved. Another pattern is the arrangement of technological networks via supply chains that involve many different firms. These chains can manifest varying degrees of relational closeness, reaching from arms-length market transactions to high levels of cooperation. For example, the modern automotive industry is characterised by a vast network of specialised producers of car parts, centring on the main producer which develops designs and eventually assembles the final product.

In the modern economy, the firm is the core organisational form of specialisation in production.

Firms embody capabilities that are distributed in the organisation and are manifest in firm-specific routines.

As we have seen, technology is enabled by various capabilities which are partly tacit or informal and which accumulate over time. The pivotal role of firms stems from the fact that they stabilise arrangements of capabilities, behaviour, and artefacts over longer time spans and independently from single members joining or leaving. A theoretical concept that covers this phenomenon is routines.[58] In joining a firm, members adopt behavioural patterns shaped by routines that improve their coordination and enable the handling of complex technologies. This puts substantial limits on technology diffusion. For example, despite tremendous efforts, China has so far not been able to develop the capabilities of producing high-quality and efficient combustion engines and, until today, has to rely on cooperation with automotive firms of other countries. Where and how routines are embodied may not be known precisely; management science is exploring these factors in great detail.

Firms also play a crucial role in technological change. Comparing an independent firm and a department with a similar task in a larger firm, the former may be better placed in developing and implementing a new technology than the latter because in the latter, the structures of tacit knowledge and experience may be distorted by the characteristics of the larger organisation.[59] The typical example today is software development and internet technology: Often, innovations are done by small start-ups which are later bought by the big incumbent firms.

Firms and their interconnections exhibit great variety, including cases where the core firm is reduced to a service firm and management unit and all material-intensive production processes are delegated to cooperating firms (for example, Apple is not directly involved in the production of smartphones, which is only the case for Foxconn). In sum, these variations imply that the boundaries of the firm and its relation to specific technologies are ambivalent and flexible:

- On the one hand, the firm is a legal and organisational construct, with borders defined via its charter and its organisational chart. From this perspective, a supplier is independent and not part of the firm.
- On the other hand, the supplier can be an essential part of the production technology, rendering the boundary of the firm fluid from this perspective. For example, whereas an energy supplier to a firm may not be seen as part of the technology, since energy is not specific to it, the supplier of a highly specific technical unit to a complex machine is a part, even if remaining legally independent.

The economic concept that allows for the analysis of firm boundaries is asset specificity, which is analogous to capability specificity.[60] Asset specificity is low when the part of the technology or input necessary for its operation is generic and non-essential. It is highest when the input can only be used in the context of this specific technology, like a component to be used for one technological device only. Many car parts have intermediate levels of asset specificity; for example, brakes, such that brakes are often supplied by independent firms which relate with various end producers of cars. Yet the brakes remain an essential part of the car technology.

The notion of supply chain often includes the distribution of the product to the end user. Asset specificity is also important here. The product may simply be sold to firms in the commercial sector, which resell to customers. But technology use may require constant maintenance and repair, which in turn may require specific knowledge and skills, such as in the case of cars. Therefore, car producers may extend their reach into the downstream part of the production chain.

As we see, many technologies are embodied in networks of tightly integrated firms. Often, such systems exhibit territorial concentration as well, resulting in the emergence of industrial clusters: For example, in Germany, many leading car producers are in the southern part, especially the state of Baden-Württemberg. We can expand the perspective to industrial systems (automotive industries) or national innovation systems when we consider all ramifications of the conditioning of certain technological trajectories.[61] An

Firms of various size and types are core units of innovation and dissemination of novelties on markets.

The boundaries of the firm are fluid and include cooperating firms in supplier networks.

Technology is embedded in networks of specialised firms.

For more detail on capability specificity, see Chapter 5, section 2.2.

Firms often concentrate spatially, thus creating geographical distributions of capabilities defining comparative advantage in higher-level patterns of specialisation.

139

important determinant is the availability of certain capabilities, which is shaped by the educational system and the system of research and development. In the long run, these shape the pattern of global specialisation of countries.[62] For example, the German system of vocational education and universities of applied sciences has laid the foundation for a car industry that excels in producing high-quality cars at the cutting edge of technology.

Although firms are organisational and institutional complements of technology, technology does not directly determine the structure of firms, which is shaped by economic forces of competition. This in turn feeds back on technological evolution. Therefore, we can speak of the co-evolution of firms and technology as a fundamental feature of the modern economy. On the level of the technosphere, this implies that one cannot approach the technosphere only in terms of its physical artefacts but must include the terms of the social relations and structures that combine with certain artefacts.

For more on
national systems
of innovation,
see Chapter 14,
section 4.1.

4.2. Technology and power in firms

On firms as
governance
structures, see
Chapter 11,
section 5.

As opposed to markets, firms are hierarchical structures which implement and monitor the application of technology in complex systems of specialisation. That means firms are institutionalised forms of forced exchange in the context of markets as domains of voluntary exchange. In a Hobbesian turn, economics mostly assumes that forced exchange within firms is based on a voluntary decision to join, mediated by labour markets.[63]

We discuss
techno-
institutional
regimes in
Chapter 13,
section 2.

In firms, humans and technology closely interact, resulting in phenomena of co-evolution of human culture and technology. For example, the new steam technology employed in factories created the need for more precise time management, thus imposing a conception of time on workers which was different from the conceptions of traditional peasants.[64] The relationship between human activity and technology is multi-valued. Consider a production technology such as the assembly line invented by Henry Ford, which revolutionised car production. The assembly line subjects workers to a strict time discipline but does not necessarily require that they specialise on one task only because they can also rotate positions. Also, there are alternatives to the assembly line. Customised luxury cars may be produced in a team of workers, as in an artisanal workshop. However, in the 20th century, many technologies evolved in the direction of mass production, which has aptly been referred to in the context of Fordism:[65] Whereas in Europe, car manufacturing initially remained in the context of a workshop; Ford's assembly line achieved a steep decline of the costs producing a car and, hence, its widespread adoption in society. This requires standardisation of products.

There are many ways technology and human work can be combined in a firm.

Consider smartphone production in Shenzhen, China.[66] The huge factories of Foxconn with hundreds of thousands of workers produce millions of smartphones a year which are identical. The peculiar design of the technology allows for customisation by end users via selection of apps which are compatible via standardised protocols and interfaces. The hardware of smart-phones is standardised, too, to the degree that core elements, such as chips, are commoditised today. Against this background, technology can have far-reaching effects on disciplining workers. In a capitalist firm, there are strong incentives to minimise labour cost and enhance efficiency as far as possible; given the nature of the capitalist work contract, contextualised (as in the Fox-conn case) by a huge oversupply of workers, there is a strong tendency to subject human labour to the discipline of the technology. Accordingly, at Fox-conn, workers are subject to a military-style disciplinary regime.

We can generalise over these observations in terms of the distinction between capabilities and functionings. Technological evolution goes hand in hand with the evolution of capabilities of human agents. Functionings are mostly implemented in the context of firms and drive the formation of capa-bilities. Therefore, specialisation in firms can be (but does not necessarily have to be) accompanied by a compression of capabilities, with direct impli-cations for outside options. This creates an apparent paradox: If functionings are uniformly standardised in firms and on labour markets, this can enhance opportunities for mobility but with a large power asymmetry between employ-ers and workers within firms. In contrast, if firms allow for the formation of diverse capabilities, this may reduce mobility because the power differential within the firm is lower, given the better outside options, and thus renders the workplace more attractive.[67]

> On capabilities
> and functionings,
> see Chapter 5,
> section 2.2.

The selection of a combination of human work and technology is often determined by power asymmetries in specialisation which eventually are endogenous to those forms.

This argument differs from the reasoning that automation directly lowers demand for labour and, hence, strengthens the power of employers versus workers. Whether automation is a necessary development during technologi-cal evolution does not only depend on technological progress per se.[68] There is a self-reinforcing tendency in automation: Partial automation (such as at the assembly line) is a means to impose labour discipline on workers and contributes to the reproduction of surplus labour on the labour market as a side effect, which may further weaken power of labour vis-à-vis capital. However, there are also technological determinants of automation, such as the technical coefficients of operating a certain process. For example, a robot can implement the same manual operation at higher speed and higher preci-sion than a human worker, can work without breaks, and so on. Humans are more effective if the tasks require high levels of flexibility, adaptation at new circumstances, and creativity.

Automation has complex effects on power relations and is driven by both social and technological forces.

In the very long run of technological evolution, as we have seen for the case of Imperial China, the crucial determinant of automation is the relative cost of energy and labour, which is evident when considering that work is exerted by both humans and machines. This perspective is hidden if we treat automation only as a substitution of labour by capital, as suggested by the standard production function approach. If both capital and labour are treated as flows that result into an output, the cost of capital is the cost of energy nec-essary to run the technology and the cost of maintaining and renewing the

From the thermodynamic perspective, energy consumption of automation and internalisation of ecological effects is an important determinant of substituting labour by capital.

technology, that is, in simplest terms, depreciation in the broad sense, hence including investment. This has consequences for the relative advantages of automation: If energy costs today fully internalised the ecological costs of energy, human labour would remain competitive, especially given the fact that the direct energy needs of labour are very low and fully externalised (daily food is normally seen as private expense of workers). This is especially true for relatively low-skilled labour, eventually requiring the adaptation of technology: Indeed, indigenous car producers in India and China adopt more labour-intensive manufacturing techniques than the established firms.

5. Conclusion

Economics mostly approaches markets as the domain of voluntary cooperation at arm's length. This introduces a hidden value statement in the analytical foundations of the discipline. As we saw in the previous chapter, this is misleading because specialisation necessarily entails the possibility of power asymmetries emerging endogenously. Yet this may result in a reconsideration of the implicit value judgement: Once we understand that specialisation and power are necessary correlates, we can explain why and under which conditions markets can indeed create and expand the reign of freedom in society. This does not happen naturally, though, but requires deliberate institutional design.

Against this background, we must acknowledge the intricate relationship between technology and power that is embodied in the modern firm. Technology is not only embodied in organised forms of cooperation, but there are also many degrees of freedom between the choice of technology and of organisational form. The modern capitalist firm is such a specific arrangement which stands in fundamental tension with markets in the sense that markets should be based on voluntary cooperation, whereas once individuals join a firm, they partly give up their freedom.

Similarly, externalities of production are deeply shaped by power relationships and, thus, are primarily determined by institutions, not technology. Yet this implies that a supposedly objectified view on production, the engineering view, can also have a substantial critical dimension in making externalities explicit and measurable. This broadens the meaning of 'engineering', as we would include aspects such as ecology, when considering environmental externalities, or psychology, when considering the human costs of forced specialisation in firms.

In an even wider perspective explored in this chapter, we recognise the deep structural relationship between technosphere evolution and markets at its core: Technology is created by humans, but humans cannot control and design its evolution. Their actions are guided by markets which connect human action with technosphere processes. Markets, in turn, are partly beyond human control and design, especially when it comes to outcomes, although we can shape their operations via rules, laws, and regulations.

Major chapter insights

- The technosphere is an emergent level of evolution that, in the Anthropocene, encompasses the biosphere. Production is a core process in the technosphere. In the ecological view, consumption is an intermediary input to human work and, hence, part of the production circle.
- Consumption is analysed in terms of the duality of wants and needs, with needs referring to adaptive functions and wants endogenously evolving on the level of culture.
- The specific form of specialisation in production can be analysed in the engineering or the economic perspective, with the former looking at material input-output relationships and the latter at the creation of market value. The economic view excludes important contributions to production, as manifest in deficiencies of GDP as a measure of production.
- Specialisation is embodied in assemblages of artefacts and capabilities, and manifest in uses of technology that are mediated by design. A special form of design is standardisation that enables productivity gains via lower cost of coordination and economies of scale in specialisation.
- Technological change is an open and indeterministic evolutionary process of recombining existing technologies in an expanding space of possibilities. The most important driver is markets, which induces special economic phenomena channelling technological change, such as path dependencies and network effects.
- In the modern economy, the firm is a core organisational form of specialisation in markets. In firms, capabilities are distributed across tightly cooperating members and embodied in firm-specific routines. Firms have fluid boundaries since technology is embodied in complex supply chains that are orchestrated by firms.
- The specific form of combining work and technology in firms is also shaped by power relations, including larger trends such as automation.

Notes

1 Hayek (1945).
2 Ziman (2000), Dosi and Nelson (2018).
3 Smil (2003).
4 For an exemplary economic analysis, see Ashraf and Galor (2013). This has been criticised on substantial grounds, see Guedes et al. (2013). However, the argument was further developed in Ashraf and Galor (2018).

5 The classical analysis is Wallerstein (1974). For an illustrative case of Brazil, see Rogers (2010).

6 Elhacham et al. (2020).

7 Smil (2008, 89ff).

8 Witt (2005).

9 Ulanowicz (1997).

10 Witt (2000, 2010).

11 Trentmann (2017, 165ff).

12 Corning (1983).

13 Glasman (2020).

14 Tsao and Waide (2010), Saunders and Tsao (2012), Montoya et al. (2017).

15 Saad (2007).

16 Smith (2015).

17 Trentmann (2017, 464ff).

18 Zahavi and Zahavi (1997), Saad (2007).

19 Petroski (1994).

20 For a classical analysis, see Galbraith (1967).

21 Miller and Blair (2009).

22 For a comprehensive introduction, see Miller and Blair (2009). A short overview is provided by Erickson and Kane (2018) with special reference to ecological economics.

23 Krausmann et al. (2015).

24 This perspective is explored in research on industrial metabolism or industrial ecology, see Ayres and Ayres (2002), Pauliuk et al. (2017).

25 Devictor (2018).

26 The classic on the economics of shortage is Kornai (1980).

27 This distinction is almost forgotten in modern economics but deserves analytical attention, see Brooks et al. (1990).

28 Stiglitz et al. (2009).

29 Coyle (2015, 106ff).

30 Costanza et al. (2014).

31 Fraser (2016).

32 Any advanced textbook of economics, microeconomics, and macroeconomics contains chapters on production functions.

33 Ayres and Warr (2005).

34 The distinction between producer and user capabilities has become crucial for modern theories of innovation; see, for instance, Baldwin and von Hippel (2011).

35 Fischer (1992).

36 This aspect has been elaborated in sociological studies of technology and the philosophy of technology, see Mitcham (1994). There are distinct traditions, such as the French philosophy of technology (Canguilhem, Sinondon, and others; see, for example, Combes, 2012) which emphasises the complex embeddedness of technology.

37 The concept of tacit knowledge, suggested by Michel Polanyi, is a central notion in modern theories of innovation; see, for example, Foray (2004).

38 Smil (2008, 228ff).

39 Simon (1996).

40 The concept of affordance was developed by Gibson (1979) and is influential in cognitive science.

41 Swann (2010).

42 Ziman (2000).

43 Buenstorf (2004, 123ff), Arthur (2009, 107ff).

44 Weitzman (1998), Kauffman (2000, 142ff).

45 Seminally, Arthur (1988, 1989).

46 Mokyr (2017), Beckert (2016).

47 Mokyr (1998, 2000).

48 Petroski (1996).

49 There is the concept of technological phylogeny, McCarthy (2005), Andersen (2003). Rose-Anderssen et al. (2017).

50 These aspects are mostly emphasised in so-called new versions of neoclassical theory, as in new growth theory (Helpman, 2004). Krugman (1996) builds the bridge to evolutionary economics.

51 Hausmann et al. (2013).

52 Hall and Khan (2003).

53 Bonneuil and Fressoz (2017, 112ff).

54 Dosi (1982), Cimoli and Dosi (1995). For an example, see Krasnodębski (2018).

55 Arthur (1988, 1989).

56 The theory of the firm is an extremely rich field in economics and management sciences, with many competing approaches (Walker, 2017). We are mainly inspired by evolutionary and transdisciplinary approaches, such as Casson (1997) and Aoki (2010).

57 Niche formation in industry evolution is the research topic of organisational demography, with seminal contributions such as Carroll and Hannan (2000), Hannan et al. (2007).

58 Nelson and Winter (1982), D'Adderio (2008), Vromen (2011).

59 The controversy over large versus small firms as drivers of innovation was famously triggered by Schumpeter (1942).

60 Williamson (1985).

61 For an influential contribution, see Lundvall (1992). On learning regions, see Rutten and Boekema (2007).

62 Hausmann et al. (2013).

63 Anderson (2018).

64 Thompson (1967). For a broader perspective, see De Vries's (2008) notion of industrious revolution.

65 These interdependencies have been systematically explored in French regulation theory; for an overview, see Boyer (1990).

66 Ngai and Chan (2012).

67 For a systematic approach towards the relationship between firms, capabilities, and labour markets, see Aoki (1988, 2010).

68 Acemoglu and Restrepo (2019).

References

Acemoglu, D. and Restrepo, P. (2019) 'Automation and New Tasks: How Technology Displaces and Reinstates Labor', *Journal of Economic Perspectives*, 33(2), pp. 3–30. DOI: 10.1257/jep.33.2.3.

Andersen, E. S. (2003) *The Evolving Tree of Industrial Life: An Approach to the Transformation of European Industry*. Available at: http://citeseerx.ist.psu.edu/viewdoc/download?doi=10.1.1.199.136&rep=rep1&type=pdf (Accessed: 23 June 2021).

Anderson, E. S. (2018) *Private Government How Employers Rule Our Lives (and Why We Don't Talk about It)*. Princeton: Princeton University Press.

Aoki, M. (1988) *Information, Incentives, and Bargaining in the Japanese Economy*. Cambridge: Cambridge University Press.

Aoki, M. (2010) *Corporations in Evolving Diversity: Cognition, Governance, and Institutions*. Oxford: Oxford University Press.

Arthur, W. B. (1988) 'Self-Reinforcing Mechanisms in Economics', in Anderson, P., Arrow, K. and Pines, D. (eds.) *The Economy as an Evolving Complex System*. New York: Addison – Wesley, pp. 9–31.

Arthur, W. B. (1989) 'Competing Technologies, Increasing Returns and Lock-in by Historical Events', *Economic Journal*, 99(394), pp. 116–131. DOI: 10.2307/2234208.

Arthur, W. B. (2009) *The Nature of Technology: What It Is and How It Evolves*. New York: Free Press.

Ashraf, Q. and Galor, O. (2013) 'The "Out of Africa" Hypothesis, Human Genetic Diversity, and Comparative Economic Development', *American Economic Review*, 103(1), pp. 1–46. DOI: 10.1257/aer.103.1.1.

Ashraf, Q. and Galor, O. (2018) 'The Macrogenoeconomics of Comparative Development', *Journal of Economic Literature*, 56(3), pp. 1119–1155. DOI: 10.1257/jel.20161314.

Ayres, R. U. and Ayres, L. W. (eds.) (2002) *A Handbook of Industrial Ecology*. Cheltenham and Northampton: Edward Elgar Publishing.

Ayres, R. U. and Warr, B. (2005) 'Accounting for Growth: The Role of Physical Work', *Structural Change and Economic Dynamics*, 16(2), pp. 181–209. DOI: 10.1016/j.strueco.2003.10.003.

Baldwin, C. and Hippel, E. von (2011) 'Modelling a Paradigm Shift: From Producer Innovation to User and Open Collaborative Innovation', *Organization Science*, 22(6), pp. 1399–1417. DOI: 10.2139/ssrn.1502864.

Beckert, J. (2016) *Imagined Futures: Fictional Expectations and Capitalist Dynamics*. Cambridge: Harvard University Press. DOI: 10.4159/9780674545878.

Bonneuil, C. and Fressoz, J.-B. (2017) *The Shock of the Anthropocene: The Earth, History and Us*. London and New York: Verso Books.

Boyer, R. (1990) *The Regulation School: A Critical Introduction*. New York: Columbia University Press.

Brooks, M. A., Heijdra, B. J. and Lowenberg, A. D. (1990) 'Productive Versus Unproductive Labor and Rent Seeking: Lessons from History', *Journal of Theoretical and Institutional Economics*, 146, pp. 419–438.

Buenstorf, G. (2004) *The Economics of Energy and the Production Process: An Evolutionary Approach*. Cheltenham, UK and Northampton, MA, USA: Edward Elgar Publishing.

Carroll, G. R. and Hannan, M. T. (2000) *The Demography of Corporations and Industries*. Princeton: Princeton University Press.

Casson, M. (1997) *Information and Organization: A New Perspective on the Theory of the Firm*. Oxford: Clarendon.

Cimoli, M. and Dosi, G. (1995) 'Technological Paradigms, Patterns of Learning and Development: An Introductory Roadmap', *Journal of Evolutionary Economics*, 5, pp. 243–268. DOI: 10.1007/BF01198306.

Combes, M. (2012) *Gilbert Simondon and the Philosophy of the Transindividual*. Cambridge: MIT Press.

Corning, P. A. (1983) *The Synergism Hypothesis: A Theory of Progressive Evolution*. New York: McGraw – Hill.

Costanza, R. *et al.* (2014) 'Development: Time to Leave GDP Behind', *Nature*, 505, pp. 283–285. DOI: 10.1038/505283a.

Coyle, D. (2015) *GDP: A Brief but Affectionate History*. Princeton: Princeton University Press. DOI: 10.1515/9781400873630.

D'Adderio, L. (2008) 'The Performativity of Routines: Theorising the Influence of Artefacts and Distributed Agencies to Routine Dynamics', *Research Policy*, 37(5), pp. 769–789. DOI: 10.1016/j.respol.2007.12.012.

De Vries, J. (2008) *The Industrious Revolution: Consumer Behavior and the Household Economy, 1650 to the Present*. Cambridge: Cambridge University Press.

Devictor, V. (2018) 'The Biophysical Realities of Ecosystems', in Spash, C. L. (ed.) *Routledge Handbook of Ecological Economics: Nature and Society*. London and New York: Routledge. DOI: 10.4324/9781315679747.

Dosi, G. (1982) 'Technological Paradigms and Technological Trajectories', *Research Policy*, 11(3), pp. 147–162. DOI: 10.1016/0048-7333(82)90016-6.

Dosi, G. and Nelson, R. R. (2018) 'Technological Advance as an Evolutionary Process', in Nelson, R. *et al.* (eds.) *Modern Evolutionary Economics: An Overview*. Cambridge and New York: Cambridge University Press, pp. 35–84.

Elhacham, E. *et al.* (2020) 'Global Human-Made Mass Exceeds All Living Biomass', *Nature*, 588(7838), pp. 442–444. DOI: 10.1038/s41586-020-3010-5.

Erickson, J. D. and Kane, M. (2018) 'Input-Output Analysis', in Spash, C. L. (ed.) *Routledge Handbook of Ecological Economics: Nature and Society*. London and New York: Routledge. DOI: 10.4324/9781315679747.

Fischer, C. S. (1992) *America Calling: A Social History of the Telephone to 1940*. Berkeley and Oxford: University of California Press.

Foray, D. (2004) *Economics of Knowledge*. Cambridge and London: MIT Press.

Fraser, N. (2016) 'Contradictions of Capital and Care', *New Left Review*, 100(9), p. 117.

Galbraith, J. K. (1967) *The New Industrial State*. London: Penguin Books.

Gibson, J. J. (1979) *The Ecological Approach to Visual Perception*. Hillsdale and London: Routledge.

Glasman, J. (2020) *Humanitarianism and the Quantification of Human Needs: Minimal Humanity*. Abingdon and New York: Routledge.

Guedes, J. *et al.* (2013) 'Is Poverty in Our Genes? A Critique of Ashraf and Galor, "The 'Out of Africa' Hypothesis, Human Genetic Diversity, and Comparative Economic Development" American Economic Review (Forthcoming)', *Current Anthropology*, 54(1), pp. 71–79. DOI: 10.1086/669034.

Hall, B. H. and Khan, B. (2003) 'Adoption of New Technology', *NBER Working Paper Series*, 9730. DOI: 10.3386/w9730.

Hannan, M. T., Pólos, L. and Carroll, G. R. (2007) *Logics of Organization Theory: Audiences, Codes, and Ecologies*. Princeton: Princeton University Press.

Hausmann, R. *et al.* (eds.) (2013) *The Atlas of Economic Complexity: Mapping Paths to Prosperity*. Updated Edition. Cambridge: MIT Press.

Hayek, F. A. von (1945) 'The Use of Knowledge in Society', *American Economic Review*, 35(4), pp. 519–530.

Helpman, E. (2004) *The Mystery of Economic Growth*. Cambridge and London: Belknap.

Kauffman, S. A. (2000) *Investigations*. Oxford: Oxford University Press.

Kornai, J. (1980) *Economics of Shortage*. Amsterdam and New York: North-Holland Pub. Co.

Krasnodębski, M. (2018) 'Throwing Light on Photonics: The Genealogy of a Technological Paradigm', *Centaurus*, 60(1–2), pp. 3–24. DOI: 10.1111/1600-0498.12172.

Krausmann, F. *et al.* (2015) 'Economy-Wide Material Flow Accounting: Introduction and Guide', *Social Ecology Working Paper Vienna*, 151.

Krugman, P. (1996) *The Self-Organizing Economy*. Cambridge and Oxford: Blackwell.

Lundvall, B. A. (1992) *National Systems of Innovation: Towards a Theory of Innovation and Interactive Learning*. London: Pinter Publishers.

McCarthy, I. (2005) 'Towards a Phylogenetic Reconstruction of Organizational Life', *Journal of Bioeconomics*, 7(3), pp. 271–307. DOI: 10.1007/s10818-005-5245-5.

Miller, R. E. and Blair, P. D. (2009) *Input-Output Analysis: Foundations and Extensions*. 2nd Edition. Cambridge and New York: Cambridge University Press. DOI: 10.1017/CBO9780511626982.

Mitcham, C. (1994) *Thinking Through Technology: The Path Between Engineering and Philosophy*. Chicago and London: University of Chicago Press.

Mokyr, J. (1998) 'Induced Technical Innovation and Medical History: An Evolutionary Approach', *Journal of Evolutionary Economics*, 8(2), pp. 119–137. DOI: 10.1007/s001910050058.

Mokyr, J. (2000) 'Evolutionary Phenomena in Technological Change', in Ziman, J. (ed.) *Technological Innovation as an Evolutionary Process*. Cambridge: Cambridge University Press, pp. 52–65.

Mokyr, J. (2017) *A Culture of Growth: The Origins of the Modern Economy*. Princeton: Princeton University Press. DOI: 10.1515/9781400882915.

Montoya, F. G. *et al.* (2017) 'Indoor Lighting Techniques: An Overview of Evolution and New Trends for Energy Saving', *Energy and Buildings*, 140, pp. 50–60. https://doi.org/10.1016/j.enbuild.2017.01.028.

Nelson, R. R. and Winter, S. G. (1982) *An Evolutionary Theory of Economic Change*. Cambridge and London: Belknap.

Ngai, P. and Chan, J. (2012) 'Global Capital, Chinese State, and Chinese Workers: The Foxconn Experience', *Modern China*, 38(4), pp. 383–410.

Pauliuk, S. *et al.* (2017) 'Industrial Ecology in Integrated Assessment Models', *Nature Climate Change*, 7, pp. 13–20. DOI: 10.1038/nclimate3148.

Petroski, H. (1994) *The Evolution of Useful Things*. New York: Vintage Books.

Petroski, H. (1996) *Invention by Design: How Engineers Get from Thought to Think*. Cambridge and London: Harvard University Press.

Rogers, T. D. (2010) *The Deepest Wounds: A Labor and Environmental History of Sugar in Northeast Brazil*. Chapel Hill: University of North Carolina Press.

Rose-Anderssen, C., Baldwin, J. and Ridgway, K. (2017) 'Manufacturing Systematics and Cladistics: State of the Art and Generic Classification', *Journal of Manufacturing Technology Management*, 28(5), pp. 655–685. DOI: 10.1108/JMTM-08-2016-0115.

Rutten, R. and Boekema, F. (2007) *The Learning Region: Foundations, State of the Art, Future*. Cheltenham and Northampton: Edward Elgar Publishing.

Saad, G. (2007) *The Evolutionary Bases of Consumption*. New York: Lawrence Erlbaum.

Saunders, H. D. and Tsao, J. Y. (2012) 'Rebound Effects for Lighting', *Energy Policy*, 49, pp. 477–478. DOI: 10.1016/j.enpol.2012.06.050.

Schumpeter, J. A. (2018[1942]) *Capitalism, Socialism, and Democracy*. Washington, DC: Wilder Publications.

Simon, H. A. (1996) *The Sciences of the Artificial, Third Edition*. Cambridge: MIT Press.

Smil, V. (2003) *The Earth's Biosphere: Evolution, Dynamics, and Change*. Cambridge and London: MIT Press.

Smil, V. (2008) *Energy in Nature and Society: General Energetics of Complex Systems*. Cambridge and London: MIT Press.

Smith, A. F. (2015) *Sugar: A Global History*. London: Reaktion Books.

Stiglitz, J. E., Sen, A. and Fitoussi, J. P. (2009) 'Report by the Commission on the Measurement of Economic Performance and Social Progress', *Commission on the Measurement of Economic Performance and Social Progress*. Available at: https://ec.europa.eu/eurostat/documents/8131721/8131772/Stiglitz-Sen-Fitoussi-Commission-report.pdf (Accessed: 29 August 29 2022).

Swann, G. M. P. (2010) 'The Economics of Standardization: An Update', *Report for the UK Department of Business, Skills and Innovation.*

Thompson, E. P. (1967) 'Time, Work Discipline, and Industrial Capitalism', *Past & Present*, 38(1), pp. 56–97. DOI: 10.1093/past/38.1.56.

Trentmann, F. (2017) *Empire of Things: How We Became a World of Consumers, from the Fifteenth Century to the Twenty-First, Penguin History*. London: Penguin Books.

Tsao, J. Y. and Waide, P. (2010) 'The World's Appetite for Light: Empirical Data and Trends Spanning Three Centuries and Six Continents', *LEUKOS*, 6(4), pp. 259–281. DOI: 10.1582/LEUKOS.2010.06.04001.

Ulanowicz, R. E. (1997) *Ecology, the Ascendent Perspective*. New York: Columbia University Press.

Vromen, J. J. (2011) 'Routines as Multilevel Mechanisms', *Journal of Institutional Economics*, 7(2), pp. 175–196. DOI: 10.1017/S1744137410000160.

Walker, P. (2017) *The Theory of the Firm: An Overview of the Economic Mainstream*. London and New York: Routledge.

Wallerstein, I. (1974) *The Modern World System: Capitalist Agriculture and the Origins of the Modern World – Economy in the Sixteenth Century*. New York and London: Academic Press.

Weitzman, M. L. (1998) 'Recombinant Growth', *The Quarterly Journal of Economics*, 113(2), pp. 331–360. DOI: 10.1162/003355398555595.

Williamson, O. (1985) *The Economic Institutions of Capitalism*. New York: The Free Press.

Witt, U. (2000) 'Learning to Consume – A Theory of Wants and the Growth of Demand', *Journal of Evolutionary Economics*, 11(1), pp. 23–36. DOI: 10.1007/PL00003851.

Witt, U. (2005) ' "Production" in Nature and Production in the Economy – Second Thoughts About Some Basic Economic Concepts', *Structural Change and Economic Dynamics*, 16(2), pp. 165–179. DOI: 10.1016/j.strueco.2003.11.001.

Witt, U. (2010) 'Symbolic Consumption and the Social Construction of Product Characteristics', *Structural Change and Economic Dynamics*, 21(1), pp. 17–25. DOI: 10.1016/j.strueco.2009.11.008.

Zahavi, A. and Zahavi, A. (1997) *The Handicap Principle: A Missing Piece of Darwin's Puzzle*. New York and Oxford: Oxford University Press.

Ziman, J. (ed.) (2000) *Technological Innovation as an Evolutionary Process*. Cambridge: Cambridge University Press.

PART III

CHAPTER SEVEN

The economic agent

1. Introduction

In this chapter, we develop the theory of the economic agent. We distinguish between individuals as organisms and agents having agential power in economic and social contexts. This further develops the co-evolutionary approach that we defined in Chapter 4: Biological evolution determines organismic properties of individuals; cultural evolution determines their acquired characteristics. Individual behaviour and choice are the outcome of a complex interaction between those two forces. Our theory aims at overcoming the current conundrum in economics where behavioural economics has definitively challenged the standard view of rational choice, while at the same time, rational choice continues to be a foundational analytical tool in many applications.

This methodological aspect is developed in section 2. In section 3, we introduce the brain as embodying human cognitive and emotional capacities for action. We look at basic structural principles of brain organisation and how we can understand brain functionings in evolutionary terms, in both senses of interpreting the brain against the background of its phylogenesis and of analysing the brain as an open adaptive and evolving system. This prepares the ground for two themes in which we depart substantially from the common economic approach to rationality: The first is the character of rationality as reason, which we define as the capability to give reasons, especially in social interaction; the second is emotions as enabling reason and, specifically, a commitment to rational action which is necessary because rationality, as commonly understood, cannot work under conditions of reflexive social interaction. In section 4, we turn to the analysis of agency, which we understand as the capacity to define and pursue meaningful goals of action. Agency deeply integrates individual drives for action with the social context and is manifest in agential power. The analysis of agency allows for reinstating the standard economic notion of rationality as an intentional stance in the context of markets: Interpreting the behaviour of others as rational results in socially performing *economic* rationality. Section 5 looks at mechanisms of choice in

We saw in Chapter 5 that social interaction is crucial for enabling specialisation.

153

DOI: 10.4324/9781003094869-11

more detail, focusing on the duality of wanting and liking which departs radically from the standard approach in dissociating ex ante valuation from ex post valuation. Section 6 concludes with a discussion of creativity and entrepreneurship.

2. Reframing rationality in economics

In recent years, one of the most significant trends in economic science has been the rise of behavioural economics challenging the standard economic model of rational choice. Behavioural economics claims to focus on real people, who are organisms in our parlance.[1] However, the standard concepts of preferences and utility functions were never intended to describe real people when it comes to empirical research but only the observed behaviour of individuals without identifying the organismic mechanism that generates this behaviour (so-called revealed preferences).[2] This methodological assumption sometimes has been justified by evolutionary arguments: Non-rational agents, in the long run, will drop out of the market process because market selection punishes non-rational behaviour.[3]

Agency is embodied in social mechanisms that connect bodies with external material entities, such as other bodies and artefacts.

Consequently, we must clearly distinguish between the notion of the individual as organism and the notion of economic agent. Individuals are biological entities having bodies and acting in the material world. Economic agents are social constructs and, even stronger, performative phenomena; in sociological terms, they are roles that individuals play in a market context, which is artificial in the sense of not being determined by biological evolution but by social interactions and institutions.[4] What is required, then, is a detailed understanding of how individuals and their roles on markets interplay. One fundamental fact is that roles are standardised to a substantial degree, in terms of behavioural expectations and identities, whereas individuals as organisms are unique and vary across a large space of properties. Individual variation induces variation and novelty in manifesting roles in the market context. Therefore, even if we concentrate on agency as manifest in roles, we must take heterogeneity of individuals into consideration. In their role, bankers may show a relatively uniform behaviour across many instances of action, but in certain instances, even individual differences count essentially, such as when it comes to risk preferences or moral commitments.

In Chapter 12, section 3.1, we discuss the heterogeneity of types of savers and investors.

One of the most important manifestations of heterogeneity on markets is entrepreneurship.[5] Many economists have asserted that entrepreneurial action cannot be explained by assuming rationality and recognise that entrepreneurs are driven by complex motives which often have no direct relation to market mechanisms, such as yearning for adventure and striving for power.[6] Hence, entrepreneurs are the archetypical manifestation of individuality on markets.

The individual matters in markets by creating heterogeneity of agents, with entrepreneurs as one of its most important manifestations.

Our take on rationality differs in principled ways from behavioural economics as emerging in the mainstream. The origin of behavioural economics lies in the accumulation of evidence for violations of the standard of rationality, defined in the mainstream model as the preferred form of behaviour because all deviations induce losses of individual welfare.[7] Current behavioural economics endorses this standard in its policy advice, such as in designing nudging strategies and tactics, and hence, blends positive and normative analysis.[8] We reject this analytical and normative stance. In developing our theory of economic agency, we interpret the concept of rationality in a sociological, not psychological way, and hence, strictly as a concept of positive analysis. This is exactly Max Weber's position in his analysis of capitalism as one essential aspect of rationalisation of Western societies: Rationality is a behaviour that is imposed on actors by a specific institutional context.[9] Emergent rationality is a social phenomenon, not a psychological one.

Behavioural economics blends positive and normative meanings of rationality.

3. Brain, reason, and human sociality

3.1. The nature of the brain: Predictive and social

The evolutionary approach to agency is two-pronged. One refers to the previous reasoning that agency evolves in interactions framed and mediated by external contexts, such as institutions. The other is that individual organisms have properties that emerged in biological evolution. The theory of economic agency is firmly grounded in the co-evolutionary framework.[10]

Starting out from biological evolution, the focus is on the brain. The brain evolved over an extremely long time span since many basic structures of the brain are shared with all vertebrates, and others, especially the human cortex, evolved during the phylogenetically recent emergence of *Homo sapiens*. An important question is whether the properties that the brain attained during its evolution are still determining individual behaviour today, a view championed by evolutionary psychologists,[11] or whether cultural evolution has enabled individuals to adopt behavioural patterns and forms of action which can be decoupled from the biological properties of the brain. We present a co-evolutionary view: An evolved fundamental property of the human brain is the capacity for culture, which functionally transforms biologically embodied properties.[12] We have specified this as a capacity to adopt behavioural patterns that are shaped by institutions.

The human brain is an extremely complex and dynamic network of various types of neurons and other somatic components that are mainly coordinated by electrical signals transmitted via synaptic connections and by chemical modulation via neurotransmitters, hormones, and other chemical substrates.[13] It is tightly integrated with the body, from which data become accessible to the brain, especially when it comes to perceiving results of actions.[14] The central notion reflecting this deep integration of brain and body is sensorimotor circuits, which constitute human cognitive capacities of acting in the world.[15]

Our approach to the brain recognises the roles of both phylogenetically evolved biological properties and culturally evolved functional transformations.

On culture, see Chapter 4, section 4.2; on institutions, Chapter 9.

Brain and body are deeply integrated. Cognition grounds in sensorimotor circuits.

The important consequence for economic analysis is that we cannot analytically separate between the information processing system and the action.[16] By extension, this implies that brain functions are partly externalised and distributed to the environment, such as the employment of artefacts for solving certain cognitive tasks (for example, numbers as embodied in written texts or in digital devices).[17]

Brains are structurally differentiated, but for the generation of action, flexible networks across various areas are crucial.

The brain does not passively respond to external sensory inputs in generating behaviour but is always active.[18] This is grounded in continuously occurring spontaneous neuronal activity (so-called firing). No human brain is identical with other brains due to path dependencies of brain ontogeny: Brains are only partly genetically determined, as most of the neuronal connections only build up after birth, in constant interaction with the environment and, most importantly, with other humans.[19] Brains have a complex internal division of labour across various parts, which are tightly integrated via many cross-connections and form higher-level functional systems. In generating action, many parts of the brain interact, resulting in larger-scale patterns of network modularisation depending on perceived contexts of action (such as distinguishing between action that involves competition over social status and choosing among alternatives of consumption).[20]

Against this background, two basic concepts have been suggested to capture the most general functions of the brain: the predictive and the social brain.

The predictive brain adopts a radical first-person view on the world.

The *predictive brain* refers to the fundamental role of the neuronal system to identify the structural patterns in the world despite the unsurmountable barrier between brain and world: The external world of events, things, processes, and so on is projected on an information processing system that, in simplest terms, is just neuronal signalling.[21] This establishes a first-person view in a thorough naturalistic definition: The brain constructs maps and models of the world which are not images or correspond in any direct way to the external world (a third-person view, like an exact map) but aim at enabling successful action in the world. For achieving this, the continuous generation of predictions about action consequences is crucial, which are checked against internal value functions: The proof of the pudding is in the eating, not in ascertaining objective features.[22]

Predictions drive actions on every time scale.

Therefore, the brain embodies a pervasive orientation towards the future at any time scale, ranging from the immediate next present to the long view. Predictions will be confirmed or refuted and, thereby, guide an equally continuous process of learning. The simplest form of learning is reinforcement learning: Successful predictions of positively valued results reinforce a behavioural tendency.[23] We gradually gain experience in using knives to cut fruit, for example, adapting to different kinds of fruit or grades of maturation. Accordingly, the most important generator of behaviour is habit, which reflects an economy of cognition: If certain actions always produce the expected results, they become habitual or even automatic.[24]

In contrast, this implies that surprise is a universal driver of learning: Neuroeconomists even argue that subjective value is determined by positive prediction errors, that is, we value what deviates positively from our expectations.[25] The predictive brain is a curious brain, always searching for novelty and, hence, generating evolutionary variation endogenously. In this context, habits save cognitive effort and work like a background against which novelty is accentuated. In the very long haul of vertebrate phylogeny, the predictive brain enabled fundamental biological functions, such as continuous foraging, venturing in unfamiliar territories, potentially facing adversaries and predators.[26] These neurophysiological dispositions provide the embodied roots of entrepreneurial behaviour on the marketplace, especially in terms of fundamental stances, such as alertness to opportunity.[27] In the same vein, they explain the value of diversity of goods in consumer behaviour: Shopping can be interpreted as a modern form of foraging in an uncertain environment full of surprises (and even predators, if we fall into traps of spending sprees and deceit).[28]

The *social brain* relates to the adaptation of humans to living in groups and to coordinate joint actions in generating adaptive performances.[29] Conditions more specific to humans include coordinated action in larger groups, such as in the group hunt, but most importantly in warfare and other forms of intraspecific collective violence, which have shaped human societies until modern times.[30]

Adaptation to sociality implies both positive and negative aspects. The positive aspect is the benefits of cooperation; the negative, in the widest sense, is cheating and expropriating other humans in asymmetric outcomes of social interaction. The fundamental problem of cooperation is that inner states of individuals are not directly observable, especially, intentions and states of information. The social brain has evolved distinct human capabilities in understanding and interpreting inner states, often referred to as mentalising or mind reading.[31] These capabilities emerge after a long process of socialisation: A distinctive feature of the human species is neoteny and the development of inborn somatic capacities into full-fledged capabilities, a process that requires time until achieving maturity in puberty. For example, the capacity for language is a biological endowment, but the capability to fully master a native language is only achieved with puberty.

The social brain must also be a predictive brain: Predicting the behaviour of others is a most complicated and difficult task in everyday life and relies on many sources of information, such as declared intentions or body language. Therefore, the two characterisations are deeply complementary. In this respect, language is both a boon and a curse: Language is as powerful in communicating truthful information as in fabricating lies.[32] This relates to the capacity for culture, where culture is the medium in which agency is expressed in a way to enable predictions of the behaviour of others and the capacity to adopt institutionalised behavioural patterns to enable behavioural coordination.

The predictive brain conditions economic phenomena, such as entrepreneurial alertness or consumers' desire for variety.

The social brain is shaped by selection of traits that relate to collective action, such as in the context of organising violence (group hunt, warfare).

The social brain is an adaptation to specialisation in groups, as outlined in Chapter 5.

A fundamental cognitive capacity is the prediction of others' behaviour without knowing their inner states.

Brains embody the capacity for culture. Culture scaffolds human cognition and shapes mutual behavioural expectations.

The role of
markets for
distributed
cognition is
explored in
Chapter 10,
section 4.

*The size of
primordial human
groups is limited by
the capacities of the
brain in processing
complex social
information.*

Groups are
analysed from a
social network
perspective
in Chapter 8,
section 3.3.

*Group-based
identity conceptually
connects brain and
agency.*

*There are
fundamental
limitations for
predicting our own
behaviour which
result from the
reflexivity of decisions
in social interactions.*

A related human capability is the capacity for mind shaping, that is, actively influencing states of minds of others.[33] All these phenomena serve to predict the flow of social interactions. In this sense, the predictive brain is scaffolded by culture, norms, and institutions such that fundamental cognitive functions are no longer confined to the somatic borders of the brain but are distributed over many brains linked up via those mediators, thus systematically grounding the second-person view beyond the apparently solipsistic first-person view of the neuronal system:[34] Human cognition is distributed cognition. Markets are an important manifestation of this fact, with market signals, most significantly prices, assuming powers in leveraging human cognition and action coordination.[35]

From the perspective of the social brain, individuals and groups are intimately fused in all forms of behaviour: Humans, therefore, are social animals. The term 'group' must be specified relative to certain biological capacities for group life embodied in the brain.[36] Our capacity to monitor and manage interactions in groups is limited: We can maintain close and intimate relations with only a small number of other individuals, roughly below 100. Groups cohere and coordinate via many forms of symbolically mediated interaction. As one form, group-based identity ties the brain with agency by shaping social roles that people fulfil in groups: A mother is expected to do mothering, a father to fathering, a trader would be expected to differ from a farmer, and so on. In many societies, such roles were institutionally fixed in a rigid way, such as in the Indian system of castes which also refers to occupational specialisations. Modern democratic and liberal societies have suppressed such institutionalisation (however, see the still lively presence of caste in India today), yet we can safely say that there are still implicit typologies of social roles that can affect markets. For example, most people would not accept that a doctor would clearly say that she is pursuing profits in treating patients: We expect a doctor to be a different type of agent than a Wall Street trader.

3.2. Reason and rationality

One precondition for joint action in groups is planning: In the example of the group hunt, group members must assign tasks to everybody and give information about future location, movements, and so on.[37] However, we cannot conclude that, therefore, planning is also a universal feature of individual behaviour. One of the fundamental problems in planning our own behaviour is that we are not perfectly informed about ourselves.[38] In other words, there are principled limits to predicting our own behaviour, for two reasons.

First, as said, the brain is spontaneously active and produces surprises including for ourselves, such as coming up with a new idea or falling into an unexpected mood. The brain is creative, and therefore, we cannot fully plan or control ourselves (see section 4.3 for further implications).

Second, there is the logical impossibility to rationally solve decision problems that are reflexive to higher degrees. We need to predict the behaviour of others, which would include the construction of models of their inner states, while these states also include models of our own internal states, and so on. Our brains cannot solve such embedded reflexive loops beyond a certain, small number of steps, especially considering time constraints.[39] Therefore, for principled reasons, it is impossible to rationally predict and plan even our own actions in the future.

Reflexivity in this sense is not only a source of paradox but also a capacity that we label as 'reason', which we define as the capability to understand and formulate reasons for action, reflecting on ourselves.[40] This is fundamentally different from the standard economic conception of rational choice where preferences directly determine choice: In our view, a preference is a reason for action that we provide to ourselves and to others. The capacity for rational reasoning, however, is not a biological given but emerges during human socialisation, especially including the formation of a reasoning subject and the recognition of others as reasoning subjects.[41] Accordingly, and contrary to a long tradition in Western philosophy, reason is not the manifestation of individual autonomy and enabled by individualised ratiocination but is a fundamentally social stance and type of behaviour: Reason is reasoning in communication with others, and individualised reasoning is the result of the internalisation of reasoning practices (silent speech).[42] The aim of reasoning is to get recognition of reasons by others as reasonable.

This allows for a restatement of the economic concept of rationality as intentional stance in interpreting the behaviour of others;[43] that is, as a powerful assumption in understanding and predicting the behaviour of others, given certain public information about the situational context. Rationality is the basic interpretive stance on part of the economic subjects in understanding the behaviour of others, that is, in the second-person view. In other words, individuals are not rational but interpret others as rational for predicting their actions. This is especially true when considering the context of markets where actions are scaffolded by many ways to imbue behaviour; for example, by calculative stances, such as projecting value on monetary standards in accounting. Economic rationality is not a given property of individuals but a mutually recognisable, reasonable behavioural stance on markets.[44]

The internalisation hypothesis implies that individuals project the intentional stance back on themselves: Children gradually learn by interpreting the behaviour of others to recognise themselves as rational agents.[45] That is, rational agency is a developmental achievement, not a given. As a result of

This is highly significant in many economic contexts, especially finance, see Chapter 12, section 3.3.

Rationality as reason is the capability to give reasons for actions that aim at recognition by others.

Economic rationality is the intentional stance contextualised by markets; and it is performative when scaffolded by rationalising media of interaction.

For more detail on the role of money, see Chapter 10, section 4.

development, humans form the capacity of rational agency in the sense of developing an impartial view on a decision situation and can reach rational conclusions for predicting and designing behaviour, including their own.[46]

Therefore, the economic theory of rationality can become performative in the strong sense because, in a reflexive context, it leverages the intentional stance. That means, if I interpret others as rational agents and also know that they interpret me as a rational being, there might be good reasons that I adopt rational means of decision making for me, too, thereby confirming the expectations of others.[47] This much depends on the availability of cognitive means to rationalise a decision problem, such as quantifying costs and benefits. But once these are available, we can assume that rationality becomes performative in the sense of a self-reinforcing behavioural pattern.

We introduced
reflexivity as a
methodological
concept in
Chapter 2,
section 6.

3.3. Emotions

Emotions are
manifestations
of inner states in
social interaction.
They enable
rational action via
valuations.

A standard lore in Western everyday worldviews and philosophy is the juxtaposition of emotions and rationality. However, this opposition does not survive the scrutiny of modern neurosciences and psychology. In evolutionary psychology, emotions are complex multilevel programs that integrate cognitive and affectual mechanisms in culturally embedded behavioural patterns that can be categorised and interpreted by the individuals and by others.[48] Most importantly, emotions include valuations and are, therefore, essential for rational behaviour.[49] Therefore, emotions not just are inner states but constitute another essential expression of the sociality of the brain. Emotions are intersubjectively accountable constructs of inner states, situational factors, and complex forms of signalling, especially via body movements, facial expressions, and specific vocal and linguistic forms.[50]

Emotions are
commitment
mechanisms that
enable rational
action.

As such, emotions can trigger functionally adaptive and efficacious behaviour and, in this sense, provide a rational response to a certain situation when decisions must be taken.[51] For example, in competing over a scarce resource, there may be two solutions: One is to share and save the cost of conflict; the other is an irrational threat of a very costly conflict about the resource, which may lead to the rationally preferred success.[52] Emotions are mechanisms that enable commitment to action and to credibly signal this commitment to others; therefore, they are an important determinant of the capability to act rationally in terms of outcomes, including the overcoming of rational stalemates (Buridan's ass starving because he cannot decide which haystack to eat) or blockades in social interactions. Lack of rational control implies that the information conveyed by emotions is credible and is perceived as committing an actor to a certain course of action.[53]

One important corollary of the role of emotions is that human decision making is contextualised. To illustrate this important point, we discuss one specific type of emotional stance that is closely related to enabling human sociality, namely empathy. Empathy is important in economics as it relates to the perennial debates over the opposition between individual and social preferences.[54] Social preferences would directly anchor human sociality in individual choice, as individuals would include other's preferences in their own preferences. Such a constellation would have consequences across all topics in economics. Therefore, empathy is a core topic in the economic theory of the individual, whereas other emotions may be less significant in economic contexts, such as grief or love. In social interaction, empathy is partly a meta-emotion in the sense that it enables the communication and even transmission of emotional states across individuals. Its central position in economics was already defined by Adam Smith in his theory of sympathy; economics has sidelined this core Smithian notion until most recently.[55]

Empathy, in this sense, is an important determinant of the human capability of cooperation. This has been systematised in the notion of modes of decision making which switch between individual and group-level identification in everyday talk referred to as team spirit,[56] which involves complex neurophysiological processes such as associated with the oxytocin hormone.[57] Humans have the capacity to switch from the individual stance towards a collective stance in which they follow group-level preferences in decision making. This fundamental fact is crucial for understanding cooperation in groups, such as when villagers collectively organise irrigation systems or workers collaborate in firms.

The upshot is that we cannot generally characterise humans as being selfish or altruistic. The switch between individual and social preferences can happen instantaneously and depends on contextual cues. Therefore, human groups spend much effort in maintaining such contexts via social norms, rituals, and institutional means. One of the most important emotional stances in markets is trust: Markets cannot work efficiently without trust among market agents.

4. The economic agent

4.1. Agency and agential power

In this section, we look in more detail at the notion of agency, which we introduced as the capacity to define and pursue meaningful goals of action. 'Agency' is a term that is not systematically employed in standard economics; however, it forms a core theoretical concept in sociology.[58] In our approach, it is essential to grasp the complex social nature of the economic agent. For example, in our discussion of emotions, we noticed that a certain behaviour may be crucial for achieving agency, although it might go along with the feeling of being overwhelmed by an emotion. Yet we can successfully realise our goals and succeed in winning over or overpowering others, thus assuming

Empathy is an emotional and cognitive capacity that is constitutive for social preferences.

On social preferences, see Chapter 3, section 2.

Empathy enables cooperation in groups via the switch to group-level shared preferences.

Humans are neither selfish nor altruistic by nature.

The notion of trust is scrutinised in Chapter 8, section 3.2.

Agency is the power to act autonomously and to be efficacious in interactions with others.

agency in relation to them. The poor crowds that angrily sacrifice their lives in battling with oppressive forces of a dictatorship gain agency and may eventually change the course of history.[59] Hence, the term catches the complex determinants of successful action in social contexts.

A most general restricting force of agency is uncertainty since facing uncertainty directly implies impotency in controlling the environment. Therefore, we can relate the notion of agency to the concept of the predictive brain: In a complex environment with endemic uncertainty, assessing and expressing forms and degrees of agency are crucial for choosing the right path of action. Therefore, we posit as general human tendency the pursuit of increasing agential powers, defined as reducing uncertainty.[60] This is in contrast with the notion of utility, even if this is defined in probabilistic terms. Whereas utility would relate with the direct benefits of a certain activity, striving for agential powers means that direct utility is secondary to orienting action towards the goal of enhancing future capacities for safeguarding benefits facing endemic uncertainty.

Agential power reduces uncertainty of future action.

Agency deeply relates with freedom. An individual has agency if she can control what she is doing in a way that a goal is achieved that she sets autonomously. Having agency means that one experiences the capability to make a difference in one's context and to influence a situation. Therefore, agency must be conceived as the elementary expression of power, in the sense of power to do, which, however, as we will discuss in the next chapter in more detail, includes power over, in certain circumstances.[61]

On the economic value stance of freedom, see Chapter 3, section 2.

One essential aspect of agency is the ability to have control over oneself. Philosophically, this means that freedom is not simply freedom to do whatever we want but to be able to take a distance to oneself and take control of ourselves.[62] For example, many forms of consumption of goods and services require the formation of skills and the imposition of certain disciplines on ourselves, eventually in the sense of building up human capital,[63] but also in terms of the role of savings in enabling future consumption, that is, trading different forms and qualities of consumption across time. Saving means to postpone current consumption for future benefit; more generally, saving creates material conditions for future agency, enlarging the standard interpretation of savings just as consumption postponed to managing agential power.

Freedom is agency in controlling oneself. This applies especially in acting towards the future and in forming time preferences.

We discuss saving extensively in Chapter 12, section 3.1.

Agency is often tied to controlling other resources beyond social relations. The most general economic institution in this context is property as defining agency via the possessions that can be controlled by an individual, especially when engaging in market interactions: What we own, we can freely offer and exchange on the marketplace.[64] Biologically, this is rooted in the almost universal tendency to occupy and defend territories as control of resources and as control of mates, including dominance over competitors.[65] These fundamental forces have also shaped the evolution of the human social brain. There are behavioural phenomena that directly reflect the connection between possession

Property establishes and embodies agency in economic interactions.

and agency, such as the endowment effect: Owners typically value the goods higher than in a position as non-owner.[66]

In human societies, property and wealth are important determinants of social status. We denote the relative endowment with agential powers as status, implying that humans universally pursue the goal of enhancing their status relative to others in human groups, similar to a central behavioural dimension in primate social interaction.[67] Notably, if humans compete over status, status-based exchange must violate the Pareto criterion in a principled way: Status is a relative category, hence, defining competition as a zero-sum game.[68] This is why small-scale human societies tend to level down social hierarchies and distinctions and why stable status hierarchies universally rely on violence and other forms of force. However, the emergence and growth of social complexity imply an increasing differentiation of social roles and associated status orders, resulting in their multidimensionality.

4.2 Identity

The concept of identity remains under-theorised in economics, although it is essential in defining preferences as stable across situations and through time. Rationality depends crucially on assuming the stable identity of the actor.[69]

There are two aspects of identity, social and personal.[70] The neuroscientific view focuses on personal identity in the first place.[71] This is the fundamental conception of the self, which is manifest in many important phenomena. Yet the self is another achievement of maturing as a human agent: Our neuronal system originally leaves the boundary between self and others porous in order to enable a most fundamental form of human learning – imitation as including the reconstruction of the intentions of others.[72] In order to coordinate our actions through time as adults, we continuously must activate memory, both short-term working memory and long-term memory.[73] The backward construction of our personal identity as agents also serves to project ourselves as agents into the future, even if we may take radical decisions, such as changing our gender identity: This decision itself is a strong expression of our agential powers and reinstates the self across this rupture.[74] The most important medium in which these continuities are expressed and created is language.

We already pointed out that language is a boon and a curse. Language creates the possibility to assume any kind of identity in social interactions: We can lie about ourselves, even to the degree of self-deceit.[75] Yet language is also the solution to this quandary since it imposes many constraints on what we can say and how. The core linguistic form in which identity is expressed in language is narratives.[76] In the neurosciences, narratives are treated as a basic form of autobiographical memory, bridging past and future in defining the self as a process.[77] Narratives create plots of events that imbue the course of actions with meanings, thereby also invoking a deep relation between past and

For a discussion of property, see Chapter 9, especially sections 3.1 and 5.1.

Agency in social interactions is embodied in status.

Status differences are a key determinant of economic inequality, see Chapter 15. For more on status, see Chapter 8, section 3.2.

Identity is essential for enabling rational action through time and in interaction with others.

Identity is mainly expressed in the medium of language, especially in the form of narratives.

Narratives create the agent in economic actions connecting past and future.

future as events are unfolding in the narrative present[78] and basically form a fictional identity of ourselves.[79]

For example, many consumption decisions are embedded into the recurrent evocation of narratives, such as listening to a specific type of music or choosing a favourite dish at the restaurant. The private dwellings of individuals, even in direst circumstances, are adorned with items that evoke memories and about which stories can be told.[80] Individuals accumulate stocks of goods that are anchors of narratives and, therefore, directly embody their identities.

Narratives build the bridge between personal identity and social identity in two senses. One is that narratives per se build on language as a social phenomenon; the other is that individuals define themselves via linguistic markers of identity. Social identity differs from personal identity in substantial respects. Most importantly, social identity creates the potential for externalities across individuals,[81] relating to the issue of social preferences as well as social discrimination and the stabilisation of status orders via both a drive and a pressure towards conformity.[82] The latter can stem from the urge to retaliate against the perceived damage of one's own identity resulting from deviant behaviour. Mechanisms to maintain social identities tied to groups are most universal characteristics of human societies. This includes the ubiquity of many forms of moral aggression against socially deviant behaviour, even if people are not affected at all, and as we saw in the discussion of empathy, a direct impact of group boundaries on behavioural stances, such as altruistic action.

In sum, identity is a two-dimensional concept (Figure 7.1): Personal identity anchors social identity and frames individual agency in referring, for

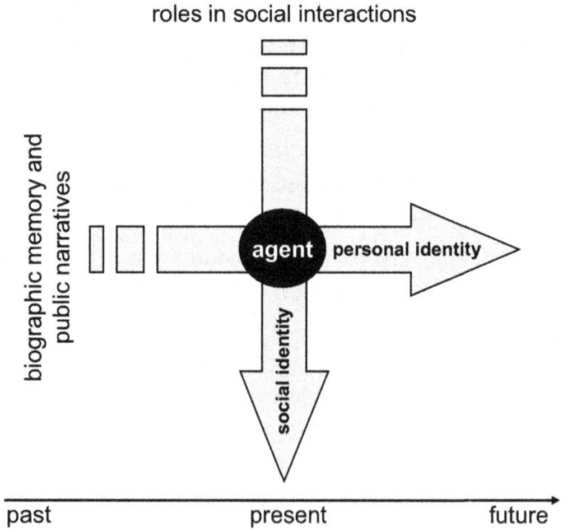

On externalities,
see Chapter 5,
section 4.

*Social identity
is the source of
discrimination in
many forms.*

roles in social interactions

biographic memory and
public narratives

agent personal identity

social identity

past   present   future

Figure 7.1 Personal and social identity

An agent's identity is constituted by the confluence of personal and social identity. Personal identity is embodied in biographic memory and its publicly shared narratives; social identity is an assemblage of roles in social interactions, which are in continuous flux, though anchored in personal identity through time.

example, to ideas about future development or emotional stances to people; social identity is more in flux, such as in the multiplicity of roles and contexts. The two can stay in a dynamic, sometimes also conflictual, relationship. For example, developing an entrepreneurial personal identity may require questioning social roles and breaking through their constraints.

4.3. Performativity

The variability of identity leads us to consider the precise mechanisms by which identity and behaviour relate to each other. In relating language and identity, we further develop our analytical toolbox introducing the notion of performativity that we already met in the context of economic methodology.

On performativity, see Chapter 2, section 6.

In current economic treatments of language, and narratives in particular, there is a tendency to reduce language to the function of representing reality.[83] However, language has many different functions, such as expressing emotions (think of cursing) or expressing commitment.[84] This multi-functionality of language has been elaborated in the theory of speech acts. An important class of speech acts is performative (or sometimes, declarative) speech acts. A simple example is declaring two individuals to be married. Performative speech acts create social facts and build on a special kind of agential powers tied to social roles, such as in this case, the priest who enacts the performation.[85]

Language has various functions beyond representing the world, including performative speech acts that create social roles.

In the current context, we focus on performing identities, which also applies in the example: Once marriage is consummated, all concerned parties form specific expectations about the behaviour of the individuals which refer to the agential powers that are shaped by the performative act. Since individuals operate in a reflective mode, they are also aware of this and adapt behaviour accordingly. That means, they assume the social identity expressed in the performation and, thereby, confirm the general social expectations that go along with it. This completes the performative mechanism.

Performativity is a key analytical concept in other contexts, too, especially institutions, see Chapter 9, section 3.

Among other applications, performativity is the analytical tool for understanding the evolution of wants. This assertion follows from a two-pronged theoretical argument based on rich empirical results from psychology and the neurosciences. The first observation is that the semantics of symbols is based on sensorimotor representations: The symbol does not simply represent an object, say, an apple, but relates to an action that integrates the sensory perception of the apple with actions involving it such that symbolic or linguistic expressions evoke those sensorimotor circuits without necessarily becoming manifest in the corresponding action.[86] The second observation is that we always experience causal impacts from the external world as symbolically mediated, as long as consciousness is involved. We cannot directly experience the amount and type of vitamins that we digest and which impact on our body. But we experience the apple as a sign of itself: the colour, the shape, the taste, and so forth. This means we need to distinguish between the causal impact of consuming the material entity, the apple, and its symbol, which is, on surface, the apple as we see and feel it.[87]

On wants and needs, see Chapter 6, section 2.2.

In consuming a good, we simultaneously consume its symbol and the meaning embodied in the sensorimotor circuits of realising the act of consumption.

See our
discussion
of sugar in
Chapter 6,
section 2.2.

*Many consumptive
actions are
markers of status
(i.e., involve
positional goods).
Consumption
involves identities
embedded in
cultural norms and
practices.*

In other words, consumption essentially involves meanings, but meanings are sensorimotor phenomena in turn: Action and meaning are deeply enmeshed.[88] For example, the human diet is deeply enmeshed with culinary culture, which is the ways to prepare and present food: A heap of nutrients reduced to chemical essentials would create a different experience of eating than a well-prepared dish with aesthetic appeal and would also produce a different somatic response.[89] This is what defines the performativity of consumption: Human consumption is mediated by meanings, and these meanings contextualise the causal impact of consumption on the body.

We can broaden the scope of performativity in considering the role of consumption in expressing and confirming status.[90] Once an act of consumption assumes the function of expressing status, it confirms status, which in turn motivates subsequent consumption decisions, thereby closing a performative loop. There are significant cultural and social phenomena that involve performative consumption, which can make up a substantial share of total consumption. Even the poor often spend extraordinary amounts of money for certain consumption activities that signal relative status.[91] For example, weddings are often extremely rare occasions of lavish consumption for the poor, where much money is spent in entertaining others. However, they are central goals in the life cycle of individuals. This reveals that, in fact, many consumption decisions are enmeshed with each other in terms of being reflections of status as a unifying pattern, such as household endowments with a home, a car, a budget for regular vacations, and so forth: Poor people maintain meagre daily food expenses in order to save for a lavish wedding that expresses their status in the community.

Reflecting the fundamental performative mechanisms, consumption is deeply shaped by social factors since performative acts are always mediated by imaginaries that are shared in communities and societies. This explains why consumption was also always and everywhere implicating moral concerns and debates.[92] This is shaped not only by long-run cultural factors but also by historical events and, therefore, cohort effects. The latter are often bolstered by the diffusion of narratives in society that foster certain behavioural stances, such as frugality after the financial crises of 2008 in the US, radically shifting savings behaviour and related attitudes.[93]

5. Mechanisms of choice and valuation

5.1. Imitation and learning

In this final section, we look at choice in more detail, which is the central concern of the standard economics approach to individual behaviour. We continue with the previous section in considering consumption in relation to the distinction of wants and needs.

As we have seen in Chapter 6, we cannot define a third-person view on wants, different from needs, as wants evolve endogenously and are only recognised in the second-person view. For example, what is regarded as poor in an advanced industrial economy is very different from what is poor in a least-developed country. Yet at the same time, perceptions of a good life as determined by material goods tend to converge worldwide, since technological development and consumption practices in advanced countries set the standard (think of the rapid growth of private passenger car use in China in recent decades). However, at the same time, we can adopt a reflective stance towards wants and consider whether they are justified and reasonable.

However, the evolution of wants is only partly determined by reasoned fixation of preferences. As our discussion of reason showed, often, reasons serve as rationalisation and justification of choices that have been determined otherwise. A basic mechanism is imitation, which builds a bridge between wants and markets. Imitation is an important means to overcome the uncertainty over one's own preferences and to express one's social identity; in other words, imitation is an essential form of a performative mechanism of choice.[94]

Wants can be determined by reasoned choice, but often, this only rationalises preferences that form by other mechanisms, especially imitation.

This is straightforward if we consider goods that have no specific function but only generic functions, such as the kind of music or the specific song that I prefer to listen, which caters my taste for music. In contrast, my need for vitamins results from specific organismic functions.[95] Music, as such, certainly responds to specific needs of humans in entertaining, distracting, and expressing or even adjusting one's mood. But we cannot relate specific kinds of music to specific functions: Clearly, there is a strong impact of collective practices, if only because I follow the crowd and imitate what people in a certain reference group prefer. This can imply that if I want to distinguish myself, I go for a minority taste: I shun the club and listen to a Bach suite at home. Still, my preference is influenced by the larger pattern, if only in distinguishing myself from it. In addition, sharing preferences with other people also opens opportunities for social interaction, as obviously in enjoying companionship in the club or when talking about favourite songs over breakfast.

To sum up, in case of hits or blockbuster movies and many other surges in demand for a particular good, we cannot argue that this happens because it is best in fulfilling a functional need, as we might argue, say, in case of a device for cleaning a window. Yet we can also assert that similar mechanisms work out in all cases when we are imperfectly informed about our own preferences in terms of such functional requirements: Food is an important case in point, which shows that rather mundane and apparently bodily needs are implicated as well. Accordingly, imitation is a major driver of wants.[96] This has far-reaching implications for market dynamics, especially if we include interaction with production and its technological characteristics. Much attention has been given to the internet business, where imitative mechanisms are even explicitly activated (likes, etc.) and interact with the network dynamics of information production and dissemination on the web.

On imitation in social networks, see Chapter 8, section 3.4.

*Learning
endogenises the
formation of wants.*

As said, imitation is a form of learning. Learning in this context is necessary because we do not know what we want or what we should want. The issue is not simply about accumulating information about objects of choice and, thereby, correcting errors individually. First, our preferences are embodied in the results and the history of our choices, or they evolve endogenously and become fixated in the consumption environment that we create.[97] Second, learning directly relates to the behaviour of others beyond imitation, as we can treat this reflexively as indicating best practices.

*Material goods
embody affordances
to consume and,
hence, are part
and parcel of
preferences.*

Taken together, these arguments imply that our preferences are externalised to a substantial degree and are scaffolded by the environment that we co-create with others in our choices. This results in an apparently paradoxical turn of the revealed preference concept: In observing our realised choices, we form our preferences.[98] An important corollary to the theory of performative consumption, which so far emphasised social mechanisms, can be added: material embodiments of consumption are part and parcel of mechanisms of choice, as they embody the information on our preferences and create affordances of consumption.[99]

5.2. Wanting, liking, and happiness

*Wanting and liking
involve different
neurophysiological
mechanisms such
that valuations ex
ante and ex post are
not identical. This is
particularly manifest
in consumption
disorders.*

For further exploring the dialectics of wants and needs in explaining choices, the distinction between wanting and liking suggested by neuroscientific research is fruitful.[100] In standard economic theory, it is taken for granted that the valuation that determines choice is identical with the evaluation during consumption. However, there are many behavioural phenomena which contradict this assumption, especially when it comes to clinical consumption disorders. The workhorse case is eating disorders, which is important as we might believe that eating is a primordial biological function such that individuals should be informed naturally about their needs. Yet modern industrial societies manifest many phenomena of dysfunctional consumption, such as overweight. Indeed, much of eating behaviour is learned, which also allows for failures in learning.

*Wanting drives
choice; liking
determines
evaluation of
outcomes.*

In principle, learning is enabled via the duality of wanting and liking. Wanting determines the choice, whereas liking is the evaluation of the consumption. In simplest terms, this creates the possibility that we want a certain food but later regret that we ate too much.[101] It is important to notice that liking is not necessarily specific, that is, we are not able to assess in detail whether a certain food intake indeed fulfilled our needs, say, for vitamins. This complicates the feedback from liking the result of a choice to the next round of wanting.

We can refer this distinction to our previous discussion of performative functions as they clearly implicate wanting but not necessarily liking: A common example is the adoption of consumption habits during transition to adulthood which often implies overcoming initial disliking, such as drinking bitter coffee or inhaling smoke.[102] Economics commonly interprets such phenomena as an expression of incomplete information (such as youth being imperfectly informed about all consequences of smoking), whereas we claim that they systematically manifest the duality of wanting and liking. One simple indication is the fact that a mere provision of information often does not change behaviour: We know very well which diet is best for us, yet we fail to follow the advice almost every day. The strongest evidence, however, is constituted by seriously dysfunctional behaviour such as addiction.[103] Addiction is often accompanied by extreme shifts in behaviour, with sudden relapses followed by deep regret; consumption of the drug may no longer be accompanied by feelings of satisfaction and elevation. In these cases, the wanting system works in a seriously dysfunctional way because what produces the reward is no longer the activity in question but the hormonal responses in the choice mechanism.

An important implication of the wanting-liking distinction is that we cannot define a quantitative measure of well-being that is utilitarian in principle and based on adding up single instances of liking an act of consumption. This has recently been recognised by economists via the strong interest in research on happiness as an indicator of subjective well-being.[104] The underlying empirical insight is that neither GDP nor quantitative indicators of living standards correlate clearly with subjective expressions of happiness, especially in the sense of a linear correlation. This does not deny that material improvements of life matter but whether people express satisfaction with their status is determined by a complex interplay of many factors. Two observations loom large against the background of this chapter. The first is that relative status matters such that, for example, growing inequality in society negatively impacts on happiness. The second is that uncertainty exerts negative impact, too, even if the measured trend of material progress is positive.[105] This can be interpreted as happiness reflecting the feeling of having agential powers. If so, this would entail important consequences for designing economic institutions and policies.

The dualism of wanting and liking explains dysfunctional forms of consumption, such as addiction.

Happiness is only partially determined by material economic factors. Inequality and uncertainty are important mediating factors.

For more on inequality, see Chapter 15.

5.3. Creativity and entrepreneurial action

The standard economic theory of the individual is heavily geared towards the theory of consumption, with the productive role of individuals mostly relegated to the abstract notion of the production function. This focus has a performative character insofar as it co-evolved with a shift in the values basis of economics, in particular, regarding the perspective on workers as the exploited class focusing on survival in the classical tradition and, subsequently, as consumers in the neoclassical tradition. In the modern economy, the distinction between consumers and producers becomes porous. For example, the new term of the 'prosumer' has been suggested with reference

Standard economic theory is performative in conceiving individuals as consumers.

*The roles of
producer and
consumer should
be synthesised for
both theoretical and
empirical reasons.*

For a discussion
of interpersonal
inequality
and its social
consequences,
see Chapter 15,
section 4.

*Creativity is a
basic mechanism
of choice, and
entrepreneurship is
its manifestation on
markets.*

We further
explore
entrepreneurship
in Chapter 11,
sections 4.1 and
5, and Chapter 12,
section 1.

to the internet economy, where users often assume productive roles when consuming a service.[106] There is a wide range of DIY activities in the household, which includes basic activities such as preparing meals or cleaning the home which are productive but are also necessary elements of consuming the goods.

This leads to an alternative conception of the individual as agent of work, with consumption only as a secondary characterisation: The *Homo faber* is one characterisation.[107] Seen from this angle, the characterisation of individuals as rational appears much more straightforward since there is a relatively clear criterion of optimality with regard to the individual organisation of work under given constraints. This link is most visible in one of the most widely used metaphorical narratives in economics, the Robinson Crusoe economy, where the lonely sailor optimises his production technology and practices to sustain and increase his levels of consumption.

In an interconnected economy, of course, this perspective points towards inequalities in consumption levels attributable to individual differences in productivity, which are partly reflected by market wages and may stem from a variety of factors, such as motivation and cognitive ability, but also socio-economic background. Here, we focus on another aspect of the *Homo faber* which tends to be theoretically marginalised in economics, namely the creative dimension of human work. In the standard view, neither consumers nor workers are creative; but this stands in contrast to the outlined fundamental creativity of the human brain, entailing activity that is autonomous from any environmental conditions and constraints. In addition, there is a basic element of playful curiosity that reflects the phylogenetic conditions of foraging in an uncertain environment full of surprises and, hence, is shared among humans and animals.[108]

As we have argued previously, the direct conceptual correspondence to creativity in economics is the entrepreneur as a type of agent. We take a broad approach and suggest that entrepreneurship is the specific form that creativity takes on markets. In fact, this is often merged, as when artists as apparently ideal typical manifestations of pure creativity act as businesspeople, as they did, for instance, in the artisanal workshops of the Renaissance. But we must also recognise entrepreneurial action by consumers. This is because entrepreneurs as producers cannot enforce innovations on consumers, unless their own creativity is driven by recognising manifest consumer wants. One pure case of this is market-seeking entrepreneurship which is creative not in terms of producing new goods but in opening new markets for existing goods. But in case of many entrepreneurial innovations, consumers must act entrepreneurially, too, in recognising this innovation, adopting it, and changing their own practices. Producers and consumers co-create innovations,[109] which is corroborated by many observations on the history of technology where users were driving the final form of adoption, even defying the original goals pursued by producers.

To conclude, psychology has established numerous factors that drive entrepreneurial behaviour, such as certain personality traits or cultural influences. However, as in general research about creativity, there is also a strong effect of environmental conditions, such as social networks, thus clearly showing that entrepreneurship is a form of agency and not simply an inborn characteristic of individuals. The heroic view on the individual as entrepreneur needs to be complemented by the environmental and social factors that create the enabling agential power.[110]

6. Conclusion

Our chapter has grounded the theory of agency on markets in co-evolutionary theory. On the one hand, we heed attention to the biopsychology of human individuals; on the other hand, we consider the performativity of agency, embodied in social roles that individuals assume, such as that of the entrepreneur. We summarise this view in Figure 7.2.

Markets are primordial drivers of performativity, in the shape of endogenously evolving economic rationality, scaffolded by both material artefacts (such as accounting systems) and social roles and institutions (such as legal

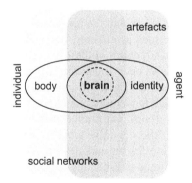

Figure 7.2 The economic agent
The brain stays at the core of the model, reaching to both body and agent identity. In both dimensions, however, the brain is complemented by extensions beyond the body. Individuals extend to artefacts in the material environment, such as their possessions or devices that enhance their capabilities (for example, the laptop). The agent extends to the social context, and the agential powers are scaffolded, for example, by assuming certain social roles. Most generally, this refers to social networks, which, however, are often institutionalised.

constructs of corporate governance). Therefore, we cannot start out from individual rationality as determining market processes but must consider the reverse causality from markets to agency. This has been dubbed ecological rationality by Vernon Smith[111] and was a defining feature of Max Weber's notion of rationalisation in modern capitalism that got lost to economics once it separated from sociology and psychology. Neither can we reduce market performance on purely generic psychological factors in the sense of genetically endowed features. A crucial characteristic of humans is their transformation of genetic endowments into socially enabled and contextualised agency. One implication is that market agents are irreducibly heterogenous.

One lesson of this chapter, therefore, is that we cannot fully develop the economic theory of the individual without analysing the complex determinants of agency, which can be organised into social networks and institutions, to be dealt with in the next two chapters. Both scaffold individual-organismic determinants of action, and they interplay in complex ways in creating the individual capabilities that enable individuals to navigate markets beyond the axiomatic theory of utility.

Major chapter insights

- The tension between the rational choice paradigm and behavioural economics can be resolved via distinguishing between the individual as living organism and the agent having agential powers in social interactions, such as markets. Rationality of agents is scaffolded by rules and structures of these interactions.
- The human brain is an open and adaptive evolutionary system that has evolved to create the capacity to predict actions and outcomes in complex and uncertain environments and to enable social coordination in human groups. The brain embodies the capacity for culture, which scaffolds its cognitive and emotional capabilities.
- Social interaction is reflexive and, therefore, hypercomplex, which puts fundamental limits to rationally determining optimal actions. Reason is the capability to rationally give reasons for actions, and especially in market contexts, rationality is the intentional stance in understanding the actions of others.
- Emotions are fundamental in enabling reason and are devices to commit the individual to rational action. Emotions connect inner states with social contexts. Empathy is a core emotional capability in enabling the coordination of action.
- Agency is determined by agential power in social interactions and is conditioned by various factors which create distinct capabilities

in relation to social functionings, such as property enabling market transactions. Agency is embodied in social status.

- Status is an important aspect of social identity which must be distinguished from personal identity. Personal identity is crucial for enabling rational action and is scaffolded by various mediators, in particular, narratives that connect past and future. Social identity is conditioned by externalities among group members who share an identity and a source of discrimination.
- Many actions are performative in creating the identity which drives action, in turn, mediated by language. Consumption is mediated by symbols whose meaning is embodied in the sensorimotor circuits of consumptive action.
- Mechanisms of choice involve the basic distinction between wants and needs, with wants having no satiation point. This allows the identification of dynamic mechanisms of learning, such as by imitation.
- The duality of wanting and liking is crucial for understanding dysfunctional mechanisms of choice, such as addiction. This also explains why happiness is not directly determined by material prosperity.
- Creativity is another basic mechanism of choice which is contextualised on markets as entrepreneurship. Both producers and consumers manifest entrepreneurial behaviour.

Notes

1 Thaler (2016) distinguishes 'ECONS' from 'HUMANS'.
2 This was seminally developed by Paul Samuelson, arguably the most influential economist of the 21st century; see Ross (2014), who reinstates this tradition as the Neo-Samuelsonian program.
3 For classical statements of the evolutionary view, see Friedman (1953) and Alchian (1977). For a critical assessment from the mechanism perspective, see Elster (2015, 205ff). The key differentiation between observed behaviour and the underlying mechanisms has been stressed by Gul and Pesendorfer (2008) for the case of neuroeconomics and vindicated by another important strand of experimental research in economics, the artificial markets paradigm: Even agents with zero intelligence generate behaviour that results in market equilibria as selected by fully rational choices, provided that the rules of the market guiding their actions are properly designed, see Plott and Smith (2008).
4 This corresponds to the externalist position developed in Ross (2014).

5 The role of the entrepreneur divides schools of thought in economics, with the standard microeconomic framework largely ignoring it and others, such as Austrian economics, putting it at the centre stage. See Kirzner (1997).

6 The locus classicus is Schumpeter (2006[1912]).

7 The most prominent example is the two systems hypothesis, with one system representing rationality and the other being the cause of deviations, see Kahneman (2012).

8 Thaler and Sunstein (2009).

9 Weber (2016[1922]).

10 A related position was maintained by Hayek (1979).

11 Tooby and Cosmides (2005).

12 Han et al. (2013), Northoff (2016).

13 The human brain is in the focus of the new research area of neuroeconomics, see Glimcher and Fehr (2013) and for a position closer to the one championed here, Harbecke and Herrmann-Pillath (2020). An important precursor is Hayek (1952); for a modern interpretation, see Herrmann-Pillath (2021).

14 An influential concept that catches this evaluative function is the somatic marker theory, Bechara and Damasio (2005), Reimann and Bechara (2010).

15 This is the view elaborated in grounded cognition theory, Barsalou (2008), Papies et al. (2020).

16 In neuroeconomics, this is reflected in the debate over the so-called good based model that is confronted with evolutionary models; see Padoa-Schioppa and Conen (2017) versus Hunt and Hayden (2017).

17 Clark (2011). North (2005, 48ff) refers to this as scaffolds.

18 This is the default mode network, Raichle (2015).

19 Edelman (2006).

20 Verschure (2016), Redcay and Schildbach (2019).

21 This was already emphasised by Hayek (1952); for a contemporary neuroscience view, see Friston (2010).

22 Clark (2013).

23 Reinforcement learning is an evolutionary mechanism, such as suggested by Cisek (2012), corresponding to the drift-diffusion model in neuroeconomics, Fehr and Rangel (2011).

24 Since Veblen (1965[1899]), habit is a central category in institutional economics, see Hodgson (2004, 2010).

25 This is the canonical model of neuroeconomics; for an overview, see Glimcher (2011).

26 Hunt and Hayden (2017).

27 Kirzner (1997).

28 This view confirms Scitovsky's (1992[1976]) seminal work.

29 Frith (2007), Alós-Ferrer (2018).

30 Tooby and Cosmides (2005), Bowles and Gintis (2011).

31 Overview in Ward (2017, 175ff).

32 Ross (2007).

33 Zawidzki (2013).

34 Hutchins (1995), North (2005, 23ff).

35 This is Hayek's (1945) classical position, restated in neuroscience terms by Basso et al. (2010).

36 Dunbar (2011).

37 Goody (1995).

38 This has been stated in principal–agent models of the brain, Brocas and Carrillo (2008), Brocas and Carrillo (2014).

39 The first argument was already suggested by Hayek (1952). For an extensive discussion of cognitive constraints on predicting others' behaviour, see Zawidzki (2013). In game theory, this is explored in the literature on higher-order beliefs, for example, Strzalecki (2014).

40 Sen (2002), Mercier and Sperber (2018).

41 Bogdan (2010).

42 This is the classical Vygotsky thesis which receives much support by recent research, for example, Tomasello (2008).

43 Dennett (2009), Zawidzki (2013).

44 This corresponds to the original position by Adam Smith, as argued in recent Smith exegesis; see, for example, Scazzieri (2006).

45 Bogdan (2010).

46 Mercier and Sperber (2018).

47 For a related argument, see Sliwka (2007).

48 Tooby and Cosmides (2005), Ward (2017, 99ff).

49 Seminally, Damasio (1995). Kirman et al. (2010).

50 Goldie (2014), Berridge (2018). Accordingly, some scholars argue that emotions are distinctively human.

51 Frank (1988).

52 This is Selten's (1978) famous chain store paradox.

53 The role of emotions in breaking up rational stalemates is the authentic meaning of Keynes's (1960[1936]) famous notion of animal spirits, contra Akerlof and Shiller (2009) who emphasise the negative effects of irrationality.

54 Fehr (2009).

55 Smith (2010[1759]), Sugden (2002).

56 Sugden (2000), Tuomela (2007).

57 Zak (2007), Declerck (2020).

58 For an integrative view, Elster (2015).

59 Tilly (2003).

60 Friston (2010).

61 Kliemt (1985) points to Hobbes as the origin of this important duality.

62 This is the Hegelian notion of freedom; for a survey, see Herrmann-Pillath and Boldyrev (2014).

63 Becker (1996).

64 Dagan (2021).

65 Davies et al. (2012).

66 Survey in Kahneman (2012).

67 De Waal (2007).

68 Hopkins and Kornienko (2004), Snower and Bosworth (2016).

69 Davis (2003). For a model of multiple selves, see, for instance, Jamison and Wegener (2010).

70 Davis (2010).

71 Damasio (2010).

72 Tomasello (2008), Hurley (2008).

73 Damasio (2010).

74 Kirman and Teschl (2006).

75 Ross (2007), Hippel and Trivers (2011).

76 For an overview on multidisciplinary approaches to narratives, see Herman et al. (2005).

77 Damasio (2010), Davis (2010).

78 Goldie (2014).

79 Beckert (2016).

80 Trentmann (2017).

81 Akerlof and Kranton (2000).

82 Kuran (1995), Bernheim (1994).

83 Kahneman (2012), Shiller (2019).

84 Pinker (2007). This is analysed formally in speech act theory, Green (2020).

85 Searle (1995).

86 Barsalou (2008).

87 Ariely and Norton (2009).

88 In economic parlance, we cannot separate preferences and action, Ariely and Norton (2007).

89 Schifferstein et al. (2020).

90 Frank (1985), Saad (2007).

91 Moav and Neeman (2012).

92 Zelizer (1997).

93 Shiller (2019).

94 Orléan (2013), Pentland (2014). This corresponds to mechanisms of non-genetic transmission explored in theories of cultural evolution, Mesoudi (2011).

95 Potts et al. (2008).

96 Orléan (2013).

97 For examples, see Trentmann (2017).

98 Ariely and Norton (2007).

99 Sobal and Wansink (2007).

100 Berridge (2009). For an economics reception, see Camerer (2006).

101 Hence, the wanting-liking duality can explain phenomena of time inconsistency and preference reversals through time which are often explained by dual systems models in behavioural economics or by distinct shapes of utility functions, see Ainslie (1992) and Kahneman (2012).

102 Wiers et al. (2007).

103 Ross et al. (2008), Herrmann-Pillath (2012).
104 This research is documented in the annual World Happiness reports; the recent one: https://worldhappiness.report/ed/2021/, accessed April 6, 2022. Davidson and Schuyler (2015) summarise the neuroscience of happiness.
105 This is salient in the data for China after 1978, see Helliwell et al. (2017).
106 Bruns (2008).
107 Arendt (2018[1958]). Compare Lucassen (2021).
108 Huizinga (1939). A distinct form of play is inter-species play, such as between humans and dogs, Merritt (2021).
109 Hartley (2008), Baldwin and von Hippel (2011).
110 Obschonka et al. (2021).
111 Smith (2003).

References

Ainslie, G. (1992) *Picoeconomics: The Strategic Interaction of Successive Motivational States within the Person*. Cambridge: Cambridge University Press.

Akerlof, G. A. and Kranton, R. E. (2000) 'Economics and Identity', *Quarterly Journal of Economics*, 115(3), pp. 715–753. DOI: 10.1162/003355300554881.

Akerlof, G. A. and Shiller, R. (2009) *Animal Spirits: How Human Psychology Drives the Economy, and Why It Matters for Global Capitalism*. Princeton and Oxford: Princeton University Press.

Alchian, A. (1977) *Economic Forces at Work*. Indianapolis: Liberty Press.

Alós-Ferrer, C. (2018) 'A Review Essay on Social Neuroscience: Can Research on the Social Brain and Economics Inform Each Other?' *Journal of Economic Literature,* 56(1), pp. 234–264. DOI: 10.1257/JEL.20171370.

Arendt, H. (2018[1958]) *The Human Condition*, 2nd Edition. Chicago and London: University of Chicago Press. DOI: 10.7208/chicago/9780226586748.001.0001.

Ariely, D. and Norton, M. I. (2007) 'How Actions Create – Not Just Reveal – Preferences', *Trends in Cognitive Science*, 12(1), pp. 13–16. DOI: 10.1016/j.tics.2007.10.008.

Ariely, D. and Norton, M. I. (2009), 'Conceptual Consumption', *Annual Review of Psychology*, 60, pp. 475–499. DOI: 10.1146/annurev.psych.60.110707.163536.

Barsalou, L. W. (2008) 'Grounded Cognition', *Annual Review of Psychology*, 59, pp. 617–645. DOI: 10.1146/annurev.psych.59.103006.093639.

Basso, F., Guillou, L. and Oullier, O. (2010) 'Embodied Entrepreneurship: A Sensory Theory of Value', in Stanton, A. A., Day, M. and Welpe, I. M. (eds.) *Neuroeconomics and the Firm*. Cheltenham and Northampton: Edward Elgar Publishing, pp. 217–234. DOI: 10.4337/9781849805605.00024.

Bechara, A. and Damasio, A. R. (2005) 'The Somatic Marker Hypothesis: A Neural Theory of Economic Decision', *Games and Economic Behavior*, 52(2), pp. 336–372. DOI: 10.1016/j.geb.2004.06.010.

Becker, G. S. (1996) *Accounting for Tastes*. Cambridge: Harvard University Press.

Beckert, J. (2016) *Imagined Futures: Fictional Expectations and Capitalist Dynamics*. Cambridge: Harvard University Press.

Bernheim, B. D. (1994) 'A Theory of Conformity', *Journal of Political Economy*, 102(5), pp. 841–877. DOI: 10.1086/261957.

Berridge, K. C. (2009) '"Liking" and "Wanting" Food Rewards: Brain Substrates and Roles in Eating Disorders', *Physiology & Behavior*, 97(5), pp. 537–550. DOI: 10.1016/j.physbeh.2009.02.044.

Berridge, K. C. (2018) 'Evolving Concepts of Emotion and Motivation', *Frontiers in Psychology*, 7 September 2018. Available at: https://www.frontiersin.org/articles/10.3389/fpsyg.2018.01647/full (Accessed: 5 April 2022).

Bogdan, R. J. (2010) *Our Own Minds: Sociocultural Grounds for Self-Consciousness*. Cambridge: MIT Press.

Bowles, S. and Gintis, H. (2011) *A Cooperative Species: Human Reciprocity and Its Evolution*. Princeton: Princeton University Press.

Brocas, I. and Carrillo, J. D. (2008) 'The Brain as a Hierarchical Organization', *American Economic Review*, 98(4), pp. 1312–1347. DOI: 10.2139/ssrn.900245.

Brocas, I. and Carrillo, J. D. (2014) 'Dual-Process Theories of Decision-Making: A Selective Survey', *Journal of Economic Psychology,* 41(4), pp. 45–54. DOI: 10.1016/J.JOEP.2013.01.004.

Bruns, A. (2008) *Blogs, Wikipedia, Second Life, and Beyond: From Production to Produsage*. New York: Peter Lang Inc.

Camerer, C. (2006) 'Wanting, Liking, and Learning: Neuroscience and Paternalism', *The University of Chicago Law Review*, 73(1), pp. 87–110.

Cisek, P. (2012) 'Making Decisions Through a Distributed Consensus', *Current Opinion in Neurobiology,* 22(6), pp. 927–936. DOI: 10.1016/j.conb.2012.05.007.

Clark, A. (2011) *Supersizing the Mind: Embodiment, Action, and Cognitive Extension*. Oxford: Oxford University Press.

Clark, A. (2013) 'Whatever Next? Predictive Brains, Situated Agents, and the Future of Cognitive Science', *Behavioral and Brain Sciences,* 36(3), pp. 181–204. DOI: 10.1017/S0140525X12000477.

Dagan, Ḥ. (2021) *A Liberal Theory of Property*. Cambridge and New York: Cambridge University Press. DOI: 10.1017/9781108290340.

Damasio, A. R. (1995) *Descartes' Error: Emotion, Reason and the Human Brain*. New York: G.B. Putnam's Son.

Damasio, A. R. (2010) *Self Comes to Mind: Constructing the Conscious Brain*. New York: Pantheon.

Davidson, R. J. and Schuyler, B. S. (2015) 'The Neuroscience of Happiness', in Helliwell, J., Layard, R. and Sachs, J. (eds.) *World Happiness Report,* pp. 88–105. Available at: http://worldhappiness.report/ed/2015/ (Accessed: 30 March 2022).

Davies, N. B., Krebs, J. R. and West, S. A. (2012) *An Introduction to Behavioural Ecology*. Oxford: Wiley-Blackwell. DOI: 10.1016/j.anbehav.2013.01.003.

Davis, John B. (2003) *The Theory of the Individual in Economics: Identity and Value*. London and New York: Routledge.

Davis, J. B. (2010) *Individuals and Identity in Economics*. Cambridge: Cambridge University Press. DOI: 10.1017/cbo9780511782237.

De Waal, F. B. M. (2007) *Chimpanzee Politics: Power and Sex among Apes*. Baltimore: Johns Hopkins University Press.

Declerck, C. (2020) 'Neuroeconomics of Cooperation Heuristics: The Role of Incentives, Social Cues, and Hormones', in Harbecke, J. and Herrmann-Pillath, C. (eds.) *Social Neuroeconomics: Mechanistic Integration of the Neurosciences and the Social Sciences*. London: Routledge, pp. 77–96.

Dennett, D. (2009) 'Intentional Systems Theory', in Beckermann, A., McLaughlin, B. P. and Walter, S. (eds.) *The Oxford Handbook of Philosophy of Mind*. Oxford: Oxford University Press, pp. 339–350. DOI: 10.1093/OXFOR DHB/9780199262618.003.0020.

Dunbar, R. I. M. (2011) 'Constraints on the Evolution of Social Institutions and Their Implications for Information Flow', *Journal of Institutional Economics*, 7(3), pp. 345–371. DOI: 10.1017/S1744137410000366.

Edelman, G. M. (2006) *Second Nature: Brain Science and Human Knowledge*. New Haven and London: Yale University Press.

Elster, J. (2015) *Explaining Social Behavior: More Nuts and Bolts for the Social Sciences*. Revised Edition. Cambridge: Cambridge University Press.

Fehr, E. (2009) 'Social Preferences and the Brain', in Glimcher, P. W. and Fehr, E. (eds.) *Neuroeconomics: Decision Making and the Brain*. Amsterdam: Elsevier, pp. 215–232. DOI: 10.1016/B978-0-12-416008-8.00011-5.

Fehr, E. and Rangel, A. (2011) 'Neuroeconomic Foundations of Economic Choice – Recent Advances', *Journal of Economic Perspectives,* 25(4), pp. 3–30. DOI: 10.1257/JEP.25.4.3.

Frank, R. H. (1985) *Choosing the Right Pond: Human Behavior and the Quest for Status*. New York and Oxford: Oxford University Press.

Frank, R. H. (1988) *Passions Within Reason: The Strategic Role of Emotions*. New York and London: Norton. DOI: 10.2307/2233985.

Friedman, M. (1953) *Essays in Positive Economics*. Chicago: Chicago University Press.

Friston, K. (2010) 'The Free – Energy Principle: A Unified Brain Theory', *Nature Reviews Neuroscience,* 11, pp. 127–138. DOI: 10.1038/nrn2787.

Frith, C. (2007) 'The Social Brain?' *Philosophical Transactions of the Royal Society B*, 362(1480), pp. 671–678. DOI: 10.1098/rstb.2006.2003.

Glimcher, P. W. (2011) *Foundations of Neuroeconomic Analysis*. Oxford and New York: Oxford University Press. DOI: 10.1093/acprof:oso/9780199744251.001.0001.

Glimcher, P. W. and Fehr, E. (eds.) (2013) *Neuroeconomics: Decision Making and the Brain*. Amsterdam: Elsevier. DOI: 10.5860/choice.51-5702.

Goldie, P. (2014) *The Mess Inside: Narrative, Emotion, & the Mind*. Oxford: Oxford University Press. DOI: 10.1093/acprof:oso/9780199230730.001.0001.

Goody, E. (1995) 'Introduction: Some Implications of a Social Origin of Intelligence', in Goody, E. (ed) *Social Intelligence and Interaction: Expressions and*

Implications of the Social Bias in Human Intelligence. Cambridge: Cambridge University Press, pp. 1–36. DOI: 10.1017/CBO9780511621710.003.

Green, M. (2020) 'Speech Acts', *The Stanford Encyclopedia of Philosophy*, Winter 2020 Edition. Available at: https://plato.stanford.edu/archives/win2020/entries/speech-acts/ (Accessed: 28 March 2022).

Gul, F. and Pesendorfer, W. (2008) 'The Case for Mindless Economics', in Caplin, A. and Schotter, A. (eds.) *The Foundations of Positive and Normative Economics*. Oxford: Oxford University Press, pp. 3–41. DOI: 10.1093/ACPROF:OSO/9780195328318.001.0001.

Han, S. *et al.* (2013) 'A Cultural Neuroscience Approach to the Biosocial Nature of the Human Brain', *Annual Review of Psychology*, 64, pp. 335–359. DOI: 10.1146/annurev-psych-071112-054629.

Harbecke, J. and Herrmann-Pillath, C. (eds.) (2020) *Social Neuroeconomics: Mechanistic Integration of the Neurosciences and the Social Sciences*. London: Routledge.

Hartley, J. (2008) 'From Consciousness Industry to Creative Industries: Consumer-Created Content, Social Network Markets and the Growth of Knowledge', in Holt, J. and Perren, A. (eds.) *Media Industries: History, Theory and Method*. Oxford: Blackwell, pp. 231–244.

Hayek, F. A. von (1945) 'The Use of Knowledge in Society', *American Economic Review*, 35(4), pp. 519–530. DOI: 10.1016/B978-0-7506-9749-1.50005-3.

Hayek, F. A. von (1952) *The Sensory Order: An Inquiry into the Foundations of Theoretical Psychology*. Chicago: University of Chicago Press. DOI: 10.4324/9781315734873.

Hayek, F. A. von (1979) *Law, Legislation and Liberty: A New Statement of the Liberal Principles of Justice and Political Economy, Volume 3: The Political Order of a Free People*. Chicago: University of Chicago Press. DOI: 10.4324/9780203103814.

Helliwell, J., Layard, R. and Sachs, J. (eds.) (2017) *World Happiness Report 2017*. Available at: http://worldhappiness.report/wp-content/uploads/sites/2/2017/03/HR17.pdf (Accessed: 28 March 2022).

Herman, D., Jahn, M. and Ryan, M.-L. (eds.) (2005) *Routledge Encyclopedia of Narrative Theory*. Abingdon and London: Routledge. DOI: 10.4324/9780203932896.

Herrmann-Pillath, C. (2012) 'Towards an Externalist Neuroeconomics: Dual Selves, Signs, and Choice, *Journal of Neuroscience', Psychology and Economics*, 5(1), pp. 38–61. DOI: 10.1037/A0026882.

Herrmann-Pillath, C. (2021) 'Evolutionary Mechanisms of Choice: Hayekian Perspectives on Neurophilosophical Foundations of Neuroeconomics', *Economics and Philosophy*, 37(2), pp. 284–303. DOI: 10.1017/S0266267120000371.

Herrmann-Pillath, C. and Boldyrev, I. A. (2014) *Hegel, Institutions and Economics: Performing the Social*. Abingdon and New York: Routledge. DOI: 10.4324/9781315848662.

Hippel, W. and Trivers, R. (2011) 'The Evolution and Psychology of Self-Deception', *Behavioral and the Brain Sciences*, 34(1), pp. 1–56. DOI: 10.1017/S0140525X10001354.

Hodgson, G. M. (2004) 'Reclaiming Habit for Institutional Economics', *Journal of Economic Psychology*, 25(5), pp. 651–660. DOI: 10.1016/J.JOEP.2003.03.001.

Hodgson, G. M. (2010) 'Choice, Habit and Evolution', *Journal of Evolutionary Economics*, 20(1), pp. 1–18. DOI: 10.1007/S00191-009-0134-Z.

Hopkins, E. and Kornienko, T. (2004) 'Running to Keep the Same Place: Consumer Choice as a Game of Status', *American Economic Review*, 94(4), pp. 1085–1108. DOI: 10.1257/0002828042002705.

Huizinga, J. (2016[1939]) *Homo Ludens: A Study of the Play-Element in Culture*. New York: Angelico Press.

Hunt, L. T. and Hayden, B. Y. (2017) 'A Distributed, Hierarchical and Recurrent Framework for Reward-based Choice', *Nature Reviews Neuroscience,* 18(3), pp. 172–182. DOI: 10.1038/nrn.2017.7.

Hurley, S. (2008) 'The Shared Circuits Model: How Control, Mirroring and Simulation Can Enable Imitation, Deliberation, and Mindreading', *Behavioral and the Brain Sciences*, 31(1), pp. 1–21. DOI: 10.1017/S0140525X07003123.

Hutchins, E. (1995) *Cognition in the Wild*. Cambridge and London: MIT Press.

Jamison, J. and Wegener, J. (2010) 'Multiple Selves in Intertemporal Choice', *Journal of Economic Psychology*, 31(5), pp. 832–839. DOI: 10.1016/j.joep.2010.03.004.

Kahneman, D. (2012) *Thinking, Fast and Slow*. London: Penguin Books.

Keynes, J. M. (1960[1936]) *The General Theory of Employment, Interest and Money*. London: MacMillan.

Kirman, A., Livet, P., and Teschl, M. (2010) 'Rationality and Emotions', *Philosophical Transactions of the Royal Society B*, 365, pp. 215–219. DOI: 10.1098/rstb.2009.0194.

Kirman, A. and Teschl, M. (2006) 'Searching for Identity in the Capability Space', *Journal of Economic Methodology*, 13(3), pp. 299–325. DOI: 10.1080/13501780600908200.

Kirzner, I. M. (1997) 'Entrepreneurial Discovery and the Competitive Market Process: An Austrian Approach', *Journal of Economic Literature*, 35(1), pp. 60–85.

Kliemt, H. (1985) *Moralische Institutionen: Empiristische Theorien ihrer Evolution*. Freiburg and München: Alber.

Kuran, T. (1995) *Private Truths, Public Lies: The Social Consequences of Preference Falsification*. Cambridge and London: Harvard University Press.

Lucassen, J. (2021) *The Story of Work: A New History of Humankind*. New Haven: Yale University Press.

Mercier, H. and Sperber, D. (2018) *The Enigma of Reason: A New Theory of Human Understanding*. London: Penguin Books.

Merritt, M. (2021) 'Dances with Dogs: Interspecies Play and a Case for Sympoietic Enactivism', *Animal Cognition*, 24(2), pp. 353–369. DOI: 10.1007/s10071-020-01468-y.

Mesoudi, A. (2011) *Cultural Evolution: How Darwinian Theory Can Explain Human Culture and Synthesize the Social Sciences*. Chicago and London: University of Chicago Press. DOI: 10.5860/choice.49-4527.

Moav, O. and Neeman, Z. (2012) 'Saving Rates and Poverty: The Role of Conspicuous Consumption and Human Capital', *Economic Journal*, 122(563), pp. 933–956. DOI: 10.2139/ssrn.1727272.

North, D. C. (2005) *Understanding the Process of Economic Change*. Princeton and Oxford: Princeton University Press. DOI: 10.1515/9781400829484.

Northoff, G. (2016) 'Cultural Neuroscience and Neurophilosophy: Does the Neural Code Allow for the Brain's Enculturation?' in Chiao, J. *et al.* (eds.) *The Oxford Handbook of Cultural Neuroscience*. Oxford: Oxford University Press, pp. 21–40. DOI: 10.1093/OXFORDHB/9780199357376.013.4.

Obschonka, M., Fritsch, M. and Stuetzer, M. (2021) *The Geography of Entrepreneurial Psychology*. Cheltenham and Northampton: Edward Elgar Publishing. DOI: 10.4337/9781788973380.

Orléan, A. (2013) *L'empire de la Valeur: Refonder L'économie*. Paris: Le Seuil.

Padoa-Schioppa, C. and Conen, K. E. (2017) 'Orbitofrontal Cortex: A Neural Circuit for Economic Decisions', *Neuron,* 968(4), pp. 736–754. DOI: 10.1016/j.neuron.2017.09.031.

Papies, E. K., Barsalou, L. W. and Rusz, D. (2020) 'Understanding Desire for Food and Drink: A Grounded-Cognition Approach', *Current Directions in Psychological Science,* 29(2), pp. 193–198. DOI: 10.1177/0963721420904958.

Pentland, A. (2014) *Social Physics: How Good Ideas Spread-the Lessons from a New Science*. Melbourne: Scribe Publications.

Pinker, S. (2007) *The Stuff of Thought: Language as a Window into Human Nature*. New York: Penguin.

Plott, C. R. and Smith, V. L. (2008) 'Markets', in Plott, C. R. and Smith, V. L. (eds.) *Handbook of Experimental Economics Results, Volume 1*. Amsterdam: North – Holland.

Potts, J. *et al.* (2008) 'Social Network Markets: A New Definition of the Creative Industries', *Journal of Cultural Economics*, 32(3), pp. 167–185. DOI: 10.1007/S10824-008-9066-Y.

Raichle, M. E. (2015) 'The Brain's Default Mode Network', *Annual Review of Neuroscience*,38(1),pp.433–447.DOI:10.1146/annurev-neuro-071013-014030.

Redcay, E. and Schildbach, L. (2019) 'Using Second-Person Neuroscience to Elucidate the Mechanisms of Interaction', *Nature Review Neurosciences*, 20, pp. 495–505. DOI: 10.1038/s41583-019-0179-4.

Reimann, M. and Bechara, A. (2010) 'The Somatic Marker Hypothesis as a Neurological Theory of Decision – Making: Review, Conceptual Comparisons, and Future Neuroeconomics Research', *Journal of Economic Psychology*, 31(5), pp. 767–776. DOI: 10.1016/J.JOEP.2010.03.002.

Ross, D. (2007) 'H. Sapiens as Ecologically Special: What Does Language Contribute?' *Language Studies*, 29(5), pp. 710–731. DOI: 10.1016/J.LANGSCI.2006.12.008.

Ross, D. (2014) *Philosophy of Economics*. New York: Palgrave Macmillan. DOI: 10.1057/9781137318756.

Ross, D. *et al*. (2008) *Midbrain Mutiny: The Picoeconomics and Neuroeconomics of Disordered Gambling*. Cambridge: MIT Press.

Saad, G. (2007) *The Evolutionary Bases of Consumption*. New York: Psychology Press. DOI: 10.4324/9780203936993.

Scazzieri, R. (2006) 'A Smithian Theory of Choice', in Brown, V. (ed.) *The Adam Smith Review, Volume 2*. Milton Park: Routledge, pp. 21–47.

Schifferstein, H. N. J., Kudrowitz, B. M. and Breuer, C. (2020) 'Food Perception and Aesthetics – Linking Sensory Science to Culinary Practice', *Journal of Culinary Science & Technology*. DOI: 10.1080/15428052.2020.1824833.

Schumpeter, J. A. (2006[1912]) *Theorie der wirtschaftlichen Entwicklung*. Berlin: Duncker & Humblot.

Scitovsky, T. (1992[1976]) *The Joyless Economy: The Psychology of Human Satisfaction*. New York: Oxford University Press.

Searle, J. R. (1995) *The Construction of Social Reality*. New York: Free Press.

Selten, R. (1978) 'The Chain Store Paradox', *Theory and Decision*, 9, pp. 127–159. DOI: 10.1007/BF00131770.

Sen, A. (2002) *Rationality and Freedom*. Cambridge and London: Harvard University Press.

Shiller, R. J. (2019) *Narrative Economics: How Stories Go Viral and Drive Major Economic Events*. Princeton: Princeton University Press.

Sliwka, D. (2007) 'Trust as a Signal of a Social Norm and the Hidden Costs of Incentive Schemes', *American Economic Review*, 97(3), pp. 999–1012. DOI: 10.1257/aer.97.3.999.

Smith, A. (2010[1759]) *The Theory of Moral Sentiments*. London: Penguin Books.

Smith, V. L. (2003), 'Constructivist and Ecological Rationality in Economics', *American Economic Review*, 93(3), pp. 465–508. DOI: 10.1257/000282803322156954.

Snower, D. J. and Bosworth, S. J. (2016) 'Identity-Driven Cooperation versus Competition', *American Economic Review*, 106(5), pp. 420–424. DOI: 10.2139/ssrn.2753488.

Sobal, J. and Wansink, B. (2007) 'Kitchenscapes, Tablescapes, Platescapes, and Foodscapes: Influences of Microscale Built Environments on Food Intake', *Environment and Behavior*, 39(1), pp. 124–142. DOI: 10.1177/0013916506295574.

Strzalecki, T. (2014) 'Depth of Reasoning and Higher Order Beliefs', *Journal of Economic Behavior & Organization*, 108, pp. 108–122. DOI: 10.1016/j.jebo.2014.09.002.

Sugden, R. (2000) 'Team Preferences', *Economics and Philosophy*, 16(2), pp. 175–204. DOI: 10.1017/S0266267100000213.

Sugden, R. (2002) 'Beyond Sympathy and Empathy: Adam Smith's Concept of Fellow – Feeling', *Economics and Philosophy*, 18(1), pp. 63–87. DOI: 10.1017/S0266267102001086.

Thaler, R. H. (2016) 'Behavioral Economics: Past, Present, and Future', *American Economic Review*, 106(7), pp. 1577–1600. DOI: 10.1257/AER.106.7.1577.

Thaler, R. H. and Sunstein, C. R. (2009) *Nudge: Improving Decisions about Health, Wealth, and Happiness*. London: Penguin Books.

Tilly, C. (2003) *The Politics of Collective Violence*. Cambridge and New York: Cambridge University Press.

Tomasello, M. (2008) *Origins of Human Communication*. Cambridge and London: MIT Press. DOI: 10.7551/mitpress/7551.001.0001.

Tooby, J. and Cosmides, L. (2005) 'Conceptual Foundations of Evolutionary Psychology', in Buss, D. M. (ed.) *The Handbook of Evolutionary Psychology*. Hoboken: Wiley, pp. 5–67. DOI: 10.1002/9780470939376.CH1.

Trentmann, F. (2017) *Empire of Things: How We Became a World of Consumers, from the Fifteenth Century to the Twenty-First*. London: Penguin Books.

Tuomela, R. (2007) *The Philosophy of Sociality*. Oxford: Oxford University Press. DOI: 10.1093/ACPROF:OSO/9780195313390.001.0001.

Veblen, T. (1965[1899]) *The Theory of the Leisure Class*. New York: Kelley.

Verschure, P. (2016) 'Synthetic Consciousness: The Distributed Adaptive Control Perspective', *Philosophical Transactions of the Royal Society B: Biological Sciences,* 371(1701), p. 20150448. DOI: 10.1098/rstb.2015.0448.

Ward, J. (2017) *The Student's Guide to Social Neuroscience*. 2nd Edition. London and New York: Routledge. DOI: 10.4324/9781315782904.

Weber, M. (2016[1922]) *Wirtschaft und Gesellschaft*. Tübingen: Mohr Siebeck.

Wiers, R. W. *et al.* (2007) 'Automatic and Controlled Processes and the Development of Addictive Behaviors in Adolescents: A Review and a Model', *Pharmacology Biochemistry and Behavior,* 86(2), pp. 263–283. DOI: 10.1016/j.pbb.2006.09.021.

Zak, P. J., Stanton, A. A. and Ahmadi, S. (2007) 'Oxytocin Increases Generosity in Humans', *PLoS ONE,* 2(11), p. e1128. DOI: 10.1371/journal.pone.0001128.

Zawidzki, T. (2013) *Mindshaping: A New Framework for Understanding Human Social Cognition*. Cambridge: MIT Press.

Zelizer, V. A. (1997) *The Social Meaning of Money*. Princeton: Princeton University Press.

CHAPTER EIGHT

Networks and social interaction

1. Introduction

Economic sociology suggests that markets are embedded in social networks.[1] In this chapter, we go one step further and treat markets *as* networks. When we skip the term 'social' here, we indicate that we focus on markets not only as forms of social interaction but also as material networks, such as geographical networks of marketplaces or the technological networks enabling human consumption (such as supermarkets and the related supply chains).[2] In a most general sense, the technosphere is a network structure, with markets being deeply shaped by technologies of transport and communication. However, in this chapter, we concentrate on the social interaction aspect. Social interaction, in turn, influences the evolution of material networks, such as the formation of cities which form the core units in the global market system and are central for understanding the interaction between markets and ecology.[3]

We will further develop a key insight on specialisation: Specialisation generates specific forms of agential power and, hence, is also a constitutive factor of forming agency, which in turn determines the evolution of the market as driven by entrepreneurial action. We refer this observation to the previous chapter in two respects. First, the formation of networks is at the same time enabled and constrained by certain capacities of the human brain. Second, our brains have the capacity for culture and language and can process any kind of symbolic media, which enables the distribution and scaffolding of cognitive performances beyond the organism. Both aspects are crucial for understanding markets as networks.

There are still difficulties in fully developing the potential of network theory in economics. One way to analytically approach social interaction is social network analysis (SNA) in quantitative sociology.[4] SNA is an analytical and quantitative theory that appears to be compatible with economic method; yet the cross-disciplinary relationship remains weak.[5] One reason

Markets are networks.

On the materiality of markets, see, for example, Chapter 1 on the Chinese market system, and Chapter 7, section 5.2, on consumption.

See Chapter 4, section 2.3, on metabolic networks and Chapter 16, section 2, on the growth of cities.

See Chapter 5, section 3, and Chapter 7, section 4.1.

185

DOI: 10.4324/9781003094869-12

for this is that SNA does not build on a theory of the individual but exclusively focuses on network structure and the corresponding dynamics. In this sense, SNA violates the principle of methodological individualism that reigns in economics. However, there are also sociological theories that emphasise the agency of individuals in networks, especially in the context of research on social capital.[6] Therefore, we think that the two fields can easily be integrated.

In section 2, we introduce basic concepts of network analysis, recognising that network positions are a crucial determinant of agential power. We sketch our own conceptual frame in highlighting three dimensions of networks that are essential for understanding the market process, namely transaction, communication, and observation. Further, we highlight the triad as elementary network structure, thus departing from the dyadic view of markets that is suggested by the supply and demand duality. Section 3 gives an overview of central topics in linking network structure to outcomes in terms of agential power and dynamics. We begin with structural determinants of agential power and continue with outlining the concept of social capital. We continue with an analysis of in-group/out-group distinctions and how they determine boundaries in networks, and the network dynamics that result from frequency-dependent mechanisms.

2. A short primer of network analysis

2.1. Fundamental types of network configurations in the context of markets

Networks are formally represented by nodes and lines that form structures of connectivity.

We start with the definition of a social network.[7] A social network is a set of nodes, the individuals or actors, which are connected by lines in a graphical representation (graph) (Figure 8.1). Sociological network analysis starts out

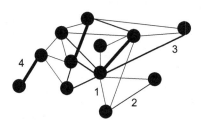

Figure 8.1 A weighted graph of a social network
Social networks can be visualised as graphs that consist of nodes (individuals) and connections between them. The connections can be further qualified in terms of intensity (weights as indicated by strength of line or by numbers).

from uni-dimensional networks which highlight a specific kind of interaction and may add further specifications, such as weighing the intensity of connections. However, for understanding economic exchange and cooperation, analysis needs to be conducted on an adequate level of complexity, given that markets are multidimensional networks.

This requires a distinction of three dimensions of networks or three layers of networks that centre on the same positions: transaction, communication, and observation.[8] These are not necessarily congruent. We can distinguish fundamental network configurations which have exemplary status in economics among the much wider range of possible configurations (Figure 8.2):

We distinguish three dimensions of networks: transaction, communication, and observation. This allows for identifying elementary configurations of networks on markets.

- Configuration A, with perfect and complete information, which means that two parties fully observe each other and communicate and transact in full transparency.
- Configuration B with asymmetric information, where at least one party imperfectly observes the other side and cannot remedy this deficit by trusted communication.
- Configuration C of an unintended externality, which figures as a transaction from individual 1 to 2, where the effect is not perceived by 1, hence including the case of unknown recipients.
- Configuration D, with intermediation by a third party and asymmetric information.

Looking at D in more detail, this configuration shows the case when two parties are brought together for exchange by a third party that knows both sides. In this case, both communication and observation may be much more limited between the two parties in comparison to the bilateral connections involving the mediator. This implies that the intermediator conveys information about the parties that enables the exchange which would be impossible otherwise.

On the pivotal role of intermediators in the Chinese market economy, see Chapter 1, section 1.2.

Based on this example, we surmise that the elementary unit of network analysis is triadic, not dyadic.[9] This is a fundamental difference to the established economic approach that typically starts out from the two market sides. The triadic structure is essential to analysing the notion of externality. In a triadic frame, an externality refers to the causal impacts of a dyadic interaction on a third party without involving a market transaction that governs this causal impact, such as in the example of pollution. This is a generalised version of case C in Figure 8.2; there, the externality is a transaction that involves just one agent as cause. In a triad, the dyadic interaction can either physically impact on a third party directly (such as noise coproduced by a group) or via being observed by the third party (such as an overheard conversation). Externalities are a universal feature of markets with respect to their information processing capacity: Every dyadic transaction may be observed by a third party which gains information from it without compensating the generating

The fundamental unit of economic network analysis is the triad, not the dyad.

On externalities, see Chapter 5, section 4.

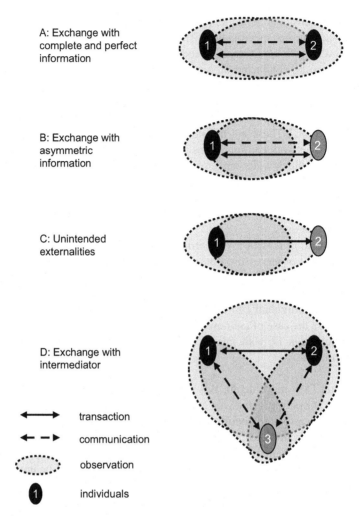

A: Exchange with
complete and perfect
information

B: Exchange with
asymmetric
information

C: Unintended
externalities

D: Exchange with
intermediator

transaction

communication

observation

individuals

Figure 8.2 Exemplary constellations of networks in economics
Basic constellations of social interaction in networks differentiate along the
three dimensions of transaction, communication, and observation which
are not necessarily congruent as in exchange with complete and perfect
information. The most important configurations are asymmetric information,
unintended externalities, and intermediation. For further detail, see main text.

agents. Figure 8.3 shows one possible configuration. More generally, when
we consider a flow of transactions through time under uncertainty, every
transaction may reveal information about market opportunity (positive externality) but, at the same time, may reduce market opportunity for the third
party (for example, successfully opening a restaurant at a particular location

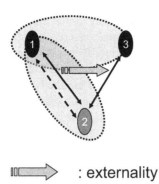

$\boxed{\text{\scriptsize 0}}\!\Longrightarrow$: externality

Figure 8.3 Triadic structure and information externality
The diagram shows an example of information externality where a third
party (3) only observes one side (1) of a transaction and extracts information
about the corresponding party (2) from it. For example, 1 buys a share from
company 2 (transaction) and communicates with 2, such as inquiring for some
information about the current status of business; 3 observes this transaction
only partially and decides to buy shares as well, without any communication
or other information flows with/from 2, as they think that 1 is well-informed.

*A fundamental
triad in economics
is constituted by
externalities of
market transactions,
such as information
externalities.*

reveals local demand as market opportunity, which, at the same time, this
restaurant may have already exhausted).

Externalities are a universal feature of markets. As we will explain in much
detail later, one channel is via wealth effects of price movements that are triggered by market transactions.[10] In the simplest triadic structure, if a third agent
owns the good that is transacted in the dyadic relation, the price emerging in
this transaction determines the value of stock held by the third party.

See Chapter 10,
section 2.2.

An important distinction in network analysis is between integral and
non-integral networks.[11] In economics, particularly in general equilibrium
analysis, networks are commonly, if implicitly, assumed to be integral. However, real-world networks are never complete; even in small communities,
some connections between agents may be lacking. The specific structure of
network holes is crucial for understanding many economic phenomena such
as information flows.[12] Most significantly, network holes may endogenously
create agential power, with the intermediator being a case in point (see next
section). If a connection between two parties is missing, the intermediator can
gain reputation, social status, and eventually, agential power in enabling the
transaction between the parties. In general, network holes often represent
market opportunity, which, therefore, drives actions that result in network
integration.

*Two fundamental
types of networks
are integral versus
non-integral
networks. In the
latter, patterns of
lacking connections
matter much for
network dynamics.*

An important corollary of considering the dimension of observation is that
we must clearly distinguish between first- and third-person views on networks: In network analysis, the first-person view is referred to as the

*In ego-centred
networks, the first-
person view obtains
causal relevance for
analysing network
dynamics.*

On these
methodological
aspects, see
Chapter 2,
section 2.

ego-centred network.[13] The difference results from the fact that network members may only have limited observational reach to overview the network with which they are indirectly connected. This was famously established in experiments about distance between any network nodes in human societies; normally, only about six steps suffice to indirectly connect everybody, without implying that those individuals know each other.[14]

Therefore, agency in networks must be distinguished from causal connectivity, such as when considering the transmission of certain items of information or indirect effects of certain actions. Yet the distinction between the first-person view and the third-person view remains of key importance because actions can only be taken based on what the actor subjectively perceives. In other words, the ego-centred network is causally relevant as a projection of the agent. This means that the external third-person view of the network cannot fully explain observed patterns without reconstructing the information and perspectives of the actors in the network (i.e., knowing the first-person view).

2.2. Dimensions of networks

We have distinguished between the three dimensions of transaction, communication, and observation. The three dimensions are often decoupled, with the precise form of decoupling being determined by market technologies. The simplest scenario is the bazaar where the three dimensions are tightly integrated: Two parties communicate, that is, they haggle over the price, they observe each other, and they eventually may realise a transaction. In modern economies, even transactions that involve transfer of ownership of huge amounts of wealth may not involve direct communication, such as in the case of a purchase of stocks of a listed company without talking to its management or its shareholders directly. In contrast, in M&A activities, the same transactions may be prepared by intensive negotiations via direct communication.

*A two-sided
transaction realises
an exchange
relation. Its form
is determined by
the technology of
exchange.*

The first network dimension, *transaction*, in the most general sense, is a one- or two-sided physical impact on an agent. On markets, it is defined as two-sided exchange that changes the states of the agents, such as the delivery of a good, the sharing of a joint product, or the provision of a service.[15] Transactions are directly shaped by the physical and technological conditions of tradability or exchangeability, which also influence network structures and processes.[16] For example, in modern economies, the place where coffee is traded can be located geographically far from the places where coffee is produced and where it is further processed.[17] The network structures of transaction on the one hand and of communication and observation on the other are dissociated: Coffee traders communicate among each other and observe each other's actions, but producers may be only dimly aware of the global market. Again, technology may change these conditions; for example, with local farmers receiving global market information via smartphone which vastly enhances transparency of the entire chain of market transactions from producer to end consumer.

We add much
detail to the
analysis of
transactions
in Chapter 14,
section 2.1.

One most significant aspect of transaction is the dissociation between material consummation and medium of transaction. An important example is the distinction between the material form of a transaction object and the claim on it, such as in formal rights of ownership. The transaction can be realised via transfer of a claim, but actual implementation may happen in another spatial and temporal setting. Once this duality is established, transactions that are realised at a specific point in time can be embedded in network processes that stretch over longer time periods.

Hence, transactions on markets are commonly realised in two complementary parts: One is the physical transaction; the other is the transfer of the ownership right. In fact, the physical transaction may only affect possession but not necessarily ownership, in case the legal claims are opaque or even non-existent. For example, in many developing countries, people possess their homes but have no enforceable legal claims which could be used in other transactions, such as mortgaging the real estate.[18] Furthermore, institutionalised networks create the conditions for reflexive transactions in which the medium of a transaction becomes the object of another transaction referring to the same original object, such as in creating financial derivatives or futures markets in hedging. For example, agents may trade coffee without effectively realising the physical transaction.

Independent from the market context, two-sided transactions manifest different degrees of reciprocity, which are related to the distinction between voluntary and forced exchange.[19] If an individual confers a certain benefit to another individual, there are three basic possibilities. The first is that this is done voluntarily because there is a present or future reverse flow which is – or is perceived as – at least equal in value. The second is that there is an altruistic motivation such that the transaction constitutes a gift relation; there is also the negative form, such as damaging someone with bad intent. In this case, the transaction tends to become one-sided, such as when the gift-giver keeps anonymity. The third is that the exchange is forced such that reciprocity no longer holds.

As has been elucidated in decades of anthropological debates, reciprocity can be governed by different principles of valuation that may differ from those of the marketplace. For example, a reciprocal gift in terms of help does not have to induce a reverse flow of the same economic value but can induce another kind of support. A gift that is small in terms of market valuation may express strong sentiments and be highly valued as such. Thus, reciprocal gift exchange does not necessarily require equality of market valuation. This also applies for modern market economies; for example, the wage relation may be complemented by a gift relation in the sense of mutual manifestations of loyalty and support.[20] Finally, the assessment of reciprocity in the third-person view is complicated by the time component and the fact that reciprocal actions can be of a very indirect nature.[21] The notion of generalised reciprocity means that the expectation of reciprocal behaviour may not even be directed at a specific person: As a member of a group, I help a group member because

In Chapter 14, we distinguish between two kinds of objects of transactions, the real and the institutional.

Market transactions distinguish between the object and the medium of transaction. In reflexive transactions, the medium becomes the object of another transaction with the same domain.

On derivatives, see Chapter 12, sections 2.1. and 4.

On voluntary versus forced exchange, see Chapter 5, section 2.

Transactions manifest different degrees of reciprocity, reaching from voluntary exchange via altruistic gift relations to forced exchange.

Reciprocity may involve multidimensional valuation and delayed indirect actions.

I expect other group members to return the favour, not necessarily because they know about my original act but because they subscribe to the same norms that motivated my action.[22]

The second network dimension is *communication*. Economics mostly focuses on the question to which extent communication between agents transmits information in the sense of conveying a truthful representation of facts. As we have seen previously, this is far too limited, as communication has many different goals and means; for example, it may include promises as well as threats. Furthermore, the scope of relevant communication is broader than the mere linguistic element. This is well recognised in the economic theory of signalling.[23] Signalling can proceed via almost any kind of action; what counts is whether the signal elicits a specific interpretation on part of the observer.

Communication does not only take place between a specific sender and a specific receiver of a message. Depending on the technology of communication, such as in the modern internet economy, communication can have various network structures, such as one-to-many, which can in turn include clearly defined audiences (such as speaking to an audience in a lecture hall) as well as an open public (such as tweeting via the internet). The communication structure can be an important aspect of business design: Advertisement is often directed at an open public, but with the internet, it is increasingly possible to direct advertisements even to single persons, based on their search history.

The economic theory of signalling highlights an important difference between language and other kinds of signals: Linguistic communication can be produced at low cost whereas other signals can be very costly.[24] The point is that a costly signal can be assumed to transfer truthful information. This follows from applying the perspective of an intentional stance of rationality on interpreting a signal independently from the true intentions of the sender. A signal that can be sent without cost can be arbitrary, whereas a costly signal will only be sent by the sender if he expects a desired effect. If the desired effect is to increase trustworthiness, the signal may be interpreted as being truthful. This argument can be employed, for example, on expensive advertising which is supposed to signal the health of the underlying business and, therefore, desirable qualities of the product.

Many signals are non-intentional.[25] For example, we might blush when lying even though we do not want it. Moreover, there is no clear separation between communication and action since the receiver can approach any kind of action as a signal and, hence, as communication. This follows from the duality of action and symbolic medium that we already highlighted in the previous chapter. For example, if I buy a sausage at the grocery, this may be interpreted as a signal that I prefer sausages, which, in turn, may motivate the

On the multi-functionality of language, see Chapter 7, section 4.3.

Communication assumes various network structures, depending on technology and media of communication.

Signalling is an important form of action in which the cost of signals conveys information.

On this understanding of rationality, see Chapter 7, section 3.2.

Communication can proceed unintentionally by means of interpreting action.

grocer to produce more of that type in the future. If I stop buying, the grocer may conclude that something is wrong with the spices (although, in fact, I turned vegetarian). More generally, actions can communicate values and identities of agents, such as in lifestyle consumption, and in this sense, support market coordination.

Markets are often explicitly designed to enable communication since the latter is essential for the preparation of many transactions. For example, if we buy a bottle of milk at the supermarket, no communication with the seller takes place, but the bottle carries labels that contain information about the product and the producer, hence, is itself a medium of communication. Many markets entail special designs for communication, such as trade fairs where potential transaction partners meet physically.[26]

We conclude that in the market context, two-sided communication is only a special case, such as in negotiations between client and banker over the conditions of a loan. This type of communication is dominated by the medium of language and, hence, is prone to the problem of trust in low-cost signals. However, at the same time, only language allows for the transmission of detailed and complex information. Therefore, linguistic communication in the market context mostly takes place in institutionalised networks, where linguistic utterances are scaffolded on a legal system which at least potentially determines meanings and consequences of actions. One medium crystallising this scaffolding is the legal contract.

The third network dimension is *observation*. Observation is a broad category and probably constitutes the most significant medium of information transfer in markets, considering that economic agents never communicate directly with most other market participants but only observe the actions that those undertake. In fact, in the marketplace it is often essential to avoid direct communication about goals and means of economic action in order to protect competitive advantage. Therefore, other actors must rely on observation to adapt their actions. Hence, a fundamental structural market pattern is the triad of two transacting parties and an observer, which we already met in discussing externalities.

These observations are crucial to understand basic patterns of information flows in competition. In modern industrial societies, many markets disentangle transactions and customer communication. If we buy a car, we talk to the dealer but not to the producer. If we buy a household kit at the hypermarket, we do not talk to anybody about this transaction. One consequence is that producers often have no direct access to information about individual consumers but only observe aggregate data about trends on the market (this is the business of market research). Therefore, an important alternative source of information is the observation of other producers' actions because these can reveal important information about what those know about consumers.[27] For example, if a producer of household kits changes colours, this might be a

The non-separability of communication and action plays a key role in fiscal and monetary policy, see Chapter 13, section 6.

Markets can require, but also enable, different ways of communication, of which two-sided communication is only a special case.

Observation is a prime mode of information transmission in markets since market agents often reveal private information via their actions only.

Observation of other producers is a key driver of imitative behaviour on markets.

On imitation, also see Chapter 7, section 5.1.

For more detail
in the context
of money and
market pricing,
see Chapter 10,
section 4.

*Technologies of
observation shape
network evolution.*

On technologies
of representation,
see Chapter 13,
section 6.1.

On arbitrage
and pricing,
see Chapter 10,
section 2.2.

signal to other producers that the new colour has become fashionable among consumers.

Observation is the primordial medium of imitation that we scrutinise in section 6. Observation entails interpretation of observed data by the observer, which may build on the rational stance that we discussed in Chapter 7: Observers employ the assumption of rationality to reconstruct revealed information of others, given knowledge about the context of their behaviour. Imitation is an important driver in competitive behaviour, as producers who mutually observe their actions are strongly biased to interpret the actions of others as profit-seeking, hence, as rational, and therefore, may imitate their actions assuming that those reflect an objectified criterion of optimality.

Observation heavily depends on the employed technology in the broadest sense, given that the natural scope of individual observation capacities is limited. Complex societies have developed various means of enhancing observational capacities, such as statistics or news reports, which are important factors of network dynamics; for example, in a large network, we can only observe the behaviour of our local neighbours in the first place but neither the behaviour of the majority nor of the average of network members. This type of information depends on certain technologies of representation. In economics, the most powerful – albeit not only – representation is the price. Observing prices is essential for triggering the core mechanism in markets, arbitrage: Individuals collect price information at various places and in various contexts such that they can exploit differences for making profits. This presupposes observational means that render those prices public.

Prices play a double role: When we perceive that a seller sets a price, this is individual information, such as in the bazaar setting where this action, however, is not treated as revealing truthful valuation in the first place but only as starting point for negotiations. Public prices have a different status even though they simply aggregate individual pricing behaviour. For example, when I am a coffee trader, I may not care for single pricing decisions but just adapt my decision to the prices listed on the coffee exchange. When I buy a car, I may directly negotiate with the dealer about discounts. Even though the listed price may appear like a collective agreement among the traders, the single trader still cannot know what kind of information has been processed during the sequence of previous market transactions among many traders.

3. Network structure and dynamics

3.1. Network structure and agential power

In this section, we further explore the fundamental relation between networks and agential power. Agential power is distributed and scaffolded beyond the boundaries of the physical individual: Network structure is a most important scaffold of agential power. As we discussed previously, the advantages of

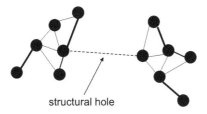

structural hole

Figure 8.4 Structural hole
A structural hole is a potential connection between two network clusters that are internally more tightly connected.

specialisation crucially depend on the degree of agents' capability specificity, which can be determined by technological properties but also by network structure: A party with more network connections to possible alternative exchange partners enjoys an advantage of agential power and can possibly enforce an unequal distribution of benefit on the other side. In addition, the factual availability of connectivity can be leveraged by sparsity in the observation dimension. For example, when I deal with a supplier and I do not know that there are other suppliers, I may have less agential power even though there would be a factual possibility to approach other suppliers. Such effects can occur in many ways because my reception of information can also be influenced by the perceived trustworthiness of sources. For example, I may only trust close friends and, therefore, remain confined to the information recycled in this small circle, which blocks me from perceiving and utilising alternative options.[28] The availability of smartphones in poor rural areas radically transformed the structures of market power in many African regions because market information was made accessible more widely.[29]

On the role of outside options in cooperation and specialisation, see Chapter 5, section 2.2.

Network structure, both realised and perceived, is a major determinant of agential power.

We can identify various general structural types of networks which, among others, impact directly on agential power.[30] We already identified one important structural type in economic relationships, namely the intermediator, which relates to structural holes in networks (Figure 8.4). As we said, completely connected networks are rare, and many connections are normally missing. However, some potential connections can be very valuable. If an individual succeeds in closing the gaps, it can reap the benefits as it enjoys a monopolistic position at least over some time.

We can distinguish between various general types of network configurations that have distinct impact on relative agential power of nodes.

Other structural types can be measured by various measures of centrality (Figure 8.5).[31] For example, in a star-like structure, the central individual will have strong agential power because she controls all indirect connections between the individuals at the periphery of the structure. As we analyse in section 3.4, some of these structures manifest the property of being self-reinforcing in the sense that the central element will accumulate an ever-increasing amount of connections, often dubbed the Matthew effect. This is of far-reaching importance, for example, in explaining agglomeration economies

On cities as networks, see Chapter 16, section 3.

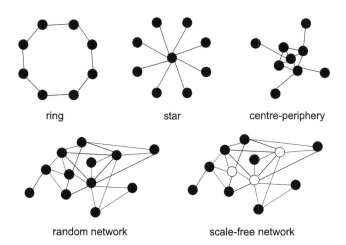

ring   star   centre-periphery

random network   scale-free network

Figure 8.5 Structural types of networks
This is a selection of ideal-typical network structures which have distinct
effects on the distribution of agential powers and network dynamics. For
explanation, see main text.

of cities, which mainly result from the intensity of spatially circumscribed
network interactions.[32]

The star structure can be extended into a centre-periphery structure, such as
when considering a city and its rural hinterland: In the city, social connections
are dense, whereas at the periphery, they are sparse. When we look at this
from the angle of agential power, it seems relatively easy to organise collective interests at the centre but much more difficult in the hinterland because
the various nodes miss interconnections and are only focused on the centre.

An important distinction in dynamic network analysis is between random networks and scale-free networks which obey a power law dynamic
(see section 3.4). Compared with network evolution governed by random
processes, scale-free networks show an emergence of hubs because of the
selective reinforcement of connections, as demonstrated in empirical distributions such as the large differences of connectivities of websites on the
internet. In epidemiology, hubs are super spreaders who speed up the diffusion of a virus.[33]

*In organisational
and institutionalised
networks, we
distinguish between
formal and informal
connections.*

Structural analysis focuses on positions in networks. In this regard, it is
partly independent from the incumbent: Different individuals may obtain the
same position and, thereby, leverage their agential power. If positions are
determined by formal rule, we speak of institutionalised networks. For example, access to certain kinds of information may only be possible for individuals holding a certain position such as that of a judge. This is also true for

networks inside organisations, such as firms. Yet we must distinguish between formal and informal networks: People in the same formal position may have structurally different agential power because of informal structures that complement or supersede the formal position. This is reflected in the duality of organisation and group in the same setting: Organisational network structures are overlaid by non-congruent group structures.[34] An important phenomenon in this context is corruption: Corruption refers to the interference between institutionalised networks and other social networks in a way that the rules governing the former erode. For example, a judge may be influenced by a rich businessman when attending the same club because the businessman offers opportunities to his children.

For the importance of informal group structures for social inequality, see Chapter 15, section 4.3.

3.2. Social capital

We have seen that agential power is a relational term in two senses. First, agential power is always relative to the agential power of others. Second, agential power is partly determined by the interests of others in certain goods or events that are under the powerful individual's control, implying that this individual may be able to demand a certain behaviour from others. If others have no interest in an individual whatsoever, the individual has a minimum of exchange opportunities or low leverage in shaping the terms of exchange. Hence, differential agential power enables exchange, and agential power can be interpreted as the capacity for social exchange.

This follows Coleman's definition of power, see Chapter 5, section 3.2.

Accordingly, economists and sociologists concur in using the term 'social capital' to conceptualise and measure agential power in social networks.[35] Social capital is a complex notion that is inspired by the economic use of the notion of capital and put aside other types of capital, such as financial assets. As in the case of agential power, it is not only determined by the properties of the individual but also by the properties of the individuals to which the individual is connected. Therefore, one essential question is what determines the scope and reliability of these connections.

Social capital is a measure of agential power of an individual or a group, as determined by social networks.

A standard distinction is between bonding and bridging types of social capital, which partly overlaps with the distinction between strong and weak ties in social networks.[36] The bonding type is based on mutual emotional commitments of individuals and recurrent, stable interactions, such as the family or a neighbourhood with a long history of joint dwelling. Humans are especially adept at actively creating such relations, such as by the establishment of clubs and associations with limited membership which hold regular meetings to maintain shared experiences and mutual commitments. Bonding builds on the capacity of the social brain to create intensive relations with a limited number of people. Extending beyond this range requires the mobilisation of symbolic media. An important example in the market context is the formation of ethnic trading networks in the diaspora, where feelings of belonging and emotional

We distinguish between bonding and bridging types of social capital.

closeness enhance trust between members and group-bounded networks enable indirect monitoring and sanctioning of behaviour.[37]

The drawback of such structures is that members share the same social capital in the sense that most information about opportunities for exchange is available to everyone and will, therefore, be exploited and exhausted. This is different in bridging social capital, which partly relies on weak ties. Weak ties are connections that extend beyond bonding types and may even be ephemeral, such as when travelling to another city, meeting a stranger, and discovering some information never heard of previously. Hence, we assume, following the famous Granovetter argument, that new information can mostly be obtained via bridging relations.[38]

Weak ties enable better access to new information than strong ties. The capacity to create and exploit weak ties is also a form of social capital.

In a third type of tie, trust in new information obtained by a weak relationship is established via recurrent interaction.

Whereas weak ties are conducive to gather new information, strong ties are conducive to trust, especially in the sense of personal trust. But how can we trust new information obtained via a network tie that does not manifest reliable social mechanisms of trust? Economic theory implicitly assumes that this builds on systemic trust, that is, institutionalised forms of guaranteeing the reliability of information (such as product quality standards). However, this cannot apply to singular tokens of information that refer to conditions specific in time and space, such as a business opportunity (where entrepreneurial judgement cannot be subject to a general quality standard). Hence, we posit another type of tie apart from the weak/strong duality: ties that are weak but still embedded in contexts of recurrent interactions. This is often expressed in notions such as acquaintance; some societies even have a special and elaborate cultural repertoire in creating such ties, such as 'guanxi' in China.[39] In comparison, there are many factors that foster trust in a bonding network, such as mutual knowledge of one's past behaviour, current observability, comprehensiveness of indirect information, and the awareness that group-based sanctioning mechanisms exist.

The distribution of agential power across individuals creates a complex interactive dynamic of mutual trust, with asymmetries eroding conditions of trust.

Like agential power, trust is a relational property and can be decomposed into two dimensions, namely trusting and trustworthiness. For example, if one party can signal trustworthiness and induce trusting of the other party, this enhances the probability of cooperation and reduces uncertainty for both parties. At the same time, however, trusting creates the opportunity for exploiting trust by opportunistic action.[40] If this is anticipated, even only as a general possibility, trusting may not emerge despite efforts to create trustworthiness. However, advantages in agential power systematically create tendencies to trust because of the assumption of control, independently from judging the trustworthiness of the other. But the same asymmetry can jeopardise trustworthiness on part of the more powerful party, as agential power enables opportunism and may even weaken the potential of retaliation on the weaker side. Thus, relationships of trust are intertwined with agential power;[41] building trust will often require convergence to similar levels of agential powers. This explains why, in general, democratic societies manifest higher levels of societal trust than authoritarian countries.[42]

Social capital cannot be consumed; it can even grow through use.[43] The more individuals mutually support each other, the larger the confidence in future interaction. At the same time, however, social capital is susceptible to the free-rider problem, especially when it comes to bonding capital. Therefore, many forms of social capital qualify as non-congestible club goods which must rely on mechanisms of sanctioning free-riders, of which the most powerful one is exclusion.

In comparison, bridging social capital is often close to a private good, as the example of the intermediator shows: The intermediator can control access to her connections, and these are susceptible to erosion via overly frequent use. However, sometimes social capital is also conceived as including public goods, such as a strong public morality.[44] Therefore, in empirical terms, it is important to clearly distinguish between levels of social capital; the most important distinction being between the social capital of an individual and the social capital of a group. This has implications for comparing social capital within groups and across groups: For example, a member of a group may have low social capital relative to high status members of the group but still may benefit from higher social capital on the group level relative to other groups (think of low-rank officials of a colonising country vis-à-vis natives).

Forms of social capital differentiate according to the criteria of excludability of network members and rivalry of uses.

We can summarise this overview by two criteria for classifying social capital in the network context (Figure 8.6). One is whether individuals can be excluded from accessing and using social capital, both on the individual and social level: An entrepreneur can protect her connections from others, a group may exclude somebody from mutual support. The other is whether the use of social capital is rivalrous or non-rivalrous: A connection can be rivalrous as a consequence of the scarcity of time and resources invested into it, whereas a high level of trust in a group can be used without limits, provided that free-riding remains rare and does not lead to an erosion of trust.

One important determinant of social capital is social status, in the sense of structural positions endowed with different levels of agential power as a result of the confluence of various social forces impacting on the network, such as wealth, political office, or leadership in religious organisations. In part, status is a direct measure of social capital and is self-reinforcing. An individual with high status needs to spend less effort in creating high-quality social relations with others, which in turn contributes to status.[45] Therefore, high status

An important aspect of social capital is social status.

We discuss social stratification in more detail in Chapter 15.

	Excludable	Non-excludable
Rivalrous	Private good (relationships)	Commons (collective safety)
Non-rivalrous	Club good (associations)	Public good (morals)

Figure 8.6 Types of social capital
See main text.

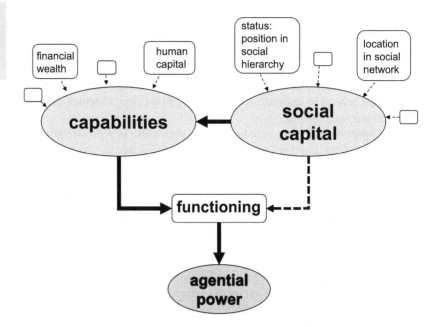

Figure 8.7 Social capital as scaffold of agential power (after Lin)
Social capital embodies the position of an agent in social networks. It is a
central determinant of capabilities that generate agential power. The latter is
embodied in functionings based on multidimensional capabilities that result
from social capital as well as other factors such as financial wealth.

*Groups sharing high
social status are
referred to as elites,
which need to be
distinguished from
social classes and
interest groups.*

On the
capabilities/
functioning
distinction,
see Chapter 5,
section 2.1.

individuals will more frequently connect with other high-status individuals
such that their status positions are mutually reinforcing. This results into the
formation of elites.

Elites are an important social network concept which differs from other
concepts, such as social classes or interest groups, and remains comparatively
underexplored in economics.[46] Elites are mainly defined via the mutual support of status as a shared interest but not necessarily via a congruence of substantive interests, such as when bankers socialise with leading politicians. In
contrast, interest groups in economics are defined by shared specific interests
tied to specific economic activities, such as farming. At the same time, by
enabling frequent social interaction and exchange, elites can be important
vehicles of interest group politics.[47]

We summarise main insights in Figure 8.7. Social capital generates agential power as determined by the capability to access other agents with high
positions in a network, the diversity of contacts that provide various benefits
and access to new information, and the value of resources that can be mobi-
lised in the interest of the agent. Status and structure result from the individual

position of the agent in the network. Social capital is one of the determinants of individual capabilities for action; others include wealth and human capital. The capabilities result in assuming a specific functioning, including, in the market context, a specific pattern of specialisation. All these determinants flow together in creating agential power.

3.3. Boundaries in networks: In-group/out-group

Today, the world is entirely covered in one universal human network.[48] This is the counterpart to the expansion of the technosphere, given that human networks are embedded in, and scaffolded by, technological artefacts. Even remote aboriginal tribes in the Amazonas region sometimes meet non-members, who in turn are connected to others, and so forth. This pattern of universal connectivity already emerged in prehistorical times in the sense of some networks starting to grow relative to others which remained isolated and can be empirically verified in the distribution of artefacts far beyond their point of origin. Network dynamics resulted in structural expansion and dominance, for example, by the early empires. The most important driver for this universal connectivity is economic action, such as migration, trade, or exchange in general, which we can observe from the earliest periods of human development.

Today's world is characterised by universal network connectivity.

Increasing network connectivity can be analysed via the so-called small-world pattern, which relates to the weak tie notion but adds distinct forms of circular closure (Figure 8.8).[49] Small worlds are clusters of tightly and almost universally connected nodes. Connections between these clusters are few but suffice to establish indirect connections across all involved individuals in the larger set. In the economy, such patterns are prevalent: The Chinese consumers of soya beans from Brazil have no direct connection to Brazilian farmers but are still linked via markets. Eventually, small worlds can undergo a phase transition to a strongly integrated network.[50] Also, depending on technology, network connectivity may take many forms. For example, smartphones have strong economic effects on less-developed countries, partly substituting the lack of adequate transport infrastructure.

Network connectivity can be specified by small-world patterns.

We distinguish between two different types of groups: primary and secondary groups. Primary groups are defined by strong and recurrent interaction between all group members, implying that everybody can observe the behaviour of others, and communication regularly takes place without bias. This implies that group members have access to all information that is transmitted via non-linguistic signals, such as body language. Primary groups correspond to the standard hunter-gatherer group in the human phylogenetic past, implying that many human emotional and cognitive capacities are adapted to managing social relationships in this pattern.[51]

We distinguish between primary and secondary groups. Primary groups activate all forms of interaction among members.

The formation of primary groups heavily relies on the social brain, see Chapter 7, section 3.1.

Secondary groups can, in principle, be of any size; there is an intermediate level which can be called a tribe.[52] Tribes are alliances of groups which share

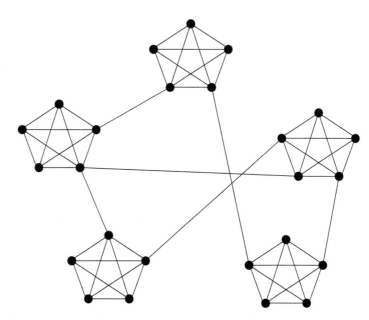

Figure 8.8 Small world

Clusters of networks are connected via sparse ties, which, however, speeds up information transmission among them such that the larger network is integrated in terms of flows of information and other elements such as the use of artefacts.

Secondary groups leverage specific symbolic media of forming group identity.

On identity, see Chapter 7, section 4.2.

Coordination in markets is often achieved via networks of groups with shared identities, such as ethnic trading networks or professional clubs.

certain markers such as local dialect, and they are small worlds in being connected across the groups via few intermediating individuals and points of contact, which, however, if being active recurrently, will diffuse shared information and markers. Tribes play an important role in modern market systems, such as by constituting professional communities (e.g., financial traders across the world).

Secondary groups build on biological mechanisms that enable group formation triggered and shaped by a symbolic repertoire that is culturally transmitted.[53] The core of this phenomenon is identity: Human identity is group-based, in the sense of requiring recurrent interaction with a group to which the individual feels to belong.[54] The important consequence is that ostracism is a powerful means to enforce group boundaries and shared norms of behaviour.[55]

The first observation is that, in economics, the claim is often made that modern market systems build on the transition to governance mechanisms applying to large groups of basically anonymous individuals that are predominantly governed by legal institutions.[56] This, however, does not depict reality. Group boundaries continue to exert a strong impact on market transactions, such as when ethnic or religious groups tend to dominate a particular trade. This is often highly visible in international trade, suggesting that a lack of efficacious institutions may force economic agents to fall back on group-level mechanisms to reduce risk.[57] This argument can be easily extended to conditions within countries and, in this case, may not only refer to strong group markers such as ethnicity or religion. For example, in China today, place of birth often serves as an anchor for group identity, and certain trades in cities are dominated by people from the same region who also tend to settle together in certain neighbourhoods, such as Hunan taxi drivers in Shenzhen.[58]

Economic agents actively foster group formation based on shared identities by which certain behavioural standards are enforced.

The second observation is that group formation is often deliberately fostered by economic agents. An important example are professional associations, such as lawyers' associations, which allow for the expression of professional identities and can also enforce certain behavioural standards on its members. Group formation can also embed economic activities in other social activities, such as the proverbial golf club as meeting ground for social elites. In the most general sense, group formation can endogenously emerge from recurrent interaction, such as in the case of old boys' networks.[59]

Negative discrimination of certain groups is a pervasive phenomenon with important economic consequences.

The third observation is the often-pervasive negative discrimination of certain groups, which can have deep effects on the distribution of income and economic achievement, including fundamental aspects such as education and health. One example is discrimination against Afro-Americans in the US and other countries such as Brazil. A typical pattern until today is that elites are predominantly white, whereas neighbourhoods with high levels of crime and bad public services and retail logistics are predominantly black.[60]

On mechanisms of discrimination, see Chapter 15.

Taken together, in real-world economies in-group/out-group boundaries shape economic activities in many ways. The general reason is that markets presuppose a high degree of voluntary cooperation to reduce transaction cost, such as by building trust and containing cheating. In other words, markets build on a strong basis of social capital both on the individual and collective level.[61] Social capital is embodied in specific social contexts which are group based. Yet there is always the possibility that existing group structures with strong social capital are undermined by free-riders. Therefore, there is a necessity of mechanisms that clearly identify group members and credibly signal their quality, which means that those signals need to be costly and difficult to imitate. This is the case if the signals do not refer to capacities, skills, or other assets that are economically functional because such markers would be prone to imitation and rapid diffusion.[62] The employment of non-functional and costly indicators of group identity can ensure an adequate mixture of rules-based market interactions and mechanisms of social capital formation that are conducive to the formation of trust in markets.

Social capital embodied in groups is a necessary condition of trust even in a rules-based system of markets.

3.4. Network dynamics and frequency-dependent mechanisms

On imitation, see Chapter 7, section 5.1.

We have already referred to dynamic features of networks, which are rooted in the human capacity to learn by imitation. Imitation fosters the emergence of frequency-dependent dynamics, which matches with epidemiological models of diffusion in social networks. There are two types of frequency dependency that correspond to different types of modelling in economics:[63]

*Global and
local frequency
dependency relate to
different categories
of models: logistic
diffusion models and
cellular automata,
respectively.*

- *Global frequency dependency* relates the frequency of a pattern to a factor that applies to the population in total. For example, individuals may have information about the average incidence of a pattern in the population (how many people buy electric cars?) and eventually adopt this average themselves (the more people buy, the more I am inclined to buy as well; for example, because I expect that there will be improvements in the availability of charging stations); or a universal constraint, such as a limited resource, affects all individuals equally (such as sellers facing the gradual satiation of the market for a particular product).
- *Local frequency dependency* means that individuals adapt to events in their neighbourhood which may be different from the average situation in other neighbourhoods (I happen to live in a posh neighbourhood, where many people buy electric cars, and buy one as well, irrespective of the general availability of charging stations). However, since neighbourhoods are contiguous, such a pattern can spread across the entire population (once the rich park their electric cars in the inner city, other people going there for shopping start to imitate).

The two types of frequency-dependent dynamics relate to different types of mathematical modelling, which are highly relevant for economics. Global frequency often results in the diffusion pattern of a logistic function (Figure 4.5), which constitutes a general description of many processes of growth in nature and the economy.[64] For example, logistic functions describe the diffusion of many innovations and technological artefacts, driven by imitation dynamics and constraints to market expansion.[65]

*Agent-based models
of markets show that
assumptions about
the rationality of
agents can be very
weak in explaining
market states.*

Local frequency dependency can be described by cellular automata (Figure 8.9), which in economics have been developed into agent-based modelling tools.[66] Cellular automata are a powerful tool to simulate economic processes, contrasting analytical solutions of highly compressed formal hypotheses as commonly used in most subdisciplines of economics.[67] Cellular automata also differ fundamentally from general equilibrium modelling in providing microfoundations for understanding macro-patterns in data. However, there are wide degrees of freedom in designing simulation models, especially with regard to the complexity of network relations that are considered. In contrast, assumptions on individual behaviour can be very parsimonious. In simulation models, economic agents just follow simple rules of contextualised decision making, and the dynamics results from structured interaction in the network.[68]

The nature of dynamics depends on the specific network structure in the three dimensions. The dimension of observation is of special interest: The

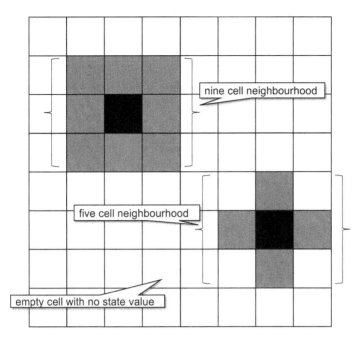

Figure 8.9 Basic construction of cellular automata
Agent-based models build on grids that consist of cells corresponding to states
of agents which are influenced by regularised neighbourhoods. Diffusion
spreads along encounters between agents. The specific dynamic is determined
by the shape of neighbourhoods. Two examples are shown.

structure of observation determines whether global or local frequency
dynamics is triggered, even if causal chains operate across the entire network, such as in transaction chains. A well-known result of cellular automata models is that outcomes can differ from what people would prefer in
terms of the average, such as in racial discrimination. Further, a crucial question is what kind of information triggers the dynamics, private or public.
One conspicuous example in economics is herding or, more generally, information cascades.[69]

Imitation can work via various channels. For example, a piano teacher
may show to a student how a piece should be performed. This would substantially differ from many imitative processes in the economy where individuals have incentives to keep information private, such as entrepreneurs
who want to protect market intelligence from diffusing easily. In this case,
individuals can only observe (subsets of) actions. As a result, there is a
possibility that false information spreads in a population of imitators, even

*Frequency-
dependent models
are essential for
understanding
imitation dynamics.*

On financial
crises, see
Chapter 13,
section 5.2.

if individuals have private information that contradicts the information deduced from observing others. The only condition is that imitators obey a certain rule, such as following a perceived majority trend. This may result in herding dynamics, such as capital flight or financial bubbles.[70] In many examples of this kind, the problem is that there is no external benchmark for assessing values so that we cannot determine whether the information driving the dynamics is true or wrong before the dynamics implodes.

A classic mechanism of statistical interactions caused by observational patterns is the lemons problem.

Another classic type of network dynamic in three dimensions is the lemons problem.[71] The original example is a second-hand car market with information asymmetries between buyers and sellers of cars: Sellers know the quality of the individual car, but buyers only know the average quality of cars. Hence, a seller of a high-quality car will not be able to fetch the adequate price. If she decides to withdraw her offer, the average quality of cars will decline, thus potentially triggering a downward spiral. This analysis applies universally to all network relations in large groups. To show this, we can translate the lemons problem into the question whether an individual knows the true level of trustworthiness of another individual. In a large group, she will only know average quality; in a small group, she may be able to assess individuals. Hence, in the large group, a similar implosion of the quality of relations can happen if trustworthy individuals cannot get proper recognition by others and withdraw. In this case, withdrawal can mean that the larger population fragments into groups with a high internal level of trust and those with a low level of trust, where endemic misbehaviour confirms expectations about a low average level of trustworthiness.[72] This is salient in the wide variations of social trust across countries that have been consistently measured in surveys, such as the World Values Survey.

We refer to the lemons model, for example, in the context of financial markets, Chapter 12, section 2.3, and Chapter 13, section 5.2.

Power laws apply across many economic domains, such as economic geography or social network markets.

A significant frequency-dependent mechanism is the power law dynamics which is characteristic for scale-free networks.[73] This results in a type of statistical distribution over a certain domain that fundamentally differs from the normal distribution (Figure 8.10). Simple mechanisms that induce a power law dynamic are of the type in which one event attracts other events of the same type, such as in citation networks, resulting in cumulative dynamics (the Matthew effect, the rich get richer).

Similar mechanisms work in many domains of the economy and markets. In economic geography, the distribution of cities converges to a power law, thus explaining an essential phenomenon in the spatial structure of the economy.[74] Many markets in which network effects are similar to citation networks (such as music) reveal that pattern. Once we consider status effects, with status working like an attractor, even financial markets can reveal a power law dynamic. The pattern observable across all these cases is that market shares are dominated by a few large entities, and many small entities make up the long tail of the distribution. Hence, power laws can have strong effects on distribution and inequality in the economy.

On status effects in market competition between firms, see Chapter 15, section 3.2.

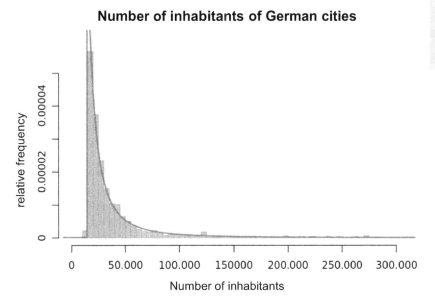

Number of inhabitants of German cities

Figure 8.10 Power law distribution
The power law distribution has a long tail and a peak, which is empirically exemplified by phenomena, such as citation networks, blockbuster movies, and the distribution of city and town sizes, shown here for Germany: There are many small towns and very few large cities.

Source: https://commons.wikimedia.org/wiki/File:German_Cities_Pareto_Density_de.svg (Credit: Accountalive)

4. Conclusion

A perspective on markets as networks entails crucial differences to the conventional equilibrium view on markets, even when considering imperfect competition. Most fundamentally, this results from considering triadic structures, as opposed to dyads, and from focusing on non-integral structures. Both endogenise the distribution of agential power in networks and, therefore, directly affect patterns of specialisation in face of the specialisation dilemma. In real-world economies, social networks are crucial for understanding, for example, the interaction of financial elites at Wall Street and government, or the extent of discrimination and segregation in residential areas. Social network dynamics drive imitation, which is a core phenomenon in explaining consumer behaviour or the diffusion of innovations in industry.

The question of how network structures become stable and sustainable through time, especially when it comes to highly complex market systems involving huge numbers of diverse agents, requires the study of institutions, which is the subject of the next chapter.

Major chapter insights

- Markets are networks, both social and physical, which mutually shape their evolution. Networks are patterns of connections between individuals and typically modelled as graphs.
- Network analysis allows for the identification of endogenous structural determinants of agential power. We distinguish between three dimensions of networks: transaction, communication, and observation. The basic unit of network analysis is the triad, which entails archetypical forms, such as third-party intermediation or externalities. Other important concepts include the degree of network integration and connectivity, and the distinction between the first-person (ego-centred) and the third-person view on networks.
- *Transactions* are shaped by the technologies of transaction and determinants, such as the distinction between object and the claim (property right), or the form and degree of reciprocity (e.g., gift exchange versus market exchange). In *communication*, apart from technology, we must consider the crucial role of interpretation on part of the receiver, which implies that communication can be non-intentional, such as in certain forms of signalling. *Observation* is important in markets, as agents often do not communicate private information, and is a driver of imitation.
- We distinguish various basic types of network structure with direct implications for the distribution of agential power across nodes and network dynamics, which are important for analysing markets, such as centre-periphery structures or scale-free networks.
- Social capital is an aggregate measure of agential power in social networks. We distinguish various forms, such as bonding versus bridging social capital, and as determined by degrees of rivalry and excludability.
- For preserving and enhancing social capital, discrimination between in-group and out-group entails the powerful mechanism of ostracism. As a result, even rule-based markets manifest a strong role of exclusive social networks, such as ethnic trading networks or professional clubs.
- There are two basic forms of frequency dependency in networks, global and local, which can be analysed by different types of models, logistic diffusion and agent-based models. Such models are applied in understanding imitation and information flows in markets, formation of trust, and concentration of market shares.

Notes

1 The classical contributions are summarised by Granovetter (2005).
2 This perspective is mostly developed in physical network analysis, which is often seen as the overarching framework of network analysis, see Newman (2010). Network analysis is a prime research method in econophysics.
3 Batty (2013).
4 For a comprehensive overview of the field, see Scott and Carrington (2011).
5 Jackson (2014).
6 A very influential view is Burt (1992, 2002).
7 Knoke and Yang (2008, 6ff), Newman (2010, 109ff).
8 Herrmann-Pillath (2002, 51ff).
9 The German sociologist Georg Simmel had forcefully argued that society is fundamentally shaped by triadic structures, see Nooteboom (2006).
10 Economists refer to this as pecuniary externalities, which, in perfect markets, would not matter for Pareto efficiency. This is not true for real-world markets, see Greenwald and Stiglitz (1986).
11 Potts (2000, 20ff).
12 Burt (1992).
13 Marsden (2011).
14 Jackson (2019, 54ff) overviews these experiments.
15 The centrality of the transaction was emphasised by the old institutionalists: Commons (1934).
16 Herrmann-Pillath (2002, 464ff).
17 Andriani and Herrmann-Pillath (2015).
18 De Soto (2001).
19 Reciprocity is a central notion in economic anthropology; for an overview of the debates, see Hann and Hart (2011). This can be traced back to Polanyi (1944).
20 Akerlof (1982).
21 This is important in the case of Chinese social networks, so-called 'guanxi', see Herrmann-Pillath (2013, 364ff).
22 There is a large literature on the evolution of generalised reciprocity, for example, Rankin and Taborsky (2009), which was inspired by Trivers (1985).
23 Seminally, Spence (1974). More recently, Skyrms (2010).
24 In game theory, this is discussed in the context of the cheap talk paradigm, Farrell and Rabin (1996), Krishna and Morgan (2008).
25 The classic on this is Ekman (1985).
26 For example, Çalışkan (2007).
27 This is a central idea in White's (1981, 2002) sociological theory of markets.
28 There is a lot of research on trust in supplier networks, with interesting cross-cultural comparisons; for a Chinese comparison, see Özer et al. (2014).
29 Aker and Mbiti (2010).

30 Social network analysis has developed various quantitative measures for those types that we do not need to scrutinise in more detail here; for a concise overview, see Knoke and Yang (2008, 51ff).

31 Hanneman and Riddle (2011).

32 Batty (2013, 47ff).

33 For these and many other applications, see Jackson (2019, 44ff).

34 For an exemplary study, Soda and Zaheer (2012).

35 There is a rich literature on social capital. Our approach is inspired by Lin (2001).

36 Putnam (2000), Dasgupta (2005).

37 Landa (1994).

38 Granovetter (1985).

39 Barbalet (2021).

40 This is emphasised by both the biological and the philosophical literature on trust as a behavioural universal, see Field (2001) or Hollis (1998).

41 Nooteboom (2002).

42 Inglehart (2018, chapter 7).

43 Solow (2000).

44 Putnam (2000).

45 This extends on Podolny (2005).

46 Acemoglu and Robinson (2009).

47 Bond and Harrigan (2011).

48 McNeill and McNeill (2003).

49 Watts (1999).

50 Newman (2010, 591ff).

51 Tooby and Cosmides (2005).

52 Kotkin (1992).

53 Bowles et al. (2003).

54 Akerlof and Kranton (2000).

55 Bowles and Gintis (2011, 24ff).

56 North (1990).

57 Landa (1994), Rauch (2001).

58 Herrmann-Pillath et al. (2020).

59 Carroll and Sapinski (2011).

60 Gagnon and Goyal (2017), Graham (2018).

61 Platteau (1994).

62 Munz (1993).

63 On diffusion models, see Newman (2010, 628ff). The economics classic on checkerboard models of local interactions is Schelling (1978). With Wolfram's (2002) monumental work, cellular automata became foundational for many scientific and technological disciplines.

64 Smil (2019, 31ff).

65 Chandrasekaran and Tellis (2017).

66 Seminally, Albin and Foley (1998).

67 Leijonhufvud (2011).

68 Plott and Smith (2008).

69 Bikhchandani et al. (1992, 1998), Raafat et al. (2009).

70 Baddeley (2010), Schmitt and Westerhoff (2017).
71 Akerlof (1970).
72 Kranton (1996).
73 Newman (2010, 247ff), Gabaix (2016).
74 Krugman (1996), Fujita et al. (1999).

References

Acemoglu, D. and Robinson, J. A. (2009) 'Persistence of Power, Elites, and Institutions', *American Economic Review*, 98(1), pp. 276–293. DOI: 10.1257/aer.98.1.267.

Aker, J. C. and Mbiti, I. M. (2010) 'Mobile Phones and Economic Development in Africa', *Journal of Economic Perspectives*, 24(3), pp. 207–232. DOI: 10.1257/jep.24.3.207.

Akerlof, G. A. (1982) 'Labor Contracts as Partial Gift Exchange', *Quarterly Journal of Economics*, 97(4), pp. 543–569. DOI: 10.2307/1885099.

Akerlof, G. A. and Kranton, R. E. (2000) 'Economics and Identity', *Quarterly Journal of Economics*, 115(3), pp. 715–753.

Akerlof, George A. "The Market for 'Lemons': Quality Uncertainty and the Market Mechanism." The Quarterly Journal of Economics 84(3) (1970): 488–500. https://doi.org/10.2307/1879431.

Albin, P. S. and Foley, D. K. (1998) *Barriers and Bounds to Rationality: Essays on Economic Complexity and Dynamics in Interactive Systems*. Princeton: Princeton University Press.

Andriani, P. and Herrmann-Pillath, C. (2015) 'Transactional Innovation as Performative Action: Transforming Comparative Advantage in the Global Coffee Business', *Journal of Evolutionary Economics*, 25(2), pp. 371–400. DOI: 10.1007/s00191-014-0388-y.

Baddeley, M. (2010) 'Herding, Social Influence and Economic Decision-Making: Socio-Psychological and Neuroscientific Analyses', *Philosophical Transactions of the Royal Society B: Biological Sciences*, 365(1538), pp. 281–290. DOI: 10.1098/rstb.2009.0169.

Barbalet, J. M. (2021) *The Theory of Guanxi and Chinese Society*. 1st Edition. Oxford: Oxford University Press. DOI: 10.1093/oso/9780198808732.001.0001.

Batty, M. (2013) *The New Science of Cities*. Cambridge and London: MIT Press. DOI: 10.7551/mitpress/9399.001.0001.

Bikhchandani, S., Hirschleifer, D. and Welch, I. (1992) 'A Theory of Fads, Fashion, Custom, and Cultural Change as Informational Cascades', *Journal of Political Economy*, 100(5), pp. 992–1026. DOI: 10.1086/261849.

Bikhchandani, S., Hirschleifer, D. and Welch, I. (1998) 'Learning from the Behavior of Others: Conformity, Fads, and Informational Cascades', *Journal of Economic Perspectives*, 12(3), pp. 151–170. DOI: 10.1257/jep.12.3.151.

Bond, M. and Harrigan, N. (2011) 'Political Dimensions of Corporate Connections', in Scott, J. and Carrington, P. (eds.) *The Sage Handbook of Social Network Analysis*. Los Angeles: Sage, pp. 196–209.

Bowles, S., Choi, J.-K. and Hopfensitz, A. (2003) 'The Co-Evolution of Individual Behaviors and Social Institutions', *Journal of Theoretical Biology,* 223(2), pp. 135–147. DOI: 10.1016/S0022-5193(03)00060-2.

Bowles, S. and Gintis, H. (2011) *A Cooperative Species: Human Reciprocity and Its Evolution.* Princeton: Princeton University Press. DOI: 10.23943/princeton/9780691151250.001.0001.

Burt, R. S. (1992) *Structural Holes: The Social Structure of Competition.* Cambridge and London: Harvard University Press.

Burt, R. S. (2002) 'The Social Capital of Structural Holes', in Guillén, M. F. *et al.* (eds.) *The New Economic Sociology: Developments in an Emerging Field.* New York: Russell Sage Foundation, pp. 148–192.

Çalışkan, K. (2007) 'Price as a Market Device: Cotton Trading in Izmir Mercantile Exchange', in Callon, M., Millo, Y. and Muniesa, F. (eds.) *Market Devices.* Hoboken: Wiley-Blackwell. pp. 241–261. DOI: 10.1111/J.1467-954X.2007.00738.X.

Carroll, W. and Sapinski, J. P. (2011) 'Corporate Elites and Intercorporate Networks', in Scott, J. and Carrington, P. (eds.) *The Sage Handbook of Social Network Analysis.* Los Angeles: Sage, pp. 180–195.

Chandrasekaran, D. and Tellis, G. J. (2017) 'A Critical Review of Marketing Research on Diffusion of New Products', in Malhotra, N. (ed.) *Review of Marketing Research*, Vol. 3. Abingdon and New York: Routledge.

Commons, J. R. (1934) *Institutional Economics: Its Place in Political Economy.* Madison: University of Wisconsin Press.

Dasgupta, P. (2005) 'Economics of Social Capital', *The Economic Record,* 81(255), pp. 2–21.

De Soto, H. (2001) *The Mystery of Capital: Why Capitalism Triumphs in the West and Fails Everywhere Else.* London: Black Swan.

Ekman, P. (1985) *Telling Lies: Clues to Deceit in the Marketplace, Politics, and Marriage.* New York: Norton.

Farrell, J. and Rabin, M. (1996) 'Cheap Talk', *Journal of Economic Perspectives,* 10(3), pp. 103–118.

Field, A. (2001) *Altruistically Inclined? The Behavioral Sciences, Evolutionary Theory, and the Origins of Reciprocity.* Ann Arbor: University of Michigan Press.

Fujita, M., Krugman, P. and Venables, A. J. (1999) *The Spatial Economy: Cities, Regions, and International Trade.* Cambridge: MIT Press.

Gabaix, X. (2016) 'Power Laws in Economics: An Introduction', *Journal of Economic Perspectives,* 30(1), pp. 185–206. DOI: 10.1257/jep.30.1.185.

Gagnon, J. and Goyal, S. (2017) 'Networks, Markets, and Inequality', *American Economic Review,* 107(1), pp. 1–30. DOI: 10.1257/aer.20150635.

Graham, B. S. (2018) 'Identifying and Estimating Neighborhood Effects', *Journal of Economic Literature,* 56(2), pp. 450–500. DOI: 10.1257/jel.20160854.

Granovetter, M. (1985) 'Economic Action and Social Structure: The Problem of Embeddedness', *American Journal of Sociology,* 91(3), pp. 481–510.

Granovetter, M. (2005) 'The Impact of Social Structure on Economic Outcomes', *Journal of Economic Perspectives,* 19(1), pp. 33–50. DOI: 10.1257/0895330053147958.

Greenwald, B. and Stiglitz, J. (1986) 'Externalities in Economies with Imperfect Information and Incomplete Markets', *Quarterly Journal of Economics*, 101(2), pp. 229–264. DOI: 10.2307/1891114.

Hann, C. M. and Hart, K. (2011) *Economic Anthropology: History, Ethnography, Critique*. Cambridge and Malden: Polity Press.

Hanneman, R. A. and Riddle, M. (2011) 'Concepts and Measures for Basic Network Analysis', in Scott, J. and Carrington, P. (eds.) *The Sage Handbook of Social Network Analysis*. Los Angeles: Sage, pp. 340–369.

Herrmann-Pillath, C. (2001) *Kritik der reinen Theorie des internationalen Handels, Band 1: Transaktionstheoretische Grundlagen*. Marburg: Metropolis.

Herrmann-Pillath, C. (2002) *Grundriß der Evolutionsökonomik*. Stuttgart: Wilhelm Fink Verlag.

Herrmann-Pillath, C. (2013) *Foundations of Economic Evolution: A Treatise on the Natural Philosophy of Economics*. Cheltenham and Northampton: Edward Elgar Publishing. DOI: 10.4337/9781782548362.

Herrmann-Pillath, C. (2016) *China's Economic Culture: The Ritual Order of State and Markets*. London: Routledge. DOI: 10.4324/9781315884653.

Herrmann-Pillath, Carsten, Man, Guo and Xingyuan, Feng. (2020) *Ritual and Economy in Metropolitan China. A Global Social Science Approach*. London: Routledge.

Hollis, M. (1998) *Trust within Reason*. Cambridge: Cambridge University Press.

Inglehart, R. (2018) *Cultural Evolution: People's Motivations Are Changing, and Reshaping the World*. Cambridge: Cambridge University Press. DOI: 10.1017/9781108613880.

Jackson, M. O. (2014) 'Networks in the Understanding of Economic Behaviors', *Journal of Economic Perspectives*, 28(4), pp. 3–22. DOI: 10.1257/jep.28.4.3.

Jackson, M. O. (2019) *The Human Network: How Your Social Position Determines Your Power, Beliefs, and Behaviors*. New York: Pantheon.

Knoke, D. and Yang, S. (2008) *Social Network Analysis*. Los Angeles: Sage. DOI: 10.4135/9781412985864.

Kotkin, J. (1992) *Tribes: How Race, Religion, and Identity Determine Success in the New Global Economy*. New York: Random House.

Kranton, R. E. (1996) 'Reciprocal Exchange: A Self-Sustaining System', *American Economic Review*, 86(4), pp. 830–851.

Krishna, V. and Morgan, J. (2008) 'Cheap Talk', in Vernengo, M. *et al.* (eds.) *The New Palgrave Dictionary of Economics*, Vol. 1. Basingstoke and New York: Palgrave Macmillan, pp. 751–756. DOI: 10.1057/978-1-349-95121-5_2525-1.

Krugman, P. (1996) *The Self-Organizing Economy*. Cambridge and Oxford: Blackwell.

Landa, J. T. (1994) *Trust, Ethnicity, and Identity: Beyond the New Institutional Economics of Ethnic Trading Networks, Contract Law, and Gift-Exchange*. Ann Arbor: Michigan University Press.

Leijonhufvud, A. (2011) 'Nature of an Economy', *CEPR Policy Insights*, 53.

Lin, N. (2001) *Social Capital: A Theory of Social Structure and Action*. Cambridge: Cambridge University Press.

Marsden, P. V. (2011) 'Survey Methods for Network Data', in Scott, J. and Carrington, P. (eds.) *The Sage Handbook of Social Network Analysis*. Los Angeles: Sage, pp. 370–388. DOI: 10.4135/9781446294413.N25.

McNeill, J. R. and McNeill, W. H. (2003) *The Human Web: A Bird's-Eye View of World History*. New York and London: Norton.

Munz, P. (1993) *Philosophical Darwinism: On the Origin of Knowledge by Means of Natural Selection*. London and New York: Routledge.

Newman, M. E. J. (2010) *Networks: An Introduction*. Oxford: Oxford University Press.

Nooteboom, B. (2002) *Trust: Forms, Foundations, Functions, Failures and Figures*. Cheltenham and Northampton: Edward Elgar.

Nooteboom, B. (2006) 'Simmel's Treatise on the Triad (1908)', *Journal of Institutional Economics*, 2(3), pp. 365–383. DOI: 10.1017/S1744137406000452.

North, D. C. (1990) *Institutions, Institutional Change, and Economic Performance*. Cambridge: Cambridge University Press. DOI: 10.1017/cbo9780511808678.

Özer, Ö., Zheng, Y. and Ren, Y. (2014) 'Trust, Trustworthiness, and Information Sharing in Supply Chains Bridging China and the United States', *Management Science*, 60(10), pp. 2435–2460. DOI: 10.1287/mnsc.2014.1905.

Platteau, J.-P. (1994) 'Behind the Market Stage Where Real Societies Exist – Part I: The Role of Public and Private Order Institutions', *Journal of Development Studies*, 30(3), pp. 533–577. DOI: 10.1080/00220389408422328; 'Behind the Market Stage Where Real Societies Exist - Part II: The Role of Moral Norms', *Journal of Development Studies*, 30(4), pp. 753–817. DOI: 10.1080/00220389408422338.

Plott, C. R. and Smith, V. L. (2008) 'Markets', in Plott, C. R. and Smith, V. L. (eds.) *Handbook of Experimental Economics Results*, Vol. 1. Amsterdam: North – Holland.

Podolny, J. M. (2005) *Status Signals: A Sociological Study of Market Competition*. Princeton and Oxford: Princeton University Press.

Polanyi, K. (2001[1944]) *The Great Transformation: The Political and Economic Origins of Our Time*. Boston: Beacon Press.

Potts, J. (2000) *The New Evolutionary Microeconomics: Complexity, Competence and Adaptive Behavior*. Cheltenham and Northampton: Edward Elgar Publishing.

Putnam, R. (2000) *Bowling Alone: The Collapse and Revival of American Community*. New York: Simon & Schuster.

Raafat, R. M., Chate, N. and Frith, C. (2009) 'Herding in Humans', *Trends in Cognitive Sciences*, 13(10), pp. 420–428. DOI: 10.1016/j.tics.2009.08.002.

Rankin, D. J. and Taborsky, M. (2009) 'Assortment and the Evolution of Generalized Reciprocity', *Evolution*, 63(7), pp. 1913–1922. DOI: 10.1111/j.1558-5646.2009.00656.x.

Rauch, J. E. (2001) 'Business and Social Networks in International Trade', *Journal of Economic Literature*, 39(4), pp. 1177–1203. DOI: 10.1257/jel.39.4.1177.

Schelling, T. C. (1978) *Micromotives and Macrobehavior*. New York and London: Norton.

Schmitt, N. and Westerhoff, F. (2017) 'Herding Behaviour and Volatility Clustering in Financial Markets', *Quantitative Finance*, 17(8), pp. 1187–1203. DOI: 10.1080/14697688.2016.1267391.

Scott, J. and Carrington, P. (eds.) (2011) *The Sage Handbook of Social Network Analysis*. Los Angeles: Sage.

Skyrms, B. (2010) *Signals: Evolution, Learning, & Information*. Oxford: Oxford University Press.

Smil, V. (2019) *Growth: From Microorganisms to Megacities*. Cambridge: The MIT Press.

Soda, G. and Zaheer, A. (2012) 'A Network Perspective on Organizational Architecture: Performance Effects of the Interplay of Formal and Informal Organization', *Strategic Management Journal*, 33(6), pp. 751–771. DOI: 10.1002/SMJ.1966.

Solow, R. M. (2000) 'Notes on Social Capital and Economic Performance', in Dasgupta, P. and Serageldin, I. (eds.) *Social Capital: A Multifaceted Perspective*. Washington: World Bank, pp. 6–10.

Spence, M. (1974) *Market Signaling: Informational Transfer in Hiring and Related Screening Processes*. Cambridge: Harvard University Press.

Tooby, J. and Cosmides, L. (2005) 'Conceptual Foundations of Evolutionary Psychology', in Buss, D. M. (ed.) *The Handbook of Evolutionary Psychology*. Hoboken: Wiley, pp. 5–67. DOI: 10.1002/9780470939376.CH1.

Trivers, R. (1985) *Social Evolution*. Menlo Park: Benjamin/Cummings.

Watts, D. (1999) *Small Worlds: The Dynamics of Networks Between Order and Randomness*. Princeton: Princeton University Press.

White, H. (1981) 'Where Do Markets Come From?' *American Journal of Sociology*, 87(3), pp. 517–547.

White, H. (2002) *Markets from Networks: Socioeconomic Models of Production*. Princeton: Princeton University Press.

Wolfram, S. (2002) *A New Kind of Science*. Champaign: Wolfram Media.

CHAPTER NINE

Institutions

1. Introduction

See Chapter 4,
section 4.2,
and Chapter 8,
section 3.3.

Institutions are key to understanding cultural evolution. Institutions are the defining feature of making humans ultra-social; it is institutions that enable and maintain extremely complex and diversified cooperative specialisation via the formation of networks that today have achieved global scale. On markets, institutions are crucial for defining economic agency, agential powers, and the mediation of transactions.

The term 'institution' covers both the rules of interaction and resulting stable patterns of interaction. We distinguish between institutions and institutionalised behaviour.

In analysing institutions, we need to distinguish clearly between the behavioural patterns as such and the generating forces.[1] Both elements are included in the term 'institution', which has resulted in different definitions of institutions: One class of definitions focuses on patterns of regularity in the behaviour of agents, another on institutions as rules governing this behaviour. Our term 'institution' covers both meanings but recognises their fundamental difference. We suggest the term 'institutionalised behaviour' as equilibrium phenomena in group behaviour, whereas the term 'institution' refers to the generating forces.[2] We treat 'institution' as an umbrella term that covers various generating forms:[3]

Fundamental types of institutions are conventions, social norms, informal institutions, and formal institutions, which differ in terms of enforcement mechanisms.

- *Conventions* are self-enforcing social practices. External enforcement is not necessary because the pay-off structure incentivises even self-interested agents to follow the convention. A game-theoretic reference is the Coordination Game.
- *Social norms* are value-driven expressions of identity that are additionally enforced by mutual sanctions in a group, such as moral aggression against norm violators. The game-theoretic reference is the battle of the sexes and the stag hunt.
- *Informal institutions* are practices that are not necessarily value-based but enforced by mutual sanctions in a group that also involve status-based

DOI: 10.4324/9781003094869-13

third-party enforcement. In game theory, this is another reference of the stag hunt but especially the prisoner's dilemma.

- *Formal institutions* are practices that are enforced by specialised third-party organisations and are written down in authoritative documents. The game-theoretic frame is the prisoner's dilemma.

The chapter proceeds as follows. In section 2, we explain the following of institutions by certain properties of the human social brain. Section 3 extends the view to the performative mechanisms of institutions that establish causal loops between institutions as external facts and institutionalised behaviour. Section 4 introduces a core economic concept in the analysis of institutions, namely transaction cost and the cost of establishing and maintaining institutions; both are essential for understanding the evolution of institutions but cannot fully explain it causally. For achieving this, in section 5, we connect the analysis of institutions with the phenomenon of power and violence, and in concluding, discuss the question how we can evaluate institutions.

The various types of institutions refer to archetypical forms of strategic interaction as analysed in Chapter 5, section 3.1.

2. Following an institution

The standard economic theory of institutions focuses on incentives. However, incentives are not physically neutral causal impacts (third-person view), as assumed in standard theory, but mediated by perceptions and interpretations (first- and second-person view). Full consideration of this distinction is necessary to explain the individual following of institutions, that is, the emergence and stability of institutionalised behaviour. Institutions gain their force via both cognitive and emotional factors that involve the social and predictive brain.[4]

On the social and predictive brain, see Chapter 7, section 3.1.

2.1. Cognitive mechanisms of institutionalisation

Humans have the cognitive capability to discover and employ regularities in social interactions. One universal principle in cognitive psychology is the Gestalt principle, namely the completion of fragmentary perceptions of larger patterns, such as recognising an object while just seeing parts of it.[5] This also applies for behaviour through time such that we tend to extrapolate fragmented information about an unfolding behaviour to a familiar pattern. Gestalt expectations coalesce into framing effects: Given some cues on the situation, agents will frame it according to a well-known pattern. Cues may be systematically prearranged in the environment and, hence, are materially embodied.

The role of embodied cues has been highlighted in game-theoretic analyses of salience and correlated equilibria: Since most social interactions are

An important cognitive driver of regularising behaviour is the Gestalt perception of behavioural patterns triggered by embodied cues of social roles.

217

exceedingly complex and may involve multiple equilibria as outcomes, cues can drive equilibrium selection in a substantial way.[6] Cues often constitute indicators for roles that individuals will assume in an interaction, such as ways of dressing or body language. They might match with certain indicators in the environment, such as the location and its architectural features. Institutions depend on material representations for triggering affordances of action via individual cognitive mechanisms.[7] This is different from both internalisation (such as automatically driving on the right hand in Germany) and incentivisation (fees punishing wrong parking).

We introduced framing in Chapter 2, section 6. For more on framing, see Chapter 10, section 3.3.

In terms of cognitive mechanisms, the Gestalt principle works as a form of rules-based induction. But there is also the possibility that, for example, the type of an agent is directly indicated by full assignment to a certain role and social position. In terms of cognitive mechanism, this is the operation of metaphor: Someone is treated as somebody; something is treated as something else.[8] Social roles are assigned via explicit metaphorical transformations: By dressing as a judge and taking a specific seat in a room, the individual assumes a full range of behavioural standards and triggers corresponding expectations about the role of a judge. Framing is a most universal form of metaphorical transfer of meaning that can affect entire settings of behaviour and their perception.

Institutions minimise surprise via the abductive formation of behavioural expectations.

Finally, individuals also have the capacity for rules-based predictions, which activates the cognitive mechanism of abduction, building on a hypothesis: Individuals observe behavioural phenomena in their environment, and they form hypotheses that best explain them as a regularity.[9] If the expectation aka hypothesis is refuted, that is a surprise which instigates further hypothesis formation. Institutions embody the minimisation of surprises, thus causally involving capacities of the predictive brain.[10] Institutions correspond to hypotheses maintained by individuals to predict future behaviour in their social context (Figure 9.1).

Institutionalisation proceeds via interlocking sequences of actions, outcomes, and expectations.

In the real world, the three types of cognitive operations work together in the formation of behavioural expectations and how expectations are coordinated across agents (Figure 9.1).[11] Institutionalisation can be conceived as a circular closure of mutually enhancing cognitive operations that relate expectations with outcomes of actions. There are various possible patterns. We start out from considering an action that produces an outcome, which triggers an inductive Gestalt formation, such as when comparing the outcome with earlier outcomes or via a metaphorical operation. The next action is based on the transformed prediction, and the outcome may now trigger an abductive process (for example, there might be surprising deviation from expectations that motivates search for hypotheses). After rounds of hypothesis testing, the result is a categorisation of action types and contexts, which we approach as institutionalisation; but as there is always variance in outcomes, the entire range of cognitive operations remains important to stabilise the institution.

We discuss specific ways expectations form in Chapter 13, section 4.

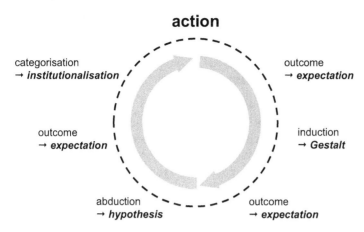

action

categorisation
→ *institutionalisation*

outcome
→ *expectation*

outcome
→ *expectation*

induction
→ *Gestalt*

abduction
→ *hypothesis*

outcome
→ *expectation*

Figure 9.1 Interlocking cognitive mechanisms of institutionalisation
Institutionalisation can be conceived as the circular and self-reinforcing closure of interlocking cognitive mechanisms. Action outcomes trigger inductive generalisations as Gestalt formations which enable the generation of hypotheses by means of abduction. Hypotheses guide choices of actions. Once hypotheses are confirmed, they result in categorisation as the cognitive complement of institutionalisation.

Consider, for example, the case of corruption, which can undermine a wide range of formal institutions simultaneously.[12] Corruption is itself an institutionalised behaviour; for example, individuals may know that in order to get an import license, they must bribe an official, and even rates may be public knowledge. Corruption is deviating from formal institutions whereas the institutionalised behaviour related to it can be interpreted as an informal institution. An individual may meet a corrupt tax officer for the first time, resulting in a surprise when a cue is produced that indicates an expectation of a bribe. The individual may pay and now believe that this particular tax officer is corrupt, thus immediately offering a payment next time. Subsequently, a mechanism of inductive learning may coalesce into a Gestalt, which after further recurrent interactions will condense into a general hypothesis that all tax officers are corrupt. Once such a regularity is abductively established, all parties will interact in maintaining institutionalised corruption. The institutionalisation of corruption can be explained by the interplay of all three types of cognitive operations.

This explains the phenomenon of hysteresis in institutional evolution: Once the formal tax code is undermined by rampant corruption, it is difficult to restore its binding powers.[13] Typically, anti-corruption initiatives only work as big push concerted actions and not gradually: The formal institutions must be undergirded by strong punishments; a new and independent anti-corruption

Corruption can be approached as a form of socially undesirable institutionalisation, mainly as an informal institution, with strong hysteresis.

219

agency must be established. Corruption remains an institutionalised feature in most of economic systems across the globe.[14]

2.2. Institutions and emotions

The institution of property is emotionally grounded, as manifest in the endowment effect.

Biologically rooted emotions undergird core institutions of the economy. Examples are emotional mechanisms connected to possession and property, which can be traced back to the universal phenomenon of territoriality.[15] In animals, territoriality combines with peculiar behavioural patterns, in particular, distinct regulations of aggression and ritual displays of dominance. This is the biological root of the so-called endowment effect: Humans value a good much higher if they possess it and, correspondingly, reveal a strong aversion against loss.[16] The endowment effect is an essential emotional anchor for stabilising the institution of property since it leads everyone to expect that there is an asymmetry in the willingness to spend effort in acquiring goods possessed by others.

On social exclusion, see Chapter 8, section 3.3.

Emotions are an important determinant of the following of institutions. This is particularly clear with respect to social norms, as these activate mechanisms of identity such as moral aggression against deviant behaviour. For example, if a country has a strong culture of civil servant discipline and loyalty, corrupt tax officers may face the moral outrage of colleagues. Similarly, if citizens are imbued by public spirit, they may not treat tax avoidance as a minor offense and shun fellow citizens who practice it. This is the mainstay of republican thinking about institutions: Institutions must be undergirded not only by rational consent but also by emotional commitments of citizens.[17]

An important example of the interaction between emotions and institutions is the sustainability of authoritarian systems, mediated by authoritarian values.

The interplay between social norms and formal institutions has a major emotional component. One example is the interaction between authoritarian values and authoritarian institutions.[18] Authoritarian values may be enshrined in many social practices, such as patriarchal conceptions of the family, the use of physical punishment in education, and strict regulation of sexual behaviour outside marriage. At the same time, authoritarian political institutions may sustain authoritarian values in society. Notably, this includes the possibility that similar performances in cooperation are achieved in different institutional regimes if there is a match between values and institutions.[19] This may be a major reason why markets appear to be compatible with different political systems, despite many liberal economists normatively claiming a necessary combination of markets and political freedom.

On trust and social capital, see Chapter 8, section 3.2.

An important example for the role of emotions in following an institution is trust. The nature and performance of institutions in a society is shaped by the distribution of social capital.[20] Even in the case of a unitary set of formal institutions or of convergence across countries, the underlying diverse values may cause differences in outcomes: Examples include divergent regional development in Italy,[21] differences in political systems in North and South

America despite the diffusion of shared constitutional models,[22] and political polarisation in the United States, where political stances towards emotionally loaded issues such as abortion systematically correlate with institutional preferences over issues such as taxation.[23]

An important mediator between emotions and institutions is ritual: Many institutions combine with certain ritual actions and are literally performed, such as a wedding ritual or courtroom proceedings.[24] Rituals often explicitly connect domains, such as singing the national anthem at a major sports event, thus associating the emotions triggered by the event with other contexts, such as pride for the nation. By means of such ritual connections, emotional stances are transferred across domains, such as the spirit of cooperation in sports to the domain of citizenship and service to the nation. Rituals regulate a certain form of externalised non-functional behaviour which causes emotional states that sustain institutionalised behaviour.

Ritual is an important mediator between emotions and institutions.

3. Performing institutions

3.1. Performative mechanisms in two dimensions

A central concept in institutional analysis is performativity.[25] In a basic sense, performativity means that institutions cannot be separated from the identity of the agents – a focus that stands in contrast to the externalised, incentives-based view of standard economic theory. A simple example for institutional performativity is a soccer player who has internalised the rules of the game such that following the rules of the game essentially *means* to be a soccer player.[26] If that is the case, the need for external supervision and sanctions is clearly much reduced: Soccer players are simply those people who, in the average, play the game in the way the rules define it. How do actors assume that property? Many economic roles are shaped by a process of self-selection and education. For example, not everyone aspires to become a CEO, and not everyone enrols in an MBA program. Only a limited subset of individuals starts this developmental track and eventually ends up as a certain type of agent, which is publicly visible, for example, in having the MBA degree, attending a golf club, and wearing a business outfit.

In other words, institutional selection enhances and scaffolds the heterogeneity of agents. At the same time, heterogeneity is regularised in terms of categorial identities or institutionalised social roles. In general terms, this relates to the distinction between capabilities and functionings, with the latter denoting institutionally defined social roles. Individuals with similar capabilities may realise different functionings particularly in the case of social stereotyping of functionings, which affects the identity of agents.[27]

One important example stems from gender research referring to the low share of women in top executive positions in the economy: The stereotyping

Performativity results in the formation of types of agents relating to institutional contexts.

We introduced the notion of performativity in Chapter 2, section 3.2, and Chapter 7, section 4.3.

On heterogeneity and dimensions of inequality, see Chapter 15, section 2.

Stereotyping of functionings is an important medium of performing types of agents, such as in gender discrimination.

The Aoki model is our key conceptual frame for understanding money in Chapter 10, section 2.1, and introducing the notion of market states in Chapter 11, section 4.2.

The Aoki model dissects the various causal factors in the emergence and stabilisation of institutions in the behavioural and the cognitive dimension, and on the individual and the population level.

of functionings in top executive positions still tends to be male-oriented. This creates conflicts with female identity, often resulting in the implicit adoption of the stereotype by women, which can lead to their self-selection into careers that do not lead to top executive positions or low levels of self-confidence in situations under stress, such as in job interviews.[28] This interaction between functionings, stereotypes, and capabilities is a performative mechanism, which results in patterns of gender discrimination that may attain the strength of informal institutions.

In order to understand performativity, it is necessary to develop a general model of a performative mechanism. In the context of institutions, we present a framework that builds on a game theoretic model of institutions suggested by Aoki (Figure 9.2).[29] Our framework approaches an institution in terms of its constitutive mechanisms, like an engine consisting of many different parts that realise different physical mechanisms. We perceive the mechanism as a circular process, as depicted in Figure 9.2.

We distinguish between two aspects of mechanism: One is the individual versus the population (i.e., the interactions); the other is the behavioural versus the cognitive. Furthermore, we distinguish constitutive mechanisms

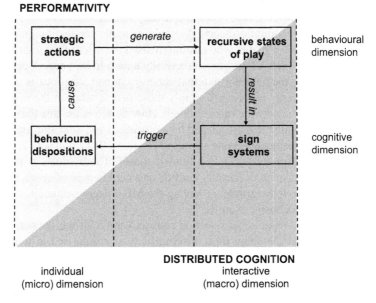

Figure 9.2 The Aoki model of institution (after Aoki)

The diagram shows a circular process of performing institutions with cognitive functions, where the latter undergird the performative generation of behavioural equilibria on the population level. For more detail, see main text.

of institutions that are either external or internal to the individual. The external mechanisms include the interactions among individuals in a population, which can be analysed with standard models of game theory (recursive states of play, upper right), and the embodied cues of institutions, which are public representations (Aoki's term), or more generally, signs (lower right). The internal mechanisms include the cognitive and emotional mechanisms that we analysed in the previous section. The two aspects connect in a propensity to act, namely a behavioural disposition (lower left), which results in institutionalised behaviour, that is, the strategic actions (upper left). Institutions never impact deterministically on behaviour but create propensities on the individual level. Thus, institutionalised behaviour entails a stochastic element, resulting in a population-level probability distribution of the behaviour which is, in turn, determined by all individual propensities. This is important for explaining frequency-dependent institutional change: A minor trigger may drive many people to more extreme poles of their individual distribution of behaviour, resulting in a strong shift of the population-level distribution.[30] On the population level, we can now apply game theoretic thinking to understand mechanisms that result in a population-level equilibrium of institutionalisation, that is, recurrent states of play with regard to manifest behaviour.

This equilibrium, in turn, includes the production of signs or public representations that embody the institutionalised behaviour. Individuals may not, and need not, have full information about equilibria and their generating forces and can just respond to the signs, cues, and embodied forms of institutions in adapting their behaviour. This is called information compression; the performative loop is thus closed.

Taking a core institution of markets, property, as an example, the formal institution is embedded in a broad range of mechanisms that reach beyond mere legal enforcement. Behavioural dispositions are grounded in the endowment effect, as mentioned in the previous section, as well as individual value stances, such as the recognition of certain expressions of inequality, as anchored in meritocratic attitudes. This level ties up with the population level via individual expectations of sanctions for deviant behaviour. There are informal sanctions resulting from social norms of respecting ownership and based on concomitant trust. The formal institution refers to the signs of property, such as land deeds, and is enforced by the threat of violence, triggering propensities by sign systems, such as fences or "no trespassing" plaques. The translation from behavioural propensities to actual (strategic) behaviour entails a stochastic element. Behavioural variation may have many sources, reaching from mere ignorance or erroneous perception to a fully rational cost-benefit calculus with respect to deviant behaviour. The recurrent states of play that will emerge, and eventually stabilise, on the population level, will realistically always include a certain share of deviant behaviour, whether sanctioned or not.

Frequency dependency is analysed in Chapter 8, section 3.4.

Institutions have the important function of information compression.

The institution of property emerges as recurrent state of play in the Aoki model, where references to formal institutions assume the role of signs.

The Aoki model can be framed in the general VSR model.

The VSR model is introduced in Chapter 4, section 3.

Path dependency of institutional evolution results from the interplay of frequency-dependent and cognitive-emotional mechanisms.

For network effects in the context of technological evolution, see Chapter 6, section 3.3.

Path dependency implies that mere change of formal institutions by political intervention may not affect institutionalised behaviour.

The Aoki model can be framed in the general evolutionary logic of the VSR mechanism, laying the ground for a general evolutionary theory of institutions.[31] Behavioural dispositions include variation, which is then subject to selection on the population level, such as in the form of sanctions or via the workings of frequency-dependent mechanisms. The generation of signs assumes the general function of retention, similar to encoding biological information in genetic endowments. For example, formal institutions enshrined in legal texts are societal repositories of past knowledge accumulating in the context of practicing the institution of property in society.

3.2. Path dependency of institutional evolution

One consequence of performativity is that institutional evolution is strongly path dependent. This implies that it is not possible to reduce the current status of institutions to a context-independent cost-benefit calculus on the individual level.[32] One cause is critical mass effects, as implicit in our analysis of corruption: Individual behaviour adapts to the observed frequency of behaviour in a population, which might be different from the factual frequency.

Another important effect is network externalities that we have already encountered in the context of technological evolution and that are particularly familiar from communication technologies. Institutions work as standardising interfaces in social interaction and their smooth functioning requires expectations of the interaction parties to converge: For example, the corrupt tax officer sends a cue, but the other side does not interpret it correctly because she does not expect to meet a corrupt officer. That may result in transaction failure, viewed from both sides. The tax officer does not obtain the bribe but now applies the tax regulations in a very strict manner which may in turn enhance incentives to bribe – and therefore, ultimately strengthen the informal institution.

Path dependency also results from cognitive mechanisms of institutions as scrutinised in section 2.1. For example, the citizen may understand the cues of the corrupt officer, as they are widely used, and maintains the expectation that almost all tax officers are corrupt. If the three types of mechanisms that we identified in section 3.1. interact, they determine a path of institutional evolution which is self-sustaining in the sense that individuals may not be able to switch to another path. Even radical reforms may not succeed, as they would only affect formal institutions but not the real institutions that result from the confluence of all forces. This argument is well known from the analysis of path dependencies in technological change, referring to the lock-in of less-than-optimal technologies.[33]

One of the most important general consequences of performativity is the impact of institutions on the balance between individual and social preferences and, hence, the degree of cooperation in society and the market.[34] In this case, the causal relationship between the institution and the identity of the agent is most visible. Consider the diffusion of corporate governance concepts which include heavy reliance on pecuniary incentives in recent decades. These concepts were mainly motivated by research in new institutional economics, which builds on common economic concepts of rationality and self-interested action.[35] Performativity implies that via the adoption of institutions, such as certain managerial compensation systems, the institution shifts the distribution of types of agents which become more similar to the assumptions of the theory. If this happens, empirical observations will confirm the theory, thus further supporting the case for this peculiar institutional design.[36]

There are various mechanisms that drive the emergence of such form of performativity. Besides self-selection of types of agents, there are population-level processes of equilibrium selection.[37] The institution also constitutes a signal indicating that presumably most agents in the population belong to a certain type – for example, in the business context, the expectation that other actors are businesspeople who are especially prone to adopting self-interested and opportunistic behaviour (which can be further accentuated by performativity of economics and management sciences postulating such types of motivation). Accordingly, reasonable individuals will tend to adopt matching behaviour which is not only beneficial to them but also minimises coordination failure. On markets more generally, however, types of agents can differ depending on the specific institutional arrangements in sectors, industries, or domains of action, such as domestic versus international. In recent decades, many institutional changes have converged on fostering a type of financial agent who focuses on the financial aspects of market transactions, thereby decontextualising economic behaviour in terms of accepted practices (such as extending financial accounting to health care).[38]

An important general conclusion from the analysis of path dependency, analogously to the point of individual cost-benefit analysis mentioned before, is the impossibility to define a decontextualised measure institutional efficiency that would allow to compare different states of the economy through time or different economies simultaneously across space (for more on that, see next section).[39] For example, for a long time, economists have argued that the enclosure of the agricultural commons was efficient in raising the productivity of agriculture and in undergirding industrialisation. However, we know by today that many commons were highly productive, especially when considering ecological aspects and externalities.[40] The enclosure, supported by new economic ideas about property and market organisation, was an element of a successful path-dependent institutional regime, the transition to which cannot be explained by a context-free measure of efficiency. Rather, the crucial factors were shifts in agential power and interests in the context of newly emerging forms of capitalist market economy.

Performativity grounds in various mechanisms, such as self-selection and signalling, and may result in the concentration of self-interested and opportunistic agents in the market context.

In Chapter 12, section 3.1, we develop a typology of savers and investors.

Path dependency implies that the measure of efficiency of institutions is endogenous and an institutional phenomenon of its own.

4. The cost of institutions

4.1. The basic setup

A core aspect of institutional variety and its connection to path dependency is the cost of institutions. We distinguish two basic categories:

- The first is the cost of transactions as governed by institutions, which we refer to as a key element of economic transaction cost.[41]
- The second is the cost of creating and maintaining (formal but also informal) institutions, which we refer to as political transaction cost.[42]

Importantly, these costs are endogenous to the institutions and, therefore, cannot be projected on a decontextualised measure of costs. Institutions and transactions are inextricably enmeshed, as we cannot posit a state of the world where transactions could be conducted free of institutions. Therefore, institutions both reduce and generate costs, and it is costly to reduce the cost of transactions itself. Further, when considering a certain institution, the cost of enforcing that institution is determined by other institutions: Hence, a principle of holism applies, which means that we cannot directly compare costs on the level of single institutions. This is well known from experience with transferring institutions across different societies: What is practicable in one society may prove to be messy in another and produce unexpected side effects there.[43]

Costs on different levels determine the evolution of institutions in a complex top-down and bottom-up causal interdependence.

In Figure 9.3 we outline a general framework for the analysis of different levels of costs of institutions. In the political dimension, we add the level of constitution.

In a natural state, as envisaged by social contract theories, transactions are imagined to be institution-free, necessitating a hypothetical constitutional stage where people agree on creating institutions. In this stage, there is direct feedback between transactions and the constitutional level which is, however, rare in practice, such as in truly revolutionary situations that are accompanied by the eruption of social chaos. The direct link between institutions and transactions runs via economic transaction costs. As we will discuss, one core hypothesis in institutional economics is that transaction costs feed back on institutional evolution, as agents strive to economise on them, and thereby may induce institutional change.[44] Political transaction costs include all costs of creating, maintaining, and enforcing institutions. They are at least partly determined on the constitutional level, or, broadly speaking, by the political system, understood in a broad sense of including informal institutions (compare, for example, Putinism as a complex of formal and informal institutions determining the power structure around the Russian president).[45]

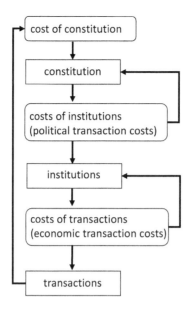

Figure 9.3 Costs of transactions and institutions
Institutions govern transactions and determine their costs. In turn, establishing
and sustaining institutions is costly. These costs relate to institutional change,
which is governed on the constitutional level, where processes also involve
costs.

We will analyse the different levels in a bottom-up fashion, that is, starting
with economic transaction costs, then proceeding to political transaction costs
and the constitutional level. In each part, we will look at basic features of the
respective category first and then relate it to institutional evolution.

4.2. Economic transaction costs

Economic transaction costs are the costs of preparing, enacting, and monitoring a market transaction ex post, given its governance by a specific institution
which manifests itself in the agreement that underlies the transaction.[46] As a
reminder, our evolutionary concept of institution is very broad and includes,
for example, social norms governing the use of language in arranging transactions, such as the general expectation that people tell the truth.[47] A significant
element of economic transaction cost is the cost of information, which directly
relate to the network dimensions outlined in the previous chapter, in particular, the dimension of observation.

*On markets,
transaction costs
combine ex ante and
ex post costs (i.e.,
preparing, enacting,
monitoring,
and enforcing a
transaction that
is governed by a
specific institution).*

The main driver of economic transaction cost is uncertainty. We can distinguish an ex ante and ex post perspective, involving screening the marketplace (ex ante), negotiating over a deal, and having possible conflicts arising from the enforcement of mutual obligations. As well, there are operational costs in conducting and monitoring a transaction. There are various ways to address these costs. For example, sellers may build reputation over time, and buyers may develop the habit to always buy with their favourite seller. If reputation is anchored in certain accepted norms of the market community, it may relate to an informal institution (for example, if the seller cheats, this might trigger ostracism by other sellers).[48]

A general economic hypothesis is that institutions evolve along the gradients of transaction costs.

A general economic hypothesis about institutional evolution is its tendency to minimise economic transaction cost. This hypothesis requires knowledge of the causal link between institutions and economic transaction cost on which a cost-efficient institutional choice could then be based. A typical example is the privatisation of state-owned industries: Economists generally argue that state-ownership goes along with high costs of monitoring and the implementation of economic transactions and recommend privatisation as the more efficient institution.[49]

However, since transaction costs are multidimensional, there is the problem of aggregating over various factors. Most importantly, there is a trade-off between ex ante and ex post transaction costs. In principle, we can minimise ex post transaction costs if we formulate complete contracts that are straightforward to enforce. However, this requires a considerable investment in ex ante transaction costs. An optimal contract would define a minimum of the aggregate costs, but there is the problem that the ex post cost is unknown.[50] Therefore, trust matters much since trust suggests lower ex post costs and, therefore, also allows for less investment in contracting, even doing without any contract.

Since institutions also determine patterns of externalisation, individual cost-benefit choices cannot necessarily lead to institutions that minimise total transaction cost.

A related perspective on institutional evolution and economic transaction cost is the character of institutions as means of internalising costs of economic decisions. Individuals will consider the costs of the transactions that they realise under a certain institution; at the same time, this institution determines which costs are included in their calculus in the first place, implying that some costs are externalised to other agents. The crucial question then is which (subset of) costs determine institutional evolution.

See our case study on the Chinese market economy, Chapter 1, section 4, and our discussion of externalities in Chapter 5, section 4.

Let us discuss this with the example of an institution that many historians regard to be a core institution of modern capitalism, limited liability.[51] Limited liability is explicitly designed as an externalisation mechanism (i.e., allocating costs of risk-taking partially to society).[52] At the same time, limited liability is mostly explained in terms of reducing economic transaction costs. Most significantly, entrepreneurs could limit their cost of gaining information about transaction partners, market potentials, and other factors since their losses are limited. This is seen as fostering innovation and growth and would count as a positive externality. However, limited liability also creates moral hazard in risk-taking.

Therefore, at first glance, limited liability can be seen as a confirmation of the hypothesis that economic transaction costs are minimised, but this happens via a partial externalisation of other costs. The key implication is that we cannot refer to transaction costs as a commensurable and objectified measure of the costs of institutions from a third-person view and establish this as a standard in the second-person view. Yet this does not mean that costs of institutions do not matter causally: What is perceived as costs in the second-person view drives institutional choices and the institutionalisation of behaviour. This implies that institutions diverge in adapting to context, time, and place, as mediated by human action contextualised by perceived costs and benefits.

Costs are causal drivers of institutional evolution, but there is no third-person concept of cost efficiency.

4.3. Political transaction costs

As said, political transaction costs are the costs of creating and maintaining institutions. There is a wide range of relevant costs, such as the cost of analysing and understanding alternative institutions, the cost of negotiating and agreeing about institutions, and the cost of installing and enforcing an institution. This involves complex interactions between various types of institutions, such as formal institutions of government and informal institutions of elite politics.

We add much detail to our analysis in the evolutionary theory of politics expounded in Chapter 17.

The cost of analysing and understanding alternative institutions is often neglected in economics but of substantial significance. In real-world societies, it is a major factor explaining that a significant part of institutional innovation is driven by imitation: While we have stressed path dependence as a major reason for institutional variety; at the same time, institutional evolution can be shaped by mutual observation and judgement that eventually results into institutional imitation.[53] Importantly, this presupposes a hypothesis about the causal relationship between institution and performance, which may even include the proper identification of the institution. There have been radical and far-reaching examples for institutional transfers, such as the Russian modernisation program under Catherine the Great and the adoption of many capitalist institutions by China after 1978. However, even today, we have only contested knowledge about the causal link to performance: For example, although patent regimes have seen convergence over the last decades, it continues to be unclear whether and how patents decisively shape and drive innovation in economic growth.[54]

Since information about the institution-performance link is limited, imitation often determines the choice of institutions, sometimes even on the societal scale.

A discussion of institutional competition between states-jurisdictions is provided in Chapter 17, section 2.5.

As on the level of economic transaction cost, therefore, the general conclusion is that a third-person view on political transaction cost cannot be defined and the causal driver of institutional evolution is perceived cost, such as exemplified earlier. At the same time, however, the efficiency of institutions may, to a certain extent, be objectified by institutional competition as a special case of group selection. Empirically, we often observe that economic agents would migrate towards, and invest in, institutional settings where both economic transaction cost and political transaction cost, such as mediated by the tax burden, are low. The ensuing possibility of a race to the bottom is an example for the potential interest of economic agents to externalise transaction cost.

Institutional evolution is driven by the perceived cost of institutions as well as institutional competition.

Another category of political transaction cost is the cost of negotiating and agreeing on institutions. On first sight, these are the costs of government, but of course, the costs of influencing government must be included. This relates to the well-established theory of rent-seeking in economics which starts out from the observation that all institutions allocate costs and benefits among agents simply because they constrain action for some and enable actions for others and that this triggers actions aiming at minimising and shifting these costs onto others.[55]

The transfer of formal institutions requires the existence of complementary informal institutions and social norms.

The costs of running an institution are basically the costs of governing. Think of a speed limit on highways: There are costs of keeping the police on watch and costs of litigation. The example shows that technology can have huge impact, such as automatic speed controls that connect with software-generated sending of tickets to violators. However, costs of government mainly refer to the enforcement of formal institutions. As we have seen, formal institutions may be undergirded or impeded by other forces of institutionalisation. Often, governing formal institutions can be supported by informal institutions, such as when compliance to intellectual property laws is supported by industry associations. Consider the transfer of institutions between countries of different levels of development: For example, the establishment of a modern system of patents requires the matching social attitudes towards respecting intellectual property and a sufficient supply of educated professionals, such as patent lawyers. If these complementary institutions are weak, transplanting the standard of patents of advanced industrialised nations may be prone to failure and even counterproductive because it triggers political tensions and waste of scarce administrative resources that could be better employed elsewhere.[56]

Connections between economic and political transaction costs are complex.

As a final observation, there is no necessary connection between the levels of economic and political transaction costs. In fact, modern legal systems are very costly in terms of maintaining the government bureaucracy, the court system, and so forth. Economists commonly assume that these costs are outweighed by the gains in lowering economic transaction cost. However, there are also the costs of influencing the government (i.e., the rent-seeking costs). Hence, the verdict is not evident: Systems that apparently contribute to efficiency in terms of lowering economic transaction cost may at the same time go together with high cost of the political production of these institutions.[57] Much depends on complementary forces, as the example of tax morale showed, where social norms and values may determine which formal institutions are more efficient.

4.4. Political transaction costs on the constitutional level and the social contract

There is a long tradition in economics and philosophy to approach institutions in contractarian terms, essentially taking a rationalist approach to institutions.[58]

The contractarian approach is ahistorical in essence, in the sense that institutions are analysed in terms of hypothetical situations in which all individuals deliberate and discuss institutions and eventually agree to establish them, including the binding commitment to accept sanctions against deviations. This approach is mostly normative, as it takes voluntary agreement as a benchmark. However, there are also many examples where such social contracts were factually concluded, such as when parliaments adopt new laws or settler communities create covenants for local governance. Once these contracts come into existence, subsequently, individuals do not have the opportunity to renegotiate but may just be free to join or not (voice versus exit[59]). This is not true for most legal regimes in the world where citizenship by birth automatically implies law enforcement without consent. Emigration is the only way to choose institutions, apart from political activism changing them. Therefore, the pure contractarian view is mostly normative: Would individuals have agreed to the current laws, if they enjoyed the opportunity for negotiating them again?[60]

The social contract is a fictitious frame of reference in which a hypothetical consent on institutions is analytically scrutinised.

See our discussion of freedom and the Pareto principle in Chapter 3, section 2.

The contractarian approach ties up with the cost of institutions approach insofar as the same problems are pertinent, that is, collecting, judging, and preparing opinions about alternative social contracts; negotiating and implementing the social contract; and monitoring observance by all parties: These are political transaction costs on the constitutional level. In principle, the resulting complexities can partly be resolved via the institution of voting because in this case, individual preferences and information are indirectly pooled such that voting compresses all the relevant information.[61] However, this only applies in case of unanimous acceptance: All kinds of majority voting imply that the chosen institution is imposed on the minority without consent. Only universal consent indicates that the institution is Pareto-efficient without further considering informational details. However, since achieving unanimous consent is costly, majority voting may save costs of decision making, which could also be in the interest of the minority if all parties bear the burden of the cost of negotiation. There are other ways to arrange acquiescence of minorities with majority decisions, such as various compensations offered to minorities.

The political transaction costs of concluding and enforcing a social contract are influenced by a variety of factors, such as the cost of organising divergent interest groups.

The imposition of results of majority voting on a minority constitutes a negative externality in the sense of Chapter 5, section 4.

However, the cost of political contracting also involves the cost of organising the interests that are involved in an institutional choice, collecting the pertinent information, and communicating the positions. A celebrated result of institutional analysis in economics is the insight that relative size of groups and related structural factors, such as spatial proximity of group members, are crucial determinants of the relative cost of organising a group (the so-called Olson hypothesis).[62] For example, a small group that is spatially concentrated can organise much more easily than a large group that is dispersed. In addition, absolute and aggregate costs and benefits of institutions have different individual impact, depending on group size. This implies that an institution may negatively affect a large group but with small average impact on the individuals, and positively affect a small group, hence, with large individual impact. Accordingly, the small group may effectively organise because individual incentives are strong, and the large group may not even expend the costs of information about the negative impact (so-called rational ignorance[63]) such that, eventually, it is the minority that dominates the voting result.

More detailed analysis on the organisation of interests is provided in Chapter 17, section 3.

Therefore, the normative application of the contractarian approach does not resolve the problem of indeterminacy in real-world scenarios of institutional choice (unless everyone would factually follow the model, hence rendering it performative). Similar to the results of the previous section, we cannot assume that institutional evolution follows an objectively determined trajectory of costs and benefits balanced over all concerned parties. But we also have reasons to give less analytical weight to the cost of social contracting since many institutions are mainly enforced and even imposed by force.

From a contractarian perspective as well, institutional choice remains indeterminate.

5. Power and institutions

On agential power, see Chapter 7, section 4.1.

In this section, we look at the relationship between power and institutions. As we clarified in earlier chapters, we use a concept of power that is grounded in a general notion of agential power, which is not inherently political in the sense of necessarily relating to government. Markets are defined by specific forms of agential power, such as constituted by property rights or freedom of contract. Market-based agential power can, but does not necessarily have to, spill over to the political realm; for example, monopolistic power can remain market-based but also assume influence on political decisions and, therefore, the evolution of formal institutions.

5.1. Institutions and endogenous agential power

A most important institutional form of agential power in markets is property rights.

Institutions involve power in two ways. First, they assign and allocate agential power to individuals, and second, asymmetry of power is necessary for making sanctions work that enforce institutions. The first perspective is most visible in some of the core institutions in the economy, property and ownership.[64] Ownership rights assign exclusive agential power over certain assets to specific individuals or groups, thus creating agential power in a double meaning: On the one hand, individuals achieve autonomy in deciding about how they use their rights, and on the other hand, they can rely on sanctioning mechanisms that protect their rights against interference from others, fore-mostly the third-party enforcement of formal institutions (i.e., government and law). However, this is often costly such that relying on other sanctioning mechanisms may dominate.[65] For example, misbehaviour among business-people may be governed by social norms in business communities and con-cerns for reputation. As a next step, individuals may rely on arbitration by insiders, which is partly informal, partly formal. Only if the conflict escalates, individuals may seek recourse with the courts.

Clear assignments of agential powers are of crucial significance for the operations of markets. Most generally, this can be analysed in terms of trans-action costs since diffused agential powers may cause tensions and conflicts in all stages of transactions. For example, institutions of corporate governance regulate agential powers of various parties engaged in a corporation, such as shareholders and management. But even if ownership is unequivocally defined, this does not determine only one and optimal distributional outcome of transactions. The Coase theorem cuts the link between initial allocation of rights and final allocation achieved via exchange, provided that transaction costs are zero. But if transaction costs are not zero, this is no longer true. This means that the initial allocation of agential powers matters crucially and that the Coase theorem is only interesting as a negative result, leaving much lee-way for real-world institutional trajectories.[66]

On the Coase theorem, see Chapter 5, section 4.

Indeed, a crucial question about agential powers is how far they go along with imposing involuntary actions on others. It is important noticing that net-work dynamics and institutions may not necessarily work in a fully congruent and unequivocal way: Often, institutions leave much leeway in determining the factual distribution of agential power. Agential power simply means that another individual cannot just impose her will, which works only via exchange. But there is the possibility that exchange is partly enforced by the other per-son. The classical example is monopolistic power: Both sides may have equal agential power as defined by formal institutions, but in fact, one side has no alternative choices so that the other side can impose non-reciprocal exchange. We have already analysed in detail that capacity specificity is a major factor in determining this relationship: The party with the higher degree of specificity will always have fewer choices and may, therefore, be forced to accept less beneficial conditions of exchange. Accordingly, aside from institutions, agen-tial power is always co-conditioned on the structure of networks and the prop-erties of the specialisation pattern and the original allocation of assets and related agential powers.

See Chapter 5, section 2.2.

The distribution of agential power is partly determined by institutions, but also by endogenous network dynamics.

5.2. Institutions and violence

We now turn to the second aspect of power and institutions, which is the fact that enforcement often means to contain deviant action by means of violence. This points to a fundamental issue in the economic theory of institutions, in

On specialisation on violence, see Chapter 5, section 3.2.

*The form of
institutionalising
violence has strong
impact on economic
institutions.*

*The presence
of the military
in institutional
development can
give rise to limited
access orders.*

*For incumbents
of political power,
power trumps
efficiency, yet
under certain
constellations, this
may include market-
friendly policies.*

particular as far as markets are concerned. Institutions are the major means to regulate and pacify endemic violent conflict over the allocation of resources. Violence breeds violence such that regulations of any kind, even if going along with some efficiency losses, may imply a gain for society.[67]

The enforcement of institutions implies the use of violence against deviators, at least in the sense of a threat that is realistic. To be realistic, this presupposes a capacity for violent action that is unequally distributed in a society because, otherwise, a deviant individual may just resort to counterviolence. In other words, institutionalisation always goes hand in hand with societal conflicts over the use of violence. Specialisation on the use of violence may guarantee the enforcement of institutions by the specialists, but at the same time, the specialists may shape institutions to their own benefit. Therefore, the socio-political institutionalisation of violence (military, taxation, police, etc.) has a deep impact on economic institutions.[68]

Remaining on an abstract level of analysis, the interest of specialists in biasing institutions is directly triggered by two connected motives. The first is that violent capacities require resources, and the second is that this need is leveraged in arms races both with internal challengers to incumbents of power, including those groups who suffer from institutional bias, and external challengers (i.e., competing groups). In a most general sense, this means that economic institutions are deeply shaped by the mechanisms of resource extraction that maintain the capacity for the use of violence in society and against external enemies. This capacity is mostly concentrated with certain groups in society, namely specialists in violence.[69]

This partly explains why the military is a powerful political force behind the screen in many countries and why its containment is a major achievement in modern liberal democracies. In fact, in many countries, this can only be achieved by giving the military access to vast economic assets, thus paying the military off by special rents. This is an important example of how the transactional level directly influences the constitutional level: Many countries of this type may have even perfectly democratic formal institutions, but still, politics is under the dark shadow of the military.[70] Such regimes are forms of so-called limited access orders because the economy is deeply divided into an elite stratum and the general population lacks access to essential political and economic assets.[71]

For the incumbents of positions of power, it does not matter in the first place whether institutions are efficient but whether they stabilise the current allocation of power and contain violence so that they can protect their appropriation of benefits. Efficiency only comes into play if benefits for the incumbents are enlarged and their power position is stabilised. This may be explained, in specific historical cases, by imitation of institutions under other regimes, which appear to be accompanied by larger economic gains that could be reaped by elites. Therefore, powerful elites may be in favour of free markets because competition limits the accumulation of power in the economy and contributes to enhanced productivity and, hence, growth of surplus that can be appropriated by the elites. There are many cases where this includes authoritarian systems in which colluding elites could even protect the economic system from arbitrary interventions to safeguard its productive potential, such as in authoritarian Asian countries which experienced rapid economic growth after WWII (e.g., Korea and Taiwan).[72]

5.3. Evaluating institutions

There are two alternatives of evaluating institutions. The first is transcendental institutionalism which argues from the vantage point of theoretically identifying the best institutional regime: This is the third-person view. The second is to inquire into the effects of the regime for concerned parties, which is realisation-focused comparisons: This is the second-person view.[73]

The first alternative is often represented by economics, which also enables its critical potential since institutions are judged independently from the current distributions of interests in society. One simple example is the tariff: The free-trade theorem, based on comparative advantage, implies that tariffs entail efficiency losses for society, with few exceptions, but certainly for the world in total. That allows to judge any step towards lowering tariffs as an improvement. But the problem is that there are always losers and winners from lowering tariffs, and therefore, in the real world, they will exert influence on the political design of institutions, which consumes resources. That means, a full economic judgement must include the costs of institutions and the degree of externalisation. As we have seen, a third-person point of view is impossible to define in this case.[74]

In principle, we distinguish two forms of evaluating institutions, transcendental institutionalism versus realisation-focused comparisons.

Therefore, the only viable and empirically operational way to judge institutions is realisation-focused comparisons. However, as our discussion of political transaction costs and contracting has shown, we cannot simply assume that real-word politics will generate a standard that comes close to an objective representation of all concerned interests since the formation of interests is endogenous and may leave out interests that are relevant but cannot find expression for whatever reasons.

Considering these difficulties, the only way to judge institutions is judging the procedure of how they come into being, how they are changed, and how they are maintained. If we maintain the normative standard of freedom and voluntary exchange, this means that we must judge how far the political systems enables participation of concerned parties, especially minority positions. However, political discrimination and elite formation in a society matters much. In many cases, we can clearly identify structures that contain and even suppress the voice of parties which are obviously concerned. For example, poor farmers in developing countries may have no voice, whereas in other countries, farmers may have disproportionate impact on policymaking.[75] We cannot explore these issues here in more detail, but we can state some general

Realisation-focused comparisons cannot establish an objective standard for evaluating institutions since inclusiveness of affected groups is endogenous.

principles. When judging institutional change in terms of realisation-focused comparisons, we must consider the following, among many other aspects:

- whether there is a bias in expressing one's voice on policies and discrimination against certain affected groups;
- whether there are explicit measures to give voice to concerned parties, beginning with offering opportunities to express concern in the first place;
- whether potentially concerned parties have the social and human capital to collect and judge information about policies, and to which extent this is supported by public policies;
- whether the provision and processing of information about policies is free and supported by the political process;
- whether there are transparent and accountable ways to process voice in the political decisions;
- whether there are feedback mechanisms after policy implementation.

In a nutshell, this means to ask whether the general principles of liberal and democratic politics apply in the single case. This cannot be taken for granted even in liberal democracies, as is evident in the complaints about elitism and lack of transparency. A case in point is the debates about trade policies which, for decades, have been mostly conducted as external diplomacy, thus explicitly referring important decisions to the domain of confidential government activities.[76] Accordingly, trade policy reforms should not only be judged from the viewpoint of how institutions affect trade but also how these institutions come into being and how they are evaluated. From the latter perspective, the current institutional setup of trade policy does not allow for a balanced and transparent process of evaluating institutions.

As said, however, we cannot simply assume that real-world politics achieves an adequate evaluation of institutions since this can only be attained from the position of impartiality. Whereas transcendental institutionalism assumes that there is a third-person external view on institutions, realisation-focused comparisons must refer to impartiality as an endogenous third-person view, which is not objective in the scientific sense but which would be potentially agreeable to all parties. This is where the economist enters the scene, and economics can offer beacons for guiding the public debate towards a position of impartiality, even though economics, as we saw, cannot define a third-person view.

We further develop these arguments in Chapter 17, section 3.

We can formulate procedural criteria to which extent a process of realisation-focused comparisons is inclusive.

For more, see Chapter 18.

Realisation-focused comparisons can refer to an impartial viewpoint ideally represented by economics.

6. Conclusion

Institutions and networks together constitute markets in terms of the structuring of transactions via the distribution of agential powers and the decisions of agents to specialise and engage in exchange. However, we have also repeatedly seen that technology is a force that impacts on the forms of embodying markets. Economics commonly emphasises production technology and new consumer products. But as we saw, for example, insofar as technology also affects enforcement mechanisms, technological change also affects institutional evolution, in the narrow sense (such as changing institutions governing fisheries if monitoring technologies change) and the wider sense (such as military technology impacting on the historical transition from feudalism to capitalism).

In emphasising costs of institutions, in the past, economists tended to marginalise the role of enforcement and, ultimately, violence and the threat of it in their explanations of institutional evolution. This artificially separates the market domain from other social domains, where social and political power loom large, and is one reason why economists often claim to achieve analytical perspectives which are less loaded with value statements. However, once we systematically include the perspective on enforcement and power, we recognise, for example, that distributional consequences of markets are not exclusively determined by forces of efficiency and economic performance.

One deeper reason for this apparent separation between economic, social, and political domains is that one key institution of markets, money, has performative powers that undergird such a constellation. Markets are defined by the use of money in transactions; money is the embodiment of value in economics. Therefore, studying money is crucial in further improving our understanding of institutions.

Major chapter insights

- The distinctive feature of the human niche in evolution is the capacity to create and follow institutions. Institutions integrate the individual level in terms of institutionalised behaviour and the level of the group, which also defines a separate process of group selection of institutions.
- We distinguish between various types of institutions: conventions, social norms, informal institutions, and formal institutions. Institutionalised behaviour is always shaped by interactions among these types, even though one type can be prominent.
- The emergence and stabilisation of institutions are grounded in various cognitive mechanisms that interlock in a circular enactment of institutions and result in the categorisation of institutionalised behaviour along types of agents. Cognitive mechanisms causally connect with embodied cues and signs in the environment.

- Emotional mechanisms undergird the conjunction of institutions and types of agents via grounding institutionalised behaviour in individual and group identity.
- Performativity links institutions and identities via specific mechanisms, such as social stereotyping. A full causal model is the Aoki model which analyses institutions in two dimensions (cognitive and behavioural) and on two levels (individual and population). The key mediator in performativity is the role of public signs that emerge endogenously as a constituent of the institution.
- Institutional evolution is strongly path dependent, which implies that measures of institutional efficiency are endogenous. This results from the complex interaction between the costs of transactions as determined by institutions and the political transaction costs of creating and maintaining institutions.
- Institutions shape the distribution of agential power in the market, most prominently in the form of property rights. But the eventual impact on institutionalised behaviour is always mediated by the endogenous forces in networks that create distributions of agential power. This must be distinguished from the analytical reconstruction of institutions as reflecting a hypothetical social contract, under the condition of political transaction costs of negotiating such a contract.
- The enforcement of institutions apart from pure conventions is ultimately determined by violent action. Therefore, social arrangements regulating violence between different groups impact on institutional evolution, as institutions determine the extent and forms in which rents can be appropriated by elites that control means of violence.
- There are two ways of evaluating institutions, transcendental institutionalism (often adopted in economics) and realisation-focused comparisons.

Notes

1 Aoki (2001, 26).
2 This distinction was introduced in Herrmann-Pillath (2013, 340ff).
3 This synthesises Elster (1989, 2015), North (1990), and Eggertsson (1990).
4 Cognitive factors have been emphasised by North (2005), see Greif and Mokyr (2017). The role of emotions is neglected in economics but has attracted much attention recently in organisation theory, see Zietsma et al. (2019).
5 Schlicht (1998).
6 Sugden (2011).

7 Aoki (2011).

8 Searle (1995).

9 Abduction is a cognitive mechanism introduced by Charles S. Peirce (see Douven 2021).

10 Friston (2010).

11 Herrmann-Pillath (2013, 358ff).

12 For a comprehensive survey, see Rose-Ackerman and Palifka (2016).

13 Schlicht (1998, 50f).

14 Rose-Ackerman and Palifka (2016) overview the policies that successfully contain corruption. On the global prevalence of corruption, see https://www.transparency.org/en/cpi/2020/index/nzl

15 Davies et al. (2012, 116ff), Bradshaw (2020, 45ff).

16 Thaler (2016, 12ff).

17 Taylor (1989) distinguishes the two traditions in modern thought, the rationalist enlightenment tradition and the romantic emphasis on emotions, which was combined in one philosophical framework in Hegel's conception of *Sittlichkeit*, "ethical life", grounded in his critique of Kant.

18 Herrmann et al. (2008).

19 Vollan et al. (2017).

20 For an exemplary study, see Rothstein and Stolle (2008).

21 The classical contribution is Putnam et al. (1994).

22 North (1990, 101ff).

23 On emotional groundings of political culture in the American South, see Nisbett and Cohen (1996).

24 Collins (2005), Zietsma et al. (2019).

25 Boldyrev and Svetlova (2016).

26 Searle (1995).

27 This is formalised in the economics of identity, Kranton (2016).

28 Bertrand (2020).

29 Aoki (2011), Herrmann-Pillath (2012).

30 Kuran (1995).

31 Hodgson (1999).

32 Kuran (1995).

33 Arthur (1989).

34 Bowles and Polania Reyes (2012).

35 Ghoshal (2005).

36 Herrmann-Pillath (2016).

37 Falk and Kosfeld (2006), Sliwka (2007).

38 Cohn et al. (2014).

39 Aoki (1996).

40 De Moor (2015).

41 North (1990).

42 Dixit (1996).

43 Zweynert (2011).

44 Eggertsson (1990).
45 Herrmann-Pillath (2018), Åslund (2019).
46 The classic is Williamson (1985).
47 This transpires when considering the pragmatics of communication, such as Grice's maxim of cooperation, Davis (2019).
48 Seminally, Milgrom et al. (1990).
49 Roland (2008) overviews the topic.
50 See, for example, Anderlini and Felli (1999).
51 Kuran (2012).
52 Pistor (2019).
53 Zweynert (2011).
54 Boldrin and Levine (2008).
55 Hillman (2013).
56 Yu (2011).
57 Seminally, Magee et al. (1989).
58 The classic is Buchanan and Tullock (1962). For a survey of the field of constitutional political economy, see Voigt (2020).
59 Hirschman (1970).
60 See the discussion in Voigt (1999).
61 Buchanan and Tullock (1962).
62 Seminally, Olson (1965).
63 Classically, Downs (1957).
64 Dagan (2021).
65 Ellikson (1991).
66 Kennedy (2013).
67 North et al. (2009).
68 See the collection of papers in North et al. (2013).
69 Mann (1986).
70 See the cases in North et al. (2013).
71 North et al. (2009).
72 The classical analysis is Amsden (1989).
73 Sen (2009).
74 For pertinent debates in the theory of tariffs, see the exemplary study by Rodrik (1986) or more recently Acharya (2018).
75 For rich empirical illustrations, see Anderson (2019).
76 Herrmann-Pillath (2019).

References

Acharya, R. C. (2018) 'Endogenous Trade Policy in General Equilibrium: An Interaction of Redistribution Rule, Trade Openness, and Labor Market Condition', *Economics & Politics*, 30(3), pp. 423–443. DOI: 10.1111/ecpo.12110.

Amsden, A. H. (1989) *Asia's Next Giant: South Korea and Late Industrialization.* New York: Oxford University Press.

Anderlini, L. and Felli, L. (1999) 'Incomplete Contracts and Complexity Costs', *Theory and Decision*, 46, pp. 23–50.

Anderson, K. (2019) *World Scientific Reference on Asia-Pacific Trade Policies, Volume 1: Political Economy of Agricultural Protection in East Asia*. Hackensack, NJ: World Scientific.

Aoki, M. (1996) 'An Evolutionary Parable of the Gains from International Organizational Diversity', in Landau, R., Taylor, T. and Wright, G. (eds.) *The Mosaic of Economic Growth*. Stanford: Stanford University Press, pp. 247–263.

Aoki, M. (2001) *Toward a Comparative Institutional Analysis*. Stanford: Stanford University Press.

Aoki, M. (2011) 'Institutions as Cognitive Media between Strategic Interactions and Individual Beliefs', *Journal of Economic Behavior and Organization*, 9, pp. 20–34. DOI: 10.1016/j.jebo.2011.01.025

Arthur, W. B. (1989) 'Competing Technologies, Increasing Returns and Lock-in by Historical Events', *Economic Journal*, 99(394), pp. 116–131. DOI: 10.2307/2234208.

Åslund, A. (2019) *Russia's Crony Capitalism: The Path from Market Economy to Kleptocracy*. New Haven: Yale University Press. DOI: 10.12987/9780300244861.

Bertrand, M. (2020) 'Gender in the Twenty-First Century', *AEA Papers and Proceedings*, 110, pp. 1–24. DOI: 10.1257/pandp.20201126.

Boldrin, M. and Levine, D. K. (2008) *Against Intellectual Monopoly*. Cambridge: Cambridge University Press. DOI: 10.1017/CBO9780511510854.

Boldyrev, I. and Svetlova, E. (2016) 'After the Turn: How the Performativity of Economics Matters', in Boldyrev, I. and Svetlova, E. (eds.) *Enacting Dismal Science: New Perspectives on the Performativity of Economics: Perspectives from Social Economics*. New York: Palgrave Macmillan, pp. 1–27. DOI: 10.1057/978-1-137-48876-3_1.

Bowles, S. and Polanía – Reyes, S. (2012) 'Economic Incentives and Social Preferences: Substitutes or Complements?' *Journal of Economic Literature*, 50(2), pp. 368–425. DOI: 10.1257/jel.50.2.368.

Bradshaw, K. (2020) *Wildlife as Property Owners: A New Conception of Animal Rights*. Chicago: University of Chicago Press. DOI: 10.7208/chicago/9780226571539.001.0001.

Buchanan, J. M. and Tullock, G. (1999[1962]) *The Calculus of Consent: Logical Foundations of Constitutional Democracy, the Collected Works of James M. Buchanan*, Vol. 3. Indianapolis: Liberty Fund.

Cohn, A., Fehr, E. and Maréchal, M. A. (2014) 'Business Culture and Dishonesty in the Banking Industry', *Nature*, 516. DOI: 10.1038/nature13977.

Collins, R. (2005) *Interaction Ritual Chains*. Princeton: Princeton University Press.

Dagan, Ḥ. (2021) *A Liberal Theory of Property*. Cambridge and New York: Cambridge University Press. DOI: 10.1017/9781108290340.

Davies, N. B., Krebs, J. R. and West, S. A. (2012) *An Introduction to Behavioural Ecology*. Oxford: Wiley-Blackwell. DOI: 10.1016/j.anbehav.2013.01.003.

Davis, W. (2019) 'Implicature', *The Stanford Encyclopedia of Philosophy*, Fall 2019 Edition. Available at: https://plato.stanford.edu/archives/fall2019/entries/implicature/ (Accessed 12 April 2022).

De Moor, T. (2015) *The Dilemma of the Commoners: Understanding the Use of Common-Pool Resources in Long-Term Perspective*. Cambridge: Cambridge University Press. DOI: 10.1017/CBO9781139135450.

Dixit, A. K. (1996) *The Making of Economic Policy: A Transaction-Cost Politics Perspective*. Cambridge: Cambridge University Press.

Douven, I. (2021) 'Abduction', *The Stanford Encyclopedia of Philosophy*, Summer 2021 Edition. Available at: https://plato.stanford.edu/entries/abduction/ (Accessed: 12 April 2022).

Downs, A. (1957) *An Economic Theory of Democracy*. New York: Harper & Row.

Eggertsson, T. (1990) *Economic Behavior and Institutions*. Cambridge: Cambridge University Press.

Ellikson, R. C. (1991) *Order without Law: How Neighbours Settle Disputes*. Cambridge: Harvard University Press.

Elster, J. (1989) *The Cement of Society: A Study of Social Order*. Cambridge: Cambridge University Press.

Elster, J. (2015) *Explaining Social Behavior: More Nuts and Bolts for the Social Sciences*. Revised Edition. Cambridge: Cambridge University Press. DOI: 10.1017/CBO9781107763111.

Falk, A. and Kosfeld, M. (2006) 'The Hidden Costs of Control', *American Economic Review*, 96(5), pp. 1611–1630. DOI: 10.1257/aer.96.5.1611.

Friston, K. (2010) 'The Free Energy Principle: A Unified Brain Theory', *Nature Reviews Neuroscience,* 11, pp. 127–138. DOI: 10.1038/nrn2787.

Ghoshal, S. (2005) 'Bad Management Theories Are Destroying Good Management Practices', *Academy of Management Learning & Education*, 4(1), pp. 75–91. DOI: 10.5465/AMLE.2005.16132558.

Greif, A. and Mokyr, J. (2017) 'Cognitive Rules, Institutions, and Economic Growth: Douglass North and Beyond', *Journal of Institutional Economics*, 13(1), pp. 25–52. DOI: 10.1017/S1744137416000370.

Herrmann, B. *et al.* (2008) 'Antisocial Punishment across Societies', *Science*, 319(5868), pp. 1362–1367. DOI: 10.1126/science.1153808.

Herrmann-Pillath, C. (2012) 'Towards an Externalist Neuroeconomics: Dual Selves, Signs, and Choice, *Journal of Neuroscience'*, *Psychology and Economics*, 5(1), pp. 38–61. DOI: 10.1037/A0026882.

Herrmann-Pillath, C. (2013) *Foundations of Economic Evolution: A Treatise on the Natural Philosophy of Economics*. Cheltenham and Northampton: Edward Elgar Publishing. DOI: 10.4337/9781782548362.

Herrmann-Pillath, C. (2016) *China's Economic Culture: The Ritual Order of State and Markets*. London: Routledge. DOI: 10.4324/9781315884653.

Herrmann-Pillath, C. (2018) 'Power, Ideas and Culture in the 'longue durée' of Institutional Evolution: Theory and Application on the Revolutions of Property

Rights in Russia', *Journal of Evolutionary Economics*, 29(5), pp. 1483–1506. DOI: 10.1007_s00191-019-00624-z.

Herrmann-Pillath, C. (2019) 'Ways out of the Globalization Trilemma: Deliberating Trade Policy', in Brousseau, E., Glachant, J.-M. and Sgard, J. (eds.) *Oxford Handbook on International Economic Governance and Market Regulation*. Oxford: Oxford University Press. Available at: https://www.oxfordhandbooks.com/view/10.1093/oxfordhb/9780190900571.001.0001/oxfordhb-9780190900571-e-14 (Accessed: 14 May 2022).

Hillman, A. (2013) 'Rent seeking', in Reksulak, M., Razzaloni, L. and Shughart II, W. F. (eds.) *The Elgar Companion to Public Choice*. 2nd Edition. Cheltenham and Northampton: Edward Elgar Publishing, pp. 307–330. DOI: 10.4337/9781849802857.00032.

Hirschman, A. O. (2004[1970]) *Exit, Voice, and Loyalty: Responses to Decline in Firms, Organizations, and States*. Cambridge: Harvard University Press.

Hodgson, G. M. (1999) *Evolution and Institutions: On Evolutionary Economics and the Evolution of Economics*. Cheltenham and Northampton: Edward Elgar Publishing.

Kennedy, D. (2013) 'Some Caution about Property Rights as a Recipe for Economic Development', in Kennedy, D. and Stiglitz, J. E. (eds.) *Law and Economics with Chinese Characteristics: Institutions for Promoting Development in the Twenty-First Century*. Oxford: Oxford University Press, pp.187–213. DOI: 10.1093/acprof:oso/9780199698547.003.0007.

Kranton, R. E. (2016) 'Identity Economics 2016: Where Do Social Distinctions and Norms Come From?' *American Economic Review*, 106(5), pp. 405–409. DOI: 10.1257/AER.P20161038.

Kuran, T. (1995) *Private Truths, Public Lies: The Social Consequences of Preference Falsification*. Cambridge and London: Harvard University Press.

Kuran, T. (2012) 'Political Consequences of Middle East's Islamic Economic Legacy', in Aoki, M., Kuran, T. and Roland, G. (eds.) *Institutions and Comparative Economic Development: International Economic Association Series*. London: Palgrave Macmillan, pp. 99–115. DOI: 10.1057/9781137034014_6.

Magee, S. P., Brock, W. A. and Young, L. (1989) *Black Hole Tariffs and Endogenous Policy Theory: Political Economy in General Equilibrium*. Cambridge: Cambridge University Press.

Mann, M. (1986) *The Sources of Social Power, Vol. I: A History of Power from the Beginning to A.D. 1760*. Cambridge: Cambridge University Press.

Milgrom, P. R., North, D. C. and Weingast, B. R. (1990) 'The Role of Institutions in the Revival of Trade: The Law Merchant, Private Judges, and the Champagne Fairs', *Economics and Politics*, 2(1), pp. 1–23.

Nisbett, R. E. and Cohen, D. (1996) *Culture of Honor: The Psychology of Violence in the South: New Directions in Social Psychology*. Boulder: Westview Press.

North, D. C. (1990) *Institutions, Institutional Change, and Economic Performance*. Cambridge: Cambridge University Press. DOI: 10.1017/cbo9780511808678.

North, D. C. (2005) *Understanding the Process of Economic Change*. Princeton and Oxford: Princeton University Press. DOI: 10.1515/9781400829484.

North, D. C., Wallis, J. J. and Weingast, B. R. (2009) *Violence and Social Orders: A Conceptual Framework for Interpreting Recorded Human History*. Cambridge: Cambridge University Press. DOI: 10.1017/CBO9780511575839.

North, D. C. *et al.* (eds.) (2013) *In the Shadow of Violence: Politics, Economics, and the Problem of Development*. Cambridge: Cambridge University Press. DOI: 10.1017/CBO9781139013611.

Olson, M. (2003[1965]) *The Logic of Collective Action: Public Goods and the Theory of Groups*. Cambridge: Harvard University Press.

Pistor, K. (2019) *The Code of Capital: How the Law Creates Wealth and Inequality*. Princeton: Princeton University Press. DOI: 10.1515/9780691189437.

Putnam, R. D. *et al.* (1994) *Making Democracy Work: Civic Traditions in Modern Italy*. Princeton: Princeton University Press.

Rodrik, D. (1986) 'Tariffs, Subsidies, and Welfare with Endogenous Policy', *Journal of International Economics*, 21(3–4), pp. 285–299. DOI: 10.1016/0022-1996(86)90041-3.

Roland, G. (ed.) (2008) *Privatization: Successes and Failures, Initiative for Policy Dialogue at Columbia*. New York: Columbia University Press.

Rose-Ackerman, S. and Palifka, B. J. (2016) *Corruption and Government: Causes, Consequences, and Reform, Second Edition*. New York: Cambridge University Press. DOI: 10.1017/CBO9781139962933.

Rothstein, B. and Stolle, D. (2008) 'The State and Social Capital: An Institutional Theory of Generalized Trust', *Comparative Politics*, 40(4), pp. 441–459. DOI: 10.5129/001041508X12911362383354.

Schlicht, E. (1998) *On Custom in the Economy*. Oxford: Clarendon.

Searle, J. R. (1995) *The Construction of Social Reality*. New York: Free Press.

Sen, A. (2009) *The Idea of Justice*. Cambridge: Belknap Press.

Sugden, R. (2011) 'Salience, Inductive Reasoning and the Emergence of Conventions', *Journal of Economic Behavior and Organization*, 79(1–2), pp. 35–47. DOI: 10.1016/j.jebo.2011.01.026.

Taylor, C. (1989) *Sources of the Self: The Making of Modern Identity*. Cambridge: Harvard University Press.

Thaler, Richard H. Misbehaving: The Making of Behavioural Economics. New York, London: W. W. Norton & Company, 2016.

Thaler, Richard H. Misbehaving: The Making of Behavioural Economics. New York, London: W. W. Norton & Company, 2016.

Voigt, S. (1999) *Explaining Constitutional Change: A Positive Economics Approach: New Thinking in Political Economy*. Cheltenham and Northampton: Edward Elgar Publishing.

Voigt, S. (2020) *Constitutional Economics: A Primer*. New York: Cambridge University Press. DOI: 10.1017/9781108764445.

Vollan, B. *et al.* (2017) 'Co-operation and Authoritarian Values: An Experimental Study in China', *European Economic Review*, 93, pp. 90–105. DOI: 10.1016/j.euroecorev.2017.01.007.

Williamson, O. (1985) *The Economic Institutions of Capitalism*. New York: The Free Press.

Yu, P. K. (2011) 'TRIPS Enforcement and Developing Countries', *American University International Law Review*, 26(3), pp. 727–782.

Zietsma, C. *et al.* (2019) *Emotions in Organization Theory*. Cambridge: Cambridge University Press. DOI: 10.1017/9781108628051.

Zweynert, J. (2011) 'Shock Therapy and the Transfer of Institutions: The New Debate and some Lessons from the post-1806 Reforms in Prussia and in South-western Germany', *Constitutional Political Economy*, 22, pp. 122–140. DOI: 10.1007/s10602-010-9095-3.

CHAPTER TEN

Money and value

1. Introduction

Money is the key institution in markets. Its use defines the scope of markets, apart from barter arrangements which still survive at the fringes of modern markets.[1] One of the most damaging misconceptions of general equilibrium theory in the 20th century was the assumption that in principle, markets could operate without money. In this perspective, money is conceived as a mere technology for implementing transactions; money is just a veil, and prices are defined in a strictly relative fashion, with the nominal price level determined by the quantity of money.[2]

Whereas economics mostly approaches money in mere technological terms, the morality of money has been a social concern since its invention.

The standard theory of money blanks out another important aspect that we tackle in this chapter: The history of money is also a history of moral debates over money.[3] This is entirely ignored in economics where money is approached as a mere technical device. The core question is whether money merely represents value, or whether it *has* value, and if the latter, whether it possibly overshadows other kinds of value. Given this, we must clearly distinguish between value in the sense of Chapter 3, where it is explicitly detached from economic contexts and is introduced as an exogenous frame of reference, and economic value as discussed in this chapter. Here, we develop a notion of economic value that explicitly recognises the diversity of values and analyses how markets create economic value as a category that combines the subjectivity of value and its framing in an objectifying medium (i.e., money).

The chapter proceeds as follows. In section 2, we first establish a general framework for the institutional analysis of money in terms of the Aoki model, highlighting the performative mechanisms that explain the emergence and stability of money. Second, we explore the role of a specific type of economic action, namely pricing or assigning money signs to objects which is constitutive for objectifying subjective value. We introduce the notion of arbitrage as relating prices, budgets, and exchange in a monetary economy. Section 3 unfolds the psychological and behavioural theory of money, which explains phenomena, such as the intrinsic value of money and the anchoring the money

246

DOI: 10.4324/9781003094869-14

institution in trust. This approach is essential for understanding why and how money objectifies subjective value. Objectification is analysed in section 4 where we relate money to the concept of economic rent in the standard view and explore Georg Simmel's idea that choice is an arbitrage process in which monetary valuation is involved. We complement these microeconomic aspects with a section that conceives of money as a form of social capital.

Our analysis of money continues in Chapter 12, where we will look at the more detailed institutions governing the production and use of money in society, often referred to as finance. To some extent, this division of chapters reflects the transition from a micro- to a macroeconomic perspective.

2. Performing money

In this section, we provide a map of the arguments presented in this chapter by applying the Aoki model of institution to the institution of money. To do this, it is necessary to distinguish between money as sign and the institution of money. The money sign takes various physical forms, such as coins, bills, and electronic entries on special accounts, and its handling is regulated by certain legal prescriptions. The institution of money is then constituted by the entire causal circuit depicted in the Aoki model. We distinguish between 'money' in the generic sense and 'money species', which refers to a specific kind of money, such as national currencies, and its physical manifestations (such as coins or electronic media).

> For the Aoki model, see Chapter 9, section 3.1.

We see the notion of price as key in highlighting the role of the money sign, that is, we approach prices as a monetary phenomenon. In the equilibrium view, absolute prices do not matter and only relative prices or scarcities are taken into account, which obliterates reference to the materiality of the price as a monetary sign.[4] The money sign is embodied in objects such as coins, and a specific action is pricing, that is, the assignment of a money sign to an object. Pricing impacts on the assessment of economic choices via their budgetary consequences: In our theory of money, the budget obtains a pivotal role in mediating effects of money on economic behaviour. This establishes the bridge between the microeconomic analysis and macroeconomics.

2.1. The institution of money

Money is a sign that relates to the agential powers of entering exchange relations with others (Figure 10.1). This sign is embedded in a complex system of institutions that governs its use across various domains, such as in accounting or government budgets. In the widest sense, we refer to this system as finance. Finance includes all institutions that govern the use of money in society, which comprises not only financial organisations in the narrow meaning, such

We employ a broad definition of 'finance' as the system of institutions that govern the use of money in society.

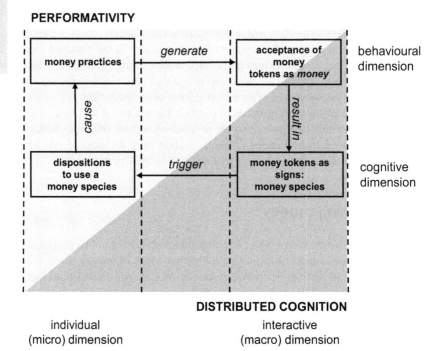

PERFORMATIVITY

Figure 10.1 Money in the Aoki model of institution
The figure is based on *Figure 9.2* and establishes a framework of various mechanisms that involve the material artefacts of money. The traditional functions of money as identified by economics relate to the cognitive functions. Behavioural and psychological aspects impact on the population-level mechanisms, where practices diffuse among market agents resulting in the universal acceptance of money as a medium of transactions. For more detail, see main text.

We develop the details on finance in Chapter 12.

In the Aoki model, network effects on the population level interact with cognitive and emotional determinants on the individual level.

as banks, but also, for example, accounting departments at companies. When a household head considers the family budget and plans expenses and savings, this is finance.

In the Aoki model, we assign the various processes of enacting the money institution to the outlined levels and dimensions of the model: individual (micro) versus interactional (macro) and behavioural versus cognitive. Thus, we include aspects of money that are rarely considered in economics, such as expressive uses of money in society. In all respects, population-level network effects of money use loom large.

For understanding the reproduction of the money institution, functional analysis is important. This ties our view back to the standard economic approach in distinguishing the common three functions of unit of account, medium of transaction, and store of value:

- As a *unit of account*, the money sign enables the quantification and comparison of values of objects, both in exchange and in stocks held by economic agents. The action of pricing assigns money signs to objects.
- As a *medium of transaction*, the money sign enables the intersubjective comparison of values of objects via prices and expands opportunities of exchange since it is universally accepted by both sides in an exchange relation.
- As a *store of value*, the money sign enables to desynchronise exchange relations even in the longer run.

These functions relate money with various uses agents make of money in interacting with each other: We refer to this as money practices, which, on the population level, result in institutionalised behaviour of individuals. Financial systems fix the special arrangements such that the equilibrium transactions may result into a diversification of the money sign, reflecting different money practices. In modern economies, this is partly grasped by different statistical measures of the quantity of money: For example, the function of storing value may be fulfilled by types of accounts with reduced fungibility (such as savings accounts), meaning that those accounts would first need to be changed into money in fully fungible forms (such as demand deposits) that allow for the function of a medium of transaction.[5]

In this sense, money is endogenous to the financial domain in the economy even if it is legally enacted by government fiat. This results from the functional forces that drive money practices: Economic agents may introduce new uses of money or even new forms of the money sign once they perceive the need to improve functional performance.

Money practices are driven by positive network externalities, analogously to communication media in general (the more a certain money species is used, the more people will also use it). Network externalities result in an evolutionary nature of the money institution, which is clearest when considering competition between different types of money (i.e., currencies). Today, this kind of competition mostly happens in the international domain, but in principle, it is possible under any circumstances, particularly in case of monetary innovation such as new digital currencies. Network externalities drive the use of a certain currency as unit of payment in international transactions: The more a certain currency is used, the lower the transaction cost, the more ample the opportunities of specialisation for the management of payments, and so on.

A fundamental element of money as an institution is trust. Trust in money is rooted in cognitive and emotional mechanisms pertaining to a disposition to use a certain money species in fulfilling the monetary functions. Vice versa, the money species in use embodies affordances of acting on money. We can refer to this as a somatic marker,[6] that is, a neurophysiologically anchored social preference for a certain money (lower-left corner of Figure 10.1) (for more on this, see section 3). This preference, in turn, creates a behavioural

The standard three functions of money (unit of account, medium of transaction, store of value) relate to the cognitive dimensions of the Aoki model.

Money practices endogenise the functions of money in society.

We explore the duality of private and sovereign money in Chapter 12, section 2.

On money in the international context, see Chapter 14, sections 2.3 and 4.3.

On network externalities, see Chapter 8, section 2.

Trust in money is a non-cognitive behavioural disposition.

We discuss trust
in Chapter 8,
section 3.4.

*Accounting and
assetification are
core performative
mechanisms in the
monetary economy.*

On assetification,
see Chapter 12,
sections 2.1 and 5.

bias, that is, a disposition to use a certain money species in exchange on the population level. This bias is the anchor for primordial trust into money, which is then bolstered by its functional performance.

However, the functions of money cannot explain why trust emerges in the first place and why money historically emerged and stabilised.[7] Mechanisms of trust are highly contextualised and relate to specific money species. The evolution of money manifests all phenomena that we highlighted in the analysis of network dynamics, in particular, path dependence (e.g., dominance of an international medium of payment) and hysteresis (e.g., hyperinflation with endemic instability of monetary reforms).

Based on the fundamental performative mechanism relating to trust in money, we can identify a range of other performative mechanisms that derive their performative power from the basis mechanism (lower-right corner of Figure 10.1). One of these mechanisms is accounting, which assigns monetary values to a certain good and, thereby, transforms it into an asset. Assetification is the precondition for creating a market for that good and conducting financial operations related to its value; one of the simplest forms is pawning that good at a pawnshop. The performativity of the money institution drives the expansion of money uses across social domains via the assetification of goods. In a monetary economy, monetary valuation is enacted by pricing an object and, thereby, enabling its exchange.

2.2. Money, prices, and arbitrage

*The act of pricing
transforms an object
into a tradable.*

In money practices, the core activity is pricing, that is, assigning a money sign to an object: This fundamental act transforms an object into a tradable or, in Marxist terms, a commodity.[8] Pricing is enabled by the institutional design of markets and specific pricing practices. There are various basic types, such as the following:

*There is a wide
range of pricing
practices and
institutional regimes
of pricing for
different categories
of goods.*

- Direct negotiating over prices. This type applies over a wide range of settings and products, such as the traditional bazaar and pricing bespoke arrangements (e.g., for tailoring and many other crafts).
- Price setting by suppliers with leaving demand to adapt. This type applies to most consumer goods.
- Auctions, which can be governed by a variety of alternative rules depending on the nature of the product.
- Exchanges of various kinds, such as for bulk resources ranging from agricultural products to oil and bourses in the financial sector.

*Pricing entails
substantial
informational
functions.*

These different regimes have implications for the way a market price is settled and becomes observable.[9] For example, bespoke arrangements mostly lack transparency; this can be remedied via a call for bids, which, however, are normally not visible for third parties. Public auctions are generally transparent but exhibit a high level of price uncertainty. Exchanges are defined outright via the public observability of prices, that is, in the second-person view. Even if prices are public, however, this does not mean that they are widely observable: There are many mechanisms that determine the degree of publicity, such as websites devoted to price comparisons.

A related issue is the question which information pricing conveys to the buyer. In the bazaar setting, the simplest form of price negotiation, both sides will aim at keeping information about their reservation price (willingness to pay) private in order to gain a maximum in rents, which grounds in their first-person view. In the case of public pricing of an object, the endowment effect implies that economic agents will tend to reveal divergent reservation prices depending on whether they are owners or buyers of an object: If they are owners, they systematically set a higher price. However, when individuals perceive themselves only as an intermittent owner of an object, which is true for most of arbitrage (see further section later), pricing will converge between the two roles of individuals. Therefore, valuation has two different sides, namely valuation in terms of the intrinsic value of an object that is owned and used, and valuation in terms of assignment of monetary value when the object is intended to be traded on the market.[10]

Another aspect of the informational function of pricing is the role of prices as indicator of hidden quality, such as most famously in the context of the lemons problem. For example, lowering a price can reveal information about self-assessed lower quality but also about a convergence to true cost (i.e., the reservation price). In all cases, information transmission by prices is driven by interpretations of receivers of price communication and, hence, multi-valent.

These considerations relate to another fundamental characteristic of pricing, namely that pricing decisions take place under radical uncertainty. This is because pricing is an inherently social and, often strategic, decision,[11] and the mutual dynamics of pricing choices of different agents can impossibly be foreseen. Against this background, pricing decisions by other agents are often a major benchmark to decide about own action, independent from accounting data.[12] There is also a distinct coordination problem that results from asymmetry of responses: Raising prices incentivises current customers to search for another alternative whereas lowering prices may not necessarily attract new customers. All this implies that prices realised at a certain point of time tend to be sticky since price changes tend to come at a cost that is difficult to predict.[13] Eventually, prices assume the status of social conventions, barring strong impacts of unanticipated events: There is a price of bread publicly considered as normal, but in the emergency of crop failure, everybody knows that prices will go up.[14]

In a production context, pricing decisions are strongly informed by accounting. If a producer follows strict principles of accounting, she might set prices according to costs, including a markup for profit. Markup pricing is a

The endowment effect creates a wedge between reservation prices for the same individual in the role of seller or buyer.

On the endowment effect, see Chapter 9, section 2.2.

See, for a depiction of the lemons problem in the context of social networks, Chapter 8, section 3.4.

Pricing decisions take place under radical uncertainty and often exhibit a strategic character in taking responses of competitors into consideration. This can result in price stickiness and a status of prices as social conventions.

widespread assumption in certain macroeconomic schools, such as post-Keynesian or stock-flow consistent modelling.[15] However, the assignment of costs to specific products can be difficult, and accounting costs only consider current costs. For example, price setting may deliberately aim at expanding sales, which in turn may impact on costs via increasing returns to scale or learning curve effects. Therefore, the role of accounting may be much less pronounced in a dynamic environment.

Arbitrage is profit-oriented exploitation of price differences. The law of one price establishes an objectified second-person view on economic value as market valuation.

If agents treat prices as givens and act as price takers, they may engage in the specific economic mechanism of arbitrage.[16] Arbitrage refers to actions of profit-seeking economic agents who exploit price differences between same goods at different points in time and space. The key effect is price equalisation, and the emergence of a unitary market price (law of one price). Therefore, whereas pricing is based on the first-person view in the first place, arbitrage generates the emergence of an objectified second-person view (see further section later).

We discuss costs of trade in much detail in Chapter 14, section 2.

The fact that arbitrage, as commonly conceived, refers to trade, both in spatial and in temporal terms, implies that the forces of price convergence depend on many other aspects that relate to the costs of trade and the technical tradability of goods.[17] Arbitrage not only works via the prices of the goods in question. In principle, competition over cost differentials constitutes arbitrage as well, as embodied in the accounting procedures: The cost-price is compared to the price obtainable on the market, and inputs are traded versus outputs.

The law of one price is performative as it also determines which goods are seen as being of the same quality and kind. Thus, pricing also performs the space of goods.

The validity of the law of one price crucially depends on the assumption that the good in question is of the same quality.[18] Therefore, the criterion of price convergence can be regarded as an indication that agents on the market approach the good in question as the same. In some markets, this is key for the information-generating function of prices, as already outlined for the lemons problem and related cases. For example, in markets for government bonds, the convergence of interest rates and bond prices is an indicator that market actors treat bonds of different countries as belonging to the same class of risks:[19] Prices are interpreted as indicators of quality. In this case, pricing becomes performative: A divergence of prices may trigger further selling of bonds, creating a self-reinforcing process that eventually moves bonds into different risk classes.

Pricing impacts on the valuation of stocks which are not transacted, depending on accounting conventions.

As a final point, pricing not only affects the value of the transacted good but also the value of stocks of goods, such as of inventories. Thus, pricing generates externalities, with the price settled in transactions also changing the value of stocks that are not being transacted. The concrete character of these externalities again depends on accounting conventions, particularly on the question whether the valuation of stocks is conducted in line with the historical cost of acquisition or production or with currently prevailing market prices. The pricing of stocks is essential for defining the category of wealth in monetary terms.

3. The psychology of money: Anchoring the performativity of monetary institutions

3.1. Agential power and the value of money

To understand money, its behavioural foundations need to be made explicit. Money is unique in being an acquired primary reinforcer:[20] There is no genetically determined valuation of money, yet neuroscience has shown that money activates the same reward mechanisms as genetic primary reinforcers such as food or sex. Indeed, from early times on, money has been experienced as being especially powerful in transforming human psychology.[21]

Money is an acquired primary reinforcer.

The special psychological role of money is evident in the phenomenon of money illusion, defined as fallacy to account for price-level-induced changes of the purchasing power of money.[22] In standard economics, money illusion is conceived as irrational because of its implication that agents fail to distinguish properly between nominal and real values: If people receive more money in nominal terms but prices adjust accordingly, they should not perceive a gain. However, this judgement depends on treating money as a mere transactional tool without intrinsic value. If money does have intrinsic value, perceiving an increase in nominal quantities with proportional price increases generates additional perceived benefit, which is vindicated by experimental data.[23]

Money illusion reflects the intrinsic value of money.

Money illusion implies that individuals assign intrinsic value to gaining money as distinct from using it for purchases of other valued goods. We suggest that this reflects the value of money as embodying the opportunity for social exchange, in the sense of being a good with lowest asset specificity and, hence, a widest range of possible transactions.[24] More specifically, the intrinsic value of money is embodied in somatic markers that relate to the human propensity to social exchange or somatic markers that value social capital (for more on that, see section 4.3). This type of reward from experiencing social exchange as such, rather than just the (material) result of the exchange itself, has early been recognised by Adam Smith in his notion of fellow feeling and has been vindicated in neuroeconomics research on social exchange and reciprocity.[25]

The valuation of money grounds in the value of generalised opportunities for social exchange.

On social capital, see Chapter 8, section 3.2.

Given its universal fungibility and use as a universal standard of value, money embodies freedom of choice and confers its owners with a generalised form of agential power. A key formal-institutional manifestation of this power is the concept of legal tender, that is, the legal obligation to accept money as a means of payment and debt cancellation. The latter is by no means universal:

On agential power, see Chapter 7, section 4.1.

For example, in many land rent arrangements in peasant societies, rent payments do not automatically nullify all other social obligations between the two sides.

In principle, money exhibits the lowest asset specificity compared to all other assets because it can be exchanged with all other goods and services. However, this property crucially depends on whether the supply of a good to be purchased by money is competitive and whether the good can be easily substituted. In a competitive market economy, this is routinely the case: The standard constellation of buyers' markets confers strong agential power to money owners. For example, consumers in their role as money holders often have stronger agential power than producers as sellers, whose goods, as a consequence of specialisation, exhibit a higher degree of asset specificity. On labour markets as well, buyers of labour services enjoy systematic advantages in agential power, given that the asset specificity of mobile financial assets is lower than that of labour services. In contrast, in a seller's market (e.g., in the monopoly case), the holding of money does not convey stronger agential power; in the extreme, money as such can become dysfunctional. This was the situation in many planning economies, given that the main criterion of access to goods was often planning orders rather than money holdings.[26]

This analysis shows the limits of purchasing power as the primary standard criterion of the value of money.[27] Purchasing power is an abstract construct by economists and statisticians that cannot directly be referred to the individual, apart from assigning individuals to certain group characteristics that correspond to types of consumption baskets.

Agential power has a clearly relational character, as it depends on the degree to which all other agents recognise the value of money. The valuation of money grounds in the shared recognition of money and, hence, constitutes an aspect of shared identity between individuals.[28] This results in an emotional loading of money as used in the group context and is a crucial factor in sustaining the performativity of money.

On the general concept of capacity specificity, see Chapter 5, section 2.2.

Money is a good with lowest asset specificity so that in a competitive market economy, owners of money enjoy an advantage in differential agential power.

The agential power embodied in money emanates from the shared recognition in a community.

3.2. Cognition and money emotions

The psychological dimensions of money have already been comprehensively analysed by the sociologist Georg Simmel, and many of his insights have been vindicated by recent psychological research.[29] We can distinguish between cognitive and emotional aspects, which must be seen in conjunction. Turning to the cognitive dimension first, new cognitive operations that are detached from the physical properties of goods become possible and allow for all operations that are feasible in natural numbers.[30] One important example is divisibility: A calf can be divided into many pieces, individuals may pool money to buy parts of a calf together, and they may later divide the profit from selling the cow based on the original division. Another operation is the addition of physically different items to a whole, such as of cows, tools, and land in assessing the value of a farm. Thus, money allows to form the abstract notion of wealth as an aggregate of many different types of goods.

Accordingly, one of the central institutional pillars of a monetary economy is accounting, as it emerged in earliest times in the context of the public economy of Sumer.[31] Accounting is the social practice that embodies cognitive functions of money and imposes a particular discipline on the way values are assigned to objects.[32]

Accounting is an essential institution in a monetary economy.

As supported by ample experimental evidence, money has strong framing effects.[33] On the most general level, money shifts the perception of a situation towards a transactional frame or frame of exchange, which can even dominate the perception in terms of hedonic or instrumental considerations.[34] One important example is the evaporation of the endowment effect: As we have already mentioned, if people perceive themselves as permanent owners, they have a higher reservation price than if acting as traders who engage in arbitrage; even though they are owners, they judge the good in terms of the price that can be obtained in exchange.[35] Another example is the fair price frame: here, the preference over alternatives is less influenced by their immediate hedonic value than by the perceived distribution of monetary gains.[36] Learning about different costs of goods can change the preference order on its own right, and agents may be willing to incur losses of hedonic benefit to realise what they classify as a fair exchange.

Money has strong framing effects making the transactional dimension more salient, de-emphasizing the dimension of preference satisfaction.

The cognitive effects of money always have emotional consequences as well, as in the case of the endowment effect. On a general level, the abstraction of assigning monetary values to goods implies a decontextualisation in terms of specific emotional linkages. We present three examples. The first is the treatment of gifts: I might assess a gift in terms of its monetary value and consider reselling; indeed, the gift-giver may anticipate this and send me money. In most societies of the world, however, this kind of behaviour tends to be seen as problematic and confined to specific settings, including the explicit ritualisation of pecuniary gift-giving.[37] The difference is that a gift expresses a mutual emotional commitment and, therefore, establishes a lasting relationship, whereas the act of market exchange is concluded by the payment.[38]

The money frame neutralises emotional context, such as in gift exchange.

The second example is blood donations, as famously analysed by Titmuss.[39] Here, money erodes commitments that root in the personal identity of individuals; blood is indeed experienced as immensely personal and, hence, should be transacted in a gift relationship rather than a market context. A third example comes from gender relations: With their growing intimacy and freedom in some Western societies, the explicit use of money in gender interactions became increasingly sensitive because of the blurred borderline to prostitution. Tellingly, in prostitution, conscious emphasis of pecuniary mediation partly protects the emotional sphere of the sex workers.[40] As a

Societies establish various institutional regimes governing emotional contextualisation of money, such as in gender and kinship.

consequence, money use in social relations is subject to institutional constraints and emotional regulation.

Further emotional effects of money include evidence that priming with money changes the feeling of pain[41] and reduces the willingness to cooperate not only in terms of helping others but also of asking for help. Accordingly, money-induced individualisation is not to be equated with the strengthening egoism, as getting help from others certainly serves self-interest.[42]

Different types of agents perform money differently, and money frames endogenise types.

Summing up, we cannot treat the psychological set up of agents independently from whether money is involved in the definition of a situation; money is not neutral in terms of being a mere technology of exchange. This is directly relevant for the distinction of economic types of agents. Business actors often deliberately define their role as partly autonomous vis-à-vis monetary valuations. For example, the owner of a family business might value her assets in terms of monetary opportunity cost, that is, approaching her business like a financial investment, but can also valuate it in terms of socio-emotional wealth, implying the sacrifice of monetary gains to keep the family business tradition intact.[43]

4. Money, arbitrage, and the objectivisation of subjective value

Since the marginalist revolution, economists have posited that economic value is not defined in monetary units but in subjective utilities. Utilities are conceived in a quantitative fashion but incommensurable across subjects. Prices do not reflect subjective utilities but market-based scarcity rather than individual valuations.

Although in economics, utilities are subjective values, the notion of economic rent allows to quantify an indirect measure in monetary terms and refers to the difference between market price and willingness to pay or reservation price.

However, economics does define a commensurable welfare measure tied to markets and money, namely economic rent.[44] The consumer rent, or more generally, economic rent on the buyer's side, is defined as the difference between willingness to pay and the actual market price; the producer rent, or more generally, economic rent on the seller's side, is defined as the difference between willingness to sell and the actual market price. Therefore, the notion of economic rent relates to market exchange and the observation that, in negotiating deals, agents may agree on a price that differs from the price that they would be still willing to accept. In other words, parties on both market sides set a reservation price, which defines the limit to their willingness to conclude a deal. For example, in price haggling on a bazaar, the two parties aim at keeping their reservation prices secret and try to find out where the limits lie. A buyer who would be able to get a lower price than she would be effectively willing to pay would gain something extra beyond the good itself, namely the economic rent. Taking into consideration markets with many agents on both

See Chapter 5, section 2.1.

sides, the same applies on a collective level and commonly defines the welfare gains of markets and specialisation.

Based on the concept of economic rent, in this section, we present a theory of market valuation as a price-based objectification of subjective values, that is, the function of modern markets to transform first-person views on valuations (subjective utility) into an objectified second-person view that renders valuations commensurable via the notions of pricing and willingness to pay. We will proceed in three steps: first, we analyse monetary valuation as a performative rationalisation of choice, with a strong (albeit not exclusive) focus on economic rent on the buyer's side. Second, we look at the sellers'/ producers' side, introducing the concept of entrepreneurial rent. Third, we analyse money as a form of social capital.

4.1. Objectification of value as performative rationalisation of choice

As mentioned, economic rent on the buyer's side (which, for reasons of simplicity, we will simply refer to as economic rent in this section) is defined as the difference between the willingness to pay and the actual market price, which can be interpreted as the benefit gained from giving up money and purchasing a good with the respective amount. This interpretation can be extended to the case where an agent already owns a good (good 1) and considers resale and usage of the monetary proceeds for the purchase of another good or bundle of goods (good 2), assuming negligible transaction cost. In this case, the price of good 1 can be interpreted as reflecting either the benefit that can be gained from reselling good 1 and using the proceeds for purchasing good 2, or alternatively, the benefit gained from holding good 1 and forgoing the benefits from purchasing good 2. Thus, the decision on resale entails a standard opportunity cost consideration: For example, assume that the economic rent from keeping good 1 (which, for consistency of exposition, can be conceptualised as a sale and subsequent repurchase of good 1 for the same price) is smaller than the economic rent from selling good 1 and using the proceeds to purchase good 2. In this case, there is an opportunity cost of holding good 1 vis-à-vis the alternative of purchasing good 2 in terms of economic rent forgone; therefore, good 1 will be sold. In the reverse constellation, it will be held. Thus, revealed preference with respect to the decision on resale is based on a comparison between economic rents, not a comparison between the absolute benefits of the two goods as conceptualised by subjective utilities.

With the rise of capitalism, monetary valuation of consumer goods diffused widely in society.

Historically, the aspect of resale loomed large for many goods that were not only seen as consumer goods but as a form of wealth (i.e., savings). For example, individuals bought valuable pocket watches or expensive cutlery that constituted a form of savings.[45] The core institution where goods could be exchanged against money while keeping property rights intact was the pawn-shop. The respective markets were highly imperfect but did reflect the intrusion of monetary valuation into the psychological process of individual goods valuation as a key characteristic of the emerging consumer culture. A visible transformation happened in the 19th century when social status was increasingly perceived in terms of financial wealth, the pursuit of which became a major driver of behaviour; for example, in the context of marriage.[46]

According to the revealed preference logic, paying the price for a good implies that at least the agent's reservation price is met and all other alternatives obtainable by money are less valuable. From the individual perspective, the price inheres a second-person view because it includes information on the valuation of the good by the other side. If prices become public, that is, are no longer assigned to specific interaction partners, the second-person view would become collective. In other words, prices are a medium through which subjective valuations are objectified in the sense of establishing a reference frame for first-person valuations.

We approach prices as mediating the objectivisation of subjective valuation.

This view is quite familiar to economists who employ cost-benefit analysis and other methods to learn about consumer valuation that is only implicit in observable behaviour, such as when considering goods with many properties that influence valuation simultaneously. There has been a development of complex methods, such as hedonic pricing, which aim at the assignment of prices to these properties as reflecting willingness to pay. A standard example is the valuation of real estate.[47] Take the case of valuing a beautiful panorama when assessing the price of a villa.[48] In the simplest case, we can assign a price to this panorama by considering the difference between the price of a villa with panorama and of a villa without it. Someone who is willing to sell her villa without panorama and use the proceeds to buy the villa with panorama – assuming that the villas are comparable in all other respects – would reveal her preference for the panorama by accepting a higher price.

Methods such as cost-benefit analysis imply that price differentials indicate relative economic rents as opportunity costs.

The opportunity cost in exchange is the differential between rents gained from the alternatives such that reservation prices indicate lower bounds for their subjective valuation.

As argued earlier, the opportunity cost of buying the other villa is neither the absolute amount of utility generated by the first villa nor its pecuniary value but the economic rent lost from holding (conceptually, selling and rebuying for the same price) the villa. Hence, the price differential refers to the differential of economic rents, and we can now assign a price to the panorama in terms of the specific gains in economic rent that it generates. Consider the owner of a villa with panorama who does not sell his villa to acquire a cheaper villa without panorama. From the revealed preference logic, we can infer that the benefit from this arbitrage over all other properties of the villa does not cover the loss in economic rent generated by the panorama forgone. Therefore, the price differential indicates the lowest bound for the monetary valuation of the gain (i.e., the difference in economic rent), which otherwise would remain fully subjective.

Taken together, we note two points. First, our argument does not refer to subjective utilities: We just argue that price differentials indicate relative gains in valuation, implying that they become commensurable across agents (second-person view). This is why techniques such as hedonic pricing can be used in designing marketing strategies that target consumers as groups. Second, the formation of preferences can itself take place via the process of comparing monetised alternatives: The homeowner learns about her valuation of the panorama by learning that he would not change to another villa at the prevailing price differential (ignoring the generic endowment effect).

Hence, we can employ the concept of arbitrage on consumer choices: Reselling a good is the cost of generating a surplus of economic rent by buying another good. Consumers, when buying a good, consider what other goods they might buy and which they give up in spending the money now. That means, following Simmel, we approach choice as an internalised arbitrage mechanism that is mediated by external economic valuation, that is, prices.[49] This type of choice is not universal: It is the frame in which we can define what rational behaviour means in economic terms. Rational behaviour in the economic sense is not a given property of an agent but only emerges in the context of markets and money as a medium of valuation. In simplest terms, rationality is tantamount to the internalisation of arbitrage on markets.

At this point, the famous parable of Lucky Hans is illuminating, which is one instance of the money pumps widely discussed in economics and philosophy.[50] As is well known, Lucky Hans barters down in a series of transactions eventually ending up with a worthless stone for a nugget of gold. The point of the parable is that Hans perceives a subjective gain at every single instance of exchange and retrospectively is happy about the process. Yet he experiences a severe financial loss, and a rational individual would have recognised in advance that upon arrival, the piece of gold could have been sold with great profit and had allowed for much greater gains. But this judgement rests upon the implicit assumption that a single exchange in the chain would only have been rational if Hans had made a monetary profit and that the entire chain is framed in one unified monetary accounting scheme, corresponding to the environment of an arbitrageur. In other words, the irrationality of Hans's behaviour only appears in the light of market valuation of goods as a standard of value in analysing Hans's behaviour rather than their subjective valuation.

As Alfred Marshall has argued,[51] money is a measure of subjective value not in terms of the content of the good but in terms of expressing the intensity of the desire for it. Simmel added the notion of opportunity cost and interpreted choice as exchange, in the sense that agents always must give up something else for achieving a certain good, creating a resistance to eventually choosing it.[52] Therefore, the subjective value assigned to a good is the surplus over that resistance.

Further, we must consider the budgetary constraint under which consumers articulate their demand. Then if an agent offers a certain amount of money for acquiring a good, this amount could also be used for other purposes. If the agent considered alternative goods and actions directly, she

This further substantiates our discission of rationality in Chapter 7, section 3.2.

The objectivisation of subjective value proceeds via the internalisation of arbitrage over a set of goods with different prices that produce satisfaction of wants.

In the fairy tale of Lucky Hans, he only appears irrational when we treat economic rent valued at price differentials as the standard of valuation.

would have to reflect upon many specific aspects of the benefits received and would likely have troubles in comparing them. If money is accepted as a generalised medium of exchange, spending money evokes a similar general notion of the value of all possible alternatives. The mediating quantity is price in monetary units: The agent may feel uncertain about the specific benefits of a good but at least knows its price, which creates a universalised notion of opportunity cost as resistance and a basis for the corresponding reflective process. I can start a reflective process in assessing what else I could buy for the price I have to pay for the current choice and only in the second step would start to consider the actual benefits. This is what could have been expected from Hans: At every instance of exchange, consider the price of the two goods and assess opportunity cost in monetary terms, thus objectifying his differential intensities of desiring the two goods. Following this, Hans would never exchange gold for a horse but sell the former to a trader and buy the latter from the proceeds, keeping the difference in cash.

Money rationalises choices under the condition of specialisation in the context of markets. This is mediated via the budget and considering opportunity costs as reflected in prices.

Thus, money is a rationalising force that objectifies opportunity cost, which is essential for enabling agents to act in a society with deep specialisation. In other words, money is a cognitive means to enable individual choices under the conditions of specialisation: Market exchange becomes the cognitive frame for individual choice as exchange among alternatives and is ultimately internalised as a universal mechanism of choice. There is strong evidence for this in experimental economics, which defines its difference to experimental psychology by the exclusive use of money as a pay-off to experimental subjects.[53] Monetary incentives are supposed to be strong enough to focus decisions of experimental subjects on the respective decision problem (i.e., act as a rationalising medium); and money would render decisions commensurable within and across subjects, objectifying valuation across experimental settings.[54]

Our approach is corroborated by the fact that experimental economics treats monetary pay-offs as representing subjective value.

Going back to our extreme scenario when all activities would be mediated by markets, the consumer would assign prices to all alternative choices, then consider the opportunity costs that the specific choice would result in, and finally, take a decision aiming at maximising surplus. This is the arbitrageur, which is less strange as it seems, when we consider someone who shops at the supermarket: This person acts like a producer who produces a basket of goods. The consumer has a budget, would screen prices, always consider alternatives as priced on the shelves, and finally, would be happy to leave the supermarket with some savings, which compare to profits made during an arbitrage over the various alternatives (for example, considering how many cheap goods one can purchase by giving up one expensive good and how the relative gains would compare). As a universal medium of exchange, money represents generalised opportunities for exchange and an indicator of economic rents that accrue from exchange.[55]

4.2. Entrepreneurial rent and exchange value

The role of arbitrage in determining valuation via economic rents is salient once we turn from consumers to other market agents, that is, producers and traders who expend money on generating supply and focus on economic rent on the seller's side. Producers' and traders' reservation prices reflect the costs of producing or acquiring the good, valued at market prices. All sellers whose reservation price (defined as break-even point for that transaction) is below the realised price on the market will make a profit (which is roughly equivalent to the economic rent on the seller's side), which they can use for other economic actions. In that sense, money is a measure of value for the seller; if prices are public and recognised by everyone, money is the objective measure of value for all agents who hold goods for the purpose of selling them on the market only.

For agents who hold goods exclusively for selling on the market, money is a direct indicator of value in terms of profits as economic rent. Marx called this exchange value.

The argument so far only applies to the present. Economic theory suggests a deeper level of analysis in introducing the future flow of benefits that a good or asset can provide. For agents that entirely specialise on markets, that is, have no own use for the good or asset in question, all future flows of benefits are monetary flows which are discounted to a present value.

Once we consider the future, monetary value of a current asset is determined by the uncertain losses of alternative opportunities for profit.

As reflecting individual expectations, opportunity costs are subjectively determined in the first place (first-person view). Analogously to our earlier argument, the current monetary value of an asset represents the gain from holding it over alternative uses, including those that pertain to the future. This defines the asset's (opportunity) cost in a way different from bookkeeping cost. In other words, while a seller may generate an economic rent because she could supply the good at a certain cost as reflected in the books, she may lose future profit flows. In this case, her opportunity cost would be defined by this lost chance and not by the costs in the books.[56]

Since future profit flows in a market setting are subject to fundamental uncertainty, the respective economic rent on the seller's side becomes an entrepreneurial rent. Insofar as current prices and costs reflect expectations, and associated opportunity costs, of market agents, the entrepreneurial rent is defined in monetary terms but remains a subjective magnitude in an essential way.[57] Therefore, even for producers, monetary values are objective quantities only if there is a market equilibrium in which the expectations of all agents are recurrently confirmed, that is, if there is no innovation and no surprise. Market prices obtain an essential role in anchoring subjective expectations by objectifying them into a second-person view and by enabling the construction of subjective valuations in the first place.

In Chapter 13, section 4, we discuss in detail how expectations are formed.

A standard example of this role is stock markets. The price/earnings ratio compares the costs of obtaining a share with the earnings per share. While in principle, the price/earnings ratio can be applied to both historical earnings and future earnings, on stock markets, the current market price of the share is

We discuss valuation on financial markets and expectations in Chapter 12, section 3.3.

routinely interpreted as an indication of earnings expectations. The entrepreneurial value investor is someone who disagrees with the market valuation.[58]

In all these considerations, accounting procedures obtain a central role in operationalising a monetary form of value. Market-based valuation has been bolstered by changes of accounting principles over recent decades, which reflect the economic theory of opportunity cost and the role of expectations.[59] Whereas traditionally, assets would be evaluated at historical cost, modern accounting marks to market, that is, it takes market valuations as a reference and considers these as true values or objectivisations of valuation. However, this only entails the intersubjective recognition of entrepreneurial valuations that are implicit in the price (i.e., the second-person view). Modern forms of accounting assume that current market prices reflect the aggregate judgements of *all* market participants about the value of the resource. This renders accounting strictly performative since future flows are co-determined by the current value of the asset.[60] On a deeper level, there is a fundamental paradox in establishing monetary valuation in competition: If the expected rate of return determines the value of the current asset (i.e., capital), the amount of capital as measured in monetary terms becomes arbitrary since its volume cannot be assessed by other measures. This is the famous Cambridge paradox in valuing capital, whose importance extends to macroeconomics and the theory of distribution.[61]

We come back on the Cambridge controversy in Chapter 12, section 3.3.

See Chapter 12, section 3.1.

4.3. Money as form of social capital

We discuss this in detail in Chapter 12, section 2.1.

Using money is extending credit to issuers and users of money, which enables its transactional functions.

So far, we considered microeconomic aspects of money and value. The question remains how value relates to aggregate monetary quantities (i.e., the budget or financial wealth in the narrow sense). Recent debates have centred around the question whether money is primarily defined by its transactional function or rather constitutes an embodied form of credit.[62] In our view, the latter perspective emanates from the transactional role itself. Suppose that in a typical market exchange, a seller accepts money in exchange for his product. If the money received has no intrinsic value, this means that he effectively provides credit to the issuer of money rather than the buyer. This is because the buyer, in realising the exchange with the seller, can rely on the respective credit to eventually be extended to somebody else (i.e., another person who accepts the money), who in turn is confident in the potential acceptance of others and so forth. In other words, the money flows associated with transactions are not simply flows of a money token that technically enable transactions but constitute trading in promises to pay. These promises are anonymous as the parties in one exchange never know in which specific second exchange the promise will be fulfilled.[63] The question, then, is how agents' trust into the flow of promises emerges. There are two aspects to consider: first, the role of money as credit in a social network context and, second, the production of money.

In traditional small-scale societies, the role of credit in transactions is not resolved by the introduction of money but by credit or, indeed, promises that are mutually given.[64] Here, credit is not a financial phenomenon but a social commitment. If there is no coincidence of wants, an individual can just accept a promise to return something valuable in the future. Indeed, in traditional societies, there is a form of exchange that is exclusively based on this mutual extension of credit, mostly referred to as reciprocal exchange as different from market exchange. For example, traditionally, there would be no markets for labour involving money wages but networks of mutual help in labour services, governed by social norms of reciprocity and moral obligation. Economists tend to confront the two regimes in a dichotomous fashion, stressing the severe constraints on freedom of action associated with the latter. However, mutual commitments, as determined by social norms, are regularly conceived as communal obligations and, hence, intersubjectively objectified: Because all individuals are members of the same community and share group identity, they can derive trust in bilateral transactions from communal trust. This corresponds to the notion of group-based social capital.

Thus, the conventional solution to the problem of barter is not money but social credit or community-bound social capital. Barter is possible if all participants commit themselves to the respective community and accept the binding force of mutual commitments to a future balancing of obligations. Money represents trusting into a community of market agents who rely on each other in terms of specialisation and who expect that mutual obligations will be met via the acceptance money as a means of payment. We call this the primary monetary community.[65] Money is an embodied form of credit that can in turn become an object of exchange. Therefore, we can interpret money as embodying a specific quantifiable form of social capital that is fungible, tradable, and commensurable across subjects. This implies that money has intrinsic value. Money is a form of credit with a maximum range and variety of potential partners of exchange; the essential point is that this credit no longer relates to individual properties of agents, that is, credit and trustworthiness is exclusively based on the ability to pay. Ultimately, trusting money becomes an institution.

This analysis is vindicated by considering the treatment of modern central bank money in accounting terms. Fiat money issued by the central bank is currently treated as a liability of the central bank and an asset of money holders. But this does not correspond to standard accounting rules: Money could only be regarded a liability of the central bank if the monetary system obliged it to change its money into another reserve medium such as gold. In contrast, money holders do not dispose of any formal claim, neither vis-à-vis the central bank nor other agents, given that those are entirely free to enter a transaction. At its core, fiat central bank money is a public good, that is, a form of social capital which manifests the willingness of all members of a market economy to mutually transact and to engage in mutual obligations.[66]

In traditional small-scale societies, the problem of trilateral exchange is solved by extending social credit to others (i.e., using social capital).

On reciprocal exchange, see Chapter 5, section 2.

On social capital, see Chapter 8, section 3.2.

We further discuss the primary monetary community in Chapter 12, section 2.

Money is fungible and tradable social capital.

5. Conclusion

In this chapter, we explored the fundamentals of the theory of money, which differ substantially from the established view in economics that treats money as a mere technology of transaction. Money is a core institution in a wide range of performative mechanisms that we will scrutinise in the subsequent chapters. Following Simmel, we showed that money is constitutive of economic rationality in the market context, eschewing reference to the concept of subjective utility. Money-based market rationality is a performative phenomenon of its own; the mode of valuation performed by money coexists with other modes. For example, if I sit at a desk inherited from my grandparents, I might not assess its value in terms of the market for antiques but in terms of my warm memories of staying with them when I was a child. Indeed, this may often be seen as irrational or emotional, yet as long as I do not intend to sell it or find myself in dire financial straits, the economic valuation does not matter, and its neglect does not impact on my welfare.

Once my actions get entangled with markets; however, the money frame becomes salient. As we saw, that is not only true for those agents who explicitly pursue profit motives as business but also for consumers who must consider their budgets when choosing among goods. The budget is the institutional mechanism that mediates performative functions of money in domains which are prima facie not organised as markets. Budgets are a central institutional phenomenon in the financial domain of the market and bridges the microeconomic and macroeconomic functions of money. This is the topic of Chapter 12. Before moving to this, we will now pull all threads of the previous chapters together in presenting our evolutionary account of what constitutes a market.

Major chapter insights

- Money is the key institution of markets and is the major distinctive feature of market exchange versus non-market exchange. The chapter approaches money as the core performative institution of the market, which we analyse in the frame of the Aoki model, where cognitive and performative mechanisms work together on the individual and the population level. The focal phenomenon is trust in money.
- Pricing assigns money signs to objects: Prices are monetary phenomena. Pricing is an entrepreneurial act since both the reactions of other agents and the future developments of parameters influencing pricing are not certain. Pricing practices and technologies of trade determine the mechanisms of the law of one price that creates the

conditions for the emergence of an objectified second-person view on valuation.

- The value of money roots in its embodying of agential power with the greatest inclusiveness of choice and its property of zero specificity to market opportunity. It is salient in the various framing effects of money which include the shift to the transactional frame, making exchange value salient rather than subjective satisfaction, as well as individualisation, social distancing, and emotional neutralisation. Societies establish social norms which regulate behaviour in the light of these effects.
- The concept of economic rent reveals the role of money in objectifying subjective valuation. For consumption choices, given a certain budget, prices convey information about lost alternatives and, thus, guide the rationalisation of choices. In exclusively market-centred action, money is the prime standard of value, and considering uncertainty in future-oriented action, the notion of entrepreneurial rent renders monetary value subjective.
- Rationalised choice is an internalised arbitrage process in which alternatives are evaluated by prices, thus anchoring subjective valuation in the objectified second-person view of the market. This is vindicated in the general rule of experimental economics to treat money values as linear correlates of subjective utility.
- Money is a form of social capital bound to communities of exchange, reflecting general opportunities for exchange, which is universally fungible and tradable. The original solution to the problem of trilateral exchange is social credit.

Notes

1 For example, countertrade in international transactions, Marin and Schnitzler (2002).
2 Classically, Arrow and Hahn (1971).
3 Walsh and Lynch (2008).
4 Hardie and MacKenzie (2012).
5 In monetary statistics, these distinctions are reflected in the M0, M1, etc. aggregates; see https://www.federalreserve.gov/faqs/money_12845.htm (Accessed 30 August 2022).
6 Bechara and Damasio (2005).
7 Ingham (2000).
8 Ertman and Williams (2005) is a rich collection on commodification.
9 Çalışkan and Callon (2010).

10 Amir et al. (2008).

11 White (2002).

12 White (2002), Taylor (2016).

13 Seminally, Negishi (1979).

14 This explains why Weyl (2019) distinguishes a separate domain of price theory in economics which combines the microanalysis of mechanisms with aggregate-level determination of stability.

15 Godley and Lavoie (2012).

16 Sugden (2018, 120ff). On the general concept, see Hausman (1989).

17 Herrmann-Pillath (2001).

18 Therefore, the LOP play a very important role in international trade law, see Hudec (2001).

19 This criterion is standard in analysing financial market integration in Europe, see, for example, Lieven et al. (2004).

20 Camerer et al. (2005), Phelps (2009).

21 Walsh and Lynch (2008). For a neuroeconomics perspective, see Bourgeois-Gironde (2021).

22 Shafir et al. (1997), Fehr and Tyran (2001).

23 Weber et al. (2009).

24 Lea and Webley (2006).

25 Fehr (2009).

26 Kornai (1980).

27 The classic is Fisher (1912). Polman et al. (2018) show that people value purchasing power more when the money is owned by themselves than by others.

28 Tuomela (2007, 182ff).

29 Simmel (1907). Simmel's ideas have been largely ignored by economists since the book was only translated into English decades later, and then highly appraised, though without echo; Laidler and Rowe (1980).

30 Seaford (2004).

31 Goetzmann (2017, 15ff).

32 Soll (2014).

33 Vohs (2015).

34 Amir et al. (2008).

35 Kahneman (2012, 297ff).

36 Kouchaki et al. (2013).

37 Zelizer (1997).

38 Hénaff (2002).

39 Titmuss (1970).

40 Zelizer (2011, 181ff).

41 Zhou et al. (2009).

42 Vohs et al. (2006, 2008).

43 Zellweger (2017, 116ff).

44 The concept of rent is a key notion in Marshall's (1920) *Principles*.

45 De Vries (2008, 4).

46 Piketty (2013 Chapter three).
47 Sirmans et al. (2005).
48 Cavailhès et al. (2009).
49 Simmel (1907).
50 Cubitt and Sugden (2001), Andreou (2020).
51 Marshall (1920, 98ff).
52 Rammstedt (2003).
53 Tyler and Amodio (2015).
54 Smith (1976).
55 This converges with Lea and Webley (2006).
56 Buchanan (1969).
57 Kirzner (1979).
58 Zuckerman (2012).
59 Perry and Nölke (2006).
60 Vosselman (2014).
61 Cohen and Harcourt (2003).
62 Martin (2014).
63 Hicks (1989, 41ff).
64 Graeber (2011).
65 Following Richter (1987).
66 Kumhof et al. (2020).

References

Amir, O., Ariely, D. and Carmon, Z. (2008) 'The Dissociation Between Monetary Assessment and Predicted Utility', *Marketing Science*, 27(6), pp. 1055–1064. DOI: 10.1287/mksc.1080.0364.

Andreou, C. (2020) 'Dynamic Choice', *The Stanford Encyclopedia of Philosophy,* Winter 2020 Edition. Available at: https://plato.stanford.edu/archives/win2020/entries/dynamic-choice/ (Accessed: 17 April 2022).

Arrow, K. J. and Hahn, F. (1971) *General Competitive Analysis*. San Francisco: Holden-Day.

Bechara, A. and Damasio, A. R. (2005) 'The Somatic Marker Hypothesis: A Neural Theory of Economic Decision', *Games and Economic Behavior*, 52(2), pp. 336–372. DOI: 10.1016/j.geb.2004.06.010.

Bourgeois-Gironde, S. (2021) 'Has Money Transformed Our Brains? A Glimpse into Stone-Age Neuroeconomics', *Annals of the Fondazione Luigi Einaudi*, 55(1), pp. 165–184. DOI: 10.26331/1139.

Buchanan, J. (1969) *Cost and Choice: An Inquiry in Economic Theory*. Chicago: University of Chicago Press.

Çalışkan, K. and Callon, M. (2010) 'Economization, Part 2: A Research Programme for the Study of Markets', *Economy and Society*, 39(1), pp. 1–32. DOI: 10.1080/03085140903424519.

Camerer, C., Loewenstein, G. and Prelec, D. (2005) 'Neuroeconomics: How Neuroscience Can Inform Economics', *Journal of Economic Literature*, 43(1), pp. 9–64. DOI: 10.1257/0022051053737843.

Cavailhès, J. *et al.* (2009) 'GIS-Based Hedonic Pricing of Landscape', *Environmental and Resource Economics*, 44(4), pp. 571–590. DOI: 10.1007/s10640-009-9302-8.

Cohen, A. J. and Harcourt, G. C. (2003) 'Whatever Happened to the Cambridge Capital Controversies?' *Journal of Economic Perspectives*, 17(1), pp. 199–214. DOI: 10.1257/089533003321165010.

Cubitt, R. P. and Sugden, R. (2001) 'On Money Pumps', *Games and Economic Behavior*, 37(1), pp. 121–160. DOI: 10.1006/game.2000.0834.

De Vries, J. (2008) *The Industrious Revolution: Consumer Behavior and the Household Economy, 1650 to the Present*. Cambridge: Cambridge University Press.

Ertman, M. M. and Williams, J. C. (eds.) (2005) *Rethinking Commodification: Cases and Readings in Law and Culture, Critical America*. New York: New York University Press.

Fehr, E. (2009) 'Social Preferences and the Brain', in Glimcher, P. W. and Fehr, E. (eds.) *Neuroeconomics: Decision Making and the Brain*. Amsterdam: Elsevier, pp. 215–232. DOI: 10.1016/B978-0-12-374176-9.00015-4.

Fehr, E. and Tyran, J.-R. (2001) 'Does Money Illusion Matter?' *American Economic Review*, 91(5), pp. 1239–1262. DOI: 10.1257/aer.91.5.1239.

Fisher, I. (2006[1912]) *The Purchasing Power of Money: Its Determination and Relation to Credit Interest and Crises*. New York: Cosimo Classics.

Godley, W. and Lavoie, M. (2012) *Monetary Economics: An Integrated Approach to Credit, Money, Income, Production and Wealth*. London: Palgrave Macmillan. DOI: 10.1007/978-1-137-08599-3.

Goetzmann, W. N. (2017) *Money Changes Everything: How Finance Made Civilization Possible*. Princeton: Princeton University Press. DOI: 10.2307/j.ctvc77dzg.

Graeber, D. (2011) *Debt: The First 5,000 Years*. New York: Melville House.

Hardie, I. and MacKenzie, D. (2012) 'The Material Sociology of Arbitrage', in Knorr-Cetina, K. and Preda, A. (eds.) *The Oxford Handbook of the Sociology of Finance*. Oxford: Oxford University Press, pp. 187–201. DOI: 10.1093/oxfordhb/9780199590162.013.0011.

Hausman, D. M. (1989) 'Arbitrage Arguments', *Erkjenntnis*, 30, pp. 5–22.

Hénaff, M. (2002) *Le Prix de la Vérité: le Don, l'argent, la Philosophie*. Paris: SEUIL.

Herrmann-Pillath, C. (2001) 'A General Refutation of the Law of One Price as Empirical Hypothesis', *Jahrbücher für Nationalökonomie und Statistik*, 221(1), pp. 45–67.

Hicks, J. (1989) *A Market Theory of Money*. Oxford and New York: Clarendon Press.

Hudec, R. E. (2001) 'Like Product: The Differences in Meaning in GATT Articles I and III', in Cottier, T. and Mavroidis, P. C. (eds.) *Regulatory Barriers and the Principle of Non-Discrimination in World Trade Law*. Ann Arbor: University of Michigan Press, pp. 101–123. DOI: 10.3998/mpub.16814.

Ingham, G. (2000) 'Babylonian Madness: On the Historical and Sociological Origins of Money', in Smithin, J. (ed.) *What Is Money?* Abingdon and New York: Routledge, pp. 16–41. DOI: 10.4324/9780203072691-6.

Kahneman, D. (2012) *Thinking, Fast and Slow*. London: Penguin Books.

Kirzner, I. M. (1979) *Perception, Opportunity, and Profit: Studies in the Theory of Entrepreneurship*. Chicago: University of Chicago Press.

Kornai, J. (1980) *Economics of Shortage*. Amsterdam and New York: North-Holland.

Kouchaki, M. *et al*. (2013) 'Seeing Green: Mere Exposure to Money Triggers as Business Decision Frame and Unethical Outcomes', *Organizational Behavior and Human Decision Processes*, 121(1), pp. 53–61. DOI: 10.1016/j.obhdp.2012.12.002.

Kumhof, M. *et al*. (2020) 'Central Bank Money: Liability, Asset, or Equity of the Nation?' *Rebuilding Macroeconomics Working Paper Series*, 20, pp. 1–44.

Laidler, D. and Rowe, N. (1980) 'Georg Simmel's Philosophy of Money: A Review Article for Economists', *Journal of Economic Literature*, 18(1), pp. 97–105.

Lea, S. G. and Webley, P. (2006) 'Money as Tool, Money as Drug: The Biological Psychology of a Strong Incentive', *Behavioral and Brain Sciences*, 29(2), pp. 161–209. DOI: 10.1017/S0140525X06009046.

Lieven, B. *et al*. (2004) 'Measuring European Financial Integration', *Oxford Review of Economic Policy*, 20(4), pp. 509–530. DOI: 10.1093/oxrep/grh030.

Marin, D. and Schnitzler, M. (2002) *Contracts in Trade and Transition: The Resurgence of Barter*. Cambridge: MIT Press.

Marshall, A. (2009 [1920]) *Principles of Economics*. 8th Edition. New York: Cosimo.

Martin, F. (2014) *Money: The Unauthorized Biography from Coinage to Cryptocurrencies*. New York: Vintage Book.

Negishi, T. (1979) *Microeconomic Foundations of Keynesian Macroeconomics*. Amsterdam: North Holland.

Perry, J. and Nölke, A. (2006) 'The Political Economy of International Accounting Standards', *Review of International Political Economy*, 13(4), pp. 559–586. DOI: 10.1080/09692290600839790.

Phelps, E. A. (2009) 'The Study of Emotion in Neuroeconomics', in Glimcher, P. W. and Fehr, E. (eds.) *Neuroeconomics: Decision Making and the Brain*. Amsterdam: Elsevier, pp. 233–250. DOI: 10.1016/B978-0-12-374176-9.00016-6.

Piketty, T. (2013) *Le capital au XXIe siècle*. Paris: SEUIL.

Polman, E., Effron, D. A. and Thomas, M. R. (2018) 'Other People's Money: Money's Perceived Purchasing Power Is Smaller for Others Than for the Self', *Journal of Consumer Research*, 45(1), pp. 109–125. DOI: 10.1093/JCR/UCX119.

Rammstedt, O. (2003) 'Wert, Geld und Individualität', in Rammstedt, O. (ed.) *Georg Simmels Philosophie des Geldes, Aufsätze und Materialien*. Frankfurt am Main: Suhrkamp.

Richter, R. (1987) *Geldtheorie: Vorlesung auf der Grundlage der Allgemeinen Gleichgewichtstheorie und der Institutionenökonomik*. Berlin: Springer Verlag.

Seaford, R. (2004) *Money and the Early Greek Mind*. Cambridge: Cambridge University Press. DOI: 10.1017/CBO9780511483080.

Shafir, E., Diamond, P. and Tversky, A. (1997) 'Money Illusion', *Quarterly Journal of Economics*, 112(2), pp. 341–374.

Simmel, G. (2009[1907]) *Philosophie des Geldes*. 2nd Edition. Cologne: Anaconda.

Sirmans, G. *et al.* (2005) 'The Composition of Hedonic Pricing Models', *Journal of Real Estate Literature*, 13(1), pp. 3–43. DOI: 10.1080/10835547. 2005.12090154.

Smith, V. L. (1976) 'Experimental Economics: Induced Value Theory', *American Economic Review*, 66(2), pp. 274–279. DOI: 10.1017/CBO9780511528354.008.

Soll, J. (2014) *The Reckoning: Financial Accountability and the Making and Breaking of Nations*. London: Penguin.

Sugden, R. (2018) *The Community of Advantage: A Behavioural Economist's Defence of the Market*. Oxford and New York: Oxford University Press. DOI: 10.1093/oso/9780198825142.001.0001.

Taylor, J. B. (2016) 'The Staying Power of Staggered Wage and Price Setting Models in Macroeconomics', in Taylor, J. B. and Uhlig, H. (eds.) *Handbook of Macroeconomics, Volume 2*. Amsterdam: North-Holland, pp. 2009–2042. DOI: 10.1016/bs.hesmac.2016.04.008.

Titmuss, R. M (2019[1970]) *The Gift Relationship: From Human Blood to Social Policy*. Bristol: Policy Press. DOI: 10.2307/j.ctv6zdcmh.

Tuomela, R. (2007) *The Philosophy of Sociality*. Oxford: Oxford University Press. DOI: 10.1093/ACPROF:OSO/9780195313390.001.0001.

Tyler, T. R. and Amodio, D. M. (2015) 'Psychology and Economics: Areas of Convergence and Difference', in Fréchette, G. R. and Schotter, A. (eds.) *Handbook of Experimental Economic Methodology*. New York: Oxford University Press, pp. 181–196. DOI: 10.1093/ACPROF:OSO/9780195328325.003.0012.

Vohs, K. D. (2015) 'Money Priming Can Change People's Thoughts, Feelings, Motivations, and Behaviors: An Update on 10 Years of Experiments', *Journal of Experimental Psychology: General*, 144(4), pp. e86–e93.

Vohs, K. D., Mead, N. L. and Goode, M. R. (2006) 'The Psychological Consequences of Money', *Science*, 314(5802), pp. 1154–1156. DOI: 10.1126/science.1132491.

Vohs, K. D., Mead, N. L. and Goode, M. R. (2008) 'Merely Activating the Concept of Money Changes Personal and Interpersonal Behavior', *Current Directions in Psychological Science*, 17(3), pp. 208–212. DOI: 10.1111/j.1467-8721.2008.00576.x.

Vosselman, E. (2014) 'The "Performativity Thesis" and Its Critics: Towards a Relational Ontology of Management Accounting', *Accounting and Business Research,* 44(2), pp. 181–203. DOI: 10.1080/00014788.2013.856748.

Walsh, A. and Lynch, T. (2008) *The Morality of Money: An Exploration in Analytic Philosophy.* Houndsmills and New York: Palgrave Macmillan.

Weber, B. *et al.* (2009) 'The Medial Prefrontal Cortex Exhibits Money Illusion', *Proceedings of the National Academy of Sciences*, 106(13), pp. 5025–5028. DOI: 10.1073/pnas.0901490106.

Weyl, E. G. (2019) 'Price Theory', *Journal of Economic Literature*, 57(2), pp. 329–385. DOI: 10.1257/jel.20171321.

White, H. (2002) *Markets from Networks: Socioeconomic Models of Production.* Princeton: Princeton University Press.

Zelizer, V. A. (1997) *The Social Meaning of Money.* Princeton: Princeton University Press.

Zelizer, V. A. (2011) *Economic Lives: How Culture Shapes the Economy.* Princeton: Princeton University Press.

Zellweger, T. M. (2017) *Managing the Family Business: Theory and Practice.* Cheltenham and Northampton: Edward Elgar Publishing.

Zhou, X. *et al.* (2009) 'The Symbolic Power of Money: Reminders of Money Alter Social Distress and Physical Pain', *Psychological Science*, 20(6), pp. 700–706. DOI: 10.1111%2Fj.1467-9280.2009.02353.x.

Zuckerman, E. (2012) 'Market Efficiency: A Sociological Perspective', in Knorr-Cetina, K. and Preda, A. (eds.) *The Oxford Handbook of the Sociology of Finance*. Oxford: Oxford University Press.

CHAPTER ELEVEN

Markets evolving

1. Introduction

Markets mediate micro and macro in conventional approaches.

This book lays out economics as a science of markets. The previous chapters have outlined the main elements needed for a comprehensive and transdisciplinary view of markets, including the general evolutionary framework, the issue of values, specialisation, production, and technology; the role of agency as embedded in individuals, networks, and institutions; and the role of money. This chapter draws these threads together to develop a systematic perspective on markets and their evolution. It is deliberately placed on what would form the borderline between a micro- and macroeconomic perspective in a standard textbook: On the one hand, it delves deeper into the analysis of market mechanisms, partly based on the evolutionary theory of the market process as developed by evolutionary economics; on the other hand, it integrates an institution that in standard analysis would mostly be dealt with in a macroeconomic context, namely money. We approach markets as mediating between the domains of micro and macro since markets are driven by individual behaviour, but market states are population-level phenomena where money mediates aggregative mechanisms, together with other population-level structures, especially social networks.[1]

Markets are regarded in an evolutionary perspective, embedded in the Darwinian paradigm.

We employ an evolutionary approach to markets.[2] Our view includes many of the main ingredients of the evolutionary economics perspective, such as the emphases on uncertainty and entrepreneurship; on endogenous technological, organisational, and institutional innovation; or on the dynamics of competition. We agree with those strands in evolutionary economics that explicitly refer to the Darwinian paradigm for understanding the accumulation of information on markets, which we have specified as the general model of variation, selection, and retention in a multilevel systemic context.

See Chapter 4, section 3.

We emphasise the explicit consideration of various temporal scopes, which was a major feature of Marshall's approach to markets. We refer to the idea of markets as information processors but extend it from the shorter-run view to the question how market dynamics coalesce into a structuration of markets in the longer run, which we will call market states. Accordingly, one question is

DOI: 10.4324/9781003094869-15

how markets support the emergence and sustainability of niche formation by innovative specialisation, that is, the emergence of increasingly complex systems of division of labour. Markets have a fundamentally temporal component both with respect to the longer-run evolution of niches and the product space, and, in the shorter run, regarding the analysis of concrete acts of exchange (i.e., the market transactions).

Emphasising the temporal dimension also means that uncertainty and risk are constitutive parts of the market process. The distribution of risk among market actors is a fundamental determinant of the structure of market transactions over time. This is a major aspect in our analysis of economic fluctuations in Chapter 13, implying that fluctuations are a necessary feature of markets. However, our notion of market states also assumes that institutionalised behavioural patterns are of great significance, an idea that Keynes had already ventilated in his famous treatment of long-term expectations that he referred to as conventions,[3] which include the role of institutions exogenous to the market process. Institutions play a fundamental role in regularising market behaviour over time and, in fact, perform markets by enabling transactions. However, as far as endogenous market evolution is concerned, the main phenomenon in processing uncertainty is the emergence of the firm. The firm is often seen as substitute of the market, defined by hierarchies and non-voluntary exchange, though – at least, ideal typically – on the basis of a voluntary labour contract.[4] We argue that the firm is complementary to the market, though under the condition of continuous technological change and novelty.

The chapter is organised as follows. Section 2 lays out the defining characteristics of markets as developed in the previous chapters. Section 3 develops an evolutionary perspective of markets, combining standard market process theory with main categories of evolutionary theory as presented in Chapter 4. Section 4 unfolds the performative function of money for the operation of markets. Section 5 presents our view on the relationship between markets and firms, and section 6 takes a look at the role of market institutions.

The temporal dimension is crucial for understanding markets.

On the division of labour, see Chapter 4, section 2.1, and Chapter 5, section 2.

Uncertainty and risk are constitutive parts of the market process that are partly addressed by institutionalised behavioural patterns.

On performative functions of institutions, see Chapter 9, section 3.

On the firm, see Chapter 6, section 4.

2. Characteristics of markets: A reprise

2.1. Elements of markets

As a social technology to allocate resources, markets are universal to human forms of life.[5] At the same time, many concrete characteristics of markets are historically and culturally contingent. Based on the previous chapters, we can identify the following universal features:

Markets share universal features.

On the example of China, compare Chapter 1.

- First, on a most general level, market transactions are a form of *exchange*. In principle, an exchange relationship implies the mutual shifting of resources of value between the transaction partners on a voluntary and non-hierarchical basis. However, the borderline to non-market transactions

Market transactions are a form of voluntary exchange.

See Chapters 3 and 5.

Markets are networks.

See Chapter 8.

See Chapters 1 and 10.

Market exchange is institutionalised.

See Chapter 9.

Markets rely on money.

See Chapter 10.

Markets address economic scarcity.

See Chapters 5 and 7.

Markets are drivers of diversification.

See Chapters 4 and 6.

is blurred: Clearly, exchange can take place on a highly asymmetric basis, implying a dilution of voluntariness and the existence of factual hierarchies, including on one market side (e.g., large producers versus small suppliers). The counterparts to voluntary exchange are, on the one hand, one-sided resource transfers, such as gift-giving (again with a blurred borderline to factual reciprocity), and on the other, forced exchange or transfer, such as in the case of taxation.

- Second, markets involve a *plurality of actors* at least on one market side. An exclusively bilateral exchange relationship with no meaningful outside options is not a market. This multilateral character is the reason why markets need to be analysed in terms of social networks and are constituted by triadic, not dyadic structures; also, markets not only coordinate between but also within the two market sides.[6] Multilateral exchange is related to the notion of a physical marketplace (both geographically specified and virtual) where many buyers and sellers meet, following certain rules governing exchange.

- Third, market exchange is *institutionalised*, that is, exhibits behavioural regularities associated with a potential of social sanctions. In modern markets, this can (but normally does not have to) imply the existence of formalised entitlements constituted by property rights. Therefore, markets can both emerge on a spontaneous basis or be created by intentional design.

- Fourth, markets, at least beyond a certain threshold of complexity, rely on a generalised medium of exchange, *money*. Money is one of the key institutions that ease the specialisation dilemma because it reduces risk associated with the production of goods and services for which the producer has no personal need. All market transactions involve the flow of money (i.e., payments) or of claims on future flows of money. The resulting budget constraints do not necessarily imply optimisation but create a behavioural stance of monetary efficacy (i.e., market actors are money minded).

- Fifth, markets are social technologies addressing economic *scarcity*. As in the general evolutionary framework, scarcity is endogenous to market evolution. The universal condition is that evolutionary competition is driven by positional advantages and disadvantages which determine the differential reproduction of certain behavioural and structural patterns. In the specific context of markets, this results from status competition, driven by the quest for profits on the side of traders and producers and the concomitant generation of wants.

- Sixth, via the creation of novelty, markets are drivers of niche diversification via comparative advantage. Diversification operates on many levels; for example, as competitive specialisation among actors internal to the market and as economic specialisation of a market community in relation to the external conditions under which the economy operates. These external conditions, or market environment, include ecological as well as institutional factors.

- Seventh, and lastly, the realm of market-based resource allocation differs widely across time periods and cultures. This is partly a question of societal values, but it also relates to the viability of markets as regimes of resource allocation vis-à-vis alternative regimes. While societies without any elements of market allocation are empirically very rare, there is no unidirectional or deterministic path towards higher degrees of commodification or marketisation. At the same time, particularly since the 19th century, the science of economics, taking a performative role, has actively contributed to marketisation.

The scope of market-based resource allocation differs.

See Chapters 2 and 3.

2.2. A simple map of a market

We systematise our approach to markets for products in Figure 11.1. On the supply side, we include two types of agents – comprising both individual and

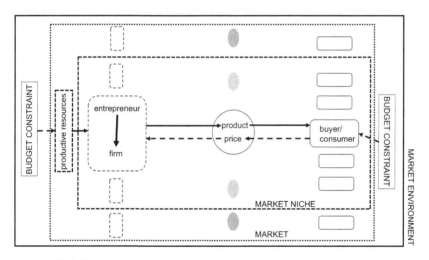

Figure 11.1 Basic constituents of markets
This simple visualisation of a market distinguishes between sellers (entrepreneurs and firms) and buyers (consumers, firms buying intermediate products, traders) and the opposite flows of products and payments (based on the pricing of products). Both sides operate under a budget constraint that reflects the pivotal role of money in realising market exchange. We distinguish between the market and the market niche, with the borderline dynamically constituted via differential degrees of substitutability of products. Markets are embedded in market systems (not shown in the graph for simplicity) and the market environment, defined by resources, networks, and institutions as most important elements.

275

collective actors – entrepreneurs and firms. Entrepreneurs are drivers of innovation in a very general sense and embody the creativity of market action. They create firms as the fundamental form of cooperation among producers (we do not show that consumers are mostly employees, hence play a double role as producers). We use the term 'firm' in a very broad sense, including, for example, the peasant household and farm in a pre-industrial economy such as China. Firms mobilise productive resources, often via other (factor) markets. On the demand side, we refer to buyers as agents that must rely on money to fulfil their wants and needs, which for most of them means earning monetary income generated by employment. Both production and consumption are not necessarily enacted via the market; in particular, consumers who can fulfil their wants independently from markets, such as subsistence farmers, would be deemed a special category of producer which does not concern us here. That is, all three categories of actors are ultimately focused on obtaining monetary income.

As we will show in the next section, markets manifest different levels of selection, which we capture by the following basic categories:

- market niches, appearing either as niche for a product or niche for an actor, such as a firm;
- markets;
- market systems;
- the market environment.

Products embody market niches.

Products embody market niches for products which emerge from various forms of institutionalised behaviour on both sides, such as specialisation and branding on the supply side and habituation on the demand side.[7] Similarly, actors carve out niches, which, in the case of firms, relate to the distinct capacities of firms and the knowledge embodied in their organisational structures and routines. Niches for actors coincide with product niches in the case of a one-product firm but diverge with the presence of multi-product firms (see further section later). The distinction between market and market niche is traditionally covered by the concept of elasticity of substitution, that is, the ease and speed how a product can be substituted by another one. Importantly, this implies a second-person perspective with a potential for performative feedback loops, that is, there is no a priori third-person definition of what constitutes a product. Market systems, in turn, are sets of markets connected by arbitrage.

The hierarchical character of these selection levels implies that niches are never disconnected to the wider market and market system; the borders are porous and dynamic. Ultimately, the reason is the universality of the budget constraint. Markets are defined by the basic transactions of delivery of a product and payment, which implies that the budget establishes universal substitutability of payments: Even if the car is not a substitute for bread, we can still

On entrepreneurs, see Chapter 7, section 5.3.

On levels of selection, see Chapter 4, section 3.2.

On arbitrage, see Chapter 10, section 2.2.

decide to eat less to save for a car. Hence, the market system is universally connected via the medium of money.[8]

Finally, markets and market systems are embedded in the environment. One important example is information externalities between actors, such as firms gaining information by observing other firms, enabled by social networks. There are many social and institutional structures that condition certain forms of market performance, such as the degrees of internalisation of environmental costs which impact on price competitiveness or the social support of workers/employees in families.

See Chapter 4, section 2.1, and Chapter 8, section 2.

3. The evolutionary market process: Competition, endogenous niche formation, and growth

We now turn to the analysis of the market process from an evolutionary perspective. There are important analytical analogies between natural evolution and market competition which have been explored extensively by evolutionary economists.[9] At the same time, markets are specific social arrangements to organise competition and enable specialisation and the division of labour, which have certain generic advantages but, at least from a conceptional point of view, are not without alternatives. Like all elements of institutional evolution, markets are ultimately grounded in biological and ecological evolution and draw on the hard-wired human capacity for culture, but they are in no way natural states of affairs in the sense that market evolution emerges directly from natural evolution.[10]

Markets are regimes of exchange which are institutionally focused on money as the relevant resource for the reproduction of market agents. Market agents are defined by certain forms of institutionalised behaviour, and market reproduction works via the diffusion and sustainability of these behavioural patterns. The key material artefact of markets is the product, which is simply defined as object of market transactions (without reference to utility, as in standard economics). As said, products are units of market selection and embody the information generated and accumulated in market evolution in two senses: Products conjugate information, first, that enables their production and, second, about wants and needs. This can be seen as a form of cooperation via information complementarities: Consumers buy products without knowing how to produce these themselves, and suppliers learn about wants and needs, hence about what they need to produce. Therefore, markets are communities of advantage based on cognitive cooperation in a context of distributed knowledge.[11]

Products increasing their market share, and therefore occurring in greater frequency, are better adapted to demand and, therefore, exhibit higher (relative) fitness whereas others undergo the opposite development (selection).[12] Entrepreneurial actors bring modified or new products to the market

On the distinction between agents and individuals, see Chapter 7.

Products are units of market selection and embody information generated in market evolution.

On this division of knowledge, see Chapter 6, section 3.2.

Product competition can be conceived along the lines of the VSR model, see Chapter 4.

On the role of consumers, see Chapter 6, section 3.2.

Multilevel selection is related to increasing differentiation and complexity of products but also to market disruption.

On the concept of affordance, see Chapter 6, section 3.2.

Niche formation is often associated with evolutionary stasis; this can be broken by entrepreneurial vision.

(variation) and keep offering them if they obtain a certain market share (retention). Over time, retention results in the formation of a niche, characterised by specialisation of its occupants to harness the available resources and a concomitant stabilisation of the resource flow. This is the classic Hayekian discovery process, placed in an evolutionary framework and eventually taking place on the different levels outlined earlier.[13]

Similar to ecology, the differentiation of niches and their interdependencies is endogenous to the evolutionary process. One implication is that the selection criteria established by niches co-evolve with inhabitant populations of products and actors. A standard case is the active generation of wants by entrepreneurial action, for example, via the establishment of a new brand which reduces readiness for substitution on the demand side for technologically very similar products. Furthermore, consumers are not only passive adopters of product innovations but generate variation themselves by creative, and possibly unanticipated, patterns of use. Finally, there is dynamic interdependence between niches for products and niches for actors, for example, in the case of successful products that attract new firms.

As said, the concept of niche implies that markets manifest different levels of selection in the sense that niches defined by products compete against other products and their niches. For example, a brand of coffee competes against another brand, but on a higher level of aggregation, coffee competes against other drinks containing caffeine, and on the next higher level, drinks containing caffeine compete against drinks without caffeine. Multilevel selection is the driving force towards increasing differentiation and complexity of products and their niches.[14] It also constitutes a major cause of what is often perceived as market disruption since agents often are cognitively focused on their closest niche. For example, in the early period of Amazon company development, observers often treated the company as a bookseller and, hence, downplayed its incipient market-disrupting role as an entirely new form of organising and governing retail transaction across a much wider range of products.[15] This establishes one fundamental form of market performativity: Cognition and manifest market structure mutually drive market evolution, and as said, there is no exogenous (i.e., third-person perspective) fixation of what constitutes a product.[16] However, this does not imply mere subjectivist constructivism: Markets are material and, hence, also influence cognition once a certain market state is established. The causal link emerges from product affordances that relate to habits and routines.

It is important to recognise that the formation of niches does not exclude, and indeed is often associated with, evolutionary stasis.[17] Consumers develop habits (i.e., behavioural regularities) in using products, which creates affordances that undergird the reproduction of products. On the supply side, as we will argue later, firms develop routines in producing and selling products. As a result, we can speak of market states as institutionalised behavioural patterns and repeated coordinated action on both sides of the market (see, for more detail, further section later).[18] More generally, static markets are characterised by a relative strength of selection forces that suppress variation. Those selection forces may be an endogenous result of market competition, but they may also stem from exogenous institutional limitations on competition, such as a presence of social norms that are directed against innovation, given its potentially disruptive effects on the existing social order. In view of cognitive inertia, entrepreneurial action is often driven by visions that do not have a direct grounding in realised market states.[19] Finally, evolutionary stasis can result from general ecological scarcity. Imperial China is an important case for evolutionary stasis of a fully developed market system, dubbed involution,[20] showing that markets can foster high efficiency of resource use while at the same time constraining innovative and risk-prone entrepreneurship.

If variation forces are sufficiently strong, the evolutionary dynamics of niche formation is the primary source of market-based endogenous growth, which is homologous to increasing complexity of ecosystems: On the supply side, there is an enormous expansion and differentiation of the product space, based on technological progress that allows for an increasingly efficient harnessing of natural (e.g., solar energy) as well as endogenously created resources. On the demand side, there is a concomitant expansion and differentiation of wants; the key driver here is positional competition for social status that is to an increasing extent (and possibly pushed by entrepreneurial action) signalled by increased consumption levels.[21] The link between material growth and market evolution is the flow of energy that is harnessed in the production process, thus creating a direct connection between ecology and market niche expansion. Energetic constraints ultimately explain evolutionary stasis in China, while releasing these constraints opened the gates for the flow of product innovations in Europe and, later, the Northern hemisphere.

Market competition is positional competition. In principle, positional competition is ubiquitous in evolution since adaptive success (i.e., fitness) is a strictly relative concept, given that the selection environment of an evolutionary unit always includes all other evolutionary units competing for resources in the respective niche and generates competing adaptations.[22] In the market sphere, this manifests itself in two main ways. First, successful innovations by necessity generate negative externalities on competing products and actors, whose resources will shrink over time.[23] With respect to entrepreneurship, this is the complementary element of Schumpeter's famous notion of creative destruction. Second, market competition entails powerful incentives for various forms of predatory strategies that directly target competitors, such as dumping or hostile takeovers. That is why stationary economies tend to restrict competition and to adopt a moral economy of stable assignments of rights to a given set of resources.[24] In growing economies, however, the positional character of competition is mitigated by the fact that absolute and relative gains and losses, defined in terms of resource flows, no longer coincide, that is, relative losses can be compensated by absolute material gains.

On involution in China, see Chapter 1, section 4.

See Chapter 4, section 2.1, and Chapter 6, section 3.3.

On wants, see Chapter 7, section 5.2.

Innovation always creates negative externalities on third parties. Material growth bolsters the acceptance of market for those who lose in relative terms.

Positional competition entails the possibility of evolutionary arms races, with two basic types of outcomes: On the one hand, adaptation on one level of selection or with respect to one niche can lead to functional or dysfunctional results on another level or niche, such as sometimes alleged in advertising,[25] but also with respect to negative effects from predatory competition or winner-take-all contests.[26] On the other hand, evolutionary arms races can create exaptations, that is functional adaptations in another context, such as opening up a new niche and thereby allowing for an expansion of the space of niches and a softening of positional competition.[27]

4. Money, prices, and market states

4.1. Entrepreneurship and pricing under the shadow of the specialisation dilemma

We discuss this role of money in Chapter 16, section 5.

Money defines and enables actions that are constitutive to market competition as outlined earlier in several respects. A major function of money is the delimitation of the realm of market-based resource allocation. What counts as a resource and as scarce in the sense of the market process – even if only indirectly attributable to it via substitutive relationships, such as in the case of public transport – is directly connected to whether the respective item is attributed a monetary value. This attribution, in turn, is related to the institutionally defined borderline between markets and non-markets, which is not fixed but can be deliberately shifted – most generally by the establishment of new legal rights and concomitant marketisation, commodification, or assetification,[28] and partly via the internalisation of externalities. Marketisation is an important aspect of market-based economic growth and can itself be driven by entrepreneurship, where entrepreneurial vision, different from other forms of cognitive creativity, is at least partly shaped by a monetary focus: Even though the original motivation of entrepreneurs may be non-pecuniary in many ways, eventually entrepreneurs must adopt a money-minded attitude to succeed on the marketplace. We may speak of imagined profits as a driver of entrepreneurship.[29]

On assetification, see Chapter 3, section 3.2, and Chapter 12, section 4.

See Chapter 5, section 2, and Chapter 10, section 3.1.

The function of money as the most universal resource of market competition and its association with its low asset specificity impacts on the structure of the specialisation dilemma. As outlined, the specialisation dilemma entails a power asymmetry between agents that exhibit different degrees of capability specificity, with the consequence that specialisation potentials may not fully be exploited. The exchange relationship between an owner of money or financial assets and a producer or trader on the seller's side in a competitive market can be regarded as a special case of this relationship, where the money-induced net effect on relative agential power strongly depends on the availability of alternatives on both market sides: From a producer-entrepreneur's point of view, the existence of money increases the number of potential transaction partners; therefore, there is a wider field of experimentation for innovative specialisation, the risk of losing out in a bilateral exchange relationship in view of the hold-up problem decreases, and the willingness to engage in risky specialisation may increase due to the expectation to gain a universal medium of value. However, the fact that the buyer holds money increases its range of alternatives as well, implying higher competitive pressure for the producer.

Money has significant effects on the structure of the specialisation dilemma.

As outlined, monetised prices allow for the operationalisation of budget constraints, which constitute the primary framework for the objectification of economic valuation as well as of scarcity, in the sense of limits on the degree to which market actors can satisfy their wants and needs or realise their plans – fully corresponding to the everyday notion of money being scarce. This remains true in a fiat money regime, where money as a resource of market competition remains scarce as long as there is a meaningful (albeit in many respects structurally specific) selection process on the side of creditors. Scarcity in this context refers not only to the command of money resources in the sense of owning them but also to the more specific concept of liquidity, that is, the ability to fulfil obligations to pay an amount of money at a certain point in time.[30]

On objectification of value, see Chapter 10, section 4.1.

Prices allow for the establishment of profits as the main performative measure of selective pressure in market competition, including markets for external finance. Profits are essentially accounting balances related to a supplier over a certain period and are established as criterion of the relative fitness of actors, and eventually, products in market competition. The profit criterion can function as a determinant of rank competition and, therefore, incentivises a differentiation of competitive strategies, including predatory competition. As outlined, the most general form of profit generation on markets is arbitrage. Arbitrage can also be regarded as a generalised form of the entrepreneurial discovery process in the sense of profit maximisation, rather than the narrower notion of introducing a new product.[31]

Profits and external finance determine the evolution of the budget constraint through time and, thereby, shape the selection process.

We discuss arbitrage in Chapter 10, section 2.2.

As outlined, market prices play a pivotal role in the market process in the sense of conveying information that is ultimately subject to various options of interpretation on the recipient's side. Consequently – and perfectly in line with real-world experience – information flows and learning related to the mitigation of fundamental uncertainty with respect to specialisation decisions will involve other channels of information than just realised transactions. This is where the role of networks becomes centre stage. For example, social capital (in this case, mainly individual social capital based on weak ties) is a central determinant of market actors' transactional capabilities, including those

In contrast to the standard view, price cannot carry the brunt of information processing in the economy but social networks.

See Chapter 8, section 3.2.

enabling the collection and processing of information about other actors, in particular, competitors and potential buyers.

4.2. Beyond equilibrium: Prices, market clearing, and market states

Markets build on cognitive cooperation in framing markets and products.

On this collective action problem, see Chapter 5, section 3.

There are two important implications of the resulting network-based view on the market process. The first is a reiteration of the point that markets entail a substantial degree of cooperation in the sense of establishing communities of advantage. In many cases, the market process will be sustained by non-market cooperative structures. Of course, those structures can themselves be subject to issues of strategic interaction, particularly the collective action problem of organising agents for cooperation, which may feed back on the workability and stability of the market process. Yet a major form of cooperation is cognitive cooperation, meaning that market participants communicate and agree at least implicitly on shared frames of markets and products which are important to give meaning to prices. The second is that the more elaborate and differentiated the information flows, the more likely potential modifications of the entrepreneur's strategy will concern not only the pricing decision but the whole range of market responses as focused on in business research. This refers in particular to the ceteris paribus assumption with respect to the identity of the offered product over time in the standard market process model.

The Aoki model is introduced in Chapter 9, section 3.1.

We now draw together the main elements of our argument in presenting a unified conceptual framework for understanding the market process, namely market states (Figure 11.2). The concept of market states can stand as a generalised alternative to textbook models, in particular, the standard supply-demand diagram.[32] Market states are conceived of as being institutionalised in the most general sense (i.e., undergirded by institutionalised behavioural patterns), following the lines of the Aoki model.

On pricing, see Chapter 10, section 2.2.

We start with prices (lower-right side). Prices are not seen as market-clearing equilibrium outcomes but as material artefacts whose emergence can be institutionalised in many different ways and which stay in a complex and bidirectional causal relationship with market-clearing. The reference is to standard product prices as well as to input prices in production, including wages. Those prices are observed by producers-suppliers and buyers and work as information-compressing cues that shape expectations and behavioural dispositions (lower-left side) but at the same time are complemented by an elaborate range of other interactions in networks. Behavioural dispositions translate into strategic actions (upper-left side) in a stochastic way; for example, if there is a change in a firm's leadership. Regarding strategic actions, then, producers-suppliers (as far as producers are present on the respective market) and buyers have to be differentiated. Whereas the latter draw the standard purchasing decision, producers have to decide simultaneously about selling their outputs, purchasing inputs, and conducting the production

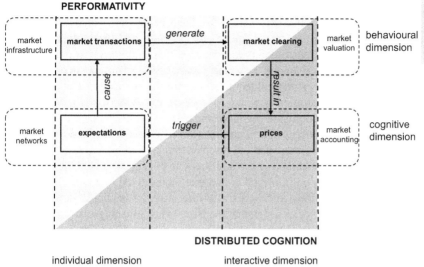

Figure 11.2 The market state as an institution
The diagram builds on the Aoki model of *Chapter 9*. A market state is conceived as an institutionalised circular causal loop between individual behaviour and population-level processes and structures. On each pole, contextual determinants play a role, such as practices of accounting, market infrastructures, social network structures, and practices of valuation. Prices are epiphenomena of market clearing and do not establish equilibrium. Yet they are important in guiding individual expectations, such as on budget constraints. For further detail, see main text.

process in a technical sense. The production process as such constitutes a spate of non-market actions but is obviously tightly related to the market, as produced products must be sold in a future round of the circuit. Transactions themselves are embedded into a market infrastructure, which includes not only the transaction technology, such as a physical marketplace, but also the institutions enabling the transaction. There are two main population-level results of all realised transactions: first, the extent to which the market has been cleared, with no presumption that it actually reaches an equilibrium; and second, the distribution of profits among producers-suppliers. These results then feed back on prices, for example, via decision making of producers-suppliers, including the respective intrafirm decision making processes as well as the population of supplying firms.

This framework describes an institutionalised process in the sense of regularised market behaviour, eventually complemented by the formation of routines in firms[33] and habits of consumers. Markets may be characterised by a relatively high amount of stability; but this is not primarily because of their

Market states are undergirded by the formation of routines in firms and habits of consumers.

See Chapter 6, section 4.1, and Chapter 7, section 5.

inherent tendency to equilibrate demand and supply but because of a more general institutionalisation of market-related behaviour, which is what ultimately constitutes the market niches for products and firms outlined in the previous section. Innovation is associated with a temporary disruption of that institutionalised behaviour, eventually re-stabilising and constituting a new niche. Thus, many structural features of institutional change are applicable to market-based innovation as well.

Divergent interpretations of prices invalidate the no trade theorem.

Market states conjugate cognitive and material states via distributed cognition and performativity. The interpretation of prices is mediated by a wide range of symbolic media and interpretive frames, and by necessity heterogenous: Indeed, the famous no trade theorem[34] suggests that if prices were exclusive carriers on information and were interpreted in a uniform way, no one would be willing to transact at all because the readiness to trade itself would be interpreted as a sign that the trade is not advantageous for the transaction partner.[35] This implies that there is no correct price as a measure to which these variety could be referred.

Prices are not a necessary medium to achieve market clearance.

The notion of market clearance relates to the concept of conjectural equilibrium, that is, a state in which agents' expectations are confirmed by recurrent market action.[36] This confirmation is a direct determinant of market stasis, as agents would not perceive the need to change future behaviour. Although market clearance can be observed as a material phenomenon, prices are by no means the necessary medium to achieve market clearance, as assumed in the standard equilibrium view. A much-cited example is the role of prices of snow shovels after a blizzard: Social conventions strongly frown on raising prices to clear the market such that other mechanisms would be active such as queuing up.

In conclusion, prices are an important element of market states and may be seen as one, but not the only one, cue on market clearing. Market clearing is mainly mediated via perceptions of costs and profits rather than direct expectations on the price responsiveness of demand. Changing prices is an entrepreneurial decision under fundamental uncertainty.

5. Entrepreneurs and firms as market makers

See Chapter 1.

On the role of firms, see Chapter 6, section 4.

The key actors on the supply side of many markets are entrepreneurs and the firms that they create.[37] At the same time, the emergence of firms is not an inevitable outcome of the market process. In principle, markets can arrange the division of labour in a flexible and efficient way while maintaining the autonomy of agents, as the example of China has shown. As we saw in discussing the relationship between technology and firms, the emergence of firms in capitalism was conditioned by the growth of modern technology, which created distinct needs to organise larger scale production processes using complex technological capital, with concomitant requirements for funding that were institutionally accommodated by the legal construct of limited liability. In general, this accentuated the role of entrepreneurs and rendered entrepreneurship riskier. Hence, entrepreneurial firms play an important role in managing and mitigating entrepreneurial risk, and they embody hierarchies and power asymmetries between (the minority of) entrepreneurs/employers and (the majority of) workers-employees. Complementing the focus on the relation between firms and technology in Chapter 6, this section briefly enlarges on those points.

There is a principal rationale for the emergence of firms in that an ex ante valuation of entrepreneurship on markets is not possible, and entrepreneurial activity, therefore, cannot become a service contracted via markets.[38] Such a valuation would only be possible for mere arbitrage activities: For example, the broker is an entrepreneur that trades his specific knowledge about market opportunities and sells his services to customers who are lacking this information. Such intermediaries are significant in both traditional markets and highly sophisticated markets such as finance. However, there are limits to contracting when it comes to true novelty, such as the introduction of an entirely new product. In this case, the Arrow information paradox[39] comes into play: If an entrepreneur wanted to sell her knowledge to another agent, the agent would only be willing to pay if she is fully informed about the nature of this novelty. However, that would imply that the entrepreneur already gives her knowledge away. Therefore, the entrepreneur cannot contract the provision of novelty as a market service but needs to exploit this knowledge by herself. Since this eventually requires expansion of scale, she must set up a firm. This establishes control over entrepreneurial knowledge (e.g., via contracting with other agents and setting up internal hierarchies) as a key function of the firm.[40]

Entrepreneurial firms exist because genuine entrepreneurial knowledge cannot be priced on markets.

Entrepreneurial advantage can be eroded over time via imitation. Therefore, entrepreneurship is only sustainable on the market if there are barriers to imitation.[41] There are two major types of barriers, apart from just keeping secretive about specific knowledge. The first is knowledge that is tacit and idiosyncratic to a degree that it cannot be imitated easily. Another type of barrier is constituted by institutions that actively restrict the utilisation of entrepreneurial knowledge by other actors, in particular, intellectual property rights.

A necessary condition for sustaining entrepreneurial advantage are barriers to imitation, embodied in firms.

On imitation, see Chapter 8, section 3.4.

The erosion of competitive advantage is one key category of entrepreneurial risk flowing from conditions of fundamental market uncertainty, as outlined in the previous sections. We can generalise this by stressing the temporal nature of entrepreneurial action and market-based feedback. Routinely, if an entrepreneur wants to introduce a new product to a market, she will have to spend resources in advance on production or at least on reaching a stage where an offer and a subsequent transaction with a buyer (e.g., in the form of an advance delivery contract) is possible. As said, this spending, and subsequently, pricing, is a decision under fundamental uncertainty and raises the specialisation dilemma in the sense of a reduction of transactional options; the

Entrepreneurial risk-taking involves the specialisation dilemma, particularly if roundabout production is involved.

285

Power- and efficiency-based approaches to the firm can be integrated, explaining the diversity of governance and compensation regimes across firms.

dilemma is aggravated by the necessity of roundabout production via building up (real) capital and investment, which implies an extended time perspective for the vulnerable position of holding specific assets.

Competitive market advantage and entrepreneurial risk are intertwined with power differentials based on the emergence of hierarchies and increasing capability specificity within those structures. This establishes an integrated evolutionary perspective on power- and efficiency-based approaches to the emergence of the firm.[42] One key aspect is the classical risk transformation inherent in the relationship between the (entrepreneurial) employer and the employee. This transformation entails an exchange of reliance on market-based, and inherently risky, profit shares against a regularisation, but also limitation, of income by receiving wages: Effectively, entrepreneurs-owners insure employees against certain categories of market risks in exchange for hierarchical command over the employee's labour power.[43] The inherent asymmetry may be exacerbated by increasing internal specialisation; for example, a long-term employee will regularly develop firm-specific expertise and experience that are not easily transferable to an alternative employer, thereby reducing his exit options and increasing the power of the hierarchical superior, ultimately leading to a hierarchical relationship involving a new specialisation dilemma *within* the firm. More generally, however, distribution of knowledge in firms exhibits wide variety, reaching from exclusive concentration on the top to dispersion across all members. All this results in a wide range of varieties of governance and compensation regimes across the spectrum of firms in the economy.[44]

On these three dimensions, see Chapter 8, section 2.2.

Firms develop organisational structures and practices that enhance cooperation, trust and knowledge sharing within the firm.

Firms constitute distinct network configurations in all three dimensions of transaction, communication, and observation insofar as they establish relatively durable vehicles of intensified interaction both between human individuals (and groups) and between humans and artefacts. Like other network structures related to markets (see previous section), firms allow for the development of cooperative patterns and, more specifically, the convergence of cognitive models of their members. In particular, firms can, again by way of their relative stability, address inherent limits of collaboration exclusively based on monetary incentives, such as the measurement of individual contributions to a cooperative endeavour, a possible orientation towards short-term profit maximisation (in the case of management), a performative increase in opportunism, and a possible self-selection of agents entering a firm in the first place. For example, firms can systematically support the formation of internal networks of trust as well as of a common (corporate) identity.[45] Leadership styles (for example, paternalistic forms as widespread in family businesses but also models of co-determination) can promote long-term loyalty and incentivise human capital formation, thus helping to find a balance between a power-based limitation of exit options and the negative effects of large power asymmetries (e.g., in terms of mutual trust).[46] Finally, intensified interaction also plays an important role in overcoming information asymmetries on individual effort; in standardising communication and interpretation (e.g., with respect to managerial orders) and stabilising mutual expectations; and in providing entrepreneurial leaders with a platform to exert persuasive influence on employees with regard to their visions and conceptions.[47]

The existence of firms also entails a signalling function. Again, given the ubiquity of asymmetric information and fundamental uncertainty, the key is the firm's relative durability as a recipient of resource flows and occupant of a niche. This may be combined with social status considerations, such as in the case of luxury brands. Potentially at least, a firm's signalling is important vis-à-vis all its (potential) transaction partners, although it may take different forms: buyers and consumers with respect to the quality, longevity, or social status accredited to a product; creditors with respect to competitiveness and financial stability; employees with respect to the quality of, and social status stemming from, an employment relationship; and competitors with respect to potentials to outcompete them. The signalling function with respect to creditors ties this approach to the firm back to the issue of time lags and the associated entrepreneurial risk.

Firms shape market niches via their communication, such as signalling by means of branding.

On social status, see Chapter 8, section 3.2.

Firms structure market competition as autonomous units of evolution insofar as they constitute organisational structures that exist, in principle, independently from the entry and exit of individuals, and as they are primary carriers of technological capabilities. But firms also sustain or even create markets, in the sense of market making:[48] The more complex the economy, the stronger the limitations on individual agency to sustain a market. Therefore, in the evolutionary view, firms and markets are complements, contrasting the theoretical stance of transaction cost theories that they are substitutes. This renders phenomena such as value chains in production networks inherently plausible on theoretical grounds.

In the evolutionary view, firms and markets are complements.

The structuring of market competition by firms also implies that niches for products do not coincide with niches of firms, if they generate multiple products: A market niche for a firm may derive from its capability to specialise into the production of a variety of products occupying different niches (e.g., by employing a baseline technology), or a product or product category may be produced by different firms, possibly employing different technologies. A divergence of niches of products and of firms may also stem from the appropriability of entrepreneurial rents and profit, given barriers to imitation as outlined earlier.

Multi-product firms operate in various market niches and create firm-specific niches via exploiting generic but firm-specific capabilities.

As far as firms are present as market actors, internal selection *within* firms and external selection pressure *on* firms as units of selection need to be distinguished. In this perspective, the entrepreneurial development of a new product is a multi-stage process, routinely starting with intrapreneurial activity within the firm and continuing with the standard entrepreneurial push on the respective market, which will again feed back to intra-organisational development and learning. In line with the general structure of multilevel selection, the organisation-level criterion of adapting to, and eventually shaping, its

We distinguish internal selection within the firm (intrapreneurship) and external selection via the market.

niche does not necessarily coincide with the motives and incentives of intra-firm groups or decision makers, a fact which may drive a wedge between internal and external selection criteria. A standard case is that a firm-level introduction of a new product based on a new technology devalues intrafirm assets related to a hitherto established technology and is, therefore, resisted by the holders and beneficiaries of those assets due to a concern with internal power and influence. Increased external competitive pressure would then tend to decrease the wedge and, by implication, limit internal power. In contrast, very high competitive intensity may dilute the firm's innovation potential, given the firm's role as core organisational form of specialisation in production.

6. Markets and institutions

Returning to the example of the entrepreneur introducing a new product, another obvious risk of building up specific assets is to be subject to theft, fraud, or similar misdemeanours. From an institutional point of view, this raises two issues. The first is the operational significance of clearly assigned, and enforceable, agential powers for the market process because of their effect on reducing transaction cost, particularly the cost of tensions and conflict. The second is the assurance of voluntary rather than forced exchange, which is at the core of the connection between markets and the value of liberty.

Markets regularly, but not necessarily evolve towards a pivotal role of the law and sovereign authority in governing transactions, especially property rights.

The first and most straightforward type of institutions addressing those issues is formal (i.e., the law). The connection between legal principles and the idea of voluntary, and eventually market-based, exchange is deeply entrenched in the Western legal tradition, based on the classic liberal idea that liberty, and therefore, any meaningful notion of voluntary choice, presupposes the availability of property rights as assignments of agential power over an asset to a specific individual or group, including the right to exclude others from its use.[49] Property rights are intimately related to contract law, which, to a large extent, defines rights and obligations around the transfer of property rights, and criminal law, which regulates the sanctioning of breaches. At their core, these formal institutions rely on the presence of a political sovereign, which both concretises and elaborates them and provides implementation and enforcement via controlled use of violence. Thus, state authority reduces entrepreneurial risk and improves the framework conditions for market-based specialisation.[50]

On emotional roots of ownership, see Chapter 7, section 3.3; on property rights as an institution, Chapter 9, section 3.1.

However, a brief glance into history suffices to see that state-enforced property rights do not constitute a generic feature of the operation of markets. Traditional Chinese contract law mainly operated as customary law that was enforced by private regulation.[51] Even in modern capitalist economies, property rights and their enforcement always need complements on the informal institutional level. For one, there is the question of values and the associated conventions and norms regarding respect of ownership. Furthermore, there are elements of tolerance of, or even respect for, material inequality, which can refer to different reference groups (reaching, e.g., from the family to the state) and be rooted in rational (e.g., the expectation of social ascendancy) as well as emotional factors (e.g., a strong commitment towards meritocratic values).[52] However, there are principled limits to the enforcement capacity of state authorities. The complementary sanctioning mechanisms will strongly depend on the associated network configurations, including technologies of network organisation: For example, online auctions for small-scale items use indirect enforcement mechanisms such as a public evaluation of traders, although they certainly continue to work under the shadow of applicable law.

However, social networks, social values and informal institutions remain important complementary elements.

Issues of voluntariness, uncertainty, and asymmetries of power on markets are pervasive in modern economic law. For example, competition law, by providing precautionary regulation against monopolisation, among others, is intended to ensure that voluntary market-based exchange is not factually transformed into forced exchange. In a general sense, rental law and employment law pursue a similar objective insofar as they try to level out systematic power asymmetries between contract partners. Regarding uncertainty and information flows, beyond standard contract law, for example, consumer protection laws increase market transparency and intend to (further) reduce fraud and cheating.[53]

Specific legal frames, such as competition law and consumer protection law, deal with ubiquitous asymmetries of power and information.

It is essential to recognise that formal institutions regulating markets render them operational not just by constraining individual behaviour but by *performing* market behaviour. This is easiest to see for the case of instituting new immaterial rights, such as intellectual property rights or emission rights. As far as those rights are tied to monetary resource flows and valuation, they essentially create new markets by acts of marketisation or commodification and, therefore, also define what would be perceived as a risk of theft in the first place.[54] But the performativity of institutions also relates to the decomposition of standard property rights, such as by rights of lien or mortgages, or financial claims as assetification.[55]

The law is a major performative medium in markets, such as in creating entirely new objects via defining new forms of property or in enabling the creation of new agents such as the corporation.

Further, the performativity of formal institutions pertains to the definition of complementary rules for non-market allocation. The most important example of this is corporate law, which defines and standardises a specific set of organisational and hierarchical positions as well as rights and obligations flowing from them (e.g., with respect to legal personality, liability, bodies and their competencies, due diligence rules, and insolvency procedures). The operation of firms on modern markets is, therefore, not a natural given but in fact performed by their underlying legal framework. This is often overlooked in the discussion of various theories of the firm, which simply take the alternative between market-based and firm-based allocation as given and tend to be vague on the concrete institutional options that are involved.

7. Conclusion

This chapter presents the core ideas of evolutionary market theory. We frame the common notion of market clearing as a market state. As a consequence, much analytical burden is relieved from prices as the pivotal means to coordinate market actions. We believe that the overemphasis on prices has created an impoverished view on markets that is far away from reality: Coordination on markets is complex and multidimensional, and prices are often just expressions of market states which have been achieved by other media of coordination.

Markets are complex evolutionary systems working on multiple levels. In this chapter, we only looked at the niche and the firm. However, there are other levels, in particular relating to the spatial nature of markets. This can often be grasped by positive externalities, such as in the case of regional economies which manifest economies of cooperation and information sharing that have been already highlighted by Alfred Marshall in his notion of industrial districts.[56] Similarly, markets are embedded in social groups, such as in ethnic trading communities.[57] The notion of levels of selection implies that in these cases market competition takes place within the respective level (such as ethnic traders competing among the group over business opportunities) and on that level (the ethnic traders as a group competing against other groups). As a result, market dynamics has a much greater complexity than normally assumed by economists and is better recognised by historians or sociologists.

One important implication is that we cannot reduce economic policy to the clarion call of getting prices right, which is mainly interpreted as liberalising the economy. Freedom of market actors is not just granted by free movement of prices but mainly be ensuring that power asymmetries are minimised. This does not mean that intervening in prices is without dysfunctional effects since, after all, pricing is a key entrepreneurial action. But we cannot expect that a perceived problem in market states can be naively resolved by getting prices right, for the simple reason that there are no right prices.

> We explore spatial aspects in Chapter 14.

> *Economic freedom cannot be achieved by getting prices right but by levelling power asymmetries on the marketplace.*

Major chapter insights

- Markets constitute the interface between the traditional delineation of micro- and macroeconomics: On the one hand, markets are driven by individual behaviour; on the other, they are population-level phenomena, with money constituting the medium of aggregation.
- Markets entail various temporal scopes, reaching from short-run price setting to longer-term structuration of market systems. Risk

and uncertainty, and their distribution across actors, are constitutive parts of the market process.

- The main actors on the market supply side are entrepreneurs and firms. Entrepreneurs can act as innovators and risk-takers, with the establishment of firms constituting a vehicle to spread risk but also to protect entrepreneurial knowledge against imitation and thereby developing and maintaining competitive advantage. Firms also serve as relatively stable vehicle of routines and as branding and signalling devices vis-à-vis different transaction partners. All those functions imply that firms regularly engage in 'making' complex markets and that firms and markets are complements rather than substitutes.
- An evolutionary view of markets looks at the market process as a multilevel phenomenon entailing niche formation on the level of products, markets, and market systems. The product space evolves according to principles of variation, selection, and retention. At the same time, the market process is frequently characterised by evolutionary stasis.
- The evolutionary counterpart to the standard notion of market equilibrium is market states. Market states conjugate cognitive and material states via distributed cognition and performativity, with expectations playing a constitutive role for realised transactions and prices constituting a material artefact around which distributed cognition is organised.
- Market states are embedded in institutions regulating market behaviour. In the Western tradition, those institutions are mostly of a formal-legal kind but always need to be complemented by conventions and informal institutions. Institutions perform and eventually create new markets by acts of marketisation and commodification.

Notes

1 Such intermediary phenomena are referred to as meso by evolutionary economists, Dopfer (2012).
2 This is closely related to, but not fully equivalent to the approach of evolutionary economics, which itself has been characterised by intellectual and conceptional fragmentation throughout its history, see Nelson (1995) and Witt (2008). There are strands focusing on competition and innovation (seminally, Nelson and Winter 1982), and strands promoting the Darwinian paradigm as a full-scale alternative to neoclassical economics (Veblen, 1898; Hodgson 1999). There are a couple of closely connected approaches, such as the old Institutional economics (Ayres,

1944), complexity theory (Anderson et al., 1988), and econophysics, which has been taken up particularly in the context of financial economics (Jovanovic and Schinckus, 2017).

3 Keynes (1960[1936], chapter 12).

4 This is in the tradition of Coase's (1937) influential contribution.

5 Smith (1776, Book I, chapter II) famously remarked that "Nobody ever saw a dog make a fair and deliberate exchange of one bone for another with another dog".

6 White (2002).

7 Although the term 'niche' is widely used in marketing, the concept does not play a systematic role in the established microeconomic theory of markets. However, it is central to economic sociology, seminally Burt and Talmud (1993) or Hannan et al. (2007).

8 Although this is taken for granted in economics, sociologists have identified this as the key to the social ontology of markets, classically Luhmann (1994).

9 For example, Metcalfe (1998), Witt (2003), or Hodgson and Knudsen (2013).

10 However, in the sense of ontological continuity, there is a notion of biological markets; some human markets, such as for marriage, refer to both social and biological reproduction, Barclay (2016).

11 Sugden (2018).

12 Evolutionary economists have explored this view in much detail; for example, see Nelson et al. (2018). It must be noted that agent-based modelling in general pursues the same mechanistic paradigm, see Hamill and Gilbert (2016).

13 Hayek (1945).

14 Hidalgo (2015), Coyle (2015, 88, 126ff).

15 Herrmann-Pillath (2011, 96f), referring to a non-published paper by Timo Ehrig.

16 This is the perspective of organisational demography; for a survey, see Hsu and Hannan (2005).

17 The concept of stasis is much emphasised by the evolutionary biologist Gould (2002).

18 This concept relates to Nelson's concept of market order, Nelson (2013).

19 Beckert (2016).

20 Huang (1990).

21 See, for the emergence of an empire of things during the Industrial Revolution, Trentmann (2017).

22 Lo (2019, 176ff).

23 Witt (2003, 310ff).

24 Seminally, Scott (1976).

25 Krähmer (2006).

26 Forsyth et al. (2018[2005]), Rietveld and Schilling (2021).

27 See, for the case of sword-making in Japan, Martin (2000).

28 Çalışkan and Callon (2010), Pistor (2019).

29 Kirzner (1979).

30 Liquidity is much emphasised by Keynes (1960[1936]).

31 Kirzner (1979).

32 This is done along the lines of Herrmann-Pillath (2013, 530f), who combines the Aoki model of institutions presented in Chapter 9 with Nelson's (2013) analysis of a market order.

33 The concept of routines is essential to the models of markets developed by Nelson and Winter (1982); for a survey, see Lazaric (2011).

34 Milgrom and Stokey (1982).

35 Lo (2019, 45ff).

36 Seminally, Hahn (1977).

37 Seminally, Casson (1997).

38 Herrmann-Pillath (2001).

39 Arrow (1962).

40 These topics have been intensively discussed in contexts such as the theory of the multinational firm, see Narula et al. (2019).

41 This was the key insight in building the theory of sustained competitive advantage in strategic management thinking, Barney (1991).

42 For efficiency-based views, see, for example, Foss (1993) and Hodgson and Knudsen (2004); on power-based views, Marglin (1991) or Anderson (2018).

43 The locus classicus is Barzel (1989).

44 Aoki (2010).

45 Roberts (2004), Henderson and van den Steen (2015).

46 Aoki (2010).

47 In management science, this is covered under the topic of corporate culture, Schein (2017).

48 Casson (1997).

49 For a modern view on this classical theme, beginning with John Locke, see Dagan (2021).

50 Barzel (2002).

51 Huang (2006).

52 Such differences are explored in large-scale surveys such as the World Values Survey, Inglehart (2018).

53 Economists differ in judging the degree of potential fraud and cheating on the marketplace. For a view emphasising the role of governance and government intervention, see Akerlof and Shiller (2015).

54 For the fascinating example of fisheries, see Holm and Nielsen (2007).

55 Pistor (2019).

56 Rutten and Boekema (2007).

57 Rauch (2001).

References

Akerlof, G. A. and Shiller, R. J. (2015) *Phishing for Phools: The Economics of Manipulation and Deception.* Princeton and Oxford: Princeton University Press.

Anderson, E. (2018) *Private Government How Employers Rule Our Lives (and Why We Don't Talk about It)*. Princeton: Princeton University Press.

Anderson, P., Arrow, K. and Pines, D. (eds.) (1988) *The Economy as an Evolving Complex System*. New York: Addison – Wesley.

Aoki, M. (2010) *Corporations in Evolving Diversity: Cognition, Governance, and Institutions*. Oxford: Oxford University Press. DOI: 10.1093/acprof: oso/9780199218530.001.0001.

Arrow, K. J. (1962) 'Economic Welfare and the Allocation of Resources for Invention', in NBER (ed.) *The Rate and Direction of Inventive Activity: Economic and Social Factors*. Princeton: Princeton University Press, pp. 609–626.

Ayres, C. E. (1944) *The Theory of Economic Progress*. Chapel Hill: University of North Carolina Press.

Barclay, P. (2016) 'Biological Markets and the Effects of Partner Choice on Cooperation and Friendship', *Current Opinion in Psychology*, 7, pp. 33–38. DOI: 10.1016/j.copsyc.2015.07.012.

Barney, J. (1991) 'Firm Resources and Sustained Competitive Advantage', *Journal of Management*, 17(1), pp. 99–120. DOI: 10.1177/014920639101700108.

Barzel, Y. (1989) *Economic Analysis of Property Rights*. Cambridge: Cambridge University Press.

Barzel, Y. (2002) *A Theory of the State: Economic Rights, Legal Rights, and the Scope of the State*. Cambridge: Cambridge University Press.

Beckert, J. (2016) *Imagined Futures: Fictional Expectations and Capitalist Dynamics*. Cambridge: Harvard University Press. DOI: 10.4159/9780674545878.

Burt, R. S. and Talmud, I. (1993) 'Market Niche', *Social Networks*, 15(2), pp. 133–149.

Çalışkan, K. and Callon, M. (2010) 'Economization, Part 2: A Research Programme for the Study of Markets', *Economy and Society*, 39(1), pp. 1–32. DOI: 10.1080/03085140903424519.

Casson, M. (1997) *Information and Organization: A New Perspective on the Theory of the Firm*. Oxford: Clarendon.

Coase, R. H. (1937) 'The Nature of the Firm', *Economica*, 4(16), pp. 386–405. DOI: 10.1111/j.1468-0335.1937.tb00002.x.

Coyle, D. (2015) *GDP: A Brief but Affectionate History*. Princeton: Princeton University Press.

Dagan, Ḥ. (2021) *A Liberal Theory of Property*. Cambridge and New York: Cambridge University Press. DOI: 10.1017/9781108290340.

Dopfer, K. (2012) 'The Origins of Meso Economics', *Journal of Evolutionary Economics*, 22(1), pp. 133–160. DOI: 10.1007/S00191-011-0218-4.

Forsyth, P. *et al.* (eds.) (2018[2005]) *Competition versus Predation in Aviation Markets: A Survey of Experience in North America, Europe and Australia*. London: Routledge. DOI: 10.4324/9781351161404.

Foss, N. J. (1993) 'Theories of the Firm: Contractual and Competence Theories', *Journal of Evolutionary Economics*, 3(2), pp. 127–144. DOI: 10.1007/BF01213830.

Gould, S. J. (2002) *The Structure of Evolutionary Theory*. Cambridge and London: Belknap.

Hahn, F. H. (1977) 'Exercises in Conjectural Equilibria', *The Scandinavian Journal of Economics*, 79(2), pp. 210–226.

Hamill, L. and Gilbert, G. N. (2016) *Agent-Based Modelling in Economics*. Chichester and Hoboken: John Wiley & Sons. DOI: 10.1002/9781118945520.

Hannan, M. T., Pólos, L. and Carroll, G. R. (2007) *Logics of Organization Theory: Audiences, Codes, and Ecologies*. Princeton: Princeton University Press.

Hayek, F. A. von (1945) 'The Use of Knowledge in Society', *American Economic Review*, 35(4), pp. 519–530.

Henderson, R. and Van den Steen, E. (2015) 'Why Do Firms Have "Purpose"? The Firm's Role as a Carrier of Identity and Reputation', *American Economic Review*, 105(5), pp. 326–330. DOI: 10.1257/aer.p20151072.

Herrmann-Pillath, C. (2001) 'A General Refutation of the Law of One Price as Empirical Hypothesis', *Jahrbücher für Nationalökonomie und Statistik*, 221(1), pp. 45–67.

Herrmann-Pillath, C. (2011) *The Economics of Identity and Creativity. A Cultural Science Approach*. St. Lucia: University of Queensland Press.

Herrmann-Pillath, C. (2013) *Foundations of Economic Evolution: A Treatise on the Natural Philosophy of Economics*. Cheltenham and Northampton: Edward Elgar Publishing. DOI: 10.4337/9781782548362.

Hidalgo, C. A. (2015) *Why Information Grows: The Evolution of Order, from Atoms to Economies*. London: Penguin Books.

Hodgson, G. M. (1999) *Evolution and Institutions: On Evolutionary Economics and the Evolution of Economics*. Cheltenham and Northampton: Edward Elgar Publishing.

Hodgson, G. M. and Knudsen, T. (2004) 'The Firm as an Interactor: Firms as Vehicles for Habits and Routines', *Journal of Evolutionary Economics*, 14(3), pp. 281–309. DOI: 10.1007/s00191-004-0192-1.

Hodgson, G. M. and Knudsen, T. (2013) *Darwin's Conjecture: The Search for General Principles of Social and Economic Evolution*. Chicago: University of Chicago Press.

Holm, P. and Nielsen, T. N. (2007) 'Framing Fish, Making Markets: The Construction of Individual Transferable Quotas (ITQs)', *Sociological Review*, 55(s2), pp. 173–195. DOI: 10.1111/j.1467-954X.2007.00735.x.

Hsu, G. and Hannan, M. T. (2005) 'Identities, Genres, and Organizational Forms', *Organization Science*, 16(5), pp. 474–490. DOI: 10.1287/orsc.1050.0151.

Huang, P. C. C. (1990) *The Peasant Family and Rural Development in the Yangzi Delta, 1350–1988*. Stanford: Stanford University Press.

Huang, P. C. C. (2006) 'Civil Adjudication in China, Past and Present', *Modern China*, 32(2), pp. 135–180. DOI: 10.1177/0097700405285397.

Inglehart, R. (2018) *Cultural Evolution: People's Motivations are Changing, and Reshaping the World*. Cambridge: Cambridge University Press. DOI: 10.1017/9781108613880.

Jovanovic, F. and Schinckus, C. (2017) *Econophysics and Financial Economics: An Emerging Dialogue*. New York City: Oxford University Press. DOI: 10.1093/acprof:oso/9780190205034.001.0001.

Keynes, J. M. (1960[1936]) *The General Theory of Employment, Interest and Money*. London: MacMillan.

Kirzner, I. M. (1979) *Perception, Opportunity, and Profit: Studies in the Theory of Entrepreneurship*. Chicago: University of Chicago Press.

Krähmer, D. (2006) 'Advertising and Conspicuous Consumption', *Journal of Institutional and Theoretical Economics (JITE)*, 162(4), pp. 661–682. DOI: 10.1628/093245606779252689.

Lazaric, N. (2011) 'Organizational Routines and Cognition: An Introduction to Empirical and Analytical Contributions', *Journal of Institutional Economics*, 7(2), pp. 147–156. DOI: 10.1017/S1744137411000130.

Lo, A. W. (2019) *Adaptive Markets: Financial Evolution at the Speed of Thought*. Princeton: Princeton University Press. DOI: 10.1515/9780691196800.

Luhmann, N. (1994) *Die Wirtschaft der Gesellschaft*. Frankfurt am Main: Suhrkamp Verlag.

Marglin, S. (1991) 'Understanding Capitalism: Control versus Efficiency', in Gustafsson, B. (ed.) *Power and Economic Institutions: Reinterpretations in Economic History*. Aldershot: Edward Elgar Publishing, pp. 107–169.

Martin, G. (2000) 'Stasis in Complex Artefacts', in Ziman, J. (ed.) *Technological Innovation as an Evolutionary Process*. Cambridge: Cambridge University Press, pp. 90–100.

Metcalfe, J. S. (1998) *Evolutionary Economics and Creative Destruction*. London and New York: Routledge. DOI: 10.4324/9780203018927.

Milgrom, P. and Stokey, N. (1982) 'Information, Trade and Common Knowledge', *Journal of Economic Theory*, 26(1), pp. 17–27. DOI: 10.1016/0022-0531 (82)90046-1.

Narula, R. *et al*. (2019) 'Applying and Advancing Internalization Theory: The Multinational Enterprise in the Twenty-First Century', *Journal of International Business Studies*, 50(8), pp. 1231–1252. DOI: 10.1057/s41267-019-00260-6.

Nelson, R. R. (1995) 'Recent Evolutionary Theorizing About Economic Change', *Journal of Economic Literature*, XXXIII, pp. 48–90.

Nelson, R. R. (2013) 'Demand, Supply, and their Interactions on Markets, as Seen from the Perspective of Evolutionary Economic Theory', *Journal of Evolutionary Economics*, 23(1), pp. 17–38. DOI: 10.1007/s00191-012-0274-4.

Nelson, R. R. and Winter, S. G. (1982) *An Evolutionary Theory of Economic Change*. Cambridge and London: Belknap.

Nelson, R. R. *et al*. (eds.) (2018) *Modern Evolutionary Economics: An Overview*. Cambridge and New York: Cambridge University Press. DOI: 10.1017/9781108661928.

Pistor, K. (2019) *The Code of Capital: How the Law Creates Wealth and Inequality*. Princeton: Princeton University Press. DOI: 10.1515/9780691189437.

Rauch, J. E. (2001) 'Business and Social Networks in International Trade', *Journal of Economic Literature*, 39(4), pp. 1177–1203. DOI: 10.1257/jel.39.4.1177.

Rietveld, J. and Schilling, M. A. (2021) 'Platform Competition: A Systematic and Interdisciplinary Review of the Literature', *Journal of Management*, 47(6), pp. 1528–1563. DOI: 10.1177/0149206320969791.

Roberts, J. (2004) *The Modern Firm: Organizational Design for Performance and Growth*. Oxford: Oxford University Press.

Rutten, R. and Boekema, F. (2007) *The Learning Region: Foundations, State of the Art, Future*. Cheltenham and Northampton: Edward Elgar Publishing.

Schein, E. H. (2017) *Organizational Culture and Leadership*. 5th Edition. Hoboken: Wiley & Sons.

Scott, J. C. (1976) *The Moral Economy of the Peasant: Rebellion and Subsistence in Southeast Asia*. New Haven: Yale University Press.

Smith, A. (1776) *An Inquiry into the Nature and Causes of the Wealth of Nations*. London: W. Strahan and T. Cadell.

Sugden, R. (2018) *The Community of Advantage: A Behavioural Economist's Defence of the Market*. Oxford and New York: Oxford University Press. DOI: 10.1093/oso/9780198825142.001.0001.

Trentmann, F. (2017) *Empire of Things: How We Became a World of Consumers, from the Fifteenth Century to the Twenty-First*. London: Penguin Books.

Veblen, T. (1898) 'Why is Economics not an Evolutionary Science?' *The Quarterly Journal of Economics*, 12(4), pp. 373–397.

White, H. (2002) *Markets from Networks: Socioeconomic Models of Production*. Princeton: Princeton University Press.

Witt, U. (2003) *The Evolving Economy: Essays on the Evolutionary Approach to Economics*. Cheltenham and Northampton: Edward Elgar Publishing.

Witt, U. (2008) 'What Is Specific about Evolutionary Economics?', *Journal of Evolutionary Economics*, 18(5), pp. 547–576.

PART IV

CHAPTER TWELVE

Money and finance

1. Introduction

A fundamental fact about real-world market economies is that private and sovereign producers of money interact in provisioning the economy with money and that the activity of finance directly influences real economic activity. Current macroeconomics distinguishes between the money market and the capital market: The former is defined as the market where the equilibrium between demand and supply of money is established; the latter, as the market where the equilibrium between saving and investment is determined.[1]

In contrast, we adopt an integrative view on the money market and the capital market which is based on a broad conception of finance and which instead disentangles the capital market into two markets, one for saving and the other for investment. This is based on the concept of the budget. The budget constraint defines the financial constraints of economic activity; finance is the domain in the economy where the budget constraint can be managed via operations involving money and assets denominated in money, especially in the intertemporal dimension.

> We introduce the budget constraint in Chapter 11.

As one central implication, we recognise the impact of accounting on economic activity.[2] Accounting is involved in a core entrepreneurial activity of finance, namely the creation and handling of assets: We define as an asset any object that embodies a monetary value and that is deployed to generate a yield measured in monetary units. We identify a universal performative mechanism, assetification, which entails use of legal means to create an institutional object in monetary terms, such as a share that represents a right on economic profits generated from the underlying real capital in productive use. Assetification puts the institutional dimension of macroeconomic analysis centre stage: Money flows are interwoven with processes of assetification and markets for assets. This complex institutional structure is what we refer to as finance.

> *We distinguish between capital and assets resulting from the legal process of assetification.*

> This distinction builds on our analysis of transactions in Chapter 8, section 2.2.

We present an evolutionary view on money and finance in the following senses.[3] First, we argue that money must be seen as inherently diversified, with various functionally adaptive forms. Second, money practices entail strong

301

DOI: 10.4324/9781003094869-17

We present an evolutionary view on money and finance that emphasises the functional diversity of money, financial innovation, and novelty in behavioural patterns coalescing into types of agencies.

performative effects, which play out in assetification and its repercussions on the financial system, where financial innovation driven by financial entrepreneurship is an important driving force.[4] Third, financial innovation creates the space for the emergence of new and variegated forms of economic agency, which we can approach in a typology of actors. Fourth, financial innovation and changes in the composition of types in the population of market agents are major determinants of behavioural patterns on markets, especially financial markets.

In the following, we will start out from exploring the production of money by private and sovereign agents. Section 3 explores money and capital, starting out from considering the relation between saving and investment, both defined as real economic activities, namely saving as intertemporal shift of consumption at a given budget constraint and investment as formation of real capital by means of reducing consumption at present, thus expanding the intertemporal budget constraint. We also consider the complex question of valuing capital. Section 4 concludes with a discussion of liability arrangements in assetification, which are central for the allocation of risk.

2. Private and sovereign money

See, for the intrinsic value of money, Chapter 10, section 3.1.

Whereas money as a generalised medium of exchange is a public good, the budget is a private good.

Money is a sign for generalised opportunities of exchange and, therefore, has intrinsic value beyond its mere contribution to improving the technology of exchange. Money is a specific form of social capital: I cannot consume money alone since its use for me is entirely dependent on others accepting it as means of payment and vice versa. At the same time, the budget (i.e., a specific amount of money available to an actor) is a private good from which others can be excluded and over which alternative uses and users rival; this explains why people are willing to pay a price for obtaining money, such as paying interest for taking a loan. The evolution of money reveals a distinct role of both private (market agents) and sovereign (government) producers of money, which are conjugated in modern monetary regimes of capitalism.

2.1. Private money as assetified debt

Early money was intimately tied to political communities, thus creating a medium of trust.

The emergence and rapid diffusion of minting and coins in the Ancient Mediterranean was directly linked to the concept of community of the Greek city state: Coins were signed by the sacred symbols of these communities, thereby imbuing them with an aura of trustworthiness.[5] This created a pattern of monetary evolution in which the institution of money was almost always placed in a political context. There is a similarity to the situation today, with states or other political bodies such as the European Union issuing the legal tender.

The question is whether the political framing of money is necessary to establish society-wide shared trust into money. Private issuance of money mostly emerged in the context of long-distance trading, involving groups who arrange tradable certificates that allow the holder to draw on an account of the issuer.[6] For example, a merchant in one city may issue an IOU that can be drawn by a fellow merchant in another city, and the two would settle accounts separately. In this case, therefore, money is backed by a group or community that specialises in organising transactions which transcend borders of primordial communities. IOUs become money when they start to circulate and people accept them without immediately cashing in.[7]

This analysis motivates a new formulation of the triangular exchange paradigm in understanding money as endogenously emerging in a market. In Figure 12.1, we look at a triangle of loan relations in the form of real borrowings, such as lending wheat to another farmer, or generally, a supplier loan. In a barter economy without prices, these loans are incommensurable; however, they create an asset, which corresponds to the debt. Once money exists, this debt can be measured in terms of the price of the item lent. This creates space for assetification as the creation of an institutional object. Assetification transforms debt into private money if agents can cancel one bilateral debt as liability with another debt as claim, such as C using $debt_2$ to pay back $loan_1$ cancelling $debt_1$.

Private money emerged in communities of traders mutually extending credit.

For triangular exchange, see Chapter 8, section 2.1.

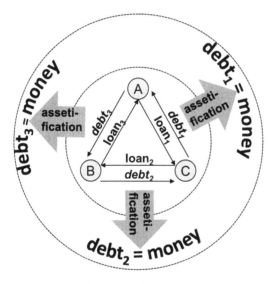

The triangular exchange paradigm is defined in terms of pairwise debt, where money enables the assetification of debt and, hence, a triangular balancing on new institutional objects.

Figure 12.1 Triangular exchange, debt and money
In this model of trilateral exchange, the triangular exchange of goods is enabled via bilateral borrowings. The introduction of prices allows to measure the debt and renders it commensurable across agents. This enables assetification of debt, which creates the possibility to balance the bilateral debts trilaterally. Assetified debts constitute money as institutional objects. The process presupposes the existence of money as an accounting standard enabling pricing.

There is a long strand of similar institutional innovations in which de facto private money is issued in the context of systems of sovereign supply of the legal tender. All these innovations are forms of assetification, establishing an asset that is tradable and assumes the functions of money.[8] Historically, the principles of sovereign and private issuance of money were merged in the 19th century, when the new central banks accepted bills of exchange in exchange for legal tender. A highly trusted bill of exchange is private money once it circulates widely and is accepted in all kinds of transactions as a means of payment. This is an evolving money practice in the sense of the Aoki model.

Private money is in fact governed by the same principles of community enforcement of promises as in the primordial communities, building on and transforming social capital of the community of producers of private money. This pattern emerged in medieval long-distance trade, where large merchant houses increasingly traded bills of exchange generated in commerce, without necessarily being directly involved in the original transactions. However, access to these circles was limited such that common network mechanisms that generate trust could apply (e.g., the threat of ostracism).

A large-scale system of private money is typically organised as a hierarchical system of networks of exchange. We can grasp this in a general fashion by complementing the concept of primary monetary community, as previously introduced, by the secondary monetary community:[9] In the primary community, money is used as a means of extending mutual credit in market exchange, such as accepting a delay in payment; the secondary community is the network of financial agents who trade with mutual promises to pay as financial assets, such as bills of exchange. The two connect via referring to the same symbolic representation of various forms of credit, which is money. One remarkable feature of modern finance is that it has not become footloose but continues to be spatially concentrated, although modern technology would certainly allow for dispersal.[10] Spatial circumscription creates the conditions for forming social capital among the members of the secondary monetary community.

The question is how far such a system of private money can go. Clearly, the problem is how to establish and maintain trust that permeates all levels of society and allows for a deep division of labour.[11] There is a fundamental tension between the use of money in society and a community-based system of generating trust. Indeed, a frequent occurrence over past centuries was a collapse of trust within the secondary community. These financial crises affected credit relations in the primary monetary communities (credit crunch).[12]

As said, one central function of money is to serve as unit of account for the assessment of debt and repayment obligations. This applies to all kinds of debt, including taxation which relates to the production of public goods.[13] If taxation takes place in monetary terms, there must be a unit of account that measures this obligation and relates to the valuation of private goods traded

On money as social capital, see Chapter 10, section 4.3.

On ostracism, see Chapter 8, section 3.3.

We distinguish between the primary community of money users in markets and the secondary community of financial agents trading with claims on money and producing private money.

Maintaining trust between the primary and the secondary communities is a key issue in stabilising the institution of money.

On financial crises, see Chapter 13, section 5.2.

on markets such that the debt can be assessed in terms of the value of income generated by market activities. This is the bridge between money as involved in taxation and money as used in the market. Thus, the value of private money as manifest in its proper functioning as a unit of account in the market is interconnected with its role as the unit of account in taxation.[14]

2.2. Sovereign money as public unit of account

Trust in sovereign money is established by enforcing the unit of account via taxation. Originally, units of account did not emerge in the market context but in the context of the public economy of the Sumerian empire.[15] A historical turning point came with the use of sovereign money as a means to procure goods and services via the market rather than via imposition of direct confiscation of goods or forced labour.[16]

This turning point did not only take place in the Western hemisphere but also in China, where it happened during Ming times (1368–1644).[17] However, China did not experience another turning point, namely the emergence of government debt which is fungible on financial markets.[18] This emergence reveals a deep relationship between money and government debt insofar as both presuppose a certain level of trust into the governments' capability and willingness to maintain its trustworthiness or creditworthiness, both as an issuer of money and of public debt.

In the European case, the emergence of government debt resulted in an intimate relationship between the secondary monetary community and the sovereigns which never emerged in China. Yet private money did not supersede sovereign money, and during industrialisation and concomitant warfare, culminating in the world wars of the 20th century, government grew to a size that made it by far the most important actor in the economy, thus further bolstering the role of sovereign money.

From the perspective of issuers of private money, there are considerable gains from leveraging public trust into private money by building on the trust that sovereign money enjoys. The disadvantage is that the sovereign may abuse its power in debasing and inflating sovereign money. From the perspective of the sovereign, by tapping financial markets via issuing bonds, it can rely on private money to leverage its own access to the resources of its jurisdiction beyond taxation. However, when sovereign money is used as a unit of account in both domains, a serious coordination problem emerges insofar as a single private actor would be strongly motivated to expand production of money in order to gain market shares, resulting in over-expansion of the total money supply.

There are two major ways to address this problem. The first is the common reference to a scarce commodity, as historically represented by the gold standard in the Western world.[19] However, the gold standard severely restricts the political autonomy of government, given that national money supply will be directly determined by international trade and investment flows.

A key mechanism in establishing trust in private money is grounding the unit of account in taxation, that is, in assessing the debt towards the sovereign.

Sovereign money emerged as unit of account in the public economy and taxation.

The emergence of government debt in Europe created a close relationship between government and the secondary monetary community (i.e., the financial sector).

See, for the case of China, Chapter 1, section 4.

Modern central banks govern monetary policy to constrain private production of money in fractional reserve regimes. Confidence into central banks derives from institutional safeguards, such as central bank independence.

The second way is the establishment of a central bank which assumes responsibility of controlling the money supply. This can, in principle, be done by private actors. Historically, that was indeed the case for the first central bank, the Bank of England, which was a private-public partnership between the secondary monetary community and the sovereign. However, a central bank without sovereign backing faces limitations to its creditworthiness. While problems of trustworthiness are also inherent to sovereign central banks, those can be addressed by institutionally containing sovereign intervention possibilities, which is routinely achieved on the constitutional level. Such a solution can be in the interest of both the sovereign, since trust in sovereign money is bolstered, and private financial actors insofar as they gain access to sovereign money.[20] In the late 19th century, this happened mainly via the possibility to discount bills of exchange at the central bank, which constituted the origin of monetary policy in which money supply is indirectly managed via a variety of tools. If banks hold fractional reserves in sovereign money, the banking system as a whole can expand the money supply since private money operates via the mutual extension of tradable credit: In accounting terms, a loan extended and put on (another) bank account is no longer earmarked as originating with the lender but counts as an asset based on which the second bank can extend a new loan to another client, and so on. Hence, the banking system has the capacity to create money, which is to a large extent private in terms of its origin but sovereign in terms of the guarantees provided by the central bank.

| The interaction between central banks and private actors is further discussed in Chapter 13, section 6.2. |

2.3. Linkages between primary and secondary monetary communities

The creditworthiness of borrowers in the primary monetary community depends on the creditworthiness of their transaction partners such that network effects loom large.

The agents in the primary monetary community are the depositors and borrowers in the financial sector (i.e., the secondary monetary community). Thereby, those agents can overcome budgetary constraints by taking out loans. In principle, agents in the primary monetary community can also provide loans to each other (e.g., in the form of trade credit taking the form of deadline extensions for payments). However, budget constraints faced by all lenders put principal limitations on this form of borrowing. Since, in contrast, the financial sector can produce money, financial agents emerge as major source of loans.

Based on this, from the perspective of the secondary monetary community, there is the problem of how to assess the creditworthiness of a borrower in a complex system of specialisation. Notably, the trustworthiness of a single lender does not only rest on his individual characteristics but the characteristics of all his market partners as well. There are strong externalities in any system of networks of mutual credit since the default of one actor can always entail the default of another actor even though this second actor may have pursued a sound business strategy that did not exceed its budget constraints.[21] Therefore, in order to judge the creditworthiness of a potential borrower, a

| For network externalities in general, see Chapter 8, section 2. |

lender does not only have to know her individual credentials but must also assess the individual creditworthiness of all members of the network in which its business relations are embedded and how specific network configurations among them affect their respective degree of creditworthiness. This creates another version of the lemons problem: Individuals can often only assess the creditworthiness of average agents in the market rather than that of other individuals. As a consequence, individuals with high creditworthiness will have to pay exceedingly high interest rates and might withdraw from the market, causing a gradual deterioration of the average quality of borrowers.[22] In contrast, lenders may interpret the willingness to pay high interest as indicator of risk and, hence, refrain from lending (credit rationing).[23] This problem is central to the market economy if we consider its core dynamic, innovation, and competition. In the primary monetary community, entrepreneurs are the group which drives this dynamic. Extending loans to entrepreneurs can be highly profitable but is risky. Therefore, entrepreneurial finance is entrepreneurial itself and requires special skills and knowledge for assessing the creditworthiness of entrepreneurs.

These capacities are embodied in the secondary monetary community where agents specialise on assessing the creditworthiness of borrowers. In practice, however, a bifurcation in the financial sector can often be observed which entails discrimination against small business and start-ups since even the banks face difficulties in assessing the creditworthiness of an individual. As a consequence, in most less developed countries, there is a large sector of the economy which is disconnected from modern finance and which still applies the original forms of credit in primary monetary communities, such as loans extended in networks of kin or rotating credit associations.[24]

Besides the provision of loans, the other key function of the secondary monetary community is to offer deposits (see next section). In standard accounting schemes, a deposit is treated like a loan extended to the bank. However, the offering of deposits also constitutes a service, which is particularly salient in the standard case that alternative forms of holding assets bear risks of losing value.[25] At the same time, depositors may also have better chances to get a loan when needed since the bank is then better informed about individual conditions.

As a consequence of the outlined arrangements between secondary and primary monetary community, there is a coordination problem in the production of private money. Financial actors stand in competition against each other with respect to handing out loans as a main source of profits; overly cautious actors can lose business to competitors. At the same time, in judging the creditworthiness of borrowers, lenders would always consider the general conditions in their business environment, connecting the decision process in the financial sector with general economic conditions as perceived by the majority of agents. This causal feedback can reinforce trends in economic activity via the expansion or contraction of loans, classically dubbed the credit cycle.[26]

On the lemons problem, see Chapter 8, section 3.4.

The financial sector develops special capacities in judging the creditworthiness of borrowers.

*The financial sector
tends to cyclical
overexpansion,
bolstered by the
leverage mechanism.*

Credit cycles
and financial
crises are further
analysed in
Chapter 13,
section 5.2.

Credit cycles can turn into full-scale boom and bust cycles driven by the leverage mechanism, that is, the increase of profitability of capital by increasing the external finance share of its acquisition,[27] a strategy that often tends to be supported by banks.[28] Via the interbank mechanism of creating deposits, leverage can then drive the expansion of credit and the production of private money. This analysis reveals the most important function of the central bank, namely the containment of dysfunctional effects of private money in case of a general loss of trust in the economy. The key is that the central bank expresses its willingness to extend sovereign money to the financial sector, effectively guaranteeing its commitments to the private money that it has produced in the past. In effectively implementing this, it is not given reserves that count but the willingness of the central bank to do 'whatever it takes' which in the first place is a commitment, not necessarily a factual creation of sovereign money.[29]

3. Money and capital

3.1. Saving and investment relating to types of agents

In the standard model, a fundamental role of finance is the coordination of saving and investment or, more generally, of intertemporal markets that cater for the need to allocate resources in time. Both saving and investment are non-monetary, hence, real activities in the intertemporal dimension:

*Saving is postponing
consumption to
the future. Given
uncertainty about
the future, future
consumption is
discounted at a
positive rate.*

- Saving means a reduction of current consumption and its shift to a later period. This can happen either in order to make up for an expected shortfall or to expand future consumption. The question is how this real intertemporal shift of consumption is enabled, given that physical transfer is constrained in many ways. Saving always faces uncertainty about the future in many forms, such as uncertainty about one's own existence as an agent and uncertainty about the sustainability and future availability of the saving medium. This is reflected in a positive discount rate for future expected consumption by saving.[30]

*Investment
enhances productive
capacities to expand
future consumption.*

- Investment means a reduction of current consumption in order to create productive capital that will increase production in the future. Hence, investment shifts the real constraints on future consumption via the expansion of the productive capital stock, whereas saving postpones consumption under a given real constraint. Since investment increases productive capacity, a positive real rate of return applies. In a dynamic market economy with high levels of uncertainty, a high rate of return relative to others can only be attained by taking risk.

In a monetary economy, money plays a crucial role in enabling both activities. Here again, the budget constraint turns centre stage: saving is interpreted as income saved; investment as money invested in the acquisition and generation of productive capacities. A consumer who wants to save reduces current expenditure and shifts the saving to the future to enable future consumption; it is not her primary goal to earn a monetary future return. In contrast, investment aims at selling products on the market such that returns are measured in pecuniary terms, even if the ultimate goal of the investor were to enhance her consumption.

In a monetary economy, an important difference between saving and investment is their relation to inflation, which we define here as a perceived loss of the purchasing power of money.[31]

- With respect to saving, inflation means that the expected postponed consumption opportunities cannot materialise. The expected rate of inflation becomes an important component of discounting the future benefits of saving.[32] Since future inflation is uncertain, inflation adds to the risk of saving. Expected inflation requires a distinction between the real and nominal interest rate, which differ in terms of including the inflation rate.
- Investment is not directly affected by expected inflation because future returns are assessed in future expected prices. Therefore, in principle, investors do not prioritise inflation in forming expectations about future returns, whereas savers do.[33] Further, as investment options are measured in monetary terms, they become universally commensurable.

In a monetary economy, the rate of inflation is a determinant of uncertainty of future consumption enabled by saving. However, investment remains neutral because future returns are measured in future prices.

A monetary economy enables the preponing of consumption: The opposite operation to saving is to take out a loan for the funding of higher present consumption. On the investment side, a corresponding difference is between the investment of own savings and investment via external finance (i.e., borrowing for investing). The budget constraint is binding and can only be overcome via financial operations, with the important consequence that anybody who takes out a loan must generate future monetary income to pay back both principal and interest. That means, independently from the original motivation to borrow, the loan imposes a financial goal on future activities. For example, a consumer must financially discipline her future consumption in view of balancing her intertemporal budget constraint.

The monetary economy creates the possibility of preponing consumption. Borrowing imposes financial goals on future activities that enable repayment.

Considering the performative impact of money on behaviour, mediated by the institution of credit, we distinguish between two ideal types of activities and the corresponding social roles in investing: The entrepreneur and the investor.

The *entrepreneur* is the ideal type of agent that predominantly aims at a real return to investment. In the Schumpeterian view, there are many forms of return which cannot easily be quantified, such as a personal ambition to push through a technological innovation, which would become the primary criterion of success. In contrast, the *investor* is an agent that exclusively pursues monetary rates of return. The difference between the two translates into different degrees of substitutability of investment options: For the ideal-typical Schumpeterian entrepreneur, there are few substitutes to the preferred option,

The basics on the performativity of agency were developed in Chapter 7, section 4.3.

On the
entrepreneur,
see Chapter 7,
section 5.3, and
Chapter 16,
section 5.

*Performative
mechanisms drive
the emergence of
types of investment
activities, which
differentiate
along subjective
substitutability of
investment options.*

*Similarly, we
distinguish between
ideal types of
savers/consumers,
depending on
the degree how
financial mediation
is used to arrange
intertemporal
allocation.*

whereas for the investor, substitutability is high. Both types of agents are ready to take risk.

There is a hybrid ideal type of entrepreneur, the financial entrepreneur. *Financial entrepreneurs* manifest a medium degree of substitutability between investment options. For example, in many family businesses, the parent founder generation commits itself to the original business whereas follower generations may focus on monetary returns and, hence, be more ready to reap higher profits by alternative investments.[34] The relative share of these types in the economy is strongly influenced by performative institutional mechanisms: Recent trends of financialising the economy have increased the scope of financial entrepreneurship.[35]

On the savings/consumption side, the primary ideal type of reference is the *real saver* who forgoes present consumption to increase future consumption but is only willing to take a minimum amount of risk in conducting this intertemporal transfer. Beyond this, savers may be willing to take a higher degree of risk in order to achieve a positive rate of return. An extreme form of this would be an outright change to entrepreneurship, such as in the phenomenon of old-age entrepreneurship.[36] However, the more developed the financial sector, the larger the scope for investment in money-denominated financial assets that carry a positive return, involving a certain risk. Therefore, another hybrid ideal type is the *financial saver* who optimises a given intertemporal budget via choosing among a wider range of financial assets and aims at generating a positive return to compensate for risks to future consumption. Although related, financial savers and financial investors differ in terms of their degree of risk aversion, their expansive motives compared to optimisation within given constraints, and the salience of the consumption motive.

When we focus on consumption and treat saving only as a derivative activity aiming at intertemporal allocation, we can include the *entrepreneurial consumer* as the third ideal type on the savings/consumption side. Entrepreneurial consumers keep the focus on specific consumption goals. They do not aim at financial returns but exploit the opportunities of finance to expand their present consumption (i.e., preponing consumption). However, this creates a financial motivation in later periods, when loans must be repaid.

We summarise this discussion in Figure 12.2. There is a strong heterogeneity of agents, which includes the six ideal types presented here. Depending on the economic context, agents can reflexively switch types, such as a consumer switching from financial saver to financial investor. The bridge between the types of investor and consumer, as said, is the switching of types of financial entrepreneur and financial saver.

From this analysis, we reach the important conclusion that macroeconomic developments will be crucially affected by the evolving composition of types of agents in the economy and their interaction.[37] For example, the creation and diffusion of dominant narratives about the state of the economy can fundamentally shift the dominance of types of consumers in the

	Main motive	Propensity to take risk	Importance of financial market conditions	Asset specificity/ substitutability	Effect on consumption	Example
Schumpeterian entrepreneur	Create productive capital to generate real return	Medium to high	Depends on degree of external finance	High	Postpone	Classic entrepreneurial pioneer
Financial entrepreneur	Generate monetary return from specific entrepreneurial projects	Medium to high	Depends on degree of external finance	Medium	Postpone	Venture capitalist
Financial investor	Generate monetary return on financial assets	Medium to High	High	Low	Postpone	Investment fund
Entrepreneurial consumer	Prepone consumption by taking out loans	Medium	High	High	Prepone	Mortgage borrower
Financial saver	Generate monetary return from low-risk saving instrument	Low to medium	Medium; depends on inflation	Medium to high	Postpone	Bond holders
Real saver	Forgo consumption to accumulate for later consumption	Low	Low to medium; depends on pressure to generate positive real returns in view of inflation	Medium to high	Postpone	Long-term savings account

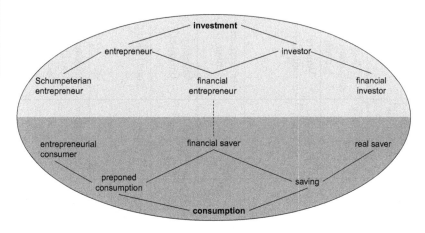

Figure 12.2 Ideal types of investment and saving

Endogenous
evolution of
types in the agent
population is a
major factor in
driving economic
fluctuations
as analysed in
Chapter 13.

economy. One example is the transition to a culture of thriftiness and constraint after the Great Depression[38]; another is the rise of the entrepreneurial
consumer before the financial crisis in 2008, which was driven by the emergence of new forms of mortgage loans and the public encouragement of
homeownership.[39]

3.2. Deconstructing the capital market

*Instead of a
capital market that
balances saving
and investment,
we analyse two
interconnected
markets for saving
and investment
instruments created
by assetification.*

In an economy with a deep division of labour, the roles of saving and investment have to be differentiated. Yet treating the capital market as one marketplace that balances the demand for real savings and real investment is a
problematic assumption. We disentangle the notion of capital market into two
analytically separate markets for saving and investment. This distinction
defines the difference between a neoclassical and what might broadly be clas-
sified as a Keynesian view. In the latter, decisions to save and decisions to
invest are taken in different segments of the economy by different actors with
specific motivations, and there is no direct mechanism that coordinates these
two decisions, such as the interest rate.

These various aspects can be analytically organised around the role of
assetification. Savers who do not want to hoard money or other precious
assets for saving purposes must approach the financial sector for an asset that
enables them to save. We call this a saving instrument (SI) and refer to the
market for SIs as the market where such assets as institutional objects are
traded. The standard saving instrument is a deposit at a bank, commonly interpreted as a loan to the bank. In fact, however, the deposit is an institutional
object created by the bank and sold to the depositor (Figure 12.3). There are

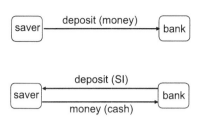

Figure 12.3 The market for saving instruments
In the conventional view (top), savers hold money balances in cash that they
deposit at the bank. In the market for saving instruments as presented here
(bottom), banks create a new kind of institutional object or asset, the deposit
which is sold to the savers at a price. The value of that asset for savers is the
reduction of risk vis-à-vis investment instruments.

other forms of saving instruments, such as most importantly, government
bonds (see later section).

Economists commonly assume that savers have a positive time preference
such that they must be incentivised to save by receiving a positive interest.
However, adopting the perspective of assetification, an SI is an asset and service offered with a positive price, which translates into negative interest.[40]
This view is especially valid for the type of the real saver. That is, the benefit
from saving at a bank is the reduced level of risk offered by the respective
deposit as a saving asset.

An agent who wants to postpone consumption always has the choice
between saving and investment, which will depend on his risk aversion. In the
case of investment, the future return is by definition uncertain whereas in the
case of saving, economic agents aim at achieving a revenue stream that is as
safe as possible. This implies a trade-off between higher returns and higher
risk, which can be addressed by splitting the roles of saving and investment
via insertion of an intermediator, namely the financial sector. Its key function
is risk transformation, that is, the financial sector offers various saving instruments and earns a profit from the difference between the interest paid on them
and the revenue from lending out the accumulated deposits. This difference,
the spread, can be interpreted as the price for saving in the sense of its opportunity cost in terms of hypothetical higher income streams from investment
opportunities forgone. The spread between interest rates on deposits and on
loans at a bank is the price to be paid by savers to the bank for offering an SI
with a lower level of risk than the investment. This implicitly constitutes negative interest from the perspective of savers.

In terms of manifest monetary flows, a positive interest regularly emerges
on the market for SIs because banks compete over attracting deposits. This,
however, does not alter the role of the spread as the opportunity cost of saving.

This builds on
the distinction
between object
of transaction
and the claim
on it that we
introduced
in Chapter 8,
section 2.2, and
pursue further
in Chapter 14,
section 2.1.

*Banks offer
assetified saving
instruments to
savers and charge
a price for the
reduction of risk,
implying negative
interest. The
negative interest is
the spread between
interest on deposits
and loans, which is
the opportunity cost
of savers preferring
risk reduction.*

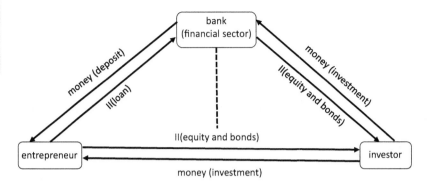

Figure 12.4 The market for II

The financial sector produces various types of investment instruments (II). Loans are an II for the financial sector by which entrepreneurs obtain deposits. Besides that, there is a large variety of bonds and other means of external finance and equity in various forms, such as shares. These can be used by investors as II that are offered by entrepreneurs, by intermediation of the financial sector. Investors can also invest into the financial sector directly, such as buying shares of banks.

In other words, via the organisation of the financial sector as a competitive market, positive rates of return achievable by investment exert an upward pull on the implicitly negative interest of deposits.[41] Typically, however, the nominal interest paid on saving deposits remains low and is often contractually fixed, which implies that even in cases of only moderate inflation, savers often accept negative real interest.[42]

On the market for investment instruments, the financial sector enables the conduct of various types of investment.

As the next step, we introduce the market for investment instruments (II), which are again understood as institutional objects. This market involves at least three poles, namely banks, entrepreneurs, and investors (Figure 12.4), and entails the exchange of investment-enabling assets that are created and traded by the financial sector. The underlying fundamental problem is the temporal coordination of expenditure and revenue. In a market economy, the former is mostly fixed and regularly must be incurred before the realisation of revenue inflows, such as by paying wages to employees. Moreover, revenue is never fully certain such that even the ordinary course of business implies risk-taking, and there is always the possibility that current revenue may not balance expenditure. As key example, an entrepreneur often may not have the financial means to launch her project or expand the size of operations. Therefore, she must rely on the financial sector to smooth out intertemporal variation in matching flows of payments with the budget constraint.[43]

The role of temporal coordination was stressed in our concept of market states, Chapter 11, section 4.2.

Loans are one form of investment instrument that in modern monetised economies are complemented by many others. Entrepreneurs can offer investment opportunities via institutionalised forms of equity, such as by issuing shares, or they might issue securitised debt, such as corporate bonds. All these IIs are created by the financial sector via assetification supported by law.[44] The financial sector can create investment instruments both for funding its own capital (i.e., issuing forms of equity) and for funding loan expansion. For example, banks may create special funds that they use to invest into shares of various companies and offer these funds to both investors and savers. Accordingly, some instruments have a hybrid nature, depending on the nature of motivation to buy them. This implies that the market for SIs and the market for IIs are connected via arbitrage mechanisms: The higher returns on the market for II, the more risk savers may be willing to take, implying the effective transformation of some IIs into SIs.

Why do banks in fiat money regimes attract saving deposits at all, given that they can produce money autonomously? Despite the systemic capacity of producing money, the individual bank still faces the budget constraint: If a borrower defaults on a loan, the bank must write off the loan and incurs losses, both in terms of principal and lost future streams of interest. Commonly, saving deposits are seen as liabilities of the bank. But once we view deposits as saving instruments (i.e., assets sold to savers), the saving deposit is in fact an asset for the bank. This is especially true if real savers prevail in the economy who are relatively insensitive to the interest rate and may agree to restrict withdrawal. Thus, there is a link between the prevalence of types of savers in an economy and the behaviour of banks: If real savers are prevalent and trust in the safety of their deposits, as in the case of Japan in recent decades, banks can cope with a large amount of fragile loans.

Banks attract saving deposits because those deposits are functional assets that maintain the solvency of banks if the type of real saver is dominant in the economy.

Finally, we already mentioned that in a fiat money regime, government bonds constitute a saving instrument. Except the obligation to pay interest,[45] government debt is not a liability of the government but an asset sold to other economic agents in need of low-risk saving instruments.[46] In principle, the government would not need to issue bonds at all since the sovereign can always cover its debt by raising taxes or issuing fresh money.[47] In contrast, although private producers of SIs are technically able to produce money as well, they entail a risk of insolvency because of latent incentives to overextend loans (see further section earlier). Therefore, via competing with other SIs, government bonds impose constraints on other suppliers of SIs regarding excessive risk-taking. In principle, issuing bonds is a commitment device of the sovereign to enhance trust into sovereign money. However, there are many cases of exploitation of both government debt and the production of money for political goals, including mere personal advantage of incumbents of power. In principle, these possibilities of misuse are diminished in monetary regimes with a commodity anchor and the universal obligation to convert sovereign money into that commodity, such as in the gold standard (see further section earlier).

Since in a fiat money regime, government could just finance expenditures by issuing money, government bonds are the SI with lowest level of risk offered to savers. Further, they are a commitment device of government to create trust into sovereign money.

3.3. Valuing capital

On the market for IIs, two dimensions of reflexivity loom large, which open much space for performative mechanisms:[48]

On reflexivity,
see Chapter 2,
section 6.

Financial markets are reflexive in two senses: one is via the role of expectations of future prices of assets; the other is reflexive assetification.

- The first dimension is the reflexivity of pricing assets, as depending on the state of expectations: If agents expect future price increases, this boosts current demand for an asset and, hence, increases its price, and vice versa.[49] Hence, current prices of assets are expectational prices (corresponding to the well-known expression that future developments have already been priced in). Expectations, in turn, are heterogenous, with market agents assessing future market trends in guessing the expectations of others, which includes their guesses about expectations of the former. In that sense, asset prices are performative; fundamentals anchor asset prices only via subjective expectations (first-person view) that are objectified by market pricing (second-person view).
- The second dimension is the reflexivity of securitisation as a specific form of assetification, which constitutes a fundamental institutional operation in finance. Any kind of object can be turned into an asset if the right to its returns is securitised: In the broadest sense, this is the deed by which the property right is proven. This security is an asset in turn such that the right to the returns of that security can also be securitised in turn (such as a mortgage loan) and so forth; we call the security of the securitised asset a financial asset. This is important when the second round involves the bundling of such rights. For example, a mortgage loan is securitised and can be packed together with other loans into a new asset which is securitised in turn. Such reflexive operations are the gist of entrepreneurship in finance.

Leverage can substantially increase profits of assets.

Assetification is directly connected with the financial mechanism of leverage (see previous section).[50] Leverage is a strong driver of market activity as profit expectations can be leveraged as well; notably, this effect also works in the opposite direction in the form of deleveraging. The leverage mechanism crucially depends on the institutional distinction between external finance and equity, which is itself performative as it depends on specific regulations on liability, priorities on claims, and others that characterise the different asset classes treated as external finance or equity (see next section).

The value of capital is a conjectural value that is fixed by accounting conventions.

Against this background, we can now take a deeper look at the valuation of capital. In a market economy, this valuation is based on the notion of yield, which encompasses changes of the value of capital as well as future income streams, as possibly discounted to the present (interest). Both pillars can be judged in widely different ways (Figure 12.5). As said, in all dimensions, expectations play an important role, which renders valuation reflexive. This implies that valuation requires institutionalisation, which takes place via the establishment of accounting principles and procedures.[51]

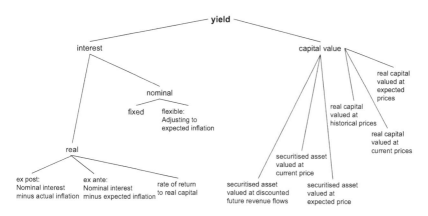

Figure 12.5 The complex determinants of yield
Yield is determined by changes in capital value and current returns, here
referred to as interest. However, there are many ways to determine these
parameters and to move from nominal to real values, that is, accounting
for inflation when valuing the future nominal interest or any component of
yield that is exclusively denominated in fixed monetary terms. For economic
decisions about buying or selling an asset, expected yields are crucial, which
refer to current prices on markets for assets. For example, holding a share
must consider expected future share prices, expected future dividends, and
expected value of the underlying real capital, that is, the business prospects of
the company. To achieve a comprehensive judgement, developments across
various stock markets and product markets must be considered.

There are different options to do this. We can look at the prices of capital
goods, such as machines, tools, and production sites, as traded on the respective markets and then simply add their market values to obtain the current
aggregate value of the capital. Another alternative is to value at historical cost:
The current value of capital can be higher or lower than at the time of its
acquisition. However, neither losses nor gains are current income and, thus,
would not be realised. Both methods do not include the synergies of compos-
ing a set of productive capital from the various elements that are priced
separately. Therefore, economics mostly refers to another method, namely
treatment of the discounted future flow of revenue generated from the capital
composite as its current value. For this, a discount factor must apply. In order
to determine this factor, if we only apply a subjective time preference
(first-person view), we cannot achieve a valuation that is commensurable
across different agents. Hence, reference to a market rate is preferable, such as
a common rate of interest.

However, this creates a fundamental problem in the valuation of capital as
related to the relationship between saving and investment.[52] If we employ the

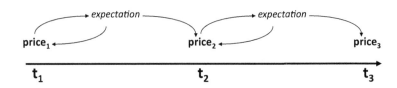

Figure 12.6 Recursive reflexivity of price expectations
In a most general way, valuation of assets is driven by recursive reflexivity reaching from the present t_1 to the future $t_2 \ldots t_\infty$. At the present, expectations refer to current prices but determine expected price, which, via market actions in the present, feeds back on current price. However, the same holds for any point of time in the future: To forecast price at t_2, one must also forecast the corresponding state of expectations and so forth.

This is the Cambridge paradox as introduced in Chapter 10, section 4.2.

Reflexivity through time implies that current expectations of future prices are expectations over expectations prevailing in the future.

market interest rate as a discount factor, and simultaneously assume that this rate reflects the equilibrium between the supply and demand of capital, we can no longer approach the quantity or volume of capital as being independent from the interest rate.

Once assets are traded independently from trading the underlying object, prices for assets and prices for the underlying real objects can differ. The consequence is that current prices of assets are mostly driven by expectations about the future yield of the underlying objects. Considering the case of real capital, there are two dimensions to take into account: one is the future price of capital; and the other is the value of the conjugated asset. However, when we ask what will determine these prices in the future, the same applies: In the future, the prices will be driven by expectations about the even more distant future. That means, the pricing of assets today is a complex reflexive operation that involves expectations about future expectations (Figure 12.6).

As we saw, expectations on future revenue streams are subjective, and once the assets are traded, a price will be established that is only indirectly related to this valuation in the sense that supply and demand are driven by differences in these expectations. At the same time, for example, someone who buys an asset will form expectations about the future price of that asset. That means, his reference is not future revenue streams as such but the expectations of others, both with respect to these streams and the future values of an asset.[53] Future yields are determined by future revenue flows and, again, by the then prevailing expectations about asset prices in the more distant future. As a result, what determines the current profits of investors in assets is whether they correctly anticipate the current and future expectations of all other investors since these drive prices on the market of assets.

This approach corresponds to our general theory of market states in Chapter 11, section 4.2.

To sum up, we eschew the equilibrium concept of yield that is fundamental for the established theory of finance. The value of capital is determined as a market state, strongly shaped by the state of expectations. We further explore this in the next chapter.

4. Assetification and liability

Given the functions of money, an asset can be any kind of composite: Assetification means that the underlying real objects are made commensurable and can be assorted in almost arbitrary ways. In a market economy, the most important type of composite asset is real capital as an assemblage of means of production. In the primordial form of economy, real capital would be owned by an entrepreneur. If size and complexity grow, and additional funding requirements emerge, real capital is corporatised in terms of a legal person, which is the condition for assetification. A most common form of corporatisation combined with assetification is the joint-stock company. Here, the assets are the shares, with a share constituting a fractional right to own a part of the company. This right includes many aspects of ownership, such as taking part in management decisions. But in the context of finance, what matters most is the fractional claim on profits.

Assetification is itself an instrument of shaping risk. This is because the concrete form of assetification entails the design and assignment of property rights. The key legal manifestation is the design of liability, which constitutes a major determinant of the inherent value of an asset. In a complex market economy, there is always the risk that non-owners, such as lenders, claimants in tort action, or the government in tax disputes, raise claims on an asset. The stronger the legal shield against such claims, the more valuable the asset.[54]

Designing liability in assetification is the major instrument of risk of an asset.

In terms of liability, it is common to distinguish between equity and external finance, with a concomitant differentiation of rights regarding priority of claims in case of bankruptcy. In primordial forms of finance, there is only the distinction between a loan and an equity partnership. A loan minimally means that the borrower is obliged to pay back the loan at maturity; mostly, interest also must be paid. A lender does not take responsibility for the business, even though there is the risk of default. The counterpart to this is the reduction of risk, which is reflected in a priority claim: If possible, the loan must be repaid first, and losses must be covered by the owners (i.e., holders of equity).

A partnership means that the provider of capital participates in risk-taking, meaning that in case of losses, she accepts her share. Normally, if the contribution is substantial, the provider would also claim participation in business decisions. However, we must distinguish between entrepreneurial provision

*Limiting liability
is the condition for
the emergence of
markets for equity
assets and shields
real capital against
changes of ownership
and claims at
shareholders.*

See, for a
discussion
of limited
liability as an
externalisation
mechanism,
Chapter 9,
section 4.2.

*Limited liability is a
specific institutional
form that emerged in
Western Europe and
is essential to defining
'capitalism' as an
economic system.*

*Limited liability
increases the
tradability of
the respective
asset, eventually
establishing a fluid
borderline between
certain assets and
private money.*

of capital and investment by investors. The former results in diverse forms of shared property rights, implying full liability. In contrast, investors aim at the reduction of liability, which combines with more limited property rights. The instrument to cater to the needs and interests of these various groups is corporatisation. Corporatisation is a form of assetification in the sense that it creates a legal person that is partly autonomous from the owners who do not directly own the real capital but own the assets that refer to it. This is the difference between a partnership and a joint-stock corporation. Assetification enables the construction of an ownership right that can be traded without trading the underlying real capital, thus shielding the capital composite against changes of fractional ownership. At the same time, creditors of owners of shares cannot reach through to the real capital of the corporation.[55]

This confirms the institutional design of liability as an important issue in finance. Economic agents will have strong preferences for institutional arrangements which protect their own capital against claimants of any kind. Financial instruments manifest a vast diversity of forms how liability is limited. However, limited liability creates systematic moral hazard in the financial sector because investors will not bear the full costs of risk-taking. Limited liability is not a necessary feature of finance in general but is certainly peculiar to the form of capitalism that emerged in Western Europe.[56] Its rapid spread since the 19th century is mostly explained by the growing clout of one group in the economy, the investors, and hence, the dominance of the monetary motive in economic activity.[57] Different from entrepreneurs, investors commonly do not pursue single investment projects but aim at managing risk via creating portfolios of assets. This implies that they would not necessarily be interested in taking part in decisions, which, however, increases risk. Limiting liability, in turn, is a means to reduce that risk. However, it also implies that the cost of risk-taking is externalised, particularly in case of forms of corporatisation that do not keep at least one owner with full liability.

One important consequence of limiting liability is to enhance the tradability of equity. Even if a partnership with full liability were assetified, tradability would likely remain low, given that there are strong information asymmetries between current owners of the asset and potential buyers. If liability is limited, this cost can be reduced. Further, an important side effect is increasing the liquidity of the asset, thus approaching a form of quasi money.

The borderline between assetification and private money is fluid, which is already evident when considering the tradable IOUs at the origin of private money. In principle, any form of asset that is universally accepted as cancelling another debt is private money. In the modern economy, mutual obligations within the secondary monetary community can become proxies of private money.[58] Since banks can create deposits via lending, there are no principled limits to expansion. This is especially problematic once we consider leverage: As long as the banks reap the spread, they can leverage the profits to their equity by reducing it to the smallest possible amount.[59] This, however, also creates huge risks in case of losses. Therefore, the simplest way to control the private production of money is increasing equity requirements (and not reserve requirements) with strong liability. Basically, this is the private banking model that was prevalent in the 19th century. This model does not entirely suppress the capacity to produce private money but minimises externalities.

5. Conclusion

Chapter 10 concluded with identifying money as a form of social capital in a complex market economy. This raises the question whether a similar judgement holds for modern finance and its different forms of assetification more generally.

It turns out that there is no clear theoretical basis for relating profits in the financial sector to positive contributions to general welfare, as commonly conceived in economics.[60] National accounting standards fail to define a convincing measure of the value added of finance; they allow for highly questionable valuations such as the measurement of a positive contribution of the financial sector in a crisis caused by it, based on services such as the restructuring companies in consequence of the crisis.[61] In addition, there are growing concerns about misbehaviour, fraud, and systematic abuse of accounting schemes in the financial sector, corroborating widespread moral concerns about the corrupting forces on money.[62] In our view, these developments arise from the performative nature of money. More specifically, trust in money and in agents responsible for handling money cannot be secured by mechanisms that are themselves mediated by money.[63] There is no way to incentivise trust in money by pecuniary means.

The contribution of profits in the financial sector to economic welfare cannot be measured conclusively. The corrupting forces of money can only be contained by mechanisms exogenous to the financial sector.

Financial markets trade divergent expectations over future flows of pecuniary returns, which implies that they are by definition zero-sum games: There is always one side who loses money, the asset with least asset specificity.[64] For other goods, even if the buyer judged the price incorrectly, she would still be able enjoy the benefits of owning the good. In the case of financial assets, benefits of owning are exclusively related to expected future value increases, realisation of which would result in another round of zero-sum transactions. Since there is no independent measure of welfare in judging financial market outcomes, the Smithian invisible hand theorem does not apply here.

Overall, ethical commitments are of paramount importance in maintaining the integrity and the performance of the secondary monetary community. Values matter for finance.

Major chapter insights

- The chapter explores the role of the financial sector in institutionalising money in the economy and enabling its dynamic capacities. The key concept is assetification, which is involved in both the private production of money and in enabling saving and investment.
- We distinguish between private and sovereign money. Private money emerges in communities of exchange where mutual claims on payments are assetified and become fungible and tradable (such as bills of exchange). This leads to the separation between primary and secondary monetary communities, the latter commonly known as the financial sector.
- Sovereign money emerged as a unit of account of the public economy and taxation. In Europe, private and sovereign money were intrinsically merged via the emergence of government debt. This fusion created incentives for the overexpansion of private money and the abuse of minting power by government. The institutional solution is the politically independent central bank.
- Creditworthiness in the primary monetary community is determined by network effects and general economic conditions. This creates a systematic tendency of cycles of economic activity, bolstered by leverage and driven by overexpansion and contraction of loans.
- The capital market is deconstructed into the two markets for saving instruments and investment instruments. Saving and investment are distinct economic processes, both institutionally and behaviourally, in particular, in terms of degrees of risk aversion and the effects on the budget constraint through time.
- In a monetary economy, there are different types of saving and investment, mostly with reference to the relative importance of monetary returns in agent decisions. The composition of these types evolves depending on the state and context of economy.
- Assetification implies that risk-averse savers demand saving instruments for risk reduction and, hence, pay negative interest in terms of the interest rate spread between deposits and loans, that is, the opportunity cost of saving and foregoing risky returns to investment. Risk-taking entrepreneurs pay positive returns to the producers of investment instruments, such as loans, equity, and bonds.
- The valuation of capital is a complex and uncertain process that is only fixed by institutionalising specific procedures in accounting rules. This results from reflexivity of both the formation of expectations over future yields and the process of assetification.
- A major mechanism of risk reduction is assetification with limiting liability.

Notes

1 The term 'money market' was used by Walter Bagehot (1857) to describe the capital market in the sense of the financial sector. Until today, the term often appears to lack a clear demarcation, even on theoretical grounds (Friedman, 1987). Our reference reflects the distinction in the original IS/LM model, where the latter strictly refers to the demand and supply of money as the most liquid asset in the economy and the former to the capital market in the sense of the equilibrium between investment and saving defined as shares of national income. However, given the specific assumptions on saving behaviour, this is effectively the goods market so that this model was superseded by the recent AD/AS framework in macroeconomics.

2 In this, we follow the approaches of stock-flow consistent modelling that has been championed by post-Keynesian theorists but was also prevalent in earlier literature, especially Stützel (1978[1958]). See Caverzasi and Godin (2015).

3 Lo (2019).

4 Ferguson (2008).

5 Goetzmann (2017, 92ff).

6 Goetzmann (2017, 203ff).

7 Hicks (1989, 47ff).

8 Martin (2014).

9 Richter (1987). Hicks (1989) introduces a similar distinction.

10 Alessandrini et al. (2009), Sassen (2018).

11 Swedberg (2012). This was the core concern in Bagehot (1857).

12 This was especially salient in the 2008 crisis, where the financial sector lost trust in the web of mutual commitments related to asset-backed securities. One form of how the loss of trust between primary and secondary communities is manifest is the bank run. Rich insight in these phenomena is provided by Calomiris and Haber (2014).

13 Ingham (2000), Chavas and Bromley (2008).

14 Hicks (1989, 41ff) argues that the fundamental function of money is being the unit of account.

15 Ingham (2000), Goetzmann (2017, 19ff).

16 Graeber (2011) shows that this happened in different periods, such as during Alexander's warfare against the Persians or in the Middle Ages.

17 Huang (1988).

18 Brandt et al. (2014).

19 Eichengreen and Flandreau (1997).

20 Walsh (2008).

21 Acemoglu et al. (2015); Glasserman and Young (2016).

22 This is a specific case of Kranton's (1996) universal mechanism.

23 Stiglitz and Greenwald (2003).

24 Djankov et al. (2007), Bond et al. (2015), Onda (2021).

25 Hicks (1989, 56).

26 In recent debates, the work by Minsky has received renewed attention, which was marginalised in macroeconomics. After the financial crisis, research into credit cycles boomed, for example, Amromin et al. (2020), with reference to the US mortgage industry or loans to SME, Rodano et al. (2020). However, there is a long tradition of Minsky-type economic analysis including influential authors such as Kalecki; for a survey, see Nikolaidi and Stockhammer (2017).

27 Geanakoplos (2010, 2011).

28 Admati and Hellwig (2014).

29 This is Bagehot's (1857) view that received renewed interest after 2008, see Bernanke (2013). For a critical assessment, see Le Maux (2021). The citation is Mario Draghi's famous statement in the Eurocrisis 2012.

30 Gesell (1916).

31 For a concise overview of the history and meaning of the concept, see Bryan (1997). Bryan shows that originally, the term referred to overexpansion of money production and only later to price increases. These two meanings coalesce in our definition.

32 Macchia et al. (2018).

33 One expression of this asymmetry is the rare use of indexation in modern market economies, even though this would be a powerful institutional means to reduce uncertainty for savers, see Allais (1999).

34 This cross-generational transition between types is a major reason of tensions and conflicts in family business succession, see Zellweger (2017, 203ff).

35 Krippner (2005).

36 Wainwright and Kibler (2014).

37 De Grauwe and Ji (2019) distinguish between two types of agents in terms of the underlying mechanisms of forming expectations. Lo (2019) argues in terms of diverse financial strategies.

38 Shiller (2017, 136ff).

39 Calomiris and Haber (2014).

40 This is the theory advanced by Gesell (1916) based on analysing a real Robinson economy. The argument has been recognised by Fisher (1930) and Keynes (1936, 353ff), yet both think that it is transformed in a monetary economy where interest is paid for money. Gesell's theory has recently received interest in the context of negative nominal interest rates, see Ilgmann and Menner (2011). Hicks (1989, 56) also recognises that negative interest is the primordial form.

41 This is Fisher's (1930) argument against negative interest as empirically valid case. Our argument is the same as in Hicks (1989, 57).

42 Recent debates about negative interest rates mostly consider a variant of loanable funds thinking, such as the savings glut hypothesis, see Galesi et al. (2017). Our use of 'natural' differs radically from Wicksell (1889), since we do not consider an equilibrium between saving and investment.

43 Godley and Lavoie (2012, 250ff).

44 Hicks (1989, 82) treats bonds and shares as belonging to the same general category of financial instruments. An important implication is that both equities and corporate

bonds must be treated as liabilities of companies. In practice, this is revealed by the dividend expectations of shareholders, as discussed in Godley and Lavoie (2012, 29f), who treat equities as liabilities in the national accounting scheme.

45 Indeed, in our interpretation, the ideal institutional form of government debt is the consol, prevalent in the 19th century, a perpetual bond with interest coupons that would never be redeemed but allow a steady flow of rent for the owner. The saver can exchange it on secondary markets when she needs money for consumption. The British consols were finally redeemed only in 2015.

46 Von Weizsäcker (2011).

47 Kelton (2020).

48 Compare Zuckerman (2012). Reflexivity has been theorised by the famous investor George Soros, see Davis and Hands (2018).

49 A self-fulfilling prophecy, as classically defined by Merton (1948).

50 Geanakoplos (2010, 2011).

51 Soll (2014).

52 Cohen and Harcourt (2003) and Pasinetti and Scazzieri (2008).

53 This is Keynes's (1936) famous theory of the beauty contest. This argument has been subject to many experimental tests and is today linked to the level-k reasoning approach in game theory, which allows for more concrete modelling, also in macroeconomics, see Mauersberger et al. (2020).

54 Pistor (2019).

55 Hansmann et al. (2006) speak of entity shielding.

56 Ireland (2010).

57 Preda (2005).

58 Martin (2014).

59 Admati and Hellwig (2014).

60 Zingales (2015).

61 Coyle (2015).

62 The data clearly show that conditions have worsened in recent decades; see Akerlof and Shiller (2015), Zingales (2015).

63 This point was classically made by Polanyi (1944).

64 Lo (2019, 296ff).

References

Acemoglu, D., Ozdaglar, A. and Tahbaz-Salehi, A. (2015) 'Systemic Risk and Stability in Financial Networks', *American Economic Review*, 105(2), pp. 564–608. DOI: 10.1257/aer.20130456.

Admati, A. R. and Hellwig, M. (2014) *The Bankers' New Clothes: What's Wrong with Banking and What to Do about It*. Princeton: Princeton University Press. DOI: 10.1515/9781400851195.

Akerlof, G. A. and Shiller, R. J. (2015) *Phishing for Phools: The Economics of Manipulation and Deception*. Princeton and Oxford: Princeton University Press.

Alessandrini, P. *et al.* (eds.) (2009) *The Changing Geography of Banking and Finance*. Boston: Springer Verlag. DOI: 10.1007/978-0-387-98078-2.

Allais, M. (1999) *La Crise Mondiale d'aujourd'hui: Pour de Profondes Réformes des Institutions Financières et Monétaires*. Paris: Juglar.

Amromin, G., Bhutta, N. and Keys, B. J. (2020) 'Refinancing, Monetary Policy, and the Credit Cycle', *Annual Review of Financial Economics*, 12(1), pp. 67–93. DOI: 10.1146/annurev-financial-012720-120430.

Bagehot, W. (2017[1857]) *Lombard Street: A Description of the Money Market*. London: White Crane.

Bernanke, B. S. (2013) *The Federal Reserve and the Financial Crisis*. Princeton and Oxford: Princeton University Press.

Bond, E. W., Tybout, J. and Utar, H. (2015) 'Credit Rationing, Risk Aversion, and Industrial Evolution in Developing Countries', *International Economic Review*, 56(3), pp. 695–722. DOI: 10.1111/iere.12119.

Brandt, L., Ma, D. and Rawski, T. G. (2014) 'From Divergence to Convergence: Reevaluating the History Behind China's Economic Boom', *Journal of Economic Literature*, 52(1), pp. 45–123. DOI: 10.1257/jel.52.1.45.

Bryan, M. F. (1997) 'On the Origin and Evolution of the Word Inflation', *Federal Reserve Bank of Cleveland, Economic Commentary*. Available at: https://www.clevelandfed.org/en/newsroom-and-events/publications/economic-commentary/economic-commentary-archives/1997-economic-commentaries/ec-19971015-on-the-origin-and-evolution-of-the-word-inflation.aspx (Accessed: 30 August 2022).

Calomiris, C. W. and Haber, S. H. (2014) *Fragile by Design: The Political Origins of Banking Crises and Scarce Credit*. Princeton and Oxford: Princeton University Press. DOI: 10.1515/9781400849925.

Caverzasi, E. and Godin, A. (2015) 'Post-Keynesian Stock-Flow-Consistent Modelling: A Survey', *Cambridge Journal of Economics*, 39(1), pp. 157–187. DOI: 10.1093/CJE/BEU021.

Chavas, J. P. and Bromley, D. W. (2008) 'On the Origins and Evolving Role of Money', *Journal of Institutional and Theoretical Economics*, 164(4), pp. 624–651. DOI: 10.1628/093245608786534631.

Cohen, A. J. and Harcourt, G. C. (2003) 'Whatever Happened to the Cambridge Capital Controversies?' *Journal of Economic Perspectives*, 17(1), pp. 199–214. DOI: 10.1257/089533003321165010.

Coyle, D. (2015) *GDP: A Brief but Affectionate History*. Princeton: Princeton University Press. DOI: 10.1515/9781400873630.

Davis, J. B. and Hands, D. W. (eds.) (2018) *Reflexivity and Economics: George Soros's Theory of Reflexivity and the Methodology of Economic Science*. Abingdon and New York: Routledge.

De Grauwe, P. and Ji, Y. (2019) *Behavioural Macroeconomics: Theory and Policy, First Edition*. New York: Oxford University Press.

Djankov, S., McLiesh, C. and Shleifer, A. (2007) 'Private Credit in 129 Countries', *Journal of Financial Economics*, 84(2), pp. 299–329. DOI: 10.1016/j.jfineco.2006.03.004.

Eichengreen, B. and Flandreau, M. (eds.) (1997) *The Gold Standard in Theory and History*. 2nd Edition. London: Routledge.

Ferguson, N. (2008) *The Ascent of Money: A Financial History of the World*. London: Penguin Books.

Fisher, I. (1930) *The Theory of Interest, as Determined by Impatience to Spend Income and Opportunity to Invest It*. New York: Palgrave Macmillan.

Friedman, B. M. (1987) 'Capital, Credit and Money Markets', in Eatwell, J., Murray, M. and Newman, P. (eds.) *The New Palgrave: A Dictionary of Economics*. 1st Edition. London: Palgrave Macmillan.

Galesi, A., Nuño, G. and Thomas, C. (2017) 'The Natural Interest Rate: Concept, Determinants and Implications for Monetary Policy', *Banco de Espana Analytical Articles*, 7(17).

Geanakoplos, J. (2010) 'The Leverage Cycle', *Cowles Foundation Paper*, 1304.

Geanakoplos, J. (2011) 'What's Missing from Macroeconomics: Endogenous Leverage and Default', *Cowles Foundation Paper*, 1332.

Gesell, S. (1916) *Die natürliche Wirtschaftsordnung durch Freiland und Freigeld*. Les Hauts-Geneveys: Selbstverlag.

Glasserman, P. and Young, H. P. (2016) 'Contagion in Financial Networks', *Journal of Economic Literature*, 54(3), pp. 779–831.

Godley, W. and Lavoie, M. (2012) *Monetary Economics: An Integrated Approach to Credit, Money, Income, Production and Wealth*. London: Palgrave Macmillan. DOI: 10.1007/978-1-137-08599-3.

Goetzmann, W. N. (2017) *Money Changes Everything: How Finance Made Civilization Possible*. Princeton: Princeton University Press. DOI: 10.2307/j.ctvc77dzg.

Graeber, D. (2011) *Debt: The First 5,000 Years*. New York: Melville House.

Hansmann, H., Kraakman, R. and Squire, R. (2006) 'Law and the Rise of the Firm', *Harvard Law Review*, 119.

Hicks, J. (1989) *A Market Theory of Money*. Oxford and New York: Clarendon Press.

Huang, R. (1988) *China: A Macro History*. London: Routledge.

Ilgmann, C. and Menner, M. (2011) 'Negative Nominal Interest Rates: History and Current Proposals', *CAWM Discussion Paper*, 43.

Ingham, G. (2000) 'Babylonian Madness: On the Historical and Sociological Origins of Money', in Smithin, J. (ed.) *What Is Money?* Abingdon and New York: Routledge, pp. 16–41. DOI: 10.4324/9780203072691-6.

Ireland, P. (2010) 'Limited Liability, Shareholder Rights and the Problem of Corporate Irresponsibility', *Cambridge Journal of Economics*, 34(5), pp. 837–856. DOI: 10.1093/cje/ben040.

Kelton, S. (2020) *The Deficit Myth: Modern Monetary Theory and How to Build a Better Economy*. London: John Murray.

Keynes, J. M. (1960[1936]) *The General Theory of Employment, Interest and Money*. London: MacMillan.

Kranton, R. E. (1996) 'Reciprocal Exchange: A Self-Sustaining System', *American Economic Review*, 86(4), pp. 830–851.

Krippner, G. (2005) 'The Financialization of the American Economy', *Socio-Economic Review*, 3(2), pp. 173–208. DOI: 10.1093/SER/MWI008.

Le Maux, L. (2021) 'Bagehot for Central Bankers', *Institute for New Economic Thinking Working Paper Series*, 147. DOI: 10.36687/inetwp147.

Lo, A. W. (2019) *Adaptive Markets: Financial Evolution at the Speed of Thought*. Princeton: Princeton University Press. DOI: 10.1515/9780691196800.

Macchia, L., Plagnol, A. C. and Reimers, S. (2018) 'Does Experience with High Inflation Affect Intertemporal Decision Making? Sensitivity to Inflation Rates in Argentine and British Delay Discounting Choices', *Journal of Behavioral and Experimental Economics*, 75, pp. 76–83. DOI: 10.1016/j.socec.2018.05.006.

Martin, F. (2014) *Money: The Unauthorized Biography from Coinage to Cryptocurrencies*. New York: Vintage Book.

Mauersberger, F., Nagel, R. and Bühren, C. (2020) 'Bounded Rationality in Keynesian Beauty Contests: A Lesson for Central Bankers?' *Economics*, 14(1), p. 20200016. DOI: 10.5018/economics-ejournal.ja.2020-16.

Merton, R. K. (1948) 'The Self-Fulfilling Prophecy', *The Antioch Review*, 8(2), pp. 193–210.

Nikolaidi, M. and Stockhammer, E. (2017) 'Minsky Models: A Structured Survey', *Journal of Economic Surveys*, 31(5), pp. 1304–1331. DOI: 10.1111/joes.12222.

Onda, M. (2021) Rotating Savings and Credit Associations as Traditional Mutual Help Networks in East Asia', *International Journal of Asian Studies*, 18(2), pp. 271–287. DOI: 10.1017/S1479591421000036.

Pasinetti, L. L. and Scazzieri, R. (2008) 'Capital Theory: Paradoxes', in Durlauf, S. N. and Blume, L. E. (eds.) *The New Palgrave Dictionary of Economics*. London: Palgrave Macmillan. DOI: 10.1057/978-1-349-95121-5_240-1.

Pistor, K. (2019) *The Code of Capital: How the Law Creates Wealth and Inequality*. Princeton: Princeton University Press. DOI: 10.1515/9780691189437.

Polanyi, K. (2001[1944]) *The Great Transformation: The Political and Economic Origins of Our Time*. Boston: Beacon Press.

Preda, A. (2005) 'The Investor as a Cultural Figure of Global Capitalism', in Knorr-Cetina, K. and Preda, A. (eds.) *The Sociology of Financial Markets*. Oxford: Oxford University Press, pp. 141–162.

Richter, R. (1987) *Geldtheorie: Vorlesung auf der Grundlage der Allgemeinen Gleichgewichtstheorie und der Institutionenökonomik*. Berlin: Springer Verlag.

Rodano, G., Serrano-Velarde, N. and Tarantino, E. (2020) 'Lending Standards over the Credit Cycle', *The Review of Financial Studies*, 31(8), pp. 2943–2982. DOI: 10.2139/ssrn.2699553.

Sassen, S. (2018) *Cities in a World Economy*. 5th Edition. Thousand Oaks: SAGE Publications.

Shiller, R. J. (2017) 'Narrative Economics', *American Economic Review*, 107(4), pp. 967–1004. DOI: 10.2139/ssrn.2896857.

Soll, J. (2014) *The Reckoning: Financial Accountability and the Making and Breaking of Nations*. London: Penguin.

Stiglitz, J. and Greenwald, B. (2003) *Towards a New Paradigm in Monetary Economics*. Cambridge: Cambridge University Press.

Stützel, W. (1978[1958]) *Volkswirtschaftliche Saldenmechanik: Ein Beitrag zur Geldtheorie*. Tübingen: Mohr Siebeck.

Swedberg, R. (2012) 'The Role of Confidence in Finance', in Knorr-Cetina, K. and Preda, A. (eds.) *The Oxford Handbook of the Sociology of Finance*. Oxford: Oxford University Press. DOI: 10.1093/oxfordhb/9780199590162.013.0028.

Wainwright, T. and Kibler, E. (2014) 'Beyond Financialization: Older Entrepreneurship and Retirement Planning', *Journal of Economic Geography*, 14(4), pp. 849–864. DOI: 10.1093/jeg/lbt023.

Walsh, C. E. (2008) 'Central Bank Independence', in Durlauf, S. N. and Blume, L. E. (eds.) *The New Palgrave Dictionary of Economics*. London: Palgrave Macmillan. DOI: 10.1057/978-1-349-95121-5_2217-1.

Weizsäcker, C. C. von (2011) 'Staatliches Gewaltmonopol, Staatsverschuldung und individuelle Vorsorge: Walter Adolf Jöhr Vorlesung 2011, Universität St. Gallen', *Volkswirtschaftliche Beiträge*, 13.

Wicksell, K. (1889) *Geldzins und Güterpreise: Eine Studie über die den Tauschwert des Geldes bestimmenden Ursachen*. Jena: Fischer. DOI: 10.11588/diglit.22270.

Zellweger, T. M. (2017) *Managing the Family Business: Theory and Practice*. Cheltenham and Northampton: Edward Elgar Publishing.

Zingales, L. (2015) 'Presidential Address: Does Finance Benefit Society', *The Journal of Finance*, 70(4), pp. 1327–1363. DOI: 10.1111/jofi.12295.

Zuckerman, E. (2012) 'Market Efficiency: A Sociological Perspective', in Knorr-Cetina, K. and Preda, A. (eds.) *The Oxford Handbook of the Sociology of Finance*. Oxford: Oxford University Press.

CHAPTER THIRTEEN

Economic fluctuations and aggregate economic evolution

1. Introduction

Macroeconomic debates have traditionally been shaped by two major schools.

Economic fluctuations are a universal phenomenon in human economic history and stand at the core of extensive macroeconomic analysis and debates.[1] Two major schools can be distinguished that have been facing each other for decades, albeit under different labels and guises: the neoclassical, later, new classical school, and the different Keynesian schools. Besides their differences, the two strands exhibit important commonalities. First, they tend to deal with economic fluctuations in a relatively compartmentalised fashion, separating theories of business cycles from theories of economic growth. Second, they primarily associate economic fluctuations with GDP and the concomitant movement of a set of other macroeconomic variables. Accordingly, macroeconomic debates have been dominated by an almost exclusive on mathematical modelling and statistical analysis. At the same time, particularly following the 2008/2009 crisis, the contribution of established macroeconomics to an understanding of economic fluctuations, including recurrent crises, has been fundamentally put into question even by leading academics in the field.[2]

Recently, heterodox streams as well as new approaches, such as behavioural macroeconomics, have been gaining influence.

Heterodox streams of macroeconomics are partly characterised by a stronger reliance on verbal arguments rather than mathematical modelling, most notably the Austrian school as epitomised by Hayek's theory of investment and credit-driven business cycles,[3] the related Schumpeterian approach,[4] Minsky's theory of the inherent instability of finance in market economies,[5] and the Marxist-inspired French regulation school.[6] Some of those perspectives have influenced new strands of macroeconomics, such as behavioural macroeconomics[7] and alternative approaches to learning and expectations formation.[8]

Against this background, we posit that the discussion of economic fluctuations necessitates a framework which incorporates the co-evolution of institutional, technological, and economic/market factors in the narrower sense, with only the latter being measured by classic aggregate statistics such as GDP. The resulting complex interactions imply that in principle, each fluctuation is

330

DOI: 10.4324/9781003094869-18

historically singular. At the same time, fluctuations exhibit a cyclical character in different time scales, with periods of relative stasis and more minor fluctuations being punctuated by ruptures of large-scale change (i.e., economic crises). We suggest an evolutionary perspective that draws on the Schumpeterian approach to business cycles, complemented by an institutional perspective as exemplified by the regulation school. Accordingly, the chapter is structured as follows. Section 2 provides a brief introduction to Schumpeterian approaches and the regulation school and, building on this, develops the notion of techno-institutional regimes and their connection to economic fluctuations. Section 3 offers a brief critique of standard macroeconomic theory and proposes a theoretical shift of focus to the evolution of monetary accounting balances on different levels of aggregation. Section 4 provides a discussion on expectations and their formation both on the individual and collective level. Section 5 analyses two key patterns of economic fluctuations, namely fluctuations induced by entrepreneurship and technological change, and financial crises. Section 6 discusses monetary and fiscal policy, introduced by reflections on the performativity of economic indicators. Section 7 draws the different threads together by analysing market fluctuations as shifts of market states.

A comprehensive view of fluctuations needs to include institutional and technological development in accordance with the general evolutionary perspective.

2. Schumpeterian dynamics and techno-institutional regimes

The standard Schumpeterian approach sees technological change as the primary driver of economic cycles. Changes of technological paradigms are at the root of longer-term economic upturns and market disruption, whereas smaller-scale technological change triggers market dynamics following a life cycle pattern. The early phase is characterised by rapid innovation and growth of the respective market niches, which subsequently attracts further market suppliers with new products and technologies; eventually, market maturity and saturation are reached, which eventually paves the way for a new change via a recession (creative destruction) and, possibly, the introduction of a new technological paradigm. The cyclical character of innovation-driven fluctuations is reinforced by the role of the financial sector, in particular, via effects of leveraging during the boom and deleveraging during the bust.[9] Schumpeter integrated the longer- and shorter-time perspective by arguing that economic cycles of different length would superimpose (Figure 13.1).[10] The superimposition of waves accounts for different amplitudes of economic fluctuations; for example, simultaneous troughs in cycles of different length can lead to major economic crises such as the 1929/1930 Great Depression.

This result is essentially confirmed when taking a broader perspective, including a connection of technological and institutional factors. The regulation school incorporates a key distinction between an accumulation regime (referring to investment) constituted by the prevailing technological and

On technological paradigms, see Chapter 6, section 3.3.

The Schumpeterian approach sees technological change as a primary driver of economic cycles on different time scales.

The superimposition of cycles accounts for different amplitudes of economic fluctuations.

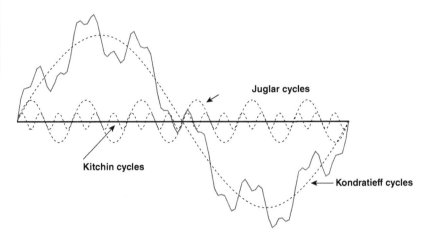

Figure 13.1 Superimposition of economic cycles according to Schumpeter[11]
Schumpeter saw cyclical economic development as a result of a superimposition
of cycles on three time scales, namely Kitchin cycles (short run, around three
years), Juglar cycles (medium run, around ten years), and Kondratieff cycles
(long run, around half a century). Superimposition determines the amplitude
of fluctuations.

*Economic crises
are associated
with institutional,
organisational,
and technological
change.*

On institutional
evolution, see
Chapter 9,
section 4.3.

*Techno-institutional
regimes are
complementary
combinations of
technological and
institutional pillars.*

organisational paradigms, and a mode of regulation in different economic policy fields.[12] Economic booms are associated with over-accumulation, which
eventually proves unsustainable and is corrected by an economic downturn.
This downturn is labelled as a minor crisis if it leads to no or only a gradual
alteration of institutional forms and as a structural crisis if it leads to a major
modification of the institutional setup because of emerging internal contradictions. Crises contribute to the path-dependent emergence and evolution of a
variety of accumulation regimes within the capitalist paradigm, corresponding to the emergence of varieties of capitalism,[13] which in turn influence how
economic fluctuations play out in concrete space and time.

We integrate these approaches via a generalised concept of techno-institutional regimes and their evolution,[14] where a 'regime', in the most general
sense, is defined as a configuration of social and material relationships that is
relatively stable over time. Techno-institutional regimes comprise the two
main pillars of technology (including technological paradigms) and institutions (including formal and informal institutions). Institutions include the economic policy framework which, in turn, is related not only to political power
constellations but also to the intellectual and academic environment, which
influences regime evolution in a performative way (e.g., Keynes's influence
on the Bretton Woods monetary regime).[15]

Techno-institutional regimes can be defined on different levels of aggregation. On the most general level, they encompass a set of complementary

institutional, technological, and organisational paradigms that, in a certain geographical space, exhibit stability over a longer time interval, which we deem as an epoch. A key example is the Fordist regime, as it emerged after WWII, which entailed a combination of economies of scale, increasing real wages, and mass consumption.[16] This level can be disaggregated, most importantly, along geographical space (e.g., the German versus the French regime) and along broad policy fields, which in the following we will label as techno-institutional sub-regimes. The most important sub-regimes are the monetary and financial regime, the fiscal policy regime, the labour market and social welfare regime, the competition regime, the international trade and investment regime, and the political regime in the general sense of different distributions of power and participatory opportunity. Those sub-regimes go beyond the notion of institutional forms in regulation theory insofar as they invariably encompass a technological component as well, albeit with varying relative importance (for example, the presence of economies of scale for the competition regime and various forms of digitalisation in the monetary and financial regime). Also, sub-regimes are internally differentiated in terms of the character of their rules and their temporal patterns of change.

Techno-institutional sub-regimes are, on the one hand, connected by institutional complementarities, such as between the competition regime and the international trade and investment regime. On the other hand, they evolve relatively autonomously such that a particular competition regime can coexist with different monetary regimes or tensions can arise between a restrictive international monetary regime (gold standard) and an expansive fiscal policy regime.

Based on this, we can distinguish different categories of economic fluctuations, understood in the broad sense outlined earlier, along the following criteria:

- *Length:* The standard indicator-based distinction between short-term, medium-term, and long-term cycles is related to regime change on different levels of aggregation. Technological and institutional paradigms on the regime level are relatively inert and, therefore, evolve in longer-term intervals, while the development of specific technologies and institutions on a sub-regime level takes place in a shorter time frame.
- *Depth and impact:* As far as the usual key statistical indicators are concerned, we concur with the standard distinctions of boom, recession, depression, and so on but at the same time include the breadth and intensity of their impact on the evolution of different sub-regimes and, eventually, regimes. An economic crisis is a recession or depression that is associated with a deep and longer-run impact on the evolution of various interconnected sub-regimes.
- *Endogenously versus exogenously caused:* The conceptual integration of regime evolution entails the endogenisation of many factors such as political business cycles (which are endogenous to the political and fiscal

Techno-institutional regimes can be defined on different aggregation levels. Sub-regimes can be identified along policy fields.

Techno-institutional sub-regimes co-evolve but not necessarily in a synchronic fashion.

For the concept of complementary institutions, see Chapter 9, section 4.1.

Economic fluctuations can be categorised along their length, depth and impact, causes, and the degree of involvement of different techno-institutional sub-regimes.

333

policy regime) or external price shocks (which are partly endogenous to the international trade and investment regime since it co-determines the extent of shock propagation). Natural influences, such as a pandemic or a natural catastrophe, count as purely exogenous causes.

- *Which regimes are causally involved to which degree?* Here, we distinguish between fluctuations that are causally confined to a specific regime, such as the monetary and financial regime, and those that are caused by a confluence of evolution of different regimes, such as by a combination of the monetary/financial regimes and technological paradigms.

Crises are singular historical events. Causal relations with regard to economic fluctuations and crises are ambiguous and subject to ex post construction.

These categories open up a very complex set of possibilities for the combination of economic fluctuations with regime evolution (Figure 13.2). In certain epochs, different sub-regimes coalesce into complementary sets but still exhibit a certain degree of autonomy such that they can experience ruptures at different points in time. Simultaneous ruptures of more than one regime are more likely to generate economic crises; the end of an epoch is likely to be associated with a major crisis. Importantly, due to the overwhelming complexity of the underlying relationships, crises are singular historical events whose causal ambiguities are subject to ex post construction. For example, it is still unclear whether the 2008 crisis was primarily rooted in the unsustainability of the US financial regime or whether there were deeper structural reasons at play, such as the structure of economic inequality in the United States or imbalances in trade and investment flows.[17]

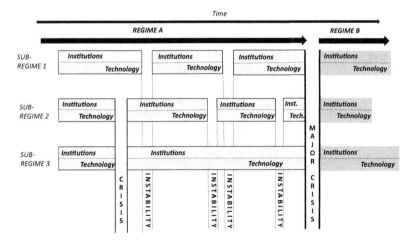

Figure 13.2 Evolution of techno-institutional (sub-)regimes and economic fluctuations

This simplified scheme visualises our perspective on the connection between changes of techno-institutional (sub-)regimes and economic fluctuations. For details, see main text.

3. Economic fluctuations of monetary aggregates: Macroeconomics and accounting balances

'Macroeconomics', by definition, is devoted to studying the economy in terms of monetary aggregates over different markets. The core of macroeconomic modelling is currently constituted by Dynamic Stochastic General Equilibrium (DSGE) models.[18] In principle, such models take a frictionless world of complete, completely integrated, and perfectly competitive markets as a benchmark and then introduce a wide variety of distortions, such as sticky prices, imperfect competition, and financing constraints. In coming to terms with the overwhelming complexity of market systems, we posit that the general equilibrium approach needs to be replaced by a taxonomy of more limited-range mechanisms. This has several implications for traditional key concepts of macroeconomics.

DSGE models exert a performative effect on economic policies, especially in the monetary realm.

First, the choice of aggregation level should avoid concealing concrete mechanisms in space and time; for example, in terms of the expectations of consumers and investors, their budget constraints, the distribution of income and wealth between different groups with different propensities to consume, and the dependence on wages and wage-setting institutions.

Overly high levels of aggregation conceal concrete mechanisms in space and time.

Second, the concept of representative agent[19] needs to be replaced by a distinction of types in a population of heterogenous agents. The population concept is also relevant for the crucial interaction between economic fluctuations and the evolution of the income distribution; for example, with regard to the propensity to consume.

The use of representative agents needs to be replaced by heterogeneity of agent types.

Third, markets are connected not only via realised (equilibrium) transactions but also via information flows and patterns of observation and interpretation of market participants.[20] Therefore, beyond pricing, the full range of social network mechanisms is relevant not only for single markets but for market systems and, therefore, macroeconomic dynamics. Market systems almost always constitute non-integral networks, implying incomplete connectivity over the different dimensions and a substantial role of the temporal element in market coordination. A standard example is the coordination between labour and product markets:[21] Unemployment can constrain suppliers of labour on the goods market, who will not be able to realise their consumption plans. The decreased revenue, in turn, will prevent employers from recruiting additional labour, which may further dampen consumption and so on.

Connections between markets are subject to the full range of social network dynamics.

Fourth, the existence of particular markets cannot just be assumed. This is of key importance; for example, with respect to insurance against risk: Since certain risks, such as the loss of employment and income, are de facto uninsurable on private markets, risk-averse households will engage in precautionary (buffer stock) saving in line with their subjective risk perception, which will in turn depend on their perception of the overall economic situation.[22]

The existence of specific markets cannot just be assumed.

Given those points, the question is which analytical framework can adequately capture the systemic complexity of macroeconomic development as relating to its key monetary aggregates, that is, going beyond the general

Our network-based perspective was developed in Chapter 8.

technological-institutional evolution outlined in the previous section. We argue that this can best be done by focusing on agents' monetary constraints and their interrelated evolution over time. This amounts to an analysis of macroeconomic relationships in terms of the mechanics of accounting balances of different market actors (*Saldenmechanik*), which is related to the more recent concept of stock-flow consistent modelling.[23] *Saldenmechanik* rests on the straightforward idea that, in a closed system of monetarily valued stocks and monetary flows over time, independent of its scope of claims and liabilities, income and expenditure over a certain period have to add up to zero and that, as a corollary, in that period, a negative or positive balance of any entity implies a reverse balance by the complementary entity that closes the system. This basic restriction structures the temporal flow of economic transactions, which is co-determined by budget constraints and the availability and provision of liquidity but at the same time fundamentally path dependent. In that sense, the mechanics of accounting balances is an example of pattern prediction in complex systems under constraints.[24]

Pattern prediction can take place on different aggregation levels insofar as *Saldenmechanik* does not entail any a priori determination in this respect; the standard microfoundations postulate is replaced by a flexible treatment of distributed agency and heterogenous agents. In this context, the distinction between individual and collective rationality becomes immediately clear once the scope of the closed system is defined: In such a system, an increase of monetary savings via a reduction of spending is possible for individual entities but not the system as a whole.[25] The analytical emphasis is on the different paths on which the necessary adjustments take place rather than on the attainment of market-clearing equilibria. Accounting balances – at least in an ex post perspective – establish a topology of network relationships via realised transactions and the associated monetary flows, which then have to be complemented by the respective patterns of information flows and observation. Over time, the resulting patterns can exhibit stability – in the sense of a coincidence of balances planned ex ante and realised ex post – without market clearing necessarily taking place. In other words, accounting balances play a key role both in fixing certain market states and in determining specific patterns of mechanisms generating aggregate phenomena.

On the mechanistic approach and the concept of agent types, see Chapter 2, section 4.

Accounting balances are the key determinant of market states and their aggregate effects.

4. Expectations as drivers of economic fluctuations

As said, the stability of market states over time is co-determined by a coincidence of planned and realised transactions. Ex ante planning, in turn, is inextricably linked to the formation of expectations, which, therefore, attains a crucial status in determining paths of macroeconomic adjustment and the associated fluctuations. The general treatment of expectations in economic thought has undergone a remarkable transition: Whereas earlier authors tended to regard expectations as a frequently volatile, incalculable, and potentially irrational component of economic behaviour, albeit potentially necessary for entrepreneurial action (epitomised by Keynes's animal spirits), the rational expectations revolution starting in the 1960s[26] has reversed this to the stance that economic actors (at least on average) are able to process all available information to form accurate predictions based on a correct model of the economy. We provide a new view based on our conceptualisation of individuals and social networks.

4.1. Individual expectations

The formation and use of individual expectations can be analytically organised into three components. First, there is the selection of informational inputs used by the economic agent; second, the process or model which transforms these inputs into expectations, including different ways to interpret the informational inputs; and third, the translation of expectations into actual behaviour.

Recent modelling has emphasised individual cost-benefit analysis both with respect to the use of information and the generation and updating of expectations. Indeed, many people tend not to take the effort, or lack the ability, to retrieve quantitative information about economic developments and infer their predictions from qualitative impressions, for example, conversations or news reports, in their social and work environment. Also, the updating of expectations can take place in a staggered or irregular fashion; for example, because people stay rationally inattentive to new information. However, the higher the expected stakes of an individual economic decision, the higher the pressure to incur the cost of learning to attain a rational decision basis.[27]

The problem with a cost-benefit-based approach to the formation of expectations is that Arrow's information paradox applies, that is, individuals cannot know in advance the benefit of the information that they incur cost for since this information is ex ante unknown. This is exacerbated by the context of fundamental uncertainty of macroeconomic development.[28] Therefore, there is no 'true' model of the economy, in the sense of a third-person view, to which subjective beliefs can eventually converge, and the heterogeneity of expectations, if only based on different interpretations of perceived economic data in a first-person view, is a fundamental regularity on the level of market systems. How, then, can individuals cope with fundamental uncertainty in expectations formation?

First, individuals connect experience into models of causality that eventually allow them to rationalise their decisions. Therefore, adaptive and iterative learning are not understood as a stepwise approximation of a true model but as an effort in line with the social stance of rationality, that is, the capability to provide reasons for behaviour in communication with others. One example is the use of probability-weighted alternative scenarios for returns that are in fact

The rational expectations revolution replaced earlier traditions relating to animal spirits.

Information and formation of expectations can be subject to individual cost-benefit analysis.

The standard cost-benefit calculus overlooks the problem of fundamental uncertainty.

Individuals rationalise expectations formation by forming subjective models of causality.

subject to fundamental uncertainty. More generally, the use of economic statistics and indicators for expectations formation, if taking place at all (see previous section), can be seen as a shared communicative anchor that allows for the emergence of a second-person view associated with a perceived higher degree of rationality.

The formation of expectations is inextricably linked to emotions.

Second, the formation of expectations is linked to emotions, that is, it integrates cognitive and affectual mechanisms.[29] This implies that the information incorporated in expectations formation is much wider than the economic realm, including situational and contextual factors and unconsciously received stimuli, and that individual selection of information used is not necessarily intentional.

Entrepreneurial expectations are based on fictionality.

Third, certain types of individuals base their expectation formation on fictionality, that is, imagined future states of the world that are not only constituted by extrapolated past trends but also by creative components.[30] These not only are pertinent for the Schumpeterian entrepreneur but can also be constructed, for example, by entrepreneurial consumers in comparing different future states of satisfaction of wants and needs in the context of developments in their social environment (such as fashion or status considerations) that influence the subjective valuation of goods. This leads to the role of collective dynamics in expectations formation.

On rationality as social stance, emotions, and entrepreneurship and creatvity, see chapter 7.

4.2. Collective dynamics

Expectations formation is of a fundamentally social nature. Since expectations are inner states, a variety of collective dynamics can arise from the formation of higher-order expectations.

The complex collective dynamics of expectations stems from the fact that the relation between the interpretation of others' behaviour, the formation of own expectations, and the consequences drawn for own behaviour is always multi-valued and, by necessity, entails the formation of higher-order expectations (Figure 13.3). The paradigmatic example is Keynes's beauty contest; but the problem applies beyond financial markets: If an employee wants to form an expectation on whether he will be fired in the foreseeable future, he has to form an expectation on the employer's behaviour based on the employer's expectations, which in turn may depend on others' expectations that are relevant for the employer (e.g., those of creditors or consumers) and further on. At the same time, the employer forms expectations about the employee's loyalty to the company and the lure of new job opportunities, which is in turn shaped by the perceptions of labour market conditions.

Keynes's beauty contest and higher-order expectations in financial markets are covered in Chapter 12, section 3.3.

This fundamental interdependence of expectations has several important implications. First, it confirms the result that a formation of rational expectations can only hold as a social stance: This is because even if a true model of the economy existed (third-person view) and agent A knew that model, she would also have to assume that agent B knows the model (second-person view), that agent B assumes that agent A as well as agent C know the model, and so on. Second, expectations are most likely to exhibit heterogeneity on the population level, even if strong shifts in a certain direction take place. Third,

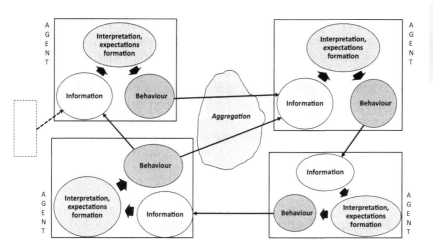

Figure 13.3 Interdependence of expectations and aggregation
Expectations are individual states that constitute necessary foundations of
economic behaviour. Their formation relies on the (conscious or unconscious)
collection of information and its interpretation. Information is derived from
the behaviour of other individuals, eventually mediated by informational cues
and/or aggregation, such as typically generated by economic statistics. Higher-
order expectations can be formed upon interpretation of others' behaviour.
Therefore, expectations do not form and stabilise on the basis of objective
economic facts but of institutionalised behavioural patterns, which may entail
a social stance of rationality.

many models of expectations formation entail a considerable potential for
purely endogenous movements of the business cycle. This is a key result of
the complex systems approach to macroeconomics, which has specified different assumptions about learning heuristics, observational patterns, and time
horizons that yield endogenous fluctuations without convergence to specific
system states.[31]

*Expectations are
fundamentally
heterogenous
and entail the
potential for
purely endogenous
movements of the
business cycle.*

As a consequence, the evolution of expectations is subject to the full range
of network analysis outlined in Chapter 8,[32] including the technology of communication. Accordingly, the formation of expectations may be influenced by
group boundaries and related social status, which may entail dynamics of
groupthink but also a hierarchical signalling of credibility, such as in the case
of expert opinion or certain news media.[33] Another implication of networked
expectations formation is the importance of frequency-dependent effects. For
example, expectational shifts in small high-status groups (e.g., high-profile
financial investors) may generate contagion effects that appear in waves,
spreading locally in communities of financial investors and savers, and then
spilling over to the general economy. These shifts, in turn, can be strongly

*The distinction
between short-
run and long-run
expectations is
endogenous to
actors' perceptions.*

influenced by the dynamics of narratives.[34] Importantly, all these effects are regularly embedded in emotional factors, such as market moods that systematically impact on the interpretation of incoming information.

Finally, an important distinction must be drawn between long-run and short-run expectations. On financial markets, this distinction is clearly endogenous to actors' perceptions:[35] In a boom, the short run ends at the time when actors expect a correction of prices to take place. More generally, the distinction associates different time horizons with different prospects of realisation of a certain state, given subjective estimates on the stability of relevant circumstances.

5. Patterns of economic fluctuations

5.1. Entrepreneurship and technological change

As said, one key source of economic fluctuations is technological change. Technology-driven fluctuations can be generated by differential changes of productivity in different sectors and industries, which are seen as exogenous by most mainstream theories, and ensuing adjustments in the production structure and on labour markets. The key to an endogenous view of the relation between technological change and short-term fluctuations is Schumpeterian entrepreneurship. The link to economic fluctuations is established via the notion of creative destruction together with a clustering of entrepreneurial activity, resulting in waves of innovation and discontinuous change.[36]

*The role of
Schumpeterian
entrepreneurship
for economic
growth is
discussed in
Chapter 16,
section 5.*

*Risk-taking
entrepreneurs,
regularly backed by
external finance,
are driven by the
potential to attain
entrepreneurial
rents, generating
positions of
temporary
monopoly.*

Schumpeterian entrepreneurial action is, to an important extent, based on the readiness to take risk based on fictional expectations – as, for example, embodied in narratives on new technologies. In a monetary economy, profit is a necessary corollary of entrepreneurial success, which primarily consists of the attainment of a temporary monopoly position. This generates incentives to overcome the problems associated with introducing a new technology. Also, the innovation may generate network-based externalities on other entrepreneurs or established firms, which eventually lead to further innovation; alternatively, other entrepreneurs (or established firms) may pursue a strategy of imitation. Innovation diffusion, then, involves a gradual evaporation of monopoly profits and an associated shift in the structure of production and demand, possibly coupled with the development of new wants and creative adaptations on the consumer side. Concomitantly, some established producers will lose competitiveness and, by way of profit-based market selection, leave the market, leading to associated changes in labour demand.

Thus, competitive entrepreneurial incentives coupled with externalities from innovation may lead a single or relatively isolated innovation to trigger an innovation wave gradually expanding to macroeconomic significance. This generates increases of income via an increase of profits, the enhancement of productivity, and the weeding out of less productive firms and outdated technologies. However, given fundamental uncertainty and the unplanned character of the process, the wave will tend to overshoot. Here, the frequency-dependent emotional side of expectations formation comes into play: In the wake of general enthusiasm, lower-quality projects enter the scene that eventually have to be liquidated, demand gets saturated, and possibilities of external finance will worsen. With respect to creative destruction, the second element gets centre stage, expectations are revised downwards, and boom turns into bust.

Overall, therefore, in modern market economies, entrepreneurship, innovation, and economic fluctuations are endogenously intertwined. The underlying relations also provide the crucial link to the longer-term perspective: Given entrepreneurship as a key driver of technological progress, economic fluctuations are a necessary corollary of economic growth in a market economy. At the same time, the shorter-run procedure of adaptation to an innovation involves losers not only on the level of single firms but also on the level of wider aggregates, such as regions, industries, or different groups and strata of the working population. The distributional effects of technology-induced fluctuations may be exacerbated by the role of the financial sector, to which we turn next.

5.2. Finance and financial crises

Financial relationships are another key source of shorter-run economic fluctuations and crises (Figure 13.4); indeed, some theoretical accounts see inherent financial sector instability as the primary source of economic fluctuations, with a possible connection to central bank policies and the modern fiat money system.[37] The underlying generative forces may vary, but as has been stressed by historical as well as theoretical accounts,[38] there are common patterns resulting from the specific structure of competition in the financial sector as well as the key role of transactions driven by expectations – including higher-order expectations – on financial markets.

A financially driven boom starts by the triggering of some credit expansion process. One standard case is the entrepreneurial need for external finance. Another more general case is the occurrence of some perceived positive changes in the economic realm – including institutional change, such as financial liberalisation – that shift expectations on the development of asset prices, such as for stocks or real estate, upward. Under the assumption that entrepreneurs and households at least to some extent rely on external finance, their expansive stance will spill over, and eventually be driven by, the financial sector. Expansion of the financial sector will generally translate into the wider economy via an increase of production and consumption. Notably, however, the effect may vary with the institutional setup; for example, an increase in house prices is likely to increase consumption in countries where

The macroeconomic significance of creative destruction stems from innovation externalities and spillovers.

Economic fluctuations induced by the financial sector can vary in their generative forces but exhibit common patterns.

Financial booms are triggered and fuelled by an expansion of external finance via loans or equity.

*Expansion can
become self-
reinforcing by an
increase of leverage
and propensity to
take risk, herding
behaviour and
bubbles, and
incentives for
financial innovation.*

See, for an
analysis of
leverage in a
specific monetary
context,
Chapter 12,
sections 2.3 and
3.2.

mortgage-backed credit financing of such expenditure is common (such as in the Anglo-American world), but it may have the opposite effect (i.e., generate an increase in savings) in countries where this is not the case (such as in most of Continental Europe).[39]

There are various mechanisms which may render this expansion a self-reinforcing process. Most importantly, an increased propensity to take risk is associated with a gradual acceptance of higher leverage, establishing the expansionary part of the leverage cycle.[40] The significance of leverage is increased by the fact that changed valuations on markets for assets generate performative feedback effects on markets for loans. For example, an entrepreneurial firm that is subject to mark to market valuation in accounting terms will gain easier access to additional loans or equity because, as a consequence of its increase in net worth, the premium of external over internal finance decreases. Also, a financial investor or household may use existing assets as collateral for (additional) loans to expand investment or consumption, while at the same time, requirements with respect to the quantity and quality of collateral tend to fall. Those mechanisms are key examples of financial accelerators in the sense of both amplifying initial impulses and reinforcing an ongoing expansion.[41]

Other important aspects are information externalities and herding behaviour: Given uncertainty on the prospects of repayment, financial investors may simply imitate others in providing preferential loans to entrepreneurs in certain industries[42] or, in a context of general optimism, metaphorically transfer eased financing conditions to other sectors. On markets for assets, the corresponding mechanism is the formation of bubbles, which constitutes a standard case of divergence between individual and collective rationality: Individual rationality dictates participation, but profits must eventually be limited by reaching a collective upper bound, which, however, is a priori unknown.

Furthermore, the expansion generates incentives for financial innovation as distinct form of entrepreneurship. Examples in the last decades abound, including junk bonds, the expansion and differentiation of derivative instruments, and credit default swaps and mortgage-backed securities that played a decisive role in the 2008/2009 crisis. In the case of a Schumpeterian upturn, therefore, there is an important co-evolution of technological/organisational innovation and financial innovation, with the latter tending to generate economic instability.[43]

For a discussion
of agent types
of consumers
and investors,
see Chapter 12,
section 3.1.

In a general perspective, these mechanisms entail a distinct institutional component insofar as they destabilise and shift a variety of rules and conventions, such as on socially acceptable degrees of risk-taking and leveraging. Concomitantly, the distribution of types of investors and consumers will change as well; in particular, a boom will likely increase the relative shares of entrepreneurial consumers and financial investors.

How would the boom end and eventually turn into bust? The principal explanation is that at some point, over-optimistic expectations on prices and profits are not met and eventually have to be revised downwards. In the case of the Schumpeterian cycle, this may happen, for example, because of a petering out of the innovation wave and an increasing dominance of lower-quality projects, as outlined in the previous section. In the case of asset bubbles, the trigger may ultimately be of minor importance, such as a bankruptcy or another piece of bad news. In general, there is always a certain degree of arbitrariness in the timing of the apex, reflecting the fundamental expectations-driven character of the process.

The mechanisms outlined earlier, then, are essentially put in reverse mode, with financial accelerators, and more specifically, deleveraging, working to speed up the contraction. The pervasiveness of externalities in actions of financial actors and the role of networks will endogenously shape information and observation flows. For example, a financial crisis is likely to intensify mutual scrutiny between banks, including their respective business partners,[44] which may constitute an autonomous factor for the downwinding of mutual credit relationships besides the revision of expectations and the generally decreasing appetite for risk. Particularly in large-scale crisis events, a higher degree of network connectivity between market actors, as driven via leveraging, may contribute to a *de*stabilisation of markets rather than stabilising them as a consequence of a wider distribution of risk.[45]

Furthermore, there is a key role of wealth effects. A sharp revaluation of asset prices enforces a fast adjustment of balance sheets, with immediate external effects to the broader economy. The key mechanism, again, is deleveraging, as particularly taking place on financial markets:[46] Since their wealth is decreasing, some market agents will have to instigate fire sales in order to meet their margin requirements. This drives down prices further, generating more sales and so forth. Another mechanism relates to (entrepreneurial) consumers, who reduce spending because the falling value of their collateral decreases their capacity to take out, and roll over, loans. For the same reason, companies reduce investment and execute lay-offs; bankruptcies increase, which then generates negative repercussions back into the financial sector. All this is likely to lead to an endogenous shortening of time horizons, given often immediate necessities of balance sheet adjustment.

The main mechanism of market adjustment depicted by standard theory, namely an increase of the interest rate, is of minor importance to the bust scenario since it does not take into account the occurrence of credit rationing.[47] The equilibration mechanism in the sense of reconciling plans and ex post results does not primarily work via the market price (i.e., the interest rate), but the adjustment of balances via quantity signals and quantity restrictions, in particular, constraints on liquidity.

The turn from boom to bust comes with a revision of expectations, which may be triggered by minor factors.

A key role is played by contractionary wealth effects, which enforce an adjustment of balance sheets.

For a discussion from the perspective of monetary communities, see Chapter 12, section 2.3.

The contractionary effect of credit rationing is more important than increases in interest rates.

On credit rationing as a lemons-type problem, see Chapter 12, section 2.3.

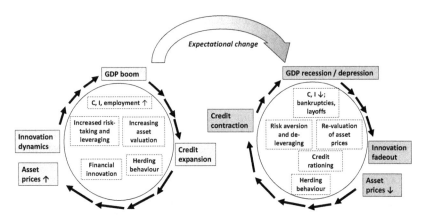

Figure 13.4 Anatomy of financial crises
Financial crises are generated by a change from an expansive market state to a contractionary one, triggered by a change in expectations that may, but does not necessarily have to, be driven by economic events, such as the fade-out of a wave of profitable technological innovation. In both states, the financial sector exhibits a trend-reinforcing and destabilising rather than a stabilising role.

To conclude, the unfolding of a financial crisis and its repercussions on the broader economy involve a combination of expectational and institutional factors that interact in complex ways. On a basic hypothetical level, for example, the crisis of 2008/2009 would not have happened if the bulk of creditors had kept a focus on longer-run expectations, with good reasons to believe that housing prices would stay on an upward trend, given, for example, demographic trends.[48] However, once the contraction was triggered, the institutional setup considerably reduced market agents' degrees of freedom in adjusting, as being reflected in their accounting balances. For example, banks faced requirements with respect to capital and the quality and valuation of collateral; rules on bankruptcies triggered immediate losses for different creditors, enforcing further downwinding. Those rules, therefore, involved performative loops with respect to market-based evaluation with a destabilising effect.

6. Fluctuations and economic policy

6.1. Performative measurement and modelling

Economic policy derives many of its decisions from systematic observation of economic statistics but also designs those decisions along (macro)economic models that rely on them. This is why an analysis of fiscal and monetary policy needs to start with the policy performativity of macroeconomic aggregate statistics as well as macroeconomic models.[49]

Analogously to the case of expectations of private actors, statistical indicators co-construct economic reality in the sense of enabling responsive policy action in the first place. For example, the expansion of public budgets and development of increasingly voluminous fiscal policy capacity from the 1930s co-evolved with the establishment of GDP in the wake of World War II and many other indicators of an even more recent date. Notably, some indicators that are systematically used by policymakers directly rely on theoretical assumptions and economic modelling, such as the output gap (the gap between current and potential output).[50]

Based on this, indicators also influence the operationalisation of economic policy interventions in many ways. First, the time scale of defining a 'fluctuation' performatively feeds back on policymakers' reaction speeds. For example, the raising of quarterly or monthly GDP data creates additional adjustment options, and incentives, for policy decisions. The construction of a distinction between fluctuations and a longer-run trend, possibly supported by the calculation of statistical-economic constructs such as the NAIRU (non-accelerating inflation rate of unemployment), may influence policymakers' perceptions and expectations; for example, when extrapolating certain trends from the past.[51] Second, economic statistics shape the level of aggregation, including geographical scope, that is commonly referred to when describing a fluctuation. For example, the territorial reference of GDP draws a delineation of national and foreign economic activity according to certain pre-established conventions. Institutions that formally or informally relate economic behaviour to a certain level of aggregation (e.g., the regular reporting of national rather than regional GDP figures) can performatively unify that level in the sense of generating increasingly correlated movements. Third, there is the issue of statistical precision and inherent measurement assumptions. For example, GDP statistics undergo ex post corrections; inflation measures and deflators can rely on different samples of market prices.

Given this, it is questionable to what extent economic indicators provide an accurate reflection of policy objectives. Economic fluctuations as measured by GDP may not adequately capture actual economic development and, therefore, provide inadequate signals to economic policy. Another problem is the inclusion of the financial sector, where modern measurement approaches have led to very questionable results particularly during the 2008/2009 crisis, in which the sector purportedly exhibited a *stabilising* role.

Macroeconomic models and statistics have complex performative effects on economic policy and market actors' behaviour.

Economic statistics co-constructs economic reality and influences policymakers' reaction speeds.

Indicators influence operative policy measures by defining time scales, levels of aggregation, and measurement conventions.

The adequacy of indicators used with respect to policy objectives is often questionable.

6.2. Monetary policy

The establishment of central banks with an official mandate to conduct monetary policy has strongly been shaped by the idea of political independence, which constitutes another important example of the policy performativity of economic science in at least two ways. First, its establishment was strongly influenced by economic ideas, such as via the policy tenets of monetarism.[52]

*The political
independence
of central banks
is related to the
performativity of
economics.*

Second, it opened the way for an essentially technocratic conception of monetary policy, which came to rely on a heavy use of quantitative macroeconomic modelling.

Modern central banks have powerful instruments at their disposal to influence economic fluctuations, as evidenced in recent financial crises where not only the classical instruments of monetary policy but also central banks' competences to regulating and supervising commercial banks were made use of. What is less clear are the longer-run effects of monetary policy interventions, particularly in terms of their impact on growth and the postulated long-run dichotomy between real and nominal values, that is, the neutrality of money and money supply with respect to the evolution and determination of supposedly non-monetary variables, such as real GDP. We reject this dichotomy perspective for two main reasons. On the one hand, the distinction between real and nominal variables is essentially a statistical construct which can itself change over time, given that measurement as such necessarily has to refer to monetary values. This applies our argument that in a market economy, money cannot just constitute a veil to the macroeconomic level. On the other hand, monetary expansion will always exhibit distributional effects by a respective adjustment of accounting balances (e.g., via different propensities to consume or increased survival rates of zombie firms in an environment of low real interest rates).[53]

*Central bank
announcements and
economic behaviour
are interrelated
in complex ways;
policy commitment
only offers a partial
solution.*

The complexity of the monetary transmission mechanism is partly constituted by performative feedback between the central bank's announcements and actions and the behaviour of market participants. In established macroeconomics, this essential point was theoretically neutralised by the rational expectations assumption, with the strong implication that monetary policy can influence economic fluctuations only by surprise measures unanticipated by market actors. Today, there is a certain consensus that a core part of central bank policy is the management of expectations of relevant market agents (e.g., by anchoring inflation expectations and providing forward guidance on estimated inflation and interest rates).[54] However, given the complexity of the interactions, there is still a plethora of constellations that can lead a central bank to failure in reaching its objectives. One reason is that market participants can extract and update information on general economic development, such as expected GDP growth, from monetary policy decisions. For example, forward guidance that, from the point of view of market participants, turns out on the pessimistic side can instigate deflationary spirals.[55]

The classic recommendation to commit a central bank to a strict rule (such as the Taylor rule) that mechanistically links policy decisions to macroeconomic indicators raises serious problems not only in terms of loss of flexibility but also with respect to credibility. This is pertinent in the well-known time-consistency problem of standard monetary and economic policy[56] as well as in the too-big-to-fail dilemma in the bailout of financial institutions during a crisis: While a pre-commitment against such bailouts is instrumental in avoiding moral hazard issues with respect to risk-taking, it can become necessary to breach that commitment during crisis due to the danger of systemic effects, which in turn will reduce the credibility of the pre-commitment.[57]

Central bank policies, including their effects on economic fluctuations, are core elements of monetary-financial regimes and entail a bundle of complementary institutions, implying that periods of stability can be followed by drift or more radical change. In the stable phase, institutions rest on patterns of central bank measures and communication which create dispositions for economic behaviour. A core example is price setting by firms; translated into action, respective dispositions generate some measure of inflation as a population-level phenomenon, which in turn serves as core informational cue for policy decisions. To an important extent, the emergence of behavioural dispositions rests on well-known elements such as trust into, and reputation of, the central bank, but those factors need to be seen in the broader context of internal and external institutional mechanisms; for example, the status of the German Bundesbank up to the 1990s was clearly embedded in broader notions of national historical experience, culture and pride (*Stabilitätskultur*).[58] Importantly, institutionalisation in this context is not to be equated with the simple imposition of policy rules in the rules-versus-discretion dimension; for example, Alan Greenspan drew part of his reputation in the 2000s from his alleged refusal to follow schematic rules, although the Fed's decisions could ex post be reconstructed to follow a modified Taylor rule.[59] In case of the no-bailout problem, market participants can hold beliefs that run counter the official rule, whose breach would then actually stabilise the institution. Institutionalisation also includes the central bank's factual relationship to fiscal institutions and policy, to which we turn next.

Central bank policies are core elements of monetary-financial regimes, for which social trust plays a crucial role.

Behavioural dispositions are key elements in our model of institution-alisation in Chapter 9, section 3.1. For more on the role of central banks for trust in economic stability, see Chapter 12, section 2.3.

6.3. Fiscal policy and reform

As in monetary policy, the influence of fiscal policy on economic fluctuations is inextricably linked to the development of the modern state – it was only in the 20th century that taxation levels as well as public expenditure reached GDP shares that would render a macroeconomic impact on a regular base – that is, except in wartime – possible. Fiscal effects are generated not only via active political decisions on government income and expenditure but also via automatic stabilisers that mainly depend on the system of taxes and (social) transfers. In that respect, the institutional framework has a direct and, at least in the short run, non-discretionary influence on patterns of economic fluctuations.

The central economic role of fiscal policies is linked to the expansion of the modern state.

Expectations of market actors play a key role for the effectiveness of fiscal policy, as in the case of monetary policy. The corollary of the rational expectations hypothesis is Ricardian equivalence (i.e., taxpayers anticipate the future tax burdens stemming from public debt repayment), with the main

Expectations and the interaction between policy and economic behaviour play a key role for fiscal policy as well.

347

theoretical alternative being posed by the Keynesian multiplier (assuming expansionary effects of government expenditures). Both accounts, again, suffer from the problem of a lack of thicker descriptions and explanations of concrete mechanisms in specific space and time,[60] and widely ignore the complexity of communication and information flows as well as the importance of institutionalised behaviour, including the level of trust into public authorities and its embeddedness in broader cultural contexts. One example is the role of the state as an insurer against economic downturns and hardship: In many countries, the unprecedented scale of anticyclical measures against the COVID-19 crisis appears to have been widely accepted despite their risks in the longer-run perspective in terms of maintaining trust in sovereign money.

See, for the
related regime
of inequality
concept,
Chapter 15,
and for the role
of government
bonds for trust in
sovereign money,
Chapter 12,
section 3.2.

Furthermore, a crucial role accrues to accounting balances together with the possibility to stretch budgetary constraints over time via the financial system; for example, the success of typical policies of austerity to consolidate public balances will not only depend on expectations-based reactions of the private sector in terms of consumption and investment in general but also on their capacity to finance those decisions, given that in the aggregate (and ignoring the open economy case, which will be the focus of the next chapter), an improvement in the public accounting balance is necessarily complemented by deterioration of the private sector balance.

Business cycles can be politically imbued.

The direct susceptibility of fiscal policy to political, and eventually democratic, decision making entails the possibility of politically imbued instability or political business cycles. These scenarios abandon the assumption of economic policymakers as benevolent stabilisers and essentially endogenise fiscal policy as responding to political-economic forces itself, again unfolding a wide variety in space and time.[61]

See, for our
underlying
theory of
economic policy,
Chapter 17.

The rules versus discretion problem is a key issue for both fiscal and monetary policy and their interrelation.

The presence of such cycles leads to the rules versus discretion problem in fiscal policy. At first glance, particularly in democracies, fiscal policy cannot be restrained by technical rules to the extent of monetary policy since devising a budget is a key political prerogative. As far as fiscal rules are in place, they mainly apply in sub-entities of currency areas, such as US federal states or German *Länder* but also the member states of the Euro area. Those rules address the coordination problem stemming from the potential of expansionary fiscal policies of a sub-unit to end up in default, which would then affect the entire currency area. Correspondingly, on the sovereign level, the absence of respective rules always raises the prospect of fiscal expansion financed by a conceptionally unlimited supply of domestic (fiat) currency. Therefore, the combination of an independent central bank and a political culture of fiscal restraint can ultimately be seen as a combined monetary-financial and fiscal regime based on the fictional narrative of a government budget constraint, which stabilises expectations regarding the maintenance of a market economy given that it limits the size of government intervention. However, a recurrent incidence of massive government bond purchases by central banks may put this narrative into question.

7. Economic fluctuations as shifts in market states

We now synthesise our view of market fluctuations by generalising the concept of market states to the case of interconnected markets. Institutionalised behavioural patterns on markets rest on different categories that will exhibit different degrees of inertia. For example, the array of formal and informal institutions around property is normally a relatively stable category, exhibiting more substantial change only in the longer run or in rare revolutionary situations, whereas expectations, seen as behavioural propensities, can change more quickly. This corresponds to the distinction between regime change and shorter-run fluctuations within a certain techno-institutional sub-regime: Market states include the institutional foundations of both categories and evolve accordingly.

The concept of market states is generalised to interconnected markets.

The concept of market states was introduced in Chapter 11, section 4.2.

Based on this, we distinguish two categories of market interconnections (Figure 13.5). First, there are realised market transactions at market prices, corresponding to the upper left and lower right of Figure 11.2. This category is analytically captured by accounting balances: In a given period of time, each realised monetary transaction, whether market-clearing or not, constitutes a change in the accounting balance of the respective market actor. These changes spill over to other markets via the budget constraint, given the respective network topology, liquidity constraints, and the possibility to shift budget constraints over time via finance and financial markets. Institutionalised behaviour implies that (i) in the stable state, there is no systematic discrepancy between realised transactions and expected results (e.g., in terms of profits or net household income) over time; and (ii) the concrete patterns of setting prices and quantities vary from market to market, including the applicable degree of price stickiness or inertia.

Markets are connected in two main ways: first, by realised market transactions and, second, by mutual expectations.

Second, markets are connected by expectations (referring now to the lower-left part in Figure 11.2). As said, expectations depend on observation and interpretation of market information relating to the other three parts of Figure 11.2, for the market in question as well as for other related markets but also a wide range of additional information, such as on economic policy measures. The structure and degree of interconnection of different markets via expectations depends on their network connections along the standard three dimensions, with the dimension of transactions as captured by accounting balances now being filtered by subjective perception and interpretation. Institutionalised behaviour implies a stabilisation in all three dimensions of expectations mentioned in section 4: The selection of information and formation of expectations follows certain conventions,[62] which entail information compression in Aoki's sense insofar as agents rely on informational cues, such as statistical information on the general economic situation. The behavioural consequences of expectations are stabilised in terms of behavioural propensities, habits, or, given the complexity of the environment, decision heuristics. These heuristics may, but do not necessarily have to, include

On information compression, see Chapter 9, section 3.1.

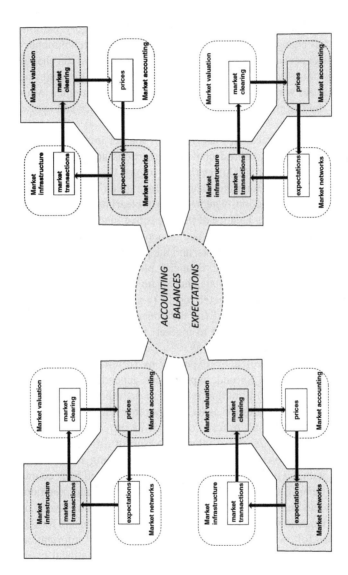

Figure 13.5 Market connections via accounting balances and expectations

Economic fluctuations are simultaneous shifts in market states, whose graphical depiction corresponds to Figure 11.2. Markets are interconnected via two main elements: first, accounting balances emerging from realised market transactions at sets of market prices; second, expectations derived from observation of other markets, including the formation of higher-order expectations (see Figure 13.3). These elements mediate exogenous changes and the evolution of techno-institutional regimes.

higher-order expectations; particularly, if related to the short run, they may just rely on trust in a general stability of the state of affairs (such as in the case of sequential market transactions). Notably, a stable state of expectational conventions does not necessarily imply homogeneity, particularly on financial markets, where prices may reflect stable distributions of expectations about yield.

Against this background, we can now look at the propagation of shocks and fluctuations as a temporal sequence of destabilisation of different market states and, eventually, a shift and re-stabilisation into new states. In principle, those processes take place on the outlined levels of aggregation in the market context (market niches, markets, and the market system), with possible sequences entailing both downward and upward causation. As a classic example, the economic crisis of 2008/2009 started on the market for US real estate finance, then spilled over to other financial markets, and subsequently extended to markets for other products and services, that is, the national market system of the US and other countries (upward causation). Vice versa, via the universality of the budget constraint, a system-level crisis is likely to spill over to a broad array of markets and market niches that were initially unaffected (downward causation).

The sequence in which shifts of market states take place depends on the intensity and speed of their connections in terms of monetary flows, mediated via accounting balances, and the determinants of expectations in both dimensions mentioned earlier. For example, the financial sector is regularly a forerunner of general economic downturns because its market depth and low transaction cost enable (and once a downturn unfolds, necessitate) a relatively rapid adjustment of accounting balances; also, the self-referentiality of financial market valuations as well as regularly high stakes of financial market actors (leading them to a more frequent update of their expectations) will lead to high expectational volatility and sensitivity against perceived external changes.

The formation of expectations as well as their translation into actual behaviour are strongly influenced by economic policy, as discussed in the previous section, as well as technological and more general institutional factors. This relates to the established differentiation between early, coincident, and lagging indicators of the business cycle. For example, decisions underlying factory orders for (intermediate) goods, an early indicator, are likely to directly reflect medium to longer expectations due to the technological nature of the production process.[63] However, employers may be able to translate deteriorating economic expectations into actual behaviour only with a significant time lag due to institutional restrictions established by employment protection laws, which is why the unemployment rate is commonly seen as a coincident

Economic fluctuations constitute a temporal sequence of shock propagation on different levels of aggregation, resulting in a shift and, eventually, re-stabilisation of market states.

For different aggregation levels in the market context, see Chapter 11.

The sequence of shifts in market states depends on the intensity and speed of connections established by monetary flows, and the determinants of expectations, particularly on financial markets.

The translation of shifted expectations into behavioural adjustment is influenced by economic policies and institutions more generally.

On price setting,
see Chapter 10,
section 2.2.

rather than a leading indicator. The most well-known example for lagged adjustment is price stickiness (which, on the aggregate level, corresponds to inflation as a lagged indicator). This is because prices de facto constitute social conventions on their own, which imbues *any* change with a significant amount of uncertainty for the price setter. Also, movements in certain prices are restricted by formal institutions that vary over space and time; for example, there are wide differences between countries in terms of rules affecting wage setting, reaching from employment protection legislation to the degree to which wage negotiations are centralised; the same is true for rules on tenant protection and rent control.

Therefore, the analysis on how changes in certain markets ripple through the economy needs to encompass the full set of relatively inert formal and informal institutions that impact on the formation of expectations and ensuing market behaviour. On the formal level, pertinent examples are competition law, as far as it concerns price setting; regulation of the financial sector (e.g., with respect to capital requirements of financial institutions); bankruptcy legislation; and the size and design of the social safety net, which can constitute an automatic stabiliser. On the informal level, there are, for example, cultural factors influencing the savings rate; the propensity to finance consumption by debt; and labour market mobility.

Economic fluctuations are path-dependent processes. As a result, economic fluctuations are path-dependent processes. The specific patterns of interaction between markets are always decisively shaped by antecedent technological and institutional conditions; in the longer run as well as for stronger fluctuations, in particular, economic crises, there is a feedback loop from market evolution to technological and institutional development which can amount to regime change. Whereas in principle, fluctuations can be rendered comparable in space and time by tracing the evolution of accounting balances of market agents on different levels of aggregation, temporal adjustment paths are highly complex and unique. Actions are intertwined in the sense that market agents, particularly in phases of instability, continuously scrutinise and interpret their environment and eventually adapt their behaviour in line with revised expectations as well as objective budget constraints, such as when faced with a change of options of external finance. Since the state space of economic activity is constantly changing, objective probabilities of future events cannot be calculated and reactions to changes are, therefore, fundamentally subjective. At the same time, market states exhibit a significant degree of inertia, including a forgetting of past crisis events, which can lead to a resemblance of historical patterns, with the most prominent example constituted by financial crises.[64] In that sense, fluctuations exhibit regularities as well as singular historical components.

8. Conclusion

Conventional economic theory analyses economic fluctuations in terms of exogenous shocks to full-employment market equilibrium and consequently puts its focus on the question of how re-equilibration is – and eventually, can be, via policy instruments – achieved. More recent approaches – in particular, the perspective of complex systems macroeconomics – have partly given up the equilibrium perspective and offer explanations of endogenous fluctuations or even chaotic outcomes, based on different assumptions on expectations formation, learning, and decision heuristics. In this chapter, we offered a generalisation of this perspective by integrating fluctuations into a larger-scale evolutionary and institutional framework. Economic fluctuations are elements of the long-term evolution of techno-institutional regimes and the complementary sub-regimes constituting them; while smaller-scale fluctuations are associated with shifts on the sub-regime level, major economic crises will normally induce a regime shift due to their institutional implications, which, to an important part, stem from economic policy measures.

Our general approach is to depict economic fluctuations as shifts of market states, that is, a change in institutionalised behavioural patterns that constitute relatively static (and interconnected) markets. Given this, specific patterns of fluctuations emerge from two main channels via which markets are connected. First, there are monetary flows, which are a function of budget constraints and over time result in accounting balances on different levels of aggregation, in line with the temporal flow of realised transactions. Second, there is the formation of expectations, taking place in an environment of fundamental uncertainty, and their translation into actual behaviour. Both are influenced by the prevailing techno-institutional regime and its sub-regimes; for example, via the speed and breadth in which an adjustment of financial sector balances translates into the overall economy (monetary and financial regime), legal restrictions on price adjustment (competition regime), and the structure of the production process. They are also influenced by economic policy, with the interaction between policy measures, their interpretation by economic actors, and the associated formation of expectations being critical to the success of both monetary and fiscal policy in terms of stabilising the economy. As we have emphasised, the scope of both fiscal and monetary policy has enormously expanded since the regime change of the Great Depression from 1929. Given this, we have argued that under a fiat money regime, the institutional separation between fiscal and monetary policy, as primarily epitomised by the political independence of the central bank, is a key feature of a market system.

> **Major chapter insights**
>
> - Economic fluctuations are embedded in techno-institutional regimes, which encompass technological paradigms as well as institutional principles, and their constituent sub-regimes. Concrete patterns of fluctuations are influenced by the co-evolution of sub-regimes, with concurrent changes in several sub-regimes commonly leading to a stronger fluctuation amplitude.
> - As an alternative to highly aggregated conventional models with *strong behavioural* assumptions, a temporal analysis of accounting balances on different levels of aggregation can account for the historicity of economic fluctuations as well as common patterns.
> - Expectations, as formed both on an individual as well as collective level, are the key subjective determinants of economic fluctuations. All three components of the evolution of expectations, that is, the selection of information, its interpretation and the formation of expectations, and the translation of expectations into actual behaviour, are contingent on individual and collective circumstances.
> - Economic fluctuations can be triggered by technological and institutional change as well as by financial sector instability, resulting in typical boom and bust cycles.
> - Monetary and fiscal policy are performatively shaped by the use of economic statistics and macroeconomic modelling. Their effectiveness in stabilising fluctuations depends on complex interactions with economic agents in terms of credibility and expectations formation. The institutional separation between monetary and fiscal policy is a specific component of post-war regimes in Western Europe and has been instrumental in keeping up the narrative of a market system.

Notes

1 A good exposition of the various schools is provided by Snowdon and Vane (2005). For the history of macroeconomics, see De Vroey (2016).
2 Buiter (2009), Romer (2016).
3 Hayek (2012 [1931]).
4 Schumpeter (2006 [1911]).
5 Minsky (2008 [1986]).

6 Boyer (1990).

7 De Grauwe and Ji (2019).

8 Hommes (2021).

9 Schumpeter (1911); Peneder and Resch (2021); Perez (2003).

10 Schumpeter (1939).

11 Geiger (2014), p. 44, taken from Schumpeter (1939), p. 213.

12 For a survey of the regulation school, see Boyer (1990); for a summary including the school's connection to Marxism, Boyer (2018).

13 Hall and Soskice (2001).

14 The concept relates to the notion of techno-institutional complexes, which was originally introduced to explain the lock-in of fossil fuel–based energy systems, Unruh (2000).

15 Cesarano (2006); Blyth (2002).

16 Boyer (1990), Freeman and Louçã (2001).

17 Rajan (2011).

18 See, for a widely cited application, Smets and Wouters (2007), and for a critique, Caballero (2010).

19 Kirman (1992).

20 This issue is recognised by the emerging complex systems approach to macro-economics, which has generated a wide range of quantitative and experimental results. See, for a survey, Hommes (2021).

21 This is the dual decision hypothesis, Clower (1965); Leijonhufvud (1967, 2011); Snowdon et al. (1994).

22 Hendry and Muellbauer (2018).

23 Stützel (1978 [1958]), Godley and Lavoie (2012).

24 Hayek (1972),

25 This, of course, corresponds to Keynes's paradox of saving, Keynes (1960 [1936]).

26 Muth (1961).

27 See, for an overview, Curtin (2019).

28 See, for example, Roos (2015).

29 Curtin (2019), chapter 5.

30 Beckert (2016).

31 De Grauwe and Ji (2019), Hommes (2021).

32 Potts (2000).

33 See, for an example, Hong and Stein (2007).

34 Shiller (2017, 2019), Herrmann-Pillath and Macedo (2021). For the example of representativeness bias with respect to certain economic news, see Kahneman and Tversky (1973).

35 Keynes (1960 [1936]), chapter 12.

36 Schumpeter (1911).

37 In particular, Hayek (see 2009 [1976]) and the Austrian school, and Minsky (2008 [1986]).

38 Tonveronachi (2020); Kindleberger and Aliber (2011); Hayek (2012 [1931]).

39 Duca and Muellbauer (2013).

40 Geanakoplos (2010).
41 Bernanke et al. (1996, 1999).
42 Baddeley (2010).
43 Minsky (2008 [1986]).
44 Caballero (2010).
45 Acemoglu et al. (2015); Stiglitz (2018).
46 Geanakoplos (2010).
47 Stiglitz (2018).
48 See, for example, Herrmann-Pillath (2018), p. 347.
49 Many of the following points are inspired by Coyle (2015).
50 In the Euro area, the output gap has direct policy significance in terms of supporting the determination of excessive fiscal deficits and, in this context, has recently been subject to intense criticism. See Tooze (2019); Buti et al. (2019).
51 For a critical review of the NAIRU concept, see Galbraith (1997).
52 See Kydland and Prescott (1977); Barro and Gordon (1983) for the theoretical foundation and Bodea and Hicks (2015) for the empirical side.
53 See, for a summary, Snowdon and Vane (2005), chapter 9, and for the example of Japan, Ahearne and Shinada (2005), Caballero et al. (2008).
54 See Cunningham et al. 2010; for recent practice of the Bank of England Tuckett et al. (2020).
55 Ahrens et al. (2017); for a similar empirical example on Germany, Enders et al. (2019).
56 Kydland and Prescott (1977).
57 For historical evidence, see Kindleberger and Aliber (2011).
58 Tognato (2012).
59 Blinder et al. (2005).
60 See, for a summary of empirical studies on Ricardian equivalence, Ricciuti (2003).
61 The classic is Nordhaus (1975). For overviews, see Snowdon and Vane (2005, 517 ff); Dubois (2016). Guo (2009) and Tsai (2016) provide Chinese examples for the presence of political business cycles in authoritarian systems.
62 The notion of expectations as conventions is also used by Keynes (1960 [1936]), chapter 12.
63 This would be in line with Austrian capital theory, as summarised in Snowdon and Vane (2005), chapter 9.
64 Kindleberger and Aliber (2011); Reinhart and Rogoff (2009).

References

Acemoglu, D., Ozdaglar, A. and Tahbaz-Salehi, A. (2015) 'Systemic Risk and Stability in Financial Networks', *American Economic Review*, 105(2), pp. 564–608. DOI: 10.1257/aer.20130456.

Ahearne, A. G. and Shinada, N. (2005) 'Zombie Firms and Economic Stagnation in Japan', *International Economics and Economic Policy*, 2(4), pp. 363–381. DOI: 10.1007/s10368-005-0041-1.

Ahrens, S., Lustenhouwer, J. and Tettamanzi, M. (2017) 'The Stabilizing Role of Forward Guidance: A Macro Experiment', *Beiträge zur Jahrestagung des Vereins für Socialpolitik 2017: Alternative Geld- und Finanzarchitekturen – Session: Monetary Policy I*, No. C06-V1.

Baddeley, M. (2010) 'Herding, Social Influence and Economic Decision-Making: Socio-Psychological and Neuroscientific Analyses', *Philosophical Transactions of the Royal Society B: Biological Sciences*, 365(1538), pp. 281–290. DOI: 10.1098/rstb.2009.0169.

Barro, R. J. and Gordon, D. (1983) 'Rules, Discretion and Reputation in a Model of Monetary Policy', *Journal of Political Economy*, 91, pp. 101–121.

Beckert, J. (2016) *Imagined Futures: Fictional Expectations and Capitalist Dynamics*. Cambridge: Harvard University Press. DOI: 10.4159/978067 4545878.

Bernanke, B., Gertler, M. and Gilchrist, S. (1996) 'The Financial Accelerator and the Flight to Quality', *The Review of Economics and Statistics*, 78(1), pp. 1–15.

Bernanke, B., Gertler, M. and Gilchrist, S. (1999) 'The Financial Accelerator in a Quantitative Business Cycle Framework', in Taylor, J. B. and Woodford, M. (eds.) *Handbook of Macroeconomics, Volume 1, Part C*. Amsterdam: North-Holland. DOI: 10.1016/S1574-0048(99)10034-X.

Blinder, A. and Reis, R. (2005) 'Understanding the Greenspan Standard', *CEPS Working Paper*, 114(September).

Blyth, M. (2002) *Great Transformations: Economic Ideas and Institutional Change in the Twentieth Century*. Cambridge: Cambridge University Press.

Bodea, C. and Hicks, R. (2015) 'Price Stability and Central Bank Independence: Discipline, Credibility, and Democratic Institutions', *International Organization*, 69(1), pp. 35–61. DOI: 10.1017/S0020818314000277.

Boyer, R. (1990) *The Regulation School: A Critical Introduction*. New York: Columbia University Press.

Boyer, R. (2018) 'Marx's Legacy, Regulation Theory and Contemporary Capitalism', *Review of Political Economy*, 30(3), pp. 284–316. DOI: 10.1080/0953 8259.2018.1449480.

Buiter, W. (2009) 'The Unfortunate Uselessness of Most 'State of the Art' Academic Monetary Economics', *VOXEU*, 06 March 2009. Available at: http://voxeu.org/article/macroeconomics-crisis-irrelevance (Accessed: 02 May 2022).

Buti, M. *et al.* (2019) 'Potential Output and EU Fiscal Surveillance', *VOXEU*, 23 September 2019.

Caballero, R. J. (2010) 'Macroeconomics after the Crisis: Time to Deal with the Pretense-of-Knowledge Syndrome', *Journal of Economic Perspectives*, 24(4), pp. 85–102. DOI: 10.1257/jep.24.4.85.

Caballero, R. J., Hoshi, T. and Kashyap, A. K. (2008) 'Zombie Lending and Depressed Restructuring in Japan', *American Economic Review*, 98(5), pp. 1943–1977. DOI: 10.1257/aer.98.5.1943.

Cesarano, F. (2006) *Monetary Theory and Bretton Woods: The Construction of an International Monetary Order*. Cambridge: Cambridge University Press.

Clower, R. W. (1965) 'The Keynesian Counter-Revolution: A Theoretical Appraisal', in Hahn, F. H. and Brechling, F. (eds.) *The Theory of Interest Rates*. London: MacMillan, pp. 103–125.

Coyle, D. (2015) *GDP: A Brief but Affectionate History*. Princeton: Princeton University Press. DOI: 10.1515/9781400873630.

Cunningham, R., Desroches, B. and Santor, E. (2010) 'Inflation Expectations and the Conduct of Monetary Policy: A Review of Recent Evidence and Experience', *Bank of Canada Review*, 2010 (Spring), pp. 13–25.

Curtin, R. T. (2019) *Consumer Expectations: Micro Foundations and Macro Impact*. Cambridge: Cambridge University Press. DOI: 10.1017/9780511791598.

De Grauwe, P. and Ji, Y. (2019) *Behavioral Macroeconomics: Theory and Policy, First Edition*. New York: Oxford University Press.

De Vroey, M. (2016) *A History of Macroeconomics from Keynes to Lucas and Beyond*. Cambridge: Cambridge University Press. DOI: 10.1017/cbo9780511 843617.

Dubois, E. (2016) 'Political Business Cycles 40 Years After Nordhaus', *Public Choice*, 166(1–2), pp. 235–259. DOI: 10.1007/s11127-016-0313-z.

Duca, J. V. and Muellbauer, J. (2013) 'Tobin LIVES: Integrating Evolving Credit Market Architecture into Flow of Funds Based Macro-Models', *ECB Working Paper*, 1581.

Enders, Z., Hünnekes, F. and Müller, G. J. (2019) 'Monetary Policy Announcements and Expectations: Evidence from German Firms', *Journal of Monetary Economics*, 108(C), pp. 45–63. DOI: 10.1016/j.jmoneco.2019.08.011.

Freeman, C. and Louçã, F. (2001) *As Time Goes By: From the Industrial Revolutions to the Information Revolution*. Oxford: Oxford University Press.

Galbraith, J. K. (1997) 'Time to Ditch the NAIRU', *Journal of Economic Perspectives*, 11(1), pp. 93–108. DOI: 10.1257/jep.11.1.93.

Geanakoplos, J. (2010) 'The Leverage Cycle', *Cowles Foundation Paper*, 1304.

Geiger, N: (2014) 'Cycles versus growth in Schumpeter', *Cahiers d'Économie Politique*, 2(2014), pp. 35–54.

Godley, W. and Lavoie, M. (2012) *Monetary Economics: An Integrated Approach to Credit, Money, Income, Production and Wealth*. London: Palgrave Macmillan. DOI: 10.1007/978-1-137-08599-3.

Guo, G. (2009) 'China's Local Political Budget Cycles', *American Journal of Political Science*, 53(3), pp. 621–632. DOI: 10.1111/j.1540-5907.2009. 00390.x.

Hall, P. A. and Soskice, D. (eds.) (2001) *Varieties of Capitalism: The Institutional Foundations of Comparative Advantage*. Oxford: Oxford University Press.

Hayek, F. A. von (1972) *Die Theorie komplexer Phänomene*. Tübingen: Mohr.

Hayek, F. A. von (2009 [1976]) *Denationalisation of Money: The Argument Refined*. Auburn: Ludwig von Mises Institute.

Hayek, F. A. von (2012 [1931]) *Prices and Production and Other Works on Money, the Business Cycle, and the Gold Standard, ed. by J. Salerno*. Auburn: Ludwig von Mises Institute.

Hendry, D. F. and Muellbauer, J. N. J. (2018) 'The Future of Macroeconomics: Macro Theory and Models at the Bank of England', *Oxford Review of Economic Policy*, 34(1–2), pp. 287–328. DOI: 10.1093/OXREP/GRX055.

Herrmann-Pillath, C. (2018) *Grundlegung einer kritischen Theorie der Wirtschaft*. Marburg: Metropolis.

Herrmann-Pillath, C. and Macedo, L. (2021) 'Narratives and Economic Policy: Theoretical Explorations and the Case of Central Bank Communication in Brazil', *Schmollers Jahrbuch/ Journal of Contextual Economics*, forthcoming.

Hommes, C. (2021) 'Behavioral and Experimental Macroeconomics and Policy Analysis: A Complex Systems Approach', *Journal of Economic Literature*, 59(1), pp. 149–219. DOI: 10.1257/jel.20191434.

Hong, H. and Stein, J. C. (2007) 'Disagreement and the Stock Market', *Journal of Economic Perspectives*, 21(2), pp. 109–128. DOI: 10.1257/jep.21.2.109.

Kahneman, D. and Tversky, A. (1973) 'On the Psychology of Prediction', *Psychological Review*, 80(4), pp. 237–251. DOI: 10.1037/h0034747.

Keynes, J. M. (1960 [1936]) *The General Theory of Employment, Interest and Money*. London: Macmillan.

Kindleberger, C. P. and Aliber, R. Z. (2011) *Manias, Panics and Crashes: A History of Financial Crises*. London: Palgrave Macmillan. DOI: 10.1057/9780230628045.

Kirman, A. P. (1992) 'Whom or What Does the Representative Individual Represent?', *Journal of Economic Perspectives*, 6(2), pp. 117–136.

Kydland, F. E. and Prescott, E. C. (1977) 'Rules Rather Than Discretion: The Inconsistency for Optimal Plans', *Journal of Political Economy*, 85(3), pp. 473–491.

Leijonhufvud, A. (1967) 'Keynes and the Keynesians: A Suggested Interpretation', *American Economic Review*, 57(2), pp. 401–410.

Leijonhufvud, A. (2011) 'Nature of an Economy', *CEPR Policy Insights*, 53.

Minsky, H. P. (2008 [1986]) *Stabilizing an Unstable Economy*. New York: McGraw-Hill.

Muth, J. F. (1961) 'Rational Expectations and the Theory of Price Movements', *Econometrica*, 29(3), pp. 315–335.

Nordhaus, W. D. (1975) 'The Political Business Cycle', *Review of Economic Studies*, 42(2), pp. 169–190. DOI: 10.2307/2296528.

Peneder, M. and Resch, A. (2021) *Schumpeter's Venture Money*. Oxford: Oxford University Press. DOI: 10.1093/oso/9780198804383.001.0001.

Perez, C. (2003) *Technological Revolutions and Financial Capital*. Cheltenham and Northampton: Edward Elgar Publishing.

Potts, J. (2000) *The New Evolutionary Microeconomics: Complexity, Competence and Adaptive Behavior*. Cheltenham and Northampton: Edward Elgar Publishing.

Rajan, R. G. (2011) *Fault Lines*. Princeton: Princeton University Press.

Reinhart, C. and Rogoff, K. S. (2009) *This Time is Different – Eight Centuries of Financial Folly*. Princeton and Oxford: Princeton University Press.

Ricciuti, R. (2003) 'Assessing Ricardian Equivalence', *Journal of Economic Surveys*, 17(1), pp. 55–78. DOI: 10.1111/1467-6419.00188.

Romer, P. (2016) 'The Trouble with Macroeconomics', *Paul Romer*, 14 September 2016. Available at: https://paulromer.net/the-trouble-with-macro/WP-Trouble.pdf

Roos, M. W. (2015) 'The Macroeconomics of Radical Uncertainty', *Ruhr Economic Papers*, 592. DOI: 10.2139/ssrn.2721683.

Schumpeter, J. A. (1939) *Business Cycles, 2 Volumes*. New York: McGraw-Hill.

Schumpeter, J. A. (2006 [1911]) *Theorie der wirtschaftlichen Entwicklung*. Berlin: Duncker & Humblot.

Shiller, R. J. (2017) 'Narrative Economics', *American Economic Review*, 107(4), pp. 967–1004. DOI: 10.1257/aer.107.4.967.

Shiller, R. J. (2019) *Narrative Economics: How Stories Go Viral and Drive Major Economic Events*. Princeton: Princeton University Press.

Smets, F. and Wouters, R. (2007) 'Shocks and Frictions in US Business Cycles: A Bayesian DSGE Approach', *American Economic Review*, 97(3), pp. 586–606. DOI: 10.1257/aer.97.3.586.

Snowdon, B. and Vane, H. R. (2005) *Modern Macroeconomics: Its Origins, Development and Current State*. Cheltenham and Northampton: Edward Elgar Publishing.

Snowdon, B., Vane, H. R. and Wynarczyk, P. (1994) *A Modern Guide to Macroeconomics*. Cheltenham and Northampton: Edward Elgar Publishing.

Stiglitz, J. E. (2018) 'Where Modern Macroeconomics Went Wrong', *Oxford Review of Economic Policy*, 34(1–2), pp. 70–106. DOI: 10.1093/oxrep/grx057.

Stützel, W. (1978 [1958]) *Volkswirtschaftliche Saldenmechanik: Ein Beitrag zur Geldtheorie*. Tübingen: Mohr Siebeck.

Tognato, C. (2012) *Central Bank Independence: Cultural Codes and Symbolic Performance*. New York: Palgrave Macmillan. DOI: 10.1057/9781137268839.

Tonveronachi, M. (2020) 'Ages of Financial Instability', *Journal of Post Keynesian Economics*, 43(2), pp. 169–209. DOI: 10.1080/01603477.2020.1734469.

Tooze, A (2019) 'Output Gap Nonsense', *Social Europe*, 30 April 2019. Available at: https://socialeurope.eu/output-gap-nonsense (Accessed: 02 May 2022).

Tsai, P. H. (2016) 'Fiscal Incentives and Political Budget Cycles in China', *International Tax and Public Finance*, 23(6), pp. 1030–1073. DOI: 10.1007/s10797-016-9392-5.

Tuckett, D. *et al.* (2020) 'Monetary Policy and the Management of Uncertainty: A Narrative Approach', *Bank of England Staff Working Paper*, 870.

Unruh, G. C. (2000) 'Understanding Carbon Lock-in', *Energy Policy*, 28(12), pp. 817–830. DOI: 10.1016/S0301-4215(00)00070-7.

CHAPTER FOURTEEN

The economics of global markets

1. Introduction

This chapter presents an introduction into what is commonly approached as 'international economics'. This term reflects the special conditions of the late 19th and the 20th century when governments of nation states emerged as central actors in national economies and adopted a powerful role in shaping the institutions of economic relations between those nation states. However, many important features of current economic developments clearly transcend the international framing, among them, the global reach of the technosphere and the global dimension of climate change together with other environmental issues. Matching with this, the term 'globalisation' mainly refers to the global reach of markets. In this sense, globalisation seems to put national governments on par with other economic actors, especially the multinational firm; the term 'global economics' is apt to catch this new reality.[1]

Nations remain important units in the global economy, but other units are on par, such as the multinational firm.

However, confining global economics only to the present overlooks the historical depth of the global economy.[2] The 19th century was the age of Empire; the Pax Britannica shaped a truly global economy, given the deep impact of global economic activities on local and regional societies and ecosystems (often dubbed the first globalisation[3]). In the first millennium, when most of Europe fell back behind the level of development achieved by the Roman Empire, the Muslim world had created a vast network of trading centres that spanned Europe, Africa, India, and China. We suggest that economic theory must cover all these phenomena in one framework, which is the economics of global markets, the title of our chapter.

Globalisation reaches far back into the past, such as the Muslim world in the first millennium.

The chapter proceeds as follows. In section 2, we develop the theory of global economic transactions. This requires three steps: first, an analytical deconstruction of transactions into their components; second, an analysis of the notion of border in a complex hierarchy of spatial scales; third, a detailed look at the activity of pricing in an international context. Section 3 explores how political borders influence global transactions, both regarding trade and monetary arrangements, and introduces the theory of market access rights. Section 4 analyses the structural evolution of locational comparative advantages, both as reflected in the position of locations in the spatial division of labour and in terms of aggregate effects relating to the balance of payments.

361

DOI: 10.4324/9781003094869-19

2. Transactions and the spatial structure of global markets

2.1. Deconstructing global transactions

A central feature of global economics is a detailed analysis of market transactions, implying their deconstruction into separate aspects (Figure 14.1):

- The first is that every transaction involves a payment. This raises the issue which currency is used in the transaction, affecting pricing and price expectations as related to the exchange rate, which is determined on markets for currencies, the foreign exchange markets.

We deconstruct transactions into the three aspects of payment, real and institutional objects, and transaction-enabling transactions.

- The second important distinction is between real and institutional objects of transactions. We interpret the term 'real object' in a broad way as being defined by the intentions of the agents of the transaction. It covers both of what is conventionally distinguished as goods versus services. Institutional objects are rights transferred with the transaction, in general, property rights, and assets, which embody monetary value and are rights to future yield.

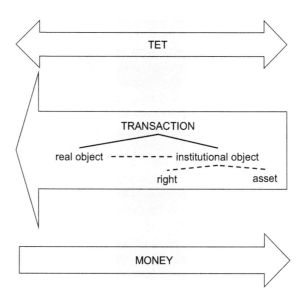

Figure 14.1 Deconstructing global transactions
We deconstruct global transactions into three aspects. The first is the flow of payments. The second is the flow of real and institutional objects, which can be tightly coupled or decoupled (for example, trading coffee at a coffee exchange involves the institutional object, whereas the coffee as real object is transacted elsewhere). We distinguish property rights (the right to own a quantity of coffee) and assets held for yield (the right to coffee becomes an asset on futures markets for coffee). The third aspect is the complementary transactions that make the transaction possible (such as trade finance in coffee trade), TET.

The distinction has increasingly gained in importance since a growing share of international trade today is value-added trade (Figure 14.2) that includes a significant share of trade in goods which embody services that are differentiated as institutional object, often via the intellectual property rights that protect this specific input in the production of the good.[4] This is a key feature of offshoring and global value chains: A company exports parts to a second country where these are assembled and exported to a third country; the second country only adds local value to the product, such as the wages of assembly line workers. The company may even arrange the production of these parts in other countries in a way that there would be no production taking place at all in the country of origin. As a result, the conventional current account and trade statistics are highly misleading insofar as they only cover the flow of physical objects across borders and not the embodied institutional objects, such as the embodied services protected by intellectual property rights in all shapes.

The third aspect in deconstructing global economic transactions is the transaction-enabling transaction (TET). For decades, conventional trade theory has ignored the real activity of trading, including transport costs but

For a related distinction in the context of social networks, see Chapter 8, section 2.2.

The distinction between real and institutional object is salient in value-added trade; in value-added trade, the flow of objects is decoupled from the payments flow.

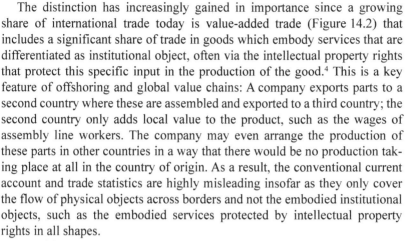

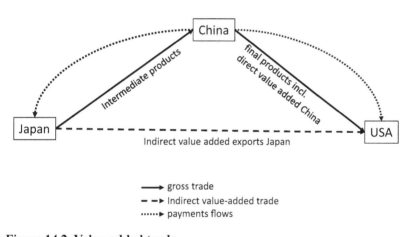

Figure 14.2 Value-added trade
Conventional current account statistics only cover the flow of real objects and the related payments (gross trade). However, if a country is mostly at an intermediate production stage, this hides the flow of embodied institutional objects which are essential for allocating the value added. The balance of payments remains binding, though misleading if only focusing on bilateral relations. In the trilateral relation between Japan, China, and the US, Japan exports intermediate products to China which are further processed and exported to the US. The processing value added can be much smaller than the former. Hence, factually, Japan exports to the US indirectly, but there is no matching bilateral payment flow so that there is a huge gap between the China–US gross trade and the underlying direct and indirect value-added exports.

also all other activities that make transactions possible.[5] This distorts basic facts about globalisation, in which the unfolding of commerce was the key driver since the earliest stages.[6] For example, the technological and organisational innovation of the container was an important driver of world trade growth after WWII.[7] Another important domain is trade finance, which was a motor of financial evolution since the Middle Ages. In a nutshell, TETs encompass all activities of trading and transactions that make trading possible.

In the case of value-added trade, the differentiation of institutional objects enables the creation of specific TETs. For example, the multinational firm creates a web of agreements between various producers in the value chain which sustains the flow of transactions and, thus, operates as a generator of TETs, such as mechanisms that reduce quality uncertainty about the product.[8] For instance, if I want to buy bananas from a country far away from my location, there are daunting difficulties in directly transacting with farmers, and a multinational firm can assume all tasks of quality control and assume legal responsibilities in the importing country, thus cutting the direct link between producer and buyer.

2.2. Spatial structure, borders, and costs of global economic transactions

Our evolutionary approach to global economics entails a multilevel model of spatial organisation, as laid out in Figure 14.3. At the core is a configuration which corresponds to a country in conventional theory; here, region, jurisdiction, and currency area are conceived as one unit. Region$_A$ is an intranational region sharing the same institutional and legal framework, including the currency, with other intranational regions. Yet region$_A$ plays a distinct role in interregional economic interactions, both within and beyond the jurisdiction, because of agglomeration effects and other externalities generated within a constricted spatial reach (see section 4).[9]

Jurisdictions define borders of markets, thus distinguishing the domestic from the international market even for the same kind of product and market niches. Borders of jurisdictions not only relate to border-related measures as such, as in case of a tariff, but to all institutional differences to other jurisdictions which increase the economic transaction cost (see later section).

We distinguish between two levels of jurisdictions, *A* and *B*, which relate to three different types of regions. Jurisdiction$_A$ can be a unitary state or a federation where the members (provinces, states, etc.) have partial autonomy in setting institutions but the federal government retains distinct central authority in important areas, such as issuing the currency or entering agreements on international trade (such as the United States or India). Jurisdiction$_B$ refers to

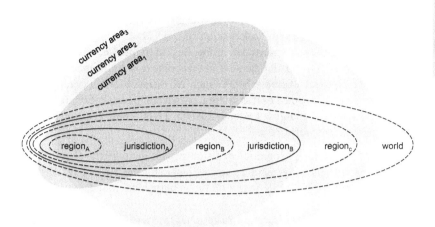

Figure 14.3 The spatial hierarchy of the global economy
We deconstruct the conventional unit of country into region, jurisdiction, and currency area, which simplifies the variety of political organisation on the globe. All three define distinct forms of borders that transactions must overcome. The spatial setting arranges for multilevel evolution, such as regions within jurisdictions becoming main export sites or larger regions clustering several jurisdictions into closer integrated economies. Regional agreements can include the establishment or enlargement of a currency area beyond national borders. In real cases, some elements of the diagram may not apply. For further detail, see main text.

institutional constructs where one jurisdiction is member of another jurisdiction, such as in the case of a trade agreement that includes various countries and establishes a certain degree of centralisation in setting institutions that impact on global economic relations; the most significant example is the European Union. Region$_B$ is a cross-border region within the higher-level jurisdiction. Region$_C$ is primarily defined by a relative closeness and clustering of economic interactions rather than by political criteria. For example, the Middle East would not count as a region$_C$ whereas that would be the case for parts of East Asia and South-East Asia; this is because the level of intra-regional trade is currently much lower in the former than the latter.[10] Often, political initiatives aim at institutionalising such regions (such as APEC), though falling short of establishing a jurisdiction$_B$. Currency areas are structures sui generis because they can be partly decoupled from other institutional determinants of transactions. In the example of the EU, the currency area is strongly integrated, but member country–level institutions can still differ in substantial respects. Beyond that, there are weaker forms of currency areas which are determined by both monetary practices and political decisions about national monetary policy (such as in the case of dollarisation[11]).

These institutional structures determine the cost of transactions across geographical space.[12] The spatial element in this context is not primarily defined in terms of physical characteristics (such as distance or topography) but defined in terms of the cost of transacting, which are, by definition, relative to agents' capacities of enabling trade, that is, the TETs. These costs include the following main categories:

The costs of global transactions cover a range of categories reaching from transportation to transaction cost in the narrow sense. All of them are relative to agents' capacities to produce TETs.

- Cost of overcoming geographical distance: This includes the classical cost of transport and movement in space, including the cost of rendering a good or service tradeable (e.g., via the geographical movement of a service provider).
- Cost of overcoming formal-institutional barriers of jurisdictions that directly relate to the movement of goods and factors: Those include classical instruments of trade policy, such as tariffs, quotas, and export restraints, but also include the opportunity cost of time and effort spent, such as for customs clearance or the acquisition of information on customs rules and investment screening procedures.[13]

For a general discussion of economic transaction cost, see Chapter 9, section 4.2.

- Cost of overcoming general institutional differences between jurisdictions: This refers to the wide notion of non-tariff barriers and domestic obstacles to exports, foreign direct investment and labour migration, both of a directly and indirectly discriminating nature.[14]
- Cost of understanding, and adapting to, informal institutions and social networks across borders: This category includes, for example, the cost of language acquisition, of adapting to different cultural circumstances, and of building up trust and status in foreign networks.
- Cost of trading in different currencies: This includes the transaction cost in the narrow sense of exchange between currencies as well as the cost of exchange rate risk, in particular, hedging against fluctuations.

For one transaction, trade costs differ for the three constituent aspects and are especially important for the complementary TET, mostly in the form of trade-enabling services transactions.

Notably, these cost categories can differ for real and institutional objects as well as for TETs. TETs are particularly important for services trade and can involve a wide set of domestic regulations and corresponding arrangements.[15] In the case of value-added trade, the institutional object of intellectual property that relates to embodied services may be an object of TETs in various senses.[16]

A corollary of this differentiation is that one cannot explain the patterns of international trade and the distribution of gains from trade by only considering relative production cost as determined by resource endowments and ignoring the capacities to produce TETs. The distribution of capacities for TETs also implies that shared properties of locations tied by transactions influence trade flows in an idiosyncratic way (such as the presence of diaspora communities).[17]

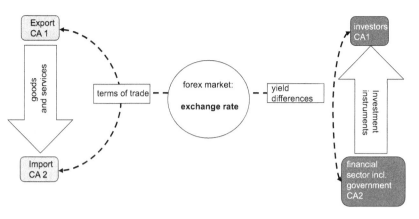

Figure 14.4 The exchange rate and global transactions
The exchange rate between two currency areas (CA) plays a central role in coordinating global transactions both of goods and services and of assets, and it is influenced by trade in both categories. In principle, given a set of market access conditions, flows are determined by differences in prices and yields for like objects. Asset flows move faster than flows of goods and services and, hence, have a more direct impact on the exchange rate (see main text for more detail). The exchange rate also co-determines the ToT. These connections result in asset flows (capital account) financing imbalances in the current account, without being necessarily tied to current account transactions directly.

2.3. The exchange rate and arbitrage

A distinct issue in transactions that cross the borders of currency areas is the exchange rate as related to pricing. An exporter that fixes a price for its product must consider the domestic price in the target market: The exchange rate determines the value of payments in terms of the domestic currency, which is what matters for the exporter's budget constraint. Similarly, importers consider foreign prices as co-determined by the exchange rate for potential comparison with domestic prices. In practice, this exchange rate pass-through leaves much leeway for pricing decisions as co-determined by standard considerations.[18]

At the same time, the exchange rate is a genuinely macroeconomic phenomenon insofar as it affects all prices in global transactions simultaneously, instantaneously, and across all trade partners (Figure 14.4). This is covered by a distinct statistical construct, the terms of trade (ToT). The ToT compare the level of export prices with the level of import prices, calculated in one currency, and therefore, reflect the quantity of imports that can be financed by a quantity of exports. For example, if a currency depreciates, and foreign exporters do not change prices in their domestic currency, importers will face price increases, which will eventually trigger adaptive responses. ToT effects depend on many contextual factors, with

The exchange rate directly impacts on pricing with substantial degrees of freedom (exchange rate pass-through); but it is also a macroeconomic phenomenon, as epitomised by the terms of trade (ToT).

For a general discussion of pricing decisions, see Chapter 11.

a specifically strong impact of relative country size, roughly approximated by GDP, and the corresponding significance of the respective locus of global transactions. ToT effects imply that transactions across currency areas can cause negative externalities on third parties. The reason is that, say, once a bilateral intervention, such as a targeted tariff, generates exchange rate effects, these effects automatically affect transactions with all other traders.[19]

The exchange rate is determined on the market for foreign exchange, where expectations about future rates are key factors.

Analysis of the determinants of the exchange rate belongs to the most challenging tasks of economics. We present a basic framework for currency markets in Figure 14.4. In those markets, expectations play a key role since traders who hold foreign currencies will consider future exchange rates and generate profits from arbitrage both in the present and over different periods.[20] This creates a problem of indeterminacy of the current exchange rate, which is formally equivalent to the problem of valuing capital and financial assets, since expectations are heterogenous and, as is discussed later, cannot be anchored in an objectified second-person view.

An important theory is Purchasing Power Parity which grounds in the law of one price and the related arbitrage mechanisms but refers to their aggregate effects on the relation between domestic and foreign price levels.

Exchange rate uncertainty can be a determinant of trade costs once we consider that export capacities will often be specific to a target location and, hence, may be devalued if the exchange rate changes unexpectedly.[21] One simple measure to reduce this uncertainty is the introduction of a fixed exchange rate by the sovereign producer (or producers, if a bilateral agreement is established) of the currency (currencies). This implies that the sovereign must act as lender of last resort for the foreign currency concerned, namely by building up international reserves. Thus, a new type of budget constraint is created, given that aggregate demand for foreign currency can lead to a depletion of reserves. As long as a market for foreign exchange exists, market agents will form expectations about the sustainability of the reserve position, which can lead to frequency-dependent effects, such as herding and contagion, and eventually, the occurrence of currency crises.

Exchange rate uncertainty cannot be completely reduced, even in a fixed exchange rate regime.

Purchasing Power Parity (PPP) cannot anchor expectations in the short and medium term.

Independently from whether the exchange rate is fixed or flexible, a crucial question is on what determines expectations over the future exchange rate. One approach is Purchasing Power Parity (PPP), a simple argument based on the law of one price. The idea is that international price differences, measured as some aggregate index, level out in the longer run via arbitrage transactions.[22] These transactions have effects on both micro and macro level: If prices deviate from the law of one price, there will be an imbalance between supply and demand for the respective products that not only triggers further price adjustments but also aggregate effects on the foreign exchange (forex) market, where imbalances across many product markets are reflected in aggregate demand and supply of the currencies that are needed for conducting the transactions. However, the scope of PPP is limited by the fact that arbitrage is a costly and potentially risky process. In particular, prices of non-tradable goods will converge only to the extent that effective arbitrage of inputs takes place, but this arbitrage may be hampered by trade cost as well as locational externalities.[23] Despite a general tendency of decreasing technological and institutional barriers to trade, then, cross-border arbitrage in goods and services is not likely to be deep enough to generate substantial price equalisation on the disaggregate level.

This leads to the second arbitrage-based model which concentrates on the capital account (i.e., relies on financial flows) and is often subsumed under the rubric of interest rate parities. Assuming free cross-border flows of financial capital, the idea is that the exchange rate corresponds to an equilibrium in which yields equalise for the same type of assets, both referred to expected values. One simple way to characterise sameness of financial assets is to consider the associated risk of the expected yield. Both expectations of the future yield and the future exchange rate must be arranged in decisions of buying and selling assets globally.[24] To this, the differences between markets for present and future transactions of foreign exchange must be added. In practice, there will be simultaneous adjustment of interest rates, exchange rates (if a flexible regime prevails), and expectations, all of which are strongly influenced by central bank policies.[25]

Overall, compared to PPP, the attractiveness of this approach comes from the fact that arbitrage is mostly low-cost and not hampered by the comparability and externality issues outlined earlier. However, its predictive power depends on the anchoring of exchange rate expectations in economic fundamentals. This entails a problem of reflexivity: Market actors would have to believe in the model itself as well as in the similarity of other actors' beliefs, which affects the financial arbitrage model and, eventually, the PPP model as well. Accordingly, exchange rate movements appear to be driven by similar expectational factors, as outlined in Chapters 12 and 13.

Since global financial flows react faster than arbitrage in goods, the exchange rate is determined by the responses to yield differences and the exchange rate expectations which level these differences.

For an analysis of reflexivity in financial markets, see Chapter 12, section 3.3.

3. Market access rights and institutions governing global transactions

The fact that established international economics mostly takes nations as units comes with a reason: National governments define the borders of jurisdictions. Although markets extend across borders, access to domestic markets is often controlled and restricted by different categories of formal-institutional trade barriers (see previous section). To understand the interplay of those restrictions with actual trade, we distinguish two levels of competition, namely the respective markets proper and the competing jurisdictions which control market access.

The latter level is the domain of international economic policy. Accordingly, we distinguish different levels of the institutional structure of the global economy (Figure 14.5).[26] There is a constitutional level, such as certain normative principles of economic liberalisation, which, however, is mostly implicit. The next level is constituted by institutions governing market access rights (MARs),[27] as enshrined in international agreements, such as the WTO/GATT and regional trade agreements. These establish the third level, namely institutions of global markets themselves, which include institutions that emerge endogenously, such as the lex mercatoria, the customary law of international traders.

All these institutions differ in two dimensions, formal versus informal and forced versus consensual. For example, many institutions of colonial imperialism

This analysis is based on our general framework of institutions as deployed in Chapter 9, section 4. The notion of competing jurisdictions is taken up again in Chapters 15 and 17.

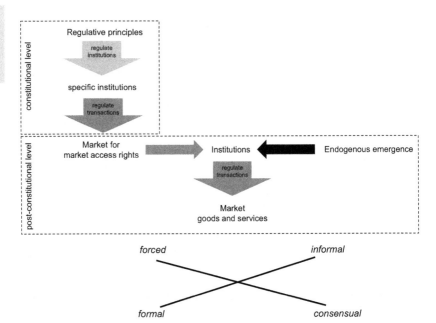

Figure 14.5 Two-level institutional structure of global economy
The institutions governing global markets are determined on two levels of
exchange: a) the political exchange of MARs between governments; and b)
market exchange, where MARs interact with endogenously evolving institutions
such as the *lex mercatoria*. Institutions can be both formal and informal, and
they reflect varying degrees of power asymmetries across countries, including
the forced imposition of institutions such as in colonialism. Institutions
governing the exchange of MARs are shaped on the constitutional level.

The institutional were coercive, whereas the WTO today operates on principles of unanimous con-
structure of the sent. US hegemony after WWII was partly informal.
global economy is   Another reason why nations stay at the centre of standard theory is that they
two level, the market often coincide with currency areas. This results in another manifestation of the
level and the level of national border in national accounts, namely the balance of payments that cov-
governments which ers cross-border flows of goods, services (current account), and financial assets,
exchange rights including monetary flows (capital account). MARs shape these flows and,
to market access, therefore, are often used as instruments to influence the balance of payments.
MARs. The BoP is an aggregate budget constraint and captures the aggregate effects of
transaction flows on the international financial position of a country.

3.1. MARs and two-level exchange

MARs encompass institutions and policies that directly regulate the cost and
conditions under which cross-border movements of goods, services, and

production factors are possible and induce specific trade costs. MARs imply that the global economy must minimally be approached as a two-level system: On one level, economic agents interact; on the other, governments establish or change MARs. The dynamics of the latter establishes the scene for international trade policy, including the WTO which aims at a coordination of national measures relating to MARs. This results in a distinct form of the general specialisation dilemma in the global division of labour.

Consider an exporter specialising into a certain market (e.g., in terms of adapting to standards or customising its products to specific buyers' needs).[28] From the point of view of the exporter, the cross-border character of the respective transaction entails a significant additional risk in terms of possible changes in the institutional framework that grants market access in the first place. Under normal circumstances, such risk will be more difficult to control for the exporter than institutional change on its home market, be it due to information asymmetries or to specific political incentives for destination countries.

Hence, the ex post power asymmetries between trading partners as a consequence of increased exporters' capability specificity result in the ex ante potential that certain specialisation engagements are avoided in the first place.[29] At the same time, since decisions on MARs are essentially in the domain of sovereign states, their structure will primarily follow a political rather than economic logic, such as domestic political competition or concerns about national security.[30] There are two main issues arising from this tension. First, how can a structure of MARs be established and upheld that enables international trade and investment flows, given the interests of governments?[31] And second, how are those interests formed themselves, that is, how does the political process within states address the tension between political and economic logic? The remainder of this section will focus on the first question.

As outlined, the specialisation dilemma on a global scale implies that full potentials of specialisation are likely to be exploited only if the recipient (or host, in case of FDI) country provides, and credibly commits to upholding, a respective MAR. However, the very definition of 'sovereignty' implies that governments can arbitrarily change the MARs regime, which leverages uncertainty in global transactions (Figure 14.6).

There are essentially three ways of how a commitment can be achieved. The first is a reciprocal exchange of MARs (Figure 14.6). In this case, MARs can be considered as representing economic value, such as export volumes, which renders them comparable in quantitative terms (corresponding to standard practice in international trade negotiations).[32] This creates the possibility to retaliate in case the recipient country decides to revoke the MAR, hence following a logic of mutual hostage taking that would render the recipient country's commitment credible.[33] Reciprocal exchange of MARs has been institutionalised in the various GATT rounds of reciprocal liberalisation.

For the specialisation dilemma, see Chapter 5, section 2.2.

Uncertainty of MARs creates additional risk for exporters.

On the role of interjurisdictional competition, see Chapter 17, section 2.5.

The formation of interests in the policy process is discussed in Chapter 17.

Uncertainty of MARs leverages the specialisation dilemma for global market transactions.

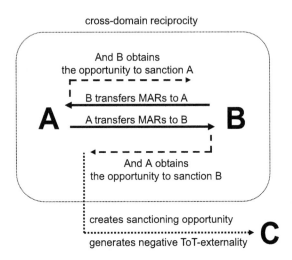

Figure 14.6 Exchange of MARs
International trade policy can be analysed as reciprocal exchange of MARs:
Transferring a MAR to a trade partner is uncertain unless violations can be
sanctioned. This is enabled by offering a MAR in return, thus creating a scene
of possible mutual sanctions. This depends on the relative value of the MARs.
Bilateral exchange can create ToT externalities on third parties, which explains
international rules, such as the most-favoured nation (MFN) principle.

*Reciprocal exchange
of MARs can
resolve the global
specialisation
dilemma and has
been practiced in
GATT rounds. It is
strongly influenced
by asymmetries of
export specificity
and relative
country size.*

Importantly, the commitment effect of MARs will vary with asymmetries
between the trading partners.[34] For example, if the degree of specificity of
mutual exports and FDI differs, the recipient of exports/FDI with higher specificity will have a relatively larger sanctioning power. More generally, if the
source country is small relative to the recipient country, its sanctioning possibilities are more limited. As a consequence, therefore, an international
exchange of MARs on a purely bilateral and reciprocal basis would presumably lead to significant differences between international market actors:
Smaller countries would face the double disadvantage of higher political risk
of specialisation and higher dependency on international trade and investment
in economic terms, given their limited market size. This is a main argument
for establishing a multilateral trade regime.

Accordingly, the second possibility to ensure country commitment with
regard to MARs is the establishment of some kind of international legal
regime.[35] This option faces the well-known problem of enforceability typical
for all international law, implying that reciprocity, based on national sovereignty, necessarily remains a regulative principle for MARs in a multilateral
context as well.[36] Based on this, ways to address enforceability in the field of
international economic relations are diverse and contingent on historical

developments. Dispute settlement in the trade field is still dominated by the WTO as a comprehensive multilateral structure, which foresees a two-level dispute settlement system explicitly authorising retaliation.[37] In the investment field, the prevailing bilateral structure is largely backed up by a system of ad hoc arbitration and the ultimate possibility to enforce damages payments from states by seizing their property on foreign territory.

The third possibility to ensure country commitment is the embedding of agreements on MARs into broader framework obligations.[38] For example, there is often a clear connection between the negotiation of trade and investment agreements and geostrategic considerations, such as in case of the recently established Regional Comprehensive Economic Partnership (RCEP) involving China, Australia, and the majority of South-East Asian states.[39] The embeddedness of MARs is akin to hegemonic theories of the international trade and investment system which essentially posit that the upholding of a free-trade regime would only work under the auspices of a dominant power that essentially enforces the granting of MARs by other countries, such as the British Empire in the 19th century.[40]

Given that the international system of MARs emerges from political decisions, MARs, if not negotiated and applied universally, generate power-based externalities of their own, most simply by excluding countries from export and investment opportunities that are deemed valuable for their market actors but also via terms of trade effects.[41] The principal way to address those externalities is to overcome the collective action problem of smaller countries, which can be achieved by the establishment of a multilateral negotiation forum. Indeed, the WTO and its predecessor, the GATT, have institutionalised the most-favoured nation (MFN) principle as key instrument to internalise terms of trade effects stemming from bilateral and plurilateral agreements and ultimately to support a multilateral expansion of MARs.[42] MFN extends bilateral trade concessions automatically to all members; however, this also creates a free-riding effect with respect to third countries and hampers countries' leeway for differential treatment of others. That is why, in practice, MFN is often superseded by conditions to establish regional trade agreements.[43]

3.2. MARs and currency areas

There are two essential monetary policy instruments that are specific to the international realm, namely the regulation of flows of financial capital, commonly in the form of capital controls, and the management of the exchange rate, commonly in the form an exchange rate regime. The degree of asset mobility roughly corresponds to MARs in the financial realm, focusing on portfolio investment; the exchange rate regime characterises the scope of policy intervention with respect to both the relative prices of goods and services, similar to, for example, a tariff, and the formation of the exchange rate as an asset price (with currencies seen as assets). Also, the degree of national

Absent a world government, multilateral rules also build on reciprocity as far as enforcement is concerned.

Exchange of MARs is often embedded in larger political and cultural frames, such as thematised in the theory of hegemony.

Externalities generated by MARs can be internalised by the most-favoured nation principle, which, however, is increasingly superseded by regional trade agreements.

Borders between currency areas can be conceptualised in terms of MARs.

On monetary
policy, see
Chapter 13,
section 6.2.

autonomy of monetary policy can be seen as the macroeconomic counterpart to the degree of autonomy of sovereign decision making with respect to issues affecting locational competitiveness.

The standard analytical framework for restrictions to national sovereignty in the international monetary context is Mundell's trilemma.[44] The trilemma essentially states that out of the three desiderata of cross-border mobility of financial capital, fixed exchange rate, and autonomy of national monetary policy, only two can be sustainably chosen simultaneously, while the respective third must be eschewed. Insofar as the liberalisation of financial capital flows and a fixed exchange rate support trade in goods and services (by ensuring the financing of current account deficits and decreasing trade costs, respectively), trade openness from a sovereign perspective would relate to a (further) sacrifice in terms of losing monetary policy autonomy. This, in turn, may partly explain the absence of a global multilateral framework comparable to the WTO for flows of financial capital and the determination of the exchange rate regime. In addition, the strategic aspects of granting MARs for financial capital turn out to be quite different from MARs for goods/services and FDI. This is because financial investors, compared to specialised exporters and providers of FDI, will be able to withdraw their investment more quickly and incur lower cost if the host state reneges on its commitment.

Mundell's trilemma is highly contingent on concrete circumstances, necessitating a more concrete specification of its mechanisms from case to case. Notably, the three choices of the trilemma rarely exist in a pure form, allowing for a plethora of policy choices on a more or less continuous scale.[45] This certainly applies to different degrees of financial liberalisation but notably to the exchange rate regimes as well, where the observation of a considerable variety of floating schemes is further complicated by the frequent divergence of formal (de jure) and informal (de facto) regimes.[46]

Analogous to the trade case, a differential granting of MARs for financial investors of different countries would generate negative externalities on market actors of other countries by restricting their options of financial investment in terms of yield, risk diversification, and so on.[47] The main issue is the influence of monetary policy on the exchange rate, which can take various forms reaching from deliberate manipulation to mere side effect (in case of a flexible exchange rate regime). The most important example of a negative externality is competitive devaluation, which in the simplest case denotes a policy coordination problem in a framework of zero-sum competition.[48] Positive externalities, however, may be generated via spillover effects of stable currencies to other currency areas. In particular, a currency peg may allow to import the monetary policy of the partner country to whose currency the exchange rate is tied. Such a regime is essentially a substitute for central bank independence and frequently used if such independence cannot be established domestically, as in the case of certain developing economies.[49]

Mundell's trilemma in global economics refers to the impossibility to realise simultaneously the institutions of fixed exchange rate, free capital flows, and autonomy of monetary policy.

Monetary policies can create significant externalities, both negative (as in currency wars) and positive (stability import).

As in the case of market access rights in trade and FDI, the chief way of internalising exchange rate–induced externalities is the establishment of a multilateral negotiation forum, eventually leading to binding commitments of its members, which in its most extreme version would entail the establishment of a world currency. Arguably, however, the longer-term institutional development (particularly in the 20th century) has pointed more in the opposite direction: Since the demise of the gold standard and the Bretton Woods system in the 1970s, the worldwide default regime with respect to exchange rates is in fact flexible and used by all major currencies except the Chinese yuan.

This is an important feature of the contemporary monetary system based on fiat money, compare Chapter 12, section 2.

4. The evolution of the global division of labour

A focal phenomenon in the global economy is the combined unfolding of global transactions and endogenous development of locations of economic activity. This is a complex process with many feedbacks and self-reinforcing mechanisms because, among other factors, both the technologies of transacting and the technologies of production can manifest increasing returns and various forms of positive externalities.[50] This renders the global division of labour fundamentally contingent and its development path dependent.

4.1. Evolving comparative advantage, capacities to trade, and locational externalities

As is well known, basic textbook explanations of international trade are based on the concepts of comparative advantage and specialisation (Figure 14.7).[51] In the standard models, comparative advantage is essentially taken as given, resulting from differential factor endowments (Heckscher-Ohlin models) or productivity differences (Ricardo). Differences in the opportunity cost of resource use then give rise to price differences, whose levelling out by arbitrage results in the effective exploitation of gains from trade via frictionless exchange. This argument can be generalised to the organisation of the production process as well as to factor movements.

Established theories start out from given comparative advantage resulting from diverse resource endowments and productivity differentials, whereas the evolutionary approach highlights the discovery and creation of comparative advantage.

Applying the market process perspective outlined in Chapter 11 to the case of international trade under the conditions outlined earlier yields a different picture.[52] Starting from a hypothetical initial no-trade situation, a commensurable set of prices that accurately reflects opportunity cost cannot just be assumed, and there is fundamental ex ante uncertainty about trade costs. Trade costs by necessity enter the profit maximisation calculus based on which an entrepreneur decides on any cross-border transaction such that a strict analytical separation of production cost and trade cost is impossible. As a consequence, comparative advantage itself is not a given but can only be revealed by concrete (entrepreneurially driven) market transactions. This point is

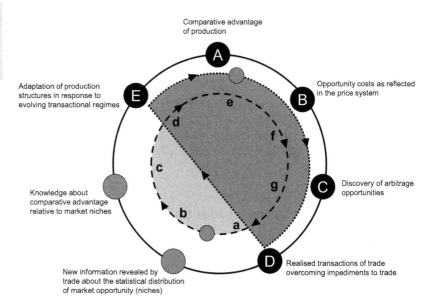

Comparative advantage
of production

Adaptation of production
structures in response to
evolving transactional regimes

Opportunity costs as reflected
in the price system

Knowledge about
comparative advantage
relative to market niches

Discovery of arbitrage
opportunities

New information revealed by
trade about the statistical distribution
of market opportunity (niches)

Realised transactions of trade
overcoming impediments to trade

Figure 14.7 Endogenously evolving comparative advantage
The standard approach is depicted as A–E, including impediments to
trade. Exogenously given comparative advantage has causal priority. The
evolutionary approach is depicted in a–g and starts out from realising trade
under uncertainty. Trade reveals information about comparative advantage
which shifts endogenously depending on the trade transactions (and foreign
investment).

reinforced when we consider an evolving economy with novelty: Technological change and other forms of innovation continuously change the conditions
of defining comparative advantage and require renewed entrepreneurial effort
to discover advantages to be reaped from exploiting the global division of
labour.

*The intensity and
direction of global
transactions is
strongly influenced
by various network
dimensions, such
as shared history,
language, culture,
or diaspora
communities.*

A more specific account of the entrepreneurial discovery process involves
the full range of the market-as-networks perspective developed in the previous chapters, emphasising that transactions are embedded in a broader framework of informational flows and observations.[53] A general conjecture is that
the degree of cross-border network integrality is lower than in the case of
standard markets. Therefore, the ability of individual firms to access new
export markets and FDI locations, and resulting patterns of trade and investment, strongly depends on the dynamics (i.e., existence and establishment) of
entrepreneurial activity in creating TETs. The capacity to create and exploit
TETs is a crucial determinant of realising comparative advantage, which can
be entirely decoupled from the other characteristics of the locations.[54] For
example, the positive relationship between the intensity of trade flows and the

geographical and cultural proximity between countries is borne out well by the continuing relevance of gravity models of international trade.[55]

Therefore, combining path dependency of trade and FDI patterns with the entrepreneurial element in international trade (and the possibility of labour migration) implies that comparative advantage evolves endogenously over time and ultimately becomes the result of a contingent historical process. Notably, networks of international trade and specialisation are far from integral and show very strong structural patterns, with huge gaps in connectivities rooting in variations in the capacity to export.[56]

For example, a country's endowment with natural resources is relevant for comparative advantage only to the extent exploited by productive activity, requiring, among others, a certain level of technological development. A country's social and organisational capital can evolve over time, particularly via the establishment of firms and, eventually, multinational enterprises (MNEs). From this point of view, and particularly in the longer run, there seem to be very few limits to the fluidity of comparative advantage – which raises the opposite question of why trade patterns in many industries have remained remarkably stable over time, such as in the automobile industry.

Here, a key question is how the different levels of spatial aggregation interact. Suppose, for example, that an exporting firm's success on a foreign market is based on a unique production technology that decreases its production cost or allows for superior quality. As already emphasised, this technology can normally not be seen in isolation from its economic and technological environment. For example, it can result from knowledge spillovers that are generated in a region or industrial district of the exporting country.[57] The consequence of this class of locational externalities is that ceteris paribus (in particular with respect to market structure), the company's export price will not reflect its market-based productivity alone but also the economic rents received via positive externalities, which are, by definition, not market-valued.[58] The same idea applies to the mirror case where an exporter generates negative externalities in its home country in the course of its production process which are not internalised (e.g., due to the lack of government measures or specified property rights).

Therefore, trade and investment flows based on comparative advantage and locational competition are intimately intertwined: Absent the theoretical borderline case of universal fully specified markets in which all externalities are internalised, competition between firms and products will always reflect specific locational patterns of externalities. This again applies to different levels of aggregation: While the country level will regularly be relevant due to its connection to the formal-institutional framework, there is a large literature on lower-level entities, such as regions, urban agglomerations, and industrial districts as well. Hence, country-level comparative advantage is the result of a complex bundle of different elements rather than factor endowments alone.

On network integrality, see Chapter 8, section 2.1.

The distribution of organisational capital of firms and of human capital also influences global transactions.

Locational externalities strongly influence firm capacities to export, are by definition external to the market, and shape comparative advantage as reflected in prices.

Compare, for the related network effects, Chapter 6, section 3.3.

Comparative advantage and locational competition are intertwined via the concept of competitive locational advantage.

As a conceptual consequence, comparative advantage needs to be widened to a more general notion of *competitive* locational advantage. Competitive advantage entails a position that, given a certain period, cannot be eroded by imitation of certain locational conditions including factor endowments.[59] Non-imitability is, therefore, not limited to the firm level but intertwined with specific features of the regional and/or national economy of origin; those interconnections, in turn, effectively establish geographical immobility of the relevant elements and, thereby, stabilise competitive advantage.

4.2. Multinational enterprises and the structure of international production

We have already argued that the MNE can be conceived as a producer of complex TETs.[60] An important corollary of this observation is that trade and investment are not substitutes but complements. In fact, for many countries and sectors, international trade is constituted by intrafirm trade to a very substantial degree, which complements the market setting as analytical reference for understanding global transactions (Figure 14.8).[61]

The MNE deconstructs traditional end product–based comparative advantage into unbundling tasks that it coordinates.

MNE as TETs have induced a major transformation of the organisation of global economic production, labelled as 'fragmentation', 'unbundling', and other terms.[62] The key observation is that the location of production follows the differentiation of tasks in production.[63] Therefore, the various governance structures of the MNE allow for a fine-graining of global production in assigning specific tasks to specific locations and orchestrating the related flows of intermediate products. By implication, we can no longer relate locational advantages to properties of end products but have to relate them to a much larger diversification of production: In particular, the MNE can complement locational advantages by moving other factors of production, especially knowledge and human capital, which potentially allows for rapid upgrading of production.

		Cross border/fragmented production structure	
		Yes	No
(Hierarchical) decision making power	Yes	Classical MNE, including vertical FDI/integration	Conglomerate, including horizontal FDI/integration
	No	Global value chain	(Portfolio investment)

Figure 14.8 Forms of international investment
We differentiate along two dimensions, hierarchical decision making and fragmented production structure. The concept of MNE only covers three combinations: If both do not apply, this is the case of international portfolio investment.

In simplest terms, we can distinguish the following forms of MNE activities, which amount to a vast space of organisational alternatives in network formations that govern intra- and extra-firm transactions with different degrees of cooperation.[64]

As observed earlier, a firm is an organisational structure including at least some amount of hierarchical, that is, non-market, decision making on economic transactions. A cross-border production process, then, can principally take place within or outside MNEs (upper- and lower-left quadrants). The former is the classic case of vertical integration; the latter implies a supply chain that is characterised by arms-length contractual relationships, that is, in principle, follows a logic of market exchange; an outsourcing decision would essentially mean a shift from the upper to the lower-left quadrant. In practice, there are intermediate forms of governance as well, such as long-term contractual relationships that are characterised by strong power asymmetries between the lead firm and the supplier, implying, for example, de facto control and command rights by the lead firm.[65] MNEs can also have a focus on horizontal integration, which in the simplest case entails a replication of production in other countries (upper-right quadrant); this may constitute an alternative to exporting as well as to other governance options, such as franchising and licensing. Both vertical and horizontal foreign direct investment can take place as greenfield investment or some form of merger or acquisition.

The logical starting point for a theory of MNEs and global value chains is the question why a national, and possibly exporting, firm would decide to engage in cross-border FDI, and the enablers and constraints of such an expansion.[66] The establishment of an MNE – and more generally, a certain governance structure of production – is an act of entrepreneurial discovery in the sense that a strict ex ante optimisation calculus based on a comparison of different governance options is analytically impossible.[67] This is because an MNE cannot be regarded as exogenous to the set of market prices based on which that comparison is supposedly conducted; a clear separation between the cost of production in a narrow sense and transactions cannot be achieved. Therefore, while the minimisation of certain categories of transaction costs may be a subjective concern (e.g., in a make-or-buy decision), it is analytically inseparable from the actual performance of the respective governance structure, which in turn is subject to evolutionary selection pressures.

Selection pressure, in turn, implies that MNEs over time need to build up competitive advantage in order to be viable. Analogously to the level of locational competition, and beyond the mere recognition of market opportunity, this rests on the development of non-imitable capabilities and routines that creatively combine factors related to locational advantages of the home/headquarter country with those of other destinations, reaching from innovation culture to low labour cost. The build-up of an MNE may start with a transfer of home-country capabilities, that is, trying to exploit a scalable advantage that the

On the firm, see Chapter 6, section 4, and Chapter 11, section 5.

MNEs orchestrate a wide variety of forms of governing global transactions, reaching from hierarchy to arms-length market exchange.

The evolutionary approach emphasises the entrepreneurial dynamics of the MNE, which faces irreducible complexity in discovering comparative advantage that is shaped by its own actions.

On this impossibility of ex ante optimisation under fundamental uncertainty, see Chapter 10, section 4.2, and Chapter 11, section 4.1.

country may have on its home market, such as technological or organisational expertise. The emergence of firm-level dynamic capabilities can lead to adaptation to destination markets as well as to more complex transfer patterns, including, for example, reverse technological transfer from a subsidiary to headquarters.

MNE activity is an evolutionary entrepreneurial process that endogenises locational advantages in exploiting firm-specific resources, especially knowledge.

Those transfers demonstrate the character of MNEs as trade-enabling and the frequently complementary relationship between market-based and intra-firm transactions. For example, MNEs provide organisational frameworks for knowledge transfer due to their capability of shifting or replicating social or technological entities that are characterised by strong internal complementarities and possibly implicit knowledge, such as expert teams. Notably, where knowledge is more standardised and costs of control as well as moral hazard issues are less pronounced, there will be a stronger tendency to outsource production with certain MNEs that have little or no in-house production; Nike and Benetton are pertinent examples.

As a result, a complex relation emerges between trade and FDI patterns generated by MNEs and country-level locational differences and competition.[68] The empirical literature clearly shows the importance of locational differences for MNEs' strategies; for example, in terms of the structure and level of taxation, the quality of institutions, the existence of trade barriers for which horizontal FDI may be a substitute, and factor endowments (e.g., in the sense of the association of headquarter locations with a certain level of human capital and the role of low labour cost). However, the way those factors play out is highly contingent on subjective perceptions and the weighting of different trade-offs by the company's management. Importantly, FDI over time tends to exhibit path dependency associated with agglomeration effects, that is, a high amount of past FDI becomes itself causal for future FDI flows. This means that once established, MNEs become determinants of locational advantage themselves. Competitive advantage of MNEs and competitive locational advantage on the country or regional level can become intertwined, such as when MNEs become part of regional systems of innovation.[69]

Ultimately, the MNE and FDI become determinants of endogenous competitive advantage of locations, such as via creating positive locational externalities.

4.3. National payment balances and their evolution over time

The balance of payments is a statistical construct that shows emergent aggregate effects of decentralised global transactions.

National accounting standards imply that the current account denotes the difference between aggregate exports and imports. A surplus means that a country, on aggregate, saves in the specific sense of building up a creditor position vis-à-vis abroad, a deficit implies the opposite. Therefore, by definition, net exports imply a surplus of savings over investment in national accounts and vice versa. Hence, two trivial but highly relevant restrictions must hold. First, in a closed system of countries, that is, the world economy, not every country can hold a current account surplus (or deficit). Second, every current account deficit needs to be financed. On the aggregate level, this can happen by internal finance – in the country case, by selling stocks of foreign assets (in the simplest case, foreign currency) – or by external finance (in the country case, by borrowing from abroad).

In the evolutionary perspective, this aggregate analysis must be deconstructed as countries are not economic agents; the balance of payments is an emergent phenomenon constructed by economic and statistical analysis. The financial connections behind financing a current account deficit can be very complex, particularly in view of the relatively high degree of integration of financial markets. That is, beyond the direct financing of transactions of goods and services, most financial flows take place *within* the capital account as financial transactions in the sense of accounting balance mechanics (e.g., via buying and selling of financial assets, or lending and borrowing). Thus, the financing of a current account deficit via capital imports always must be seen in the context of the complementary group as a whole (the rest of the world in established theory) rather than the purely bilateral relationship.

In other words, while in principle, every country faces a budget constraint in the sense that an infinite building up of financial claims or debt vis-à-vis the rest of the world is logically impossible, the concrete mechanisms as well as time perspective under which the budget constraint is enforced are highly contingent. Notably, the current account as a statistical indicator can itself become performative given that it may shape investors' perceptions of the general external financial position of the country, beyond what they could see based on their individual networks and transaction partners, resulting in phenomena such as contagion across countries.[70] Given short-run pressure to decide whether to disengage from certain markets, investors often rely on simplified categorisations, transferring economic judgements from one country to another based on limited sets of indicators, as what happened, for example, in the Asian financial crisis in the late 1990s.

Textbook theory offers some standard mechanisms of current account adjustment. The simplest works via the exchange rate; for example, a current account deficit would be associated with an increasing demand for foreign currency, leading to depreciation and respective improvement. Another – supposedly longer-run – mechanism works via relative price levels, implying improvement of the ToT. From an accounting balances perspective, these mechanisms are too general and too specific at the same time. With respect to generality, the criticism on business cycle theory outlined in the previous chapter fully applies, particularly with respect to the interest rate, which is a highly abstract notion ignoring the various differentiations that real-world financing decisions are subject to. But the mechanisms are also too specific, postulating deterministic aggregate relationships that need not hold in practice – which is clear even from standard theory if a broad enough perspective is taken. For example, given respective elasticities of demand and/or conditions with respect to market structure, a depreciation can lead to a higher, not lower, current account deficit. The truly general point stems from the income-expenditure logic: On the country level, this means that a negative accounting balance (i.e., a current account deficit) is only

The financial flows that sustain an aggregate deficit are decoupled from the current account transactions to a large degree.

Balance of payments statistics can induce performative effects on behaviour of market agents, such as contagion across countries.

The sustainability of current account deficits depends on the market agents' perceptions of financial conditions. This renders aggregate conditions path dependent and endogenously determined, as manifest in the phenomenon of current account reversals.

sustainable if market actors in the complementary country group perceive their return on (financial) investment – understood in a broad sense of including the interest rate, default risk, exchange rate expectations, maturity structures, and so on – to be more favourable than the alternatives, including their respective home markets.[71]

The empirical literature has identified several factors that seem to favour current account reversals (i.e., relatively rapid episodes of a decrease and, eventually, elimination of current account deficits), including a high initial deficit, low per-capita income, and low growth rates.[72] Similar to the case of fiscal policy and state debt, attempts were also made to identify specific thresholds beyond which a current account deficit would become unsustainable. Unsurprisingly, those attempts have met little success, revealing great variance in country cases instead.[73]

The balance of payments interacts with the government deficit. Adjustment mechanisms depend on whether government can issue debt instruments globally in own currency.

A current account deficit is often linked to a (public) budget deficit, resulting into the constellation of a twin deficit which increases the prospect of a current account reversal. From an accounting balances perspective, this implies a disaggregation of the country into (at least) two sub-sectors, namely the state and the private sector. Depending on the degree to which the current account deficit is induced by the budget deficit (normally, via different channels of expansionary fiscal policy), the sustainability of both become tightly interrelated. Here, the role of the secondary monetary community with respect to the international finance of sovereigns gets centre stage, and economic aspects are again strongly interrelated with political constellations. The most obvious example is the ability of some countries to issue sovereign debt in their own currency as well as the usability of this currency for international transactions. In the case of the United States, the role of the dollar is sometimes seen as conferring an exorbitant privilege, including the possibility to keep up a current account deficit for decades.[74] There is certainly an economic background to the privilege, given the strength and size of the US economy which renders its government bonds an attractive saving instrument for global investors.

On sovereign debt, see Chapter 12, section 2.2.

Autonomous capital flows and the specific dynamics of financial markets play a crucial role in determining the BoP in countries with liberalised capital account.

A characteristic of increasing market openness for portfolio investment is that financial flows that are not directly induced by current account transactions are massively gaining in importance.[75] Autonomous capital flows within the capital account (e.g., a foreign investor buying domestic stocks) are only indirectly related to current accounts but, due to their relatively larger volume, can still substantially affect them, mainly via inducing (additional) exchange rate volatility. International financial flows exhibit many similarities to the financial boom and bust cycles outlined in the previous chapter, but there are also points specific to the international realm. Notably, stock valuation and balance sheet effects can be amplified by the role of the exchange rate: The classic case is that capital outflows (often deemed sudden stops) lead to a depreciation, increasing the debt burden of domestic actors (private actors as well as the state) indebted in foreign currency.[76] This puts a specific twist on the role of central bank credibility and financial investors' expectations, with the latter potentially betting on the former's eventual running out of reserves.

Accordingly, absent a world central bank, a central measure in global institution building has been the creation of institutions and agreements on providing international liquidity to debtor countries which approach the situation of unstainable deficits. Originally, these were oriented towards maintaining a fixed exchange rate regime, but these functions remained important in the flexible and hybrid regimes after the collapse of the Bretton Woods system in the early 1970.

5. Conclusion

One of the core tenets of economics, often even seen as defining characteristic of being an economist, is endorsing the case for free trade, meaning that borders of jurisdictions would not interfere with cross-border market transactions and would not discriminate between foreigners and domestic citizens.[77] Stated as such, the doctrine is misleading, absent a world government or identical institutional preferences across all people on the globe. As long as these conditions do not hold, there will always be cross-border institutional differences and, hence, border effects on transactions.

Therefore, the principle of free trade should be conceived as a value proposition in the sense of endorsing cosmopolitanism in the global economy.[78] Cosmopolitan values include non-discrimination between foreigners and domestic citizens, a principled openness to global exchange in any sense, and a recognition of the autonomy of market agents not only vis-à-vis the domestic government but also any other government. This also means, however, that in principle, domestic institutional standards should apply globally: For example, domestic laws on corruption, product safety, or the environment should apply everywhere and for all agents, independent of their status as citizen. The phenomena discussed in this chapter reveal the deeply political nature of the global economy. The evolutionary approach leads to a genuine political economy of processes and outcomes on an international scale. Elaborating this approach further requires a close cross-disciplinary integration between economics and political science.

Major chapter insights

- Global transactions are analytically deconstructed into the aspects of payments flows, transactions of real and institutional objects, and transaction-enabling transactions (TETs). Via TETs, the spatial structure of the global economy is endogenous in terms of the costs of overcoming distance and borders.
- In the payments dimension, the exchange rate is a determinant of transactions while also creating genuinely macroeconomic phenomena via affecting all prices across all transacting agents and via

the aggregate budget constraints of domestic agents vis-à-vis the
rest of the world, the balance of payments.

- Global transactions unfold in a two-level regime, where the market
level is shaped by the level of market access rights that are exchanged
between governments of jurisdictions. Exchange of MARs contributes to overcoming the global specialisation dilemma when jurisdictions maintain full sovereignty in controlling market access.

- In the evolutionary view, comparative advantage is not given but
discovered and created by evolving transactions. This reflects
uncertainty about spatially distributed economic conditions and
spatially heterogenous innovation. The global distribution of production is path dependent, with a strong impact of the spatial distribution of capacities of producing TETs, specifically the MNE. In
addition, there is the effect of spatially circumscribed externalities
on locational advantages.

- MNEs play a central role in governing and conducting global
transactions, affirming the complementarity of firm and market
on a global scale. MNEs further strengthen endogenous feedbacks
between transactional patterns and locational advantages.

- Despite the growing complexity of global transactions, the balance
of payments remains a strict accounting constraint that drives emergent aggregate phenomena, such as deficits and surpluses in trade.
However, the globalisation of financial markets results in a decoupling between financial flows and the financing of trade flows.

Notes

1 This decoupling of the global division of labour from a given structure of nation
states is a key point in Baldwin (2016).
2 Explored in much detail by Findlay and O'Rourke (2007).
3 Chilosi and Federico (2021).
4 On calculating value-added trade, see Aslam et al. (2017). The OECD publishes special statistics: https://stats.oecd.org/Index.aspx?DataSetCode=TIVA_2018_C1
5 For example, Feenstra (2004) introduces 'traders' only in one of the final chapters of his advanced textbook.
6 For the Middle Ages, a classic is Lopez (1973).
7 Bernhofen et al. (2016).
8 Gibbon et al. (2008).
9 The integrative treatment of interregional and international trade was seminally
suggested by Ohlin (1967) but only revived in the "New Economic Geography",
as established by Fujita et al. (1999).

10 WTO (2011).

11 Alesina and Barro (2001).

12 Anderson and Wincoop (2004).

13 Moïsé and Le Bris (2013).

14 This was a salient topic in the Japan–US economic relations at the turn of the millennium, see Lincoln (1999). The American side had complained for decades that despite low formal trade barriers, market access is limited.

15 Hence, the entire range of services trade–related issues is pertinent here; for a survey, see WTO (2019).

16 This explains why the WTO includes an arrangement on intellectual property, the TRIPS, which was seen as systematically flawed by many trade economists, for example, Bhagwati (1996).

17 This is well established in the rich research on gravity models of international trade. For the example of the Chinese diaspora, see Martínez-Zarzoso and Rudolf (2020).

18 Campa and Goldberg (2005).

19 The ToT play a central role in Bagwell and Staiger (2002) because the negative externalities create the need for international trade regulation that internalise them.

20 Jongen et al. (2008).

21 The empirical evidence is mixed, though, regarding aggregate effects; see, for example, Lin (2012). This shows the heterogeneity of agent-level responses (exchange rate pass-through) that cancel out in the aggregate.

22 Taylor and Taylor (2004).

23 Bordo et al. (2017).

24 For example, Ames et al. (2017) who refer to the phenomenon of carry trade.

25 Engel et al. (2019).

26 Snidal and Thompson (2004).

27 Originated with Hillman and Moser (1996) and received as a fundamental concept in analysing the international trade system in Hoekman and Kostecki (2001). The concept was systematised and elaborated in more detail in Herrmann-Pillath (2004, 2008).

28 The recent literature has explored these matters as fixed costs of market entry; see, for example, Medin (2003) or Steingress (2019).

29 Seminally, McLaren (1997).

30 WTO (2007).

31 This perspective is much emphasised in international political economy research, especially by the so-called realist school, see Mansfield (1994).

32 This is emphasised by Hoekman and Kostecki (2001).

33 Yarbrough and Yarbrough (1992), Sykes (1996).

34 This already transpires in the standard view which states that tariffs can even be welfare enhancing in the case of a large country.

35 This is the gist of Bagwell and Staiger (2002) but is most extensively discussed as the intersection of economics, international law, and political science; see, for example, Trachtman (2011).

36 Schwartz and Sykes (1996), Herrmann-Pillath (2008).

37 Seminally, Petersmann (1997).

38 Yarbrough and Yarbrough (1992).

39 ADB (2020).

40 Mansfield (1994) shows that the hegemonial theory is difficult to assess empirically.

41 Bagwell and Staiger (2002).

42 Bagwell and Staiger (2011).

43 WTO (2011).

44 Boughton (2002).

45 For example, Aizenman (2019).

46 Rose (2011).

47 Eichengreen et al. (2011).

48 This was the (in)famous constellation on the eve of WWII, labelled as 'beggar thy neighbour' policies, Eichengreen (1995).

49 Yeyati (2019).

50 Surveyed in Krugman (1991).

51 Eaton and Kortum (2012).

52 This was developed in Herrmann-Pillath (2001) and Andriani and Herrmann-Pillath (2015).

53 There is a distinct literature featuring as Scandinavian approach to international business, see Johanson and Vahlne (2009).

54 These factors have been scrutinised mainly in the context of the relationship between quality and trade; see, for example, Brambilla et al. (2010). An early and seminal contribution is Burenstam (1961). Another pertinent literature is on market entry costs which are relative to capacities to reduce them; for example, Melitz and Trefler (2012).

55 For a survey, see Baier and Standaert (2020).

56 This is empirically documented in the Atlas of Economic Complexity, Hausmann et al. (2013); see also the website https://atlas.cid.harvard.edu/.

57 Rutten and Boekema (2007).

58 Seminally, Storper (1995).

59 Storper (1995).

60 The mainstream literature has mostly referred to this as headquarter services; for example, Ekholm (1998).

61 Lanz and Miroudot (2011).

62 Jones et al. (2005), Baldwin (2016).

63 Grossman and Rossi-Hansberg (2008).

64 Giroud and Scott-Kennel (2009).

65 Strange and Humphrey (2019).

66 There is a rich literature on the theory of the MNE, overviewed by Hennart (2009). Our approach is mainly inspired by Dunning's (1993, 2001) influential work.

67 Riviere and Romero-Martínez (2021).

68 For a survey, see Paul and Feliciano-Cestero (2021).

69 A case in point is the complex patterns that have emerged in the Asia-Pacific, see Zhao et al. (2021).
70 Agénor et al. (1999) on the paradigmatic case of the Asian crisis 1998.
71 Stützel (1978[1958]).
72 Aristovnik and Kumar (2006), De Haan et al. (2008).
73 For example, Freund (2005).
74 Eichengreen (2011).
75 Sahin (2014).
76 Eggertsson and Krugman (2012).
77 Irwin (1996).
78 Charnowitz (2002), Kumm (2009).

References

ADB (2020) *Regional Comprehensive Economic Partnership: Overview and Economic Impact*, Asian Development Bank Policy Brief No. 164, Manila: ADB.

Agénor, P. R. *et al.* (eds.) (1999) *The Asian Financial Crisis: Causes, Contagion and Consequences*. Cambridge and New York: Cambridge University Press.

Aizenman, J. (2019) 'A Modern Reincarnation of Mundell-Fleming's Trilemma', *Economic Modelling*, 81(C), pp. 444–454. DOI: 10.1016/j.econmod.2018.03.008.

Alesina, A. and Barro, R. J. (2001) 'Dollarization', *American Economic Review*, 91(2), pp. 381–385. DOI: 10.1257/aer.91.2.381.

Ames, M. *et al.* (2017) 'Violations of Uncovered Interest Rate Parity and International Exchange Rate Dependences', *Journal of International Money and Finance*, 73(A), pp. 162–187. DOI: 10.1016/j.jimonfin.2017.01.002.

Anderson, J. E. and Wincoop, E. van (2004) 'Trade Costs', *Journal of Economic Literature*, 42(3), pp. 691–751. DOI: 10.1257/0022051042177649.

Andriani, P. and Herrmann-Pillath, C. (2015) 'Transactional Innovation as Performative Action: Transforming Comparative Advantage in the Global Coffee Business', *Journal of Evolutionary Economics,* 25(2), pp. 371–400. DOI: 10.1007/s00191-014-0388-y.

Aristovnik, A. and Kumar, A. (2006) 'Some Characteristics of Sharp Current Account Deficit Reversal in Transition Countries', *South-Eastern Europe Journal of Economics*, 1, pp. 9–45.

Aslam, A., Novta, N. and Rodrigues-Bastos, F. (2017) 'Calculating Trade in Value Added', *IMF Working Papers*, 178. DOI: 10.5089/9781484311493.001.

Bagwell, K. and Staiger, R. W. (2002) *The Economics of the World Trading System*. Cambridge and London: MIT Press.

Bagwell, K. and Staiger, R. W. (2011) 'What Do Trade Negotiators Negotiate About? Evidence from the World Trade Organization', *American Economic Review*, 101(4), pp. 1238–1274. DOI: 10.1257/aer.101.4.1238.

Baier, S. and Standaert, S. (2020) 'Gravity Models and Empirical Trade', *Oxford Research Encyclopedia of Economics and Finance*. Available at:

https://oxfordre.com/view/10.1093/acrefore/9780190625979.001.0001/
acrefore-9780190625979-e-327

Baldwin, R. E. (2016) *The Great Convergence: Information Technology and the New Globalization*. Cambridge: The Belknap Press of Harvard University Press.

Bernhofen, D. M., El-Sahli, Z. and Kneller, R. (2016) 'Estimating the Effects of the Container Revolution on World Trade', *Journal of International Economics*, 98, pp. 36–50. DOI: 10.1016/j.jinteco.2015.09.001.

Bhagwati, J. (1996) 'The Demands to Reduce Domestic Diversity Among Trading Nations', in Bhagwati, J. and Hudec, R. E. (eds.) *Fair Trade and Harmonization: Prerequisites for Free Trade? Volume 1*. Cambridge: MIT Press, pp. 9–39.

Bordo, M. *et al.* (2017) 'The Real Exchange Rate in the Long Run: Balassa-Samuelson Effects Reconsidered', *Journal of International Money and Finance*, 75(C), pp. 69–92. DOI: 10.1016/j.jimonfin.2017.03.011.

Boughton, J. M. (2002) 'On the Origins of the Fleming-Mundell Model', *IMF Staff Papers*, 50(1).

Brambilla, I., Lederman, D. and Porto, G. (2010) 'Exports, Export Destinations, and Skills', *American Economic Review*, 102(7), pp. 3406–3439. DOI: 10.1257/aer.102.7.3406.

Burenstam, L. S. (1961) *An Essay on Trade and Transformation*. Stockholm: Almqvist & Wiksell.

Campa, J. M. and Goldberg, L. S. (2005) 'Exchange Rate Pass-Through into Import Prices', *Review of Economics and Statistics*, 87(4), pp. 679–690. DOI: 10.1162/003465305775098189.

Charnowitz, S. (2002) 'WTO Cosmopolitics', *Journal of International Law and Politics*, 34(2), pp. 299–354. DOI: 10.1142/9789814513258_0004.

Chilosi, D. and Federico, G. (2021) 'The Effects of Market Integration during the First Globalization: A Multi-Market Approach', *European Review of Economic History*, 25(1), pp. 20–58. DOI: 10.1093/ereh/heaa009.

De Haan, L., Schokker, H. and Tcherneva, A. (2008) 'What Do Current Account Reversals in OECD Countries Tell Us About the US Case?', *World Economy*, 31(2), pp. 286–311. DOI: 10.1111/j.1467-9701.2007.01070.x.

Dunning, J. H. (1993) *Multinational Enterprises and the Global Economy*. Reading: Addison Wesley.

Dunning, J. H. (2001) 'The Eclectic (OLI) Paradigm of International Production: Past, Present and Future', *International Journal of the Economics of Business*, 8(2), pp. 173–190. DOI: 10.1080/13571510110051441.

Eaton, J. and Kortum, S. (2012) 'Putting Ricardo to Work', *Journal of Economic Perspectives*, 26(2), pp. 65–90. DOI: 10.1257/jep.26.2.65.

Eggertsson, G. B. and Krugman, P. (2012) 'Debt, Deleveraging, and the Liquidity Trap: A Fisher-Minsky-Koo Approach', *The Quarterly Journal of Economics*, 127(3), pp. 1469–1513. DOI: 10.1093/QJE/QJS023.

Eichengreen, B. (1995) *Golden Fetters: The Gold Standard and the Great Depression, 1919–1939, NBER Series on Long-Term Factors in Economic Development*. New York: Oxford University Press.

Eichengreen, B. (2011) *Exorbitant Privilege: The Rise and Fall of the Dollar and the Future of the International Monetary System*. Oxford: Oxford University Press.

Eichengreen, B. *et al.* (2011) *Rethinking Central Banking: Committee on International Economic Policy and Reform*. Washington, DC: Brookings Institution.

Ekholm, K. (1998) 'Headquarter Services and Revealed Factor Abundance', *Review of International Economics*, 6(4), pp. 545–553. DOI: 10.1111/1467-9396. 00124.

Engel, C. *et al.* (2019) 'The Uncovered Interest Parity Puzzle, Exchange Rate Forecasting, and Taylor Rules', *Journal of International Money and Finance*, 95, pp. 317–331. DOI: 10.1016/j.jimonfin.2018.03.008.

Feenstra, R. C. (2004) *Advanced International Trade*. Princeton: Princeton University Press.

Findlay, R. and O'Rourke, K. H. (2007) *Power and Plenty: Trade, War, and the World Economy in the Second Millennium*. Princeton: Princeton University Press.

Freund, C. (2005) 'Current Account Adjustment in Industrial Countries', *Journal of International Money and Finance*, 24(8), pp. 1278–1298. DOI: 10.1016/j. jimonfin.2005.08.014.

Fujita, M., Krugman, P. und Venables, A. J. (1999) *The Spatial Economy: Cities, Regions, and International Trade*. Cambridge: MIT Press.

Gibbon, P., Blair, J. and Ponte, S. (2008) 'Governing Global Value Chains: An Introduction', *Economy and Society*, 37(3), pp. 315–338. DOI: 10.1080/0308514080 2172656.

Giroud, A. and Scott-Kennel, S. (2009) 'MNE Linkages in International Business: A Framework for Analysis', *International Business Review*, 18(6), pp. 555–566. DOI: 10.1016/J.IBUSREV.2009.07.004.

Grossman, G. M. and Rossi-Hansberg, E. (2008) 'Trading Tasks: A Simple Theory of Offshoring', *American Economic Review*, 98(5), pp. 1978–1997. DOI: 10.1257/aer.98.5.1978.

Hausmann, R. *et al.* (eds.) (2013) *The Atlas of Economic Complexity: Mapping Paths to Prosperity, Updated Edition*. Cambridge: MIT Press.

Hennart, J.-F. (2009) 'Theories of the Multinational Enterprise', in Rugman, A. M. (ed.) *The Oxford Handbook of International Business, Second Edition*. Oxford: Oxford University Press. DOI: 10.1093/oxfordhb/9780199234257.003.0005.

Herrmann-Pillath, C. (2001) *Kritik der Theorie des internationalen Handels, Band I: Transaktionstheoretische Grundlagen*. Marburg: Metropolis.

Herrmann-Pillath, C. (2004) *Kritik der Theorie des internationalen Handels, Band II: Evolutionäre Politische Ökonomie*. Marburg: Metropolis.

Herrmann-Pillath, C. (2008) 'International Market Access Rights and the Evolution of the International Trade System', *Journal of Theoretical and Institutional Economics*, 164(2), pp. 302–326. DOI: 10.1628/093245608784 514518.

Hillman, A. and Moser, P. (1996) 'Trade Liberalization as Politically Optimal Exchange of Markets', in Canzoneri, M., Ethier, W. and Grilli, V. (eds.)

The New Transatlantic Economy. Cambridge: Cambridge University Press, pp. 295–316.

Hoekman, B. M. and Kostecki, M. M. (2001) *The Political Economy of the World Trading System, the WTO and beyond*. Oxford: Oxford University Press.

Irwin, D. A. (1996) *Against the Tide: An Intellectual History of Free Trade*. Princeton: Princeton University Press.

Johanson, J. and Vahlne, J. E. (2009) 'The Uppsala Internationalization Process Model Revisited: From Liability if Foreignness to Liability of Outsidership', *Journal of International Business Studies*, 40(9), pp. 1411–1431. DOI: 10.1057/jibs.2009.24.

Jones, R., Kierzkowski, H. and Lurong, C. (2005) 'What Does Evidence Tell Us about Fragmentation and Outsourcing?', *International Review of Economics & Finance*, 14(3), pp. 305–316. DOI: 10.1016/J.IREF.2004.12.010.

Jongen, R. *et al.* (2008) 'Foreign Exchange Rate Expectations: Survey and Synthesis', *Journal of Economic Surveys*, 22(1), pp. 140–165. DOI: 10.1111/j.1467-6419.2007.00523.x.

Krugman, P. (1991) *Geography and Trade*. Cambridge: MIT Press.

Kumm, M. (2009) 'The Cosmopolitan Turn in Constitutionalism: On the Relationship between Constitutionalism in and beyond the State', in Dunoff, J. L. and Trachtman, J. P. (eds.) *Ruling the World? Constitutionalism, International Law, and Global Governance*. Cambridge: Cambridge University Press, pp. 178–205.

Lanz, R. and Miroudot, S. (2011) 'Intra-Firm Trade: Patterns, Determinants and Policy Implications', *OECD Trade Policy Papers*, 114. DOI: 10.1787/5kg9p39lrwnn-en.

Lin, C.-Y. (2012) 'Exchange Rate Uncertainty and Trade', *The B.E. Journal of Macroeconomics*, 12(1), pp. 1–37. DOI: 10.1515/1935-1690.2389.

Lincoln, E. J. (1999) *Troubled Times: U.S.-Japan Trade Relations in the 1990s*. Washington, DC: Brookings Institution Press.

Lopez, R. S. (1973) *The Commercial Revolution of the Middle Ages: 950–1350*. Cambridge: Cambridge University Press.

Mansfield, E. D. (1994) *Power, Trade, and War*. Princeton: Princeton University Press.

Martínez-Zarzoso, I. and Rudolf, R. (2020) 'The Trade Facilitation Impact of the Chinese Diaspora', *World Economy*, 43(9), pp. 2411–2436. DOI: 10.1111/twec.12950.

McLaren, J. (1997) 'Size, Sunk Cost, and Judge Bowker's Objection to Free Trade', *American Economic Review*, 87(3), pp. 400–420. DOI: 10.7916/D8M90H55.

Medin, H. (2003) 'Firms' Export Decisions – Fixed Trade Costs and the Size of the Export Market', *Journal of International Economics*, 61(1), pp. 225–241. DOI: 10.1016/S0022-1996(02)00076-4.

Melitz, M. and Trefler, D. (2012) 'Gains from Trade When Firms Matter', *Journal of Economic Perspectives*, 26(2), pp. 91–118. DOI: 10.1257/jep.26.2.91.

Moïsé, E. and Le Bris, F. (2013) 'Trade Costs – What Have We Learned? A Synthesis Report', *OECD Trade Policy Papers*, 150. DOI: 10.1787/5k47x2hj fn48-en.

OECD (2022) 'Trade in Value Added (TiVA) 2018 ed: Principal Indicators', *OECD. Stat.* Available at: https://stats.oecd.org/Index.aspx?DataSetCode=TIVA_2018_C1

Ohlin, B. (1967) *Interregional and International Trade*. Cambridge: Harvard University Press.

Paul, J. and Feliciano-Cestero, M. M. (2021) 'Five Decades of Research on Foreign Direct Investment by MNEs: An Overview and Research Agenda', *Journal of Business Research*, 124, pp. 800–812. DOI: 10.1016/j.jbusres.2020.04.017.

Petersmann, E.-U. (1997) *The GATT/WTO Dispute Settlement System: International Law, International Organizations and Dispute Settlement*. London, The Hague and Boston: Graham Trotman Limited.

Riviere, M. and Romero-Martínez, A. M. (2021) 'Network Embeddedness, Headquarters Entrepreneurial Orientation, and MNE International Performance', *International Business Review*, 30(3). DOI: 10.1016/j.ibusrev.2021.101811.

Rose, A. K. (2011) 'Exchange Rate Regimes in the Modern Era: Fixed, Floating, and Flaky', *Journal of Economic Literature*, 49(3), pp. 652–672. DOI: 10.1257/jel.49.3.652.

Rutten, R. and Boekema, F. (2007) *The Learning Region: Foundations, State of the Art, Future*. Cheltenham and Northampton: Edward Elgar Publishing.

Sahin, B. (2014) *Zur Kausalität in der Zahlungsbilanz – der Zusammenhang zwischen (reinen) Finanz- und Leistungstransaktionen in einer Währungsunion*. Chemnitz: PhD Dissertation/ Technische Universität Chemnitz.

Schwartz, W. F. and Sykes, A. O. (1996) 'Toward a Positive Theory of the Most Favored Nation Obligation and Its Exceptions in the WTO/GATT System', *International Review of Law and Economics*, 16(1), pp. 27–51. DOI: 10.1016/0144-8188(95)00053-4.

Snidal, D. and Thompson, A. (2004) 'International Commitments and Domestic Politics: Institutions and Actors at Two Levels', in Drezner, D. W. (ed.) *Locating the Proper Authorities: The Interaction of Domestic and International Institutions*. Ann Arbor: University of Michigan Press, pp. 197–233.

Steingress, W. (2019) 'Market Size and Entry in International Trade: Product versus Firm Fixed Costs', *Review of International Economics*, 27(5), pp. 1351–1370. DOI: 10.1111/roie.12427.

Storper, M. (1995) 'The Resurgence of Regional Economies, Ten Years Later: The Region as a Nexus of Untraded Interdependencies', *European Urban and Regional Studies*, 2(3), pp. 191–221. DOI: 10.1177%2F096977649500200301.

Strange, R. and J. Humphrey (2019) 'What Lies Between Market and Hierarchy? Insights from Internalization Theory and Global Value Chain Theory', *Journal of International Business Studies*, 50(8), pp. 1401–1413.

Stützel, W. (1978 [1958]) *Volkswirtschaftliche Saldenmechanik: Ein Beitrag zur Geldtheorie*. Tübingen: Mohr Siebeck.

Sykes, A. O. (1996) 'The Economics of Injury in Antidumping and Countervailing Duty Cases', *International Review of Law and Economics*, 16, pp. 5–26.

Taylor, A. M. and Taylor, M. P. (2004) 'The Purchasing Power Parity Debate', *Journal of Economic Perspectives*, 18(4), pp. 135–158. DOI: 10.1257/08953 30042632744.

Trachtman, J. (2011) 'Constitutional Economics of the World Trade Organization', in Dunoff, J. L. and Trachtman, J. P. (eds.) *Ruling the World? Constitutionalism, International Law, and Global Governance*. Cambridge: Cambridge University Press, pp. 206–231. DOI: 10.1017/CBO9780511627088.009.

WTO (2007) *World Trade Report 2007: Six Decades of Multilateral Trade Cooperation: What Have We Learnt?* Geneva: WTO.

WTO (2011) *World Trade Report 2011: The WTO and Preferential Trade Agreements: From Co-Existence to Coherence by World Trade Organization*. Geneva: WTO.

WTO (2019) *World Trade Report 2019: The Future of Services Trade*. Geneva: WTO.

Yarbrough, B. V. and Yarbrough, R. M. (1992) *Cooperation and Governance in International Trade: The Strategic Organizational Approach*. Princeton: Princeton University Press.

Yeyati, E. L. (2019) 'Exchange Rate Policies and Economic Development', *Oxford Research Encyclopedia of Economics and Finance*.

Zhao, W. and Ruet, J. (2021) 'Managing the "Post Miracle" Economy in China: Crisis of Growth Model and Policy Responses', *Post-Communist Economies*, 33(7), pp. 820–841. DOI: 10.1080/14631377.2020.1867427.

CHAPTER FIFTEEN

Markets and inequality

1. Introduction

Individuals in human populations are characterised by a variety of traits, reaching from those that are predominantly defined biologically, such as height and proneness to certain illnesses, to complex social-institutional types, such as entrepreneurs and investors. The question arises of which dimensions and levels of diversity are deemed as inequality with economic relevance and why. Standard economic theory takes a clear stance, using indicators related to monetary income and wealth as key measures of inequality between individuals and households (e.g., income or wealth deciles, poverty thresholds), firms (profits), and regions and countries (e.g., GDP or GDP per capita). Economic explanations of inequality are grouped around the respective indicators.

In this chapter, we develop a broader theoretical framework for the analysis of economic inequality based on a sub-regime of techno-institutional regimes that we will call a 'regime of inequality'. A regime of inequality is a combination of technologies and institutions that generates a relatively stable pattern of distribution of different resources, which, besides material wealth and income, includes agential power and social status. Regimes of inequality can be defined on different levels of aggregation, reaching from the family to the global economy. A focus on regimes of inequality has the following key implications.

First, the specific dimensions and levels of inequality are endogenous to regime evolution. They reflect societal values, importantly in terms of the perceived fairness of social outcomes.

Second, the economic dimension of inequality is embedded in other dimensions, including social capital and status, agential power, health, happiness, life satisfaction, the exposure to risk, and on the collective level, endowments with human and real capital, including the capacity for organising violence. Those dimensions interact in complex ways.

Third, regimes of inequality entail a set of informal institutions and conventions related to subjective values and fairness notions. Legitimacy is a crucial determinant of the sustainability of the regime, mainly in the sense of the containment of social and political forces for change. Legitimacy concerns

Inequality is a corollary of diversity unfolding on markets.

On agency types, see Chapter 12, section 3.1.

Economics mostly refers to monetary measures of inequality.

Techno-institutional regimes were introduced in Chapter 13, section 2.

Regimes of inequality generate relatively stable distributional patterns and exist on different levels. They reflect social values.

Economic inequality is embedded in other dimensions of inequality.

393

DOI: 10.4324/9781003094869-20

*Legitimacy
is a crucial
determinant of an
inequality regime's
sustainability.*

*Regimes of
inequality co-evolve
on different levels.*

are a key reason why economics as a discipline of markets has to deal with the topic of inequality in the first place: Without a general acceptance of the market process and unequal market outcomes in various dimensions, markets as social technologies are not sustainable over time.[1]

Fourth, regimes of inequality imply that different levels and their evolution need to be viewed in an integrated fashion rather than analysing them separately. For example, a firm-level inequality regime that legitimises high pay differences is difficult to reconcile with a jurisdiction-level regime that emphasises social solidarity and equality of outcomes.

Obviously, there is a great variety of inequality regimes over space and time. Some of them are largely exogenous to market competition while at the same time allowing for it; for example, traditional European aristocratic societies or the Indian caste system. The focus of this chapter, however, will be on inequality regimes that are endogenously generated by, or at least co-evolve with, market competition. In doing this, we proceed as follows. In section 2, we deepen the conceptional analysis of inequality by introducing the distinction between structural-positional and interpersonal inequality, specifying levels of aggregation, and exemplifying measurement issues together with their potential performative effects. Section 3 provides an analysis of the evolution of market-based structural-positional inequality, focusing on the level of formal-institutional development first and then providing an analysis of inequality within firms and in competition between firms. Section 4 relates this to an analysis of interpersonal inequality, with a dynamic focus on path-dependent individual mobility over the life cycle as well as intergenerational mobility. Section 5 discusses key aspects of the legitimacy of market systems.

2. Concepts and measurement of inequality

This section provides a brief overview of three core topics for the conceptualisation and measurement of inequality, namely the distinction between structural and interpersonal concepts of inequality, the level of aggregation for comparing different social entities, and building on this, the key dimensions of inequality and their interrelationship.

The distinction between structural-positional and interpersonal inequality is a fundamental element of inequality analysis. Conceptionally, although their degree of formalisation can vary, positions are independent from concrete individuals occupying them and can differ in key dimensions, such as income, power, and social status. A typical market-related example is a hierarchical structure within a firm: Assuming that this structure is static for a certain period, individuals may move into, out of, and between the positions – which captures the essence of modern labour markets as distinguished from entrepreneurial behaviour. This can be generalised in terms of the social mobility concept: Structural-positional inequalities are associated with certain

*Structural-positional
and interpersonal
inequality need to
be distinguished and
are intertwined in
a co-evolutionary
relationship.*

degrees of social mobility, which in turn (at least in modern contexts) enjoy certain degrees of legitimacy.

Structural-positional and interpersonal inequality are intertwined in a co-evolutionary relationship over time. For example, intra-organisational entrepreneurial behaviour may lead to the creation of new positions, and individual social mobility in a generalised sense would be directly associated with positional change. Another example is elite closure: In such a scenario, elites create positional niches to which they, and possibly their offspring, have – de facto or de jure – privileged access, ultimately reducing social mobility. However, there is also the reverse possibility that high structural-positional dynamics may be associated with low social mobility, which may be a result of educational stratification (see further section later).

See, for the definition of 'elites', Chapter 8, section 3.2.

As said, there is a wide range of options as to the level of aggregation and choice of collective entities for the conceptualisation of economic inequality, with social classes, the capital-labour antagonism, ethnic groups, demographic cohorts and generations, gender, and firms being prominent examples. As in the analysis of business cycles, then, the analysis of inequality is shaped by the concrete measures and statistical indicators that are available. For example, one of the most influential accounts of the evolution of inequality over the last 200 years was driven by improved data availability and estimation techniques (e.g., with respect to the refined splitting up of income percentiles).[2] Similar issues exist for gender inequality, the distinction between households and individuals,[3] wealth inequality,[4] and individual and intergenerational social mobility.[5] A specific domain is the measurement of inequality between regions and countries, which has traditionally been done via GDP but increasingly relies on alternative, subjective measures, such as life satisfaction and happiness.[6] All those measures are potentially performative, both with respect to the perception of inequality and the (policy) measures that are derived from it. Ultimately, they become key elements of inequality regimes themselves.

The choice of aggregation level of comparisons can be performative.

Based on this, in order to capture the evolution of market-related regimes of inequality in a parsimonious way, we will distinguish four co-evolving levels of structural-positional inequality regimes (Figure 15.1):

- First, sub-regimes of inequality *within* firms, encompassing dimensions of income, status, and power of individual positions.
- Second, sub-regimes of inequality *between* firms and their evolution, which encompasses the emergence of new (entrepreneurial) firms, disappearance of existing firms, and boundary shifts, such as by mergers and acquisitions but also by a change in competitive intensity and substitutability on both labour and product markets.
- Third, country (in the sense of national state)-level inequality regimes.
- Fourth, interjurisdictional regimes on an international and global level, encompassing institutions of international trade and investment, and of locational competition.

Those levels are an adapted version of the co-evolving levels defined in Chapters 11, 13, 14, and 17.

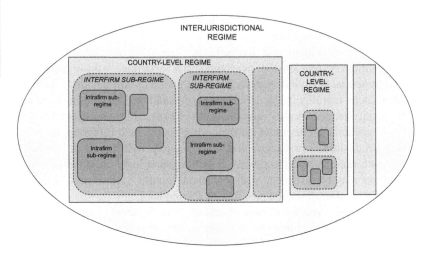

Figure 15.1 Levels of inequality regimes
We distinguish four levels of co-evolving structural-positional regimes of
inequality, namely regimes within firms, between firms, within countries, and
between countries. For more detail, see text.

For our analysis
of different
levels of market
competition,
see Chapter 11;
for the
distribution of
political power,
Chapter 9,
section 5.

The first and second level cover voluntary market exchange and, thus, extend
the framework developed previously both in terms of a deeper analysis of
competition between firms, as mediated by their profitability on product markets, and the analytical inclusion of labour markets. The third and fourth level
are primarily of a political nature and, therefore, refer to the distribution of
power in society.

3. Structural inequality and multilevel market selection

We now proceed by focusing on the evolution of market-related structural-positional inequality before complementing this by an analysis of interpersonal
inequality in the following section.

3.1. Country-level inequality regimes and formal institutions

With respect to market competition, country-level regimes of inequality
exhibit two main pillars. First, they define political power positions and rules
of the game for political competition. Second, they define rules of the game

for market competition, most generally by establishing a regulatory framework for the build-up or reduction of inequality of income and wealth but partly also of human capital. An immediate implication is that a full analysis of market-based inequality is only possible when taking into account the interaction with inequality in the political realm.

The establishment of systems with an institutionalised separation between the political realm and markets is historically an exception rather than the rule.[7] In liberal democracies, this separation is achieved in two main ways. First, certain core institutions ensuring the functioning of the market economy, above all the institution of property rights, are enshrined on the constitutional level and associated with the more general idea of limiting political power by establishing different branches and a corresponding checks and balances system. Second, decision making is principally based on a one-person-one-vote principle whereas market allocation is directly related to monetary resources (i.e., follows a one-dollar-one-vote principle). Beyond this ideal-typic distinction, however, modern democracies are characterised by substantial spillovers between the two levels. Spillovers from the economic to the political realm take the form of lobbying and interest group politics, partly categorised as rent-seeking. Interest group competition will often lead to a formation of relatively stable distributional coalitions and, therefore, tends to cement structural inequality, relating to the concept of political institutions as truces between different interest groups. In contrast, some of the regulative institutions mentioned earlier can be interpreted as spillovers from the democratic-political to the market realm; for example, in the form of redistributive policies, anti-discrimination rules, or the introduction of democratic elements into intrafirm decision making (workers' councils).

The formal institutions regulative of market competition are constitutive of country-level inequality regimes insofar as they define a framework in which material differences in terms of wealth and income – both on the individual/household and firm level – can be built up and retained. In addition, there is the large category of institutions that directly influence, and mostly mitigate, the interpersonal inequality of market outcomes.[8] These institutions include rules on direct redistribution of income and wealth (classically, by a combination of taxation and transfers) but also of other capital assets that are relevant for the distribution of income and wealth (most importantly, human capital in the form of education or health services). Institutions also provide direct rules on certain structural power positions in markets. The key example is corporate governance; for instance, in most jurisdictions the institutional power of a CEO of a limited liability company is relatively strictly circumscribed. Finally, regimes of inequality entail substantial institutional complementarities. Such complementarities can occur, for example, between the setup of educational systems and skills-based wage differentials as possibly emerging from wage bargaining, or between the level of redistributive

For a full analysis of political competition and the distinction of regulatory levels, see Chapter 17. For the formal institutions of market competition, see Chapter 11, section 6.

Liberal democracies exhibit an institutional separation between the political realm and markets.

On checks and balances, see Chapter 17, section 3.5; on rent-seeking, Chapter 17, section 3.3.

Spillover effects between the political and economic level include rent-seeking and anti-discrimination legislation.

taxation and the restrictiveness of employment legislation, both exemplified by the traditional contrast between US-style capitalism and the German social market economy.

In terms of their evolution, country-level regimes of inequality are contested both from within and outside. There is a close relationship between interjurisdictional and country-level regimes of inequality insofar as a certain degree of country-level inequality can be functional with respect to competitiveness and an improved position on the interjurisdictional level – which was a classic issue, for example, in the systemic competition between capitalist and socialist economies. External competitive success of a regime can stabilise internal inequalities due to the provision of a 'rising tide' that makes everyone better off and increases the acceptance of inequality.[9] However, interjurisdictional competition does not necessarily lead to a convergence of market-based country-level inequality regimes. Varieties of capitalism have not been eliminated, and the equity-efficiency trade-off has played out in very different ways; for example, by partly substituting high-powered financial incentives for entrepreneurship in the Anglo-American system by a better health, mobility, and educational infrastructure in the European social market economies.[10] In contrast, interjurisdictional competition, particularly in the context of modern globalisation, tends to exhibit certain standardising effects on country-level regimes of inequality, including patterns of income distribution. Those effects can play out on the formal-institutional level, such as the universally recognised ban on child labour, as well as endogenously emerge from market competition, such as the fair trade movements.

The two classic mechanisms of interjurisdictional competition are exit and voice. The institutional degree of availability of the two options is itself part of the regime: Both can be severely restricted but may also be kept open for non-economic power-based reasons – for example, the emigration of certain groups may have a stabilising effect on an existing distributional coalition. With respect to voice, the key issue is to what extent subjective discontent with the existing distributional situation can be transformed into a change of the extant power coalition, which depends on political transaction cost and the associated collective action problems.

Taken together, those factors will contribute to a high degree of inertia of country-level inequality regimes; the relative persistence, and eventual accumulation, of inherited wealth over generations is an important manifestation.[11] In fact, it can be argued that entrenched patterns of structural and interpersonal inequality can only be upset by extreme events, such as war, revolution, or pandemics.[12]

3.2. Firms and interfirm competition

Firms represent sub-regimes of inequality insofar as they constitute hierarchical organisations that are relatively stable in time, allowing for the emergence

---

Interjurisdictional competition does not necessarily result in convergence of intrajurisdictional inequality regimes but can have standardising effects.

On the structure of interjurisdictional competition, see Chapter 17, section 3.4.

The internal stability of country-level inequality regimes is determined by exit and voice mechanisms.

In general, country-level inequality regimes exhibit a high degree of inertia.

of intrafirm structures, both formal and informal, that underlie positions and individual differences in power, status, and income. At the same time, they are, to a varying degree, under external competitive pressure, resulting in patterns of evolution of populations of firms over time. Large parts of income flows are generated by wages; of those, most come from employee positions in firms.

Starting with the intrafirm level, why are hierarchical power and stratified incomes prevalent in firms in the first place? As explained previously, technological requirements can only provide a very rough answer insofar as there is a likely need to reward indispensable, and at the same time scarce, human qualifications. Beyond that, the relation between human activity in firms and technology is multi-valued, and contingent effects of power and competition get centre stage, for which we have already presented an integrated approach.

In the classic power-oriented perspective, the firm primarily serves as a device to establish institutionalised control over the surplus-generating production process. The control position is originally taken by the owner(s) and, subsequently, with the separation of ownership and control in the modern corporation, complemented by executive management. In the first place, workers draw a voluntary decision to become firm employees and, therefore, submit themselves to the intrafirm hierarchy, as a consequence of differential endowments (in particular, with respect to financial capital) and risk aversion. A subsequent increase of capability specificity of employees' human capital (e.g., via Marxian deskilling) can then endogenously reinforce the hierarchy.

Payment differentials in firms are frequently defined over positions rather than individuals, rendering them an element of structural-positional inequality. Those positions are not only defined along economically rational productivity criteria: organisational structures, including internal positional differentials, often spread according to a logic of appropriateness, implying that populations of firms may exhibit similar inequality regimes following certain role models, such as incentivised schemes of wage payments.[13] Positional payment differences address patterns of status and group differentiation, including issues of interpersonal comparisons and envy.[14] Also, firms constitute, or are composed of, primary groups, which tend to develop internal relationships of hierarchy, status, and mutual ascriptions that are supported by emerging cognitive patterns and mutually stable behavioural expectations; those, in turn, may notably correlate with larger-scale in-group–out-group boundaries as described in the next section.[15] These patterns will also be embodied in the firm's organisational routines, establishing a – albeit ambiguous – link to patterns of specialisation and embodied technical and organisational knowledge.[16]

As on the country level, intrafirm sub-regimes of inequality encompass many elements that are highly complementary, such as differences in pay, working conditions, categories of employment contracts, internal social status, and patterns of external finance. Also, they often constitute truces between

Firms are key elements of regimes of inequality on markets.

On power and efficiency in firms, see Chapter 6, section 4.2, and Chapter 11, section 5.

Payment differentials are a manifestation of structural-positional inequality insofar as they are defined over positions rather than individuals.

Intrafirm sub-regimes of inequality are characterised by complementarities.

*The evolution
of intrafirm
sub-regimes of
inequality may
manifest ossification
and ageing.*

See, for the
role of stasis in
market evolution,
Chapter 11,
section 3.

*Interfirm sub-
regimes of
inequality are often
characterised by
relative stasis, with
a key role of status
orders.*

*The relationship
between intrafirm
and interfirm sub-
regimes of inequality
is mediated by
labour markets.*

different intrafirm groups, such as the management and workers, regional or technical departments, but also shareholders: In that respect, intrafirm sub-regimes of inequality are not only important with regard to the inequality of labour income but also to capital income, with the shareholder value movement of the 1980s and onwards being a case in point.[17]

Although, as a consequence of the previous point, intrafirm sub-regimes of inequality tend to exhibit inertia, they nevertheless evolve. One classic topic of organisational demography is organisational ageing and its possible association with structural ossification.[18] An important correlate of this in terms of intrafirm sub-regimes of inequality is the well-known transition from auto-cratic-charismatic to bureaucratic leadership,[19] or more generally, an increasing degree of formalisation with respect to the rules of the game of intrafirm competition. For example, it has long been hypothesised (but remained ambiguous in empirical terms) that bureaucratic firms with highly formalised internal assessment procedures reduce intrafirm income disparities because they create better standing for less powerful (groups of) employees.[20]

Turning to inequality sub-regimes between firms, we can directly build upon our previous result that markets are frequently characterised by evolutionary stasis due to their distinctly institutionalised character. Market stasis can entail inequality between firms not only due to technological variability but also due to the emergence of status orders, which contribute to persistent differences in profitability.[21] Status orders are social network phenomena insofar as they coordinate and enhance information flows between firms as well as between firms and the demand side. In both cases, the key point is the signalling function of status: For the demand side, status is a key signal of product quality.[22] As a consequence, for example, a high-status firm is unlikely to enter a supply chain with a lower-status supplier. Advertisements exhibit an information function not only with respect to a product's concrete attributes but also the firm's status vis-à-vis other firms, both from the perspective of these and the consumers.

Accordingly, there is a complex dynamic relationship between intrafirm and interfirm sub-regimes of inequality (Figure 15.2). In general terms, the question is, to what extent competition between firms, with the profit criterion as its yardstick, constrain the variety of intrafirm inequality sub-regimes, and how those inequality sub-regimes themselves contribute to competitive success on the interfirm level. A core role is, therefore, played by labour markets, including interfirm competition on those markets. In this regard, the standard economic approach focuses mainly on intrafirm monetary incentives (i.e., wage and earnings differentials). The baseline model of relative remuneration postulates a correspondence of wage differences with differences in individual productivity, which, besides constituting a profit maximisation criterion, can be interpreted as a competitive constraint on intrafirm wage equalisation. Limits to intrafirm wage equalisation can also be established by, for example, the relative scarcity of different categories of skills,[23] compensation

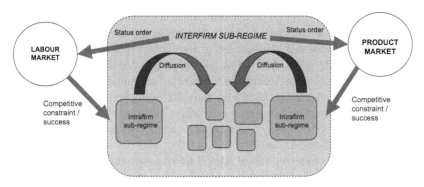

Figure 15.2 Interplay of inequality sub-regimes on interfirm and intrafirm level
Intrafirm sub-regimes of inequality are constrained by competition on both product and labour markets, with competitive success partly determined by status orders. Successful sub-regimes will tend to diffuse and eventually shape the interfirm sub-regime. However, diffusion can also take place endogenously, following a logic of appropriateness.

aspects (e.g., for the relative difficulty or risk of certain tasks), and the establishment of monetary incentives for intrafirm careers.[24]

Monetary incentives can be directly linked to firms' relative success on product markets rather than to internal differences. For example, some modern high-tech firms, such as Microsoft or Google, entail relatively egalitarian and less formalised working cultures than those of many competitors but offer very competitive salaries, thus effectively siphoning off high-qualified employees from the labour market.[25] This is one example for the repercussions of the entrepreneurial establishment of a new intrafirm inequality sub-regime to the interfirm inequality sub-regime. Evidently, an important status element is entailed here: The dominant status of these companies on their respective product markets would then stand in a mutually reinforcing relationship with their status on labour markets.

Firms' statuses on product and labour markets are interrelated, with the possibility of mutual reinforcement.

Finally, the interfirm inequality regime is also influenced by firm boundaries; for example, the trend to outsource parts of production activities to separate entities in local or international supply chains can be interpreted as a shift in inequality regimes, implying higher inequality between the workforce of a privileged core and the periphery.[26]

The way the outlined mechanisms on the intra- and interfirm level play out is inextricably linked to the higher-order inequality regime on the country level. The most obvious examples are regulations directly impacting on wage differentials, such as minimum wages and rules pertaining to the organisation and bargaining power of trade unions. Other crucial fields of regulations are employment protection regulation and corporate governance,

Intra- and interfirm sub-regimes of inequality are deeply influenced by country-level regimes.

which will both impact on patterns of intrafirm income differentials and the relative extent to which voice and exit options are used as a response to intrafirm distributional conflict. These formal institutions, in turn, will be complemented by more informal categories, such as conventions on expected degrees of loyalty and emotional attachment in the employer–employee relationship. Those factors are used to explain, for example, the much-discussed divergence of executive and average workers' pay that took place in the US and the UK over the last decades, quite contrary to developments in the European Union and Japan.[27]

To conclude, the evolution of market-based structural-positional inequality, as, for example, reflected in inequality of incomes, is decisively influenced by the co-evolutionary development of intrafirm- and interfirm sub-regimes of inequality. This competitive process determines the relative significance of technological and economic efficiency criteria and of structures of social power for income inequality. In principle, these factors are complementary insofar as market-based interfirm competition will establish limits to the extent to which intrafirm inequality can be based on purely power-related factors, such as cronyism, but also the extent to which intra-organisational stratification in firms will be streamlined by external competition. Overall, the competitive process is strongly influenced by the politically determined framework of formal institutions, which have a standardising effect on some features of intrafirm sub-regimes of inequality, such as in the case of a minimum wage, as well as interfirm sub-regimes, such as in the case of restrictions posed by competition law. Similar standardisation processes apply with respect to technology but not in any deterministic sense; our general conclusion continues to hold that specialisation and exchange, together with the underlying technological structure and its evolution, can go along with very different social structures, including different distributions of power, income, and wealth.

Results of market competition are ambivalent insofar as there is a strong chance element but also a high degree of structural persistence.

Based on this, the overall results of market competition in terms of economic inequality exhibit an important ambivalence. On the one hand, decentralised agency, distributed knowledge, and the outlined co-evolutionary process inevitably introduce an important chance element to competition results.[28] It is, therefore, not possible to relate certain structural characteristics, such as specific intrafirm sub-regimes of inequality, to market outcomes in a deterministic way, which holds a fortiori for the emergence of new firms. Therefore, the indeterminacy of market results should, at least in the longer run, keep a market system and the regimes of inequality that it encompasses fluid. On the other hand, market inequality tends to exhibit a remarkable degree of structural persistence, given the outlined reasons for the inertia of inequality regimes both on the political and firm level (in some sectors, large-scale enterprises persist over generations).[29]

4. Interpersonal inequality: Individual differences, networks, and social mobility

We now turn to a more explicit focus on interpersonal inequality, concentrating on its dynamic aspect, namely individual mobility over the life cycle and intergenerational social mobility, and highlighting some further aspects of the co-evolution with structural-positional inequality. The analysis here starts with a focus on individuals and individual differences over the life cycle. We then widen the scope to social interaction, with a focus on various influences of social networks. Conceptually, social mobility can be conceived of as the unfolding and outplay of different categories of capital – in particular, human capital, social capital, and wealth as summarising financial and real capital (such as shares or real estate) – and their differential distribution over individuals in market processes. Notably, there is generally a close co-evolution of the market-based distribution of income and wealth (i.e., financial and real capital) and the distribution of human and social capital. For example, a given distribution of income and wealth will put significant constraints on the evolution of the human capital distribution, most importantly via the stratification of educational opportunity. Conversely, the distribution and specific manifestations of human capital will clearly affect market-based income and wealth, such as by driving technological change and, thereby, devaluing existing assets. As has been stressed in section 3, a key role in this co-evolutionary process is played by firms.

For the network perspective, see Chapter 8, section 3.2.

4.1. Individual differences, nature versus nurture, and path dependency

The logical starting point of a discussion of evolving individual differences in capital endowments is genetic variation. The basic argument on genetically determined capacities and propensities and their phenotypic expression via individual characteristics and behavioural patterns follows the lines of Chapters 7 to 9 but with the crucial twist that the focus is now on interpersonal differences, not evolutionary human universals. This raises the important issue of the extent differences in individual outcomes on the social level, such as income and wealth, but also crime rates or happiness, can be related to genetic variance in a certain population. The distinction between genetic and environmental influences, or nature and nurture, is, of course, a classical theme in human medicine, including the field of mental illnesses, but also of behavioural genetics and, to an increasing extent, psychology in general; it is also used in empirical studies on labour market outcomes.[30] The key concept used is heritability, which measures the extent to which the variance of a phenotypic (human) trait can*not* be explained by environmental differences in a specific population.[31]

Heritability measures the extent to which the variance of a phenotypic trait cannot be explained by environmental differences.

On the evolutionary background, see Chapter 4, section 3.

The importance of genetic factors for market outcomes appears to be relatively clear as long as the focus is on differences in traits of a primarily biological nature, such as height, the proneness to certain (including mental) illnesses, but also physical attractiveness.[32] The picture appears to be less clear when it comes to more complex traits, such as attitudes towards risk, altruism, political preferences, creativity, and cognitive ability. Indeed, there is an increasing literature in economics, but also political science and sociology, that tries to identify the heritable components of such traits,[33] which in the case of high levels of heritability would exhibit considerable inertia across generations that are relatively independent of their respective socio-economic environment. The economic and social implications of such a scenario would be particularly far-reaching for the case of cognitive ability. There is a relatively widely established consensus in psychology on how to measure cognitive ability[34] and an important correlation of cognitive ability with a broad range of stratified outcomes in modern market economies, including educational attainment and job productivity,[35] which can be interpreted as a measure to which those economies indeed exhibit a meritocratic structure.[36] If those results are combined with a sufficiently high level of heritability of IQ, the prospect of a genetically stratified, caste-like society as an endogenous result of meritocratic competition would arise.[37] Unsurprisingly, this scenario has sparked significant concerns and controversy.

Particularly with respect to complex traits, the phenotypic expression of genetic differences is always tied to different levels of environmental influences – starting with the cell and reaching to the social level – that interact and accumulate in highly complex ways. As a consequence, a strict additive separation between nature and nurture is not possible, and the strive for clean experimental conditions that would allow for a complete isolation of all environmental factors is faced with conceptual obstacles. The developmental process needs to be traced in terms of causal chains on different levels, including variation in the creative use of non-shared environments.[38]

Against this background, we conceptualise the unfolding of interpersonal inequality in terms of path-dependent development. For the human individual, the interaction between different levels, including the genetic in the sense of DNA sequence, leads all the way from conception to mature professional life and beyond, including, for example, conditions in the maternal womb, early childhood environment, schooling, and professional conditions. A fundamental property of path dependency is that antecedent conditions do not determine but constrain posterior paths of development. The concrete degree of rigidity of those constraints will differ from case to case and itself depend on external conditions; ultimately, it can only be determined empirically. To return to the issue of cognitive ability, it appears improbable, for example, that the phenomenon of extremely high ability (genius) can be explained by variability on levels that go much beyond biological genes, including early childhood conditions.[39] In that sense, it would indeed be correct that the deep genetic level

A high heritability of certain traits, such as cognitive ability, raises the prospect of a genetically stratified society.

The distinction between nature and nurture with respect to more complex traits is fraught with difficulties.

Individual development is a path-dependent process that includes both genetic differences and environmental influences in a non-deterministic fashion.

puts constraints on individuals' cognitive potentials. At the same time, cognitive ability seems to be relatively fluid until the age of around eight and only then tends to crystallise, which implies that the complex interactions of childhood development would be both an enabler and a constraint of later individual development.[40] While ageing, individuals to an increasing extent engage in cognitive niche formation, that is, they create a social and material environment corresponding to their cognitive ability, which then may generate feedback loops.[41] At the same time, similar to technological and institutional development, there is a possibility of formative events/shocks which may change the developmental path (e.g., traumatic experiences that reduce cognitive ability).

Thus, an evolutionary approach to interpersonal economic inequality includes differences with respect to the degree to (and the point in individual lifetime in) which certain traits are prone to social influence. Certain relevant traits may exhibit intergenerational persistence that is relatively independent of environmental influences, which in turn may be a partial explanandum of lower-than-expected (or desired) social mobility in market competition. In contrast, the path-dependent character of the underlying multilevel developmental mechanisms by necessity attributes a large role to environmental-social factors, to which we now turn.

This specifies the path dependency of brain ontogeny, see Chapter 7, section 3.1.

4.2. Human capital: Educational stratification and labour markets

As mentioned, a given distribution of wealth and income will have a strong impact on the potential of individuals and groups to accumulate human capital. Inequality already sets in with the maternal womb (e.g., by negative impacts of maternal stress on the embryo) and continues into early childhood.[42] A key connection to markets then appears via the educational system: If schooling is provided via markets or at least offers a respective private option for richer parts of the population, the further development of individual differences is likely to be tied more strongly to socio-economic family background.[43] This is one of the key rationales for building up a public schooling system based on equality of opportunity, providing children with the same learning environment irrespective of their socioeconomic background. Whether equality of opportunity alone can level out pre-existing differences is questionable, however, since advantaged children will tend to be better able to benefit from given learning environments for their further development.[44]

Stratification of educational opportunity tends to promote divergence of path-dependent individual development.

In modern market economies, educational systems have become pre-screening devices for labour markets, implying that educational stratification is, to an important extent, transformed into wage differentials and skills premia, which, in turn, co-evolve with skills-based technological change.[45] The transformation of educational stratification into wage differentials also works via signalling:[46] Educational attainment serves as a general signal of

Education can serve as pre-screening and signalling device for labour markets, resulting in regular occurrence of skills premia.

405

desirable characteristics of the employee, such as cognitive ability and the capacity to learn, energy, perseverance, and motivation. Costlier signals (e.g., in terms of effort, time, but also financial resources) would be the more credible ones; at the same time, the informational accuracy of a formal educational attainment varies over space and time, depending, for example, on the structure of national education systems in terms of selectivity and diversity of different streams.

Intrafirm wage differentials can become self-reinforcing due to managerial power and arms races.

There are important channels of co-evolution between educational stratification and the evolution of inter- and intrafirm sub-regimes of inequality. First, employees will tend to actively shape their environments (i.e., engage in niche formation), for example, by channelling technological change or product innovation in firms to their favour.[47] Second, the signalling perspective on education implies that the remuneration effect of educational attainment has a strongly relative component, as exemplified by the recent upward shift of educational requirements for very similar occupations,[48] and there is a potential of Red Queen effects, as exemplified by the divergence of top managerial incomes taking place in the US and Britain over the last decades.[49]

The accumulation of wealth and human capital can lead to divergence over generations.

A generalised scenario for the co-evolution between educational stratification and the distribution of income and wealth is a divergent and mutually reinforcing accumulation of human capital and wealth: (Parental) wealth enables accumulation of human capital, which, in turn, increases prospects of higher earnings; the accumulated wealth is then used for equipping the next generation with superior human capital endowment, and so forth. This accumulation process clearly depends on institutional preconditions, such as an absence of strong redistribution measures relating to income and bequests, and allowance for a stratified educational system. The likely result is decreased social mobility, even if hereditary components of human capital transmission are not assumed to play any significant role.

4.3. Social capital: Interaction in social networks and divergence

A basic characteristic of human social behaviour is homophily, that is, the tendency of individuals who share important traits and behaviours to interact more intensely among each other than with others. Homophily may constitute

Group formation based on homophily entails a vertical component of social and status differentiation.

an underlying force of horizontal variety in group formation, but it also has a key vertical component, with endowment levels in different capital assets constituting the differentiating criterion, such as in the case of elites. In fact, horizontal and vertical criteria may intersect, such as in golf clubs with high membership fees.

In the educational system, homophily may already be structurally preordained, such as in elite universities or a stratified system of primary or secondary schooling. But even in more uniform, public-dominated systems, there is a tendency of youths with similar socio-economic backgrounds to group together or attend educational options beyond the basic curriculum in selected groups. A related example is geographical agglomeration, given, for example, the strongly vertical character of residential differentiation in urban areas. Finally, there is professional and vocational interaction, where vertically homophilous communication can be observed both as an intra- and interorganisational phenomenon and may, among others, affect patterns of recruitment and wage setting.[50]

A key point for the formation and stabilisation of vertical groups is the emergence of group markers, such as indicators of elite education.[51] One example is dialect and vocabulary, which may serve as a delineating criterion for elites as well as for lower social strata. A related point are differences in cultural capital and certain attached behavioural patterns (habitus) that form the core of Bourdieu's approach to social inequality.[52] Other standard signals directly relate to financial and real wealth, such as expensive consumption or leisure habits. In the longer run, a classical mechanism of group stabilisation is marriage: While limits on out-group marriage have been a key institutional element of most traditional societies, a modern counterpart is the assortative mating of partners with similar socio-economic, in particular, human capital, backgrounds, which can exacerbate the process of divergent capital accumulation.[53] The same is true for the intergenerational transmission of individual vocations and professional specialisations, sometimes dubbed as the emergence of microclasses.[54]

Homophilous group formation can be fostered by educational and spatial factors as well as group markers (e.g., cultural habits).

For group markers, see Chapter 8, section 3.3.

Important parts of vertical differentiation and signalling are mediated via markets and market pricing. This is straightforward for status goods but also relevant for cultural capital as far as its accumulation is related to costly activities, such as the attendance of expensive events. Furthermore, market mechanisms are crucial for geographical differentiation: In fact, the extent to which urban areas are split into vertically (and not just horizontally, in the sense of diverse) segregated areas is directly related to the cost of buying or renting real estate. Finally, as discussed previously, in many societies, the marriage market is not only a metaphor but taken quite literally, again tending to solidify social differentiation.

Vertical group differentiation can endogenously result from the market process.

There is a striking human capability to recognise social inequality as well as a tendency to internalise and adapt to it in social interaction.[55] Experiments show that humans can draw very quick and reliable conclusions on social status from observing traits, such as language, clothing, and habits of interaction. Also, interaction is connoted with emotional states; for example, communication between individuals from lower and higher social strata regularly invokes feelings of inferiority or anxiety in the former – which has been hypothesised, among others, to contribute to weaker performance in educational institutions but also to weaker career prospects of lower-class individuals in firms even when controlling for educational attainment.[56] Interaction between individuals of similar strata is more likely to be associated with positive elements, such as mutual trust, and eventually, reciprocal behaviour.

Humans have high capability in recognising and internalising differences in social status.

In sum, there are important behavioural propensities that may lead to a hardening of individual endowment differentials into group differences. A common hypothesis on market economies is that those identities will tend to lose importance due to the corrosive effect of structural change on established vertical groups, such as the aristocracy. However, we already showed that there are endogenous mechanisms that tend to stabilise the role of groups for market transactions.

A hardening of vertical group boundaries can diminish social mobility via divergent accumulation of social capital and imitation processes.

There are various mechanisms how group-based inequality can rise over time. One works via the accumulation of social capital, both in its collective and individually appropriable sense. With respect to the former, for example, the development of trust and bonding capital between elite members can increase their external agential power by reducing political and economic competition and, eventually, limiting potentials of network entry. Differences in individually appropriable social capital may be exacerbated by their effects on job market and career opportunities: As many studies have shown, the majority of positions in firms, particularly the higher hierarchical ranks, are not advertised in a publicly accessible way, rendering the role of network-based information flows crucial.[57] If social referrals on average provide a better source of information on productivity for employers than alternatives (such as formal education), then a divergent process of capital accumulation may be triggered even if initial differentials in individual social capital are small. Furthermore, obtaining a position higher up in a hierarchy augments the social status of the holder such that an increase in the number of social connections is obtainable at relatively low cost. Also, the occupation of a central structural position provides its holder with superior information about lower-ranked networks and, associated with that, a higher degree of control of these networks.[58] All these factors favour not only divergence in general but an accumulation of social capital with a limited group of high-status individuals.

For the role of group boundaries in market transactions, see Chapter 8, section 3.3.

Another class of mechanisms relates to imitation or, more generally, the adoption of practices that contribute to the (continued) accumulation of capital assets.[59] Here, inter-group inequality is exacerbated if initial groups are characterised by homophily and adoption exhibits local frequency dependency, that is, the probability of adoption is not only a function of individual endowments (whose initial differences may be small) but also of the extent to which other peers in the homophilous network have already adopted the practice.

For a discussion of elites and social status, see Chapter 8, section 3.2.

The contribution of those mechanisms to increasing inter-group inequality crucially depends on the assumptions drawn on the degree of homophily as well as the density of ties between vertical groups. For example, human capital externalities may contribute to divergence not only between groups but also on the level of regions (e.g., cities versus rural areas) and countries (via higher growth rates from social returns to education).[60] In contrast, they may also generate equalising effects, most importantly via labour markets (e.g., in terms of an increasing scarcity of low-skilled labour in urban areas) and firms (by enabling spillover effects from high-qualified to less-qualified staff).

4.4. Entrepreneurship and risk-taking

Entrepreneurship is a standard way to disrupt not only existing technological but also social structures, with a potentially lasting effect on structural inequality as well as the income distribution.

Entrepreneurial success involves a substantial element of idiosyncratic chance, which contributes to keeping markets fluid. This element tends to be exacerbated by modern communication technology: The superstar hypothesis posits that relatively minor initial differences in certain products, such as a song, can be massively amplified by frequency-dependent effects on the demand side enabled by technology, differentiating the average musician from the star.[61] However, there are individual and social circumstances that render entrepreneurial success more likely in the first place and are unequally distributed across the population.

Starting with individual traits, the psychological literature has identified relatively stable general personality dimensions that are strongly correlated with entrepreneurial behaviour and performance, in particular, self-efficacy, achievement motivation, persistent risk propensity, innovativeness, autonomy, as well as cognitive ability and creativity (as far as it is understood as an individual capacity).[62] Although there are studies showing significant heritable components of entrepreneurial behaviour, given its complexity, the more important link between entrepreneurship and interpersonal inequality appears to be established by systematic endowment differentials in social and real/financial capital.[63] The first and most obvious is related to the necessity of external finance, which not only is crucial with respect to the availability of resources in the first place but also influences risk tolerance. From this perspective, the efficiency and extent of venture capital finance constitutes an important element of country-level inequality regimes. The second is that the entrepreneurial capacity to fill structural holes will not only depend on individual characteristics but also on the amount of individual social capital, which in turn can be a function of vertical group differentiation as discussed in the previous section. Information and learning pertain to the transfer of expertise and experience, although there may, of course, be limits to informational exchange posed by competitive relationships. Finally, network-based learning and knowledge spillovers may also be embedded in specific entrepreneurial cultures, which can constitute a source of economic divergence between countries and regions but also ethnic groups.[64]

Overall, the relation between economic inequality and entrepreneurial activity appears to be ambiguous. On the one hand, entrepreneurship is a potential source of structural change and of upward social mobility. On the other hand, given that the prospect of entrepreneurial success varies along

On entrepreneurship, see Chapter 7, section 5.3; Chapter 11, section 5; and Chapter 16, section 5.

Entrepreneurial success involves idiosyncratic chance.

Attributes systematically related to entrepreneurial success are unequally distributed across the population.

On structural holes in networks, see Chapter 8, section 3.1.

differences in capital endowments, an entrepreneurial regime of inequality is not necessarily associated with more interpersonal equality or social mobility. In fact, extant studies show that higher shares of self-employment (a concept broader than, but still associated with, entrepreneurship) tend to go along with *higher* degrees of interpersonal inequality.[65] For example, particularly in poorer countries, more people have to resort to necessity entrepreneurship to make a living. Also, however, the mentioned insurance element of employment in firms will play a lesser role in such a regime, exposing a higher share of individuals to the vagaries of market development and business risk.

The relation between economic inequality and entrepreneurship is ambiguous.

5. Legitimacy and performativity of regimes of inequality

The legitimacy of inequality can be grounded in a wide array of narratives, ranging from the notion of a divine order to a meritocracy with a strict social ranking according to capability and effort.[66] Markets have traditionally been associated with a disruption of traditional social orders and a greater fluidity of social stratification. At the same time, as we have shown, a regularity of market competition is a pronounced inequality of outcomes – more pronounced than most people seem to prefer in smaller group settings. Still, a market-based allocation of resources as such seems to enjoy a high degree of popular acceptance in many countries.

The legitimacy of modern markets rests on a combination of the entrepreneurial element of chance associated with upward social mobility and the meritocratic ideal.

In modern markets, there are two main sources of the legitimacy of market-based inequality of outcomes. The first is acceptance for the chance element of market outcomes, particularly if, in specific cases, they imply very large discrepancies stemming from relatively minor initial differences, such as in the case of entrepreneurship or a star-based resource allocation. The second source is a perception that markets achieve at least a rough correspondence of capabilities and functionings, for example, that professional positions with a higher income profile entail e.g., more responsibility, expertise, or qualification requirements than those with a lower profile. This establishes a key link to a specific subjective notion of fairness, namely the idea of meritocracy.[67] In the last decades, the meritocratic ideal has become a widely accepted hallmark of the justification of inequality in the market sphere of Western democracies.[68] The meritocratic principle in modern market economies is intertwined with the evolution of intrafirm inequality regimes insofar as firms establish relatively stable, possibly bureaucratised, structures of intra-organisational inequality that are perceived as merit-based. In contrast, if intrafirm inequalities become dominated by power structures (section 2) and/or persistent patterns of external social stratification (section 3), this may contribute to a delegitimisation of the market system as a whole.

In Western democracies, a key underlying idea of accepting market-based inequality of outcomes is equality of opportunity. One possibility to concretise this principle is the distinction between circumstances and responsibilities.[69] Equality of opportunity would then be seen as established if inequality of outcomes can exclusively be attributed to responsibilities (i.e., to individual decisions and individual effort) and their consequences. However, the ensuing necessity of equalising circumstances raises serious problems; for example, from what point in individuals' biographies should equality of opportunity apply – in particular, should it only apply with the beginning of schooling (corresponding to the meritocratic idea that educational opportunity should be equally open to everyone) or at an earlier stage, that is, would equal opportunity imply active redistribution to make up for parental investment (e.g., in terms of time and educational effort) or even differential genetic endowments? This has immediate economic policy consequences; for example, the political left would traditionally take an expansive view on circumstances whereas the right would emphasise the responsibilities side.

Narratives are not only key contributors to the stabilisation or destabilisation of regimes of inequality, but they are also performative insofar as they pre-shape basic perceptions of the dimensions and levels of inequality and are, thereby, intimately linked to basic societal values. For example, some religious philosophies relate the notion of inequality primarily to subjective happiness and render the struggle for material differentiation entirely secondary. Marxian economics famously called for the development of class consciousness in order to make people aware of pervasive inequality and determine the objective interests of the working class vis-à-vis the capitalists.[70] In a similar vein, the feminist movement advocates the identification of females as a separate social group to be compared to males in terms of economic and social outcomes. There are various channels by which those movements eventually gained performative effects on Western market economies (and beyond). One is the definition a collective identity in line with the in-group–out-group mechanisms described in section 3 and the subsequent provision of a basis for collective mobilisation. Another very important channel is measurement: The 20th century concept of GDP includes a distributional pillar which allows for a statistical differentiation between labour and capital income, thus institutionalising the Marxist dichotomy at least to a certain extent. In a similar vein, modern measurement of economic activity increasingly differentiates between men and women, and includes areas traditionally regarded as a non-economic female realm.[71]

The performativity of the meritocratic narrative strongly relies on its inherently individualistic nature: Insofar as wages in a market economy roughly correspond to effort and capability which are believed to be in the realm of individual responsibility, subjective work incentives will partly be shaped by a prospect of upward mobility for everyone. This is why the degree of redistribution in democratic constituencies is generally lower than could be expected, despite the fact that medium income and wealth are regularly below their arithmetic means in market economies.[72] A case in point is the American dream as a

Equality of opportunity is a widely accepted legitimisation of inequality of outcomes, but its operationalisation is fraught with ambiguities.

On narratives, see Chapter 7, section 4.2.

The performativity of the meritocratic narrative with respect to the stabilisation of market economies depends on a credible prospect of upward social mobility.

stabilising factor of the comparatively high degree of income and wealth inequality that has been characteristic for the US economy since the 1970s. However, the American dream may also be an example of a narrative that is evolving,
with citizens updating their beliefs on social mobility as a consequence of perceived empirical change (falling social mobility)[73] and an increasing focus on
identity-based structural discrimination along gender and ethnicity.[74]

6. Conclusion

After taking a relatively marginalised position in economic theory and empirics
for a long time, the analysis of social and economic inequality in market economies has recently gained prominence. A key reason is that traditional policies
focused on market-based economic growth and development – as driven, for
example, by national and international market liberalisation and a stress on the
promotion of research and innovation – have not generated the expected results
in terms of more egalitarian resource distributions, for example, as a consequence of trickle-down effects. In our account, we have stressed the multidimensional character of inequality in two respects: On the one hand, there is the
co-evolution of different techno-institutional regimes of inequality, reaching
from firms to the international level; on the other hand, there is a concomitant
dynamic of structural-positional and interpersonal inequality. While the outcomes of this co-evolutionary process are in principle indeterminate, there are
inherent and intertwined forces on the structural-positional as well as interpersonal level that drive divergence between a minority of individuals and positions, and the rest of the regarded population. A certain degree of inequality may
be functional in terms of competitive success on the respective level: Firms
keep competitive in markets by productivity-based remuneration schemes in
interfirm competition; countries/jurisdictions attract labour and capital by putting limits on redistributional taxation and other policies. However, the sustainability of the respective regime crucially depends on its legitimacy, that is, a
broad acceptance of procedural rules and outcomes that at least prevents the
concerned population from effective collective action towards system change.

In this context, markets exhibit an ambiguous character. On the one hand, a
market-based allocation of different categories of resources and capital tends to
have disruptive effects on more traditional, static patterns of stratification and,
therefore, may generate an equalising effect. On the other hand, market competition inheres a tendency towards concentration both in terms of structures
(e.g., the distribution of firms/suppliers in a certain market) and individuals
(e.g., the concentration of wealth over generations). Moreover, the adherence of
market systems to a meritocratic ideal is incomplete at best, with a strong role
of sheer luck and possibly small discrepancies in initial conditions. Given this,
a key role of both stabilising distributional patterns and legitimising them in
terms of practicing an internal meritocratic ideal is played by firms. Thus, intra-
and interfirm market competition for resources is a driving force not only of
market competition in general but also for regimes of inequality.

Major chapter insights

- Social and economic inequality is a corollary of diversity and can be defined in a great variety of dimensions and on many levels. The choice of which dimensions and levels to focus on, which comparisons to draw, and which results to deem problematic and eventually prone to policy measures, is based on societal values.
- The traditional economic inequality measures of income and wealth are embedded into broader structures of inequality, as most prominently constituted by agential power, social capital and status, and human capital. This is subsumed as a regime of inequality.
- Regimes of inequality are located on different levels that co-evolve. Focusing on market-based inequality, intra- and interfirm subregimes can be distinguished. These are complemented on the political level by country-level and interjurisdictional regimes. In all regimes, there is an interrelated evolution of structural-positional inequality and interpersonal inequality, which, over time, manifests itself as individual mobility over the life cycle as well as intergenerational mobility.
- Country-level regimes of inequality are shaped by various categories of formal institutions determining the rules of the game of political and market competition. Intra- and interjurisdictional competition are linked insofar as the latter can put both upper and lower limits on the country-level inequality of resource distribution. The same logic holds for the relation between intra- and interfirm competition.
- The evolution of interpersonal inequality can be perceived as a path-dependent process in which different, including genetic, potentials are transformed into different categories of capital. These are translated into differential social and economic outcomes via the educational system, labour markets, intrafirm decision making processes, and the political process.
- The sustainability of market-based inequality depends on its legitimacy, defined as broad acceptance of procedures and outcomes relevant for the emergence and stabilisation of inequality. In modern market economies, core concepts legitimising market-based inequality are equality of opportunity, meritocracy, and a related expectation of social mobility. Markets are not inherently meritocratic since entrepreneurship entails a significant amount of luck. However, intrafirm regimes as well as public educational systems can eventually act as credible merit-based regimes.

Notes

1 This is a key argument on its own right for a transdisciplinary approach to the topic, which, however, remains rudimentary in practice. For an exception, see Piketty (2019).
2 Piketty (2013).
3 For example, OECD (2011).
4 One of the main critiques of Piketty (2013) pointed out that his presentation of the evolution of inequality of wealth did not take account of the distribution of human capital (Blume and Durlauf 2015).
5 Solon (2002).
6 For example, the OECD Better Life Index, see https://www.oecdbetterlifeindex. org/topics/life/satisfaction/.
7 For an extensive historical account, see Scheidel (2018).
8 Presently, those institutions exhibit remarkable variety even among countries with a democratic setup and comparable stage of economic and technological development. One widely discussed example is the evolution of top 1 percent income and wealth shares, see Alvaredo et al. (2013).
9 Dale (2018). However, the empirical relationship between economic growth and inequality is contested; see, for example, Chambers (2010).
10 This is a key tenet of the literature on the 'European Social Model(s)', see, for example, Sapir (2006); Weidenholzer and Aspalter (2008).
11 Piketty (2013).
12 Scheidel (2018), 5ff.
13 For example, Powell and DiMaggio (2012).
14 Cobb (2016); Piff et al. (2018).
15 Avent-Holt and Tomaskovic-Devey (2019).
16 Aoki (2010).
17 See, for an overview, Fligstein and Goldstein (2022).
18 Hannan (2005).
19 The classic source on this is Weber (1922/1985).
20 Avent-Holt and Tomaskovic-Devey (2019).
21 Podolny (2005).
22 Podolny (1993).
23 See, for a standard argument on the increasing scarcity of high-skilled labour, Goldin and Katz (2010).
24 For an overview, see Lazear (2018).
25 Avent-Holt and Tomaskovic-Devey (2019).
26 Avent-Holt and Tomaskovic-Devey (2019).
27 Cobb (2016).
28 Sugden (2018), chapter 8; Hayek (1976), 70ff.
29 Seminally, Chandler (1962).
30 For example, Sacerdote (2002).
31 See, for example, Murray (2020), 210 ff.

32 For example, Pfeifer (2012).

33 For example, Funk (2013).

34 See, for an overview of the recent state of art, Sternberg (2018) and Floyd et al. (2021).

35 Murray (2020), 231 ff; Ones et al. (2012); Gensowski (2018); Strenze (2015).

36 For example, Hunt (1995), Neisser et al. (1996).

37 Herrnstein and Murray (1994), part I; Young (1958); Young (2020).

38 Downes and Matthews (2020); Danchin et al. (2019).

39 Simonton (2005).

40 Deary et al. (2009); Sternberg (2020).

41 Plomin (2018), chapters 3 and 4.

42 For example, with respect to vocabulary; Piff et al. (2018).

43 See, for a case study of market-oriented school segregation, Valenzuela et al. (2014). However, the decisive influence of educational segregation is contested by a school arguing for the importance of genetic potentials; Plomin (2018).

44 See, for a discussion, Plomin (2018), Chapter 9.

45 For example, Juhn (1999).

46 Seminally, Spence (1974).

47 Markovits (2019), 71ff.

48 Piketty (2013).

49 See, for this, Kaplan and Rauh (2013); for a general theoretical overview, Edmans et al. (2017).

50 See, for a comprehensive survey of those effects, DiMaggio and Garip (2012).

51 Dacin et al. (2010); for an overview, see van Zanten (2010).

52 See, for an empirical application to the recruitment of German CEOs, Hartmann (1996).

53 For example, Greenwood et al. (2014).

54 Jonsson et al. (2009).

55 Piff et al. (2018).

56 Pitesa and Pillutla (2019).

57 For example, Beaman and Magruder (2012).

58 Lin (1999).

59 DiMaggio and Garip (2012).

60 For example, Moretti (2004).

61 Seminally, Rosen (1981).

62 Frese and Gielnik (2014).

63 Anderson and Miller (2003).

64 See, for example, Stuetzer et al. (2018).

65 Lippmann et al. (2005).

66 Young (1958).

67 Historically, the meritocratic ethic has been primarily related to the military and public sphere, but it has also been associated to the market sphere in cultural terms. Weber (1905/2010).

68 Markovits (2019); Young (2020).

69 Roemer (2012); Roemer and Trannoy (2016).
70 Carvacho and Alvaréz (2019); Lukács (1972).
71 Compare, for example, the Gender Data Portals run by the OECD (www.oecd.
org) and the World Bank (https://genderdata.worldbank.org). Another example is
the emerging practice of gender budgeting, see Alonso-Albarran et al. (2021).
72 Putterman (1997); Benabou and Ok (2001).
73 Piketty (1995).
74 For an overview from an economic perspective, see Bohren et al. (2022).

References

Alonso-Albarran, V. *et al.* (2021) 'Gender Budgeting in G-20 Countries', *IMF Working Paper*, 2021(269).

Alvaredo, F. *et al.* (2013) 'The Top 1 Percent in International and Historical Perspective', *Journal of Economic Perspectives*, 27(3), pp. 3–20. DOI: 10.1257/jep.27.3.3.

Anderson, A. R. and Miller, C. J. (2003) '"Class Matters": Human and Social Capital in the Entrepreneurial Process', *Journal of Socio-Economics*, 32, pp. 17–36. DOI: 10.1016/S1053-5357(03)00009-X.

Aoki, M. (2010) *Corporations in Evolving Diversity: Cognition, Governance, and Institutions*. Oxford: Oxford University Press. DOI: 10.1093/acprof:oso/9780199218530.001.0001.

Avent-Holt, D. and Tomaskovic-Devey, D. (2019) 'Organizations as the Building Blocks of Social Inequalities', *Sociology Compass*, 13(2), e12655.

Beaman, L. and Magruder, J. (2012) 'Who Gets the Job Referral? Evidence from a Social Networks Experiment', *American Economic Review*, 102(7), pp. 3574–3593. DOI: 10.1257/aer.102.7.3574.

Benabou, R. and Ok, E. A. (2001) 'Social Mobility and the Demand for Redistribution: The POUM Hypothesis', *The Quarterly Journal of Economics*, 116(2), pp. 447–487. DOI: 10.1162/00335530151144078.

Blume, L. E. and Durlauf, S. N. (2015) 'Capital in the Twenty-First Century: A Review Essay', *Journal of Political Economy*, 123(4), pp. 749–777.

Bohren, J. A., Hull, P. and Imas, A. (2022) 'Systemic Discrimination: Theory and Measurement', *National Bureau of Economic Research (NBER) Working Paper*, 29820. DOI: 10.3386/w29820.

Carvacho, H. and Alvaréz, B. (2019) 'Inequality and Class Consciousness', in Jetten, J. and Peters, K. (eds.) *The Social Psychology of Inequality*. Cham: Springer, pp. 333–348. DOI: 10.1007/978-3-030-28856-3_19.

Chambers, D. (2010) 'Does a Rising Tide Raise all Ships? The Impact of Growth on Inequality', *Applied Economics Letters*, 17(6), pp. 581–586. DOI: 10.1080/13504850802046971.

Chandler, A. (1962) *Strategy and Structure: Chapters in the History of the American Industrial Enterprise*. Cambridge: MIT Press.

Cobb, A. J. (2016) 'How Firms Shape Income Inequality: Stakeholder Power, Executive Decision Making, and the Structuring of Employment Relationships', *Academy of Management Review*, 41(2), pp. 324–348. DOI: 10.5465/amr.2013.0451.

Dacin, M. T., Munir, K. and Tracey, P. (2010) 'Formal Dining at Cambridge Colleges: Linking Ritual Performance and Institutional Maintenance', *Academy of Management Journal,* 53(6), pp. 1393–1418.

Dale, G. (2018) 'A Rising Tide Lifts Us All; Don't Rock the Boat! Economic Growth and the Legitimation of Inequality', in Fagan, G. H. and Munck, R. (eds.) *Handbook on Development and Social Change.* Cheltenham and Northampton: Edward Elgar Publishing, pp. 151–170. DOI: 10.4337/9781786431554.

Danchin, É., Pocheville, A. and Huneman, P. (2019) 'Early in Life Effects and Heredity: Reconciling Neo-Darwinism with Neo-Lamarckism under the Banner of the Inclusive Evolutionary Synthesis', *Philosophical Transactions of the Royal Society*, B 374, p. 20180113. DOI: 10.1098/rstb.2018.0113.

Deary, I. J., Whalley, L. J. and Starr, J. M. (2009) *A Lifetime of Intelligence: Follow-up Studies of the Scottish Mental Surveys of 1932 and 1947.* Washington, DC: American Psychological Association.

DiMaggio, P. and Garip, F. (2012) 'Network Effects and Social Inequality', *Annual Review of Sociology*, 38, pp. 93–118. DOI: 10.1146/annurev.soc.012809.102545.

Downes, S. M. and Matthews, L. (2020) 'Heritability', *The Stanford Encyclopedia of Philosophy,* Spring 2020 Edition. Available at: https://plato.stanford.edu/archives/spr2020/entries/heredity/ (Accessed: 18 March 2022).

Edmans, A., Gabaix, X. and Jenter, D. (2017) 'Executive Compensation: A Survey of Theory and Evidence', in Hermalin, B. E. and Weisbach, M. S. (eds.) *The Handbook of the Economics of Corporate Governance*, *1*. Amsterdam: North-Holland, pp. 383–539. DOI: 10.1016/bs.hecg.2017.11.010.

Fligstein, N. and Goldstein, A. (2022) 'The Legacy of Shareholder Value Capitalism', *Annual Review of Sociology*, 48. DOI: 10.1146/annurev-soc-030420-120827.

Floyd, R. G. *et al.* (2021) 'Theories and Measurement of Intelligence', in Glidden, L. M. *et al.* (eds.) *APA Handbook of Intellectual and Developmental Disabilities: Foundations.* Washington, DC: American Psychological Association, pp. 385–424. DOI: 10.1037/0000194-015.

Frese, M. and Gielnik, M. M. (2014) 'The Psychology of Entrepreneurship', *Annual Review of Organizational Psychology and Organizational Behavior,* 1, pp. 413–438. DOI: 10.1146/annurev-orgpsych-031413-091326.

Funk, C. L. (2013) 'Genetic Foundations of Political Behavior', in Huddy, L. *et al.* (eds.) *Oxford Handbook of Political Psychology, Second Edition.* Oxford: Oxford University Press, pp. 237–261. DOI: 10.1093/oxfordhb/9780199760107.013.0008.

Gensowski, M. (2018) 'Personality, IQ, and Lifetime Earnings', *Labour Economics*, 51, pp. 170–183. DOI: 10.1016/j.labeco.2017.12.004.

Goldin, C. and Katz, L. F. (2010) *The Race Between Education and Technology*. Harvard: Harvard University Press.

Greenwood, J. *et al.* (2014) 'Marry Your Like: Assortative Mating and Income Inequality', *American Economic Review*, 104(5), pp. 348–353. DOI: 10.1257/aer.104.5.348.

Hannan, M. T. (2005) 'Ecologies of Organizations: Diversity and Identity', *Journal of Economic Perspectives*, 19(1), pp. 51–70.

Hartmann, M. (1996) *Topmanager: Die Rekrutierung einer Elite*. Frankfurt and New York: Campus.

Hayek, F. A. von (1976) *Law, Legislation and Liberty – Volume 2: The Mirage of Social Justice*. London: Routledge.

Herrnstein, R. J. and Murray, C. (1994) *The Bell Curve: Intelligence and Class Structure in American Life*. New York: Free Press.

Hunt, E. (1995) *Will We Be Smart Enough? A Cognitive Analysis of the Coming Workforce*. New York: Russell Sage Foundation.

Jonsson, J. O. *et al.* (2009) 'Microclass Mobility: Social Reproduction in Four Countries', *American Journal of Sociology*, 114(4), pp. 977–1036. DOI: 10.1086/596566.

Juhn, C. (1999) 'Wage Inequality and Demand for Skill: Evidence from Five Decades', *ILR Review*, 52(3), pp. 424–443. DOI: 10.1177%2F001979399905200304.

Kaplan, S. N. and Rauh, J. (2013) 'It's the Market: The Broad-Based Rise in the Return to Top Talent', *Journal of Economic Perspectives*, 27(3), pp. 35–56. DOI: 10.1257/jep.27.3.35.

Lazear, E. P. (2018) 'Compensation and Incentives in the Workplace', *Journal of Economic Perspectives*, 32(3), pp. 195–214.

Lin, N. (1999) 'Social Networks and Status Attainment', *Annual Review of Sociology*, 25(1), pp. 467–487. DOI: 10.1146/annurev.soc.25.1.467.

Lippmann, S., Davis, A. and Aldrich, H. E. (2005) 'Entrepreneurship and Inequality', in Keister, L. A. (ed.) *Entrepreneurship (Research in the Sociology of Work, Vol. 15)*. Bingley: Emerald Group Publishing Limited, pp. 3–31. DOI: 10.1016/S0277-2833(05)15002-X.

Lukács, G. (1972) *History and Class Consciousness: Studies in Marxist Dialectics*. Cambridge: MIT Press.

Markovits, D. (2019) *The Meritocracy Trap*. London: Penguin Books.

Moretti, E. (2004) 'Human Capital Externalities in Cities', in Vernon Henderson, J. and Thisse, J.-F. (eds.) *Handbook of Regional and Urban Economics, Vol. 4*. Amsterdam: Elsevier, pp. 2243–2291. DOI: 10.1016/S1574-0080(04)80008-7.

Murray, C. (2020) *Human Diversity – the Biology of Gender, Race, and Class*. New York and Boston: Twelve.

Neisser, U. *et al.* (1996) 'Intelligence: Knowns and Unknowns', *American Psychologist*, 51(2), pp. 77–101. DOI: 10.1037/0003-066X.51.2.77.

OECD (2011) *Divided We Stand – Why Inequality Keeps Rising*. OECD: Paris.

OECD (2022a) 'Better Life Index', *OECD Better Life Index*. Available at: https://www.oecdbetterlifeindex.org/topics/life-satisfaction/ (Accessed: 06 May 2022).

OECD (2022b) 'Gender Equality', *OECD*. Available at: https://www.oecd.org/gender/data/ (Accessed: 06 May 2022).

Ones, D. S. *et al.* (2012) 'Cognitive Abilities', in Schmitt, N. (ed.) *The Oxford Handbook of Personnel Assessment and Selection*. Oxford: Oxford University Press.

Pfeifer, C. (2012) 'Physical Attractiveness, Employment and Earnings', *Applied Economics Letters*, 19(6), pp. 505–510. DOI: 10.1080/13504851.2011.587758.

Piff, P. K., Kraus, M. W. and Keltner, D. (2018) 'Unpacking the Inequality Paradox: The Psychological Roots of Inequality and Social Class', in Olson, J. M. (ed.) *Advances in Experimental Social Psychology, Volume 57*. Amsterdam: Elsevier, pp. 53–124. DOI: 10.1016/bs.aesp.2017.10.002.

Piketty, T. (1995) 'Social Mobility and Redistributive Politics', *The Quarterly Journal of Economics*, 110(3), pp. 551–584. DOI: 10.2307/2946692.

Piketty, T. (2013) *Le Capital au XXIe Siècle*. Paris: Seuil.

Piketty, T. (2019) *Capital et Idéologie*. Paris: Seuil.

Pitesa, M. and Pillutla, M. (2019) 'Socioeconomic Mobility and Talent Utilization of Workers from Poorer Backgrounds: The Overlooked Importance of Within-Organization Dynamics', *Academy of Management Annals*, 13(2), pp. 737–769. DOI: 10.5465/annals.2017.0115.

Plomin, R. (2018) *Blueprint – How DNA Makes Us Who We Are*. Boston: Allen Lane.

Podolny, J. M. (1993) 'A Status-Based Model of Market Competition', *American Journal of Sociology*, 98(4), pp. 829–872.

Podolny, J. M. (2005) *Status Signals: A Sociological Study of Market Competition*. Princeton and Oxford: Princeton University Press.

Powell, W. W. and DiMaggio, P. J. (eds.) (2012). *The New Institutionalism in Organizational Analysis*. Chicago: University of Chicago Press.

Putterman, L. (1997) 'Why Have the Rabble not Redistributed the Wealth? On the Stability of Democracy and Unequal Property', in Roemer, J. E. (ed.) *Property Relations, Incentives and Welfare*. London: Palgrave Macmillan, pp. 359–393. DOI: 10.1007/978-1-349-25287-9_13.

Roemer, J. E. (2012) 'On Several Approaches to Equality of Opportunity', *Economics & Philosophy*, 28(2), pp. 165–200. DOI: 10.1017/S0266267112000156.

Roemer, J. E. and Trannoy, A. (2016) 'Equality of Opportunity: Theory and Measurement', *Journal of Economic Literature*, 54(4), pp. 1288–1332. DOI: 10.1257/jel.20151206.

Rosen, S. (1981) 'The Economics of Superstars', *American Economic Review*, 71(5), pp. 845–858.

Sacerdote, B. (2002) 'The Nature and Nurture of Economic Outcomes', *American Economic Review*, 92(2), pp. 344–348. DOI: 10.1257/000282802320191589.

Sapir, A. (2006) 'Globalization and the Reform of European Social Models', *JCMS: Journal of Common Market Studies*, 44(2), pp. 369–390. DOI: 10.1111/j.1468-5965.2006.00627.x.

Scheidel, W. (2018) *The Great Leveler*. Princeton: Princeton University Press.

Simonton, D. K. (2005) 'Putting the Gift Back into Giftedness: The Genetics of Talent Development', *Gifted and Talented International*, 20(1), pp. 15–18. DOI: 10.1080/15332276.2005.11673053.

Solon, G. (2002) 'Cross-Country Differences in Intergenerational Earnings Mobility', *Journal of Economic Perspectives*, 16(3), pp. 59–66. DOI: 10.1257/089533002760278712.

Spence, M. (1974) *Market Signaling: Informational Transfer in Hiring and Related Screening Processes*. Cambridge: Harvard University Press.

Sternberg, R. J. (ed.) (2018) *The Nature of Human Intelligence*. Cambridge: Cambridge University Press. DOI: 10.1017/9781316817049.

Sternberg, R. J. (2020) *The Nature of Intelligence and its Development in Childhood*. Cambridge: Cambridge University Press. DOI: 10.1017/9781108866217.

Strenze, T. (2015) 'Intelligence and Success', in Goldstein, S., Princiotta, D. and Naglieri, J. A. (eds.) *Handbook of Intelligence: Evolutionary Theory, Historical Perspective, and Current Concepts*. New York: Springer, pp. 405–413. DOI: 10.1007/978-1-4939-1562-0_25.

Stuetzer, M. *et al.* (2018) 'Entrepreneurship Culture, Knowledge Spillovers and the Growth of Regions', *Regional Studies*, 52(5), pp. 608–618. DOI: 10.1080/00343404.2017.1294251.

Sugden, R. (2018) *The Community of Advantage: A Behavioural Economist's Defence of the Market*. Oxford: Oxford University Press. DOI: 10.1093/oso/9780198825142.001.000.

Valenzuela, J. P., Bellei, C. and Ríos, D. D. L. (2014) 'Socioeconomic School Segegation in a Market-Oriented Educational System: The Case of Chile', *Journal of Education Policy*, 29(2), pp. 217–241. DOI: 10.1080/02680939.2013.806995.

Van Zanten, A. (2010) 'The Sociology of Elite Education', in Apple, S. B, Ball, S. J. and Gandin, L. A. (eds.) *The Routledge International Handbook of the Sociology of Education*. London and New York: Routledge, pp. 329–339.

Weber, M. (1905/2010) *Die protestantische Ethik und der Geist des Kapitalismus, Herausgegeben und eingeleitet von Dirk Kaesler, 3. Auflage*. München: C.H. Beck.

Weber, M. (1985 [1922b]) *Wirtschaft und Gesellschaft, Studienausgabe, 8. Auflage*. Tübingen: Mohr.

Weidenholzer, J. and Aspalter, C. (2008) 'The American and the European Social Dream: The Competition of Welfare Regimes', *Journal of Comparative Social Welfare*, 24(1), pp. 3–11. DOI: 10.1080/17486830701848662.

World Bank (2022) 'Gender Data Portal', *The World Bank*. Available at: https://genderdata.worldbank.org (Accessed: 06 May 2022).

Young, M. (1958) *The Rise of the Meritocracy 1870–2033: An Essay on Education and Society*. London: Thames and Hudson.

Young, T. (2020) 'The Rise of the Genotocracy', *The Political Quarterly*, 91(2), pp. 388–396. DOI: 10.1111/1467-923X.12831.

CHAPTER SIXTEEN

Global economic growth in the Earth system

1. Introduction

This chapter explores economic growth. We approach growth primarily as a physical and biological phenomenon, with growth of economic value only playing a secondary role. In doing so, we tackle one of the most challenging economic issues of our times: So far, growth of economic value goes along with serious damage to the biosphere and future generations of humans. However, we do not share the position of many ecological economists of discarding GDP as a measure of economic activity[1]: GDP does measure an important aspect of growth as mediated and enacted by markets, that is, what is valued in the second-person view. Overall, we must strike a proper balance between different perspectives on growth.

The distinction between pre-modern and modern growth is commonly defined in terms of growth of per-capita value added:[2] Pre-modern growth is essentially constituted by population growth, with almost no improvements of average biological indicators apart from small elites that appropriate a disproportionally large share of economic output. Modern growth is defined by growth of output and value added per capita, and goes along with the demographic transition which implies a reduction of the rate of population growth.[3] Against this background, we interpret GDP in terms of the growth of markets. This is implicit to national income conventions since they directly relate value added to market pricing.[4] GDP growth, in turn, can be seen as growth of complexity in the sense that market growth implies growth of the division of labour in society.[5] This is manifest in the growth of types of products as well as of production chains. Growth of markets also means the growth of possible choices in the first-person view. This suggests that economic growth should not mainly be seen as a reflection of material conditions but as growth of the state space of individual choice, as measured, for example, by the available (rather than factually acquired) variety of goods.[6] This interpretation directly reflects valuation in terms of individual freedom, as freedom expands via the growing complexity of alternatives for individual choices.

We approach growth primarily in material terms and secondarily in value terms.

On growth as a physical and biological phenomenon, see Chapter 4, section 2.3.

Pre-modern growth is population growth without growth of average GDP per capita; modern growth is growth of average GDP per capita, recently combined with a decline of population growth rate.

On the limits of GDP as a measure of production, see Chapter 6, section 3.1.

421

DOI: 10.4324/9781003094869-21

The chapter proceeds as follows. In section 2, we present a bird's-eye view on the growth of the human economy. Section 3 looks at the growth of the technosphere as core phenomenon in a materialist conception of growth, which we combine with the growth of population. The two perspectives are inherently connected as the technosphere is defining the human niche and, hence, enables the expansion of the human species. Section 3 explores the central role of energy in enabling growth, including growth of information. Section 4 analyses markets as drivers of growth. Section 5 discusses the distinction between anthropocentric and geocentric conceptions of growth and consequences for valuation.

2. The evolution of the human economy

Economic growth unfolded in three stages: pre-agrarian, agrarian, and industrial.

In simplest terms, we can distinguish between three stages of the evolution of the human economy (Figure 16.1): the pre-agrarian, the agrarian, and the industrial.[7] We can relate these stages to transitions in the functions of markets. In the pre-agrarian stage, markets were marginal since reciprocal social exchange (gift, barter, loans, etc.) was the dominant form of transactions. In the agricultural stage, markets expanded considerably, first in long-distance trade and then increasingly on the local level (China was our case study). In the industrial stage, markets became the dominant form of organising the economy, with concomitant growth in the size of government. Historically, non-market economies or planned economies had existed in various forms, such as in Ancient Egypt, but did not persist. The 20th century even saw a systemic competition between newly founded socialist planned economies and market economies. Yet these were dismantled or transformed into market economies, as in the case of China.

The pre-agrarian stage continued with production methods common to animals (foraging) but deployed the human capacity for culture in enabling niche construction with wide scope and variety, thus driving the global spread of the human species.

The pre-agrarian economy relied on harvesting resources in the same way all living systems do, such as by hunting and gathering as forms of human foraging. However, humans could exploit their capacity for culture already at this stage, launching the primordial stage of technosphere evolution: First, humans were extremely flexible in adapting to various environments via culturally transmitted features, which vastly enhanced the space for migration. Human populations live in highly diverse ecological niches, compared to the rigid specialisation of most animals, and they can adapt to changing conditions with much higher speed. This enabled the global spread of human populations.[8] Second, humans could develop specific skills for cooperating in groups, mediated by language and symbolic behaviour, and leveraging genetically endowed cognitive capacities of mind reading.[9] These behavioural innovations created substantial competitive advantages for humans over other animals, especially large ones, leading to a wave of mass extinctions via complex forms of group hunting that were technologically leveraged by early tools and weapons, such as spears.[10] Human groups evolved an internal

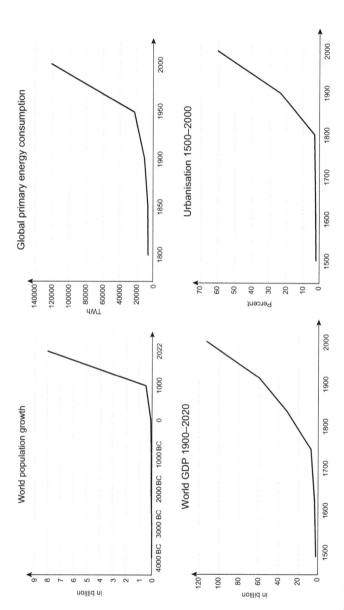

Figure 16.1 Economic growth in the long run

The four diagrams present a bird's-eye view on economic growth in various dimensions and time frames. The growth of world population is a long-term process that was sped up by industrialisation but also took off in non-industrial societies such as Imperial China. Urbanisation was launched by industrialisation and stalled in non-industrialised countries. Energy and GDP manifest the pattern of the Great Acceleration in the 20th century.

The legacy of
this period is
embodied in
the social brain,
Chapter 7,
section 3.

The theoretical
significance
of this
specialisation
on violence
was explored
in Chapter 5,
section 3.2,
and Chapter 9,
section 5.3.

*The agrarian
stage features the
co-evolution of
humans and other
living systems, partly
driven by cultural
design and enabled
the production of
surplus that could
be invested in the
formation of capital
and larger-scale
socio-political units.*

division of labour in producing joint activities and output, in particular, the gendered division of labour and the division of expertise in dealing with hunting.[11] This division of labour was associated with a relatively egalitarian social structure; yet there was a high incidence of inter-group conflict and violence.[12]

The slow growth of human populations triggered the transition to agriculture in the BCE millennia in different areas, such as the Fertile Crescent in the Middle East and Yellow River in China. Thus, a new ecological niche was created, based on the co-evolution of humans and other living systems, especially plants.[13] Humans developed the cultural capacity for artificial selection, which resulted in the emergence of large populations of domesticated animals and plants that depend on humans for their survival.[14] Co-evolution mainly relates with cultural evolution of humans and genetic evolution of plants and animals, but there are also aspects of genetic co-evolution (the most well known being lactose intolerance of certain human populations[15]). The most important intermediate form between the pre-agrarian and the agrarian ideal types is nomadism, which based on conviviality of humans and herds of animals, defining distinct ecological niches that separate nomadic peoples and agriculturalists (this shaped Chinese history over millennia and still drives ethnic conflicts in Africa).[16] Agriculture is a complex social technology that allows for a much more intensive exploitation of solar energy via photosynthesis, including the generation of partly artificial food chains (e.g., growing fodder for husbandry). Large-scale agrarian economies went hand in hand with the emergence of hierarchical state organisation and steep social stratification between ruling elites and producers (peasants). Stratification was conditioned by the emerging surplus from agricultural production that could be appropriated by investing into means of violence.[17] The division of labour became more complex, especially with regard to the production of goods for elite needs (luxury, policing, architecture, etc.). The gendered division of labour was further pronounced.[18]

Turning to the industrial stage, the fundamental distinction between agriculture and industry is that the former feeds on the continuous flow of solar energy into the Earth system whereas the latter exploits and depletes stocks of solar energy stored in fossils.[19] These stocks enabled the exponential growth of energy throughputs in the past three centuries. The carbon economy still dominates the world, with other energy sources, mainly nuclear energy and renewables, remaining marginal.[20] The industrial economy supports the technological transformation of agriculture, first by new inputs such as artificial fertilisers and the whole range of agrotechnology, and more recently in the development of biotechnological forms of directly intervening in the genetic information of plants and animals. The industrial economy was combined with the emergence of capitalism as an institutionalised form of the division of labour organised via markets and firms, and the diffusion of participatory forms of government which diminished the all-encompassing role of social and political hierarchies in society. Gradually, the gendered division of labour has been retreating, with women entering the formal workforce of the industrial economy. Capitalism manifests the combination of growth of markets and of energy throughputs enabled by technological progress, reflected by the growth of GDP per capita. However, a persistent feature of capitalist growth is the divergence of per-capita GDP across world regions (both across countries and within countries).[21]

Another important difference between the industrial society and the agricultural economy lies in their distinct forms of information generation and transmission. The agricultural economy mainly builds on the transmission of information via oral traditions and practices; only few traditional societies, such as China, developed forms of written information transmission, such as via pamphlets describing agro-technologies distributed by the government. In contrast, industrial economies build on the systematic exploration and storage of written information, most importantly via the social system of science.[22] Although in the field of engineering, there is also a certain role of routines and practices; most knowledge is transmitted via symbolic media of storage. Further, technological artefacts become indirect transmitters and storages of information in fundamentally shaping the niche in which humans live today. This role of formal information processing also shapes economic activities: The industrial economy is based on comprehensive and complex forms of quantifying economic activity (i.e., accounting in the wide sense).[23] In the agrarian economy, economic valuation was limited to specific areas, especially long-distance trade and surplus production above subsistence production in the peasant economy, which, however, was mostly extracted via taxation and forced labour.

The industrial society was originally confined to certain world areas and was combined with a colonial system of agricultural production that had emerged in the 16th century: European countries, and then the United States, became industrial economies as parts of a global division of labour that assigned most other countries to the role of agricultural production bases, such as the plantation economies of Latin America.[24] Given that this development resulted in stark asymmetries of wealth and military power, from the late 19th century onwards, many countries pursued government-led industrialisation strategies, starting with Russia and Japan, and followed by many others after decolonisation, especially after World War II. As a result, the industrial economy has spread to most regions of the world, with the exception of less and least developed countries, such as in Sub-Saharan Africa, which are still mainly agricultural economies. However, many agricultural economies are locations of rich deposits of natural resources, thus combining traditional or even subsistence agriculture with strong resource extraction industries.

Until today, the industrial stage is shaped by the exponential growth of fossil-fuelled energetic throughputs, resulting in divergent growth of per-capita GDP across the globe.

The industrial and the agrarian stage differ in terms of media and means of information processing and transmission.

On the knowledge structure of technology, see Chapter 6, section 3. On the fundamental performative role of accounting for money-based market economies, see Chapter 10, section 2.2, and Chapter 12, section 3.3.

After the age of colonialism, industrial society was further spread by government-led catch-up development in many parts of the world.

3. Economic growth and the technosphere

The standard neoclassical model of economic growth explains growth as the reflection of savings that are channelled into investment up to the point where investment equals depreciation.[25] Until this point is reached, the per-capita stock of capital, and hence the per-capita GDP, will grow. In this model, the only source of continuous growth is exogenous productivity growth driven by information or knowledge generation, namely technological progress. Modern growth theory has advanced in endogenising growth of knowledge via assuming endogenous generation of positive externalities of knowledge creation and human capital formation but keeps the basic modelling approach.[26]

Positive externalities are the central concept relating economic growth theory to the notion of the technosphere. The pertinent empirical phenomenon is the growth of cities. Cities are an indispensable aspect of technosphere growth; at the same time, they constitute the key spatial configurations for generating and sustaining positive externalities of knowledge production (Figures 16.1 and 16.2).[27] Therefore, cities are crucial for understanding economic growth.

Cities are the key spatial configuration generating positive externalities of knowledge production that drives economic growth of markets.

The neoclassical growth model suggests that economic activities disperse in space as a consequence of diseconomies of agglomeration. Those diseconomies are reflected, among others, in the necessary build-up of a capital stock that counters them, such as infrastructure for water and wastewater management. However, cities also feature growing returns to scale in essential domains. Their primary manifestation are network effects in social interaction, relating to the generation of information.[28] Via spatial proximity, cities allow for superlinear growth of network connections and of opportunities for generating new combinations of existing information. Together with higher diffusion speed, this drives the ongoing urbanisation of human ways of life, reaching to growth of megacities via enhanced agglomeration.[29]

Positive agglomeration economies outweigh negative effects, with superlinear productivity of social network generating knowledge growth as key factor.

Regional economics has shown many ways these effects work out, such as via the intensifying flow of people between firms.[30] As a result, the growth of cities can take a hyperbolic form, such as in the extremely rapid growth of megacities in China in the past three decades.[31] Yet important material aspects of urban infrastructure do not manifest increasing returns, such as transport networks or water and waste disposal networks. Therefore, urban growth takes various forms which mix agglomeration effects and dispersal, such as manifested in suburbanisation. The growth of cities is a core driver of CO_2 emissions in the global economy, in particular, via the production of steel and cement. This shows how urbanisation and technosphere growth are closely related.

These patterns differ from biosphere growth patterns, see Chapter 4, section 2.3.

There are important indicators demonstrating the close congruence of material growth of cities and economic growth; for example, the strong correlation of lighting and GDP growth.[32] Lighting is an important aspect of the human niche in the technosphere; it decouples human activities from the circadian circle as determined by nature. Another example is the role of heating

Figure 16.2 Share of urban population in world population (2018)
The diagram shows that in the more developed regions of the world, the majority of population lives in urban areas. This trend continues in less developed regions as they further grow.
Source: https://commons.wikimedia.org/wiki/File:Urbanized_population_2018.png
(Credit: Wikignuthor)

and cooling. In case of lighting, the correlation with GDP can be explained by two-directional causality: More lighting expands the time available for productive activities and social encounters, and intensification of these drives demand for more lighting. Today, about 16 percent of total electricity consumption is driven by lighting, and energy savings did not result in slowing down the absolute growth of energy for lighting.[33]

Technosphere growth is driven by the growth of artefacts. Even though miniaturisation is often emphasised, drivers of growth include the growth of mass of single units. Salient examples include the difference in the mass of slum dwellings compared to a middle-class home which is equipped by all amenities of modern urban life or the increasing mass of cars.[34] This puts the emphasis on consumer society in degrowth scenarios into perspective, considering the fact that in less developed countries, urbanisation proceeds mainly via the formation of slums and other substandard dwellings.[35]

Technosphere growth materialises via the growth of mass of types of artefacts.

As mentioned, one method that allows for a quantification of the relationship between economic growth and technosphere growth is material flows analysis (MFA). MFA allows to calculate material intensities of GDP growth, which exhibit large variety such as in the case of structural change towards services. Urbanisation is extremely material intensive; therefore, China has been leading the world in the consumption of steel and cement in recent decades. In all cases, however, the relationship between economic growth and the technosphere can only be assessed on the global level due to interdependencies; for example, structural change towards services can go hand in hand with the relocation of material intensive production to other countries.[36] MFA data do not cover this today. Yet in principle, we can indirectly measure the growth of the technosphere as a material stock fed by input flows and subtracting waste.[37]

On MFA see
Chapter 6,
section 2.2.

On the aggregate and global level, we can speak of the growth of technomass, corresponding to the growth of biomass in the biosphere. The measure is physical growth of the technosphere, that is, of all artefacts that relate to the human economy including substantial parts of the biosphere, such as managed forests or animal husbandry. Depending on the measurement approach, the technomass has grown beyond the biomass in the early 2020s and certainly will surpass it in 2040.[38]

4. Energy and limits to growth

The correlation of energy consumption and economic growth has been scrutinised by many studies. Results are mixed and depend on the period and region considered.[39] However, in the long run, the stage of industrialisation features an important role of both technological progress and the growth of energy throughputs, where the latter is often driven by technological advances in harnessing and utilising energy.

However, most of this (econometric) research faces a deep methodological issue. In the standard growth theory framework, energy does not have theoretical status but just constitutes one input factor necessary for production; in models with high levels of abstraction which only consider capital, labour, and technology, energy as an input becomes implicit altogether.[40] This approach implies that energy is substitutable by other production factors, in particular, by technological progress embodied in capital: The more advanced the capital stock, the looser the correlation between energy and growth, which is advanced as the hypothesis of decoupling.[41]

The methodological stance of the thermodynamic perspective developed in this book is entirely different: Energy is a universal factor of production and, hence, cannot be substituted at all. For example, capital cannot substitute energy because the production of capital also involves energy inputs. This is captured by the concept of embodied energy which is a full energetic account of all intermediary energetic transformations of a specific artefact. For example, the embodied energy of a smartphone must include energy use of the production of all inputs, such as chips.[42] The embodied energy of a packed cheese is not the caloric content indicated as nutritional value but the entire energetic input needed to make it available to the consumer, such as the energy in producing the packaging, in transporting it from factory to shop, and in its agro-industrial processing. Modern agriculture and food processing is energy-intensive production beyond the energetic needs of the autotrophic plants and the energy stored in them.

The embodiment perspective avoids a flaw in growth accounting methods to test for the correlation of energy and growth, which is to take the low contribution of the energy sector to GDP as a measure, relying on a market framework for estimating the production function.[43] However, this only reflects the lack of internalisation of the true cost of energy via a proper pricing of externalities, such as CO_2 emissions of fossil energy. Further, the contribution of capital is overestimated since it is not conceived as embodying energy.

Contrary to neoclassical assumptions, energy is the primordial production factor that cannot be substituted by other factors, especially capital.

A correlation of energy use and growth does not per se imply causality, raising the question of concrete causal mechanisms. Those must be treated on two levels. One consists of the mechanisms that relate production and consumption of energy, covering a wide range of rebound effects that are, to a large extent, mediated by markets. The other refers GDP growth to the material growth of the technosphere and asks for the direction of causality of thermodynamic processes.

Rebound effects are the core mechanisms in relating increases of energy efficiency to the growth of demand and, eventually, absolute amounts of energy consumed.

Rebound effects relate efficiency improvements to the expansion of energy demand or throughputs, which are often mediated by prices.[44] If efficiency improves, this is reflected in lower costs and lower prices which enhance demand; in addition, there are budgetary effects if demand has reached saturation. Taking lighting as an example, rapidly improving energy efficiency of lighting has triggered a secular decline of costs of lighting. However, this has not resulted in a levelling off of total demand and not even of the absolute amount of energy consumed in lighting because the saturation point is still far away.[45] Declining costs even result in the growth of energy demand for lighting, corresponding to a rebound effect larger than one. Furthermore, even if the share of lighting in total expenditures declined, this would potentially release demand for other energy-intensive goods.

In general, an analysis of efficiency for single artefacts will reveal that rebounds are mostly less than one, that is, that energy savings are realised in terms of lower absolute energy demand. For example, heating a room may approach a satiation point (although in wintertime, many people would heat more to be able to wear summer shirts at home); hence, efficiency gains in heating would result in absolute energy savings. Still, the question remains on what is done with the budget that is freed up. There are activities that are closely related in technological terms such that rebounds include complementarities. We can assume that rebound effects larger than one are characteristic for all general-purpose technologies that create circular feedback mechanisms. The classical example is Jevons's 'coal question', the first statement of rebound mechanisms in the economic literature.[46] Jevons showed that lower prices for coal boost demand for coal in steel production, which is also used for building railways that lower the costs of transporting coal. In other words, this type of rebound is a circular autocatalytic mechanism which eventually triggers continuous growth of energy throughputs in the entire technological system involving mining, transport, and uses of coal. Today, information technology fits the bill, too. The general growth model that reflects such a circular interdependence stipulates that efficiency gains result in demand growth that further feeds growth of production.[47] This process is constrained by two factors: resources on the production side, and satiation on the demand side.

The Great Acceleration can be explained as a release of both constraints. On the production side, Jevons's mechanism can be generalised: The release of technological constraints on exploiting fossil fuels fed the growth of the technosphere and, hence, further eased constraints, such as in the recent case of fracking in the US: Technological progress causes a cost decline of producing oil and gas in the United States and, therefore, drastically reduces economic incentives for shifting to renewables, as long as externalities of carbon fuel are not fully internalised. On the demand side, cultural creativity drives the growth of wants and the emergence of new wants.

Against this background, unequal world development factually implies a shift of satiation points further into the future. This is even true for basic needs, such as the need for communication as now met by smartphones, that is, highly sophisticated artefacts with high embodied energy (stemming from chip production). Considering this endogenous dynamics, there appear to be no principled constraints on aspirations to economic growth.

Taking the fundamental thermodynamic constraints into account, in principle, the energy balance of the Earth system would allow for a vast expansion of the human share of solar energy and the exportation of entropy to outer

Economic growth is driven by cyclical interdependences between efficiency gains and demand expansion.

On autocatalytic mechanisms, see Chapter 4, section 4.1.

On externalities and internalisation, see Chapter 4, section 2.1, and Chapter 6, section 2.2.

space.[48] However, competition between technosphere and biosphere proceeds within a range of other constraints that are defined in structural terms in the Earth system. This has been theorised and measured in terms of planetary boundaries:[49] Given certain current forms of technology use, technosphere growth may result in a violation of structural constraints that jeopardise the biosphere. One example is nitrogen concentration resulting from agriculture, which is one of the salient forms in which technosphere, human niche construction, and biosphere interact. Nitrogen fertilisers and associated technologies have vastly increased the energy intensity of agriculture, which increases productivity and, hence, releases constraints of population growth.[50] Population growth, in turn, further enhances food demand and intensification of agriculture, leading into another autocatalytic feedback. However, this results into growing concentration of nitrogen in water ecosystems, thus overstretching structural constraints.

The planetary boundaries concept highlights non-linearities and irreversibilities in approaching boundaries, which may be invisible when only considering the aggregate level. For example, with growing nitrogen concentrations, local ecosystems may approach tipping points where catastrophic decay unfolds in very short time spans, resulting in ecosystem degradation that cannot be simply recovered (the proverbial scrambled egg that cannot be remade into an egg). An example is water ecosystems, where the transgression of certain temperature thresholds may lead to the collapse of coral populations. The climate system is highly complex and non-linear; for example, local temperature changes can result in changing wind flows that cannot be predicted by climate models which can only extrapolate past data.

What, then, is the ultimate driver of growth? The circularity of growth mechanisms explains why the correlation between growth and energy can be interpreted in both directions. Thermodynamics suggests causality from energy to growth, with the connection established via the role of information in living systems.[51] If we approach energy as ultimate constraint and enabler of the survival and reproduction of living systems, it follows that biological information evolves in the direction of harnessing energy in competition with other living systems, powered by autocatalytic mechanisms. This is the maximum power principle. The maximum power principle reflects the second law in its manifestation for nonlinear dynamic systems (i.e., the maximum entropy production principle). In this sense, we can say that economic growth is rooted in fundamental thermodynamics and directly reflects the second law. The second law introduces a principle of stochastic finality, given certain constraints, meaning that complex systems evolve towards states of highest probability, which represent maxima of entropy production. The physical manifestation is the long-term trend in growing energetic throughputs and increasing energy intensities of the technosphere.

These principles unify economic growth across different evolutionary stages of the human economy. The Great Acceleration is distinct from

On MPP and MEPP, see Chapter 4, section 2.2.

Economic growth is the physical manifestation of the second law in the economy.

previous stages because of the peculiar effects of the sudden (in geological time scales) technological overcoming of the physical constraints on the release of stored solar energy in fossils.[52] In previous stages, the slow-moving manifestation of growth was population growth (i.e., the growth of human biomass and associated domesticated animal and plant biomass).

As a result, releasing economic constraints never results in a state where living systems simply come to rest in a land of plenty. Rather, those systems relentlessly grow towards new boundaries, as was evident in both the transition to agriculture and to industrialisation for the human economy. This growth imperative is also manifest in the growth of the biosphere. Therefore, when considering limits to growth, we must clearly distinguish between economic growth and material growth. There are physical determinants of growth in the complex non-linear and non-equilibrium Earth system which are also manifest in the human economy. Yet this does not mean that any form of growth is ecologically sustainable. The question is how far the market system can direct technosphere growth and energetic transformation in a way that the biosphere is not jeopardised.

5. Markets as drivers of growth

We analysed technological evolution in Chapter 6, section 3.3.

According to the neoclassical model, economic growth is driven by technological innovation. As we have seen earlier, technological evolution is commonly perceived as linear progress, but in fact, it explores a growing state space that we cannot oversee in advance. That means, we do not know whether technological evolution just proceeds to local optima, that is, improvements relative to the concrete context, or whether there are forces that move towards global optima, that is, the objectively best technology, which are, however, unknown from a third-person perspective. We can only adopt a second-person view on past developments and judge the current status from hindsight. Technological evolution, insofar it proceeds gradually, would certainly approach local optima as the most probable pattern and only accidentally hit global optima. Yet there are forces that may break up such trajectories and make global optima accessible. Most importantly, this is imagination and science, in modern times, sometimes combined in the genre of science fiction.[53]

Human imagination allows for the free combination of existing entities via their mental representations without observing actual physical constraints. For example, from early times on, people imagined to be able to fly, and eventually, this imagination drove technological tinkering and innovation realising that vision. That means, in imagining futures, the search can be directed towards new goals despite being currently not accessible as local optima. When we include markets here, however, another specific constraint has to be taken into account, namely the budgetary constraint. The role that bridges these various domains is the entrepreneur, often designated as Schumpeterian by economists.[54]

The entrepreneur is a type of agent that has risen to prominence during industrialisation, as far as the combination of market prowess and technological ingenuity is concerned. However, as the case of Imperial China demonstrates, this linkage is not necessary since, under certain economic incentives, entrepreneurship can only focus on market opportunity in the narrow sense and sideline the role of technology.[55] In fact, entrepreneurship that is oriented towards monopolisation as a means of profit generation can form a barrier to innovation since monopolisation becomes entrenched in barriers to market access for new competitors. There are also cultural constraints on entrepreneurship, such as risk aversion against innovation in most peasant societies.[56]

Imagination is a driving force of entrepreneurship, and entrepreneurially driven research and technological tinkering may allow to overcome physical constraints. This often renders entirely new kinds of products possible, such as CD players based on laser technology, and thus, drives economic growth. As said, however, entrepreneurship also faces a budgetary constraint (i.e., limits in the availability of capital), for example, in the form of making loans available for one technology but not the other.[57] This implies a complementary force of path dependency of technological change, as profit expectations indirectly reinforce the budgetary constraints. Thus, there is no necessary connection between what is deemed possible in imagination and factually possible trajectories that approach global optima. Budgetary constraints may simply reinforce one particular local trajectory against another: There was no binding technological constraint on adopting electrical motorisation at the end of the 19th century, but there were economic motives that favoured the carbon-fuelled engines.

Why do entrepreneurs pursue technological goals at all? Concentrating on efficiency as a generic parameter of competition determined by technology, an arms race dynamic applies.[58] Consider the situation of a producer who knows that cost advantages will determine competitive success. Since the producer does not know whether and when other producers will innovate, she is forced to invest in improving efficiency, thus entering a race in which everybody continuously strives to improve efficiency, pushing technological progress. In this sense, competition comes close to a prisoner's dilemma: Even if most entrepreneurs are happy with the status quo, they cannot be sure whether others still strive to disrupt it; hence, they are forced to take precautionary measures. Economics regards this as a case of prisoner's dilemma that is socially desirable, as the result is enhancing aggregate efficiency of the economy. However, this argument is only true if all relevant externalities, such as distributional effects, or the consequences of a relentless acceleration of change and intensification of effort, are internalised.[59]

Therefore, markets are indeed drivers of growth, yet there are important structural constraints that determine the direction of evolution. A foremost example is the comparison of Western Europe and China, given that in both cases, market systems were developed early. China evolved towards a pattern

Imagination is a force that can overcome path dependencies and lock-in in local optima.

See Chapter 7, section 5.3, and Chapter 11, section 5.

The entrepreneur is a type of agent emerging in the industrial stage who combines market prowess with technological imagination.

We discuss these various aspects extensively in Chapter 11.

Entrepreneurs are pushed by an arms race dynamic of the market process towards relentless acceleration of innovation.

433

of intensifying land use by means of growing labour inputs, whereas Western Europe evolved towards a pattern of capital deepening and increasing labour productivity. In addition, China evolved towards increasing energy efficiency, whereas Europe moved into the direction of expanding energy throughputs. In both cases, we can assert that the pattern was efficient in the sense of being driven by markets, given differences in exogenous parameters:

For background
information, see
Chapter 1.

- In China, social norms of family formation established a direct causal connection between economic growth and population growth. Once surplus increased, family size increased, too, thus generating a Malthusian growth pattern which sustained a low relative price of human labour that, in turn, fostered labour intensity of production in both agriculture and industry.[60] In Europe, social norms emerging in medieval times (especially those that discriminated against the extended family) caused a transition to late marriage and reduced numbers of children, which motivated the transition to more capital-intensive production technology (proto-industrialisation).[61]

Markets motivated divergent technological trajectories of economic growth in China and Europe.

- In China, coal deposits were located far away from economic centres, whereas especially in England, they were relatively close, resulting in differences in transportation cost.[62] By implication, in China, energy was relatively more expensive than labour, whereas in England, the opposite relation prevailed.[63]
- In China, the vast size of the Empire implied that the centre of economic activity was in the South, beyond the frost line separating rice and wheat areas.[64] Therefore, in the South, agricultural production could take place throughout the year, whereas in Western Europe, the harvest time was tightly constrained by winter frost. By implication, in Western Europe, there were strong incentives to speed up harvesting techniques and intensify agricultural production, which implied capital intensification. In Chinese rice agriculture, capital was mostly formed in the shape of irrigation systems and expansion of land (such as terracing), which required intensive labour input, such as in maintaining terraces.

As a consequence, despite entirely different technological trajectories, both China and Europe experienced economic growth in the material sense, manifesting as capital formation in Europe and population growth in China and, in this sense, representing the market-framed logic of neoclassical substitution in both cases. However, China did not exhibit growth in terms of GDP per capita. The crucial difference was not markets but the transition to fossil fuels in Europe and the immense growth of the material intensity of the economy in the technosphere. The different trajectories reflect different forms of adaptive efficiency.

For an analysis
of the role of
transaction cost
in comparative
institutional
analysis, see
Chapter 9,
section 4.

In more recent perspectives on growth, economists have mostly emphasised the role of institutions. This is because institutions determine transaction costs and the time horizon of investors: In an economy shaped by weak institutions and political instability, entrepreneurs face high risks, especially when committing to large investments. Regarding the global dimension of entrepreneurship and market dynamics, the distinction between voluntary and forced specialisation is of essential importance. Historians comparing China and Europe have emphasised the distinct role of colonialism in accessing the resources for European industrialisation and in opening markets for capitalist expansion, whereas China (and Japan) adopted a deliberate policy of closure.[65] As said, European colonialism had long-run effects on the distribution of per-capita GDP across the world, but it also entailed ecological changes (plantation agriculture) as well as institutional effects in both the economy and political systems.[66] The result has been a fragmentation of the global economy into so-called convergence clubs, that is, clusters of countries which share certain characteristics establishing specific path dependencies of market evolution (e.g., the clusters of the Asia-Pacific, of Latin America, and of Sub-Saharan Africa).

6. Anthropocentric versus geocentric conceptions of growth

The legacy of colonialism is the formation and persistence of convergent country groups with similar trajectories of growth.

Is economic growth desirable? In an anthropocentric perspective, this is certainly the case, given that externalities are taken into consideration that affect human well-being: Green growth would be a goal worthwhile to pursue. In the geocentric perspective, however, this is by no means warranted. We discuss this in turn.

6.1. The anthropocentric perspective

To achieve convergence of economic conditions across the globe, growth remains a necessary economic goal, given that billions of humans still live in poverty and economic distress. However, convergence implies that there must be a positive difference between the growth rates of low-income and high-income countries, including the option of levelling off growth in the most prosperous countries.[67] This idea has famously been stated by John Stuart Mill in his conception of the stationary state.[68] Mill envisaged that in this state, societies would focus on non-economic aspects of a good life, an idea that matches with later ideas such as Maslow's hierarchy of needs which assumes that after material needs are fulfilled, humans will switch to catering other needs, such as spiritual ones.[69] Accordingly, some visions of degrowth would imply that after achieving a certain level of prosperity, societies will endogenously slow down economic growth.

In some visions of growth, market growth will subside as humans focus on non-market wants.

In judging this possibility, it is necessary to consider how growth is measured. The distinction between consumption and production in GDP is mainly conventional and itself determined by market constructs. For example, human capital formation is conventionally approached as production, but we can also treat it as consumption if we assume that people enjoy their growth of skills and knowledge.[70] Education would then be included in the value added, and education is less energy intensive than other forms of consumption. In other words, even when maintaining the same rate of GDP growth, the qualitative and structural characteristics of demand can be vastly different. European growth since industrialisation was geared towards material consumption, especially in status competition.[71] In a general sense, this applies for the question of labour versus leisure time. Reduction of growth is feasible via increasing leisure time, while also renouncing further growth of material complements: We would love to hike in our spare time but do not indulge in car racing for which we need powerful cars.

This discussion shows that the connection between GDP growth and material growth is not necessarily proportional because GDP measures market transactions independently from their physical characteristics; the key criterion is the fulfilling of demand as expressed by monetary flows. Therefore, to a certain extent, decoupling is possible once the structure of consumption changes. Yet as we noticed, this is not realistic for the majority of the world population which still has a far way to go to reach the living standards of an average citizen in industrialised countries. Therefore, we cannot expect dematerialisation to happen within a foreseeable future, as far as human needs are concerned.[72]

The structure of consumption partly determines the material consequences of growth such that partial decoupling is feasible.

We can further approach this question by relating aggregate growth to individual growth. In this context, organismic aspects of growth are connected to the first-person view in the most direct way and implicit in alternative development indicators which refer to prolongation of life spans, improved health status, and increasing body height as indicating improvements of the human condition.[73] Growth of individual organisms is mostly constrained, which is certainly true in case of mammals.[74] Industrial growth has resulted in phenomena of individual growth that are not desirable even in the first-person view, namely obesity. However, obesity does not directly imply that food consumption has reached a satiation point, as may be derived from Engel's curve which states the statistical regularity that in the course of economic development, the share of food expenditures in total expenditures is declining.[75] For example, we might start to consume food that cannot be locally provided but must be transported from far away, or we start to prefer luxury items with sophisticated preparation. Modern economic growth has created the phenomenon that individual growth is increasingly realised via possessions that enable daily individual consumption acts, most visible in the environment of our homes and the artefacts of our daily use, such as cars. These offer scope for individual growth, for example, by buying a larger and more powerful car, or moving into a larger home. The lifestyles of the rich reveal that satiation points are rarely physically

Individual growth of consumption is mostly limited by satiation points, yet there are no limits to expanding possession of consumption opportunities.

defined; we may be only able to drive one car at the same time yet still enjoy possessing many of them.

Hence, as thematised by many world religions, the question of limits to individual growth is mainly about the distinction between use and possession. In principle, possession can grow without limits, whereas actual consumption defined in terms of use eventually reaches satiation points. Hence, one way of decoupling GDP growth from material growth is the institutional decoupling of possession and consumption. This increasingly happens in modern markets via sharing models of many kinds. Those models increase the efficiency of using the stock of consumption capital (such as the stock of fancy cars), while at the same time creating value added via the services that enable the sharing.[76]

Individual growth must be considered together with the aggregate form of organismic growth, namely population growth which is biologically related to the reproduction of the single organism. Until today, population growth has repeatedly been identified as a major threat to long-run sustainability of the human economy, even though doomsday scenarios often failed to materialise.[77]

Demographic growth is a central phenomenon in both the agricultural and the industrial transition, which, to a certain extent, reflects the two types of reproductive strategies defined in ecology: The reaction to an expansion of a resource space can be either to grow the number of progeny or to reduce their number to enhance quality.[78] Human demography clearly shows similar mechanisms, but those depend on social and economic contexts of competition and are, therefore, primarily cultural, not biological. Human reproductive strategies are mainly determined by culture, more specifically, by culturally mediated economic factors, especially the value of children and their role in the economy. There are direct causal mechanisms that relate reproduction, status, and economic inequality.[79]

The costs of children are mainly determined by education in the broadest sense, together with a delay in entering production, and by status competition, including competition for mates. A pertinent example is demographic decline in modern China: Even a softening of the one-child policy could not stop this trend because even in many rural areas, the cost of education and marriage have been rising relentlessly, thus motivating a reduction of family size. Economic development creates many socio-economic mechanisms that result in a lower reproductive rate of human populations, mainly via the extension of the time and investment necessary to raise children. This combines with cultural forces; for example, the question of whether children are regarded as an essential form of fulfilling individual life. An important role is played by gender power relations: In the past, most of the care work was externalised to women, whereas in many advanced industrial societies, women can now decide with greater autonomy whether they assume these tasks. These demographic changes interact with the progress in hygiene and medicine that have

A sharing economy institutionally decouples consumption and possession.

Human reproductive strategies are, to a large extent, culturally determined, with strong impact of patterns of inequality in status and wealth.

Economic growth and status competition increase the costs of raising children and, hence, reduce family size, interacting with cultural changes, in particular, in gender relations.

drastically reduced child mortality and prolonged human life, resulting in the peculiar pattern of demographic aging that shapes almost all advanced industrial economies today.

To summarise, in the anthropocentric perspective, economic growth is conceived as desirable, once we recognise that the market economy allows for a wide range of structural adaptations of consumption and ways of life that would be compatible with establishing a better balance with ecological goals. Yet the question remains of how far this still implies growth of the technosphere in material terms, relative to the biosphere, and what the consequences for the Earth system are.

6.2. The geocentric perspective

In the geocentric perspective, GDP growth is relevant only to the extent that it reflects technosphere growth more generally. We approach the human economy in terms of its effects on Earth system regulation, taking a third-person view on growth which encompasses the distinction between human parameters of action in the market system and externalities.

In principle, economic growth reflects the trajectory of growing thermodynamic productivity of the Earth system, manifest in the growth of the biosphere.

It is important to recognise that this view does not necessarily imply an irresolvable tension of economic growth with Earth system sustainability. Many notions of sustainability erroneously suggest that the Earth system stays in a kind of equilibrium that is disturbed by economic growth. That might be true when considering single ecosystems, but it is wrong for the overall system. A defining feature of the biosphere is that it has been growing for billions of years, exhibiting growing thermodynamic productivity fed by the continuous inflow of solar radiation.[80] Insofar as economic growth reflects the unfolding of MPP and MEPP, there is no principled contradiction between Earth system finalities and economic growth.

A geocentric view on growth would suggest that, in principle, human aspirations would be secondary to Earth system regulatory objectives. Given the continuous and open interaction between biosphere and technosphere, how can we specify such objectives?

Considering the biosphere, one central issue is that we cannot specify biospheric objectives as such but only objectives of components. Take, for example, the relationship between living systems and humans in agriculture: Human economic objectives partly converge with the goals of domesticated plants and animals, such as sustaining populations and their reproduction. This domain has been growing to the detriment of wildlife, but we cannot simply say that there is a fundamental conflict with the biosphere. Consideration of non-anthropocentric goals means that we would heed attention, for example, to the dignity of domesticated animals in considering their natural preferences of ways of life. Yet this does not resolve the conflict, say, between wolves and sheep, as salient in restoration agendas and wildlife protection. In other words, we cannot define a third-person view on the biosphere beyond highly aggregated views, such as the planetary boundaries concept: We can safely say that the very high levels of nitrogen production by human industrialised agriculture jeopardise ecosystems, but it is more difficult to evaluate specific losses of biodiversity which result from unavoidable competition between domesticated species and wildlife.

Therefore, the adoption of a geocentric view requires institutional solutions that translate biospheric goals into the human domain as interests and establish procedures to negotiate those interests, given the fact that the biosphere is a competitive regime.[81] This is not primarily a policy measure but a means to achieve an inclusive second-person view on the Earth system, that is, one that takes into consideration the biosphere in terms of its systemic complexity and plurality and aims at approaching an objective view in terms of impartiality, including humans and the biosphere. One intermediate way is the ecosystem services concept, which still refers the biosphere to human needs and interests but internalises all externalities and indirect ecological connectivities.[82] The ecosystems services concept implies a hybrid objective in the sense that ecosystems are eventually seen in an anthropocentric perspective, yet the fundamental dependence of humans on the biosphere is recognised and a balance between biospheric interests and human interests is struck.

Given the persistent conflictual nature of interests in a geocentric perspective, the economy can only be approached in terms of ecological (eventually, physical) regulatory requirements which can be deduced from the planetary boundaries concept. For example, the switch to organic agriculture does not take specific biospheric interests into consideration but mainly reflects the need to protect regulatory biosphere mechanisms that are clearly destabilised by human interventions. A similar argument applies to the need to internalise the costs of carbon: There is widespread scientific agreement that all current price assignments are too low to avoid regulatory collapse of the global climate.

We mentioned previously that a geocentric perspective includes the insight that the growth of the human economy also contributes to the thermodynamic productivity of the Earth system. This can be translated to a reversal of the ecosystem services concept: We may ask how the human economy contributes to the flourishing of the biosphere, going beyond mere protection and restoration and including the possibility of a symbiotic relationship between biosphere and technosphere evolution. This requires new imaginaries of technological innovation that would not put human needs at the centre. A simple example is terracing of high-rise buildings that would include spaces for wildlife.[83]

7. Conclusion

Economic growth has been the subject of extensive debates in economics, society, and politics for decades. With the rise of capitalism, ecological

We can establish a third-person view on conflicts between technosphere and biosphere on a general level but cannot ultimately specify trade-offs in concrete contexts.

On the importance of impartiality for economic judgement and valuation, see Chapter 3 and Chapter 9, section 5.4.

concerns have become particularly prominent.[84] However, economics has mostly adopted the view that economic growth is desirable as it improves the human lot via technological progress. This view has been shared by both pro-market economists and its critics: Marxism is a pro-growth theory that predicts revolutionary change only once a certain level of economic progress is achieved. Hence, in the 20th century, growth was an imperative until the 1970s, when the oil crisis and the emergent green movements raised public concern.

We did not discuss wider ramifications of growth, such as military competition as a driver of growth. The simple connection is surplus that can be appropriated by political entities in order to mobilise resources for war: Designing new financial instruments for funding the British navy was essential for establishing British supremacy in the 19th century. The Cold War included competition between the economic models of the US and the USSR; there are many other examples. Military competition creates a strong incentive for pursuing growth by government policies.

In this chapter, we focused on the Earth system dimension, thus closing the circle to Chapter 4. One key insight is that economic growth is growth of markets and, if analysed in material terms, is a manifestation of the universal phenomena of growth in the biosphere and the Earth system: Growth is a disequilibrium phenomenon, and the Earth is a disequilibrium system. In this view, growth is a natural process, that is, undergirded by human aspirations on progress, both individually and in society. However, the recent centuries have seen special conditions of growth that was fuelled by fossil energies. The current focus on climate change tends to overlook that the fundamental issue in judging growth is the relative growth of the technosphere vis-à-vis the biosphere, which can be fuelled by any kind of energy: Indeed, earlier futuristic visions of human society highlighted the role of nuclear energy, which is carbon neutral. Technosphere growth is a material phenomenon. By implication, our core concern should be the material side of economic growth and not simply the way it is measured.

Major chapter insights

- We approach economic growth in material terms primarily and, secondarily, as growth of GDP. GDP measures the growth of markets, whereas material growth is manifest in the growth of the technosphere. Pre-modern growth is growth of population without growth of GDP per capita; modern growth is growth of GDP per capita. In the long run, we distinguish three technologically mediated human niches and related stages of growth: the pre-agrarian (simple tools), agrarian (co-evolution of human culture and domesticated plants and animals), and industrial (rapid expansion of technosphere).

- The standard economic model of growth is basically an accounting framework that relates saving, investment, depreciation, and population growth in explaining persistent growth by technological progress. Endogenous technological progress is generated by positive externalities of knowledge production and diffusion. The material setting is the city: Modern economic growth centres on urbanisation as key structure of the technosphere.

- In cities, super-linearities of information processing in human social networks drive persistent economic growth despite growing costs of agglomeration. This is reflected in the growing material and energetic flows of urbanisation, such as energy needed for lighting, heating, and cooling, or cement and steel for construction.

- Energy is the key driver and enabler of growth that cannot be substituted by other factors of production since these also embody energy. Growth of energy throughput and economic growth are tightly correlated in the long run, which can be conceived as manifestation of fundamental thermodynamic principles as established in Chapter 4. Via the release of stored solar energy in fossils, the Great Acceleration was triggered which has already transgressed some planetary boundaries, thus potentially reaching tipping points that would result in irreversible damage of the biosphere.

- Market-driven entrepreneurship motivated by imagination is a force that can overcome path dependencies of technological evolution, yet we are not able to assess technological change from a third-person perspective. Depending on structural constraints on the economy, markets generate divergent trajectories of technological evolution, as the comparison between China and Europe demonstrates.

- In judging whether economic growth is desirable or not, we distinguish the anthropocentric and the geocentric view. In the anthropocentric view, growth is desirable as it improves the human condition, such as prolonging life or improving living conditions for the substantial share of global human population who still live in poverty. One factor of making growth sustainable is a reduction of the material intensity of consumption. A geocentric view asks for the effects of technosphere growth for Earth system regulation and establishes criteria for orienting the technosphere towards a positive contribution to biosphere evolution.

Notes

1 Costanza et al. (2014).
2 Jones (1988).
3 Rosenberg and Birdzell (1986).
4 Stiglitz et al. (2009).
5 Hidalgo (2015).
6 Coyle (2015, 88ff).
7 Lenton et al. (2016).
8 McNeill and McNeill (2003); Henn et al. (2012).
9 Bowles and Gintis (2011).
10 Van der Kaars et al. (2017).
11 Lucassen (2021: 44ff).
12 Pinker (2012, 36ff).
13 Altman and Mesoudi (2019).
14 Smil (2003).
15 Wiley (2020).
16 Qing et al. (2019).
17 Mann (1986).
18 Alesina et al. (2013).
19 Smil (2008).
20 IEA (2021).
21 Johnson and Papageorgiou (2020).
22 Rosenberg and Birdzell (1986), Mokyr (2017).
23 The role of accounting in the rise of the modern economy was seminally emphasised by Max Weber. For a recent comprehensive account, see Soll (2014).
24 The classic is Wallerstein (1974). This picture is confirmed by Findlay and
O'Rourke (2007).
25 This is standard textbook lore, for example Jones and Vollrath (2013).
26 Helpman (2004).
27 Glaeser (2011), Batty (2013).
28 Bettencourt (2013), West (2017, 209ff).
29 Glaeser (2011).
30 This builds on Marshall's notion of industrial districts and is elaborated in modern spatial economics, seminally Fujita et al. (1999).
31 Guan et al. (2018).
32 Henderson et al. (2012).
33 Tsao and Waide (2010), Zissis et al. (2021).
34 Smil (2019, 460ff, 492ff).
35 Trentmann (2017, 679ff).
36 Krausmann et al. (2017).
37 Zalasiewicz et al. (2017).
38 Elhacham et al. (2020).
39 Among many, see Stern (2011), Omri (2014), Azam (2020).

40 Kümmel (2011).

41 Sharma et al. (2019).

42 The concept has been systematically introduced by Odum (2007), summarising his early work.

43 Ayres and Warr (2005).

44 Sorrell et al. (2009), Azevedo (2014).

45 Tsao and Waide (2010), Saunders and Tsao (2012).

46 Sorrell (2009).

47 Ayres and Warr (2009) refer to this as Salter cycle.

48 Kümmel (2011), Kleidon (2016).

49 Folke et al. (2021).

50 Smil (2008, 291ff).

51 Lahav et al. (2001), Kolchinsky and Wolpert (2018).

52 Haff (2014).

53 Beckert (2016, 169ff).

54 Schumpeter (1911).

55 Elvin (1973).

56 Mendola (2007).

57 This tension was classically analysed by Veblen (1921).

58 Binswanger (2013).

59 Rosa (2010).

60 Chao (1986).

61 Goody (1983).

62 Pomeranz (2000).

63 Allen (2009).

64 Hesse (1982).

65 Pomeranz (2000).

66 Acemoglu et al. (2002).

67 Survey in Kallis et al. (2018).

68 Mill (1871).

69 Maslow (1943).

70 Llavador et al. (2015).

71 De Vries (2008), Trentmann (2017).

72 Smil (2019, 492).

73 The Human Development Index published by the UNDP strongly correlates with life expectancy. Body height is widely used in economics as indicator of development and inequality, see, for example, Cámara et al. (2019).

74 West (2017).

75 Chai and Moneta (2010).

76 Acquier et al. (2017).

77 The problem is complex because Malthusian constraints can even hold when population growth rates decline, see Naso et al. (2020).

78 Davies et al. (2012, 223ff).

79 Seminally, Veblen (1899).

80 Kleidon (2016).
81 Herrmann-Pillath (2021).
82 Dasgupta (2021).
83 Recently, such ideas have been put into the policy concept of nature-based solutions; for a survey and extension, see Herrmann-Pillath et al. (2022).
84 Plumpe (2019, 279ff).

References

Acemoglu, D., Johnson, S. and Robinson, J. A. (2002) 'Reversal of Fortune: Geography and Institutions in the Making of the Modern World Income Distribution', *The Quarterly Journal of Economics*, 117(4), pp. 1231–1294. DOI: 10.1162/003355302320935025.

Acquier, A., Daudigeos, T. and Pinkse, J. (2017) 'Promises and Paradoxes of the Sharing Economy: An Organizing Framework', *Technological Forecasting and Social Change*, 125, pp. 1–10. DOI: 10.1016/j.techfore.2017.07.006.

Alesina, A., Giuliano, P. and Nunn, N. (2013) 'On the Origins of Gender Roles: Women and the Plough', *The Quarterly Journal of Economics*, 128(2), pp. 469–530.

Allen, R. C. (2009) *The British Industrial Revolution in Global Perspective*. Cambridge: Cambridge University Press. DOI: 10.1017/CBO9780511816680.

Altman, A. and Mesoudi, A. (2019) 'Understanding Agriculture within the Frameworks of Cumulative Cultural Evolution, Gene-Culture Co-Evolution, and Cultural Niche Construction', *Human Ecology*, 47, pp. 483–497. DOI: 10.1007/S10745-019-00090-Y.

Ayres, R. U. and Warr, B. (2005) 'Accounting for Growth: The Role of Physical Work', *Structural Change and Economic Dynamics*, 16(2), pp. 181–209. DOI: 10.1016/j.strueco.2003.10.003.

Ayres, R. U. and Warr, B. (2009) *The Economic Growth Engine: How Energy and Work Drive Material Prosperity*. Cheltenham and Northampton: Edward Elgar Publishing. DOI: 10.4337/9781848445956.

Azam, M. (2020) 'Energy and Economic Growth in Developing Asian Economies', *Journal of the Asia Pacific Economy*, 25(3), pp. 447–471. DOI: 10.1080/13547860.2019.1665328.

Azevedo, I. M. L. (2014) 'Consumer End-Use Energy Efficiency and Rebound Effects', *Annual Review of Environment and Resources*, 39, pp. 393–418. DOI: 10.1146/annurev-environ-021913-153558.

Batty, M. (2013) *The New Science of Cities*. Cambridge and London: MIT Press. DOI: 10.7551/mitpress/9399.001.0001.

Beckert, J. (2016) *Imagined Futures: Fictional Expectations and Capitalist Dynamics*. Cambridge: Harvard University Press. DOI: 10.4159/9780674545878.

Bettencourt, L. M. A. (2013) 'The Origins of Scaling in Cities', *Science*, 340(6139), pp. 1438–1441. DOI: 10.1126/science.1235823.

Binswanger, H. C. (2013) *The Growth Spiral: Money, Energy and Imagination in the Dynamics of the Market Process*. Berlin and Heidelberg: Springer. DOI: 10.1007/978-3-642-31881-8.

Bowles, S. and Gintis, H. (2011) *A Cooperative Species: Human Reciprocity and Its Evolution*. Princeton: Princeton University Press.

Cámara, A. *et al.* (2019) 'Height and Inequality in Spain: A Long-Term Perspective', *Revista De Historia Económica/Journal of Iberian and Latin American Economic History*, 37(2), pp. 205–238. DOI: 10.1017/S0212610919000089.

Chai, A. and Moneta, A. (2010) 'Retrospectives: Engel Curves', *Journal of Economic Perspectives*, 24(1), pp. 225–240. DOI: 10.1257/jep.24.1.225.

Chao, K. (1986) *Man and Land in China: An Economic Analysis*. Stanford: Stanford University Press.

Costanza, R. *et al.* (2014) 'Development: Time to Leave GDP Behind', *Nature*, 505, pp. 283–285. DOI: 10.1038/505283a.

Coyle, D. (2015) *GDP: A Brief but Affectionate History*. Princeton: Princeton University Press. DOI: 10.1515/9781400873630.

Dasgupta, P. (2021) *The Economics of Biodiversity: The Dasgupta Review*. Available at: https://www.gov.uk/government/collections/the-economics-of-biodiversity-the-dasgupta-review (Accessed: 22 March 2022).

Davies, N. B., Krebs, J. R. and West, S. A. (2012) *An Introduction to Behavioural Ecology*. Oxford: Wiley-Blackwell.

De Vries, J. (2008) *The Industrious Revolution. Consumer Behavior and the Household Economy, 1650 to the Present*. Cambridge: Cambridge University Press.

Elhacham, E. *et al.* (2020) 'Global Human-Made Mass Exceeds All Living Biomass', *Nature*, 588(7838), pp. 442–444. DOI: 10.1038/s41586-020-3010-5.

Elvin, M. (1973) *The Pattern of the Chinese Past*, Stanford: Stanford University Press.

Findlay, R. and O'Rourke, K. H. (2007) *Power and Plenty: Trade, War, and the World Economy in the Second Millennium*. Princeton: Princeton University Press.

Folke, C. *et al.* (2021) 'Our Future in the Anthropocene Biosphere', *Ambio*, 50(4), pp. 834–869. DOI: 10.1007/s13280-021-01544-8.

Fujita, M., Krugman, P. und Venables, A. J. (1999) *The Spatial Economy: Cities, Regions, and International Trade*. Cambridge: MIT Press.

Glaeser, E. L. (2011) *Triumph of the City: How Our Greatest Invention Makes Us Richer, Smarter, Greener, Healthier, and Happier*. New York: Penguin Press

Goody, J. (1983) *The Development of the Family and Marriage in Europe*. Cambridge: Cambridge University Press.

Guan, X. *et al.* (2018) 'Assessment on the Urbanization Strategy in China: Achievements, Challenges and Reflections', *Habitat International*, 71, pp. 97–109. DOI: 10.1016/j.habitatint.2017.11.009.

Haff, P. K. (2014) 'Maximum Entropy Production by Technology', in Dewar, R. C. *et al.* (eds.) *Beyond the Second Law: Understanding Complex Systems*. Berlin and Heidelberg: Springer, pp. 397–414. DOI: 10.1007/978-3-642-40154-1_21.

Helpman, E. (2004) *The Mystery of Economic Growth*. Cambridge and London: Belknap.

Henderson, J. V., Storeygard, A. and Weil, D. N. (2012) 'Measuring Economic Growth from Outer Space', *American Economic Review*, 102(2), pp. 994–1028. DOI: 10.1257/aer.102.2.994.

Henn, B. M., Cavalli-Sforza, L. L. and Feldman, M. W. (2012) 'The Great Human Expansion', *PNAS*, 109(44), pp. 17758–17764. DOI: 10.1073/pnas.1212380109.

Herrmann-Pillath, C. (2021) 'A Copernican Moment: Engaging Economic Ethics in Orchestrating the Geocentric Turn in Economics', in Bohle, M. and Marrone, E. (eds.) *Geo-societal Narratives – Contextualising Geosciences*. Cham: Palgrave Macmillan, pp. 105–126. DOI: 10.1007/978-3-030-79028-8_8.

Herrmann-Pillath, C, Hiedanpää, J. and Soini, K. (2022) 'The Co-Evolutionary Approach to Nature-Based Solutions: A Conceptual Framework', *Nature-Based Solutions*, 2, p. 100011. DOI: 10.1016/j.nbsj.2022.100011.

Hesse, G. (1982) *Die Entstehung industrialisierter Volkswirtschaften: Ein Beitrag zur theoretischen und empirischen Analyse der langfristigen wirtschaftlichen Entwicklung*. Tübingen: Mohr Siebeck.

Hidalgo, C. A. (2015) *Why Information Grows: The Evolution of Order, from Atoms to Economies*. New York: Basic Books.

IEA (2021) *Global Energy Review 2021*. Paris: IEA.

Johnson, P. and Papageorgiou, C. (2020) 'What Remains of Cross-Country Convergence?', *Journal of Economic Literature*, 58(1), pp. 129–175. DOI: 10.1257/jel.20181207.

Jones, C. I. and Vollrath, D. (2013) *Introduction to Economic Growth*. New York and London: W.W. Norton & Company.

Jones, E. (1988) *Growth Recurring*. Oxford: Oxford University Press.

Kallis, G. *et al.* (2018) 'Research on Degrowth', *Annual Review of Environment and Resources*, 43(1), pp. 291–316. DOI: 10.1146/annurev-environ-102017-025941.

Kleidon, A. (2016) *Thermodynamic Foundations of the Earth System*. Cambridge: Cambridge University Press. DOI: 10.1017/cbo9781139342742.

Kolchinsky, A. and Wolpert, D. H. (2018) 'Semantic Information, Autonomous Agency and Non-Equilibrium Statistical Physics', *Interface Focus*, 8(6). DOI: 10.1098/rsfs.2018.0041.

Krausmann, F. *et al.* (2017) 'Material Flow Accounting: Measuring Global Material Use for Sustainable Development', *Annual Review of Environment and Resources*, 42(1), pp. 647–675. DOI: 10.1146/annurev-environ-102016-060726.

Kümmel, R. (2011) *The Second Law of Economics: Energy, Entropy, and the Origins of Wealth*. New York: Springer.

Lahav, N., Nir, S. and Elitzur, A. C. (2001) 'The Emergence of Life on Earth', *Progress in Biophysics and Molecular Biology*, 75(1–2), pp. 75–120. DOI: 10.1016/S0079-6107(01)00003-7.

Lenton, T. M., Pichler P-P. and Weisz, H. (2016) 'Revolutions in Energy Input and Material Cycling in Earth History and Human History', *Earth System Dynamics*, 7(2), pp. 353–370. DOI: 10.5194/ESD-7-353-2016.

Llavador, H., Roemer, J. E. and Silvestre, J. (2015) *Sustainability for a Warming Planet*. Cambridge: Harvard University Press.

Lucassen, J. (2021) *The Story of Work: A New History of Humankind*. New Haven: Yale University Press. DOI: 10.12987/9780300262995.

Mann, M. (1986) *The Sources of Social Power, Vol. I: A History of Power from the Beginning to A.D. 1760*. Cambridge: Cambridge University Press.

Maslow, A. H. (1943) 'A Theory of Human Motivation', *Psychological Review*, 50(4), pp. 370–396.

McNeill, J. R. and McNeill, W. H. (2003) *The Human Web: A Bird's-Eye View of World History*. New York and London: Norton.

Mendola, M. (2007) 'Farm Household Production Theories: A Review of "Institutional" and "Behavioral" Responses', *Asian Development Review*, 24(1), pp. 49–68.

Mill, J. S. (1871) *Principles of Political Economy with Some of Their Applications to Social Philosophy, Seventh Edition*. London: Longmans, Green, Reader & Dyer.

Mokyr, J. (2017) *A Culture of Growth: The Origins of Modern Economy*. Princeton: Princeton University Press. DOI: 10.1515/9781400882915.

Naso, P., Lanz, B. and Swanson, T. (2020) 'The Return of Malthus? Resource Constraints in an Era of Declining Population Growth', *European Economic Review*, 128, p. 103499. DOI: 10.1016/j.euroecorev.2020.103499.

Odum, H. T. (2007) *Environment, Power, and Society for the Twenty-First Century: The Hierarchy of Energy*. New York: Columbia University Press.

Omri, A. (2014) 'An International Literature Survey on Energy-Economic Growth Nexus: Evidence from Country-Specific Studies', *Renewable and Sustainable Energy Reviews*, 38, pp. 951–959. DOI: 10.1016/j.rser.2014.07.084.

Pinker, S. (2012) *The Better Angels of Our Nature: Why Violence Has Declined*. New York: Penguin Books.

Plumpe, W. (2019) *Das kalte Herz: Kapitalismus, die Geschichte einer andauernden Revolution*. Berlin: Rowohlt.

Pomeranz, K. (2000) *The Great Divergence: China, Europe and the Making of the Modern World Economy*. Princeton: Princeton University Press. DOI: 10.1515/9781400823499.

Qing, P. *et al.* (2019) 'Climate Change, State Capacity and Nomad – Agriculturalist Conflicts in Chinese History', *Quaternary International*, 508, pp. 36–42. DOI: 10.1016/j.quaint.2018.10.022.

Rosa, H. (2010) *Alienation and Acceleration: Towards a Critical Theory of Late-Modern Temporality, NSU Summertalk*. Natchitoches: NSU Press.

Rosenberg, N. and Birdzell, L. E. (1986) *How the West Grew Rich: The Economic Transformation of the Industrial World*. New York: Basic Books.

Saunders, H. D. and Tsao, J. Y. (2012) 'Rebound Effects for Lighting', *Energy Policy*, 49, pp. 477–478. DOI: 10.1016/j.enpol.2012.06.050.

Schumpeter, J. A. (2006 [1911]) *Theorie der wirtschaftlichen Entwicklung.* Berlin: Duncker & Humblot.

Sharma, N., Smeets, B. and Tryggestad, C. (2019) 'The Decoupling of GDP and Energy Growth: A CEO Guide', *McKinsey Quarterly*. Available at: https://www. mckinsey.com/industries/electric-power-and-natural-gas/our-insights/the-decoupling-of-gdp-and-energy-growth-a-ceo-guide (Accessed: 11 May 2022).

Smil, V. (2003) *The Earth's Biosphere: Evolution, Dynamics, and Change.* Cambridge and London: MIT Press.

Smil, V. (2008) *Energy in Nature and Society: General Energetics of Complex Systems.* Cambridge and London: MIT Press.

Smil, V. (2019) *Growth: From Microorganisms to Megacities.* Cambridge: The MIT Press.

Soll, J. (2014) *The Reckoning: Financial Accountability and the Making and Breaking of Nations.* London: Penguin.

Sorrell, S. (2009) 'Jevons' Paradox Revisited: The Evidence for Backfire from Improved Energy Efficiency', *Energy Policy*, 37(4), pp. 1456–1469. DOI: 10.1016/j.enpol.2008.12.003.

Stern, D. I. (2011) 'The Role of Energy in Economic Growth', *Annals of the New York Academy of Sciences*, 1219, pp. 26–51. DOI: 10.1111/j.1749-6632. 2010.05921.x.

Stiglitz, J. E., Sen, A. and Fitoussi, J. P. (2009) 'Report by the Commission on the Measurement of Economic Performance and Social Progress', *Commission on the Measurement of Economic Performance and Social Progress*. Available at: https://ec.europa.eu/eurostat/documents/8131721/8131772/Stiglitz-Sen-Fitoussi-Commission-report.pdf (Accessed 31 August 2022).

Trentmann, F. (2017) *Empire of Things: How We Became a World of Consumers, from the Fifteenth Century to the Twenty-First, Penguin History.* London: Penguin Books.

Tsao, J. Y. and Waide, P. (2010) 'The World's Appetite for Light: Empirical Data and Trends Spanning Three Centuries and Six Continents', *LEUKOS*, 6(4), pp. 259–281. DOI: 10.1582/LEUKOS.2010.06.04001.

Van der Kaars, S. *et al.* (2017) 'Humans Rather Than Climate the Primary Cause of Pleistocene Megafaunal Extinction in Australia', *Nature Communications*, 8, 14142. DOI: 10.1038/ncomms14142.

Veblen, T. (1965[1899]) *The Theory of the Leisure Class.* New York: Kelley.

Veblen, T. (1983[1921]) *The Engineers and the Price System.* New Brunswick: Transaction.

Wallerstein, I. (1974) *The Modern World System: Capitalist Agriculture and the Origins of the Modern World–Economy in the Sixteenth Century.* New York and London: Academic Press.

West, G. B. (2017) *Scale: The Universal Laws of Growth, Innovation, Sustainability, and the Pace of Life in Organisms, Cities, Economies, and Companies.* New York: Penguin Press.

Wiley, A. S. (2020) 'Lactose Intolerance', *Evolution, Medicine, and Public Health*, 2020(1), pp. 47–48.

Zalasiewicz, J. *et al.* (2017) 'Scale and Diversity of the Physical Technosphere: A Geological Perspective', *The Anthropocene Review*, 4(1), pp. 9–22. DOI: 10.1177/2053019616677743.

Zissis, G., Bertoldi, P. and Serrenho, T. (2021) 'Update on the Status of LED-Lighting World Market Since 2018', *European Commission (Joint Research Centre)*. DOI: 10.2760/759859.

PART V

CHAPTER SEVENTEEN

Economic policy

1. Introduction

As emphasised throughout this book, markets cannot be regarded as stand-alone social phenomena. Instead, they are part of larger-scale social structures, in particular, social networks and institutions. They are also subject to political intervention, whose significance in Western market economies has substantially increased since the Great Depression and World War II. Political intervention and institutional structures overlap insofar as economic policy is mostly conducted via the setting of formal institutions – predominantly, legislation – and takes place via an institutionalised policy process. This chapter focuses on the economic policy process both from a positive and a normative perspective. The positive perspective develops an evolutionary framework for political competition in different realms; the normative perspective relates this framework to the exogenous values of inclusive deliberation and human freedom and dignity. Our approach builds on, and extends, previous work on evolutionary public choice and evolutionary political economy. These perspectives, in turn, were developed as counterparts to neoclassical public choice theory which emerged as an economic theory of politics based on standard assumptions of rationality and fixed preferences. In contrast, the evolutionary approach presented here provides a process-based perspective stressing the endogeneity of political preferences and the role of political entrepreneurship.[1] One implication is the rejection of a textbook technocratic approach to economic policy, which derives necessities for policy intervention from theoretical criteria, such as the presence of public goods and externalities. While those criteria can become performative elements of the policy process, they cannot be established from an exogenous third-person view.

Economic policy constitutes an integral part of the embedding of markets in (formal) institutions.

On normative aspects regarding values and institutions, see Chapter 3, section 4, and Chapter 9, section 5.4.

The chapter is organised as follows. Section 2 outlines the theoretical framework, starting with the regulatory role of the state and different levels of regulation and outlining the application of a framework of multilevel variation, selection, and retention to the policy realm. Section 3 discusses different realms of political competition, namely competition for public opinion,

453

DOI: 10.4324/9781003094869-23

competition for democratic votes, and competition between interest groups; interjurisdictional competition; and political decision making, including policy implementation, which constitutes the domain of the bureaucracy. Section 4 discusses exogenous criteria along which policy results can be judged and posits that such criteria can be formulated in procedural terms, based on the more fundamental values of freedom and human dignity.

2. Economic policy and political competition: An evolutionary approach

2.1. Economic policy and the state

The main carriers of economic policy are states, that is, territorial entities which can enforce formal rules by monopolised violence.

There is a variety of organisational frameworks for economic policy; for example, the federal state and the separation of powers.

Economic policy as political intervention requires the existence of a state structure. In line with previous chapters, we define a state as a territorially defined jurisdiction with the capacity to impose formal rules on its subjects, which can be enforced by monopolised violence. Imposition and enforcement can vary along different dimensions, notably their legitimisation and organisation. In terms of legitimisation, we can roughly distinguish democratic and authoritarian regimes, where the former applies the principle of voluntary decision making to an institutionalised choice of an electorate between parliamentary alternatives in regular intervals. In terms of organisation, there is a large variety in the vertical as well as horizontal dimension. Vertically, we can distinguish between centralised and federal states, and the degree to which regulatory competence is located on a national, international, or supranational level, such as in the European Union Internal Market. Horizontally, imposition and enforcement may be allocated in different ways, in particular, between the legislative, executive, and judicative branch. Also, certain non-state actors may effectively be tasked with economic policy decision making, such as employer and employee organisations in collective wage bargaining or professional organisations in setting technical standards.

In practice, factual enforcement by physical means will only be effectuated in a small minority of cases, but key categories of state intervention take place, and obtain their effectiveness from a credible threat of physical enforcement as an instrument of last resort. The most important example is, of course, taxation as a financial basis of state activity. Modern states also engage in a broad variety of other regulative measures, reaching from the protection of property and freedom of contracts to more specific measures, such as price controls, standard setting, or restrictions on certain types of agreements, such as rental contracts, labour contracts, or cartels. Apart from this, the state can influence the market process by generating income (by social transfers, subsidies, and wages to state employees) or engage in the provision of products itself, which in modern welfare states covers vast areas, such as health, education, and physical infrastructure, but can also pertain to standard areas of

See, for the role of violence in enforcing institutions, Chapter 9, section 5.2.

industrial production. Embedded in this, there is a wide array of measures trying to influence citizens' behaviour by both financial and non-financial means, such as nudging. Monetary policy has emerged as a separate field of economic policy that manages the supply of fiat currencies via separate institutions, namely central banks.

Roughly, economic policy measures can be located on three levels. The first level is constituted by discretionary measures intervening in the market process, such as a decision on anti-cyclical fiscal policy or a subsidy of a firm. Such interventions can, in principle, take place on a micro level, such as the latter, or the macro level (i.e., encompassing the overall economy), such as the former. The second level concerns measures that set and change the rules of the game of market behaviour, including policy principles, such as the commitment to a market economy and respect of private property, or constraints to economic policy, such as expropriation. The third level encompasses measures to set and change the rules of the game of the policy process themselves; for example, the system of government, the structure and appointment of government (e.g., via elections, party systems, and federalist structures), and the distribution of power between different political organisations. The third level is often not dealt with under the category of economic policy; in our account, however, it will play an important role as the self-regulating character of political competition:[2] Unlike in economic competition, political decision makers can alter the rules pertaining to their decisions themselves; in other words, there is a recursive relationship between economic policy and its institutional constraints. Taken together, the second and third level, including the international level, constitute the institutional framework of the economic order, both in the international and intrajurisdictional perspective.

These three levels overlap with the distinction between a constitutional and institutional level with reference to transaction cost: Discretionary measures and rules of the game for markets directly concern economic transaction cost and are, therefore, attributable to the institutional level whereas the rules of the game of the political process are of a constitutional nature. However, this distinction needs to be complemented by the hierarchy of the legal-formal framework by which economic policy is normally conducted.[3] Here, constitutional norms refer to formal institutions with high barriers to change (in democracies, requirements of parliamentary super-majorities beyond 50 percent) and a high level of generality; they can be found on the second as well as the third level; for example, in the case of constitutionally enshrined property rights. Ordinary laws (with a standardised change requirement of a 50 percent parliamentary majority) can vary widely in terms of their level of generality and can, therefore, be found on all three levels. Executive orders, implemented by the administration/bureaucracy, regularly relate to concrete circumstances or groups and are, therefore, restricted to the first level.

Economic policy can impose a wide variety of regulations, including those backed by threat of physical enforcement, but also soft influence, such as nudging, and generate income for market actors.

Economic policy can be conducted on three levels, namely discretionary measures, rules of the game for market behaviour, and rules of the game for the political process.

Political competition is self-regulating since participants can actively change the rules of the game.

2.2. Political competition as an evolutionary process

By necessity, economic policy is constituted by concrete policy decisions (which encompass the enactment of a measure as well as a possible active decision to leave rules unchanged). These decisions are distilled from a larger pool of what we call policy proposals, to which resources aimed at their adoption are directed. This is the most basic reason why the policy process can be conceptualised in terms of evolutionary political competition: Among a large variety of proposals for policy measures, only a few will be selected in terms of being realised and implemented, and eventually, retained in terms of being kept in the established set of formal institutions. Concomitantly, there is competition for institutionalised power positions which – besides potentially conferring other advantages, such as access to financial resources or social status – increase the potential of realising such proposals.

Evolutionary political competition is defined as concomitant competition between policy proposals and for institutionalised power positions.

Therefore, policy proposals are subject to an evolutionary process of variation, selection, and retention (VSR), where retention in the political context primarily denotes the implementation and, eventually, enforcement of the respective (bundle of) measure(s). Generalising existing theories of the policy process,[4] competition between proposals is assumed to take place in different interconnected realms and related VSR processes (Figure 17.1). Relating to the state/jurisdiction as the core entity of reference, we distinguish three realms of internal selection, namely competition for public opinion, competition for votes, and competition for organised bottom-up influence on political decision makers, in particular, competition between interest groups. External selection is generated by the realm of institutional competition, which takes place between geographical entities (i.e., interjurisdictional competition). Internal and external selection criteria intertwine at the level of preparation, adoption, and implementation/enforcement of policy proposals: For example, decision makers have to balance pressure from internal interest groups and concerns with respect to external competitiveness. Here, we distinguish two realms: first, decision making on adoption of policy measures; second, the realm of the bureaucracy, whose formal responsibility is the preparation, technical concretisation, and implementation of proposals.

Political competition takes place in different interconnected realms.

The policy process does not take place in a linear temporal fashion; rather, the generation of economic policy decisions results from a complex co-evolution of competitive processes in the outlined competitive realms. In these processes, two categories of selective hierarchies can be distinguished. First, there are political organisations, mainly interest group organisations and political parties, where competition between policy proposals takes place on both an intra- and interorganisational level. Second, there is locational competition on different levels reaching from competition between jurisdictions, which is the focus of our framework, to competition between subnational regions (in the context of federalism) or urban agglomerations.

Political competition entails selective hierarchies both in terms of geographical entities and political organisations.

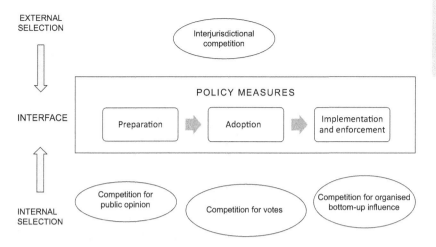

EXTERNAL
SELECTION

INTERFACE

INTERNAL
SELECTION

Interjurisdictional
competition

POLICY MEASURES

Preparation → Adoption → Implementation
and enforcement

Competition for
public opinion

Competition for votes

Competition for organised
bottom-up influence

Figure. 17.1 The structure of evolutionary political competition
Political competition is conceptualised as competition between policy
proposals taking place in different competitive realms. Relating to the state
as the core entity of economic policy, internal VSR processes for proposals
take place for public opinion, votes (electoral competition), and organised
bottom-up influence on political decision makers. External selective forces
stem from interjurisdictional competition. Both levels intertwine in the actual
adoption of proposals by political decision makers, which is complemented
by preparation and implementation by the bureaucracy.

As in market competition, the structure and outcomes of political competition are heavily shaped by its institutional rules of the game. Those rules tend
to be highly formalised in the case of liberal democracies, where they are
based on rule of law-principles, with the outlined hierarchy of legal norms as
a key example. Notably, however, except competition for votes in the narrower sense, political competition takes place in authoritarian regimes as well,
given that even a dictatorship has to rely on a minimum amount of support in
its constituency.[5] The key difference to democratic regimes is that authoritarian elites have more discretionary leeway in balancing internal and external
selection: internally because the competition of factions or interest groups –
which can factually be intense – is less institutionalised and imbued with
higher risk, including violent repression, than in democracies; externally
because authoritarian regimes have more extensive scope to control exit and
voice as the classic mechanisms of institutional competition (see further section later).

The self-regulating character of political competition implies that unlike in
economic competition, political actors have the possibility to create formal-
institutional niches, in the sense of stabilising their power position, for

*Structure and
outcomes of political
competition depend
on its institutional
rules of the game.*

*The self-regulating
character of political
competition entails
the formation of
institutional niches.*

themselves or other political and economic actors; for example, by creating and/or occupying positions in the bureaucracy or, in a more extreme case, by changing from a democratic to an authoritarian regime. Those niches are contested both by pressures of external selection (for example, a patronage-based bureaucracy needs to be replaced by an expert-based one in the context of interjurisdictional competition) and internal selection (for example, the respective bureaucratic organisation is abolished by a new government). Ultimately, therefore, policy measures, power positions and their occupation, and rules of the game co-evolve on the different levels.

The policy process is shaped by knowledge asymmetries and differences in interpretation. This applies to policy measures ex ante and their effects ex post.

As in the case of markets, the economic policy process is characterised by a principally decentralised distribution of knowledge.[6] There are knowledge asymmetries in various constellations between different parts of the constituency, in particular, citizens-voters, political decision makers, (organised) supporters, and political entrepreneurs. How these asymmetries develop over time – for example, whether diffusion of knowledge and standardisation of interpretation of certain issues takes place as a consequence of political competition – will depend, among others, on the following:

- Underlying structures of social networks: for example, diffusion will work differently in a society structured by strong rather than weak ties; the degree of polarisation may be influenced as well.[7]
- Information and communication technologies: for example, opinion polls and related (online) methods to obtain knowledge about prospective voting behaviour; the presence and role of economic statistics in the policy debate.
- The role and availability of (incomplete) expert knowledge on substantive as well as procedural issues with respect to the propagation of policy proposals.[8]

Third-person view rankings of policies are not feasible.

This corresponds to the analysis of Chapter 9, sections 4.2 and 5.4.

See, for the performative role of economic statistics Chapter 13, section 6.1.

The effects of policy measures are ex ante unclear and ex post subject to – possibly differential – interpretations in the first- and second-person view.[9] The fundamental implication is that the traditional notion of an objective – that is, third-person view – ranking of different economic policy measures along their capacity to maximise a certain criterion of welfare is misplaced, even if we abstract from the impossibility of aggregating heterogenous preferences into a coherent social ordering or welfare function.[10] This is not only because of ex ante uncertainty regarding policy outcomes but also because complexity leaves leeway for subjective ex post interpretations of those outcomes that cannot be falsified in an objectified sense. The continuous feedback between policy measures and their contested interpretation implies that the notion of economic welfare is itself endogenous to the policy process and subject to targeted influence.[11] This is one reason why an (international- or national-level) comparison of institutional arrangements along objectified welfare criteria is not possible. At the same time, such criteria can play a performative role in the policy process, primarily via the influence of theory-based economic advice. Performativity can also pertain to the establishment of beliefs on causal relations, for example, between a progressive income tax and the distribution of income and wealth, and the standard differentiation between policy objectives and instruments.

As in economic competition, a key driver of political competition is entrepreneurship.[12] Political entrepreneurs are similar to their economic counterparts in engaging into a risky discovery process, testing hypotheses on the adoption of policy proposals and attainment of power positions, and receiving feedback in a context of fundamental uncertainty, which, similar to markets, will be strongly influenced by concrete network structures of communication and observation. In line with this, entrepreneurial activity pertains to actively influencing actors' perceptions (public opinion in the political context, see further section later). They differ from the market realm, however, in lacking a direct financial measuring rod (i.e., profit) for their evolutionary success. Rather, relations between political power and the acquisition of financial capital are complex and highly dependent on concrete circumstances: For example, certain contexts at least indirectly allow for vote-buying whereas others strictly rule it out; similarly, the attainment of political power positions will be associated with the acquisition of financial capital to a strongly varying degree. In fact, in political competition, the role of idealistic entrepreneurship involving a decoupling of evolutionary success (in terms of political influence and the eventual adoption of a policy proposal) and the appropriation of material resources is likely to be more important than in the economic realm.

3. Realms of political competition

3.1. Competition for public opinion

Political beliefs are fluid and subject to a continuous network-based process of change. Given that policy decisions are inevitably based on those political beliefs, competition for influencing beliefs is a fundamental component of the policy process.[13]

In principle, subjective views on economic policy held by the public can be organised into two categories of political beliefs: first, *normative* beliefs with respect to the desirability of certain states of the economic/social system (e.g., a more egalitarian income distribution); and second, *positive-causal* beliefs on how such a state can best be achieved (e.g., a progressive income tax).[14] Taken together, these beliefs constitute a category of narratives, as related to the political realm: Political events (understood in a general sense) are imbued with meaning, both in constructing causal relations and in judging them against a normative ideal.

Political competition is driven by political entrepreneurs. Contrary to economic competition, there is no direct financial measuring rod for evolutionary success.

Political beliefs contain normative and positive-causal elements. They are fluid and subject to competition for influence.

Attention is a key resource in competition for public opinion. Its zero-sum character entails a potential for evolutionary arms races, which conflicts with the one-person-one-vote principle.

Political (or, in this case, issue) entrepreneurs will compete to influence both categories of political beliefs in their preferred direction. In this, they face complex feedback mechanisms: For example, journalists may prima facie act as idealistic issue entrepreneurs but may also face sanctions and rewards in a market setting of competition between mass media.[15] One element that is likely to be exacerbated in the political realm is competition for attention, given limited incentives of citizens to acquire information in light of, for example, the paradox of voting, and possibly, limited cognitive and educational capacity to understand the relevant issues.[16] Given that recipients' resources for attention are principally limited in terms of time (combined with cognitive capacity), competition for attention is one example for a feature that is characteristic of wide parts of political competition, namely its character as a zero-sum game, possibly with a winner-takes-all-structure, creating a potential for evolutionary arms races.[17] Arms races exhibit a specific problem in a democratic environment organised around the one-person-one-vote principle insofar as the implied transformability of unequally distributed financial capital into political influence endangers the political competitive level playing field. Therefore, some democracies intervene in market-based competition for public opinion via the payment of subsidies to smaller publications, such as newspapers.[18] In theory, public service broadcasters are supposed to serve a similar purpose via the provision of unbiased information and the neutral reflection of a variety of standpoints. In practice, however, these organisations tend to be subject to targeted political influence.

Political beliefs are relatively inert but can be subject to frequency-dependent change.

A further characteristic of political beliefs is that they tend to be relatively inert. Positive beliefs on economic policy (proposals) are almost exclusively situated in a second-person view and, in general, less easily testable than in the economic realm (e.g., with respect to the ability of an entrepreneurial service to satisfy a consumer's needs or wants). Also, political beliefs are often deeply rooted in social identity and tend to be transmitted from one generation to the next such that a fundamental revision of beliefs on the individual level tends to be relatively rare.[19] Finally, as a category of narratives, political beliefs tend to exhibit a highly collective character, if only because some individuals may use others' beliefs as a shortcut for forming their own, but also possibly driven by collective dispositions, such as conformity pressure, which may drive a wedge between publicly voiced and privately held beliefs. As a consequence, the evolution of beliefs can be driven by frequency dependence, with the possibility of tipping points in case of a discrepancy between publicly voiced and privately held beliefs.[20] A case in point are revolutionary situations, such as in Eastern European countries in 1989 where both the Communist elites and Western observers were caught by surprise by the swiftness and strength of the public turnaround.

For the definition and role of narratives in the economic realm, see Chapter 7, section 4.2, and Chapter 13, section 4.2.

3.2. Competition for votes within jurisdictions

Competition for votes can take place as a contest for political decision making positions (electoral competition) or with respect to concrete policy decisions (direct democracy).[21] Electoral competition can essentially be viewed as the institutional attribution of a temporary monopoly for political decision making power (although based on election results, there remains significant discretionary leeway for political decision makers, for example, in terms of establishing party coalitions).[22] In that context, it exhibits important similarities to market competition, with political entrepreneurs offering bundles of policy proposals to prospective voters under conditions of fundamental uncertainty.[23]

In almost all democratic constituencies, electoral competition is structured by political parties.[24] There are strong endogenous forces that compartmentalise electoral competition into political parties, with the arguments partly resembling those of the theory of the firm. Party organisations serve as repositories of knowledge and routines for the propagation of (bundles of) policy proposals and, by internal specialisation and a respective pooling of resources, can eventually obtain a competitive advantage over the hypothetical alternative of an individual entrepreneur or an ad hoc social movement.[25] Parties also function as political brands, providing simplifying cues to prospective voters on their political programs and identities.[26] A further incentive for the establishment of political parties can result from institutional exigencies; for example, the conditioning of public subsidies on the existence of a party structure.[27] Those rules are important examples for the self-regulating character of political competition, given that the establishment of such regulations by incumbent parties will tend to increase competitive entry barriers for newcomers.

Given the endogeneity of political beliefs in the contest for public opinion, an important function of political parties is the organisation of the electorate into relatively stable segments of systems of beliefs or ideologies. These segments frequently correspond to social cleavages.[28] Party system alignment along those cleavages exhibits a parallel to market competition insofar as it is characterised by relative stasis and a low contestability of competitive positions, with oligopolistic parties concentrating on their – cognitively relatively inert, see previous section – segments of the electorate. This stasis, in turn, can be punctuated by relatively rapid change, such as when highly endowed political entrepreneurs exploit new socio-economic problems, as, for example, resulting from migration movements.

In sum, rather than just aggregating political preferences, the organisational structure of electoral competition co-evolves with political beliefs, mediated by entrepreneurial effort both on the intra- and interparty level. Also, it is shaped by, and at the same time influences, the formal-institutional framework of political competition. Electoral competition stands in a partly complementary, partly substitutive relationship to bottom-up competition for political influence between interest groups, to which we turn next.

Electoral competition resembles market competition in that political suppliers offer bundles of policy proposals to gain a temporary monopoly of political power.

There are strong endogenous forces to structure electoral competition as competition between political parties.

Party systems can align with social cleavages, but this is subject to endogenous change, partly depending on the electoral system.

For the role of stasis in market competition, see Chapter 11, section 4.2.

3.3. Competition for (bottom-up) influence on political decision makers

This realm of political competition covers the full range of formation and competition of interest groups and social movements with different degrees of

*Given fundamental
uncertainty on the
effects of policy
measures, interests
are not objectively
given but emerge
from the policy
process.*

*The organisation
of interests faces
several obstacles,
resulting in an
uneven degree of
organisation of
different interests.*

For the role
of emotions
and identity in
group formation,
see Chapter 8,
section 3.3.

*Competition
between interest
groups resembles
competition between
firms in terms of its
multilevel nature, its
potentially predatory
character, and the
role of product
differentiation.*

organisation, including lobbies and advocacy organisations, but also NGOs. Interests, like political preferences, are not objectively given but emerge from a communicative process.[29] For example, it is not a priori clear which groups in a constituency will benefit from the introduction of a regime of free capital movement: The domestic financial industry may gain from enlarged investment opportunities abroad but also face increased competition on its own terrain.

The shaping and organisation of interests by political entrepreneurs are inherently problematic for several reasons. First, there is standard entrepreneurial risk, posed by fundamental uncertainty on political impact, and the risk of repression in case of an authoritarian regime. Second, there is a collective action problem, given that the marginal prospect of influencing the policy process from an individual perspective is minuscule, measured by the gains that can be won.[30] However, in many (although not all) political contexts, membership of a group and group-based activity have strong emotional components and can become part of personal identity. Incentivisation for participation is generally easier in small rather than large groups, as classically emphasised on the discussion around lobbying for and against free trade.[31]

Competition between policy proposals in this competitive realm is of a multilevel nature, encompassing the exit versus voice decision on the inter- versus intra-organisational level. Given that criteria of success are much fuzzier for interest groups than for business firms (except that they must keep up a minimum of financial income in order to survive), intra-organisational elites have significant leeway to promote or block bottom-up proposals from their membership or other actors. On the inter-organisational level, competition between interest groups will sometimes entail a predatory character, with certain groups trying to monopolise the representation of certain interests; in the context of the self-regulating character of political competition, this can also be supported institutionally, such as via an introduction of obligatory membership to certain (professional) organisations.[32]

Many interest group organisations engage in political branding and product differentiation. Accordingly, the degree of organisation of different interests is not only relevant with respect to their eventual clout to influence the policy process but also their potential to attract new supporters who may initially be undecided or even opposed vis-à-vis the policy proposals. Analogously to party competition, many interest group organisations face a choice between a polarising (in the party context: partisan) and an integrating (in the party context: catch-all) strategy. On the one hand, there is an incentive to polarise since too much of a consensus with established policies essentially takes away their business rationale; on the other hand, there may be substantial gains from cooperation – and eventually compromising – between interest groups in the propagation of policy proposals.[33]

A standard economic critique of interest group competition refers to unproductive rent-seeking in the political realm. The argument is that lobbying and related activity of interest groups constitutes a waste of resources, given that it purportedly aims at mere redistribution of an already existing economic product.[34] But this view ignores the potential knowledge-generating function of rent-seeking to policymakers – most commonly via the provision of substantive expertise but also of grassroots information on political beliefs and their evolution.[35] Also, both economic and political competition are inevitably associated with the occurrence of winners and losers, at least in terms of their relative positions; there is no ex ante criterion with respect to which winner-loser constellation is preferable. Rather, the criterion is itself a result of the policy process, part of which is endogenously driven by interest groups (see, for the role of political leadership, further section later).

Despite these points, there remains a concern with the amount of resources devoted to interest group activity, namely with respect to the potential for arms races. This is because unlike competition between firms, whose state space can be expanded by economic growth and technological progress, policy space is limited and not all – in particular, of course, substantively contradictory – policy proposals can be realised at the same time (with legislators facing similar issues with respect to attention and time as in the case of competition for public opinion outlined earlier). Indeed, presumedly excessive financial resources flowing into lobbying, particularly by business organisations, are a political concern in almost all Western democracies, given the tension with the one-person-one-vote principle.

This issue is exacerbated by the general tendency towards a progressive organisation of interests, which is historically observable in many democracies and also manifested by phenomena of mobilisation and counter-mobilisation in the context of social movements.[36] Given this, the institutional approach to regulating interest group competition in democracies is ambiguous: On the one hand, there are institutional limits to certain categories of interest group activity that are deemed undemocratic, such as using donations to legislators as a lobbying device. On the other hand, the influence of certain interest groups can be highly institutionalised; for example, in the case of wage bargaining in corporatist states.

In sum, the role of interest groups in the overall setup of competition for economic policy measures is ambiguous and context dependent. Interest groups may play an important connecting role between political elites and their constituencies that, in bridging informational asymmetries and signalling preferences of different parts of the electorate, may constitute a more fine-grained democratic feedback mechanism to decision makers than elections. In contrast, competition between interest groups in a wide range of contexts – including trade unions and social movements – may endogenously contribute to polarisation and almost inevitably leads to differential weights of interests that does not correspond to the one-person-one-vote principle.

The depiction of rent-seeking as economically unproductive disregards its knowledge-generating function.

Arms races in interest group competition can be economically rational but conflict with the one-person-one-vote principle.

Political competition creates endogenous forces towards a progressive organisation of interests.

3.4. Interjurisdictional competition

Interjurisdictional competition is the main source of external selection pressure on economic policy decisions. In a system of international relations that allows for cross-border movements of goods and services, capital, and labour (and notably, information flows), jurisdictions explicitly or implicitly compete for economic resources which can eventually be translated into political power – mediated, for example, by the build-up of military capacity (hard power) or higher persuasiveness of that country's (socio-)economic model in the context of international institutional diffusion and learning (soft power). For both forms of power, gains will increase the prospect of respective policy measures to be adopted in other countries.[37]

Interjurisdictional competition for resources eventually translates into changes of international power positions.

Given the possibility of cross-border movements, interjurisdictional competition is driven by the exit and voice mechanism: Exit works via migration and capital movements as a consequence of perceived institutional (dis)advantages; voice, via so-called yardstick competition in which economic actors are assumed to benchmark the institutional performance of their jurisdiction against others.[38] Exit and voice can lead to institutional innovation and imitation, which we already mentioned as a significant driver of institutional evolution. Interjurisdictional competition, like all evolutionary competition, is a struggle for relative rank and, as such, does not depend on objective conditions. At the same time, the presence of interjurisdictional competition as a level of selection implies that criteria of internal and external selective success are interdependent and can diverge. The most general level on which this manifests itself is Rodrik's trilemma of globalisation, democracy, and the nation state.[39] Its implicit assumption is that the internal selection criteria of a national-level democratic policy process contradict the external criteria stemming from necessities and consequences of globalisation; for example, with regard to protectionist measures or tensions between redistributional demands and the need to keep the jurisdiction attractive for foreign investors.

See Chapter 9, section 4.3, and Chapter 14, section 4.1.

The selection criteria of inter- and intrajurisdictional competition can diverge, raising Rodrik's globalisation trilemma.

Rodrik's trilemma needs to be complemented by a more concrete depiction of the complex ways in which internal and external selection play out, and interact, in the policy process. This is particularly relevant with regard to the tightness of external selection criteria on internal economic policy measures, which can vary greatly from country to country and institution to institution. For example, if a domestic policy process generates a consensus that openness to goods/services and factor movements is overall beneficial (as prevalent, for example, in small open economies such as Switzerland and Sweden), then selection pressure as such may not be felt and the tension between globalisation and sovereign democracy may at least go unrecognised for a significant amount of time. Also, the reaction speed of international financial markets, another standard restriction for national policymakers, can vary greatly and is imbued with uncertainty.

Although interjurisdictional competition is of a continuous nature, it is a highly inaccurate signal with respect to concrete policy change since its workability depends on a number of relatively strong conditions.[40] First, the rules of the game for interjurisdictional competition need to be designed in a way to allow for a sufficient degree of mobility to render the exit threat credible. Second, labour and capital must exhibit a sufficient amount of factual mobility, which is problematic particularly for labour where significant social, cultural, and other obstacles for free movement exist. Third, complex institutional differences and their consequences must be interpreted by constituencies and political elites in a relatively uniform way, which again is ambiguous in practice: For example, it is a priori unclear how multinational enterprises react to changes in corporate taxation or labour standards since those measures are routinely part of a larger package of complementary institutions that are relevant for a locational decision. In line with this, race to the bottom concerns with respect to labour standards have often proved unfounded; for example, high standards of employment protection can be complementary to a well-developed educational system, fostering the development of firm-specific human capital and trustful employment relationships.[41]

The policy consequences of interjurisdictional competition are uncertain and highly context dependent, given the bundled character of relevant measures.

3.5. Occupation of political elite positions and political decision making

The interface between internal and external selection criteria of the policy process is constituted by political elite positions and decision making, together with the complementary tasks of the bureaucracy which is covered in the next section. In principle, decision makers can be assumed to strive for attainment and maintenance of political power positions and, with that, for an increase of their potential to get policy proposals adopted. In doing this, they essentially have to balance selection pressure from the outlined four realms of political competition and face two major constraints. First, there are multiple, and partly overlapping, principal agent relationships (for example, most ministers have simultaneous roles as heads of a bureaucratic organisation and party members; members of parliament, albeit normally endowed with free mandates, have to manage relations to their democratic constituencies) that are endowed with sanctioning potential in case of non-compliant behaviour (party membership can be removed; re-election can fail). Second, there are the rules of the game of the decision making process itself, which, in most democracies, entail a system of checks and balances.

Political decision making constitutes the interface between internal and external selection criteria.

Decision makers are constrained by multiple principal–agent relationships as well as the rules of the game of the policy process.

At the same time, political decision makers routinely enjoy – and in the context of the self-regulating character of political competition, create – significant discretionary leeway in decision making. Sanctions in the context of principal–agent relationships frequently only come with a time lag, with the most important case constituted by election intervals. Such lags form the

See, for the
role of time
consistency
in fiscal and
monetary policy,
Chapter 13,
section 6.

*Within their
constraints,
decision makers
enjoy significant
decisional leeway,
which necessitates
an analysis of
political leadership.*

*A key function of
political leadership
is to establish shared
notions of economic
and social welfare.*

*The welfare concept
determines the
categorisation of
certain interests as
particularistic.*

*Political decision
making entails a
Coasean framework
of internalising
externalities by
negotiations, albeit
under conditions
of fundamental
uncertainty.*

basis of the time inconsistency problem of economic policy, which is built on the potential of elected politicians (or other decision makers receiving fixed appointments for certain periods) to renege from previous promises in order to achieve certain policy results. Also, decision makers as well as their principals are faced with constitutive uncertainty on the effects of policy measures as well as their interpretation, which allows decision makers to attribute different weights to different interests. In this context, decision makers routinely engage in actively influencing political beliefs in the sense outlined earlier.

As a consequence, a theory of economic policy needs to include the phenomenon of political leadership.[42] One of the most important functions of political leadership is the establishment of shared notions of economic and social welfare. The welfare concept here is not understood in the traditional sense of aggregating individual preferences and the determination of Pareto optimal results, which is barred by the problem of fundamental uncertainty, the principal interdependence of preferences, and the transaction cost of eventual lump sum transfers. Rather, it relates to the establishment of an autonomous construct that is widely shared by the constituency, in Rousseau's sense of a *volonté générale* that goes beyond the *volonté de tous*. Examples are the notion of a social welfare state, coupled with acceptance of higher levels of taxation and redistributive activity, and the notion of openness to international trade and investment in which material well-being is at least implicitly traded off against higher dependence on international openness and, potentially, higher economic inequality.[43] These concepts, possibly coupled with the development of relevant economic statistics (see previous section), can eventually assume a performative role in shaping economic policies.

In democracies, such notions of welfare involve a large-scale process of communication and negotiation in the context of the competitive realms outlined earlier. In negotiations with interest groups, the general welfare concept and the definition of 'particularistic' interests are then interdependent.[44] Consider again the example of opening up to trade (e.g., by lowering a tariff barrier). If a welfare definition is established along conventional economic lines, opposition by interests of import-competing industries would count as particularistic and likely be framed along the lines of the general welfare concept (e.g., by stressing trust and higher certainty on quality for consumers). In contrast, if the welfare definition emphasises national security and autonomy, the attribution of particularism would more likely be directed to the groups of consumers who benefit from cheaper imports.

In this context, one main component of economic policy is the conduct of negotiations in a Coasean framework of internalising externalities. Returning to the earlier example, and assuming that (at least implicitly) the standard economic welfare definition prevails, one typical government task is to broker a compensatory agreement which secures the overall welfare gains while avoiding the occurrence of losses for specific groups.[45] Notably, however, these negotiations again take place under conditions of fundamental uncertainty, particularly on the actual gains to be won, the derived compensation, unintended side effects of the redistributional measures, and at least indirectly, the transaction cost of the negotiations themselves, including the cost of organising interests in the first place. This reinforces the role of discretionary decisional leeway in the political process.

3.6. Policy implementation and the bureaucracy

Policy measures, particularly in legislative form, while implemented, habitually leave significant leeway of interpretation and concretisation. As said, there is a distinct organisational structure, the bureaucracy, which normally bears responsibility for this stage. In fact, measures taken on the legislative and top executive (i.e., government) level and the bureaucracy often do not follow a strictly sequential fashion but are substantively and temporally intertwined.

Given significant leeway on the implementation of policy measures, political and bureaucratic decision making is often intertwined.

In the traditional separation of powers setup, the bureaucracy is mostly seen as a technocratic structure commanding expertise on the technical and operational aspects of policy implementation. It is thus supposed to address knowledge deficits on the political level (given that in democracies, there are no substantive requirements for decision makers in terms of education or experience to be elected to office) and to stabilise the policy process against the vagaries of the electoral cycle and interest group influence.[46] In policy practice, however, the bureaucratic process exhibits a political character in several respects. Bureaucracies are regularly involved in the preparation of laws, pre-structuring options for political decision makers and often largely controlling the interaction with interest groups. Second, the level of factual, and sometimes formal-legislative, decision making power can shift between the political (i.e., legislative-governmental) and the bureaucratic level depending on its degree of politicisation.[47] Furthermore, in many countries, the occupation of bureaucratic positions is subject to political influence (e.g., via party patronage).[48]

Despite the intended stabilising function of substantive expertise, the bureaucratic process exhibits a political character in several respects.

Discretionary leeway of bureaucrats vis-à-vis its political principals is supported by the frequent occurrence of lifetime tenure or similar constructs, the lack of a pecuniary performance criterion comparable to profits, and relatively high organisational stability based on the reliance on revenue enforced by state power (i.e., taxation). Given this, behavioural assumptions on members of the bureaucracy obtain central significance, which range from the standard public choice approach of maximising internal power and budget allocation to intrinsic motivation for public service.[49] Against this background, we stress the performative potential of compensation schemes, both in terms of manifested behaviour and the types of agents attracted by public service. An excessively performance-oriented approach in New Public Management may crowd out more public-spirited behaviour with concrete impacts (e.g., on the

Bureaucratic behaviour can be performatively influenced by models of management stressing pecuniary incentives.

level of corruption or the creaming of unemployed recipients of reintegration support).[50]

4. Deliberation, values, and economic policy

4.1. Inclusive deliberation as a procedural criterion

The quality of the policy process can be improved by ensuring broadest possible inclusion.

For a discussion of evaluating institutions, see Chapter 9, section 5.4.

Inclusion is unlikely to be an endogenous result of the policy process, including in democracies.

Given the endogenous analysis of the policy process in the previous section, the question arises for exogenous criteria by which this process could be judged. We have argued that in terms of comparative institutional analysis, a realisation-focused comparison is necessary which focuses on procedural criteria assuring the inclusivity of participation.[51] In principle, these criteria apply fully to the domain of economic policy measures. This is because inclusivity makes sure that economic policy acts on a broad informational basis. In view of the relative coarseness of democratic feedback via electoral competition, it also ensures that policies are subject to a constant test of legitimacy and can, therefore, evolve in a relatively continuous manner, as opposed to disruptive change that potentially follows a growing gap between (political) elites and their constituencies.

At the same time, it is clearly unlikely that the required conditions for broad inclusivity will emerge endogenously even in a democratic policy process. A core reason for this is the existence of pervasive collective action problems, given that the perceived individual prospect of influencing policy results will normally be very small: Rational ignorance may render the informational basis of collective decision making very weak;[52] the paradox of voting raises the possibility of high rates of abstention from the electoral process; as well, individual cost benefit analysis may lead to an avoidance of engagement in interest group activity (see previous section).

Part of those problems may be overcome by cultural norms, such as a civic duty to vote, and a consumption character of, or positive emotional attachment to, political activity.[53] But since those are informal institutions that may be shared only by subsets of the constituency, the deliberative process may still be distorted, at least against the benchmark of full inclusivity. The same is true with respect to unequal resource endowments: Some people may lack educational or cognitive capacities to judge policy-related issues; others may simply lack time due to work-related or other requirements. Finally, there are issues of frequency dependence and conformity pressure, which may prevent people from revealing their private preferences.[54] This means that even the results of a deliberative process that prima facie fulfils criteria of inclusivity may be distorted in terms of adequately reflecting the full range of concerned interests.

From these points, quality criteria for the policy process can be derived. On a basic level, we can provide a re-confirmation of the classic ideal of free speech, including freedom of the press and the right to organise interests, which establishes the policy process as competitive. However, political competition may result in large asymmetries of power and influence and, therefore, needs to be embedded in institutions that enforce openness and a level playing field. This means that the principle of one-person-one-vote should, mutatis mutandis, extend to all realms of political competition, in the sense of a democratic competition policy which levels out the effects of economic inequality on political participation as far as possible. This implies an equalisation of financial endowments of political competitors, meaning, for example, that small political parties should be subsidised and the lobbying power of financially strong interests curtailed. Also, the state can directly relate inclusivity of deliberation to the internalisation of the Coasean externalities mentioned earlier. For example, if negotiations between two parties, such as employees and employers, generate external effects on third parties that negotiators do not realise or care about, such as pollution on nearby inhabitants, it would be the state's task to provide an obligatory negotiation role for third parties or at least decrease the political transaction cost of their participation. Effectively, therefore, the state would engage in democratic competition policy by organising certain interests.

Another issue is the question of whose interests are represented in the policy process in the first place. Although in the history of democracies, we have seen a gradual extension of suffrage to men of lower social classes and women, this is not true for children, although the factor of externalities generated by other groups clearly applies. There is, therefore, a strong economic argument for providing vicarious suffrage to parents and/or to establish an institutionalised representation of children, and possibly, future generations yet unborn, in interest group competition.[55] A related argument can be made for animals and other living beings.[56]

Inclusivity is weakened by collective action problems and unequal resource endowments.

Assuring inclusivity entails conduct of a democratic competition policy.

The scope of represented interests needs to be extended to groups whose members cannot participate on an individual basis, in particular, children and future generations.

4.2. Freedom and human dignity as substantive criteria

As we have shown, there is no substantive exogenous third-person criterion by which the economic policy process can be judged. Correspondingly, there is a priori no way to distinguish revealed from true interests. However, we can ask which conditions best enable individuals to identify those interests for themselves. This directly relates back to the concept of freedom as constituted by a degree of self-control and power to rather than just freedom from in the negative sense. The procedural criteria outlined earlier correspond to this notion of freedom: Only participation in the political process that is possible in a fashion widely independent from economic (and other) inequalities will grant the freedom to individuals to reflect their interests and choose accordingly. In that sense, the normative criterion of freedom in economic decision making, which is one of the constitutive elements of a market economy, dovetails with political freedom.

'Freedom to' grants individuals the potential to reflect their needs and interests and to choose accordingly.

*The key implication
of ensuring
freedom in a
meaningful sense
is the limitation
of political and
economic power.*

For more on
the connection
between markets
and authoritarian
systems, see
Chapter 9,
section 2.2.

*The emotional
counterpart of
freedom is the
principle of human
dignity, whose
respect is a universal
human desire.*

Maximisation of the individual domain of power to has a fundamental economic policy implication in limiting political and economic power. Democratic and economic competition policy both appear to serve this objective, and there are implications for a wide range of economic policy fields. For example, insofar as power to (as well as power over) is an inherent characteristic of private property, redistributional policies, in particular with respect to the wealth distribution, are a consequence of the pursuit of freedom rather than contradicting it. Indeed, classic market liberals and German ordoliberalism have always stressed this aspect and, therefore, for example, advocated a steep inheritance tax.[57] Power-equalising measures also encompass the amelioration of inequalities in capability specificity and of certain categories of hold-up problems that result from these inequalities. This would include, for example, the establishment of an educational system that provides universal access to broad education.

Furthermore, a focus needs to be on the tight interrelation between political and economic power. A core result of German ordoliberal thinking was that a centrally planned economy is irreconcilable with the principles of a liberal democracy since the power of decision making over core parts of economic dispositions is effectively relegated to the state.[58] In a similar vein, a widely monopolised industry is unlikely to form a solid basis of an inclusive democracy.[59] In contrast, there are certainly examples of authoritarian systems under which markets economies can thrive. But since economic liberties in such systems lack an institutional foundation controlling and limiting governmental power, markets in such systems remain ultimately precarious.

The focus on individual liberty needs to be complemented by a second principle that centres more on the emotional component of human and social life. The necessity of this comes from the intertwined character of rationality and emotions: A rational process of deliberation based on the principle of freedom requires an emotional grounding if it is to be viable. We propose the underlying principle to be human dignity. Dignity, first, implies to respect other humans in their full individuality, including their bodily existence and needs. Recognition of participation in democratic deliberation is then built on this respect, including in situations of inequality in economic or other dimensions.

A focus on dignity entails policy-related implications in several instances. One is the requirement to generally reject exploitative labour relations (e.g., in the form of extreme specialisation and deskilling of employees). Another is the connection of the emotionally grounded recognition of a person as an individual to social solidarity: The relation between the high- and low-skilled would then not be framed in terms of (perceived and/or measured) productivity differentials but as a complementary work-sharing arrangement in which each party plays an indispensable role. Such an approach is, for example, implied in the German model of workers' co-determination (*Mitbestimmung*), but it is also related to the social welfare state, where a sense of solidarity of upper-class social strata with lower classes has been shown to increase the acceptance of redistributive activity.[60] This solidarity, in turn, may decrease with the heterogeneity of the population resulting from immigration. Indeed, as a consequence of the human propensity for group formation, increasing diversity renders the recognition of dignity more salient as a normative principle but also more difficult to realise, particularly in emotional terms.[61]

Dignity and social solidarity are tightly interrelated, raising challenges for heterogenous societies.

4.3. The deliberative policy process in interjurisdictional competition

An inclusive policy process may generate superior results in terms of interjurisdictional competition but only under certain conditions.

While values are, in principle, open to deliberate societal choice, they are also subject to external selection in various contexts. The question here is whether inclusive deliberation and a substantive stress on freedom and human dignity can be viable in a context of interjurisdictional competition.[62] Of course, such viability can ultimately only be judged in a concrete historical and geographical setting. In this section, therefore, we restrict ourselves to a short focus on general properties of the competitive economic policy process that can support the normative stance taken earlier.

As shown, a standard argument for the use of markets to address the key questions of allocation is their capacity to distribute and generate knowledge in overwhelmingly complex social systems. In principle, a similar reasoning can be established for political competition, as structured by democratic competition policy to constitute inclusive deliberation: In theory, such a process would bring in a maximum amount of knowledge to be moulded into a reasonable consensus that ultimately everyone would be able to agree to, upon reflection and eventual revision of own preferences and beliefs.[63] Therefore, compared to the alternative of centralised authoritarian decision making, this process would generate competitively superior results.

However, this perspective can be contested on several grounds. First, the political transaction cost of reaching consensus is high, all the more so since the deliberative process foresees a possible revision of individual views instead of just identifying possible compromises on the basis of given preferences. Second, similar to markets, there is no guarantee against a prevailing of factually false beliefs and/or the reaching of a consensus (or at least, a majority) that contradicts the majority views of a political or expert elite. Third, a possible alternative to the knowledge-generating function of broad-based deliberation and negotiations is constituted by policy experimentation, which, contrary to deliberation, is also open to authoritarian regimes.

On political transaction costs, see Chapter 9, section 4.

The second and third argument have been used to defend authoritarian regimes in Asia, such as in Singapore or, more recently, China:[64] The idea is that a political elite which is selected along meritocratic rather than democratic criteria is better able to exert political leadership, particularly if the country has no democratic tradition and/or is characterised by sharp social

*Institutional stability
on key principles
is a precondition
of external
competitiveness.*

cleavages. Policy experimentation, in turn, has been extensively used by the Chinese administration on a regional basis without losing its grip to power.[65]

The first argument, of course, is an important reason why most democracies foresee an institutional differentiation between rules whose change requires broad participation and consensus and those that can be imposed or altered relatively quickly, and possibly in a semi-authoritarian fashion, such as executive orders. In the context of jurisdictional competition, this can be related to a combination between stability and flexibility, or evolvability in terms of institutional change. On a very general level, then, economic policy would, on the one hand, build upon a stable framework of fundamental institutions that result from a deliberative process set up as broadly as possible. This framework would entail basic normative choices that do not necessarily focus on jurisdictional competition as a priority but allow the actors driving jurisdictional competition to build up trust into its stability. On the other hand, more flexibility would be attributed to specific policy areas, where negotiations for change could be set up along the externality principle outlined earlier. In those areas, the constituency would also have to decide in which areas to delegate competencies to a meritocratically selected expert bureaucracy and where/how to use policy experimentation.

5. Conclusion

This chapter took a process-based perspective on economic policy, understood as an alternative to two established approaches to economic policy in economic science: The traditional perspective is essentially technocratic, regarding economic policy as the result of a rational calculation of instruments to reach certain exogenously given objectives, possibly summarised in a social welfare function. The other perspective, epitomised by the fields of public choice and political economy, essentially looks at economic policy as the result of interaction of self-interested individuals with fixed preferences in different institutional settings, above all, the electoral process, interest group politics, and the political decision making process; for example, in terms of coalition building or interaction between different branches of government. Against this, our basic argument is that social welfare concepts, the evaluation of measures against these concepts, and political preferences/beliefs are endogenous outcomes of the policy process – indeed, it can be argued that the constant evolution of those elements by negotiation, persuasion, social organisation, and ultimately, political decision making itself constitutes the essence of what politics is about.

We introduced a novel conceptualisation of the policy process that stresses its competitive nature, understood as concomitant competition between policy proposals (with the objective of their political adoption) and for political power positions. Framing this competition in evolutionary terms allows a direct comparison to other forms of evolutionary competition. It turns out that economic and political competition exhibit important similarities in terms of their function of coordinating knowledge and decision making in an environment of fundamental uncertainty and the role of entrepreneurship in both realms. However, there are also important differences, notably the self-regulating character of political competition, the prevalence of zero-sum constellations and the associated potential of arms races in political competition, and the lack of a unified monetary measure of evolutionary success in the political realm. These points can be analysed in several competitive realms that, while conceptionally distinct, interact in the policy process in complex ways.

In previous chapters, we stressed the unique capacity of competitive markets to adapt and self-organise in hypercomplex environments, so the question is to what extent political competition can fulfil a similar criterion in the political realm. There is a commonality of both domains in terms of the necessity to limit power relations in order to unfold the full adaptive potential of evolutionary competition. However, the difference between an economic and democratic competition policy is that the latter must flow directly from the one-person-one-vote principle, which leads to the requirement of maximum inclusiveness of the policy process, enabling policy decisions to be grounded in a broad informational base and a high degree of legitimacy beyond mere electoral results. The substantive counterparts to this procedural criterion are freedom, in the sense of enabling individuals to choose among alternatives and unfold their full potential, and human dignity, in the sense of mutual respect irrespective of social and other differences.

Major chapter insights

- In modern market economies, economic policy is inextricably intertwined with the setting and changing of formal institutions. We can distinguish three levels of institutional change, namely the setting of discretionary measures, such as anticyclical fiscal policy; the setting of rules of the game for market activity, such as the respect of property rights; and the setting of rules of the game for the policy process itself, which is subject to the self-regulatory character of political competition.
- The economic policy process can be seen as evolutionary competition between policy proposals as well as for political power positions. Basic features similar to market competition, in particular, fundamental uncertainty ex ante (on the effect of policy measures) and ex post (on the interpretation of those effects) apply. As a

consequence, welfare concepts as well as political beliefs of the constituency are subject to continuous endogenous change. This change, in turn, is to a large extent driven by political entrepreneurs.

- Political competition takes place in different realms, notably competition for public opinion, electoral competition, competition between interest groups (understood in a general sense), and interjurisdictional competition. Different selective criteria in those realms have to be balanced by political decision makers, who are subject to complex principal–agent relationships. Given large leeway in the implementation of policy decisions, an additional and separate realm of political competition is constituted by the bureaucracy.
- The quality of the economic policy process depends on its inclusivity, given that only maximum inclusivity can ensure a full exploitation of informational sources by political decision makers and increase the legitimacy of their decisions. The substantive counterparts to this procedural criterion are freedom, in the sense of enabling individuals to choose among alternatives and unfold their full potential, and human dignity, in the sense of mutual respect irrespective of social and other differences.

Notes

1 For a – still authoritative – survey on standard public choice theory, see Mueller (2003). More recently, public choice has been developed further in line with the emergence of behavioural economics, Schnellenbach and Schubert (2015). For evolutionary public choice and political economy, see, for example, Witt (2003); Wohlgemuth (2002a); Cantner and Wohlgemuth (2014); Herrmann-Pillath (2004, chapters 1 and 2), and Slembeck (1997).
2 Wohlgemuth (2000).
3 In legal science, the underlying notion is a hierarchical pyramid of norms, with the lower level legally derived from the higher one; seminally, Kelsen (1960).
4 See, for an overview, Weible and Sabatier (2018). Our approach is closest to the multiple streams framework, see Kingdon (1984), Zahariadis (2007).
5 Razo (2013).
6 Wohlgemuth (2002b); Boettke and Storr (2016).
7 Wohlgemuth (2003); Prasetya and Murata (2020).
8 For a recent case study on the generation and diffusion of economic expert knowledge, see Flickenschild and Afonso (2019).
9 Hays (2011).

10 Arrow (1951).

11 Endogenising welfare as a cognitive and discursive construct is the key differ-ence between our approach and general equilibrium approaches to political com-petition; seminally, Grossman and Helpman (1996).

12 For a survey of concepts of political entrepreneurship, see Hederer (2010). Notably, the terminology varies, with the notions of 'policy' or 'issue' entrepre-neurship frequently used as well. A comprehensive overview of policy entrepre-neurship is provided by Mintrom (2019).

13 For the related literature on the role of ideas in the policy process and institutional change, see, for example, Béland (2019).

14 Mehta (2011).

15 On the role of mass media for agenda setting, see McCombs and Valenzuela (2020).

16 For the paradox of voting, seminally Downs (1957); Riker and Ordeshook (1968).

17 Seminally, Zhu (1992).

18 See, for an overview, Ots and Picard (2018).

19 See, for example, Sears and Brown (2013).

20 Kuran (1995), Noelle-Neumann (1991).

21 This stays at the centre of neoclassical theories of political competition, in terms of a political support function, Grossman and Helpman (1996).

22 Wohlgemuth (2000).

23 Hederer (2010); Wohlgemuth (2002b).

24 With respect to their organisational form, political parties exhibit great variety; see, for a survey including the regulatory framework, Van Biezen and Romée Piccio (2013).

25 Lynch et al. (2006); O'Cass (2009).

26 Smith and French (2009); Tomz and Sniderman (2005).

27 Nassmacher (2009).

28 The classic is Lipset and Rokkan (1967). For a more recent account on the con-tingency of cleavages, see Mair (2006).

29 Blyth (2002). For the related discussion on the role of ideas in different institu-tionalisms, see Schmidt (2008).

30 Seminally, Olson (1965).

31 Rodrik (1995).

32 See, for an overview of the European case, Dür and Mateo (2016).

33 For an overview, see Berry and Wilcox (2018).

34 Bhagwati (1982).

35 Mansbridge (1992); Wittman (1995).

36 See, for example, Clemens (1997); McFarland (1991); Abrahamsson (1993) for Sweden.

37 For an overview, see, for example, Bernholz and Vaubel (2007).

38 Salmon (2019).

39 Rodrik (2011).

40 Siebert (2006), Kaufmann and Arnold (2018).

41 Such institutional complementarities are theorised and richly illustrated in Aoki (2001).
42 For the case of world trade politics, see Deese (2008).
43 This has been emphasised in the literature on the role of ideas in politics, with seminal contributions such as Goldstein (1993). See the collection of papers Bèland and Cox (2011).
44 Herrmann-Pillath (2004).
45 Grossman and Helpman (1994), WTO (2007).
46 Weber (1922/1985).
47 See, for an empirical survey, Cooper (2021).
48 See, for example, Colonnelli et al. (2020).
49 The classic contribution for the public choice approach is Niskanen (2017/1971). For an overview of alternative approaches, see Wise (2004).
50 Maesschalck (2004).
51 Sen (2009).
52 Caplan (2001).
53 For example, François and Gergaud (2019); Riker and Ordeshook (1968).
54 Kuran (1995).
55 For example, Lecce (2009).
56 See, for example, Brown (2018).
57 For example, Rüstow (1949).
58 Eucken (1952).
59 See, for a recent US account, Teachout (2021).
60 For example, Alesina et al. (2021).
61 An influential but controversial recent contribution is Putnam (2007).
62 Herrmann-Pillath (2018).
63 Elster (1998), Wohlgemuth (2002b).
64 Bell (2015).
65 Teets and Hasmath (2020).

References

Abrahamsson, B. (1993) *Why Organizations? How and Why People Organize.* Newbury Park and London: Sage.

Alesina, A., Murard, E. and Rapoport, H. (2021) 'Immigration and Preferences for Redistribution in Europe', *Journal of Economic Geography,* 21(6), pp. 925–954. DOI: 10.1093/jeg/lbab002.

Aoki, M. (2001) *Toward a Comparative Institutional Analysis.* Stanford: Stanford University Press.

Arrow, K. J. (1951) *Social Choice and Individual Values.* New York: Wiley.

Béland, D. (2019) *How Ideas and Institutions Shape the Politics of Public Policy.* Cambridge: Cambridge University Press. DOI: 10.1017/9781108634700.

Béland, D. and Cox, R. H. (eds.) (2011) *Ideas and Politics in Social Science Research.* Oxford: Oxford University Press.

Bell, D. A. (2015) *The China Model*. Princeton: Princeton University Press.

Bernholz, P. and Vaubel, R. (eds.) (2007) *Political Competition and Economic Regulation*. London: Routledge.

Berry, J. M. and Wilcox, C. (2018) *The Interest Group Society*. New York: Routledge. DOI: 10.4324/9781315534091.

Bhagwati, J. (1982) 'Directly Unproductive, Profit-Seeking (DUP) Activities', *Journal of Political Economy*, 90(15), pp. 988–1002.

Blyth, M. (2002) *Great Transformations: Economic Ideas and Institutional Change in the Twentieth Century*. Cambridge: Cambridge University Press.

Boettke, P. J. and Storr, V. H. (2016) *Revisiting Hayek's Political Economy*. Bingley: Emerald Publishing Limited. DOI: 10.1108/S1529-2134201721.

Brown, M. B. (2018) 'Speaking for Nature: Hobbes, Latour, and the Democratic Representation of Nonhumans', *Science & Technology Studies*, 31(1), pp. 31–51. DOI: 10.23987/sts.60525.

Cantner, U. and Wohlgemuth, M. (2014) 'Evolutionary Public Choice', in Reksulak, M., Razzanoli, L. and Shughart III, W. F. (eds.) *The Elgar Companion to Public Choice*. Cheltenham: Edward Elgar Publishing, pp. 427–449.

Caplan, B. (2001) 'Rational Ignorance versus Rational Irrationality', *Kyklos*, 54(1), pp. 3–26. DOI: 10.1111/1467-6435.00138.

Clemens, E. S. (1997) *The People's Lobby: Organizational Innovation and the Rise of Interest Group Politics in the United States, 1890–1925*. Chicago: University of Chicago Press.

Colonnelli, E., Prem, M. and Teso, E. (2020) 'Patronage and Selection in Public Sector Organizations', *American Economic Review*, 110(10), pp. 3071–3099. DOI: 10.1257/aer.20181491.

Cooper, C. A. (2021) 'Politicization of the Bureaucracy Across and Within Administrative Traditions', *International Journal of Public Administration*, 44(7), pp. 564–577. DOI: 10.1080/01900692.2020.1739074.

Deese, D. A. (2008) *World Trade Politics: Power, Principles, and Leadership*. London and New York: Routledge.

Downs, A. (1957) *An Economic Theory of Democracy*. New York: Harper & Row.

Dür, A. and Mateo, G. (2016) *Insiders versus Outsiders: Interest Group Politics in Multilevel Europe*. Oxford: Oxford University Press. DOI: 10.1093/acprof:oso/9780198785651.001.0001.

Elster, J. (ed.) (1998) *Deliberative Democracy*. Cambridge: Cambridge University Press.

Eucken, W. (1952) *Grundsätze der Wirtschaftspolitik*. Bern and Tübingen: Mohr Siebeck.

Flickenschild, M. and Afonso, A. (2019) 'Networks of Economic Policy Expertise in Germany and the United States in the Wake of the Great Recession', *Journal of European Public Policy*, 26(9), pp. 1292–1311. DOI: 10.1080/13501763.2018.1518992.

François, A. and Gergaud, O. (2019) 'Is Civic Duty the Solution to the Paradox of Voting?', *Public Choice*, 180(3), pp. 257–283. DOI: 10.1007/s11127-018-00635-7.

Goldstein, J. (1993) *Ideas, Interests, and American Trade Policy*. Ithaca and London: Cornell University Press.

Grossman, G. M. and Helpman, E. (1994) 'Protection for Sale', *American Economic Review*, 84(4), pp. 833–850.

Grossman, G. M. and Helpman, E. (1996) 'Electoral Competition and Special Interest Politics', *Review of Economic Studies*, 63(2), pp. 265–286. DOI: 10.2307/2297852.

Hays, C. (2011) 'Ideas and the Construction of Interests', in Béland, D. and Cox, R. H. (eds.) *Ideas and Politics in Social Science Research*. Oxford: Oxford University Press, pp. 65–82.

Hederer, C. (2010) 'Political Entrepreneurship and Institutional Change: An Evolutionary Perspective', *International Journal of Public Policy*, 6(1), pp. 87–103.

Herrmann-Pillath, C. (2004) *Kritik der Theorie des internationalen Handels, Band II: Evolutionäre Politische Ökonomie*. Marburg: Metropolis.

Herrmann-Pillath, C. (2018) *Grundlegung einer kritischen Theorie der Wirtschaft*. Marburg: Metropolis.

Kaufmann, D. and Arnold, T. (2018) 'Strategies of Cities in Globalised Interurban Competition: The Locational Policies Framework', *Urban Studies*, 55(12), pp. 2703–2720. DOI: 10.1177%2F0042098017707922.

Kelsen, H. (1960) *Reine Rechtslehre*. Vienna: Deuticke.

Kingdon, J. W. (1984) *Agendas, Alternatives, and Public Policies*. Boston and Toronto: Little, Brown and Company.

Kuran, T. (1995) *Private Truths, Public Lies: The Social Consequences of Preference Falsification*. Cambridge and London: Harvard University Press.

Lecce, S. (2009) 'Should Democracy Grow up? Children and Voting Rights', *Intergenerational Justice Review*, 4, pp. 133–138. DOI: 10.24357/igjr.4.4.510.

Lipset, S. M. and Rokkan, S. (1967) 'Cleavage Structures, Party Systems, and Voter Alignments: An Introduction', in Lipset, S. M. and Rokkan, S. (eds.) *Party Systems and Voter Alignments: Cross National Perspectives*. New York: The Free Press, pp. 1–64.

Lynch, R., Baines, P. and Egan, J. (2006) 'Long-Term Performance of Political Parties: Towards a Competitive Resource-Based Perspective', *Journal of Political Marketing*, 5(3), pp. 71–92. DOI: 10.1300/J199v05n03_04.

Maesschalck, J. (2004) 'The Impact of New Public Management Reforms on Public Servants' Ethics: Towards a Theory', *Public Administration*, 82(2), pp. 465–489. DOI: 10.1111/j.0033-3298.2004.00403.x.

Mair, P. (2006) 'Cleavages', in Katz, R. S. and Crotty, W. (eds.) *Handbook of Party Politics*. London: Sage, pp. 371–375.

Mansbridge, J. J. (1992) 'A Deliberative Theory of Interest Representation', in Petracca, M. P. (ed.) *The Politics of Interests*. New York: Routledge, pp. 32–57.

McCombs, M. and Valenzuela, S. (2020) *Setting the Agenda: Mass Media and Public Opinion, Third Edition*. Hoboken: John Wiley & Sons.

McFarland, A. S. (1991) 'Interest Groups and Political Time: Cycles in America', *British Journal of Political Science*, 21(3), pp. 257–284. DOI: 10.1017/S0007123400006165.

Mehta, J. (2011) 'The Varied Roles of Ideas in Politics: From "Whether" to "How"', in Béland, D. and Cox, R. H. (eds.) *Ideas and Politics in Social Science Research*. Oxford: Oxford University Press, pp. 23–46.

Mintrom, M. (2019) *Policy Entrepreneurs and Dynamic Change*. Cambridge: Cambridge University Press. DOI: 10.1017/9781108605946.

Mueller, D. (2003) *Public Choice III*. Cambridge: Cambridge University Press.

Nassmacher, K.-H. (2009) *The Funding of Party Competition – Political Finance in 25 Democracies*. Baden-Baden: Nomos.

Niskanen, W. A. (2017 [1971]) *Bureaucracy and Representative Government*. New York: Routledge.

Noelle-Neumann, E. (1991) *Öffentliche Meinung – die Entdeckung der Schweigespirale*. Frankfurt and Berlin: Ullstein.

O'Cass, A. (2009) 'A Resource-Based View of the Political Party and Value Creation for the Voter-Citizen: An Integrated Framework for Political Marketing', *Marketing Theory*, 9(2), pp. 189–208. DOI: 10.1177%2F1470593109103066.

Olson, M. (2003 [1965]) *The Logic of Collective Action: Public Goods and the Theory of Groups*. Cambridge: Harvard University Press.

Ots, M. and Picard, R. G. (2018) 'Press Subsidies', in Nussbaum, J. F. (ed.) *Oxford Research Encyclopedia of Communication Oxford*. Oxford: Oxford University Press. DOI: 10.1093/acrefore/9780190228613.013.861.

Prasetya, H. A. and Murata, T. (2020) 'A Model of Opinion and Propagation Structure Polarization in Social Media', *Computational Social Networks*, 7(1), pp. 1–35. DOI: 10.1186/s40649-019-0076-z.

Popper, Karl R. (1983), *Realism and the Aim of Science*, London: Hutchinson.

Putnam, R. D. (2007) 'E Pluribus Unum: Diversity and Community in the Twenty-First Century the 2006 Johan Skytte Prize Lecture', *Scandinavian Political Studies*, 30(2), pp. 137–174. DOI: 10.1111/j.1467-9477.2007.00176.x.

Razo, A. (2013) 'Autocrats and Democrats', in Reksulak, M., Razzaloni, L. and Shughart II, W. F. (eds.) *The Elgar Companion to Public Choice, Second Edition*. Cheltenham and Northampton: Edward Elgar Publishing, pp. 83–109.

Riker, W. H. and Ordeshook, P. C. (1968) 'A Theory of the Calculus of Voting', *American Political Science Review*, 62(1), pp. 25–42.

Rodrik, D. (1995) 'Political Economy of Trade Policy', in Grossman, G. M. and Rogoff, K. (eds.) *Handbook of International Economics, Vol. 3*. Amsterdam: Elsevier, pp. 1457–1494.

Rodrik, D. (2011) *The Globalization Paradox: Democracy and the Future of the World Economy*. New York: Norton.

Rüstow, A. (1949) *Zwischen Kommunismus und Kapitalismus*. Godesberg: Küpper Verlag.

Salmon, P. (2019) *Yardstick Competition among Governments: Accountability and Policymaking When Citizens Look across Borders*. Oxford: Oxford University Press. DOI: 10.1093/oso/9780190499167.001.0001.

Schmidt, V. A. (2008) 'Discursive Institutionalism: The Explanatory Power of Ideas and Discourse', *Annual Review of Political Science*, 11, pp. 303–326. DOI: 10.1146/annurev.polisci.11.060606.135342.

Schnellenbach, J. and Schubert, C. (2015) 'Behavioral Political Economy: A Survey', *European Journal of Political Economy*, 40(B), pp. 395–417. DOI: 10.1016/j.ejpoleco.2015.05.002.

Sears, D. O. and Brown, C. (2013) 'Childhood and Adult Political Development', in Huddy, L., Sears, D. O. and Levy, J. S. (eds.) *The Oxford Handbook of Political Psychology, Second Edition*. Oxford: Oxford University Press. DOI: 10.1093/oxfordhb/9780199760107.013.0003.

Sen, A. (2009) *The Idea of Justice*. Cambridge: Cambridge University Press.

Siebert, H. (2006) 'Locational Competition: A Neglected Paradigm in the International Division of Labour', *The World Economy*, 29(2), pp. 137–159. DOI: 10.1111/J.1467-9701.2006.00775.X.

Slembeck, T. (1997) 'The Formation of Economic Policy: A Cognitive-Evolutionary Approach to Policy-Making', *Constitutional Political Economy*, 8(3), pp. 225–254. DOI: 10.1023/A:1009027913985.

Smith, G. and French, A. (2009) 'The Political Brand: A Consumer Perspective', *Marketing Theory*, 9(2), pp. 209–226. DOI: 10.1177%2F1470593109103068.

Teachout, Z. (2021) 'Monopoly versus Democracy: How to End a Gilded Age', *Foreign Affairs*, 100(1), pp. 52–60.

Teets, J. C. and Hasmath, R. (2020) 'The Evolution of Policy Experimentation in China', *Journal of Asian Public Policy*, 13(1), pp. 49–59. DOI: 10.1080/17516234.2020.1711491.

Tomz, M. and Sniderman, P. M. (2005) 'Brand Names and the Organization of Mass Belief Systems', *Working Paper/ Stanford University*. Available at: https://drive.google.com/file/d/1YIKTPENmjuCbDT2FWrDTlippiICXPpII/view

Van Biezen, I. and Romée Piccio, D. (2013) 'Shaping Intra-Party Democracy: On the Legal Regulation of Internal Party Organizations', in Cross, W. P. and Katz, R. S. (eds.) *The Challenges of Intra-Party Democracy*. Oxford: Oxford University Press.

Weber (1922 [1985]) *Wirtschaft und Gesellschaft, Eighth Edition*. Tübingen: Mohr Siebeck.

Weible, C. M. and Sabatier, P. A. (2018) *Theories of the Policy Process*. New York: Routledge. DOI: 10.4324/9780429494284.

Wise, L. R. (2004) 'Bureaucratic Posture: On the Need for a Composite Theory of Bureaucratic Behavior', *Public Administration Review*, 64(6), pp. 669–680. DOI: 10.1111/j.1540-6210.2004.00414.x.

Witt, U. (2003) 'Economic Policy Making in Evolutionary Perspective', *Journal of Evolutionary Economics*, 13(2), pp. 77–94.

Wittman, D. A. (1995) *The Myth of Democratic Failure. Why Political Institutions Are Efficient*. Chicago and London: University of Chicago Press.

Wohlgemuth, M. (2000) 'Political Entrepreneurship and Bidding for Political Monopoly', *Journal of Evolutionary Economics*, 10(3), pp. 273–295. DOI: 10.1007/s001910050015.

Wohlgemuth, M. (2002a) 'Evolutionary Approaches to Politics', *Kyklos*, 55(2), pp. 223–246. DOI: 10.1111/1467-6435.00184.

Wohlgemuth, M. (2002b) 'Democracy and Opinion Falsification – Towards a New Austrian Political Economy', *Constitutional Political Economy*, 13(3), pp. 223–246. DOI: 10.1023/A:1016156332351.

Wohlgemuth, M. (2003) 'Democracy as an Evolutionary Method', in Pelikan, P. and Wegner, G. (eds.) *The Evolutionary Analysis of Economic Policy*. Cheltenham and Northampton: Edward Elgar Publishing, pp. 96–127.

WTO (2007) *World Trade Report 2007: Six Decades of Multilateral Trade Cooperation: What Have We Learnt?* Geneva: WTO.

Zahariadis, N. (2007) 'The Multiple Streams Framework – Structure, Limitations, Prospects', in Sabatier, P. A. (ed.) *Theories of the Policy Process*, *Second Edition*. Boulder: Westview Press, pp. 65–92.

Zhu, J. H. (1992) 'Issue Competition and Attention Distraction: A Zero-Sum Theory of Agenda-Setting', *Journalism Quarterly*, 69(4), pp. 825–836. DOI: 10.1177/107769909206900403.

CHAPTER EIGHTEEN

Epilogue: The economist as adviser

But, chiefly, do not let us overestimate the importance of the economic problem, or sacrifice to its supposed necessities other matters of greater and more permanent significance. It should be a matter for specialists-like dentistry. If economists could manage to get themselves thought of as humble, competent people, on a level with dentists, that would be splendid!

John Maynard Keynes[1]

Die Kunstfehler von Ärzten können das Leben einzelner Menschen beenden. Die Kunstfehler von Nationalökonomen können Katastrophen für ganze Völker zur Folge haben.

Hans Willgerodt[2]

Keynes's famous final lines of his essay "Economic Possibilities of Our Grandchildren" must be complemented by another citation (the German motto earlier) of the late German economist Hans Willgerodt, who once observed that errors of physicians affect single individuals, but errors of economists, millions. Indeed, since the rise of economics as a science, economists have had a mixed record in policy advice, for two reasons. First, economics entails a wide range of opinions which are often outright contradictory. Second, economics changes over time. Taking up the comparison to medicine, the first point does not apply to the same degree since medicine entails a rather undisputed body of knowledge. In contrast, in many fields of economics, despite impressive work on theory and analytical methods, even basic facts and hypotheses are open to debate. At the same time, economics evolves without clear direction whereas most fields of medicine follow a relatively well-defined line of advancing knowledge. One challenge is that the nature of economic problem co-evolves with economics as a discipline: The Great Depression triggered the rise of Keynesianism, the stagflation of the 1970s pushed so-called neoliberalism, and post-2008 is still in search for a paradigm. For medicine, this would amount to a paradigm change with the emergence of every new major disease. In contrast, there are important economic questions that do manifest progress despite diversity of views. The

The record of economics in policy advice is mixed due to diversity of opinions and change of the discipline over time.

482

DOI: 10.4324/9781003094869-24

most significant example is the final demise of theories on central planning of complex market systems. But even here, doubts remain: Perhaps climate change will eventually require the adoption of a war economy, aptly dubbed Climate Leviathan.[3]

What is the lesson that we can draw and teach the young economist who aspires to improve the world? In this chapter, we present some thoughts. We start with a sketch of theoretical issues resulting from the reflexivity of economics. Economists as advisers may employ economics to understand and define their own position in interacting with the person who receives advice. If they adopt the endogenous policy framework that we unfolded in the previous chapter, economists must recognise that in the status quo, all determinants of political choices are likely to already have worked out their effects, in the sense that not only the options as such but also their political costs have been explored and included.[4] For example, in considering a tariff, the status quo would not only entail the standard welfare effects but also reflect the fact that consumer-voters may not deem it worthwhile to even process the information necessary to take a decision. This amounts to a Panglossian problem in economic advice: If policy formation is endogenous, the status quo is already determined and, hence, cannot be changed by advice. If the economist sticks to the rational choice paradigm, she would deem it likely that all relevant information has already been processed in the status quo.

This reasoning still leaves much room for advice if there are important changes in the context of the status quo such that the economist would directly be involved in the process of generating new information. For example, the Great Depression enhanced space for economists as advisers.[5] However, in such a situation, another problem looms large. The idea of advisership presupposes to take a position of impartiality, as defined earlier in this book. But can the advisee assume that this is really the case? How far is the adviser disinterested herself?[6] Indeed, this is true also for Keynes's dentist: The dentist may suggest expensive therapies without real need, and the patient cannot judge the recommendation. Knowing this, she might not fully trust the advice. Economists receive many benefits from advice, such as honoraria, reputation, or other fringe benefits. How far does that impact their advice, beginning with the definition of the problem? To which extent do the incentives in the process of advisership lead to misallocation of resources, such as often criticised in audits of government organisations splashing money on professional advisers?[7] The Arrow information paradox suggests that advised persons cannot judge the appropriate size of investing in advance since they would need to know that advice already; hence, there is much room for dysfunctional phenomena, such as using advice just for legitimising one's own beliefs. Some cases of economic advisership throw suspicion on entire groups: For example, the use of auctions created many job opportunities for game theorists on both sides of the market. Game theorists advised governments, and companies hired game theorists to optimise their strategy in the auctions, with both sides cooperating in making auctions work.[8]

Given the reflexivity of economics, in a given status quo, economic advice faces a Panglossian problem.

The notion of impartial economic advice raises serious informational issues.

On impartiality, see Chapter 3, section 5.

On the Arrow information paradox, see Chapter 11, section 5.

Impartiality may also be hampered by beliefs.

In the 20th century, economics established itself as an influential epistemic community.

Economic reasoning and rhetoric has widely diffused to politic and the law.

Interests can have many different shapes beyond direct personal advantage. One especially sensitive issue is beliefs of any kind, political, religious, and others, which might undermine the impartiality of advice. Therefore, the advised person may reflexively downplay the significance of the advice. One solution to this problem is an invitation of outright advocacy: The advised person invites many advisers who are explicitly encouraged to take a partisan position.[9] Ultimately, the advisee decides on his own. One version of this is the invitation of advisers who share the same opinion with the advisee such that the advice just becomes a rationalisation of what would have been done anyway.

In the course of the 20th century, economics has arguably become the most influential social science. One important aspect is that economics and economists emerged as an epistemic community,[10] such as in international organisations where economists frequently hold top positions. Organisations with a significant role of economists will also invite external economic advice, thus creating an attractive job market for economists. This pattern was driven by strong historical trends: first, the Great Depression that revealed the centrality of economics for the fate of modern societies; then World War II, even dubbed a war of economists by Paul Samuelson; subsequently, the rise of Keynesianism.[11] Later, representatives of the new neoclassical or neoliberal turn started to occupy the institutional infrastructure despite their advocacy of a purely rules-based policy which, strictly speaking, would have rendered them superfluous.

One factor that undergirded the role of economic advisership is the diffusion of economic reasoning and rhetoric in politics, beyond the direct role of economists. An important example is the economisation of legal language in US law, especially with regard to legal domains for which economics is directly relevant, such as property law or competition law, but also with regard to, for example, criminal law.[12] The growing diversification of economics tends to drive this further, as shown by the example of nudging which reflects the diffusion of behavioural economics into the wider policy discourse.[13] Another important vehicle of economisation is the use of decision support systems which originally have been devised by economists. The most important example is cost-benefit analysis, which may even be legally binding for decisions about public infrastructure projects and which has been expanded, for example, into the domain of ecology.[14] All this prepares a rich and fertile ground that nurtures the role of economists as advisers.

Given this background, how can economists be good and trusted advisers? We start by the simple fact that economists should know their object of study. This can by no means taken for granted: Modern economics does not have a strong tradition of collecting facts about the economy. Historically, this neglect emerged with the separation of university departments of economics and applied schools for commerce and business. In the 1920s, it was still debated, and American institutionalists emphasised the study of real-world economic practices and facts.[15] However, this tradition only survived in the focus of economics on data, meaning statistical numbers. Economists ignored practices and institutions for many decades, analytically substituting real-world behaviour by the figure of the rational agent. For example, for a long time, there was no recognition of the need to study how expectations are factually formed. The ignorance of simple facts how markets work became particularly evident in the neglect of the financial sector in macroeconomics before the 2008 financial crisis.[16]

The economist as adviser must be trained as economic naturalist and must know the details about her object. Often, economists just collect facts about a case and then employ a generic theoretical frame to reach policy conclusions. In contrast, good advice must ground in deep familiarity of the case, including knowledge of the law, culture, and precise market arrangements and practices. Economists have often denigrated this work as mere descriptions; economics departments shunned area studies economics as less reputable and rarely admitted research on countries beyond the standard-setters (such as the US) to top journals. This attitude proved to be particularly problematic after the collapse of the socialist planned economies, when high-flying economic advisers to transition countries did not even know how the alleged centrally planned economies really worked and sold the market as a panacea to solve all social and economic issues. In Russia, this resulted in the emergence of a new form of state capitalism married with oligarchy, a far cry from the market visions of the early years of transition.[17]

However, there are limitations of accumulating more and more factual knowledge about markets. In this respect, there is much to learn from the debates about the Historical School in the late 19th century.[18] Given that markets are hypercomplex systems, a mere collection of facts without good theory will lead nowhere. But how can we equip the economist-adviser with good theory? In the past, this concern was key in arguing for mainstream-style economic modelling, in particular, the general equilibrium approach.

We agree to one of the pivotal insights of general equilibrium thinking, which is simple and challenging at the same time: The economy is a tightly interconnected system; therefore, the leeway for unintended consequences of policy interventions is wide. The disclosure of unintended consequences of any kind of policy intervention has always been a primary achievement of economists' advice. The classic case is the tariff, with the latest episode constituted by Trumpian tariffs directed at China that are eventually paid for by US citizens. However, we do not necessarily need the full edifice of general equilibrium to understand the mechanisms by which real economic actors respond to tariffs and try to shift costs on others. In fact, economist-as-naturalist knowledge to understand the specific reactions may be more useful since much depends on specific business strategies in specific sectors. The overall logic, however, would remain in the general equilibrium frame. This is also true for enlightening political actors about the possible follow-up of

Economists and economic advisers need to know their object of study in a naturalistic sense, beyond analysis of statistical data.

The collection of facts should be guided by medium-range theories, taking into account unintended consequences of policy measures on the systemic level.

*An evolutionary
framework can
reveal causal
mechanisms but
does not provide
direct policy
recommendations.*

interventions and regulations, aptly labelled 'regulatory spirals', or addressing the cost of overly complex regulatory measures in terms of counter-strategies that eventually outsmart cognitively constrained policymakers with cognitive limitations.

Of course, we present theories in this book which we deem better than the previous ones. But we refrain from drafting a framework that compares with the compelling logic of general equilibrium. Evolutionary theory cannot directly generate policy recommendations, although there are important shifts of perspectives and priorities (for example, emphasising biodiversity as a policy goal). But as we argued, the evolutionary framework creates explanatory patterns into which we can locate specific causal mechanisms. This difference is salient in recent economics research, such as in finance: Conventional economic theory employs the efficient markets framework, whereas behavioural finance focuses on mechanisms; evolutionary theory adds a broader theoretical frame to the latter.[19] This means, however, that advice must be based on an empirical diagnosis of mechanisms that work at the moment of intervention. An example in finance is the understanding of the precise effects of new technologies on behaviour and market performance. This requires moving away from the efficient markets framework and inclusion of psychology and sociology.[20]

The focus on mechanisms dovetails with the rise of mechanism design in economics, which is major field of economic advice today. Economists are experts on markets; based on deep knowledge of real markets, they can help to improve or even create them.[21] Here, economics comes close to engineering or, in fact, medicine. But this analogy raises the question of for which purpose the engineering knowledge is employed. In other words, are economists in a position to give privileged advice on whether and how markets should be used? If so, what exactly are the criteria?

*The preference to
markets vis-á-vis
alternatives forms
of allocation tends
to be confirmed by
the evolutionary
approach.*

Many economists propagate the market as the best of possible worlds in many circumstances. They recognise possible drawbacks but at the same time argue that alternatives would work even less well. To a certain extent, this is true from the evolutionary perspective. Perhaps committing Pangloss's error to regard as efficient what succeeded to survive, we may just notice that markets diffused all over the globe, and radical alternatives on a societal scale failed (as evident, for example, in the example of 20th-century China). But we also diagnose that there are strong performative phenomena and vigorous interests driving their spread. Therefore, economists should take a distanced view, which we labelled 'impartial'; they should not recommend markets for the market's sake.

One key question related to a decision for or against markets is whether markets are the most powerful means to generate the societal capacities to make markets work in the first place. For example, property rights are an indispensable precondition of markets. There are also markets for property rights, of course. But can we envision that the institution of property as such can be generated and maintained by markets or that markets could even substitute for property? Such questions are also pertinent when it comes to specific forms of property: Should we adopt the criterion of making markets work in creating and assigning property rights?

We think that economists can advise societies and governments about the consequences of installing markets by creating property rights but should refrain from adopting a prescriptive stance. A good example is the instalment of markets for emission rights. Forty years ago, this was a fringe position in economics, and the Pigouvian tax was the mainstream. Today, the market solution is even pursued in China. Many economists pushed the case with a vengeance, praising the market forces of innovation and flexibility. However, until now, we have no experience that this solution will effectively address the challenge of climate change, as these markets are still not of global reach, and emissions grow relentlessly. Economists simply do not know whether markets for emission rights are the best solution to our climate quandaries. At the same time, any policy proposal will be subject to the messy forces of interest group politics (the first stage of the EU trading system for emission rights is a lesson[22]). There is no guarantee that the economist's advice will be realised in its original meaning.

As we have emphasised, any recommendation for markets has a normative basis, which is constituted by the principle of voluntary exchange combined with a recognition of individuals as decision makers who are endowed with the corresponding rights and dignity. This normative basis extends to the deliberative process in making policy decisions. In the case of greenhouse gas emissions, if a Pigouvian tax on pollution as an act of governmental force is preferred to the market alternative on the basis of an inclusive process of deliberation, there is no fundamental normative reason why the market should be preferred over the tax.

The normative ideal of the market implies that economists should be strongly concerned about power. This establishes a reason to mistrust government from an economic perspective, given that government is endowed with power to a degree that surpasses all other actors in society. However, this does not imply that markets are better than government since apart from few exceptions, markets without government are not conceivable. Yet government is a domain where power easily coalesces into dysfunctional forms that hamper the workings of markets and, in the worst case, marries government power with market power. Therefore, while power is often indispensable for implementing society-wide solutions, such as imposing a pollution tax, economists must keep their distance to powerful institutions, groups, and individuals. This is how the role of the economist as a critical adviser should be understood.

Governmental power relates to the difficult question of how political decisions for or against markets are actually drawn and how they are related to other political concerns and values. For example, liberal economists often

The self-sustaining character of markets is questionable, for example, with respect to property rights.

Recommendations for markets are invariably normative but imbued with fundamental knowledge problems.

A central concern for policy advice should be power, in particular, governmental power.

The normative basis of markets is explained in Chapter 3. On deliberative processes, see Chapter 9, section 5.4, and Chapter 17, section 3.

*A political decision
for markets can be
motivated by broader
value stances.*

*Markets for
economic advice
can enhance
a combination
of advice and
persuasion,
concealed by
quantitatively
backed expertise.*

argue that markets are a means to protect minorities against majorities not only in the economic domain but also beyond markets, such as when markets empower the free pursuit of individual lifestyles. This connection is often overlooked by market critics. In fact, even a tax such as the Pigouvian tax leaves much freedom on how to adapt to it; in that respect, it is explicitly distinct from direct government interventions such as the prescription of a certain technology for reducing CO_2 emissions. Direct interventions clearly stay in conflict with the principle of voluntary exchange because they manifest an exertion of force on individuals.

In this context, one problem is that there is a market for advice: The economist as adviser mostly is paid for her services, just as an engineer is paid for his design of the bridge. However, engineers rarely proselytise people building bridges (though, for example, they proselytised skyscrapers) whereas economists believing in markets often do. This combination of advice and persuasion tends to be concealed by the extensive use of quantitative methods and a strong tendency among economists to claim the authority of the expert.[23] The evolutionary perspective suggests that this is a pretence of knowledge. Whereas, for example, physicians know how the heart works, economists are not even sure about the nature of concepts such as capital and how to measure them. Economists claim to know that once OPEC decides to throw more oil on the market, prices will decline. But do they know when this will happen and how sustainable the drop will be, given the reactions of market actors?

Applying the principle that markets cannot produce the conditions for their existence, then, given that economic science is necessary for improving markets, it should not be subject to market forces itself. This is equivalent to postulating that economists should act as independent advisers, implying they should not be paid for their services.

Of course, this principle can only apply for academia, not for professionals. With respect to academic economists, however, another problem arises, namely the steep status order of the profession. The Harvard or Tsinghua professors' advice must be more valuable and more reliable than the advice of the professor at a regional university. This points to the role of the demand side in shaping the behaviour of economists as advisers.

*Economic advice
from academia is
fraught by status
considerations.*

As economists often lament, the relationship between economics and professional politics is fraught with tensions. Economists frequently complain about politicians asking for advice but then ignoring it. Politicians often complain about the lack of precise directions given by economists ("it depends"). At the end of the day, politicians do what they deem in their interest and refer to those economists whose advice fits the bill. Such a climate of mutual distrust tends to promote cynicism in advisership on both sides. Yet the primary criterion turns out to be status in a self-reinforcing process: Being asked for advice gives prestige; surrounding oneself with illustrious advisers sends strong signals on the quality of policies.

Therefore, the steep status order in economics departments and journals is by no means an institutional setup that fosters good advice. As said, if people in demand for advice lack the necessary knowledge themselves, they cannot judge the quality of advice either. Even ex post, many factors may interfere with implementation in an unforeseen way. Hence, the signalling of quality by other means than actual performance emerges as an institutional solution. However, this says nothing about the real quality of the advice, albeit about the general capacity to provide advice.

Hence, economics needs fundamental reforms of its academic institutions to create a new context for the role of economic advisership. One necessary reform is an institutionalised recognition and promotion of pluralism, both in terms of opinions and in terms of methods, at economics departments and economic journals. This includes a transdisciplinary perspective: Understanding financial markets should not be left to financial economists but must include the perspectives of sociologists, anthropologists, and even philosophers. This corresponds to the object-centred methodology that we advocate in this book. Further, the plurality of opinions must also be reflected in a more transparent process of research evaluation. For example, the review system in journals should be transformed into a forum of open discussion, thus making dissent more visible while sustaining the important role of the review process in raising the quality of research.

All this contributes to the most important ingredient of good economic advice, humbleness and intellectual modesty, as advocated by John Maynard Keynes. His great intellectual rival, Friedrich Hayek, admonished economists to avoid pretence of knowledge. Intellectual hubris is a sure recipe to concoct harmful advice.

For the fundamental role of ex post interpretation in the policy process, see Chapter 17, section 2.

Economics needs fundamental reform of its academic institutions.

Notes

1 Keynes (1963), p. 373.
2 Cited after Molsberger (2014).,
3 Wainwright and Mann (2018).
4 O'Flaherty and Bhagwati (1997) refer to this issue as the determinacy paradox.
5 Hirschman and Berman (2014) offer a rich survey of research on economic advisership.
6 Basu (1997).
7 Heine and Mause (2004).
8 Mirowksi and Nik-Khah (2017), p. 207ff.
9 Dewatripond and Tirole (1999).
10 Haas (1992).
11 Hirschman and Berman (2014).
12 For a survey, see Weigel (2008).
13 Kühne (2020).

14 The concept of ecosystem services is informed by economics, see Dasgupta (2021).
15 Hodgson (2004).
16 Caballero (2010).
17 Åslund (2019).
18 This refers to the *Methodenstreit* between Gustav Schmoller and Carl Menger; see Dopfer (1988).
19 Lo (2019).
20 Preda and Gemayel (2020).
21 This is recognised by Nobel awards, see Roth (2018) and Milgrom (2021).
22 Fuss et al. (2018).
23 Hopewell (2017).

References

Åslund, A. (2019) *Russia's Crony Capitalism: The Path from Market Economy to Kleptocracy*. New Haven: Yale University Press.

Basu, K. (1997) 'On Misunderstanding Government: An Analysis of the Art of Policy Advice', *Economics and Politics*, 9(3), pp. 230–250. DOI: 10.1111/1468–0343.00032.

Caballero, R. J. (2010) 'Macroeconomics After the Crisis: Time to Deal with the Pretense-of-Knowledge Syndrome', *Journal of Economic Perspectives*, 24(4), pp. 85–102. DOI: 10.1257/jep.24.4.85.

Dasgupta, P. (2021) *The Economics of Biodiversity: The Dasgupta Review*. Available at: https://assets.publishing.service.gov.uk/government/uploads/system/uploads/attachment_data/file/962785/The_Economics_of_Biodiversity_The_Dasgupta_Review_Full_Report.pdf

Dewatripond, M. and Tirole, J. (1999) 'Advocates', *Journal of Political Economy*, 107(1), pp. 1–36. DOI: 10.1086/250049.

Dopfer, K. (1988) 'How Historical Is Schmoller's Economic Theory?', *Journal of Institutional and Theoretical Economics,* 144(3), pp. 552–569.

Fuss, S. *et al.* (2018) 'A Framework for Assessing the Performance of Cap-and-Trade Systems: Insights from the European Union Emissions Trading System', *Review of Environmental Economics and Policy*, 12(2), pp. 220–241. DOI: 10.1093/reep/rey010.

Haas, P. M. (1992) 'Introduction: Epistemic Communities and International Policy Coordination', *International Organization*, 46(1), pp. 1–35. DOI: 10.1017/S0020818300001442.

Heine, K. and Mause, K. (2004) 'Policy Advice as an Investment Problem', *Kyklos*, 57(3), pp. 403–428. DOI: 10.1111/j.0023-5962.2004.00260.x.

Hirschman, D. and Berman, E. P. (2014) 'Do Economists Make Policies? On the Political Effects of Economics', *Socio-Economic Review,* 12(4), pp. 779–811. DOI: 10.1093/SER/MWU017.

Hodgson, G. M. (2004) 'Reclaiming Habit for Institutional Economics', *Journal of Economic Psychology*, 25(5), pp. 651–660. DOI: 10.1016/J.JOEP.2003.03.001.

Hopewell, K. (2017) 'Invisible Barricades: Civil Society and the Discourse of the WTO', *Globalizations*, 14(1), pp. 51–65. DOI: 10.1080/14747731.2016.1162984.

Keynes, J. M. (1963) *Essays in Persuasion*. New York: W.W. Norton & Co.

Kühne, M. (2020) 'The Application of Descriptive Theories of Human Cognition and Decision Making in Policy Making and Regulation', in Harbecke, J. and Herrmann-Pillath, C. (eds.) *Social Neuroeconomics: Mechanistic Integration of the Neurosciences and the Social Sciences*. London: Routledge, pp. 205–220. DOI: 10.4324/9780429296918-14.

Lo, A. W. (2019) *Adaptive Markets: Financial Evolution at the Speed of Thought*. Princeton: Princeton University Press. DOI: 10.1515/9780691196800.

Milgrom, P. (2021) 'Auction Research Evolving: Theorems and Market Designs', *American Economic Review*, 111(5), pp. 1383–1405. DOI: 10.1257/aer.111.5.1383.

Mirowski, P. and Nik-Khah, E. M. (2017) *The Knowledge We Have Lost in Information: The History of Information in Modern Economics*. New York City: Oxford University Press.

Molsberger, J. (2014) 'Hans Willgerodt – Ordnungspolitik als Berufung', *ORDO*, 65(1). DOI: 10.1515/ordo-2014-0123.

O'Flaherty, B. and Bhagwati, J. (1997) 'Will Free Trade with Political Science Put Normative Economists Out of Work?', *Economics and Politics*, 9(3), pp. 207–219. DOI: 10.1111/1468-0343.00029.

Preda, A. and Gemayel, R. (2020) 'Scopic Systems and Decision Making in Financial Markets', in Harbecke, J. and Herrmann-Pillath, C. (eds.) *Social Neuroeconomics: Mechanistic Integration of the Neurosciences and the Social Sciences*. London: Routledge, pp. 262–274. DOI: 10.4324/9780429296918-17.

Roth, A. E. (2018) 'Marketplaces, Markets, and Market Design', *American Economic Review*, 108(7), pp. 1609–1658. DOI: 10.1257/AER.108.7.160.

Wainwright, J. and Mann, G. (2018) *Climate Leviathan: A Political Theory of Our Planetary Future*. London: Verso.

Weigel, W. (2008) *Economics of the Law: A Primer*. London and New York: Routledge.

INDEX

abduction 218–220, 239n9
accelerator, financial 342–343
accounting 31, 159, 171, 225, 247–248,
  250–252, 255, 259, 283, 301, 306, 425,
  442; balances 281, 331, 335–336, 344,
  346, 348–354, 381–382; national 263,
  321, 325, 380; standards 32, 252, 262, 303,
  307, 316–317, 429
adaptation 19, 69, 77–79, 81, 84–86, 91n43,
  124, 128–129, 136, 141, 157, 279–280
addiction 35, 37, 43n32, 169, 173
advertisement 192, 400
affordance 133, 168, 218, 249, 278
Africa 124, 195, 361, 424, 425, 435
agency 153–155, 157–159, 161–164,
  171–172, 185–186, 190, 216, 272, 287,
  302, 336, 402
agent, autonomous 71
agent, economic 67, 153–154, 161, 171, 193,
  203–204, 229–230, 249, 251–252, 313,
  315, 320, 337, 371, 381; representative
  335; types 15, 33, 36, 37, 39, 154,
  221–222, 225, 256, 275, 302, 309–312,
  324, 335, 338, 342, 467
agglomeration 195, 364, 377, 380, 407, 426,
  441, 456
aggregation, levels 5, 68, 131, 331–333, 335,
  345, 351–354, 377, 393–394
agriculture 31, 55, 69, 70, 80, 83, 114–115,
  125–126, 225, 424–425, 429, 431–432,
  434–435, 438–439
altruism 81, 404
anthropocene 67, 68, 143
anthropocentrism 55, 67, 89n2, 112, 126, 422,
  435, 437, 438–439, 441
Aoki, Masahiko 145n56, 146n67, 222–223,
  293, 349, 414
Aoki model 222–224, 238, 246–249, 264,
  282–283, 293, 304
appropriateness, logic of 399, 401

arbitrage 14–15, 194, 246–247, 250–252,
  255–261, 263, 265, 276, 281, 285, 315,
  367–369, 375–376
arbitration 233, 373
Arrow, Kenneth 285, 337, 483
artefact 32, 69, 73, 77, 82, 84–88, 123,
  125, 133–136, 138, 140, 154, 156, 171,
  201, 204, 248, 277, 282, 286, 291, 425,
  428–430, 436
asset 13, 103–104, 136–137, 203, 232–234,
  250, 256, 261–262, 286, 288, 301, 319,
  323, 341–343, 362, 367, 403, 408;
  financial 197, 254, 263, 280, 304, 307,
  310, 314–315, 368–370, 373, 381, 397;
  specificity 104, 118n16, 139, 253–254, 280,
  288, 321; valuation 32, 316–319, 342–343
assetification 250, 280, 289, 301–304,
  312–313, 315–316, 319–321
auction 262, 289, 483
authoritarianism 116, 198, 220, 235, 454,
  457–458, 462, 470–471
autocatalysis 89
automation 123, 141–143
autonomy, individual 51, 53–54, 58, 159

Bagehot, Walter 323–324
bailout 346–347
balance sheet adjustment 343
bank, central 263, 304, 306, 308, 341,
  343–348, 353, 369, 374, 382–383, 455;
  in China 19; commercial 248, 306–307,
  312–315, 320–321, 323, 346
Bank of England 306, 356
barter 9, 246, 259, 263, 303, 422
bazaar 10, 190, 194, 250–251, 256
behaviour, institutionalised 87, 157, 216–217,
  219, 221, 223, 249, 273, 276–278, 282,
  284, 339, 348–349, 353
bicycle 136
bills of exchange 304, 306, 322

biodiversity 55, 114, 439, 486
biosphere 34, 55, 68, 72–73, 76, 112–113, 123–125, 131, 135, 143, 421, 426, 428, 431–432, 438–441
blood donation 255
bonds 252, 305, 313–315, 322, 342, 348–349, 382
boundaries: firm 139, 395, 401; group 81, 86, 164, 186, 201–203, 339–340, 399, 408; living system 68–70, 76–79, 81; market 34; mechanism 34–35; planetary 77, 431–432, 439; self 163, 194
brain 77, 87, 153–158, 160, 162, 170–171, 174n13, 175n38, 185, 405; predictive 156–158, 162, 217–218; social 84, 156, 157, 158, 162, 197, 201, 217, 424
bubble (financial) 206, 342–343
budget constraint 274–276, 281, 283, 301–302, 306, 308–309, 314–315, 322, 335–336, 348–349, 351–353, 367–368, 370, 381, 384
business, family 57, 256, 286, 310
business cycle 11, 330–331, 333, 348, 351, 381, 395, 459; political 333, 348

Cambridge controversy 262
capabilities 36, 80, 86, 100, 102–104, 111, 116–117, 132–134, 138, 140–141, 143, 144n34, 146n67, 157, 171–172, 200–201, 221–222, 281, 287, 379, 410
capital: human 162, 200, 201, 236, 286, 377–378, 380, 397, 399, 403, 405–408, 413, 426, 436, 465; real 286, 301–302, 317–320, 393, 403; social 104, 186, 197–200, 203, 208, 210n35, 220–221, 247, 253, 257, 262–263, 265, 281, 302, 304, 321, 393, 403, 406, 408–409, 413; value of 316–319
capitalism 18–19, 31, 37, 155, 172, 228, 237, 332, 398, 424–425, 439, 485; and China 9, 12, 18, 19, 20, 21, 284, 302, 320; and market economy 9, 19, 20–21, 398
carbon fuel 126, 430, 433
car, electric 134, 136–137, 204
care 55, 58, 111, 131, 194, 225, 437, 469
carrying capacity 76
cellular automata 204–205
central bank see bank, central
central political independence 345–346, 353
centre-periphery 196, 208
chiefdom 101, 108
China 38, 57, 69, 73, 138, 140, 142, 167, 177n105, 198, 203, 229, 363, 373, 426, 428, 437, 471, 485–487; imperial 9–24, 31, 33, 141, 276, 279, 284, 305, 361, 422, 424–425, 433–435

choice, rational 51–52, 153–154, 159, 172–173, 483
city 10, 14–15, 53, 125, 131, 185, 196, 198, 204, 207, 302, 372, 408, 426, 441
civil rights 50
class, social 17, 52, 200, 395, 469
climate change 56, 69, 77, 361, 440, 483, 487
CO2 71, 113, 115, 130, 426, 429, 488
Coase theorem 114, 117, 233, 467
co-evolution 67–68, 80–81, 112, 153, 155, 171; of economics and economy 31; firm/ technology 140; gene/culture 85–87, 424; inequality 395, 402–403, 406, 412; institutions/technology 330, 342; technosphere/ economy 133, 137; wants/needs 129
coffee 169, 190–191, 194, 278
cognition, distributed 158, 222, 248, 283–284, 291
cognitive ability 404
coin 16, 247, 302
Coleman, James 109, 115, 197
collateral 342–344
collective action problem 282, 373, 398, 462, 468–469
commodification 275, 280, 289, 291, 337
communication 28, 159, 161, 201, 287, 407, 430, 466; market (prices) 251, 286, 347–348, 409; network dimension 186–190, 192–193, 459; technology 15, 125, 133, 185, 224, 249, 339, 458
community of advantage 9, 277, 282
company, joint stock 319–320
comparative advantage 100–103, 109, 114, 116, 132, 140, 235, 274, 361, 375–379, 384
compensation systems 225
competition: for attention 460; democratic 469, 471, 473; electoral 457, 460–461, 474; of interest groups 397, 454, 456, 457, 461–463, 466–467, 474; interfirm 400, 402, 412, 413; interjurisdictional 317, 398, 413, 454, 456, 464–465, 471, 474; intrafirm 400; intrajurisdictional 464; law 289, 352, 402, 484; locational 114, 377–379, 395, 456; market 56, 60, 79, 80, 116, 207, 277, 279–281, 287, 290, 394, 396–398, 402, 405, 410, 412–413, 456–457, 461, 473; policy 469–471, 473; political 371, 396, 397, 453–463, 465, 467, 469, 471, 473–475; positional 279, 280; for public opinion 453, 456–457, 459–460, 463, 474; status 79, 128, 274, 436–438; systemic 398, 422; yardstick 464
complementarities, institutional 333, 397, 476

493

complexity 27, 33, 41, 74, 77, 86, 104, 130, 163, 187, 204, 274, 278–279, 290, 292, 319, 334–335, 346, 348–349, 379, 384, 386, 409, 421, 439, 458
complex systems approach 339, 355
conformity 460, 468
confucianism 15, 18
constitution 34, 39, 221, 226–227, 231, 234, 240n58, 306, 369–370, 397, 455
constitutional level 226–227, 231, 234, 306, 369–370, 397
constructal law 90n24
consumer, entrepreneurial 310–312, 338, 342
consumer sovereignty 50
consumption 11–12, 16, 26, 29, 50, 71, 104, 126–130, 142–143, 156, 162, 164–170, 173, 185, 193, 254, 265, 276, 279, 302, 308–313, 325, 333, 335, 341–342, 348, 352, 407, 423, 428, 429, 435–438, 441, 468
contagion 52, 339, 368, 381
container 137, 364
continuity, ontological 67, 88–89, 292
contract 99, 101, 226, 231–232, 238; arms-length 379; in China 13, 16; freedom of 232, 454; labour 273, 454
convention 5, 29, 36–37, 126, 131, 137, 207, 216, 238, 251–253, 263, 272–273, 284, 289, 291, 313, 317, 342, 345, 349, 351–354, 356, 362–365, 393, 402, 412, 436, 466, 486
cooking 85, 131
cooling 428, 441
corporate governance 172, 225, 233, 397, 401
corporation 14, 19, 31, 233, 289, 320, 399; separation of ownership and control 399
corporatisation 319–320
corruption 197, 219–220, 224, 239n14, 383, 468
cosmopolitanism 383
cost 11, 49, 52, 55, 100, 107, 111, 115, 130, 132, 160, 223–225, 251–252, 277, 284, 317, 320, 337, 380, 407, 439, 468, 484; capital 141–142; children 437; energy 141–142, 429; external 50, 99, 112–114; institutions 226–227, 231–232; labour 141, 379–380; opportunity 101–102, 106–110, 115, 256–262, 313, 375, 377; production 57, 78, 86, 112–113, 134, 136, 140, 375, 433; signal 192–193, 203, 406; trade 14, 366, 368, 370, 374–375, 385–386; transaction (*see* transaction cost); transport 14, 104, 137, 363, 366, 434
country size 368, 372
creative destruction 279, 331, 340–341
creativity 128, 141, 154, 169–171, 173, 276, 280, 338, 404, 409, 430

credibility, of monetary policy 339, 346–347, 354, 382
credit, social 263, 265
credit cycle 307–308, 324
credit rationing 307, 343–344
crime 56, 203, 403
crisis: balance of payments 284, 361, 363, 370, 380–382; economic 333, 351; structural 332
cue 161, 217–219, 223–224, 237, 282, 284, 339, 347, 349, 461
currency area 348, 364–365, 367–368, 370, 373–374, 380
currency peg 374
current account 363, 367, 370, 374, 380–382
current account reversal 382
cycle: economic/business 104, 331–332, 339, 351, 395, 459; political 333, 348, 356, 381

Darwin, Charle 3, 98
Darwinism 78, 84, 90n12, 136, 272, 291
debt 253, 303–305, 320, 352, 381–383; government 19–21, 315, 325, 347
decoupling, of energy and economic growth 190, 384, 429, 436–437, 459
deficit: budget 382; current account 374, 380–382
degrowth 428, 435
deliberation 453, 468–471, 487
democracy 460, 464, 470
demographic transition 421
demography 145n57, 292, 400, 437
deposit 19, 249, 306–308, 312–315, 320, 322, 425, 434
design: institutional 56, 142, 225, 235, 320; market 40, 56, 58, 110, 250; technology 133–135, 136, 138, 142–143, 155, 160, 169, 488
deskilling 53, 102, 399, 470
devaluation 374
dichotomy, of real and nominal variables 346, 411
dignity, human 454, 469–471, 473–474
discount rate 56, 308
discovery process, entrepreneurial 281, 376
discrimination 128, 164, 173, 203, 205, 207–208, 222, 236, 307, 383, 397, 412
distribution: of agential power 196, 198, 207–208, 232–233, 236–238; of income and wealth 335, 397, 403, 406, 459
diversification 83, 249, 274, 374, 378, 484
division of knowledge 277
division of labour 277, 284, 304, 312, 361, 371
dress code 50
dyad 186–187, 189, 207, 274

Dynamic Stochastic General Equilibrium (DSGE) models 335

Earth system 55, 67–74, 77, 80, 82, 83, 90n16, 112, 123, 125–126, 131, 421–422, 424, 426, 428, 430–432, 434, 436, 438–441
East Asia 365, 373
economics: academia 59; behavioural 26, 42n25, 52, 153–155, 172, 176n101, 474, 484; definition 116; economies of scale 132–134, 136, 143, 333; experimental 1, 260, 265; international 361, 369, 388, 389; see also macroeconomics
economic sociology 32, 42n3, 185, 292
economics of identity 51, 239n27
economisation 32, 44, 70, 484, 496
economist, as adviser 4, 482–489
economy 201, 437–439; agrarian 11, 422–423, 425; Chinese 9, 434; circular 84, 92n76; and ecosystem 68–71, 82–84; evolution 421–426; global 361, 426; industrial 128, 167, 276, 424–425; market 9, 12, 18–21, 37, 57, 131, 254, 263, 307–308, 314, 316, 319, 321, 341, 346, 348, 397–398, 411, 438, 455, 469; as object 29–31; planned 54, 470; pre-agrarian 422; subsystem of society 26; systems 57
ecosystem 67–70, 74, 76–78, 80–84, 89, 106, 114, 124, 126, 129–130, 279, 361, 431, 438–439, 490
ecosystem services 55, 114, 439, 490
education 17, 44, 54, 59, 131, 140, 203, 220–221, 395, 397–398, 403–408, 411, 413, 415, 436–437, 454, 460, 465, 467–468, 470
educational system 140, 397, 405–406, 413, 465, 470
efficiency 15, 49, 56–57, 76, 78, 100, 102, 115, 138, 141, 235, 237, 279, 286, 398, 402, 409, 433–434, 437; engineering 79; institutions 229–230, 234; measures 113–115, 225; of specialisation 111–115; thermodynamic incl. energy 71, 429–430; as value 54–55, 58
Egypt, Ancient 110, 112, 422
eigentime 74, 82, 84
electricity 137, 428
elite 200, 406–407
emission rights 32, 289, 487
emotion 52, 128, 153, 160–161, 165, 172, 175n50, 53, 197, 201, 217, 220–224, 238–239, 248, 254–256, 264–265, 288–289, 338, 340–342, 407, 462, 468, 470–471

empathy 161, 164, 172
empire 14, 17, 20, 101, 108, 110, 201, 292, 305, 361, 373, 434
employment 57, 156, 203, 276, 287, 289, 335, 344–345, 351–323, 398–399, 401, 410, 465
employment protection 351–352, 401, 465
employment relation 287, 465
endowment 403, 406, 408–409, 411, 468; factor/resource 166, 366, 375, 377–378, 380, 393, 399, 468–469; genetic 84, 172, 224, 411
endowment effect 39, 163, 220, 223, 251, 255, 259
energy 19, 74, 80, 82, 90n16, 128, 132, 139, 141–142, 355, 428, 434, 440; embodied 429–430; fossil 24, 76, 115, 126, 355, 429–430, 440; and growth 279, 422, 428–432, 436; solar 74, 77, 82–83, 126, 279, 424; throughput 72–73, 133, 425; and work 71
Enlightenment 27, 50, 54, 60n8, 239n17
enterprise, social 56
entrepreneurship: and creativity 46, 169–171, 280, 338, 433; financial 301–302, 307, 310–312, 314, 316, 342, 398; and firm 285, 319, 342, 401; and individuality 154, 185; and inequality 409–410; and innovation/novelty 157, 277–278, 285–286, 340, 433; in international trade 375–376, 379; and knowledge 198, 262, 285; political 453, 459, 461, 473; and profit/rent 261–262, 280–281, 287, 433; and risk/uncertainty 261, 272–273, 285–288, 337, 376, 409–410, 459, 462; Schumpeterian 279, 309, 311–312, 338, 340–341, 432; and social networks 104, 199, 409; types of 310–312
entropy 70–71, 73, 90n16, 127, 430–431
environment (ecology) 51, 55, 57, 68–71, 74, 76–82, 84–85, 99, 112–114, 116, 124–125, 131–132, 142, 156–157
envy 51, 399
epidemiology 196
equality of opportunity 405, 410–411
equity 18, 55, 314–316, 319–322, 342, 398
equity-efficiency trade-off 55, 398
ethics, professional 59, 61n38
ethnicity 203, 412
ethnic trading networks 197, 202, 208
European Union 302, 365, 402, 454
evolution 67–68, 76–77, 116, 162, 185, 196, 250, 302, 335–336, 346, 361, 364–365, 375–376, 380, 383, 394–395, 398, 463; biological 55, 77–84, 127, 153–155, 277; competition 57, 77, 80; cultural 84–88,

110, 127, 153, 155, 216; economic 79, 82–88, 99, 330, 422–432; inequality 393–396, 402, 405, 409–410; institutional 87–88, 124, 217, 219, 224, 226, 227–232, 237, 332–334, 353, 393, 464; markets 31–32, 80, 272–297, 352, 435; physical 70–74; politics 453–459, 473; preferences 51, 165–167; technological 123–124, 126–127, 129, 134–137, 140–142, 224, 422, 424, 432; theory of 78, 84, 88, 99, 224, 272–273, 486

evolutionary economics 5, 67, 80, 88, 145n50, 272, 291, 294

evolvability 81, 472

exchange: gift 56, 191, 208, 255; forced 100–101, 111, 140, 191, 274, 288–289; triangular 303; voluntary 100–101, 140, 191, 235, 273–274, 487–488

exchange rate 367–369, 381–382; determinants 368–369; fixed 368, 374; flexible 374; regime 373–374, 383; risk 366, 368

exit and voice 231, 286, 398, 402, 457, 462, 464–465

expectations: as animal spirits 337–338; collective 338–340; exchange rate 362, 368–369, 382; fictional 338, 340, 433; and fiscal policy 348, 351; frequency dependent 339, 341; higher-order 325, 338–339, 351; individual 223, 261, 283, 337–339; inflationary 346; and institutionalised behaviour 217–218, 224–225, 349–350, 352; and learning 157; and (financial) market prices 261, 282–284, 316, 341, 343–344, 349–350; rational 41, 160, 337–338, 346–347; reflexive 39, 165; and social network analysis 339–340; temporal dimension 273, 340, 351; theories of 39, 336–337; and valuation of capital 316–318

experiment, economic 39

experimentation, political 281, 471–472

explanation: causal 27, 29, 34, 40; constitutive 34; mechanistic 27, 33, 35

export 363, 365–368, 371–374, 376–377, 379–380, 430

externalisation 99, 111, 114, 116–117, 126, 128, 130, 228–229, 235, 320

externality 50–51, 55, 69, 107, 187, 369, 472; information 189; negative 50, 112, 231, 374; positive 188, 228; terms of trade 372

extinction 55, 74, 422

factory 13–14, 109, 112, 114–115, 130–131, 138, 351, 429

fairness 53–54, 393, 410

family 56–57, 113, 115, 131, 197, 220, 248, 256

family business 57, 256, 286, 310, 324

federalism 456

federation 364

feminism 411

fictionality 164, 340, 348

finance 4, 19–20, 30, 39, 57, 247–248, 281, 285, 301, 304, 307–311, 316, 319–321, 330, 341–342, 348–349, 351–352, 364, 367, 380, 382, 399, 409, 486

fire 85, 106–107, 123

firm 57, 114, 141–142, 276, 289, 342, 399–401, 455, 465; boundary 139, 401; governance/corporate 172, 225, 233, 286, 378–379, 397, 401; inequality 398–402; and market 273, 287; multinational 361, 364, 378–380; organisation 286, 394; production 123, 138–142; see also multinational enterprise

fitness 78, 81, 277, 279, 281

fluctuations, economic 4, 273, 330–336, 340–341, 345–347, 349, 352–354

foreign direct investment (FDI) 371–372, 374–380

fossils 72, 76, 115, 126, 355n14, 424–425, 429–430, 432, 440–441

fragmentation, of global production 291, 378, 435

frame, money 255–256, 264

framing, frame 39, 130, 154, 217–218, 246, 255, 265, 282, 302, 361, 472

freedom 17, 48–53, 58–60, 101–102, 110, 128, 135, 142, 162, 175n62, 204, 220, 231–232, 235, 253, 255, 263, 290, 344, 367, 421–422, 453–454, 469–471, 473–474, 488; as agential power 162, 253, 421, 469–470; of consumption 49–51, 128; of exit/opting out 101–102, 110; and markets 17, 58, 255, 290; and money 253, 255; and Pareto criterion 50, 101; and performativity 48; political 220, 454, 469–470; and rationality 51–53; and social justice 53–54, 58–61; as value 49–51, 235

free-rider problem 199, 203

frequency-dependency 78, 81, 203–204, 206–207, 223–224, 339–341, 368, 408–409, 460, 468

functionings 79–80, 86, 102, 116, 123, 141, 153, 173, 200, 221–222, 410

game: battle of the sexes (game) 105–106, 117, 216; coordination 105–107; of difference 105; ultimatum 109; zero-sum 163, 321, 374, 460, 473

game theory 3, 104, 175n39, 209n24, 217, 223, 325

GATT 369, 371–373

GDP 113, 131, 143, 169, 330, 344–347, 368, 393, 395, 411, 421–423, 429, 435; growth 346, 421, 426, 428–429, 436–438; per capita 29, 393, 421, 425–426, 434–435, 440
general equilibrium theory 33, 246
generations, future 56, 421, 469
genetics: behavioural 403; genetic endowment (*see* endowment, genetic); and genetic variation 403–404; importance for behaviour and social outcomes 80, 84–86, 88, 157, 172, 253, 404, 424–425
Georgescu-Roegen, Nicholas 90n15, 92n72
geostrategy 373
Germany 137, 139, 207, 218, 356n55
Gestalt principle 217–218
gift 56, 255, 274, 422; exchange 56, 208; relation 191, 255
globalisation 15, 68, 361, 364, 384, 398, 464
global value chains 363, 378–379
gold standard 305, 315, 333, 375
good: club 199; public 15, 18, 199, 263, 302, 304, 453; status/positional 38, 128, 137, 166, 407
government 101, 113–115, 132, 135, 207, 229, 232–233, 236, 319, 361, 364, 369–361, 377, 383, 422, 440, 455, 470, 483, 487–488; budget 247, 347–348; bureaucracy 458, 466–467; China 10, 12, 14–18, 20, 425; cost of 230; GDP 131; money 249, 302, 305, 315
graph 186, 208
Great Acceleration 68, 76, 125, 423, 430–431, 441
Great Depression 312, 331, 353, 453, 482–484
greenhouse gas 69, 113, 487
group: hunt 100, 107, 157–158, 422; markers 203, 407; small 116, 206, 232
growth 67, 74, 77, 137, 284, 346, 408, 421–448; biology 74–78, 428, 436, 440; complexity 163; demographic 19, 421, 437; economic 9, 15, 229, 235, 279, 330–331, 341, 346, 382, 412, 421, 426, 431, 434–438, 463; and energy 428–430; hyperbolic 76, 426; logistic 76, 204; market 19, 277, 280, 421, 432; modern 126, 421, 424–425; population 81, 86, 88, 424, 431–432, 434; pre-modern 421–424; technosphere 426–428, 430, 440; theory 145n50, 426
guanxi 12, 22n18, 198, 209n21
guilds 16, 18

habit 156–157, 174n24, 228, 278, 349; consumption 16, 168, 283–284, 407; food 77

happiness 29, 54, 61n24, 168–169, 173, 177n104, 393, 395, 403, 411
Hayek, Friedrich 49, 88, 174n21, 175n35, 39, 330, 489
health care 55, 58, 225
heat engine 70–72
heating 426, 430, 441
hegemony 31, 370, 373, 386n40
herding 205, 342, 344, 368
heredity/heritability 402–404
hog cycle 104
hold-up problem 281, 470
homo faber 170
homophily 406–408
hormones 155, 169
hostage 371
household 12, 21, 22n15, 166, 170, 193, 248, 335, 341–342, 393, 395, 397; production 131
housing 36, 53, 344
Human Development Index 29, 443n73
humanities 27, 41
hunter gatherer 108, 201
hunting 107–108, 110, 422, 424
hypercycle 92n75

identity 58, 163–165, 216, 220–221, 225, 254, 286, 412; economics of 51; group, social 51, 158, 164–165, 167, 171, 202–203, 263, 411, 460; personal 51, 163, 255, 462
ideology 19, 461
imitation 34, 86, 133, 163, 166–168, 173, 194, 203–205, 207–208, 229, 234, 285, 287, 291, 340, 378, 408, 464
impartiality 48–49, 59–60, 236, 439, 483–484
imperialism 18, 29, 369
import 219, 367, 374, 466
inclusion 236, 453, 468–471, 487
increasing returns to scale 132, 252, 375, 426
India 142, 158, 361, 364
indicators: expectations formation 338; business cycle 351
individualism 37, 411; methodological 186
induction 218–219
industrial district 290, 377, 442
industrial economy 128, 167, 276, 424–425
industrialisation 9, 18–20, 53, 83, 111, 135, 225, 305, 423, 425, 428, 432–436
industrial revolution 112, 138
industry: automobile 377; chemical 138; pharmaceutical 135
inequality: and capital accumulation 405–406, 409; and chance 410–411; dimensions of 393, 395; and education 403, 405–406; and

efficiency 55–56; and entrepreneurship 409–410; gender 395, 411; in human groups 106–108, 406–408; income 395, 400–401, 406; and individual development 403–405; interfirm 395–396, 400–402; interjurisdictional 364–365, 398, 464–466; interpersonal 394–395, 403; intrafirm 395–396, 398–400; intrajurisdictional 395–398; and labour markets 400–401, 406, 408; and legitimacy/ market stability 17, 58, 289, 393, 410–412, 469–470; and narratives 411–412; and 'nature vs. nurture' 402–404; and power laws 206; and signalling 405–407; and social capital 406; and status 80, 105–107, 134, 163, 166, 169, 199, 258, 279, 287, 394, 399, 400–401, 406–408, 437; structural-positional 394–395, 396–398; wealth 395, 398, 406; and well-being/happiness 128, 169

inflation 19, 250, 309, 311, 314, 345–347, 352; expected 309, 317

information 51, 105, 157–160, 167, 169, 187, 189–190, 196, 204, 217, 223, 229, 231–232, 289, 337–340, 346, 366, 400, 406, 409, 426, 464; Arrow paradox 285, 337, 483–484; asymmetric 187–188, 206, 286–287, 320, 383, 463; biological 68, 71–72, 77, 79–83, 91n39, 224, 424, 431; brain 156; cascades 205; cost of 228; embodied 72, 77, 80, 168; externality 189, 277, 290, 342–343; market 11–12, 32, 188, 190, 193–195, 198, 272, 277, 335, 349, 376; non-genetic transmission 84–87; perfect/ complete 187–189, 194, 251–252, 258, 281–282, 284; in politics 236, 347–348, 460, 463, 468, 483; technology 430, 458; transmission 192–194, 201–202, 408, 425

infrastructure 14–15, 18, 21, 33, 77, 201, 398, 426, 454, 484

in-group 69, 86, 92n79, 186, 201, 203, 208, 216, 399, 406, 411, 462

inheritance 16, 87; tax 470

innovation 34, 56, 58, 59, 144n34, 145n37, 261, 276, 278, 288, 307, 331, 340–341, 343, 376, 406, 412, 464, 487; behavioural 79, 85–86, 100, 284, 422; constraints 279, 433; consumer 170, 278; diffusion 204, 207, 340; financial 249, 302, 342, 344, 364; institution 229, 304, 464; system of 139–140, 380; technological 19, 87, 123, 132, 135, 139, 272, 309, 344, 364, 432, 439

input-output analysis 129

institution: Aoki model 223; Chinese development 19; co-evolution 86–88; and cognition 217–219; competition among 56–57, 398, 464–465, 471;

contractarian view 231–232; cost of 225–227; economic, political and economic policy 455; and emotion 220–221; enforcement 216–217, 223, 228, 230, 233–234, 237, 288–289, 304, 373, 454–457; evaluation of 235–236; formal 15, 216, 219–220, 223–224, 229–230, 232–233, 234, 253, 288–289, 352, 366, 369, 394, 396–398, 402, 453, 455–456, 461; imitation 229; and inequality (regimes) 393–394; informal 216, 219, 222, 224, 226, 228–230, 288–289, 332, 349, 352, 366, 393, 468; international borders 364–366; international 369–370; liability 319–321; and markets 274, 277, 282, 288–290, 397; money 247–250, 304–306; objects 362; path dependency 224–225; performativity 222–224; and power 232–233; and technology (regimes) 332–333; types of 216–217; types of agents 221, 309–312; and values 58; and violence 233–235; see also transaction cost

institutionalisation 158, 217–219, 223, 229–230, 234, 284, 316, 347

instrument: investment 312–315, 322, 367; saving 311–313, 315, 322, 349, 382

insurance 52, 54, 335, 410

interest group 231, 454, 456–457, 461–463, 466–469, 474; in economics 200; politics 200, 397, 472, 487; in society 59

interest rate 252, 307, 309, 312–313, 315, 318, 322, 343, 346, 369, 381–382; negative 324; parity 369

intermediation 12, 21, 187–188, 208, 314

intermediator 12, 15, 187–189, 195, 199, 313

internalisation 69–70, 107, 112–115, 123, 130, 142, 218, 277, 280, 429–430, 469

interpretation 287, 335, 338–340, 349; policies 353, 458, 466–467; prices 251, 282, 284; signals, data 192, 194, 217, 281, 337

investment 125, 136–137, 142, 286, 301–302, 308–315, 317, 320, 323n1, 324n42, 330–331, 342–343, 348, 366–367, 371–374, 376–380, 411, 426, 435, 441, 466; capabilities 102; financial 256, 382, 395, 462; infrastructure 10, 15; international 305, 366–367, 371–374, 376–380, 466; parental 411, 437; real estate 36; regime 333–334; risk 19

investment, portfolio 373, 378, 382

investor 104, 154, 225, 262, 309–312, 314–315, 318, 320, 335, 342, 367,

381–382; financial 310, 339, 342, 374, 382, 393, 434, 464
invisible hand theorem 99, 321
Islam 30, 50

Japan 292, 315, 356, 363, 385, 402, 425, 435
Jevons, W. Stanley 430
jurisdiction 229, 305, 364–366, 369, 380, 383–384, 394, 397, 412, 454, 456, 460, 464

Keynes, John Maynard 175n53, 273, 324, 325, 336–338, 344, 351, 355, 356, 482, 483, 489, 504
Keynesianism 39, 51, 312, 342, 348, 482, 484; post- 264, 335
knowledge 33, 194, 198, 219, 224, 228, 307, 378, 425, 436, 458, 461, 463, 471; distributed 277, 286, 402; embodied 80, 276, 399; entrepreneurial 285; externalities 426; objective 27, 29, 30, 32; producer 134, 136, 139, 380; spillovers 377, 409; tacit 133, 138, 145n37, 285
Korea 235

labour exchange 56
lactose intolerance 424
language 81, 86, 157, 163–165, 173, 185, 192–193, 201, 218, 227, 366, 376, 407, 422, 484; ordinary 2, 40–41, 455
law 18, 230–231, 233, 288–289, 315, 351, 383, 455, 467, 484–485; civil 16; competition 289, 352, 402; customary 16, 288, 369; international 372, 385n17
law, scientific: natural 27, 34; of comparative advantage 100; of demand 35, 38; of one price 2, 31, 252, 264, 368; power 196–197; thermodynamics 71–73, 90n16, 431
leadership 199, 282, 286, 400; political 463, 466, 471
learning 77, 80, 84–86, 102, 134, 136, 156–157, 163, 166–168, 174n23, 219, 252, 281, 287, 330, 337, 339, 353, 405, 409, 464
legitimacy 53, 58, 393–395, 410–413, 468, 473–474
lemons 206, 251–252, 307, 343
level playing field 460, 469
leverage cycle 342
leveraging 308, 316, 331, 342–344
lex mercatoria 369–370
liability 289, 302, 316, 319–320; (accounting) 263, 303, 315, 322; limited 19–20, 229, 285, 320, 322, 397
liberalisation 40, 341, 369, 371, 374, 412
liberty 288; individual 49–50, 470

life cycle 52, 71, 74, 82, 84, 166, 331, 394, 403, 413
lighting 128, 426, 428–430, 441
liking 154, 168–169, 173
liquidity 281, 292, 320, 336, 343, 349, 383
lobbying 397, 462–463, 469
lock-in 111, 218–219, 224, 237, 355, 433
logistic curve 76, 204
long-distance trade 9, 14, 16, 19, 304, 422, 425
Lotka, Alfred 73, 90n25
love 52, 127, 161, 436
loyalty 17, 57, 191, 220, 286, 338, 402
lucas critique 39, 43n45
luxury goods 38, 128

machine 54, 72, 132–134, 139, 141, 317
macroeconomics 41, 43n45, 247, 262, 301, 323n1, 324n26, 325n53, 330, 335, 339, 346, 355n20, 485; behavioural 330; Keynesian school of (see Keynesianism)
management 10, 13, 102, 138–140, 145n56, 190, 225, 233, 249, 286, 293, 319, 346, 373, 380, 399–400, 426, 467–468
marginalist turn 49, 256
market: capital 19, 301, 312, 322–323; clearing 282–284, 290, 336, 349–350, 372; foreign exchange 362, 367–368; investment instruments II 314–316; labour 13, 37, 53, 56, 104, 111, 123, 140–141, 254, 333, 338, 340, 352, 394, 396, 400–401, 403, 405, 408, 413; making 287; money 301, 323; niche 11, 136, 275–276, 276, 279, 284, 287, 331, 351, 364, 376; for saving instruments 312–313, 315; society 11, 13, 21; stasis 284, 400; state 204, 222, 272–273, 278–284, 290–291, 314, 319, 331, 336, 344, 349–353; system 3, 10–12, 14–16, 19–21, 33–34, 68, 73, 185, 202, 207, 275–277, 279, 290, 335, 337, 351, 353–354, 394, 402, 410, 412, 432–433, 438, 483, 486
market access right MAR 361, 369–372, 373, 375, 384
marketisation 32, 58, 275, 280, 289, 291
marketplace 9–15, 21, 126, 157, 162, 185, 191, 193, 228, 274, 280, 283, 290, 312
market-town 10–11, 21
marriage (markets) 11–12, 16, 52, 165, 220, 258, 407, 434, 437
Marshall, Alfred 1–3, 6, 40–43, 259, 290, 442
Marx, Karl 2, 30, 261
Marxism 131, 250, 330, 355, 411, 440
Maslow, Albert 435
mass media 460, 475

material flows analysis (MFA) 90n14, 428
materiality 26, 31, 33, 35, 41–42, 67, 185, 247
Matthew effect 195, 206
maximum entropy production principle 73, 431–434, 438
maximum power principle 73, 90, 431, 438
medium-range theory 33–34, 40, 42n26
merchant, medieval 10, 14, 16–18, 302, 304
meritocracy 58, 223, 289, 404, 410–412, 471–472
metabolism 67, 71, 74–75, 77, 89, 126–127, 144n24
Middle East 365, 424
middleman 12–13, 16; *see also* intermediator
migration 17, 53, 88, 125, 201, 366, 377, 422, 461, 464
military 15, 18, 105, 132, 141, 234, 237, 415, 425, 440, 464
Mill, John Stuart 21n1, 435
mind reading 157, 422
Minsky, Hyman 324
mobilisation (social) 411, 463
mobility 56, 141, 352, 373–374, 398; intergenerational 403–405; social 394–395, 408
model, in economics 33, 35–37, 41, 154, 344, 440–441, 464
monetary community: primary 263, 304, 306–307, 322; secondary 304–307, 320–321, 382
monetary policy 193, 306, 344–348, 353, 366, 373–374, 455, 466
money: Aoki model of 248–250; in China 16, 305; and cognition 254–255, 260; and credit 263, 303–304; fiat 31, 249, 263, 281, 315, 341, 348, 353, 455; functions 248–250, 255, 264, 304–305, 319; illusion 253; neutrality of 346; performativity (framing) 255, 309; private 302–308, 320–322; psychology 253–256; pump 259; purchasing power 253–254, 266n27, 309, 368; quantity 31, 246, 249, 260, 265n5; sign 247, 249–250; as social capital 247, 257, 321; sovereign 249, 302–303, 305–308, 315, 322, 348; trust 250–251, 305; value of 246, 253–254, 302; as veil 246, 346
monopoly 18, 109–110, 254, 340; government 18; temporary 340–341, 461
moral hazard 228, 320, 347, 380
mortgage 311–312, 316, 324, 342
most favoured nation principle MFN 372–373
multilateralism 274, 372–375

multinational enterprise MNE 364, 377–380, 384, 386
multiplier, Keynesian 348

NAIRU (non-accelerating inflation rate of unemployment) 345, 356
narrative 20, 39–40, 163–166, 170, 173, 176n76, 310, 328, 340, 348, 354, 410–412, 459–460
nature *vs.* nurture 403–404
needs 28, 36, 78–79, 123, 127–129, 137, 143, 166–168, 173, 276–277, 281, 284, 320, 338, 371, 424, 435, 460, 470; basic 430; energetic 142, 429; hierarchy of 435; human 127, 436, 439
negotiations 10, 104, 110, 113–115, 117, 190, 193–194, 231, 351–352, 371, 373, 375, 466–467, 469, 471–472
neighbour(hood) 194, 197, 204–205
neoliberalism 1, 40, 482, 484
network: ego-centric 190, 208; metabolic 75, 185; non-integral 189, 207, 335; random 196; scale-free 196, 208
network effects 206, 248, 322, 426; technology 136, 143, 426
neuroeconomics 173n3, 175n13, 16, 23, 25, 253, 266n21
neuron 29, 155–156, 158, 163
neuroscience 174n21, 175n35, 177n104, 253
niche 57, 74, 84, 90n2, 138, 145n57, 273, 395, 406, 457; cognitive 405; construction 3, 68, 128, 423, 431; ecological 68, 73, 77–78, 80–83, 90n2, 124, 422, 424; human 3, 68–69, 71, 85, 100, 128–129, 237, 422, 425–426, 431; market 11, 136, 274–276, 278–280, 284, 287, 290, 292, 331, 351, 364, 376
node (social network) 186, 190, 195–196, 201, 208
nomadism 69, 424
norm, social 15, 35, 116, 161, 216, 220, 223, 227, 230, 233, 237, 263, 265, 279, 434
novelty 33–34, 79–80, 83, 154, 157, 273–274, 285, 302, 376
nudging 155, 455, 484

obesity 129, 436
object, institutional 301, 303, 312–314, 362–364, 366, 383
objectivity, objective 26–30, 32–33, 42n4, 48–49, 61n22, 156, 232, 235–236, 261, 339, 352, 411, 458, 464
observation 28, 85, 101, 133, 186–194, 204, 227, 229, 286, 335–336, 343, 349, 459
offshoring 363
Olson, Mancur 118n35, 232, 469

ontogeny 77, 80, 84, 156, 405
opportunity cost 52, 101–102, 106–110, 115, 256–262, 313, 322, 366, 375–376
organisation 139–140, 272, 287–289, 333, 379–380, 399, 454, 461, 467; ageing 400; demography 145n57, 292, 400; forms 13, 138, 142–143; innovation 342, 364; networks 197; political 101, 365, 455–457
organism 68, 74, 76–77, 79, 81, 85, 126, 153–155, 167, 172, 185, 436–437
ostracism 16, 202, 208, 228, 304
out-group 86, 186, 201, 203, 208, 399, 407, 411
outside options 101–102, 110–111, 115–116, 141, 195, 274
outsourcing 379

pandemic 334, 398
Panglossian problem 483
paradigm: institutional 333; technological 137, 331–332, 334, 354
pareto criterion 50, 60, 101, 106–109, 111, 116, 118n9, 163, 231, 466
parliament 231, 454–455, 465
party, political 456, 461, 469, 475
patent 230
path dependency 137, 224–226, 229, 250, 377, 380, 403–405; institutions 224, 226; technology 433, 441
Pax Britannica 361
peasant 15–16, 254, 276, 425, 433
performativity 27, 459; agency 165–166, 171, 309; economics 31, 39, 48, 225, 331, 344–345; institutions 221–225, 248, 250, 253–254, 289, 410–411; market 278, 283–284
photosynthesis 72, 82–83, 126, 424
phylogeny 77, 82, 100, 124, 145n49, 157
planet, hybrid 68, 90n28
planetary boundaries 77, 431, 439, 441
plantation 125, 425, 435
polarisation (political) 221, 458, 463
policy: austerity 348; discretionary measures 455, 473; economic 349, 353, 455, 458, 463–464, 468; fiscal 331, 333, 345, 347–348, 353–354, 382, 455, 473; implementation 467, 474; monetary 193, 306, 344–348, 353, 366, 373–374, 455, 466; proposal 456–459, 461–463, 465, 472–473, 487; rules *vs.* discretion 347–348
political business cycle 333, 348, 356
political economy 383, 472, 474; constitutional 240n58; evolutionary 453
pollination 55, 106
pollution 69, 112–115, 131, 137, 187, 469, 487

possession 13, 162, 171, 191, 220, 436–437
poverty 17–18, 48, 54, 393, 435, 441
power: agential 53, 103–104, 153, 161–162, 171, 185–186, 189, 194–201, 207, 232–233, 253–254, 281, 288, 393, 408; asymmetry 101, 112, 115, 117, 141–142, 280, 285–286, 289–290, 370–371, 379; definition 109, 115; in firms 140; market 17, 195, 487; military 425; political 234, 237, 332, 396–397, 459, 461, 464–465, 472–473
preferences 49–53, 129, 154, 159, 161–163, 167–168, 176n88, 221, 231, 259, 320, 383, 458, 468, 471–472; meta 51, 60n14; political 404, 453, 461–463, 466; revealed 101, 154; social 51, 161, 164, 224, 249; subjective 49, 131
price 194, 281–284, 343, 345, 368; asset 316–318; and efficiency 113–115; fair 255; human life 54; as monetary phenomenon 250–252; objectivization of value 255–260; reservation 256–258; second person view 32; stickiness 251, 349, 352; uncertainty 251
pricing 10, 20, 35, 194, 246–247, 249–253, 264, 275, 280, 282–283, 285, 290, 303, 316, 335, 361–362, 367, 407, 421; environmental resources, ecosystem services 69–70, 114, 429; hedonic 258–259
prisoner's dilemma (game) 106–107, 117, 217, 433
product 11, 78, 83, 101, 103, 126, 130–132, 138–139, 204, 250, 262, 276–278, 281–282, 285–288, 363, 367–368, 383, 395, 401, 406; joint 103, 105, 110–111, 190; quality 15, 192–193, 198, 364, 400; space 273, 279; use 79
production 26, 123–150, 425, 428–429; ecological concept 127–129; economic concept 126; engineering concept 129–130; firm as unit of production 136–140; GDP as measure of 131; for market 102–103; metabolism 76
production function 131–132, 141, 144n32, 169, 429
profit 14, 18, 56–57, 78–80, 116, 131, 134, 136–137, 158, 194, 251–252, 254, 259–261, 264, 274, 280–281, 283–284, 286–287, 301, 307–308, 310, 313, 316, 318–319, 321, 340, 342–343, 349, 368, 375, 393, 396, 400, 433, 459, 467
progress 9, 19–20, 35, 40, 54–58, 60, 135, 141, 432, 437, 482; material 54–56, 169; technological 279, 341, 425–426, 428–430, 433, 440–441, 463

property 13, 16, 69, 81, 155, 159, 162–163, 173, 220, 223–225, 232, 254, 349, 373, 454, 486–487; intellectual 230, 285, 289, 363, 366, 385; law 484; private 20, 455, 470

property rights 13, 16, 20–21, 232, 238, 258, 274, 285, 288–289, 319–320, 362–363, 377, 397, 455, 473, 486–487

psychology 33, 35, 142, 165, 171–172, 217, 253, 260, 403–404, 486; evolutionary 155, 160

public choice 453, 467, 472, 474, 476

public opinion 27, 453, 456–457, 459–461, 463, 474

Purchasing Power Parity (PPP) 368–369

Putinism 226

race to the bottom 114, 230, 465

rational ignorance 232, 468–469

rationality 35, 51–54, 56, 58, 60n14, 153–155, 158–160, 163, 171–172, 174n7, 192, 194, 204, 225, 259, 264, 337–339, 453, 470–471; individual vs. collective 172, 336, 342; as reason 159

real estate 36, 104, 112, 191, 258, 341, 351, 403, 407

realisation-focused comparisons 235–236, 238

reason 153, 155, 158–159, 167, 172

rebound effect 429–430

reciprocity 101, 116, 191–192, 208–209, 253, 263, 274; (trade policy) 372–373

Red Queen 78, 406

reflexivity 27, 38–39, 41, 159, 316, 322, 369, 483

regime: of accumulation 332; Fordist 333; of inequality 53, 393, 396–401, 410–412; monetary 302, 332–333; techno-institutional 331–335, 350

region 13–15, 68, 100, 115, 125, 136, 145n61, 203, 220, 290, 341, 345, 364–365, 369, 377–378, 380, 384n9, 393, 395, 408–409, 426, 456

Regional Comprehensive Economic Partnership (RCEP) 373

regulation school 330–331, 355

religion 29, 32, 42n13, 49, 54, 203, 437

renewables 424, 430

rent: economic 247, 256–261, 265, 377; entrepreneurial 257, 261, 265

rent-seeking 230, 397, 462–463

republicanism 220

reputation 38, 189, 228, 233, 483; of central bank 347

reserves, international 368

resources, natural 81, 377, 425

retaliation 198, 373

retention 67–68, 80, 88–89, 224, 272, 278, 291, 453, 456

revolution 16, 41, 50, 53, 112, 138, 145n64, 256, 292, 337, 398

Ricardian equivalence 347, 356

Ricardo, David 375

rice 14–15, 69, 77, 434

risk: aversion to 310, 313, 322, 344, 399, 433; perception of 335

ritual 220–221

Robinson Crusoe 100, 102–103, 170, 324

routine 138, 143, 276, 278, 283–284, 291, 293, 379, 399, 425, 461

rules of the game 221, 396, 400, 413, 455, 457–458, 465, 473

Russia 226, 229, 425, 485

Saldenmechanik (mechanics of accounting balances) 336

Samuelson, Paul 173n2, 484

saturation 331, 429–430

saver: financial 310–312; real 310–313, 315

saving 162, 301–302, 308–315, 317, 322–324, 336, 342, 349, 352, 380, 382, 426, 428, 430, 441; paradox of 355; precautionary 335

scarcity 13, 28, 54, 76–78, 89, 199, 256, 274, 279, 281, 400, 408, 414

Schumpeter, Joseph A. 88, 145n59, 174n6, 279, 309, 311–312, 330–333, 338, 340, 342–343, 355, 432

second law (of thermodynamics) 71, 90n16, 431

security 15, 54, 316, 371, 466

selection 73, 76, 77–81, 85, 128, 135, 141, 157, 218, 221, 224, 281, 379, 424, 453; external 79, 287–288, 456–458, 464–465, 471; group 81, 86–88, 110, 229; internal 81, 287–288, 456–458, 464, 468; market 154, 276–280, 340, 396–402; multilevel 68, 129, 278, 287; natural 77, 79, 81, 124; self 221–222, 225, 286; signal 81, 290

self 163

sensorimotor circuits 155–156, 165, 173

separation of powers (legislative, executive, judicative) 454, 467

services (vs. goods) 11–14, 129, 263, 274, 362–363, 366–367, 370, 374, 381, 397, 428, 437, 464

shareholders 190, 233, 320, 325, 400

sharing 437

shock, macroeconomic 334, 351

signalling 38, 81, 160, 166, 192, 194, 198, 203, 225, 400, 406–407, 465

silver 16

Simmel, Georg 209n9, 247, 254, 259, 264, 266n29
singularity, historical 334, 352
sink 69–70, 90n14, 127
skills premium 405
small business 307
small open economy 464
small world 201–202
smartphone 129, 139–140, 195, 201, 430
Smith, Adam 2, 27, 60n8, 161, 175n44, 55, 253
Smith, Vernon 172
social market economy 57, 398
social movement 461, 463
social network analysis (SNA) 185–186, 210n30, 340
social welfare state 52, 466, 470
socio-economic background 170, 406
solidarity, social 394, 470–471
somatic marker 174n14, 249, 253
sovereignty 288, 305–306, 371–372, 374, 464
space, resource 76, 82–84, 86, 89, 124, 437
specialisation 10, 12, 58, 99–104, 108–111, 116, 129–130, 132–133, 157, 185, 195, 201, 216, 234, 249, 254, 257, 260, 263, 272–273, 276–278, 281, 288, 306, 399, 402; ecological 82–83, 422; efficiency 111–115; firms 138–141, 286–288, 461, 470; forced 108, 142, 435; global 140, 375, 377; violence 110, 234, 424; voluntary 101
specialisation dilemma: general 12, 99–100, 102–104, 115, 117, 207, 274, 280–281, 285–286, 371–372, 384; global 135, 371–372, 384
specificity: asset 104, 139, 253–254, 280, 311, 321; capability 103–104, 111, 117, 139, 195, 280, 286, 371, 399, 470
speech act 165, 176n84
spillovers 232, 341, 349, 351, 374, 377, 397, 409
spread, interest 313, 322
stagflation 482
stag hunt (game) 107–108, 117, 216–217
standardisation 133–134, 140, 143, 224, 287, 398, 402, 458
stasis 278–279, 284, 291–292, 331, 400–401, 461
state 18–19, 57, 139, 288–289, 302, 347–348, 364, 374, 382, 395, 424, 453–456, 464, 467, 469–470; China 18–19
stationary state 435
status: competition (*see* competition); good 38, 407; order 163–164, 400–401, 488; social 80, 88, 128, 134, 156, 163, 166, 169,

189, 199–200, 206, 216, 258, 279, 287, 339, 393–395, 399–400, 408, 437, 456
steam engine 133, 137
stock-flow consistent modelling 252, 336
stratification: educational 395, 403, 405–406; in firms 402; social 410, 424
structural hole 195, 409
structure, social 56–57, 116, 132, 402, 409, 424, 453
subjectivity 27–28, 49–50, 60, 246, 278
subsidy 455
subsistence economy 12
substitutability, of production factors 275
suffrage, democratic 469
sugar 127–129, 166
Sumer 255
superstar hypothesis 409
supply chains 130, 138–139, 143, 185, 379, 400–401
sustainability 15, 57, 76, 82–84, 86, 99, 114, 116, 207, 220, 273, 277, 282, 308, 368, 382, 393–394, 412–413, 432, 437–438, 441, 488

Taiwan 235
tariff 235, 241n74, 364, 366, 368, 373, 385, 466, 483, 485
tax 18, 57, 113, 115, 219–220, 224, 230, 319, 347, 459, 470, 487–488
taxation 15–17, 19, 221, 234, 274, 304–305, 322, 347, 380, 397–398, 412, 425, 454–455, 465–467
Taylorism 102
Taylor rule 346–347
technology 55, 72, 74, 80, 84–87, 123, 126, 138, 142, 194, 230, 237, 340–341, 431–433, 488; communication 15, 190, 192, 224, 409, 458; and energy 141; evolution 136–138; financial 304; and firms 138–140, 284–288, 399, 402; general purpose 137, 430; and markets 79; and power 140–142; production 19, 132–135, 170, 377, 429, 434; regime (*see* regime); techno-institutional states/space 82; social 9, 32, 273, 424; transaction 256, 264, 283; and wants 129
technosphere 68–69, 74–75, 77, 87, 112, 123–129, 133, 135, 137, 140, 142–143, 185, 201, 361, 422, 426–432, 434, 438–441
telephone 132
tenancy 13
terms of trade (ToT) 367–368, 372–373, 381, 385
Tesla 134, 137
thermodynamics, laws of 70, 90n16

ties: strong 198; weak 197–198, 281, 458
time consistency, of economic policy
    346, 466
time horizon 114, 339–340, 343, 434
time preference 162, 313, 317
tipping points 76–77, 431, 441, 460
too-big-to-fail dilemma 346
tool 2, 48, 103, 132–133, 153, 165, 204, 253,
    255, 306, 317, 422, 441
trade, value-added 37–38, 363–364, 366,
    384
trade agreements 365, 369, 373
trade barriers 369, 380, 385; non-tariff 366
trade fairs 193
trade policy 236, 366, 371–372
trade union 59, 401, 463
trading, long-distance 9, 14, 16, 19, 302, 304,
    422, 425
transaction 28, 32, 209n15, 216, 224, 226,
    233, 237, 246, 248–249, 253, 259,
    262–263, 303–304, 321, 341, 379–381,
    422; international/global 249, 361–373,
    375, 378, 382–383; market 10, 12, 15, 50,
    53, 103, 138, 187, 189, 191, 202, 225, 226,
    273–274, 276, 281, 283, 285, 335–336,
    349, 353, 408, 436; network 186–194, 286
transaction cost: economic 114, 203, 217,
    227–229, 230, 249, 257, 287, 288, 351,
    364, 379, 434, 455, 466–467; political 226,
    229–232, 235, 398, 469, 471
transaction enabling transaction TET
    362–364, 366, 376, 378, 383–384
transcendental institutionalism 235, 236, 238
transfers 20, 229, 274, 347, 372, 380, 397,
    454, 466
transmission mechanism, monetary 346
transport 11–15, 72, 74–75, 79, 115, 133,
    137, 185, 201, 280, 363, 366, 426, 430, 434
tree of life 76, 82, 124
triad 186–187, 189, 193, 207–209, 274
trial and error 135–136
triangulation 29, 37–38, 41
tribe 201–202
trilemma: Mundell 374; Rodrik 464
trust 12, 106, 116, 161, 187, 193, 198–199,
    203, 206, 209n28, 210n40, 220, 223, 228,
    247, 262–263, 286, 315, 323, 348, 351,
    366, 407–408, 465, 472, 484, 488; into
    money 249–250, 263, 302, 304–306, 315,
    321, 347–348
trustworthiness 192, 195, 198, 206, 263, 302,
    305–306

ultra-sociality 68, 81, 84, 86, 89, 100
unbundling 378

uncertainty, fundamental 261, 281, 284–285,
    287, 337–338, 341, 353, 379, 459,
    461–462, 466–467, 473
unemployment 345, 351, 468
United States 124, 133, 221, 334, 364, 382,
    425, 430
urbanisation 15, 423, 426, 428, 441
utility, subjective 256–258, 264–265

valuation: mark-to market 342; of stocks
    252–253
value 30, 37, 40, 48–59, 86, 128, 142, 162,
    193, 216, 220, 223, 230, 237, 275, 288,
    321, 383, 393, 411, 453–454, 468–471,
    487; authoritarian 220; capital 316–319;
    economic 31–32, 55, 130, 191, 206,
    246, 249, 371, 421; exchange 131,
    261; monetary 114, 131, 159, 250, 252,
    255–258, 261–262, 280, 301, 336, 346,
    362; of money 246, 253–254, 263, 302,
    305; nominal 346; subjective 28–29, 50,
    157, 246, 257, 259; use 131, 251
value-added trade 37–38, 363–364, 366, 384
value chains 37, 169, 287, 363, 379
value change 57
variation 57, 67–68, 70–89, 101, 132,
    135, 139, 154, 157, 206, 223–224, 272,
    278–279, 291, 314, 377, 403–404,
    453, 456
varieties of capitalism 37, 332, 398
Veblen, Thorstein 79, 88, 174n24, 291, 443
Verstehen 'understanding' 27
view, first person 26–29, 41, 101, 111–113,
    156, 158, 189–190, 217, 251–252, 257,
    261, 316–317, 337, 421, 436, 458
view, second person 26–28, 30–33, 39–40,
    42n7, 51, 69, 88, 101, 109, 111–113,
    127, 131, 158–159, 167, 217, 229, 235,
    251–252, 257–259, 261–262, 265, 316,
    338, 368, 421, 432, 439, 458, 460
view, third person 26–33, 38–39, 41–42,
    48–49, 54, 59, 67, 69, 71, 88, 101,
    112–113, 127, 131, 156, 167, 189–191,
    208, 217, 229, 235, 236, 337–338,
    438–439, 453, 458
violence 108–111, 116, 157, 163, 217, 223,
    233–234, 237–238, 288, 393, 424, 454
votes, in democracy 454, 456–457, 460
voting paradox 460, 468, 475
VSR mechanism 67, 80, 88–89, 123, 224,
    278, 456–457

wage 112, 170, 263, 282, 286, 314, 333, 335,
    363, 399, 401, 411, 454; minimum wage
    401–402; wage differentials 397, 401, 405

wage bargaining 397, 454, 463
wanting 154, 168–169, 173, 176n101
wants 28, 36, 57, 127–129, 143, 165–168, 170, 173, 259, 263, 274, 276–279, 281, 285, 338, 340, 430, 435, 460
war 17, 69, 88, 111, 157, 305, 323, 354, 374, 398, 440, 483–484
war finance 19
waste 54, 69–71, 80, 83–84, 89, 106–107, 126–127, 130–131, 138, 230, 428, 463; disposal 69, 74, 130, 426; products 83, 126; water 426
wealth, inherited 398

wealth effects 189, 343
Weber, Max 31, 116, 155, 172, 415, 442
welfare: economic 321, 458, 466; shared notions of 466
well-being 29, 51, 54–56, 128, 169, 435, 466
Willgerodt, Hans 482
wind 71–72, 431
winner-takes-all 280, 460
World Trade Organization (WTO) 43n43, 369–371, 373–374, 385–386, 476
World War 2, 7, 305, 345, 425, 453, 484

yield 301, 316–319, 339, 351, 362, 367, 369, 374

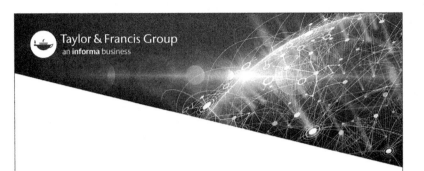

Printed in the United States
by Baker & Taylor Publisher Services